A CONCISE
GUIDE TO THE
TORAH

RABBI ADIN
EVEN-ISRAEL
STEINSALTZ

A Concise Guide to the Torah
First edition, 2020

Koren Publishers Jerusalem Ltd.
POB 8531, New Milford, CT 06776-8531, USA
& POB 4044, Jerusalem 91040, Israel

www.korenpub.com

Original Hebrew Edition © Adin Even-Israel Steinsaltz, 2018
English translation © Adin Even-Israel Steinsaltz 2020
Steinsaltz Humash translation text © 2018

This book was published in cooperation with
the Israeli Institute for Talmudic Publication.
All rights reserved for Rabbi Adin Even-Israel Steinsaltz.

The right of Adin Steinsaltz to be identified as the author
of this work has been asserted by him in accordance
with the Copyright, Designs & Patents Act 1988.

Steinsaltz Center is the parent organization of institutions
established by Rabbi Adin Even-Israel Steinsaltz
POB 45187, Jerusalem 91450 ISRAEL
Telephone: +972 2 646 0900, Fax +972 2 624 9454
www.steinsaltz-center.org

ISBN 978-1-59264-566-4, *hardcover*
Printed and bound in the United States

The Erez Series

Dedicated in loving memory of

Joseph "Erez" Tenenbaum

Whose love of learning, endless curiosity and zest for life
Survived the Destruction
And found full expression in his ultimate return to Zion.

By his son Zisman Tuvia

～～～

סדרת ארז

מוקדש לעלוי נשמת

יוסף צבי בן טוביה זיסמן טננבואם

(המכונה ארז)

"אוד מוצל מאש"

שלא נכבה בו אהבת לימוד, סקרנות אין-סופית, ושמחת חיים

ע"י בנו זיסמן טוביה

Contents

Numbers

Deuteronomy

Foreword

The Bible, also called the five books of Moses, is the foundation of all Jewish culture. Our ancestors throughout the generations studied this book and taught it to their children. This book includes the stories of the origin of the entire world and of our ancestors, from the Garden of Eden to the exodus from Egypt, the giving of the Torah at Sinai, and the subsequent sojourn in the desert. It contains the laws which are the basis for Judaism. It is not a book of history nor a book that is meant to be read casually, but rather a holy book. Therefore, it is fitting that one not merely peruse it, but rather read with the intention of seeking guidance for one's life and one's path therein.

Each of the five books of Moses has a unique nature: Genesis is the book that tells of the creation of the world and its aftermath, and in doing so addresses some of the most fundamental topics that humankind has thought about. Nevertheless, it is mostly narrative, with the stories of Adam and Eve, the flood and Noah, and the accounts of the patriarchs: Abraham, Isaac, and Jacob.

The second book of Moses, Exodus, is the book of redemption and revelation. It contains the description of Israel's enslavement in Egypt and of the miracles through which our ancestors were redeemed and escaped Egypt. It tells of the great revelation at Sinai and of the subsequent sins of Israel. It concludes with an elaborate description of the construction of the Tabernacle.

The book of Leviticus has been referred to as the *Torat Kohanim*, the priests' law. It mostly is concerned with the service in the Tabernacle and the priestly rites, but also with the obligations of all of Israel to live a life of holiness and purity.

The book of Numbers relates the story of our ancestors' sojourn in the desert for forty years, the difficulties they encountered, and their ultimate arrival at the banks of the Jordan, preparing to enter the land.

The book of Deuteronomy is called *Mishneh Torah*, the review of the Torah. Nearly all of it consists of long speeches made by Moses to Israel at the end of the forty years in the desert. He tells the children of the generation that left Egypt of the great events that their parents experienced, reminds them of a selection of the mitzvot, most of which were previously recounted, and concludes with a poem and a blessing. The final passage relates the death of Moses.

The five books of Moses are accessible to all. The Torah can be read by small children who are just learning to read and is also the object of deep scrutiny by the greatest of scholars. It was originally written in biblical Hebrew and contains a wide range of content – everything from stories to practical instructions. It is fitting that every person has this book in his or her possession so that he or she can read from it whenever the opportunity arises, either for the purpose of study or even simply to take pleasure in reading it.

In order to make the text more accessible, we have added, beyond the traditional divisions into *parashot*, topical sub-headings, each followed by a few sentences of explanation. At the beginning of each *parasha* we have inserted a brief summary of its contents.

The primary goal of this edition of the five books of Moses is that the book be available in every Jewish home so that everyone, man or woman, boy or girl, can take advantage of it. Anyone who takes the time to study it will gain wisdom and, from time to time, may also have an original insight. At the beginning of the volume we have added a detailed table of contents. At the end we have added an appendix containing maps and charts, which are not meant to be merely decorative but to aid in making the Torah accessible to all.

Rabbi Adin Even-Israel Steinsaltz

Introducing the Erez Concise Guides

A Jewish home, at any time or place, cannot be maintained based on the mere identity of its residents as Jews. Whether they conceive of themselves as religious, traditional, or secular, people need to have access to written expression of their tradition through which they can come to know, understand, and "enter" their tradition.

"To enter the tradition" can mean something different for each person. Some are simply curious, others have a particular interest, and there are undoubtedly many Jews who just do not want the worlds of the Jewish spirit to be closed to them. People therefore require bridges and gates to gain access. There is no obligation to use these, but their existence makes it possible for anyone – when that person so desires, to enter, or even to glance within – the way is clear and he or she can do so.

We have thus produced the Erez series which provides different gates by which one can enter the Jewish tradition. Just as it is told about Abraham's tent that it was open from all four directions in order to welcome guests from everywhere, these books allow anyone, whenever he or she feels like it or finds something interesting, to enter into the tradition.

There are thousands of books that cover, in various ways and at different levels, the materials presented here. However, most of them require prior knowledge and no small amount of effort to be understood. In these volumes, we have striven to give anyone who seeks it a paved road into the riches of the Jewish world. More than merely a gate, we hope that these books can be said to offer their readers a "ride" into the tradition. Each person can get off whenever he or she desires and continue traveling when their interest is reawakened.

These volumes contain some of the fundamentals of Judaism. In each of them there are elements that can be considered hors d'oeuvres that can be snacked upon and others that are more comparable to entrees, that require more time for digestion. In either case, the invitation offered by *A Concise Guide to the Sages* in Proverbs (9:5) is relevant: "Come, partake of my bread, and drink of the wine that I have mixed." The books were deliberately designed to be accessible to everyone, whether he or she is highly educated or someone whose source of intellectual stimulation consists in occasionally reading the newspaper. Anyone can enjoy something, whether by means of an occasional taste, or by sitting down to a hearty meal. The way is open and anyone can find the gate appropriate for him or her, without effort.

We have aimed to keep the translation as true to the original Hebrew and Aramaic as possible. As some of these texts are not easy to understand, we have added clarifying comments in square brackets where appropriate. Further explication is appended in notes at the end of certain passages. When we have felt it appropriate to use a transliteration, the term transliterated is first explained and then followed by the transliteration in square brackets. At the end of each book we have provided a glossary of Hebrew terms mentioned in the series. Some of the terms found there may not be found in this book, as we have used the same glossary for all the volumes of the Erez series. *The Reference Guide to the Talmud* has a far more extensive glossary as is necessary for that work.

Given the antiquity of the texts collected here, there are many occasions where it was impossible to avoid gendered usage and we have followed the texts themselves in using the male gender as the default.

Each of the volumes in this series stands alone, with only occasional citations connecting them. The first volume, *A Concise Guide to the Torah*, contains the translation of the Torah taken from the *Steinsaltz Humash*; we have abridged the commentary that can be found there. One can take this volume to the synagogue but also peruse it in the comforts of one's home.

The second volume, *A Concise Guide to the Sages*, is an anthology of rabbinic literature, organized by topics. One part includes rabbinic thinking associated with the Torah, while other topics are also addressed: the cycle of the Jewish year, the cycle of life in rabbinic eyes, as well as other topics where a person can find something that fits his or her needs.

The third volume, *A Concise Guide to Mahshava*, addresses spiritual matters. It contains an anthology of non-halakhic literature from the Jewish spiritual tradition: kabbala, Jewish philosophy, the Musar tradition, and hasidic writings. Here too, the texts are presented in a manner that is accessible to all, in clear English. This volume addresses a broad array of topics: Besides comments and explanations on the Torah, there are sections devoted to the cycle of the Jewish year, the life cycle, and fundamental questions of human life such as parenthood, marriage, and death. There are many other topics addressed in this volume and one can open it at random and find wisdom that touches the soul.

The fourth volume, *A Concise Guide to Halakha*, is a survey of practical *halakha*. It does not delve into the sources of *halakha* and provide an opportunity for intensive study but serves rather as a guidebook to what the *halakha* instructs one to do in various situations. In this way the book offers

a summary of the *halakhot* of Shabbat and the holidays, of life cycle events, and of those mitzvot that any Jew is likely to encounter. If one wishes to act in accordance with the *halakha*, he or she will know what to do with the help of this volume. It is written in clear English with a minimum of technical language so that it is accessible to anyone, man, woman, or child. And if he or she decides to act accordingly, may he or she be blessed.

The fifth volume, *Reference Guide to the Talmud* is a reprint of the work that was issued as a companion to the *Koren Talmud Bavli*. It is an indispensable resource for students of all levels. This fully revised, English-language edition of the *Reference Guide* clearly and concisely explains the Talmud's fundamental structure, concepts, terminology, assumptions, and inner logic; it provides essential historical and biographical information; it includes appendixes, a key to abbreviations, and a comprehensive index.

For improved usability, this completely updated volume has a number of new features: topical organization instead of by Hebrew alphabet, re-edited and revised text to coordinate with the language used in the *Koren Talmud Bavli*, and an index of Hebrew terms to enable one seeking a Hebrew term to locate the relevant entry.

These books are certainly not the entire Torah, but they are beneficial for any Jew to have in his or her home. If one finds something interesting, or is curious about something, these books offer a resource to investigate that topic. Even if one opens one of these volumes by chance, he or she will gain from reading them, both intellectually and spiritually. In short, these are books that it is convenient to have in one's home.

Our thanks are extended to all the people who participated in the project of writing these books, editing them, and finding the sources therein. We likewise would like to thank the publisher, and those first readers who offered helpful criticism and advice, and finally to those good people whose donations made it possible to create these books.

The Editors

Genesis

Parashat Bereshit

Parashat Bereshit – and therefore the entire Torah – opens with a description of the creation of the world. It first offers a brief description of the hierarchical order of creation – the heavens and the earth, the sea and the land, and the plants, animals, and humanity. This is followed by a more specific account of the process.

Adam is placed in the garden of Eden and commanded not to partake of the fruit of the tree of knowledge, but the snake seduces his wife into disregarding the commandment; they are punished and banished from the garden. They have two children, Cain and Abel, and Cain's jealousy of Abel gives rise to the first murder in human history.

Human beings, the children of Adam, begin to proliferate and develop a culture and civilization, but "the wickedness of man was great on the earth, and…every inclination of the thoughts of his heart was only evil all the time" (6:5), causing humanity to become corrupt. The *parasha* concludes with the Creator's decision to wipe the human race off the face of the earth, with the exception of Noah, who "found favor in the eyes of the Lord" (6:8).

Light and Dark

The initial account of Creation is quite general, and is divided into discrete units of time – days. In addition to describing each act of creation, the narrative also introduces an evaluative element, establishing that Creation was a positive act.

1 **¹In the beginning, God created** *ex nihilo* **the heavens and the earth. ²The earth was** initially **unformed and empty. And darkness was upon the face of the deep,** referring to deep waters, or to the unstructured universe. **And the spirit of God hovered over the surface of the water. ³God said: Let there be light, and there was light. ⁴God saw the light, that it was good. And God divided between the light and the darkness. ⁵God called the light day, and the darkness He called night. It was evening and it was morning,** concluding **one day.**

📖 **Further reading:** Why does the Torah open with the letter *bet*? See *A Concise Guide to the Sages*, p. 3. For more on the age of the universe and its manner of creation, see *A Concise Guide to Mahshava*, p. 291.

The Heavens

The water mentioned earlier constitutes the fundamental material of Creation. It must be divided before Creation can progress.

⁶God said: Let there be a firmament in the midst of the water. And let it divide between water and water. ⁷God made the firmament and divided between the water that was under the firmament and the water that was above the firmament; and it was so. ⁸God called the firmament heavens. It was evening and it was morning, a second day.

Land and Vegetation

The water is collected in specific areas, exposing the land underneath and enabling the creation of grass, trees, and other vegetation.

⁹God said: Let the water under the heavens be gathered to one place, and let the dry land appear. And it was so. ¹⁰God called the dry land earth, and the gathering of the waters He called seas. And God saw His creation, that it was good. ¹¹God said: Let the earth sprout grasses: vegetation yielding seed, and fruit trees bearing fruit in its kind, in which there is its seed, upon the earth. And it was so. ¹²The earth produced grasses, vegetation yielding seed in its kind, and every tree bearing fruit in which there was its seed, in its kind. And God saw that it was good. ¹³It was evening and it was morning, a third day.

The Heavenly Bodies

God establishes the orbits of the heavenly bodies, thereby arranging the structure of the universe. These are important to people chiefly for their use in measuring time.

¹⁴God said: Let there be lights in the firmament of the heavens, to distinguish between the day and the night. Let them be for causing signs, phenomena in the heavens and on Earth, and for establishing the seasons, and for marking days and years. ¹⁵Let them be for lights in the firmament of the heavens, to give light upon the earth. And it was so. ¹⁶God made the two great lights, those greatest as seen from Earth: the greater light, the sun, to rule the day, and the lesser light, the moon, to rule the night, and He also created the stars. ¹⁷God set them in the firmament of the heavens to give light upon the earth ¹⁸and to rule during the day and during the night. And these lights also serve to divide between the light and the darkness. And God saw that it was good. ¹⁹It was evening and it was morning, a fourth day.

Populating the Seas and Skies

The first creatures with a measure of will are created within the water. Since they need to act in order to reproduce, they receive a blessing from above to do so.

²⁰God said: Let the water swarm with swarms of living creatures. And let birds fly above the earth on the face of the firmament of the heavens. ²¹God created the great serpents, unidentified aquatic creatures, **and every living creature that crawls, with which the water swarmed in their kinds, and every winged bird in its kind. And God saw that it was good. ²²God blessed them, saying: Be fruitful, and multiply, and fill the water in the seas, and let birds multiply on the earth.** In contrast to vegetation, which propagates automatically, animals must actively search for a mate in order to reproduce. Consequently, they required a special blessing that would instill within them the drive to be fruitful and multiply. **²³It was evening and it was morning, a fifth day.**

Land Creatures

The land animals are fashioned from the ground.

²⁴God said: Let the earth produce living creatures in its kind, animals, and crawling creatures, and beasts of the earth in its kind. And it was so. ²⁵God made the beasts of the earth in its kind, and the animals in its kind, and every creature that crawls upon the ground in its kind; and God saw that it was good.

Creation of Man

Human beings are the culmination of the entire process of creation. As they are created in the image of God, they are given free will. They are also given dominion over all other entities.

²⁶God said: Let Us make Man in Our image, in Our likeness; sharing God's essence. **And let them dominate over the fish of the sea, and over the birds of the heavens, and over the animals, and over all** the inanimate substances of **the earth, and over every crawling creature that crawls upon the earth. ²⁷God created man in His own image,** granting him freedom and the capacity to expand and alter his surroundings; **in the image of God He created him.** The verse notes: **Male and female He created them. ²⁸God blessed them and God** also **said to them: Be fruitful, and multiply, and fill the earth;** populate it **and subdue it. And rule over the fish of the sea, and over the birds of the heavens, and over every living creature that crawls upon the earth. ²⁹God said** to them: **Behold,**

I have given you all seed-yielding vegetation that is upon the face of all the earth, and every tree in which there is seed-yielding fruit of a tree; to you it shall be for food. ³⁰And to every beast of the earth, and to every bird of the heavens, and to everything that crawls upon the earth, in which there is a living soul, I have given all green vegetation for food. And it was so. ³¹God saw everything that He had made, and behold, it was very good. It was evening and it was morning, the sixth day.

The Seventh Day

The final day is not just the day on which the labor of creation ceases. It has a distinctive character, incorporating blessing, wholeness, and holiness.

2 ¹The heavens and the earth and their entire host, everything within them, were completed. ²God completed on the seventh day His works that He had made; He rested on the seventh day from all His works that He had made. ³God blessed the seventh day and sanctified it, because on it He rested from all His labor that God had created to act.

The Second Account of Creation

The second account of Creation comprises a more detailed description of the process of forming the various living creatures. Furthermore, whereas in the first version God is called *Elohim*, expressing His all-encompassing, impersonal essence, here God is called *YHVH Elohim*, the Lord God, adding God's personal name, as it were.

Second aliya ⁴This is the legacy of the heavens and of the earth when they were created, on the day that the Lord God made earth and heaven. ⁵No shrub of the field was yet in the earth, and no vegetation of the field had yet sprouted, because the Lord God had not caused it to rain upon the earth, and there was no man to till the ground. ⁶A mist would rise from the earth, and water the entire surface of the ground. ⁷The Lord God formed man of dust from the ground, and breathed into his nostrils the breath of life. Man became a living creature, with special vitality and the ability to speak.

The Garden of Eden

While the Garden of Eden is described as a physical place, various details of the story render it mysterious, suggesting it is a lost world, outside the realm of our current experience.

⁸The Lord God planted a garden in the place known as Eden, to the east. He placed there the man whom He had formed. ⁹The Lord God grew from the ground every tree that is pleasant to the sight and good for

food, and the tree of life, in the midst, the center, of the garden, and the tree of the knowledge of good and evil. ¹⁰A river emerged from Eden to water the garden; and from there it, the river, would part, and would become four headwaters. ¹¹The name of the one is Pishon; it is that which encircles the entire land of Havila, where the gold is found. ¹²The gold in the deposits of that land is of particularly good quality; there is also bdellium and the onyx stone. ¹³The name of the second river is Gihon; it is that which encircles the entire land of Kush. ¹⁴The name of the third river is Tigris; it is that which goes east of Ashur. And the fourth river is Euphrates. ¹⁵The Lord God took the man, and placed him in the Garden of Eden, to cultivate it and to keep it. ¹⁶The Lord God commanded the man, saying: From every tree of the garden you may eat, ¹⁷but of the tree of the knowledge of good and evil you shall not eat, for on the day that you eat of it you shall die.

Creation of Woman

According to the straightforward meaning of the verses, the woman was formed from one of the man's ribs [tzela]. But as tzela also means side, the Sages interpreted the story as suggesting that before woman was created as a separate being, the first human comprised two sides, male and female. These were separated into a man and a woman, each an independent entity.

¹⁸The Lord God said to Himself: It is not good that the man shall be alone. I will make for him a helper alongside him, a partner who completes him. ¹⁹The Lord God formed from the ground every beast of the field and every bird of the heavens and brought them to the man, to see what he would call it. Whatever the man would call every living creature, that was its name. ²⁰The man called names for every animal, and for the birds of the heavens, and for the beasts of the field; but for Adam, he did not find a helper to be alongside him. This is the first time Adam is used as a name rather than as a word meaning 'the man.' ²¹The Lord God cast a deep sleep upon the man, and he slept; He took out one of his sides, and closed with flesh in its place, where He had removed this side. ²²The Lord God built the side that He took from the man into the form of a woman, and brought her to the man. ²³The man said: This time, this particular entity, is a bone from my bones, and flesh from my flesh. This shall be called woman [isha], because this was taken from man [ish]. ²⁴Therefore, a man shall leave his father and his mother, and he shall cleave, connect, to his wife, and they shall become

Third aliya

one flesh. ²⁵They were both naked, the man and his wife, and they were not ashamed.

Eating from the Tree

The woman heard about the prohibition against eating from the tree of the knowledge of good and evil only from an intermediary, her husband, rather than directly from God. Therefore it was easier for the primeval serpent, who is described as possessing intelligence, to arouse her curiosity and incite her into transgressing the prohibition.

3 ¹**The serpent was more cunning than any beast of the field that the Lord God had made. He said to the woman: Did God actually say: You shall not eat of any tree of the garden?** ²**The woman said to the serpent: From the fruit of the trees of the garden we may eat.** ³**But from the fruit of the tree that is in the midst,** the middle, **of the garden, God said: You shall not eat of it, nor shall you touch it, lest you die.** ⁴**The serpent said to the woman: You will not die.** Rather, this is the motivation for the divine prohibition: ⁵**For God knows that on the day you eat from it, then your eyes shall be opened** to understanding, **and you shall be as God, knowers of good and evil.** ⁶**The woman saw that the tree was good for eating, and that it was an enticement to the eyes, and that the tree was attractive to apprehend;** it was tempting to acquire understanding from the tree. **She took from its fruit and ate; she also gave to her husband with her, and he ate.** ⁷**The eyes of both of them were opened, and they knew** the significance of the fact **that they were naked.** Consequently, **they sewed fig leaves, and made themselves loincloths.**

The Punishment

Everyone who participated in this sin receives a punishment, which will also apply to all future generations.

⁸**They heard the voice of the Lord God** as though it were **moving in the garden with the day breeze,** before evening. **The man and his wife hid from the presence of the Lord God among the trees of the garden.** ⁹**The Lord God called to the man, and said to him: Where are you?** ¹⁰**He,** the man, **said: I heard Your voice in the garden, and I was afraid because I was naked, and** therefore **I hid.** ¹¹**He,** God, **said: Who told you** that it was wrong **that you were naked? Did you eat from the tree from which I commanded you not to eat?** ¹²**The man said: The woman whom You gave to be with me, she gave me from the tree, and I ate.** ¹³**The Lord God said to the woman: What is this you have done? The woman said:**

The serpent enticed me, and I ate. [14]The Lord God said to the serpent: Because you did this, cursed are you from among all the animals, and from all the beasts of the field; upon your belly shall you go, and dust shall you eat all the days of your life. [15]Additionally, I will place enmity between you and the woman, and between your descendants and her descendants. He, her descendant, shall strike, step on, your head, and you shall strike, bite, his heel. [16]To the woman He said: I will increase your suffering and the difficulty of your pregnancy; in pain you shall give birth to children. And furthermore, your desire shall be for your husband, and he shall rule over you. [17]And to Adam He said: Because you heeded the voice of your wife and succumbed to temptation, and because you ate from the tree that I commanded you, saying: You shall not eat from it; cursed is the ground on your account. Only in suffering, through toil, shall you eat of it, all the days of your life. [18]And thorns and thistles shall it grow for you; and you shall eat the vegetation of the field. [19]Only by the sweat of your brow, by exerting great effort, shall you eat bread, until you return to the ground; for from it were you taken. For you are dust, and to dust shall you return at your death.

[20]The man called the name of his wife Eve [Ḥava], because she was the mother of all living [ḥai] beings. [21]The Lord God made for Adam and for his wife hide tunics, and clothed them.

Expulsion from the Garden of Eden

Having eaten from the tree, man not only comprehends his mortal nature, but his capacity for free will has expanded. He is likely to try various ploys to avoid death, and he must therefore be prevented from doing so.

Fourth
aliya

[22]The Lord God said: Behold, the man has become as one of us, like one of the heavenly beings, as he has the capacity to know good and evil. And now steps must be taken lest he put forth his hand and take also from the tree of life, and eat, and live forever. [23]Therefore, the Lord God sent him out from the Garden of Eden, to cultivate the ground from which he was taken. [24]He, God, banished the man; He stationed the cherubs, a type of angel, east of the Garden of Eden. And He placed the blade of the ever-turning sword to guard the path to the tree of life.

Cain and Abel

Adam and Eve begin a new life, with all its complexities. Their family must deal with one of the fundamental issues that face humanity: Sibling rivalry.

4 ¹The man had been intimate with Eve his wife, and she conceived and gave birth to Cain and said: I have acquired [*kaniti*], merited, a man with the Lord. ²She gave birth again, to his brother Abel. Abel was a shepherd, and Cain was a cultivator of the ground. ³It happened, after some time; Cain brought from the fruit of the ground an offering, a gift, to the Lord. ⁴And Abel, he too brought an offering to God, from the firstborn of his flock and from the choicest of them; and the Lord turned toward Abel and to his offering. ⁵But toward Cain and to his offering He did not turn. Cain was very incensed, and his face and mood became downcast. ⁶The Lord said to Cain: Why are you incensed, and why did your face become downcast? ⁷Truly, if you do good, you will be elevated. And if you do not do good, remember that sin crouches at the entrance, to entrap you. And its, sin's, desire is for you, but you may rule over it if you so desire.

Cain Kills Abel

Cain's jealousy leads to hatred, which in turn leads to fratricide. God sentences Cain, a farmer, to wander the earth.

⁸Cain said to Abel his brother. It happened when they were in the field that Cain arose against Abel his brother and killed him. ⁹The Lord said to Cain: Where is Abel your brother? He said: I do not know; am I my brother's keeper? ¹⁰He, God, said to Cain: What have you done? The voice of your brother's blood cries out to Me from the ground. ¹¹Now, cursed are you from the ground that opened its mouth to take your brother's blood from your hand. ¹²When you cultivate the ground, it shall not continue giving its strength to you. The ground is cursed on your account; it shall cease to be a source of life for you. Instead, restless and itinerant shall you be on the earth. ¹³Cain said to the Lord: My punishment [*avoni*] is greater than I can bear. ¹⁴Behold, You have banished me this day from the face of the land, and from Your face shall I be hidden. I shall be restless and itinerant on the earth, and anyone who finds me will kill me. ¹⁵The Lord said to him: Therefore, anyone who kills Cain, vengeance shall be taken on him sevenfold. The Lord placed a sign for Cain, so that anyone who finds him shall not smite him. ¹⁶Cain departed from the presence of the Lord and lived in the land of Nod, east of Eden.

Cain's Descendants

It is Cain and his descendants who express human creativity, both in building cities and in shaping the developing culture.

¹⁷Cain was intimate with his wife, and she conceived and gave birth to Hanokh. He, Cain, was the builder of a city, and he called the name of the city after the name of his son Hanokh. ¹⁸Irad was born to Hanokh; and Irad begot Mehuyael; and Mehuyael begot Metushael; and ^{Fifth aliya} Metushael begot Lemekh. ¹⁹Lemekh took for himself two wives. The name of one was Ada, and the name of the other Tzila. ²⁰Ada gave birth to Yaval; he was the forerunner of those who dwell in tents, nomads, and who raise livestock. ²¹And the name of his brother was Yuval; he was the forerunner of all those who grasp the harp and pipe; the first musician and inventor of musical instruments. ²²And Tzila, she too gave birth, to Tuval Cain, forger of every sharp instrument of bronze and iron, the first metalworker. And the sister of Tuval Cain was Naama.

Lemekh's Confession

A midrash relates that Lemekh killed Cain unwittingly, and that this poem is his expression of remorse.

²³Lemekh said to his wives: Ada and Tzila, hear my voice; wives of Lemekh, listen to my speech. For have I slain a man for my wound, willfully? No, and I did not purposely kill a child for my injury. ²⁴Therefore, as Cain, who killed intentionally, shall be avenged sevenfold, and accordingly, Lemekh will be avenged seventy-seven-fold.

²⁵Adam was intimate with his wife again, and she gave birth to a son, and she called his name Seth [Shet]: As God has provided [shat] me with another offspring in place of Abel, as Cain killed him. ²⁶And to Seth too a son was born; and he called his name Enosh. Then commenced [huhal] proclaiming the name of the Lord, in organized prayers and religious rituals.

The Descendants of Adam

This passage presents a brief chronology of the first ten generations of man.

5 ¹This is the book, the story, of the legacy of Adam. On the day that God created man, in the likeness of God He made him. ²Male and female He created them. He blessed them, and He called their name Man [Adam] on the day they were created. ³Adam lived one hundred and thirty years, and begot a son in his likeness, after his image. And he called his

name Seth. ⁴The days of Adam after he begot Seth were eight hundred years, and during this time he begot sons and daughters. ⁵All the days that Adam lived were nine hundred and thirty years; and he died.

⁶Seth lived one hundred and five years, and he begot Enosh. ⁷Seth lived after he begot Enosh eight hundred and seven years; and he begot sons and daughters. ⁸All the days that Seth lived were nine hundred and twelve years; and he died.

⁹Enosh lived ninety years, and he begot Kenan. ¹⁰Enosh lived after he begot Kenan eight hundred and fifteen years; and he begot sons and daughters. ¹¹All the days of Enosh were nine hundred and five years; and he died.

¹²Kenan lived seventy years, and he begot Mahalalel. ¹³Kenan lived after he begot Mahalalel eight hundred and forty years; and he begot sons and daughters. ¹⁴All the days of Kenan were nine hundred and ten years; and he died.

¹⁵Mahalalel lived sixty-five years, and he begot Yered. ¹⁶Mahalalel lived after he begot Yered eight hundred and thirty years; and he begot sons and daughters. ¹⁷All the days of Mahalalel were eight hundred and ninety-five years; and he died.

¹⁸Yered lived one hundred and sixty-two years, and he begot Hanokh. ¹⁹Yered lived after he begot Hanokh eight hundred years; and he begot sons and daughters. ²⁰All the days of Yered were nine hundred and sixty-two years; and he died.

²¹Hanokh lived sixty-five years, and he begot Methuselah. ²²Hanokh walked with God, worshipping Him, after he begot Methuselah, three hundred years; and he begot sons and daughters. ²³All the days of Hanokh were three hundred and sixty-five years. ²⁴Hanokh walked with God and he was not in the world any longer, for God took him into His court.

Seventh aliya ²⁵Methuselah lived one hundred and eighty-seven years, and he begot Lemekh. ²⁶Methuselah lived after he begot Lemekh seven hundred and eighty-two years; and he begot sons and daughters. ²⁷All the days of Methuselah were nine hundred and sixty-nine years; and he died.

²⁸Lemekh lived one hundred and eighty-two years, and he begot a son. ²⁹He called his name Noah, saying: This son shall comfort us from the suffering of our work, and from the misery of our hands, from the ground, which the Lord has cursed. ³⁰Lemekh lived after he begot

Noah five hundred and ninety-five years; and he begot sons and daughters. [31]All the days of Lemekh were seven hundred and seventy-seven years; and he died.

[32]Noah was five hundred years old; and Noah begot Shem, Ham, and Yefet.

Humanity Disappoints

As human society expands, it becomes apparent that people's desires and choices are directed primarily to evil.

6 [1]It was, when men, the human race, **began to multiply on the face of the earth, and daughters were born to them;** [2]**the sons of the great ones,** either the upper classes, or angels, **saw that the daughters of man were fair, and they took for themselves wives from whomever they chose.** [3]**The Lord said: My spirit shall not abide in man forever, for he too is** only flesh, like the animals; **and his days shall be one hundred and twenty years.** [4]**The giants were on the earth in those days, and also thereafter, when the sons of the great ones consorted with the daughters of man, and they bore them children.** They, the children, **were the mighty who** *Maftir* **were** known **from ancient times as the men of renown.** [5]**The Lord saw that the wickedness of man was great on the earth, and that every inclination of the thoughts of his heart was only evil all the time.** [6]**The Lord regretted that He had made man on the earth. And He was saddened in His heart.** [7]**The Lord said: I will obliterate man, whom I have created from the face of the earth; from man to animal, to crawling creatures, to birds of the heavens; for I regret that I made them.** [8]**But Noah found favor in the eyes of the Lord.**

📖 **Further reading:** For more on people's inclinations toward good and evil, see *A Concise Guide to Mahshava*, p. 219.

Parashat
Noah

God chooses Noah to continue the human race, and commands him to build an ark. Noah is to bring into the ark animals of every kind, to save each species from extinction in the flood. The deluge covers the entire world and lasts for several months. When the humans and animals aboard can finally disembark, God forms a new covenant with His world.

Noah's descendants attempt to build a single city for all of humanity, with an immense tower. This attempt fails, their common tongue splits into many different languages, and they become dispersed all over the earth, becoming progenitors of separate nations.

The *parasha* concludes by introducing Abram. He and his father leave their land and set out on a long journey, which ends when they settle in Haran.

Noah and His Generation

Noah's generation has degenerated to the point that even the animals have become depraved. Noah alone chooses a better path.

6 ⁹**This is the legacy of Noah; Noah was a righteous, wholehearted man in his generations; Noah walked with God,** in His ways, and had a special relationship with Him. ¹⁰**Noah begot three sons: Shem, Ham, and Yefet.** ¹¹**The earth was corrupted before God, and the earth was filled with villainy.** ¹²**God saw the earth, and behold, it was corrupted, as all flesh corrupted its path upon the earth,** everyone behaved in a warped manner.

 Further reading: For more on the heinous sins of the generation of the flood, see *A Concise Guide to the Sages*, p. 12.

The Ark

The ark that God commands Noah to build is not in the shape of a boat; it has no mast, sails, or oars for advancing on the water, and possesses no helm for steering. This is because the ark is not meant to sail in any particular direction, but merely to float, and thereby save its inhabitants from the flood.

¹³**God said to Noah: The end of all flesh has come before Me,** I have decided to annihilate all living creatures, **as the earth is filled with villainy because of them,** their sins; **and behold, I will destroy them with the**

earth. However, you have been chosen to continue humanity. [14]Therefore, **make for you an ark of** the relatively light **gopher wood;** separate **compartments shall you make** within **the ark, and you shall coat it within and without with pitch,** as a waterproofing substance. [15]**And this is how you shall make it: Three hundred cubits shall be the length of the ark, fifty cubits its breadth, and thirty cubits its height.** [16]**You shall make a window for the ark, and you shall complete it at the top, up to** the width of **a cubit**, as the roof is to be sloped in two directions, with a flat portion one cubit wide in the middle. **And the entrance of the ark you shall place in its side. Lower, second, and third stories you shall make it;** the ark must have three floors. [17]**And behold, I am bringing the flood,** or judgment, in the form of **water, upon the earth, to destroy all flesh in which there is the breath of life from under the heavens. Everything that is on the earth shall perish.** [18]**But I will keep My covenant with you. You shall come to the ark: you, and your sons, and your wife, and your sons' wives with you.** [19]**From every living being of all flesh, two of each** species **you shall bring to the ark to keep alive with you; they shall be male and female.** [20]**From the birds according to their kind, and from the animals according to their kind, from every crawling creature of the ground according to its kind, two of each shall come to you, to keep** them **alive.** [21]**You, take for you from all food that is eaten,** edible food, **and gather it to you; and it shall be for you and for them for food.** [22]**Noah did according to all that God had commanded him; so he did.**

Pure and Impure Animals

God elaborates on His command to Noah to save all living creatures. He is to distinguish between the impure animals and the pure ones; that is, those that would later be considered pure, or kosher, according to *halakha.*

7 [1]**The Lord said to Noah: Come you and your entire household into the ark, for I have seen you to be righteous before Me in this genera-tion.** [2]**From every pure animal you shall take to you seven pairs, a male and his mate. And of the animals that are not pure, two, a male and his mate.** [3]**Also from the birds of the heavens** take **seven each, male and female,** in order **to keep offspring alive on the face of all the earth,** to repopulate the land. [4]**For in seven more days, I will make it rain upon the earth forty days and forty nights, and I will obliterate all existence that I made,** everything that lives, **from the face of the earth.** [5]**Noah did according to all that the Lord had commanded him.**

Entering the Ark

When the flood starts in earnest, water rises from underground and a deluge of water falls from the heavens. Noah and his family enter their "lifeboat," the ark, along with all the animals.

⁶**Noah was six hundred years old** at that time, **and the flood,** or sentence of judgment, **was water upon the earth.** ⁷**Noah, and his sons, and his wife, and his sons' wives with him, came into the ark, because of the water of the flood.** ⁸**From the pure animal, and from the animal that is not pure, and from the birds, and from every creature that crawls upon the ground,** ⁹**two at a time they came to Noah into the ark, male and female, as God had commanded Noah.**

¹⁰**It was after the passage of seven days that the water of the flood was upon the earth.** ¹¹**In the six hundredth year of the life of Noah, during the second month** of the year, **on the seventeenth day of the month, on that day all the fountains of the great deep erupted, and the windows,** the orifices, **of the heavens were opened.** ¹²**The rain was upon the earth forty days and forty nights.** ¹³**On that very day,** at midday on the seventeenth day of the month, **Noah, and Shem, and Ham, and Yefet, the sons of Noah, and Noah's wife, and the three wives of his sons with them, entered into the ark;** ¹⁴**they, and every beast according to its kind, and every animal according to its kind, and every crawling creature that crawls upon the earth according to its kind, and every flying thing according to its kind, every bird,** and **every** other **winged creature.** ¹⁵**They came to Noah, to the ark, two each from all flesh in which there is the breath of life.** ¹⁶**And they that came, male and female from all flesh came, as God had commanded him; and the Lord shut it for him** to prevent water from penetrating inside.

The Flood

No land animal is spared from the deluge that inundates the world. All life on the earth is annihilated.

Third aliya ¹⁷**The flood was forty days upon the earth, and the water increased, and lifted the ark, and it was raised above the earth.** ¹⁸**The water accumulated and increased greatly upon the earth, and the ark went,** drifted, **upon the face of the water.** ¹⁹**The water accumulated exceedingly upon the earth, and all the high mountains under the entire heavens,** everywhere, **were covered.** ²⁰**Fifteen cubits upward,** above the mountaintops, **the water accumulated, and the mountains were covered.** ²¹**All flesh**

that crawls upon the earth, of the birds, and of the animals, and of the beasts, and of all the swarming creatures that swarm upon the earth, and all mankind, perished. ²²**All in whose nostrils was the breath of the spirit of life,** every living creature **from all that was on the dry land, died.** ²³He obliterated all existence that was upon the face of the earth, from man, to animal, to crawling creature, to birds of the heavens; they were obliterated from the earth. Only Noah remained, and they that were with him in the ark. ²⁴The water accumulated upon the earth for one hundred and fifty days.

The Flood Abates

Even after the rain ceases and the fountains of the deep are again sealed, the water recedes only gradually. The mountaintops are the first pieces of land to be exposed.

8 ¹**God remembered Noah and all the beasts and all the animals that were with him in the ark; God caused a wind to pass over the earth, and the water subsided.** ²**The fountains of the deep and the windows of the heavens were dammed,** closed, **and the rain from the heavens was terminated.** ³**The water receded from upon the earth gradually. And the water was diminished at the end of one hundred and fifty days.** ⁴Then the ark rested, during the seventh month, on the seventeenth day of the month, upon the mountains of Ararat. ⁵And the water gradually receded until the tenth month; during the tenth month, on the first of the month, the peaks of the mountains were** revealed and **seen.**

The Raven and the Dove

In order to determine if the water had receded from the land, Noah first sends out a raven. Afterward he sends out a different bird, a dove.

⁶**It was at the end of forty days** from the time that the tops of the mountains could first be seen; **Noah opened the window of the ark that he made.** ⁷**He sent the raven, and it went** flying **to and fro until the drying of the water from upon the earth.**

⁸**He then sent the dove from him, to see if the waters** had **abated from upon the surface of the ground.** ⁹**But the dove did not find** a place of **rest for its foot, and it returned to him to the ark, as water was on the face of the entire earth, and he extended his hand and took it, and brought it to him to the ark.** ¹⁰**He waited yet another seven days and again sent the dove from the ark.** ¹¹**The dove came in to him at evening time, and behold, it had plucked an olive leaf in its mouth. And Noah knew that the**

waters had abated from upon the earth. ¹²He waited yet another seven days and sent the dove, and it did not return again to him anymore.

¹³It was in the six hundred and first year of Noah's life, during the first month, on the first of the month; the water dried from upon the earth. Noah removed the cover of the ark, and he saw, and behold, the surface of the ground had dried; it was visible but still sodden. ¹⁴During the second month, on, by, the twenty-seventh day of the month, the earth dried fully.

Noah Leaves the Ark

Noah remains in the ark even after the ground has fully dried. Just as he did not enter the ark on his own initiative, so too, now he waits for a divine command to exit it.

Fourth aliya ¹⁵God spoke to Noah, saying: ¹⁶Go out of the ark: You, and your wife, and your sons, and your sons' wives with you. ¹⁷Every living being that is with you from all flesh, of the birds, and of the animals, and of every crawling creature that crawls on the earth, bring out with you. And they will teem on the earth, reproduce, and be fruitful and multiply upon the earth. ¹⁸Noah emerged, and his sons, and his wife, and his sons' wives with him. ¹⁹Every beast, every crawling creature and every bird, everything that crawls on the earth, according to their families of species, emerged from the ark.

> 📖 Further reading: A midrash relates that it was not only living creatures that were rescued in the ark; see the story "Falsehood and Oblivion" in *A Concise Guide to the Sages*, p. 14.

Reconciliation

Now that the sinners have perished, God reconciles with His world. Whereas before the flood, man's evil inclination was the reason for his annihilation, after the flood this same inclination prompts God to forgive and to exercise compassion.

²⁰Noah built an altar to the Lord, and he took from every pure animal and from every pure bird, and sacrificed burnt offerings on the altar. ²¹The Lord smelled the pleasing aroma; He was satisfied. And the Lord said in His heart: I will not continue to curse the ground anymore on account of man, as the inclination of man's heart is evil from his youth, and therefore I will not continue to smite every living being anymore, as I did. ²²As long as the earth endures, the seasons of planting and harvest, and cold and heat, and summer and winter, and day and night, shall not cease.

Hierarchy of Humans and Animals

Before the flood, humans were forbidden to eat meat; apparently even shepherds were vegetarians. Now God both permits people to eat animals, and reiterates the prohibition against spilling the blood of another person.

9 ¹**God blessed Noah and his sons, and He said to them: Be fruitful and multiply, and fill the earth. ²Fear of you and dread of you shall be upon every beast of the earth, upon every bird of the heavens, upon all that crawls on the ground, and upon all fish of the sea. Into your hand they are** all **given. ³Every crawling creature that lives shall be yours for food; like green vegetation I have given you everything** in the world to eat. ⁴**But flesh** from an animal **with its life, its blood,** i.e., from a living animal, **you shall not eat.** This is the prohibition against eating a limb cut from a living animal. ⁵An additional limitation: **But I will demand your blood for your lives; from every beast I will demand it, and from man, from every man for his brother, I will demand the life of man.** A person or animal that spills human blood must be punished. ⁶**One who sheds the blood of man, by man shall his** own **blood be shed, as He made man in the image of God.** ⁷**And you, be fruitful and multiply; teem on the earth,** populate it, **and multiply on it.**

The Rainbow

As part of the rejuvenation of the world after the flood, God renews His connection to humanity and all other living beings by establishing a covenant never to bring another flood of these proportions again. He designates the rainbow, a natural phenomenon, as the sign of this covenant.

Fifth aliya ⁸**God spoke to Noah, and to his sons with him, saying:** ⁹**And I hereby establish My covenant with you, and with your descendants after you, ¹⁰and with every living soul that is with you, with the birds, and with the animals, and with every beast of the earth** that is **with you, from all that emerged from the ark,** extending **to every beast of the earth.** ¹¹**And I will establish My covenant with you,** that **all flesh shall not be excised again by water of the flood; there shall not be a flood anymore to destroy the earth.**

¹²**God said: This is the sign of the covenant that I place between Me and you and every living soul that is with you, for eternal generations:** ¹³**My rainbow I have set in the cloud, and it shall be as a sign of a covenant between Me and the earth.** ¹⁴**It shall be when I bring a cloud over the earth, and the rainbow will be seen in the cloud,** ¹⁵**I will remember My**

covenant that is between Me and you and every living soul of all flesh, and the water shall not become a flood anymore to destroy all flesh. ¹⁶The rainbow shall be in the cloud, and I will see it, to remember the eternal covenant between God and every living creature of all flesh that is upon the earth. ¹⁷God said to Noah: This is the sign of the covenant that I have established between Me and all flesh that is upon the earth.

Ham's Violation of Noah

Ham sees his father drunk, asleep, and exposed, and tells his brothers, who cover Noah in a respectful manner. When Noah awakens, he blesses Shem and Yefet and curses Canaan, Ham's son. Noah's response suggests that Ham or Canaan may have performed a sexual act upon him. This understanding is supported by the description of Ham as seeing his father's nakedness and the fact that the phrase "to reveal nakedness" is the expression used elsewhere in the Torah to refer to forbidden sexual contact.

Sixth aliya ¹⁸The sons of Noah, who emerged from the ark, were Shem, and Ham, and Yefet; and Ham was the father of Canaan. ¹⁹These three were the sons of Noah, and from these the whole earth was filled, with people dispersed all over it. ²⁰Noah, man of the soil, began to descend spiritually, and he planted a vineyard. ²¹He drank of the wine and became drunk, and he was exposed, lying naked inside his tent. ²²Ham, father of Canaan, saw the nakedness of his father and told his two brothers outside. ²³Shem and Yefet took the garment, and they placed it upon both their shoulders. They walked backward, and they covered the nakedness of their father, preserving his dignity. They faced backward, and they did not see the nakedness of their father.

²⁴Noah awoke from his wine and knew what his youngest son had done to him. ²⁵He, Noah, said: Cursed be Ham's son Canaan; a slave of slaves shall he be to his brothers. ²⁶He said: Blessed be the Lord, God of Shem; and Canaan shall be their servant, a servant to the descendants of Shem. ²⁷May God expand [*yaft*] the inheritance of Yefet, and He, God, shall dwell in the tents of Shem; and Canaan shall be their servant, to the descendants of Yefet. ²⁸Noah lived after the flood three hundred and fifty years. ²⁹All the days of Noah were nine hundred and fifty years; and he died.

Noah's Descendants and the Development of the Nations
The Torah lists Noah's descendants, who are considered the founders of nations, and specifies some of the lands in which they settle. Some of these nations and lands are familiar from other biblical contexts, whereas others have not been identified.

10 ¹This is the legacy of the sons of Noah, Shem, Ham, and Yefet; sons were born to them after the flood. ²The sons of Yefet: Gomer, Magog, Madai, Yavan, Tuval, Meshekh, and Tiras. ³The sons of Gomer: Ashkenaz, Rifat, and Togarma. ⁴And the sons of Yavan: Elisha, Tarshish, Kitim, and Dodanim. ⁵From these the island nations were divided into their lands, each after its language, after its families, in their nations.

⁶The sons of Ham: Kush, Mitzrayim, Put, and Canaan. ⁷The sons of Kush: Seva, Havila, Savta, Raama, and Savtekha; and the sons of Raama: Sheva and Dedan. ⁸Kush also begot Nimrod. He, Nimrod, began to be a mighty one on the earth. ⁹He was a mighty hunter before the Lord on a global scale. Therefore it is said, as a folk saying about champions: Like Nimrod, a mighty hunter before the Lord. ¹⁰The beginning of his kingdom was Babel, Erekh, Akad, and Kalne, in the land of Shinar in Mesopotamia. ¹¹From that land Ashur emerged; and he built Nineveh, the city of Rehovot, Kalah, ¹²and Resen, a city between Nineveh and Kalah; that, Nineveh, is the great city. ¹³Mitzrayim begot Ludim, Anamim, Lehavim, Naftuhim, ¹⁴Patrusim, and Kasluhim, from which lands the Philistines emerged, and Kaftorim.

¹⁵Canaan begot Sidon his firstborn, and Het, ¹⁶and the Yevusite, the Emorite, the Girgashite, ¹⁷the Hivite, the Arkite, the Sinite, ¹⁸the Arvadite, the Tzemarite, and the Hamatite; and then the families of the Canaanite dispersed. ¹⁹The border of the Canaanite was from Sidon and as you come toward Gerar until Gaza, and as you come toward Sodom, Gomorrah, Adma, and Tzevoyim, until Lasha. ²⁰These are the sons of Ham, after their families, after their tongues, in their lands, in their nations.

²¹And to Shem, father of all the children of Ever, brother of Yefet, the eldest, children were also born. ²²The sons of Shem: Elam, Ashur, Arpakhshad, Lud, and Aram. ²³The sons of Aram: Utz, Hul, Geter, and Mash. ²⁴And Arpakhshad begot Shela, and Shela begot Ever. ²⁵And to Ever were born two sons; the name of the one was Peleg, as in his days the earth was divided [*niflega*] into nations, and the name of his brother was Yoktan. ²⁶Yoktan begot Almodad, Shelef, Hatzarmavet, Yerah,

²⁷Hadoram, Uzal, Dikla, ²⁸Oval, Avimael, Sheva, ²⁹Ofir, Havila, and Yovav; all these were sons of Yoktan. ³⁰Their dwelling was from Mesha, as you come toward Sefar, on the mountain of the east. ³¹These are the sons of Shem, after their families, after their tongues, in their lands, and after their nations.

³²These are the families of the sons of Noah, in their legacy of descendants, in their nations, and from these the nations were dispersed on the earth after the flood.

The Tower of Babel

A group of people decides to congregate in a metropolis and build a lofty tower that will be seen from afar and which will be their haven. They may also have intended thereby to stage a rebellion against Heaven.

11 ¹The entire earth was of one language and of common words, intentions.
Seventh aliya ²It was as they, a large group, traveled from the east, and they found a plain in the land of Shinar, Babylon, and they settled there. ³Each man said to his counterpart: Come, let us make bricks and burn them thoroughly. The brick was for them hard as stone, and the clay was for them as mortar for cementing bricks and plastering walls. ⁴They said: Come, let us build a city for ourselves, and a tower with its top in the heavens, and let us make a name, glory and promotion for ourselves, lest we be dispersed abroad upon the face of the entire earth, without a common center.

Confusion of Tongues

God wants humanity to settle the whole world and to build productive, creative, and diverse societies. Therefore, He frustrates the people's plan and disperses them all over the earth. According to the opinion that the people were trying to rebel against God, this dispersal is their punishment.

⁵The Lord came down close, as it were, to see the city and the tower that the children of man built. ⁶The Lord said: Behold, they are one people, and there is one language for them all, and building this city is what they have already begun to do. Now nothing of all that they plotted to do will be prevented from them. ⁷Come, let us descend and muddle their language there, so that one will not understand the language of his counterpart. ⁸The Lord dispersed them from there upon the face of the entire earth, and they ceased to build the city. ⁹Therefore, its name, the city's name, was called Babel, because the Lord confounded [*balal*]

the language of all the earth there; and from there the Lord dispersed them on the face of the entire earth.

📖 **Further reading:** For more on the motivations and punishment of the builders of Babel, see *A Concise Guide to the Sages*, p. 16.

From Shem to Abram

The lifespans of people in the generations after the flood are shorter than those of people who lived before the flood. Perhaps the world contains more disease than before.

¹⁰This is the legacy of Shem. Shem was one hundred years old, and he begot Arpakhshad, two years after the flood. ¹¹Shem lived after he begot Arpakhshad five hundred years; and he begot sons and daughters.

¹²Arpakhshad lived thirty-five years, and he begot Shela. ¹³Arpakhshad lived after he begot Shela four hundred and three years; and he begot sons and daughters.

¹⁴Shela lived thirty years, and he begot Ever. ¹⁵Shela lived after he begot Ever four hundred and three years; and he begot sons and daughters.

¹⁶Ever lived thirty-four years, and he begot Peleg. ¹⁷Ever lived after he begot Peleg four hundred and thirty years; and he begot sons and daughters.

¹⁸Peleg lived thirty years, and he begot Re'u. ¹⁹Peleg lived after he begot Re'u two hundred and nine years; and he begot sons and daughters.

²⁰Re'u lived thirty-two years, and he begot Serug. ²¹Re'u lived after he begot Peleg two hundred and seven years; and he begot sons and daughters.

²²Serug lived thirty years, and he begot Nahor. ²³Serug lived after he begot Nahor two hundred years; and he begot sons and daughters.

²⁴Nahor lived twenty-nine years, and he begot Terah. ²⁵Nahor lived after he begot Terah one hundred and nineteen years; and he begot sons and daughters.

²⁶Terah lived seventy years, and during those years he begot Abram, Nahor, and Haran.

📖 **Further reading:** For more on the challenges that faced Abram in his early years, see *A Concise Guide to the Sages*, p. 18.

Family Odyssey

Terah embarks on a long family journey to Canaan but halts in Haran, well before he reaches his destination.

²⁷This is the legacy of Terah: Terah begot Abram, Nahor, and Haran; and Haran begot Lot. ²⁸Haran died during the lifetime of Terah his *Maftir* father, in the land of his birth, in Ur of the Chaldeans. ²⁹Abram and Nahor took wives for themselves; the name of Abram's wife was Sarai; and the name of Nahor's wife was Milka, daughter of his brother Haran, who was the father of Milka and the father of Yiska. ³⁰Sarai was barren; she had no child. ³¹Terah took Abram his son, and Lot son of Haran, who was the son of his son, and Sarai, his daughter-in-law, the wife of his son Abram, and they departed with them from Ur of the Chaldeans to go to the land of Canaan. And they came until Haran, and settled there. ³²The days of Terah were two hundred and five years; and Terah died in Haran.

Further reading: While the Torah provides few details about Abram's life in Haran, the Sages flesh out the narrative in midrashim. See *A Concise Guide to the Sages*, p. 19.

Parashat Lekh Lekha

Abram is commanded to go to Canaan, and upon arriving there with his family, God promises that He will give the land to his descendants, who will become a great nation. Subsequently, famine compels Abram to journey to Egypt, where Sarai is seized and taken to Pharaoh's palace. God punishes Pharaoh, and she is returned to her husband. When Abram returns to Canaan, wealthy, with much livestock and other property, fights break out between his shepherds and his nephew Lot's shepherds, and they part ways. Still, Abram hastens to help when Lot is taken captive, and succeeds in freeing him. He is granted a special prophetic revelation from God, who establishes a covenant with him and again promises him sons and the inheritance of the land. Sarai's maidservant Hagar bears Abram a son, Ishmael. When Abram is ninety-nine years old, God changes his name to Abraham and commands him to circumcise himself and the males of his household.

Abram's Journey

The Torah relates nothing about Abram's personality before God reveals Himself to him and commands him to travel to an unidentified destination. For his part, Abram knows only that he must set out on this journey, and that God promises him great blessings.

12 **¹The Lord said to Abram: Go you from your land, and from your birthplace, and from your father's house,** your family, **to the land that I will show you. ²I will make you** into **a great nation, and I will bless you, and I will make your name great,** you will be renowned, **and you shall be** a paradigm for **a blessing. ³I will bless those who bless you, and he who curses you I will curse; and all the families of the earth shall be blessed through you. ⁴Abram went, as the Lord had spoken to him. And Lot went with him. Abram was five years and seventy years old upon his departure from Haran. ⁵Abram took Sarai his wife, and Lot, son of his brother, and all their property that they had acquired, and the people,** slaves, **that they had acquired in Haran; they departed to go to the land of Canaan; and they came to the land of Canaan.**

⁶Abram passed through the land to the place of, area around, **Shekhem, until the plain** [elon] **of Moreh. And the Canaanites were then in the**

land. ⁷The Lord appeared to Abram upon his arrival in Canaan, and said: To your descendants I will give this land. He built there an altar to the Lord, who had appeared to him. ⁸He moved from there to the mountains east of the city of Beit El, and he pitched his tent there. Beit El was to the west of his place of encampment, and the Ai to the east. He built there an altar to the Lord, and proclaimed the name of the Lord. ⁹Abram journeyed, steadily journeying south, to the Negev.

Sarai in Pharaoh's Palace

Sarai, who possesses great beauty and nobility, is seen by the Egyptians as worthy of marriage to Pharaoh, and is seized and taken to his palace. The Sages count this event, and the famine that spurred Abram and Sarai's trip south, to be among the physical and emotional trials designed to test Abram's faith.

¹⁰There was famine in the land, and therefore Abram descended to Egypt to reside there temporarily, as the famine was severe in the land. ¹¹It was when he drew near to come to Egypt, that he said to Sarai his wife: Behold, I know now that you are a beautiful woman. ¹²It will be when the Egyptians see you that they will say among themselves: This is his wife, and then they will kill me and keep you alive. ¹³Please say to them that you are my sister, so that it may be well with me for your sake; as your brother, no one will have cause to harm me. And my soul shall live because of you.

Second aliya ¹⁴It was upon Abram's arrival in Egypt, the Egyptians saw the woman, that she was very fair. ¹⁵Pharaoh's officers saw her, and they praised her to Pharaoh, and the woman was taken to Pharaoh's house. ¹⁶And he, Pharaoh, benefited Abram for her sake; he, Abram, acquired sheep, oxen, donkeys, slaves, maidservants, female donkeys, and camels.

¹⁷But the Lord afflicted Pharaoh and his household with great afflictions over the matter of Sarai, Abram's wife. ¹⁸Pharaoh called Abram, and he said: What is this that you have done to me? Why did you not tell me that she was your wife? ¹⁹Why did you say: She is my sister? I took her for myself as my wife. And now, here is your wife; take her and go. ²⁰Pharaoh commanded men regarding him, assigned him escorts, and so they sent forth him, and his wife, and everything that was his.

Further reading: For more on Sarai's beauty and Abram's attempts to conceal her from the Egyptians, see A Concise Guide to the Sages, p. 21.

Return to Canaan

Abram retraces his steps north, to Canaan. Everywhere he travels, he continues to publicize God's name and presence.

13 ¹**Abram ascended from Egypt, he, and his wife, and everything that was his, and Lot with him, to the Negev.** ²**And Abram was very wealthy in livestock, in silver, and in gold.** ³**He went on his journeys from the Negev to Beit El, to the place where his tent had been initially, between Beit El and the Ai,** ⁴**to the place of the altar that he prepared there at first;** and **Abram proclaimed** to the people **there the name of the Lord,** praying to Him.

Abram and Lot Part Ways

Abram and Lot live as nomads, migrating from place to place with their flocks and cattle. Although at the time the land was relatively uninhabited, with large areas available for pasture, there is not enough land available for both of them and for the locals.

Third aliya ⁵**Lot, who went with Abram, also had flocks, and cattle, and tents.** ⁶**And the land could not support** both of **them to live together, as their property was substantial, and they were unable to live together.** ⁷**There was** also **a quarrel between the herdsmen of Abram's livestock and the herdsmen of Lot's livestock. And the Canaanites and the Perizites then lived in the land,** posing a potential threat and competition for resources. ⁸**Abram said to Lot: Please, let there be no quarrel between me and you and between my herdsmen and your herdsmen, for we are brethren.** ⁹**Isn't the whole land** available **before you? Please, part from me: If** you go **to the left, I will go** to the **right, and if** you go **to the right, I will go left.**

¹⁰**Lot raised his eyes, and saw the entire plain of the Jordan,** the southern Jordan Valley, **that it was all** well **watered. Before the Lord destroyed Sodom and Gomorrah,** the area of what is today called the Dead Sea was **like the garden of the Lord, like the land of Egypt as,** until, **you come to Tzoar.** ¹¹**Lot chose for himself all the plain of the Jordan. Lot journeyed from the east** of the place where he and Abram were situated, **and they parted one from another.** ¹²**Abram lived in the land of Canaan, and Lot lived in the cities of the plain and pitched his tent as far as Sodom.** ¹³**And the men of Sodom were** known to be **extremely wicked and sinful to the Lord.**

Genesis

The Promise Is Repeated

After Lot departs it becomes evident he is not Abram's heir and will not receive a portion in the land. God therefore reiterates His promise to Abram, of land and offspring.

¹⁴**The Lord said to Abram, after Lot parted from him: Raise now your eyes, and look from the place where you are, northward, southward, eastward, and westward;** ¹⁵**for all the land that you see, I will give to you and to your descendants forever.** ¹⁶**I will render your descendants** numerous **like the dust of the earth; if a man could count the dust of the earth, so shall your descendants be counted.** ¹⁷Therefore **arise, walk in the land to its length and to its breadth, as to you I will give it.** ¹⁸**Abram pitched his tent, and came and settled in the plains of Mamre, which are in Hebron. And he built there an altar to the Lord,** publicizing the name of God.

The Northern Kings' Campaign of Conquest

Despite their great distance from Canaan, the kings who rule over Mesopotamia are the dominant forces in the Land of Israel. They conduct a punitive campaign to defeat the local rulers who rebel against their supremacy.

14 ¹**It was in the days of Amrafel king of Shinar,** Babylon; **Aryokh king of**
Fourth **Elasar,** northeast of Babylon; **Kedorlaomer king of Elam,** also northeast
aliya of Babylon; **and Tidal king of Goyim,** or of several small nations [*goyim*]. ²**They waged war with Bera king of Sodom, and with Birsha king of Gomorrah, Shinav king of Adma, and Shemever king of Tzevoyim, and the king of Bela, which is** also called **Tzoar.** ³**All these,** the kings of Sodom, Gomorrah, Adma, Tzevoyim, and Bela, **joined forces at the valley of Sidim, which is** later called **the Dead Sea.**

⁴For **twelve years they** had **served Kedorlaomer,** the strongest northern king. **And in the thirteenth year, they rebelled.** ⁵**And in the fourteenth year, Kedorlaomer and the kings that were with him came and smote** the **Refaim in Ashterot Karnayim, and the Zuzim in Ham, and the Eimim in Shaveh Kiryatayim.** The Refaim, Zuzim, and Eimim were ancient tribes of giants. ⁶They then advanced south **and** smote **the Horites in their mountain, Se'ir, until Eil Paran, which is adjacent to the wilderness** of Sinai. ⁷**They** then **turned back** north **and came to Ein Mishpat, which is Kadesh, and smote the entire field of the Amalekites,** the region where the tribe of Amalek would later settle. **And** they **also** smote **the Emorites, who lived in Hatzatzon Tamar.**

The Four Kings Versus the Five Kings

Although the local kings outnumber the foreign ones, the actual balance of power dramatically favors the kings of the north, whose imperial forces are far superior to those of the local small fiefdoms.

[8]The king of Sodom, the king of Gomorrah, the king of Adma, the king of Tzevoyim, and the king of Bela, which is Tzoar, went out to the northern kings, **and they waged a war with them in the valley of Sidim.** [9]They fought **with Kedorlaomer king of Elam, and Tidal king of Goyim, and Amrafel king of Shinar, and Aryokh king of Elasar; four kings against the five.** [10]**The valley of Sidim was full of clay pits, and the kings of Sodom and Gomorrah fled, and they fell there,** into the pits, **and those who remained** of the defeated army **fled to the highlands.** [11]**They,** the four northern kings, **took all the property of Sodom and Gomorrah and** looted **all their food** for their own armies. **And** then **they went,** heading back to Mesopotamia. [12]**They took Lot,** who was the **son of Abram's brother, and** took **his property, and they went; and** although he did not take part in the war, nevertheless, because **he lived in Sodom** he was taken **captive.**

Surprise Attack

In the midst of the northern kings' triumphant march back, Abram and his retainers mount a surprise attack. The four kings abandon their booty and flee.

[13]**The** battle **survivor came and told Abram the Hebrew** [*Ivri*], a descendant of Ever; **and he was dwelling on the plains of Mamre the Emorite,** who was the **brother of Eshkol, and the brother of Aner, and they were** all **allies of Abram.** [14]**Abram heard that his brother,** Lot, his nephew, **had been taken captive. And he marshaled his retainers** to battle**,** some of whom had been **born in his house** and grown up in his camp; **three hundred and eighteen** soldiers in all. **And** Abram **pursued** the kings' camp **until** the region of **Dan.** [15]**He, Abram, arrayed his men against them at night, he and his servants, and smote them, and pursued them until Hova, which is to the left,** north, **of Damascus.** [16]**He brought back all the goods, and also his brother Lot and his property he returned, and also the women and the** other **people** taken captive.

Abram Is Greeted as Victor

Two people come to greet Abram upon his return to the Hebron area. The first is Malkitzedek, who is both a king and a non-idolatrous priest, one of the few believers in monotheism.

Genesis

The second is the defeated king of Sodom, who attempts to negotiate with Abram over the plunder.

¹⁷**The king of Sodom went out to meet him, after his return from smiting Kedorlaomer and the kings who were with him, to the valley of Shaveh, which is the valley of the king.** ¹⁸**And Malkitzedek king of Shalem,** another name for Jerusalem, **brought out bread and wine,** for a ritual greeting. **And he,** Malkitzedek, **was** not only a king, but also **a priest of God the Most High,** not of pagan gods. ¹⁹**He,** Malkitzedek, **blessed him, and he said: Blessed is Abram to God the Most High, master of heaven and earth,** ²⁰**and blessed is God the Most High, who delivered your enemies into your hand. He,** Abram, **gave him a tenth of all** the booty.

Fifth aliya ²¹Seeing Abram's generosity, **the king of Sodom said to Abram: Give me the people, and take the property for yourself.** ²²**Abram said to the king of Sodom: I have raised my hand** to swear **to the Lord God Most High, master of heaven and earth.** ²³**Surely, be it** even **a thread** of a garment **or a shoelace, I will not take of anything that is yours,** that I returned to you, **so that you will not say: I made Abram rich.** ²⁴Distribute the booty **without regard to me,** with the exception **only of that which the young men have** already **eaten** from the property we have restored, **and** also **the portion of the men who went with me: Aner, Eshkol, and Mamre; they shall take their** rightful **portion.**

Assurance of Progeny

After Abram's war with the great kings of the north, he may have been concerned that they would return to Canaan to avenge their losses. He receives a revelation from God, who reassures him.

15 ¹**After these matters, the word of the Lord came to Abram in a** prophetic **vision, saying: Fear not, Abram, I am a shield,** protection, **for you.** Additionally, **your** future **reward** for your deeds **is very great.** ²**Abram said: My Lord God, what will You give me** that is meaningful, given that **I go childless? And the steward of my house** and business dealings, in absence of a son, **is Eliezer of,** from, **Damascus.** ³**Abram said: Behold, to me You have not given descendants, and a member of my household,** not my child, **is my heir.** ⁴**Behold, the word of the Lord came to him, saying: This** man, Eliezer, **shall not be your heir; rather, one who shall emerge from your loins, he shall be your heir.** ⁵**He took him outside** the tent, **and said: Look now toward the heavens, and count the stars;** see **if**

you can count them. And He said to him: So shall be your descendants; they will be as numerous as the stars. **⁶He, Abram, believed in the Lord, and He considered it for him as righteousness;** God saw Abram's believing in Him as a fitting and upright act.

> 📖 **Further reading:** For more on the significance of the blessing, "So shall be your descendants," see *A Concise Guide to the Sages*, p. 22.

The Covenant between the Parts

God's promise is enshrined in a covenant through the symbolic act of bisecting animals. This ritual underscores the connection between the two parties to the covenant, as though they are two halves of one whole. God also reveals to Abram that his descendants will be exiled and then will return to Canaan to inherit the land.

Sixth aliya **⁷He said to him: I am the Lord who took you out of Ur of the Chaldeans, to give you this land to inherit it. ⁸He said: My Lord God, how shall I know that I shall inherit it?** Please give me a sign. **⁹He said to him: Take for Me a triple heifer,** three heifers, **and a triple female goat, and a triple ram, and a dove, and a young pigeon. ¹⁰He took all these** slaughtered animals **for Him, divided them in the middle, and placed each half opposite the other. But the birds,** the dove and young pigeon, **he did not divide. ¹¹The birds of prey,** carrion-feeding birds, **descended onto the carcasses. And Abram drove them away. ¹²It was when the sun was setting; a deep sleep fell upon Abram. And behold, a dread, a great darkness,** a terrible, unexplained fear, **fell upon him. ¹³He,** God, **said to Abram: Know that your descendants shall be strangers in a land that is not theirs. And they shall be enslaved to them,** to the inhabitants of that foreign land, **and they shall oppress them for four hundred years. ¹⁴And also that nation that they shall serve, I will judge, and afterward, they,** your children, **will emerge** from there **with great property. ¹⁵And** before this occurs **you shall go to your fathers,** you will die and be united with your ancestors **in peace,** and **you shall be buried at a good old age. ¹⁶And the fourth generation** of your descendants **shall return here** to inherit the promised land, **for the iniquity of the Emorite is not complete until then,** their sin will not yet be sufficient to incur punishment. **¹⁷It was when the sun had set, and there was extreme darkness, and behold, a smoking furnace,** a thick cloud of smoke, like the smoke that emerges from a furnace, **and a flaming torch that passed between those pieces,** the animal halves. The smoking furnace and smoking torch represent the Divine Presence passing between the pieces, thereby completing the covenantal ritual. **¹⁸On**

that day, the Lord established a covenant with Abram, saying: **To your descendants I have given this land,** according to my promise, **from the river of Egypt,** the Nile, **until the great river, the Euphrates River.** [19]This includes the lands of **the Kenites, the Kenizites, the Kadmonites,** [20]**the Hitites, the Perizites, the Refaim,** who were giants, [21]**the Emorites, the Canaanites, the Girgashites, and the Yevusites.**

Illustrations: See map of the Promised Land, p. 521.

Hagar Is Given to Abram

Sarai offers her maidservant Hagar to Abram as an additional wife, to bear him children, an act that was considered auspicious for her own fertility. When Hagar becomes pregnant, she treats Sarai contemptuously.

16 [1]**And Sarai, Abram's wife, bore him no children. And she had an Egyptian maidservant, and her name was Hagar.** [2]**Sarai said to Abram: Please, behold, the Lord has kept me from bearing** children; I cannot give birth. **Please, consort with my maidservant; perhaps I shall be built** and have children **through her,** or following her pregnancy. **Abram heeded the voice of Sarai.** [3]**Sarai, Abram's wife, took Hagar the Egyptian, her maidservant, at the conclusion of ten years of Abram's residence in the land of Canaan. And she gave her to Abram her husband as a wife.** [4]**He consorted with Hagar, and she conceived; she saw that she conceived, and** the status of **her mistress was diminished in her eyes.**

[5]**Sarai said to Abram: The villainy done to me is on you;** you have done me wrong. **I gave my maidservant into your bosom** as a wife, **and then she saw that she conceived, and I was diminished in her eyes.** Therefore, **the Lord shall judge between me and you.** This was not an outright accusation that Abram had harmed her, but a demand that he stand by her side in a more conspicuous manner. [6]**Abram said to Sarai: Behold, your maid is in your hand. Do to her that which is favorable,** appropriate, **in your eyes. Sarai treated her harshly, and she,** Hagar, **fled from her.**

The Vision and Ishmael's Birth

Hagar is more than a lowly maidservant; she is a woman who merits a prophetic revelation. Apparently she absorbed some understanding of God's ways from living in Abram's household. She recognizes that an angel is merely an agent of God, and cannot act independently.

⁷The angel of the Lord found her in the wilderness at or next to the spring of water on the way to Shur, in the Negev. ⁸He said: Hagar, Sarai's maidservant, from where did you come, and where will you go? She said: From my mistress Sarai I flee. ⁹The angel of the Lord said to her: Return to your mistress, and suffer under her hands; accept her treatment of you. ¹⁰The angel of the Lord said to her: I will greatly multiply your descendants, and they shall not be counted due to their great number. ¹¹The angel of the Lord said to her: Behold, you are with child, and shall bear a son. You shall call his name Ishmael, as the Lord has heard [shama] your suffering. ¹²He shall be a wild, uncontrolled, man, with a reputation as an unsettled figure. His hand shall be against everyone, and everyone's hand against him; he will be drawn to banditry and continually involved in quarrels and wars. And yet he shall dwell among all his brethren, achieving the highest status among them. ¹³She called, described, the name of the Lord who spoke to her as: You are the God of my vision, the God who reveals Himself. For she said: Have I seen a revelation here too, after my vision, in addition to those I saw in Abram's house? ¹⁴Therefore, one called the cistern Be'er Lahai Ro'i, meaning the well [be'er] of the living [ḥai] God of my vision [ro'i]. Behold, it is located between Kadesh and Bered, south of Canaan.

¹⁵Hagar returned home and bore to Abram a son; Abram called the name of his son, whom Hagar bore, Ishmael. ¹⁶And Abram was eighty-six years old when Hagar bore Ishmael to Abram.

A Personal Covenant

God had already established the Covenant between the Parts with Abram, a covenant that consisted of the eternal acquisition of the land of Canaan, and the continuation of his lineage. Now God establishes a more personal covenant with him.

17 ¹Abram was ninety-nine years old, and the Lord appeared to Abram; He said to him: I am God Almighty. Walk before Me, serve Me, and be wholehearted in your faith. ²I shall establish My covenant between Me and you, and will multiply you exceedingly. ³Abram fell upon his face in awe, due to the prophecy, and as an expression of his submission to God. And God spoke with him, saying: ⁴I, My covenant is hereby being established with you, and you shall be the father of a multitude of nations. ⁵To match your new status, your name shall no longer be called Abram, meaning lofty father. But rather, your name shall be Abraham, for I have made you the father of a multitude of nations, the meaning

of the name Abraham. **⁶I will make you exceedingly fruitful, I will make you into** the progenitor of various **nations, and kings shall emerge from** *Seventh aliya* **you** and rule, each in his own realm. **⁷I will establish My covenant,** a private, personal connection, **between Me and you, and your descendants after you throughout their generations, for an eternal covenant, to be your God, and for your descendants after you.** ⁸As part of this covenant, **I will give to you and to your descendants after you the land of your residence, the entire land of Canaan, for an eternal portion. And I will be their God.**

The Command to Circumcise

The covenant constitutes God's relationship with Abraham and his descendants, while the circumcision serves as a concrete symbol. It is both an indication of the covenant and a reminder to uphold it.

⁹God said to Abraham: And you, you shall observe My covenant, you and your descendants after you, throughout their generations. ¹⁰This is My covenant that you shall observe, between Me and you and between your descendants after you: Circumcise every male among you. ¹¹You shall circumcise the flesh of your foreskin, and it, this act, **shall be a mark of a covenant between Me and you. ¹²And one who is eight days old shall be circumcised among you, every male throughout your generations,** whether he is **born in the house** as a member of the family or household, **or** whether he is **purchased with silver** as a slave, **from any foreigner, who is not of your descendants. ¹³Circumcise those born in your house, or those purchased with your silver, and** the mark of **My covenant shall be in your flesh for an eternal covenant** throughout the generations. **¹⁴And the uncircumcised male** among your descendants **who shall not circumcise the flesh of his foreskin, that soul shall be excised from his people** and from its source, as **he has breached My covenant.**

Prophecy about Isaac and Ishmael

God announces that Sarai's name will be changed as well. From now on she will be called Sarah, meaning "dignitary," instead of Sarai, meaning "my dignitary." This is a sign of her new status, as she is to give birth to Abraham's spiritual and material heir.

¹⁵God said to Abraham: Sarai your wife, you shall not call her name Sarai, as Sarah is her name. ¹⁶I will bless her with various blessings, **and I will also give you a son from her; I will bless her, and she** too **shall become** the mother of **nations. Kings of peoples shall be** descended

from her. [17]Abraham fell upon his face in submission, **and he laughed** with joy. Nevertheless, **he said in his heart: Shall a child be born to one who is one hundred years old?** Will I become a father again at age one hundred? **And if it is Sarah, shall a ninety-year-old woman give birth?** [18]**Abraham said to God: If only Ishmael shall live before You.** Give him Your blessing, as my son.

[19]**God said: But** indeed, **Sarah your wife shall bear you a son, and you shall call his name Isaac. And I will keep My covenant with him for an eternal covenant for his descendants after him.** [20]**And as for Ishmael, I have heard you,** and your wish will be partially fulfilled. **Behold, I** have **blessed him, I will make him fruitful, and I will multiply him exceedingly; twelve princes shall he beget, and I will make him** too into **a great nation.** [21]**But My covenant I will keep with Isaac, whom Sarah shall bear** to **you at the designated time,** on this same date, **in another year,** next year. [22]**He,** God, **concluded speaking with him, and God ascended from upon Abraham** back to heaven, as it were.

Abraham Is Circumcised

Abraham circumcises himself on the same day he receives God's command to do so. This incident and others demonstrate his character as one who obeys God without delay.

[23]**Abraham took Ishmael his son, and all those born in his house, and all those purchased with his silver, every male among the people of Abraham's household, and he circumcised the flesh of their foreskin on** *Maftir* **that very day, as God had spoken with him.** [24]**Abraham was ninety-nine years old when he was circumcised in the flesh of his foreskin.** [25]**And Ishmael his son was thirteen years old when he was circumcised in the flesh of his foreskin.** [26]**On that very day, Abraham was circumcised, and** so was **Ishmael his son.** [27]**And all the people of his household,** whether **born in the house or purchased with silver from a foreigner, were cir- cumcised with him.**

📖 **Further reading:** For more on the inner significance of circumcision, see *A Concise Guide to the Sages*, p. 144; *A Concise Guide to Mahshava*, p. 9. The ceremony of circumcision and the manner in which circumcision is performed are described in *A Concise Guide to Halakha*, p. 5.

Parashat Vayera

Three angels presenting themselves as travelers arrive at Abraham's tent and Abraham welcomes his guests warmly. After they inform him that he will father a son, two of the angels continue to the city of Sodom, which is about to be destroyed. Abraham prays to God and requests His mercy for the city, but he is ultimately unable to stop the decree from being carried out; only Lot and two of his daughters are saved from the calamity. Abraham travels to Gerar, where Sarah is again taken into the household of the local king, but once the king discovers the truth of her identity he returns her to Abraham. After the prophecy of Yitzchak's birth is fulfilled, Sarah demands that Abraham expel Hagar and her son Ishmael, who has become a negative influence. The *parasha* concludes with the dramatic story of the binding of Isaac.

Abraham's Hospitality

Shortly after Abraham circumcises himself, God again appears to him, but immediately afterward, visitors arrive at Abraham's tent. Eager to welcome them and show them honor, he entreats God to wait for him until he has fulfilled his duty as a host.

18 ¹**The Lord appeared to him in the plains of Mamre, and** this occurred when **he,** Abraham, **sat at the entrance of the tent as the day grew unusually hot.** ²**He,** Abraham, **lifted his eyes and saw, and behold, three men were standing before him.** He saw them, **ran toward them from the entrance of the tent, and prostrated himself to the earth.** ³**He said: My Lord, please, if I have found favor in Your eyes,** if You wish, **please do not depart from upon your servant,** from me. ⁴Abraham turned to the men and said: **Please, let a little water be taken, and wash your feet** and rest. **And recline beneath the tree,** in the shade. ⁵**I will take a portion of bread** for you, **and you shall sustain your heart** by eating, and only **thereafter depart; as for this** opportunity **you have happened** to come **upon your servant. They said: Do so, as you have said.**

⁶**Abraham hurried to the tent, to Sarah, and said: Hurry** and take **three se'a,** a significant amount, **of choice flour, knead** dough, **and make cakes,** bread. ⁷**Abraham ran to the cattle, took a** choice **bullock, tender and good, and gave it to the** serving **lad; and he,** the lad, **hurried to prepare**

it. **⁸He took butter, milk, and the bullock that he prepared, and placed it before them,** the visitors. **He stood over them beneath the tree,** standing by to serve them, **and they ate.**

📖 **Further reading:** Who were the three guests who visited Abraham? See *A Concise Guide to the Sages,* p. 26.

Prophecy about Isaac's Birth

Abraham's guests not only know his wife's name, they bring incredible news, which Sarah can scarcely credit. Clearly, they are angels, not ordinary men.

⁹They said to him: Where is Sarah, your wife? He said: **Behold,** she is **in the tent.** **¹⁰He,** the leader of the guests, **said: I will return to you at this time next year, and behold,** there will be **a son for Sarah, your wife. And Sarah was listening at the entrance of the tent, and it,** the entrance, **was behind him,** the guest. **¹¹**The Torah notes: **Abraham and Sarah were old, advanced in years. It had ceased to be with Sarah the manner of women,** meaning that she no longer experienced a menstrual cycle. **¹²Sarah laughed inside herself,** silently, **saying: After my languishing** and old age, **shall I have youth** and fertility? **And my lord** Abraham **is old** too. **¹³The Lord said to Abraham: Why is it that Sarah laughed, saying: Shall I indeed bear a child, and I have grown old? ¹⁴Is any matter beyond the power of the Lord? At the designated time I will return to you, at this** time next year, **and Sarah shall have a son. ¹⁵Sarah denied it, saying: I did not laugh, for she was afraid** to admit to doubting God's promise. **He said: No, but you did laugh.**

Second aliya

Abraham Attempts to Save Sodom

Wickedness has become pervasive and institutionalized in Sodom, a flourishing city in the Jordan Valley. God decrees that He will destroy the city, and informs Abraham, as it is part of the land He promised him. Abraham intercedes on behalf of Sodom.

¹⁶The visiting **men arose from there and looked** out from the hills **toward Sodom. And Abraham was walking with them to see them off. ¹⁷The Lord said** to Himself: **Shall I conceal from Abraham that which I am doing? ¹⁸And Abraham shall become a great and mighty nation.** He will be a central figure in history, **and all the nations of the earth shall be blessed through him. ¹⁹For** since **I love him,** I will not conceal what I am doing **so that he shall command his children and his household after him, and they will observe the way of the Lord, to perform righteousness and justice; so that the Lord will bring upon Abraham**

that which He spoke of and promised him. ²⁰The Lord said: Because the outcry of the oppressed individuals in **Sodom and Gomorrah is great** and increasing, **and because their sin is very heavy,** ²¹**I will descend now and see; if they have acted** wickedly, **in accordance with the outcry that has reached Me,** I will bring **destruction** upon them, **and if not, I will know** how to deal with them.

📖 Further reading: For more on the severe sins of the residents of Sodom, see *A Concise Guide to the Sages*, p. 27.

²²**The men turned from there and went to Sodom, and Abraham was still standing before the Lord,** receiving His revelation about Sodom. ²³**Abraham approached, and he said: Will You destroy even the righteous with the wicked?** ²⁴**Perhaps there are fifty righteous people within the city** of Sodom; **will You even destroy, and not tolerate,** or forgive, **the place for the sake of the fifty righteous people who are within it?** ²⁵**It is inconceivable for You to do a** disgraceful **thing like this, to kill the righteous with the wicked, and** that **the righteous shall be** given the same fate **as the wicked. It is inconceivable for You; shall the Judge of all the earth not practice justice?** ²⁶**The Lord said: If I find in Sodom fifty righteous people within the city, I will tolerate** and forgive **the entire place for their sake.** ²⁷**Abraham responded and said: Behold, I have presumed** to begin **to speak to my Lord, and yet I am** as **dust and ashes.** ²⁸**Still, perhaps the fifty righteous people will lack five;** there might be only forty-five righteous people in Sodom. **Will You destroy the entire city for the** lack **of five? He,** God, **said: I will not destroy** it **if I find there forty-five.** ²⁹**He continued to speak to Him and said: Perhaps forty** righteous people **shall be found there. He said: I will not do it;** I will spare the city even **for the sake of the forty.** ³⁰**He said: Let my Lord please not be incensed, and I will** continue to **speak. Perhaps thirty shall be found there. He said: I will not do it, if I find thirty there.** ³¹**He said: Behold, I have presumed to speak to my Lord; perhaps twenty shall be found there. He said: I will not destroy, for the twenty.** ³²**He said: Please, let my Lord not be incensed, and I will speak only this time. Perhaps ten shall be found there. He said: I will not destroy, for the ten.** ³³**The Lord went when He concluded speaking to Abraham, and Abraham returned to his place.**

Lot Welcomes the Angels

As yet, only one of the angels visiting Abraham has performed a task, informing Abraham and Sarah of their forthcoming son. The other two angels set off for Sodom, where they are to fulfill their mission of punishing the city of evildoers.

19 ¹**The two angels came to Sodom in the evening. And Lot was sitting**
Third
aliya **at the gate of Sodom,** as a judge. **Lot saw them and rose to meet them, and he prostrated himself with his face to the earth.** ²**He said: Behold now my lords, please turn aside to your servant's house; stay the night, and wash your feet, and you shall awaken early and go on your way. They said: No, for we will stay the night in the street.** ³**He implored them greatly, and they turned aside to him and entered his house. He prepared a feast for them, he baked unleavened bread, and they ate.**

The Residents of Sodom Mob Lot's House

Visitors are unwelcome in Sodom; the residents demand that Lot hand over his guests to them so that they can dishonor and abuse them. While Lot defends his guests to the best of his ability, his response demonstrates that his moral sense has nevertheless become corrupted.

⁴**Before they,** the angels, **lay down** to sleep, **the men of the city, the men of Sodom, surrounded the house, from young to old, all the people from every quarter.** ⁵**They called to Lot, and said to him: Where are the men who came to you tonight? Bring them out to us, and we will be intimate with them,** exploit them sexually. ⁶**Lot went out to them,** the residents of the city, **to the entrance** of his home, **and he closed the door behind him.** ⁷**He said: Please, my brethren, do not do evil.** ⁸**Here now are my two** virgin **daughters who have not been intimate with a man; I will now bring them out to you, and you may do to them as is fit in your eyes,** whatever you want. **Only to these men do nothing, as for this they came under the shelter of my roof.** ⁹**They said: Move aside. And they said: This one came to reside, and he sits in judgment? Now** if you insist on protecting them **we will treat you worse than them. They implored the man, Lot, and they approached to break the door.**

Lot Is Rescued

The angels reveal to Lot the dual purpose of their arrival: To destroy the city and to rescue Lot and his family. Lot dithers, perhaps still unsure of his guests' identity. Finally, the angels shepherd him out of Sodom by force and instruct him where to flee.

¹⁰The men, the angels, extended their hand and brought Lot to them, to the house, and closed the door. ¹¹They smote the men who were at the entrance of the house with blindness, from small to great, so that they, the residents, were unable to find the entrance. ¹²The men, the angels, said to Lot: Who else have you here? Do you have any family in the city? A son-in-law, and your sons, and your daughters, and everyone whom you have in the city, remove from the place. ¹³For we are destroying this place, as their outcry, that of the oppressed and ill-treated in the city, has amassed before the Lord, and the Lord sent us to destroy it. ¹⁴Lot came out, and spoke to his sons-in-law, who had betrothed his daughters. And he said: Arise, depart from this place, for the Lord is destroying the city. But he seemed as only one who jests, in the eyes of his sons-in-law.

¹⁵About when the dawn broke, the angels urged Lot, saying: Arise; take your wife and your two daughters who are present in the house, lest you too be destroyed in the iniquity of the city. ¹⁶But he hesitated, and the men forcefully grasped his hand, the hand of his wife, and the hand of each of his two daughters, saving them out of the compassion of the Lord for him. They took him out and placed him outside the city. ¹⁷It was when they took them out that he, one of the angels, said: Flee for your life; do not look behind you and do not stay in the entire plain of the Jordan. Flee to the highlands, lest you be destroyed.

¹⁸Lot said to them: Please, no, my lords. ¹⁹Please, behold, your servant has found favor in your eyes, and you have increased your kindness that you have done with me to save my life. But I will not be able to flee to the highlands, lest the evil overtake me on the way and I die. ²⁰Here now, this city is near to flee there, and it is small; please, I will flee there, and perhaps there my life will be saved. ²¹He, the angel, said to him: Behold, I have granted your request for this matter as well, not to overturn the city of which you spoke. ²²Hurry and flee there, as I will not be able to do anything until your arrival there. The Torah notes: Therefore, he called the name of the small [mitz'ar] city Tzoar.

Fourth aliya

Sodom and Gomorrah Are Destroyed

Lot's wife, who may have been a native of Sodom, disregards the angel's instruction during the family's flight from Sodom. Whether out of curiosity, compassion, or emotional distress, she turns to look back while Sodom is overturned, and she immediately dies.

²³The sun rose upon the earth, and Lot came to Tzoar. ²⁴The Lord rained brimstone and fire upon Sodom and upon Gomorrah, from the Lord, from the heavens. ²⁵He overturned those cities, the entire plain, all the inhabitants of the cities, and the vegetation of the earth. ²⁶His, Lot's, wife looked behind him, and she became a pillar of salt. ²⁷Abraham arose early in the morning, to the place where he stood before the Lord. ²⁸He looked over Sodom and Gomorrah, and over all the land of the plain of the Jordan, the region that is currently the Dead Sea. And he saw that behold, the smoke of the earth rose thickly, like the smoke of a kiln. ²⁹The Torah summarizes the previous events: It was when God destroyed the cities of the plain, Sodom, Gomorrah, Adma, and Tzevoyim, that God remembered Abraham. And due to Abraham's merit, He sent Lot from the midst of the upheaval, as He overturned the cities in which Lot lived.

Lot's Daughters' Plan

Lot's daughters assume that a global catastrophe like the flood has occurred and that they are the only survivors. Believing that the continuation of the human race depends on them, and embarrassed to discuss the particulars with their father, Lot's daughters devise a plan to procreate with him, without his awareness.

³⁰Lot ascended from Tzoar and lived in the hills, and his two daughters with him, because he feared to live in Tzoar. And he lived in a cave, he and his two daughters. ³¹The elder daughter said to the younger: Our father is old, and there is no other man left on the earth to consort with us in the way of the world. ³²Let us give our father ample wine to drink, and we will lie with him, and we will give life to offspring from our father. ³³They gave their father wine to drink that night. The elder came and lay with her father, and in his drunken state he did not know when she lay or when she arose.

³⁴It was the next day, and the elder said to the younger: Behold, I lay last night with my father. Let us give him wine to drink tonight as well, and you come and lie with him; and we will give life to offspring from our father. ³⁵They gave their father wine to drink that night as well. The younger arose and lay with him, and he did not know when she lay or when she arose.

³⁶Lot's two daughters conceived from their father. ³⁷The elder gave birth to a son and called his name Moav, meaning: From father [me'av]; he is the ancestor of the Moavites to this day. ³⁸The younger too gave

birth to a son, and called his name Ben Ami. He is the ancestor of the descendants of [*benei*] Amon to this day.

Sarah Is Taken to the King of Gerar

Abraham and Sarah migrate to Philistine territory, where they find themselves in a predicament similar to that which they experienced in Egypt with Pharaoh. Abraham adopts the same precautions he used there, and does not admit that he and Sarah are married.

20 ¹Abraham journeyed from there to the land of the south; he lived between Kadesh and Shur, in the Negev; and he resided in Gerar, a Philistine city. ²Abraham said of Sarah his wife: She is my sister. Avimelekh king of Gerar sent messengers and took Sarah as a wife.

³God came to Avimelekh in a dream at night, and He said to him: Behold, you shall die, because of the woman that you have taken, and she is married to a husband. ⁴Avimelekh had not approached her sexually, even before God spoke to him. He said: Lord, will You kill me when I am a nation, a king, who is also righteous? ⁵Did he, Abraham, not say to me: She is my sister? And she, Sarah, she too said: He is my brother. In the innocence of my heart and in the cleanliness of my hands I did this; I behaved honorably. ⁶God said to him in the dream: I also knew that in the innocence of your heart you did this, and I also prevented you from sinning to Me. Therefore, I did not allow you to touch her. ⁷Now, restore the man's wife, as he is a prophet, and he shall pray for you, and you will live. And if you do not restore her, know that you shall die, you and all relatives that are yours.

Avimelekh Returns Sarah

Avimelekh, who sees himself as an upright and noble king, claims that he is innocent of any wrongdoing and demands an explanation from Abraham. After Abraham justifies his actions, Avimelekh invites him to settle in his land. Avimelekh's behavior contrasts to that of Pharaoh, earlier, as after Pharaoh's household was afflicted following his seizing of Sarah, Pharaoh became frightened and expelled Abraham from Egypt.

⁸Avimelekh rose early in the morning, and he called all his servants and spoke all these matters in their ears; and the men were very frightened due to the threat to their king's life. ⁹Avimelekh called Abraham, and said to him: What have you done to us, and how have I sinned against you, that you have brought upon me and upon my kingdom a great sin? Deeds that may not be done, you have done to me. ¹⁰Avimelekh said

to Abraham: What did you see that you did this thing? What were you thinking? [11]Abraham said: Because I said to myself: **Surely, there is no fear of God in this place, and they will kill me over the matter of my wife.** [12]**Also, she is indeed my sister, the daughter of my father, but** she **is not the daughter of my mother; and she became my wife.** [13]**It was, when God caused me to wander from my father's house** as a nomad, that I said to her: This is your kindness that you shall perform for me; at every place that we shall come, say of me: He is my brother.

[14]**Avimelekh took flocks and cattle, and slaves and maidservants, and he gave them to Abraham, and he restored his wife Sarah to him.** [15]**Avimelekh said: Behold, my land is before you: Live where it is fit in your eyes.** [16]**And to Sarah he said: Behold, I have given your brother Abraham a thousand of silver; behold, it is a covering of the eyes for you to all who are with you;** it will protect you from criticism, **and to all you are vindicated.**

[17]**Abraham prayed to God, and God healed Avimelekh, his wife, and his maidservants, and they bore children.** [18]**For the Lord had obstructed all wombs of the house of Avimelekh,** over the matter of taking **Sarah, Abraham's wife.**

Isaac's Birth and Weaning

The birth of a child in a parent's old age comes as a joyous surprise; this is expressed in the poetic manner and celebratory mood of the Torah's report of Isaac's birth.

21 [1]**The Lord remembered** [pakad] **Sarah** for good, **as He had said** through the angels, **and the Lord did to Sarah as He had spoken.** [2]**Sarah conceived, and bore Abraham a son in his old age, at the designated time that God had told him,** one year after the angels had visited his tent. [3]**Abraham called the name of his son that was born to him, whom Sarah bore to him, Isaac.** [4]**Abraham circumcised his son Isaac when he was eight days old, as God had commanded him.**

Fifth aliya [5]**Abraham was one hundred years old when his son Isaac was born to him.** [6]**Sarah said: God has made laughter for me.** This is an unusual and happy occurrence, prompting laughter. **Everyone who hears will laugh for me** and share in my joy. [7]**She said: Who would have said of Abraham that Sarah would nurse children, as I bore** him **a son for his old age?** [8]**The child grew and was weaned, and Abraham made a great feast on the day Isaac was weaned.**

📖 **Further reading:** For more on the miraculous events surrounding Isaac's birth, see *A Concise Guide to the Sages*, p. 28.

Banishment of Hagar and Ishmael

Sarah is concerned about Ishmael's problematic conduct and demands that Abraham exile him and his mother. Since God concurs, Abraham banishes them. Nevertheless, Ishmael is not abandoned or forgotten; he is miraculously saved in the wilderness, and Hagar receives a prophecy about his illustrious future.

⁹**Sarah saw the son of Hagar the Egyptian, whom she,** Hagar, **bore to Abraham, playing,** engaging in immoral behavior. ¹⁰**She said to Abraham: Banish this maidservant and her son, for the son of this maidservant shall not inherit with my son, with Isaac,** or grow up as his brother. ¹¹**The matter was very grave in the eyes of Abraham,** and he was pained **on account of** the misconduct of **his son.** ¹²**But God said to Abraham: Let it not be grave in your eyes about the lad and about your maidservant. Everything that Sarah says to you, heed her voice, for it is through Isaac that descendants will be accounted to you;** only Isaac will be your heir and successor. ¹³**Also the son of the maidservant I will make** the patriarch of **a nation.**

¹⁴**Abraham rose early in the morning;** he **took bread and a skin of water and gave it,** the provisions, **to Hagar, placed it on her shoulder, and** gave her **the child, and sent her away. She went and wandered in the wilderness of Beersheba.** ¹⁵**Eventually, the water in the skin was finished, and she cast the child** into the shade **beneath one of the bushes.** ¹⁶**She went and sat herself down at a** far **distance, approximately a bowshot removed,** around 170 m. **For she said** to herself: In this way **I will not see the death of the child. She sat at a distance, raised her voice, and wept.**

¹⁷**God heard the voice of the lad; the angel of God called to Hagar from the heavens and said to her: What is it with you, Hagar?** What happened to you? **Fear not, as God has heard the voice of the lad as he is there,** in any place or circumstance. ¹⁸**Rise, lift up the lad, and hold him with your hand, for I will make** of him **a great nation.** ¹⁹**God opened her eyes, and she saw a well of water; she went and filled the skin with water, and gave the lad to drink.** ²⁰**God was with the lad, and he grew; he lived in the wilderness and became an archer,** skilled at hunting with bow and arrows. ²¹**He lived in the wilderness of Paran, and his mother took him a wife from the land of Egypt.**

📖 **Further reading:** For more on the circumstances prompting Ishmael's exile, see *A Concise Guide to the Sages*, p. 29.

Abraham and Avimelekh Seal a Covenant

Once Abraham has an official heir his status among the Philistines rises, as they recognize that the tribe he establishes will endure for generations. Avimelekh proposes that they solidify their relationship through an oath and a covenant.

Sixth aliya ²²**It was at that** same **time** that **Avimelekh and Pikhol, the captain of his guard, said to Abraham, saying: God is with you in all that you do.** ²³**Now take an oath to me here by God that you shall not deceive** or betray **me, or my son, or my son's son; like the kindness that I have done with you** in allowing you to live within my territory, **do with me** personally, **and** also **with the land in which you** have **resided.** ²⁴**Abraham said: I will take an oath,** pledging to be trustworthy in my relations with your people and country. ²⁵**On this same occasion, Abraham reprimanded Avimelekh with regard to the well of water** Abraham dug **that Avimelekh's servants had stolen.** ²⁶**Avimelekh said: I do not know who did this thing; and you also did not tell me** it had happened, **nor did I hear of it, other than today.**

²⁷**Abraham took flocks and cattle and gave them to Avimelekh, and the two of them established a covenant.** ²⁸**Abraham placed,** set aside, **seven ewes of the flock by themselves.** ²⁹**Avimelekh said to Abraham: What are these seven ewes that you have placed by themselves?** ³⁰**He,** Abraham, **said: Because you shall take seven ewes from me** as a gift, **so that it will be for me as a testament, that I dug this well.** ³¹**Therefore he called that place Beersheba, because both of them took an oath there.** The name evokes both the oath [*shevua*] about the well [*be'er*] and the number seven [*sheva*]. ³²**They established a covenant in Beersheba.** Then **Avimelekh and Pikhol, the captain of his guard, arose, and they returned** from the place of Abraham's encampment **to the land of the Philistines.** ³³**He,** Abraham, **planted a tamarisk in Beersheba, and he proclaimed** to the local people **there the name of the Lord,** publicizing that He is the **God of the Universe.** ³⁴**Abraham resided in the land of the Philistines** for **many days** and years.

God Commands Abraham to Sacrifice Isaac

At this point, when Abraham's life is finally peaceful and stable, God tests him with a command to sacrifice his only son and heir. The difficulty for Abraham is not only that he must slaughter his only remaining son, but also that he must participate in the Canaanites'

practice of child sacrifice, which he presumably regarded as morally repugnant. Beyond the personal anguish involved for Abraham, he must also overcome his reluctance to adopt the Canaanites' debased practice of child sacrifice.

22 **¹It was after these matters** that **God tested Abraham and said to him:** *Seventh aliya* **Abraham; and he said: Here I am,** ready to listen and obey. **²He,** God, **said: Take now your son, your only one, whom you love: Isaac. And go you to the land of Moriah,** the area of Jerusalem, **and offer him up there as a burnt offering upon one of the mountains that I will tell you.**

Father and Son Journey Together

Abraham and Isaac walk together to Mount Moriah. Their thoughts and feelings are left to the reader's imagination; the Torah shares no details beyond brief snatches of dialogue.

³Abraham awoke early in the morning and saddled his donkey, to carry the items he required for the journey. **He took two of his young men,** his servants, **with him, and Isaac his son; and he cleaved the wood for the burnt offering. He arose and went to the place that God told him. ⁴On the third day Abraham lifted up his eyes and saw the place from afar. ⁵Abraham said to his young men: Stay here with the donkey** and wait for me, **and I and the lad will go there; we will prostrate ourselves** in prayer and service to God, **and will** then **return to you. ⁶Abraham took the wood of the burnt offering and placed it upon Isaac his son. He,** Abraham, **took in his hand the fire,** the kindling, **and the knife, and the two of them went together.**

⁷Isaac said to Abraham his father; he said: My father. He, Abraham, **said: Here I am, my son,** ready and attentive. **He,** Isaac, **said: Here are the fire and the wood, but** if our intention is to sacrifice an animal, **where is the lamb for a burnt offering? ⁸Abraham said: God will see for Himself the lamb for a burnt offering, my son; and the two of them went together.**

Binding of Isaac

Abraham demonstrates absolute obedience to God, even willing to sacrifice his only son if he is so commanded. The test reveals that he is truly God-fearing.

⁹They came to the place that God had told him. Abraham built the altar there, arranged the wood, and bound Isaac his son; and he placed him on the altar upon the wood. ¹⁰Abraham raised his hand and took the knife to slaughter his son. ¹¹The angel of the Lord called to him from the heavens and said: Abraham, Abraham. Again, **he,** Abraham, **said: Here I am. ¹²He said: Do not raise your hand to the lad, and do not do**

anything to him, not even a symbolic cut; for now I know that you are God-fearing, and you did not withhold your son, your only one, from Me. [13]Abraham lifted his eyes and saw that behold, there was a ram there after the angel spoke to him; it had been caught in the thicket by its horns. Abraham went, took the ram, and offered it up as a burnt offering in place of his son. [14]Abraham called the name of that place: The Lord will see, or the ever-seeing Lord, as it is said to this day with regard to that mountain: On the mount where the Lord will be seen in revelation.

📖 Further reading: Abraham and the angels shed tears during the binding of Isaac; see *A Concise Guide to the Sages*, p. 32.

The Angel Blesses Abraham

Abraham receives an additional blessing marking this turning point in human moral progress. Afterward, Abraham and Isaac return to Beersheba with the young men, who are unaware of the dramatic events that have occurred.

[15]The angel of the Lord called to Abraham a second time from the heavens. [16]He said: By Myself I have taken an oath – the utterance of the Lord – for because you have done this thing, and did not withhold your son, your only one, [17]for that I will bless you and multiply your descendants as the stars of the heavens and as the sand that is upon the seashore, and your descendants shall inherit the gate of their enemies, conquer their cities; [18]and all the nations of the earth shall bless themselves by your descendants, blessing themselves that they be like your descendants, since you heeded My voice. [19]Abraham returned to his young men, and they arose and went together to Beersheba; and Abraham lived in Beersheba.

📖 Further reading: For more on martyrdom, see *A Concise Guide to Mahshava*, p. 199.

The Descendants of Nahor

Immediately following the binding of Isaac, Abraham receives a report about his brother Nahor's family, and especially news of the birth of Nahor's granddaughter, Rebecca, who could be a worthy match for Isaac and enable the continuation of Abraham's line.

Maftir [20]It was after these matters that it was told to Abraham, saying: Behold, Milka, wife of Nahor, she too has borne children to your brother Nahor, just as Sarah has borne children to you. [21]Nahor fathered several sons: Utz, his firstborn; Buz, his brother; and Kemuel, father of Aram, an

important Aramean leader; [22]and **Kesed; Hazo; Pildash; Yidlaf; and Betuel,** Nahor's youngest son. [23]**Betuel begot Rebecca. These eight** sons **Milka bore to Nahor, Abraham's brother.** [24]**And his,** Nahor's, **concubine, and her name was Re'uma, she too bore** sons: **Tevah, Gaham, Tahash, and Maakha.**

Parashat Hayei Sarah

After Sarah dies, Abraham enters into negotiations to purchase the Cave of Makhpela as her burial place. Afterward he sends his servant to his family in Haran, to find a wife for Isaac. The servant experiences extraordinary success in his mission; he finds Rebecca immediately, she and her family consent to the marriage, and she returns with him to Canaan. When Abraham himself dies, he too is buried in the Cave of Makhpela. The *parasha* concludes with a list of Ishmael's descendants and the tribes he fathered.

Sara's Death and Burial

Sarah dies in Hebron, without her husband present, as Abraham is in Beersheba.

23 ¹**The lifetime of Sarah was one hundred and twenty-seven years, the years of the life of Sarah. ²Sarah died in Kiryat Arba, which is Hebron, in the land of Canaan; Abraham came to lament Sarah and to weep** and mourn **for her.**

Abraham Seeks a Burial Place

Abraham, who does not wish to bury Sarah among the local Hittites, decides to acquire land in perpetuity for a family burial plot. He engages in a semiformal meeting with the Hittites, asking that they enable him to purchase the Cave of Makhpela.

³**Abraham arose from before his dead, and he spoke to the children of Het, saying: ⁴I am a foreigner** here, **and a resident alien with you;** I do not have rights in this place, but I am an old acquaintance of yours. **Give me** land as **a burial portion with you, and I will bury my dead from before me.**

⁵**The children of Het answered Abraham, saying to him: ⁶Hear us, my lord: You are a prince of God in our midst,** a person of high status. **In the choicest of our graves bury your dead; none of us shall withhold his grave from you** or prevent you **from burying your dead** anywhere you desire. ⁷**Abraham arose and prostrated himself before the people of the land, before the children of Het. ⁸He spoke with them, saying: If you are willing to** help me **bury my dead from before me, heed me,**

Genesis

and intercede for me with Efron son of Tzohar, ⁹that he will give me the Cave of Makhpela, the double [*kefula*] cave, that is his, which is at the edge of his field; he shall give it to me for a full price, in your midst, for a burial portion.

Negotiations with Efron

Efron names an exorbitant price for the land. He expects Abraham to counter with a much lower offer, in accordance with the custom, but Abraham surprises everyone by immediately agreeing to pay the sum Efron proposes.

¹⁰And Efron was living among the children of Het; and Efron the Hitite answered Abraham in hearing of the children of Het, of all those coming to his city gate, the city elders, saying: ¹¹No, my lord, I cannot accept your proposal. Rather, heed me: The entire field I have given to you as a gift, and the cave that is in it, I have given it to you; in the eyes of my people I have given it to you publicly; go bury your dead. ¹²Abraham prostrated himself before the people of the land. ¹³He spoke to Efron in the hearing of the people of the land, saying: Rather, if only you will heed me and accept my proposal. I have given you, that is, I am giving you, the silver for the field, in order to purchase it; please take it from me, and I will bury my dead there. ¹⁴Efron responded to Abraham, saying to him: ¹⁵My lord, heed me. This land is worth four hundred shekels of silver; between me and you, of what importance is it? And therefore, bury your dead, and let us not suffer delays over the price. ¹⁶Abraham heeded Efron; and Abraham weighed for Efron the silver that he spoke in the hearing of the children of Het, four hundred shekels of choice silver, ready currency that would be accepted anywhere.

Sarah Is Buried

Because this is the first official foothold in the land for Abraham and his descendants, the Torah enumerates the terms of the transaction, specifying that Efron voluntarily sold his field with the consent of the local people.

Second aliya

¹⁷The field of Efron that was by the Cave of Makhpela, that was before Mamre, a place name, the field, and the cave that was in it, and every tree that was in the field, that was within its border all around, were established as Abraham's property. ¹⁸All of this was transferred as a possession for Abraham in the eyes of the children of Het, of all those who come to the gate of his city, the city elders. ¹⁹And thereafter, after the property was transferred to his ownership, Abraham buried Sarah his wife in the

cave of the field of Makhpela opposite Mamre, which is Hebron, in the land of Canaan. ²⁰The field and the cave that was in it were established as an ancestral burial portion for Abraham, which he had purchased from the children of Het.

Abraham Administers an Oath to His Servant

Abraham does not know how many years he has left, and he wishes to see to his son married. He therefore administers an oath to his senior attendant, who functions as his steward, to seek a non-Canaanite wife for Isaac, and sends him to the land where he, Abraham, came from.

24 ¹And Abraham was old, advanced in years. And the Lord blessed Abraham in everything. ²Abraham said to his servant, the elder and most important of his household, who oversaw everything that he had as the general administrator of finances in Abraham's household: Please, place your hand under my thigh, a ceremonial act signifying the taking of an oath. ³And I will administer an oath to you by the Lord, God of the heavens and God of the earth, that you shall not take a wife for my son from the daughters of the Canaanites, in whose midst I live. ⁴Rather, you shall go to my land, Aram Naharayim, and to my birthplace, Haran, where my extended family is located, and take a wife from there for my son, for Isaac. ⁵The servant said to him: Perhaps the woman will not wish to follow me to this land. Shall I return your son to the land from which you departed? ⁶Abraham said to him: Take care not to return my son there. ⁷The Lord, God of the heavens, who took me from my father's house, and from my birthplace, and who spoke to me in a prophecy, and who took an oath to me, saying: To your descendants I will give this land; He will send His angel before you, to assist you, and you will successfully find and take a wife for my son from there. ⁸And if the woman will not wish to follow you, you shall be absolved from this oath of mine, only you shall not return my son there. ⁹The servant placed his hand under the thigh of Abraham his master, and took an oath to him with regard to this matter.

The Servant's Prayer

Instead of knocking on doors to search for an appropriate wife for Isaac when he arrives in Aram Naharayim, Abraham's servant waits near the well, as the local girls will be likely to pass by. He prays for success in his mission, and decides on a sign: A girl who demonstrates exceptional hospitality toward him, a foreign visitor, will be suitable to join Abraham's family, who are noted for generously accommodating guests.

Third aliya **¹⁰The servant took ten of his master's camels, and he went with all of his master's goods in his hand,** gifts and ornaments that conveyed Abraham's status and power. **He arose and went to Aram Naharayim, to the city of** his master's brother **Nahor. ¹¹When he arrived, he had the camels kneel outside the city by the well of water, at evening time, at the time the women who draw water come out. ¹²He said** in prayer: **Lord, God of my master Abraham, please arrange it for me today, and perform kindness with,** for, **my master Abraham. ¹³Behold, I stand by the spring of water,** the water source; **and the daughters of the men of the city come out to draw water. ¹⁴It shall be that the girl to whom I shall say: Tilt your jug please, that I may drink, and she shall say: Drink, and I will also give your camels to drink;** I will know thereby that **it is she You have confirmed** to be a wife **for Your servant, for Isaac; and through her** actions **I shall know that You have shown kindness to my master.**

Rebecca's Generosity

Rebecca approaches the well while the servant is still praying. She impresses him as a suitable-looking match for Isaac. When he poses his request to her, she fulfills it with alacrity and energy, while he looks on and marvels.

¹⁵It was before he concluded to speak his prayer; **behold, Rebecca was coming out,** the same Rebecca **who was born to Betuel, son of Milka wife of Nahor, brother of Abraham. And her jug was** carried **on her shoulder. ¹⁶And the girl was good-looking, a virgin, and a man had not been intimate with her. She descended to the spring, she filled her jug, and ascended. ¹⁷The servant ran toward her, and he said: Please allow me to sip a little water from your jug. ¹⁸She said: Drink, my lord, and she hurried and lowered her jug from her hand, and gave him to drink** his fill. **¹⁹She concluded giving him to drink, and she said: I will draw** water **for your camels as well, until they conclude to drink. ²⁰She hurried, emptied her jug into the trough, ran again to the well to draw** more, **and drew** the enormous amount of water required **for all ten of his camels. ²¹The man was astonished at her. He was** still **silent,** waiting **to know whether the Lord had made his journey successful or not.**

The Servant Inquires into Rebecca's Background

Although Rebecca has fulfilled the sign the servant prayed for, he is unsure if this is the girl destined to marry Isaac. Only when he learns that she is Abraham's close relative does he realize that he has received heavenly assistance.

²²**It was when the camels finished drinking; the man took a gold nose ring whose weight was one half shekel, and two bracelets** for putting **on her arms, whose weight was ten gold shekels.** ²³**He said: Whose daughter are you; please tell me.** And **is there room in your father's house for us to stay the night?** ²⁴**She said to him: I am the daughter of Betuel, son of Milka, whom she bore to Nahor.** ²⁵**She** then **said to him: Both straw and feed is plentiful with us, as well as room to stay the night.** ²⁶**The**

ourth
aliya

man bowed and prostrated himself to the Lord. ²⁷**He said: Blessed is the Lord, God of my master Abraham, who did not withhold His kindness and His truth from my master. I have been guided by the Lord on** the right **way, to the** very **house of my master's brethren.**

Laban Greets the Servant

Rebecca's older brother, Laban, the dominant member of the family, comes to meet the man who has given his sister gifts. When he sees the laden camels, he welcomes the servant warmly.

²⁸**The girl ran and told her mother's household,** or her mother at home, **about these matters.** ²⁹**Rebecca had a brother and his name was Laban. And Laban ran out to the man, to the spring.** ³⁰**It was when he saw the nose ring and the bracelets upon his sister's hands, and when he heard the words of Rebecca his sister, saying: So spoke the man to me,** that he, Laban, **came to the man, and behold, he was standing beside the camels at the spring.** ³¹**He,** Laban, **said: Come, blessed of the Lord; why do you stand outside when I have cleared the house** to make room for you and your entourage, **and** even a **place for the camels.** ³²**The man came to the house, and he,** Laban, **unloaded the camels** or released the muzzles that prevented them from eating in others' fields; **he gave straw and feed for the camels, and water to wash his feet and the feet of the men who were with him.**

The Servant's Account

The servant wishes to avoid conflict and to maximize the likelihood of the match being agreed. Therefore, when he relates his story to Rebecca's family, he emphasizes Abraham's wealth and high status, his motivation in instructing him to find Isaac a wife in Haran, and the divine assistance he received in carrying out his mission.

³³**Abraham's** servant entered the house. **Food was placed before him to eat, and he said: I will not eat until I have spoken my words.** He, Laban, **said: Speak.** ³⁴**He said: I am Abraham's servant.** ³⁵**The Lord has**

greatly blessed my master; and he became wealthy. He, God, gave him flocks and cattle, and silver and gold, and slaves and maidservants, and camels and donkeys. ³⁶Furthermore, Sarah, my master's wife, bore a son to my master after her old age. And he gave to him everything that he has. ³⁷My master administered an oath to me, saying: You shall not take a wife for my son from the daughters of the Canaanites, in whose land I live. ³⁸Rather, you shall go to my father's house and to my family, and take a wife for my son from there.

³⁹I said to my master: Perhaps the woman will not follow me. ⁴⁰He said to me: The Lord, before whom I walked, whom I served, will send His angel with you and will make your path successful; and you shall take a wife for my son from my family, and from my father's house. ⁴¹If you take such a wife, then you shall be absolved of my oath, when you come to my family and request from them a wife for my son; and if they do not give her to you, you shall likewise be absolved of my oath.

⁴²I came this day to the spring, and I said: Lord, God of my master Abraham, if You would please make the path upon which I am going successful. ⁴³Behold, I am standing beside the spring of water; and there will be the young woman who comes out to draw, that I say to her: Please give me a little water to drink from your jug; ⁴⁴and she will say to me: You too drink, and I will draw for your camels as well; she is the woman whom the Lord has confirmed for my master's son.

⁴⁵Before I concluded to speak to my heart, behold, Rebecca came out with her jug on her shoulder; and she descended to the spring, and drew water. I said to her: Please give me drink. ⁴⁶She hurried and lowered her pitcher from her shoulder, and said: Drink, and I will give to your camels to drink as well. I drank and she gave to the camels to drink as well. ⁴⁷I asked her and said: Whose daughter are you? She said: Daughter of Betuel, son of Nahor, whom Milka bore to him. I consequently placed the ring on her nose, and the bracelets on her arms. ⁴⁸I bowed and prostrated myself to the Lord, and blessed the Lord, God of my master Abraham, who guided me in the true path to take the daughter of my master's brother for his son.

⁴⁹And now, if you will do kindness and truth with my master, tell me you agree to the match. And if you do not desire this match, likewise tell me; and I will turn to the right or to the left, to search elsewhere for a wife for the son of my master.

The Match Is Approved

The family, led by Laban, confirms that Rebecca is intended for Isaac.

⁵⁰Laban and Betuel answered and said: The matter comes from the Lord; we can speak to you neither bad nor good; we have nothing to add or comment. ⁵¹Behold, Rebecca is before you, available; take her, and go, and she shall be a wife for your master's son, as the Lord has spoken. ⁵²It was when Abraham's servant heard their statement he prostrated himself to the earth to the Lord, again expressing his thanks *Fifth* for the success of his mission. ⁵³The servant produced vessels of silver, *aliya* vessels of gold, and garments, and he gave them to Rebecca; and he gave her brother and her mother precious objects, food or gifts.

📖 **Further reading:** This is the first time the Torah depicts matchmaking. For more on the male-female relationship, on couple bonding, and on married life, see *A Concise Guide to the Sages*, p. 376; *A Concise Guide to Mahshava*, pp. 16, 179.

Rebecca Accompanies the Servant to Canaan

The servant hastens to return to his master and report on his success in fulfilling his request. Rebecca agrees to accompany him immediately, exemplifying the independence and decisiveness that will characterize her later as well.

⁵⁴He and the men who were with him ate and drank and stayed the night. They arose in the morning, and he, the servant, said: Send me to my master; allow me to return now, with Rebecca. ⁵⁵Her brother and her mother said: Let the girl remain with us for one year, or ten months; afterward she shall go. ⁵⁶He said to them: Do not delay me, as the Lord has made my path successful; send me and I will go to my master. ⁵⁷They said: We will call the girl and ask her response. ⁵⁸They called Rebecca and said to her: Will you go with this man? She said: I will go. ⁵⁹They therefore sent Rebecca their sister, and her nursemaid, and Abraham's servant, and his men. ⁶⁰They blessed Rebecca, and said to her: Our sister, may you become thousands of ten thousands, may a nation of millions come from you, and let your descendants inherit the gate of their enemies, conquer their cities. ⁶¹Rebecca and her young women rose, and they rode upon the camels and followed the man. The servant took Rebecca himself, and went.

Isaac and Rebecca's Marriage

The servant brings Isaac his bride, and he takes her to the tent that had been his mother's. Rebecca's presence in Sarah's tent and in Isaac's life fills the emotional void left by Sarah's passing.

⁶²Isaac came from going to visit the area of Be'er Lahai Ro'i; and he, Isaac, was living in the land of the South. ⁶³Isaac went out to walk in the field toward evening; and he lifted his eyes, and behold, he saw camels coming. ⁶⁴Rebecca lifted her eyes; she saw Isaac, and she fell from the camel, or leaned forward. ⁶⁵She said to the servant: Who is that man who walks in the field toward us? The servant said: He is my master, Isaac. She took the veil and covered herself. ⁶⁶The servant related to Isaac all the matters that he had done. ⁶⁷Isaac brought her into the tent of his mother Sarah. He took Rebecca, she became his wife, and he loved her. Isaac was comforted after the demise of his mother.

Abraham's Final Years

Toward the end of his life, Abraham remarries and fathers many children. In order to preserve Isaac's status as his only heir, he sends his other sons away, to the east.

25 ¹Abraham took another wife, and her name was Ketura. ²She bore
Sixth him Zimran, and Yokshan, and Medan, and Midyan, and Yishbak, and
aliya Shuah. ³And Yokshan begot Sheva and Dedan. And the sons of Dedan were the tribes Ashurim, and Letushim, and Le'umim. ⁴And the sons of Midyan: Ephah, and Efer, and Hanokh, and Avida, and Eldaa. All these were the children of Ketura. ⁵Nevertheless, Abraham gave all the property that was his to Isaac. ⁶And to the sons of the concubines of Abraham, Hagar and Ketura, Abraham gave gifts, in the form of money or valuables. And he sent them away from Isaac his son, while he was still alive, eastward, to the east country.

⁷These are the days of the years of Abraham's life that he lived, one hundred and seventy-five years. ⁸Abraham expired and died at a good old age; his later years were pleasant. He was aged in years and content with his life. And he was gathered to his people, meaning that he died. ⁹Isaac and Ishmael, his eldest sons, buried him in the Cave of Makhpela, in the field of Efron son of Tzohar the Hitite, that is located before the place called Mamre. ¹⁰The field that Abraham purchased from the children of Het, there Abraham was buried, and Sarah his wife. ¹¹It was after the death of Abraham, God blessed Isaac his son; and Isaac lived beside Be'er Lahai Ro'i.

Ishmael's Descendants

The list of Ishmael's descendants completes the account of Abraham's life. Here Ishmael is not portrayed negatively; apparently, he has reconnected to his father's spiritual legacy.

eventh *aliya* **¹²These are the descendants of Ishmael son of Abraham, whom Hagar the Egyptian, Sarah's maidservant, bore to Abraham. ¹³And these are the names of the sons of Ishmael, by their names, according to their birth: The firstborn of Ishmael was Nevayot, and then Kedar, Adbe'el, Mivsam, ¹⁴Mishma, Duma, Masa, ¹⁵Hadad, Temah, Yetur, Nafish, and** *Maftir* **Kedma. ¹⁶**These are the sons of Ishmael and these are their names. They dwelled **in their enclosures,** which were semi-permanent living spaces, **and in their fortifications.** They were **twelve princes of their** respective nations. **¹⁷These are the years of the life of Ishmael:** He lived for **one hundred and thirty-seven years; and he expired and died, and he was gathered to his people. ¹⁸**They, the sons of Ishmael, **dwelled from Havila until Shur that is adjacent to Egypt, and all the way to Ashur; he ruled over all his brethren.**

Parashat Toldot

Isaac and Rebecca suffer a long period of infertility, which finally ends with the birth of twins: Jacob and Esau, who develop in different directions. The older of the twins, Esau, does not value his birthright, and sells it to Jacob in exchange for red lentil stew.

When famine strikes, Isaac migrates to the land of the Philistines, as Abraham had done, and there he becomes wealthy. However, he becomes embroiled in conflicts with the Philistines, primarily over water rights, and is compelled to leave.

When Isaac grows old, he tells Esau that he wants to bless him. Jacob, following his mother's instructions, takes advantage of his father's failing eyesight and pretends to be Esau, thereby securing the blessing for himself. When Esau discovers that he was denied his blessing, he becomes enraged and decides to kill Jacob. Again following Rebecca's advice, Jacob leaves his home to go to his mother's family in Haran.

Rebecca's Pregnancy

Rebecca experiences a difficult pregnancy, prompting her to request divine guidance. She is told that she is carrying twins, that each of them will become patriarch of a nation, and these two nations will have divergent characteristics.

¹⁹**And this is the legacy,** the story of the descendants **of Isaac, Abraham's son: Abraham begot Isaac.** ²⁰**Isaac was forty years old when he took Rebecca, daughter of Betuel the Aramean from Padan Aram, and sister of Laban the Aramean, to be his wife.** ²¹**Isaac entreated** and prayed fervently to **the Lord on behalf of his wife, because she was barren. The Lord acceded to his entreaty, and Rebecca his wife conceived.** ²²**The children were agitated within her** womb, **and she said: If so, why am I like this,** why am I suffering? **And she went to inquire of the Lord.** ²³**The Lord said to her** through a prophet: **Two peoples,** or national leaders, **are in your womb, and two nations shall be separated from your innards. One nation will** struggle with and **prevail over the other nation, and the elder** twin **shall serve the younger.**

📖 **Further reading:** For more on Rebecca's pregnancy and the differences between the twins, see *A Concise Guide to the Sages*, p. 39.

Esau and Jacob

The diverse natures of Esau and Jacob become evident. Each parent is drawn to a different twin.

²⁴Her days to give birth were complete, the time came to give birth; **and behold, there were twins in her womb. ²⁵The first emerged with red skin, all of him like a cloak of hair,** he was very hairy. **And they called his name Esau. ²⁶And thereafter his brother emerged, his hand grasping Esau's heel** [*akev*]; **and he called his name Jacob** [Ya'akov]. **Isaac was sixty years old when she bore them. ²⁷The lads grew,** and **Esau was a man who knew** all about **hunting, a man of the field,** of the open plains. **And Jacob was a guileless man, living in tents,** staying home and learning Torah. **²⁸And Isaac loved Esau because of the game in his mouth,** as Esau would bring his father game to eat, **and Rebecca loved Jacob.**

Esau Sells His Birthright

Although Esau is the older son, his birthright is of little importance to him. By contrast, Jacob considers it a matter of great significance, and offers to purchase it from Esau, who assents.

²⁹One day Jacob cooked a stew. Esau came from the field, and he was weary. ³⁰Esau said to Jacob: Feed me please from that red, red [*adom ha'adom*] **dish,** as I am weary. **Therefore his name is called Edom. ³¹Jacob said: Sell me your birthright this day,** meaning now. **³²And Esau said: Behold, I am going to die** from exhaustion; **for what do I need a birthright? ³³Jacob said: Take an oath to me this day. He took an oath to him, and he sold his birthright to Jacob. ³⁴And Jacob gave Esau bread and a stew of lentils. He,** Esau, **ate, he drank, he arose, and he went; and Esau scorned the birthright.**

God Blesses Isaac

In response to a drought in Canaan, Isaac sets out, presumably to go to Egypt, as his father had done under similar circumstances. He has reached the land of the Philistines, the southernmost part of Canaan, when God instructs him not to go to Egypt, but to stay in the Land of Israel. He then bestows a blessing upon Isaac.

26 **¹There was a famine in the land, besides the first famine that was during the days of Abraham. Isaac went to Avimelekh king of the Philistines, to** the city of **Gerar. ²The Lord appeared to him, and said: Do not go**

down to Egypt. Dwell in the land that I will tell you; stay here. ³Reside in this land, and I will be with you, and I will bless you; for I will give all these lands to you and to your descendants, and I will keep the oath that I took to Abraham your father. ⁴And I will multiply your descendants like the stars of the heavens, and I will give to your descendants all these lands; and all the nations of the earth shall be blessed through your descendants. ⁵This is because Abraham heeded My voice, and kept My commission, My commandments, My statutes, and My laws.

Isaac and Rebecca in Gerar

Isaac's misgivings about the moral probity of the residents of Gerar prompt him to present his wife as his sister, as Abraham had done before him. This time, however, the king of Gerar discovers the truth only when he happens to see Isaac and Rebecca engaging in conjugal relations.

Second aliya ⁶**Isaac lived in Gerar,** and as God had commanded, did not go down to Egypt. ⁷**The men of the place asked him with regard to his wife. He said: She is my sister,** as he was afraid to say: She is **my wife,** for he said to himself: **Lest the men of the place kill me over Rebecca, because she is of fair appearance.** ⁸**Yet, it was when the days he was there were extended,** and Isaac was less careful; **Avimelekh king of the Philistines looked out through the window, and behold, he saw Isaac** in his house, **playing,** engaging in physical intimacy, **with Rebecca his wife.** ⁹**Avimelekh summoned Isaac and said: Behold,** I have seen that **she is your wife; how did you say: She is my sister? Isaac said to him: Because I said,** or I thought to myself: **Lest I die over her.** If I reveal that she is my wife, they might kill me and take her. ¹⁰**Avimelekh said: What is this that you have done to us? One of** the men of **the people almost lay with your wife; you would have brought guilt,** sin, **upon us.** ¹¹**Avimelekh commanded all the people, saying: Anyone who touches this man or his wife shall be put to death.**

Conflict with the Philistines

Isaac engages in a new agricultural venture in Gerar. He is immensely successful, earning both great wealth and the envy of the Philistines. Conflict arises over wells that Abraham had dug which the Philistines had since sealed.

¹²**Isaac sowed in that land, and found in that year,** when he measured his yield, that he reaped **one hundredfold** of the typical yield. **And** this was because **the Lord blessed him.**

Third aliya ¹³The man grew wealthy, and continued to grow wealthy until he became extremely wealthy. ¹⁴He had livestock of flocks, and livestock of cattle, and a great household with extensive staff; the Philistines envied him. ¹⁵The Torah notes: And all the cisterns that his father's servants dug in the days of Abraham his father, the Philistines had sealed them and filled them with earth. ¹⁶Avimelekh said to Isaac: Leave us, for you have grown much mightier and much richer than we.

¹⁷Isaac left there, and he encamped in the Valley of Gerar, and settled there. ¹⁸Isaac again dug the cisterns of water that they had dug in the days of Abraham his father and that the Philistines had sealed after the death of Abraham. He gave them names like the names that his father had given them. ¹⁹Isaac's servants dug in the valley, and they found there a well of fresh water. ²⁰The herdsmen of Gerar quarreled with Isaac's herdsmen, saying: The water is ours, since this area is our territory. He, Isaac, called the name of the well Esek, because they involved themselves [hitasseku], fought, with him. ²¹They, Isaac's servants, dug another well, and they, the Philistines, quarreled over it as well. He called it Sitna, accusation. ²²Again he, Isaac, moved from there and dug another well, and they did not quarrel over it. He called its name Rehovot, and he said: For now the Lord has expanded space [hirhiv] for us, and we shall be fruitful in the land; now we can dwell in peace and expand outward.

Covenant with the Philistines

Isaac settles in Beersheba, and the Philistines again approach him. This time it is Avimelekh and the captain of his guard who come, and they declare their wish for a covenant with Isaac. Apparently his prosperity has prompted them to forge better relations with him.

Fourth aliya ²³He, Isaac, ascended from there to Beersheba. ²⁴The Lord appeared to him that night and said: I am the God of Abraham your father. Fear not, as I am with you; I will bless you and multiply your descendants for the sake of My servant Abraham. ²⁵He built an altar there and proclaimed the name of the Lord, performing a ceremony in which he publicly invoked God's name. And he pitched his tent there, and Isaac's servants dug a well there.

²⁶Avimelekh king of the Philistines went to him from Gerar with a group of his associates, and Pikhol, the captain of his guard. ²⁷Isaac said to them: Why did you come to me? After all, you hated me, and you sent me from among you. ²⁸They said: We saw that the Lord was with you,

and therefore **we said: Let there please be an oath** of a covenant **between us, between us and you; we will establish a covenant with you:** ²⁹**If you will do us no harm when we have not touched you,** or, so that you will not harm us just as we have not harmed you, **and when we have done only good with you, and we sent you in peace.** We see that **you are now the blessed of the Lord,** and therefore we wish to establish a covenant with you.

Fifth ³⁰Isaac agreed, and **he made a feast for them, and they ate and drank.**
aliya ³¹**They awoke in the morning and took oaths to one another; Isaac sent them** off, **and they went from him in peace.**

³²**It was on that day** that **Isaac's servants came and told him with regard to the well that they had dug; they said to him: We have** again **found water.** ³³**He called it Shiva,** in allusion to the oath [*shevua*]; **therefore, the name of the city is Beersheba to this day.**

Esau Marries

³⁴**Esau was forty years old, and he took as a wife Yehudit, daughter of Be'eri the Hitite, and Basmat, daughter of Eilon the Hitite.** ³⁵The Torah attests: **They,** Esau's Hitite wives, **were a source of bitterness to Isaac and to Rebecca.**

Isaac's Request

When Isaac grows old, he decides to grant a special blessing to his favorite son, Esau.

27 ¹**It was when Isaac was old, and his eyes dimmed from seeing,** his vision was weak; **he summoned Esau, his elder son, and said to him: My son. He,** Esau, **said to him: Here I am.** ²**He,** Isaac, **said: Behold, I have now grown old; I do not know the day of my death.** ³**Now, please take your** hunting **gear, your quiver, and your bow, and go out to the field and hunt game for me.** ⁴**Prepare for me tasty food** from game **such as I like, and bring it to me, and I will eat, so that my soul will bless you;** I will bless you **before I die.**

Rebecca Commands Jacob

Rebecca, who wishes Isaac's blessing to be given to Jacob instead of to Esau, coaxes Jacob to impersonate his brother. As this is a complicated and ostensibly questionable maneuver, Rebecca invokes her authority to convince Jacob, and assists him in disguising himself.

⁵**Rebecca heard as Isaac spoke to Esau his son. Esau went to the field to hunt game** in order **to bring** it to Isaac. ⁶**Rebecca said to Jacob her son,**

saying: Behold, I heard your father speak to Esau your brother, saying: [7]Bring me game and prepare for me tasty food, and I will eat, and I will bless you before the Lord before my death. [8]Now, my son, heed my voice, to do that which I command you. [9]Please go to the flock and take for me from there two fine goat kids. And I will make them into tasty food for your father, such as he likes. [10]You shall bring it to your father and he will eat, so that he will bless you before his death. [11]And Jacob said to Rebecca his mother: Behold, Esau my brother is a hairy man, and I am a man of smooth skin. [12]Perhaps my father will feel me, and I shall be in his eyes as a deceiver, and I shall bring upon myself a curse and not a blessing. [13]His mother said to him: Your curse is upon me, my son; I will be responsible, so you will not be cursed. Only heed my voice, and go take the goat kids for me. [14]He went, and took the kids, and brought them to his mother; and his mother made tasty food, such as his father liked. [15]Rebecca then took the fine garments reserved for special occasions of Esau, her elder son, that were with her in the house, and she dressed Jacob, her younger son, in them. [16]The hides of the goat kids she placed on his arms and on the smooth part of his neck. [17]She gave the tasty food and the bread that she prepared into the hand of Jacob her son.

Isaac Blesses Jacob

Hearing Jacob's voice from the son who is purportedly Esau, Isaac is uncertain of his identity. His suspicions are eventually overcome when he feels Jacob's now-hairy arms, tastes the specially prepared food, and smells the scent of Esau's clothes. He gives Jacob a blessing similar to the blessings Abraham had received from God.

[18]He came to his father and said: My father. He, Isaac, said: Here I am; who are you, my son? [19]Jacob said to his father: I am Esau your firstborn; I did as you spoke to me, as you requested of me. Arise now, sit and eat from my game, so that your soul will bless me. [20]Isaac said to his son: How is it that you hastened the hunt so to find it, my son? He, Jacob, said: Because the Lord your God coordinated it so that the game appeared before me without delay. [21]Isaac said to Jacob: Please approach, that I may feel you, my son. Are you truly my son Esau, or not? [22]Jacob approached Isaac his father, and he, Isaac, felt him. He said: The voice is the voice of Jacob, but the hands are the hands of Esau. [23]He did not recognize him as Jacob because his hands were hairy like the hands of his brother Esau; and he blessed him. [24]He said: Are you my

son Esau? He said: I am. ²⁵He said: Serve me, and I will eat from my son's game so that my soul will bless you. He served him, and he ate, and he brought him wine, and he drank. ²⁶Isaac his father said to him: Approach and kiss me, my son. ²⁷He, Jacob, approached and kissed him. He, Isaac, smelled the scent of his, Esau's, fine garments, and he blessed him and said: See, the scent of my son is as the scent of a field that the Lord blessed. ²⁸God will give you from the dew of the heavens, from the fat of the earth, and an abundance of grain and wine. ²⁹Peoples will serve you, and nations will prostrate themselves to you. Be a lord and a leader to your brethren, conquer them, and your mother's sons, descendants, will prostrate themselves to you. Cursed be one who curses you, and blessed be one that blesses you.

Sixth aliya

Esau's Anguish

When Esau discovers his brother's deception he cries out in rage and disappointment. Isaac, however, quickly accepts the situation and declares that Jacob's blessing has taken effect and cannot be retracted. The fact that the Torah does not report that Isaac later reproves Jacob may indicate that Isaac concluded that he had given the blessing to the correct son.

³⁰It was when Isaac concluded blessing Jacob, and Jacob had just departed from the presence of Isaac his father, that Esau his brother came from his hunt. ³¹He too made tasty food, and brought it to his father. He said to his father: Let my father arise, and eat from his son's game, so that your soul will bless me. ³²Isaac his father said to him: Who are you? He said: I am your son, your firstborn, Esau. ³³Isaac was overcome with great trembling, and he said: Who is it then who hunted game and brought it to me? I ate from it all before you came, and I blessed him; indeed, he shall be blessed.

³⁴When Esau heard the words of his father, he cried a very great and bitter cry. And he said to his father: Bless me too, my father. ³⁵He, Isaac, said to him: Your brother came with deceit, and he took your blessing. ³⁶He, Esau, said: Is it for this that his name was called Jacob [Ya'akov]? As he deceived me [*vayakeveni*] these two times: He took my birthright, and behold, now he took my blessing. And he said: Have you not reserved a blessing for me? ³⁷Isaac answered and he said to Esau: Behold, I have made him a lord to you; I have given to him all his brethren as servants, and I have supported him, blessed him, with grain and wine. For you then, what shall I do, my son? ³⁸Esau said to his father: Have you but one blessing, my father? Bless me too, my father; and Esau

raised his voice and wept. [39]And Isaac his father answered and said to him: Behold, from the fat of the earth shall be your dwelling, you shall inherit a fertile portion, and you shall receive from the dew of the heavens above. [40]By your sword you shall live, and you shall serve your brother. But it will be when you revolt, or when your brother's descendants stray from the proper path, you will remove his yoke from your neck.

Rebecca's Advice

Filled with fury, Esau resolves to kill his brother. Nevertheless, he decides to delay his revenge until after his father's death, out of respect for him.

[41]Esau hated Jacob because of the blessing that his father blessed him. Esau said in his heart: When the days of mourning for my father will approach, when my father will die, then I will act, and I will kill my brother Jacob. [42]The words of Esau her elder son were told to Rebecca; she sent and summoned Jacob her younger son and said to him: Behold, your brother Esau consoles himself about you by planning to kill you. [43]Now my son, heed my voice and arise, flee to Laban my brother, to Haran. [44]Live with him a few years, until your brother's anger subsides, [45]until your brother's anger subsides from you, and he forgets that which you did to him. At that point, I will send a messenger and take you from there, from Haran. Leave now; why should I be bereaved of both of you on one day, if you fight and kill each other?

[46]Rebecca then said to Isaac: I loathe my life, I am tired of life, due to the daughters of Het, whom Esau married. If Jacob takes a wife from the daughters of Het like these, a woman from the daughters of the land, why do I need life?

Isaac Sends Jacob to Haran

Whereas the patriarchs felt the local Canaanite nations to be alien to them, they considered Nahor's family to be close relatives. Therefore, Isaac expects Laban's daughters to be suitable wives for Jacob, although he has never met them. He hopes that such a marriage will reinforce the unique character of his family.

28 [1]Isaac summoned Jacob. He blessed him, and he commanded him; he said to him: Do not take a wife from the daughters of Canaan, as your brother did. [2]Arise, go to Padan Aram, to the house of Betuel, father of your mother, and take yourself a wife from there, from the daughters of Laban, brother of your mother. [3]And may God Almighty bless you, and make you fruitful and strong, and multiply you; may you be an

Genesis

assembly of peoples,** the patriarch of a great nation. **⁴May He give you the blessing of Abraham – to you, and to your descendants with you –** in order **to inherit the land of your residence, which God gave to Abraham.** *Seventh aliya* **⁵Isaac sent Jacob, and he went to Padan Aram, to Laban, son of Betuel the Aramean, brother of Rebecca, mother of Jacob and Esau.**

Esau Takes an Additional Wife

Until this point, Esau thought that the main objection to his marrying women from Canaan came from his mother. Now that Esau sees that his father wishes his sons would marry relatives, he takes an additional wife from among his Ishmaelite cousins.

⁶Esau saw that Isaac blessed Jacob and sent him to Padan Aram, to take himself a wife from there. In blessing him he commanded him, say- *Maftir* **ing: Do not take a wife from the daughters of Canaan. ⁷Jacob heeded his father and his mother, and he went to Padan Aram. ⁸Esau saw that the daughters of Canaan were objectionable in the eyes of Isaac his father. ⁹Therefore, Esau went to** his uncle **Ishmael, and took Mahalat, the daughter of Ishmael son of Abraham, sister of Nevayot,** Ishmael's first-born, **in addition to his** previous **wives, as his wife.**

Parashat Vayetze

On his way to Haran, Jacob experiences a prophetic dream in which God encourages him and promises the land to him. He reciprocates by making a vow of commitment to God. He continues to Haran, where he finds his mother's family, and proposes to his uncle Laban that he work for him for seven years in exchange for the hand of his daughter Rachel in marriage. Laban assents, but when the wedding finally takes place, he deceives Jacob by substituting Leah for Rachel, in order to extract an additional seven years of labor from Jacob. Later Jacob also marries Bilha and Zilpa, Leah and Rachel's maidservants, and he fathers eleven sons and one daughter with his four wives. After the fourteen years of labor for his wives, Jacob remains in Haran for an additional six years, and grows wealthy. As he is concerned about his uncle's reaction to his wealth and the possibility that Laban will again try to cheat him, when he returns to Canaan he departs surreptitiously from Haran with his entourage of family members and livestock.

Jacob's Dream

While Jacob dreams, he experiences a vision and receives a revelation in which God makes far-reaching promises to him. Jacob will discover, upon his return to Canaan, that all the promises have been fulfilled.

¹⁰**Jacob departed from Beersheba and went to Haran. ¹¹He came upon the place,** which will be identified later, **and stayed the night** and slept **there, because the sun had set** and it would have been dangerous to travel at night. **And he took one of the stones from the place, and placed it beneath his head** as a pillow, **and lay in that place. ¹²He dreamed, and behold,** in his dream, **a ladder was set on the earth, and its top** was **reaching to the heavens; and behold, the angels of God were ascending and descending on it. ¹³And, behold, the Lord,** without the angels, **stood over him,** Jacob, **and said: I am the Lord, God of Abraham your father, and God of Isaac. The land upon which you lie,** the land of Canaan, **to you I will give it, and to your descendants. ¹⁴Your descendants will be as** innumerable as **the dust of the earth, and you shall spread** out **to the west, to the east, to the north, and to the south. And all the families,** the nations, **of the earth shall be blessed in you and your descendants.**

¹⁵**And, behold, I am with you; I will keep you wherever you go, and I will bring you back** from Haran **to this land** of Canaan. **For I will not leave you until I have done that which I spoke to you** with this promise.

📖 **Further reading:** For more on Jacob's slumber and dream, see *A Concise Guide to the Sages*, p. 44.

Jacob Makes a Vow

Jacob memorializes his experience of revelation by establishing a monument and making a vow.

¹⁶**Jacob awoke from his sleep, and he said: Indeed, the Lord is in this place,** causing me to have a revelatory vision. **And I did not know** this. ¹⁷**He was awestruck, and he said: How awesome is this place; this is nothing other than the House of God, and this is the gate of the heavens.** ¹⁸**Jacob awoke early in the morning, and he took the stone that he had placed beneath his head and established it as a monument, and poured oil on the top of it,** to anoint and sanctify it. ¹⁹**He,** Jacob, **called the name of that place Beit El,** meaning house of God, from that point onward. **However, Luz was the name of the city initially.** ²⁰**Jacob took a vow, saying: If God will** indeed **be with me,** as I heard in my dream, **and He will keep me on this path that I go, and will give me bread to eat and a garment to wear,** ²¹**and I return to my father's house in peace, the Lord shall be my God,** ²²**and this stone that I have established as a monument shall be the house** of worship **of God. And everything that You will give me I will tithe to You.**

Jacob Reaches Haran

Jacob had left Beersheba as a refugee, rather than of his own volition, but after the transcendant vision he receives in Beit El, he senses God's constant protection, and his mood lifts.

29 ¹**Jacob lifted his feet, and** he went **to the land of the people of the east,** specifically, the Arameans. ²**Nearing Haran, he saw, and behold, a well in the field, and behold, three flocks of sheep lying alongside it,** the well, **since from that well they watered the flocks, and the great stone was on the mouth of the well.** ³**All the** shepherds with their **flocks would gather there, and** together **they would roll the stone from the mouth of the well and give the sheep to drink, and** then **they would put the stone back on the mouth of the well, in its place.**

Second aliya

⁴Jacob said to them: My brethren, from where are you? They said: We are from Haran. ⁵He said to them: Do you know Laban son of Nahor? They said: We know him. ⁶He said to them: Is he well? They said: He is well, and here is Rachel his daughter coming with the sheep. ⁷He said: Behold, the length of **the day** before night falls **is still great; it is not time for the livestock to be gathered.** Why don't you **give the sheep to drink, and go and herd?** ⁸They said: We cannot, as the stone is too heavy. We must wait **until all the flocks are gathered, and they,** the shepherds of all the flocks, **will** together **roll the stone from the mouth of the well; then we** will **give the sheep to drink.**

Jacob and Rachel Meet

After his journey of hundreds of miles, on foot, spending each night in a different place, Jacob is excited to finally meet a member of his family.

⁹**He was still speaking with them, and Rachel came,** arriving **with her father's flock, for she was a shepherdess.** ¹⁰**It was when Jacob saw Rachel, the daughter of Laban his mother's brother, and** saw **the flock of Laban his mother's brother, that Jacob approached and rolled the stone from the mouth of the well, and gave the sheep of Laban his mother's brother to drink.** ¹¹**Jacob kissed Rachel, and he raised his voice and wept** from emotion. ¹²**Jacob told Rachel that he was her father's brother,** kinsman, **and that he was Rebecca's son; and she ran and told her father.**

Jacob's Contract with Laban

Laban brings Jacob to his house, and Jacob immediately begins assisting with the household labor as he feels a familial obligation. After a while, they agree to formalize the arrangement.

¹³**It was when Laban heard the news of** the arrival of **Jacob, his sister's son,** that **he ran to meet him,** and he **embraced him, kissed him, and brought him to his house. He,** Jacob, **related to Laban all these matters** that had happened to him. ¹⁴**Laban said to him: Indeed, you are my bone and my flesh,** a close relative. **And so he lived with him a month's time.**

¹⁵At that point **Laban said to Jacob:** Merely **because you are my brother,** my kinsman, **shall you work for me for nothing? Tell me, what is your salary?** ¹⁶The Torah notes: **Laban had two daughters: The name of the elder was Leah, and the name of the younger was Rachel.** ¹⁷**Leah's eyes were delicate,** from frequent crying. **And Rachel was of fine form, and** *Third* beautiful. ¹⁸**Jacob loved Rachel, and he said: I will work for you seven**
aliya

years for the hand of **Rachel your younger daughter** in marriage. **¹⁹Laban said: Better that I give her to you, than** that **I give her to another man; live with me.**

Jacob's Marriages

When seven years are up, Laban deceives Jacob at his wedding and gives him Leah instead of Rachel. Jacob has no choice but to accept Laban's terms if he wants to ultimately marry the woman of his choice.

²⁰Jacob worked seven years for Rachel; they were in his eyes but a few days, in his love of her. ²¹Jacob said to Laban: Give me my wife, as my time is fulfilled, and I will consort with her. ²²Laban gathered all the people of the place, and made a wedding **feast. ²³It was in the evening, and he,** Laban, **took Leah his** older **daughter and brought her to him,** Jacob; **and he consorted with her,** assuming that she was Rachel. **²⁴Laban gave Zilpa, his maidservant, to his daughter Leah as a maidservant.**

²⁵It was in the morning and Jacob discovered: **Behold, she was Leah. He said to Laban: What is this that you did to me? Wasn't it for Rachel that I worked with you? Why did you deceive me? ²⁶Laban said: It is not done thus in our place, to give the younger** sister in marriage **before the elder. ²⁷Complete the** wedding **week for this one** bride, **and we will give you that one too,** the other sister, in exchange **for the work that you will work with me another seven additional years. ²⁸Jacob did so, and** he **completed that week** for the marriage of Leah, **and he,** Laban, **gave him Rachel his daughter for a wife. ²⁹Laban gave Bilha his maidservant to his daughter Rachel as a maidservant. ³⁰He also consorted with Rachel; he also loved Rachel more than Leah. And** Jacob **worked with him,** Laban, **another seven additional years,** as he had agreed.

Leah's First Set of Sons

Jacob openly prefers Rachel, who is unable to bear children. Leah, by contrast, gives birth to several sons in succession. Through the names she gives her sons, Leah reveals her longing for her husband's love.

³¹The Lord saw that Leah was hated, and therefore **He** came to her aid and immediately **opened her womb,** and she conceived. **And Rachel was barren. ³²Leah conceived and bore a son, and she called his name Reuben; she said: Because the Lord saw** [ra'a] **my affliction; for now my husband will love me,** for I am the mother of his son. **³³Soon after-ward, she conceived again and bore a son, and said: Because the Lord**

heard [*shama*] that I am hated, He gave me this son as well. She called his name Simeon [Shimon]. ³⁴She conceived again and bore a son, and said: Now, this time, my husband will certainly accompany [*yillaveh*] and become close to me, as I have borne him three sons. Therefore, he, Jacob, called his name Levi. ³⁵She conceived again and bore a son, and said: This time I will thank [*odeh*] the Lord; therefore, she called his name Judah. And she ceased bearing for a time.

Jacob's Family Expands

Rachel tries to remedy her infertility by using the same technique Sarah had tried, giving her maidservant to her husband. After Bilha bears two sons, Leah also gives her maidservant, Zilpa, to Jacob. Not only does Zilpa bear two sons, Leah herself bears more children. Rachel, by contrast, remains childless.

30 ¹Rachel saw that she did not bear for Jacob. Rachel envied her sister, and she said to Jacob: Give me children, and if I will not bear children I am as one dead. ²Jacob was incensed at Rachel; he said: Am I in place of God, who withheld from you the fruit of the womb, children? ³She said: Here is my maid Bilha. Consort with her and she shall bear upon my knees, and I shall be built through her; I hope this act will be auspicious for my own fertility. ⁴She gave him Bilha, her maidservant, as a wife, and Jacob consorted with her.

⁵Bilha conceived and bore Jacob a son. ⁶Rachel said: God judged me [*dananni*], and also heard my voice and gave me a son; therefore she called his name Dan. ⁷Bilha, Rachel's maidservant, conceived again, and bore Jacob a second son. ⁸Rachel said: I engaged in a great, primal struggle [*naftulei*] with my sister, and I also prevailed. She called his name Naphtali.

⁹Leah saw that she had ceased bearing after the birth of Judah; she took Zilpa her maidservant and gave her to Jacob as a wife. ¹⁰Zilpa, Leah's maidservant, bore Jacob a son. ¹¹Leah said: Fortune [*gad*] has come; she called his name Gad. ¹²Zilpa, Leah's maidservant, bore a second son to Jacob. ¹³Leah said: He is born in my happiness [*be'oshri*], as women will be happy for me and praise me for my many children. She called his name Asher.

Genesis

Mandrakes and Fertility; Rachel Gives Birth

Rachel adopts any measure she can to conceive. When Leah's oldest son Reuben brings mandrakes from the field, Rachel is willing to pay for them, hoping they will engender the pregnancy she yearns for.

Fourth aliya **¹⁴Reuben went during the days of wheat harvest, found mandrakes,** a fragrant wild plant known as a folk remedy for barrenness, **in the field, and brought them to Leah, his mother. Rachel said to Leah: Please give me from your son's mandrakes. ¹⁵She,** Leah, **said to her: Is the taking of my husband insignificant?** Is it not enough for you that you have taken my husband's affections? **And** you wish **to take also my son's mandrakes? Rachel said: Therefore, he shall lie with you tonight** instead of me, **in exchange for your son's mandrakes. ¹⁶Jacob came** home **from the field in the evening. Leah came out to meet him and said: You will consort with me, for I have hired you** from my sister **with my son's mandrakes. He lay with her that night.**

¹⁷God heeded Leah in her prayers, **and she conceived and bore Jacob a fifth son. ¹⁸Leah said: God has given** me **my reward** [*sekhari*], due to the fact **that I gave my maidservant to my husband. She called his name Issachar. ¹⁹Leah conceived again and bore a sixth son to Jacob. ²⁰Leah said: God has granted me a fine gift; now my husband will reside** primarily **with me** [*yizbeleni*], **because I bore him six sons. She called his name Zebulun. ²¹And then she bore a daughter, and she called her name Dina.**

²²God remembered Rachel, and God heeded her, and He opened her womb. ²³She conceived and bore a son, and said: God has removed [*asaf*] **my disgrace. ²⁴She called his name Joseph, saying: May the Lord add** [*yosef*] **another son for me** after Joseph. This name alludes both to the removal of her disgrace and her wish for another son.

Jacob's Wages

Cognizant of Laban's devious nature, Jacob wants a contract that will benefit both parties, but will also prevent any cheating. He asks to receive payment for his work in the form of certain types of animals, in order to ensure transparency and clear standards.

²⁵It was when Rachel bore Joseph that Jacob said to Laban: Release me, and I will go to my place and to my land. ²⁶Give me my wives and my children, wives **for whom I have worked for you** faithfully, **and I will go; for you know my labor that I performed for you.** I have fulfilled all my obligations. **²⁷Laban said to him: If now I have found favor in your eyes,**

I have divined, and I have discovered that the Lord has blessed me on *Fifth aliya* your account. ²⁸He, Laban, said: Stipulate your wages for me, and I will give it, pay it.

²⁹He, Jacob, said to him: You know how I have served you, and how your livestock was with me. ³⁰For the little that you had before me, before my arrival, has increased abundantly, and the Lord has blessed you on my account. And now, when shall I provide for the needs of my household as well?

³¹He, Laban, said to Jacob: What shall I give you? Jacob said: Do not give me anything. Do not pay me with silver or the equivalent. If you will do this matter for me, I will return to my work and herd your flock and guard it: ³²I will pass, with you, through all your flock today; remove from there every speckled and spotted lamb. And, likewise, remove every brown lamb among the sheep that you find, and also the spotted and speckled among the goats, and give them to someone else to herd. And it, any of these unusual animals that are born subsequently, shall be my wages. ³³My honesty shall speak on my behalf, be proven, on a future day, when you shall go over my wages before you; every one that is not speckled and spotted among the goats, and brown among the sheep, is to be regarded as stolen if it is with me. ³⁴Laban said: Indeed, I agree, may it be so, in accordance with your statement.

Jacob's Flock

Jacob succeeds in breeding a particular type of animal. While it is unclear how the peeled rods stimulate the animals to birth offspring with the desired appearance, Jacob's flock grows immensely.

³⁵He, Laban, removed that day the streaked, those with stripes near the ankles, and spotted, older, goats, and all the speckled and spotted birthing female goats, each black goat that had a white spot in it, and all the brown among the sheep, and gave them into the possession of his sons, so that similar animals would not be reproduced among the rest of the flock. ³⁶He established a path, a distance, of three days between himself and Jacob. And Jacob herded the remaining flock of Laban.

³⁷Jacob took for himself rods from trees: of fresh poplar, and almond, and plane; he peeled white streaks in them by removing some of the bark, thereby exposing the white of the tree that was in the rods. ³⁸He displayed the rods that he peeled in the receptacles, in the water troughs from which the flocks would come to drink, facing the flocks.

And **they,** the flock, **would come into heat,** and mate, **when they came to drink.** ³⁹**The flocks came into heat due to the rods, and the flocks gave birth to streaked, speckled, and spotted** young. ⁴⁰**And Jacob separated the lambs** with this unusual appearance, **and he placed the faces of the flocks toward** all **the streaked and all the brown in the flocks of Laban,** meaning that he positioned them at the head of the flock, **and he established for himself droves alone, and did not place them with the flocks of Laban.**

⁴¹**And it was, whenever the strong flocks,** the most fertile animals, **would come into heat** during that season, that **Jacob would place the rods before the eyes of the flocks at the troughs, to have them come into heat with the rods,** when they saw them. ⁴²**When the flocks were feeble** and less fertile, **he would not place them,** the rods. **The feeble were for Laban, and the strong** and fertile animals were **for Jacob.** ⁴³**The man,** Jacob, **became exceedingly prosperous, and he had many flocks, and** used some to buy **maidservants and slaves, and camels and donkeys.**

Jacob Prepares to Leave Haran

When Laban and his sons become displeased about Jacob's wealth, Jacob consults secretly with his wives to secure their agreement to return to his homeland.

31 ¹**He,** Jacob, **heard the words of Laban's sons, saying: Jacob has taken everything that is our father's, and from that which is our father's he has accumulated all this wealth.** ²**Jacob** also **saw the countenance of Laban, and behold, it was not** friendly **toward him, as in the past.** ³At this point, **the Lord said to Jacob: Return to the land of your fathers, and to the land of your birth, and I will be with you,** I will watch over you.

⁴**Jacob sent and summoned Rachel and Leah to the field, to his flocks.** ⁵**He said to them: I see your father's countenance, and it is not toward me as in the past. And the God of my father was with me;** He promised to watch over me. ⁶**And you know that with all my strength I have served your father.** ⁷**But your father has cheated me, and changed** the conditions of **my wages ten times. But** even so, **God did not allow him to harm me.** ⁸**If,** when, **he,** Laban, **said this: The speckled** animals **shall be your wages;** then all the flocks bore speckled offspring, and I gained. **And if,** when, **he said this: The streaked shall be your wages;** all the flocks bore streaked offspring. ⁹**It has been God** who **has diverted the livestock of your father and given it to me.**

¹⁰It was at the time that the flock was in heat, I lifted my eyes, and saw in a dream, and behold, the males that mounted and impregnated the flock were streaked, speckled, and mottled. They were a variety of mixed colors, even if that was not always the case in reality. ¹¹The angel of God said to me in the dream: Jacob, and I said: Here I am; I am listening. ¹²He said: Please lift your eyes, and see, all the males that mount the flock are streaked, speckled, and mottled, for I have seen all that Laban is doing to you, and therefore I have come to help you. ¹³I am the God of your encounter in Beit El, where you anointed a monument and where you took a vow to Me. Now arise, leave this land, and return to the land of your birth.

¹⁴Rachel and Leah answered and said to him: Is there still a share or inheritance for us in our father's house? ¹⁵Are we not considered foreigners by him, as he sold us to you like merchandise? And he also consumed our silver by appropriating our dowry money for himself. ¹⁶For all the wealth that God salvaged from our father, it is for us and for our children, we deserve it. And now, everything that God said to you, do.

Jacob Flees

When Laban goes off to shear his sheep, Jacob seizes the opportunity to depart in his absence, with no advance notice. As they leave, Rachel steals her father's household idols, to prevent him from worshipping them.

Sixth aliya ¹⁷Jacob arose immediately and placed his sons and his wives upon the camels. ¹⁸He led all his livestock and all his property that he had attained, his acquisitions that he had acquired, which he attained in Padan Aram, to come to Isaac his father, to the land of Canaan. ¹⁹Laban was absent, as he went to shear his sheep. And Rachel stole the household idols that were her father's. These were used for sorcery or religious rites. ²⁰Jacob deceived Laban the Aramean, in that he did not tell him that he was fleeing. ²¹He fled, he and all that he had, his family and possessions; and he arose and crossed the river, the Euphrates, and headed toward the highlands of Gilad.

²²It was told to Laban on the third day after his departure that Jacob had fled. ²³He took his brethren with him, and pursued him a distance of seven days. He, Laban, reached him in the highlands of Gilad. ²⁴God came to Laban the Aramean in a revelatory dream of the night, and He said to him: Beware lest you speak to Jacob from good to bad; make neither seductive offers nor threats. ²⁵Laban caught up with Jacob. Jacob

had pitched his tent in the highlands of Gilad, and Laban also pitched the tents of his brethren in the highlands of Gilad.

Laban Searches for the Idols

As Laban is prohibited from hurting Jacob, he indulges his anger by hurling accusations at him, the chief one being that Jacob stole his idols. Jacob, unaware that Rachel took the idols, assumes that Laban is accusing him falsely, and invites him to inspect all his tents.

26Laban said to Jacob: What did you do, that you deceived me and led my daughters like captives of the sword, like prisoners of war? 27Why did you flee surreptitiously and deceive me and not tell me you were leaving? I would have sent you on your way in a dignified, celebratory manner, with joy and with songs, with drum and with harp. 28You did not allow me to kiss my daughters' sons, and my daughters. Now you have acted foolishly. 29It is in my power to do you harm, but the God of your father said to me last night, saying: Beware of speaking with Jacob, from good to bad. 30And now, even if you have gone because you longed for your father's house, why did you steal my gods?

31Jacob answered and said to Laban: I fled because I feared you, because I said to myself: I must flee lest you rob me of your daughters. 32And I did not rob you; with whomever you find your gods, he shall not live, but will be put to death. Before our brethren, search and identify what property of yours is with me, and take it back for yourself. And Jacob did not know that Rachel stole them.

33Laban came into Jacob's tent to search, and into Leah's tent, and into the tent of the two maidservants, but he did not find the idols; he emerged from Leah's tent and came into Rachel's tent. 34Rachel took the household idols, placed them in the cushion of the camel, and sat upon them. Laban felt throughout the tent and did not find them. 35She said to her father: Let my lord not be angry, as I cannot arise before you in respect, because the manner of women is upon me; I am menstruating. He searched the tent, but did not find the household gods.

Jacob Reproaches Laban

Convinced that there was no basis for Laban's accusation of theft, Jacob feels dishonored by Laban's intrusive search through his and his wives' tents. He goes on the offensive, reminding Laban of the unreasonable working conditions he endured without complaint. Nevertheless, Laban neither acknowledges his grievance nor apologizes.

36Jacob was angry and quarreled with Laban. Jacob responded and said to Laban: What is my transgression, what is my sin, that you have

pursued after me? [37]For you felt all my vessels; what have you found of all the vessels of your household? Place it, whatever you found, here before my brethren and your brethren, and they will determine the rightful owner, between the two of us. [38]These twenty years I have been with you; your ewes and your female goats have not miscarried. And the rams of your flock I have not eaten. [39]I did not bring the remains of a mauled animal, one torn apart by wild beasts, to you, with the claim that it was not my fault. I bore its loss and would pay for it; from me you could demand it. Whether an animal was stolen from me by day or stolen from me by night, I accepted responsibility for all damages. [40]Thus I was: When I shepherded your flock in the day dehydration consumed me, and so did the frost by night; and my sleep fled from my eyes. [41]These are twenty years for me in your house: I worked for you fourteen years for your two daughters, and six years for a portion of your flocks; and you changed my wages ten times. [42]If the God of my father, the God of Abraham, and the Fear of Isaac, God, whom Isaac feared, had not been with me then to assist me, you would have sent me away now empty-handed. God saw my hardship and the faithful toil of my hands, and proved it last night when He spoke to you.

enth
aliya

[43]Laban responded and said to Jacob: The girls, your wives, are my daughters, and the boys, their children, are my sons, and the flocks are descended from my flocks, and everything that you see is mine. And to my daughters, what can I do to them today, or to their children whom they have borne? I would not harm my family. [44]And now come, let us establish a covenant, I and you, and let it be as a witness between me and you.

Jacob and Laban Establish a Covenant

Although they will be far from one another, Jacob and Laban wish to maintain better relations in the future. The ritual they conduct to establish a covenant includes building a monument, listing their mutual responsibilities, and sharing a meal.

[45]Jacob took a stone and established it as a commemorative monument. [46]Jacob said to his brethren, his sons and other members of his camp: Gather stones. And they took stones, and made a pile around the pillar, and they ate there on the pile. [47]Laban called it Yegar Sahaduta, meaning "pile of testimony" in ancient Aramaic, and Jacob called it Gal'ed. [48]Laban said: This pile [gal] is witness [ed] between me and you today. Therefore he called its name Gal'ed; [49]and the Mitzpa, a nearby place, will also serve as testimony, as he, Laban, said: The Lord will observe

[*yitzef*] conduct **between me and you, because we will be concealed one from another** due to distance. [50]God will know **if you shall afflict my daughters, or if you shall take** more **wives in addition to my daughters,** thereby depriving them of their share. While **no man is with us** to report back to me, **see, God is witness between me and you.** [51]**Laban said to Jacob: Here is this pile and here is the monument that I have established between me and you.** [52]**This pile is witness, and the monument is witness, that I will not pass this pile** on my way **to you, and that you shall not pass this pile and this monument** on your way **to me, for harm,** as belligerents. [53]**The God of Abraham, and the God of Nahor,** and also **the God of their father** Terah, **shall judge between us. And Jacob took an oath by the Fear of his father Isaac,** meaning God, whom Isaac feared. [54]**Jacob slaughtered for a feast on the highland, and summoned his brethren to eat bread,** to join in the festivities. **They ate bread, and stayed the night on the highland.**

Maftir [55]**Laban awoke early in the morning, and kissed his sons and his daughters,** i.e., his grandchildren and daughters, **and blessed them,** and then **Laban went and returned to his place.**

Jacob Encounters Angels

Jacob continues in the direction of his father's home. When he encounters a large group of angels, he understands that God continues to accompany and preserve him wherever he goes.

32 [1]**Jacob went on his way, and angels of God encountered him.** [2]**Jacob said when he saw them: This is the camp** [*maḥaneh*] **of God.** Therefore, **he called the name of that place Mahanayim,** meaning "two camps," in reference to his camp and God's camp.

Illustrations: See map of Jacob's route back to Canaan, p. 522.

Parashat Vayishlah

As Jacob nears Esau's territory, on his way back from Haran, he sends him gifts and respectful messages, hoping to appease him. The night before Jacob expects to encounter his brother, while he is alone, a heavenly being accosts him, and they wrestle together all night; Jacob emerges wounded, but victorious. After his meeting with Esau passes without incident, Jacob parts from him and settles in Shekhem. Jacob's daughter Dina is raped and kidnapped by a local prince; her brothers avenge her honor by raiding the town, killing all the men, and returning Dina to her family. Afterward, Jacob leaves the area and heads toward his father's home, in Hebron. On the way, Rachel dies while giving birth to Jacob's twelfth son, whom Jacob names Benjamin. The *parasha* ends by detailing the saga of Esau's clan, which ultimately settles in the land of Se'ir and becomes the nation of Edom.

Jacob Sends Messengers to Esau

As Jacob approaches Canaan, he lets Esau know that he is coming, and expresses a desire to reconcile with him. After so many years apart, he does not know how his brother will react to his overtures, or if he still harbors the desire to kill him.

³Jacob sent messengers before him to Esau his brother, to the land of Se'ir, the field, region, **of Edom. ⁴He commanded them, saying: So shall you say to my lord, to Esau: So says your servant Jacob: I have resided with Laban, and tarried until now. ⁵I have oxen, donkeys, flocks, slaves, and maidservants. And I have sent** these messengers **to tell my lord,** so **that I may find favor in your eyes. ⁶The messengers returned to Jacob, saying: We came to your brother, to Esau; moreover he is coming to meet you, and four hundred men** are with him.

Further reading: For more on Jacob's messengers and his preparations for the encounter with Esau, see *A Concise Guide to the Sages*, p. 50.

Jacob Prays and Prepares for Battle

The report of Esau's approaching troop seems to confirm Jacob's worst fears. In the face of Esau's clear numerical advantage, Jacob prepares for battle, both tactically and by requesting divine assistance.

Genesis

⁷Jacob was very frightened and distressed. He divided the people who were with him, his family, slaves, and companions, and also the flocks, the cattle, and the camels, into two camps. ⁸He said: If Esau will come upon the one camp, either camp, and smite it, the remaining camp will be able to escape.

⁹Jacob then prayed, and said: God of my father Abraham, and God of my father Isaac, Lord, who says to me: Return to your land, and to the land of your birth, and I will benefit you; ¹⁰I am unworthy of all the kindnesses and of all the truth that You have performed for Your servant, for me; for I had with me only my staff when I crossed this Jordan River when I fled from Canaan, and now I have become numerous enough to fill two camps. ¹¹Deliver me please from the hand of my brother, from the hand of Esau, for I fear him, lest he come and smite me, mother and children alike. ¹²And You said in the vision of the ladder at Beit El, promising: I will benefit you, and render your descendants as numerous as the sand of the sea, which are so many they cannot be counted.

Jacob Sends Esau Gifts

Jacob sends Esau a large gift of livestock, staggering the arrival of the animals and structuring their composition for maximal effect. He hopes that the impressive gift might blunt Esau's anger toward him and even arouse fraternal feelings.

Second
aliya

¹³He stayed there that night; he took from that which was in his possession a gift for Esau his brother: ¹⁴Two hundred female goats and twenty male goats, two hundred ewes and twenty rams, ¹⁵thirty nursing camels and their offspring, forty cows and ten bulls, twenty female donkeys and ten male donkeys, males and females of every species, for breeding. ¹⁶He placed them in the charge of his servants, each herd of animals separately, and he said to his servants: Go to Esau ahead of me, and make space between each and every herd.

¹⁷He commanded the shepherd of the first herd, saying: When Esau my brother meets you, and asks you, saying: To whom do you belong, and where are you going, and whose are these animals before you? ¹⁸You shall say: They are from your servant, Jacob, and as for this collection of animals, it is a gift sent to my lord, to Esau, and behold, he, Jacob, too, is behind us. ¹⁹He commanded also the second, and also the third, and also all that followed the herds, saying: In this manner shall you speak to Esau when you find him. ²⁰You shall say: Moreover, here is your servant Jacob coming behind us to meet you. The Torah notes: He, Jacob,

said to himself: **I will appease him,** Esau, **with the gift that goes before me, and thereafter I will see his face; perhaps he will favor me** and forgive me. ²¹**The gift went before him, and he stayed that night in the camp.**

Nocturnal Wrestling

During the night before his encounter with Esau, Jacob must contend with a mysterious angelic figure. The Sages saw Jacob's struggle as a symbol of his mental and spiritual preparation to face Esau, and referred to the angelic figure as Esau's minister.

²²**He,** Jacob, **arose during that night, and he took his two wives, his two maidservants, and his eleven children, and crossed the ford of the Yabok.** ²³**He took them and brought them over the stream, and brought over that** property **which he had.**

²⁴Afterward, **Jacob remained alone** on the riverbank, **and a** mysterious **man,** an angel, **wrestled with him until dawn.** ²⁵**He,** the angel, **saw that he could not prevail against him,** Jacob, **and** therefore **he touched,** struck, Jacob, and injured **the joint of his thigh; and the joint of Jacob's thigh was dislocated as he wrestled with him.** ²⁶While the two were grappling with each other, **he,** the angel, **said: Release me, for the dawn has broken. He,** Jacob, **said: I will not release you unless you bless me.** ²⁷**He,** the angel, **said to him: What is your name? He said: Jacob.** ²⁸**He,** the angel, **said: No more shall Jacob be said to be your name; rather,** you **shall be called Israel; for you have striven** [*sarita*] **with God** [*elohim*], meaning with angels, **and** striven **with men, and you have prevailed.** ²⁹**Jacob asked and said: Tell me, please, your name,** your essence or function. **He said: Why is it that you ask my name? And he,** the angel, **blessed him there** again.

³⁰**Jacob named the place Peniel: For I have seen God,** angels, **face-to-face** [*panim el panim*], **and my life was saved.** ³¹**The sun** then **rose upon him,** shined for him, **as he passed Penuel, and he was limping on his thigh.** ³²**Therefore, the children of Israel do not eat the sciatic nerve** of animals, the large nerve that extends along the entire thigh and leg all the way to the heel, **and which is upon the joint of the thigh, to this day, because he,** the angel, **touched the joint of Jacob's thigh at the sciatic nerve.**

Third aliya

Jacob and Esau's Reunion

Jacob attempts to honor and appease Esau in several ways. Whatever Esau's private feelings toward his brother, the two have an emotional, familial meeting, with no trace of enmity.

33 ¹After sunrise, **Jacob lifted his eyes and saw, and behold, Esau came, and with him four hundred men.** He divided the children among Leah, Rachel, and the two maidservants. ²**He placed the maidservants and their children first, Leah and her children next, and Rachel and Joseph last.** ³**And he,** Jacob, **passed before them, and** as he walked toward Esau he **prostrated himself earthward seven times, until his approach to his brother.** ⁴**Esau ran to meet him, embraced him, fell upon his neck and kissed him; and they wept.**

⁵**He,** Esau, **lifted his eyes, saw the women and the children** walking behind Jacob, **and said: Who are these?** What is their relationship **to you? He,** Jacob, **said: These are the children with whom God has graced your** *Fourth aliya* **servant.** ⁶**The maidservants approached, they and their children, and they prostrated themselves.** ⁷**Leah, too, and her children approached, and prostrated themselves, and afterward Joseph and Rachel** also approached, and prostrated themselves.

⁸**He,** Esau, **said: For whom do you intend this entire camp** of livestock **that I met;** why did you send it? **He,** Jacob, **said: To find favor in the eyes of my lord.** ⁹**Esau said: I have plenty** of property, **my brother. That which is yours shall be yours.** Keep the gift for yourself. ¹⁰**Jacob said: Please do not** refuse my gift; **if I have now found favor in your eyes, receive my gift from me, for truly, I have seen your face, like the sight of the face of angels, and you welcomed me,** and reconciled with me. ¹¹**Please, take my gift that was** given to me and that I **brought to you, as God has graced me, and because I have everything** I need. **He,** Jacob, **urged him** to accept his present, **and he took it.**

Esau and Jacob Part

Despite Esau's affection toward him, Jacob thinks it best for each brother to go his own way. Esau leaves him, and Jacob returns to Canaan and settles there.

¹²**He,** Esau, **said: We will travel, and we will go** on together, **and I will go along with you.** ¹³**He,** Jacob, **said to him: My lord knows that the children are tender and that** the needs of **the nursing flocks and cattle,** with their offspring, **are upon me; if they drive them hard one day, all the flocks will die.** ¹⁴**Please, my lord will pass before his servant.** You go first, **and I will**

advance slowly, according to the pace of the property, livestock, **that is before me, and according to the pace of the children, until I will come to my lord, to** Mount Se'ir. **¹⁵And Esau said:** If so, please, **I will place with you some of the people who are with me** to protect you and your family. **He,** Jacob, **said: Why do that? I will find favor in the eyes of my lord;** do not trouble yourself for me. **¹⁶Esau returned on that day,** going on his **way to Se'ir. ¹⁷Jacob traveled to** a place named **Sukot, and built himself a house, and established booths** [*sukot*] **for his livestock. Therefore, he called the name of the place Sukot.**

¹⁸Jacob came unharmed and without losses **to the city of Shekhem, which is in the land of Canaan, upon his arrival from Padan Aram. And he encamped before the city. ¹⁹He purchased a tract of the field where he had pitched his tent, from the possession of the children of Hamor;** Hamor was the head of the city and the **father of Shekhem; for one hundred kesita,** a certain sum of money. **²⁰He established there an altar, and called it El Elohei Israel,** meaning the Strong God of Israel.

Dina Is Abducted

When Shekhem, the son of the local leader, sees an unfamiliar young girl, Jacob's daughter, Dina, he seizes her and rapes her. Afterward he becomes smitten by her and wishes to marry her.

34 **¹Dina, the daughter of Leah, whom she bore to Jacob, went out to see**
Fifth
aliya **the daughters of the land. ²Shekhem, son of Hamor the Hivite, prince of the land, saw her; and he took her, and lay with her, and raped her. ³His soul was drawn to Dina daughter of Jacob, and he loved the young woman and spoke soothingly to the young woman,** to entice and persuade her. **⁴Shekhem spoke to his father Hamor, saying: Take for me this girl as a wife.**

Hamor Negotiates with Jacob's Sons

Hamor offers commercial and social benefits to Jacob in exchange for his consent to marry off Dina to his son Shekhem. He presents Shekhem's marriage proposal as a routine matter, and does not mention the appalling incident that led to it. But Jacob's sons, who conduct the negotiations, are insulted and angry.

⁵Jacob heard that he, Shekhem, **had defiled Dina his daughter.** The news reached him at home, **and his sons were with his livestock in the field, and Jacob kept silent until their arrival. ⁶Meanwhile, Hamor, father of Shekhem, went out to Jacob to speak with him. ⁷The sons of Jacob came**

from the field immediately **when they heard** what had happened to Dina, **and the men were saddened and became very angry, as he,** Shekhem, had **done an abomination against** the family of **Israel to lie with Jacob's daughter; and so shall not be done.**

[8]**Hamor,** the prince of the land, **spoke with them, saying: The soul of my son Shekhem longs for your daughter. Please, give her to him as a wife.** [9]**And marry with us; give your daughters to us, and take our daughters for you.** [10]**And you shall live with us** permanently, **and the land shall be** open **before you; live and trade in it** freely, **and settle in it.** [11]**Shekhem said to her father and to her brothers:** Please, **let me find favor in your eyes, and that which you shall say to me I will give.** [12]**Inflate upon me the bridal payment and gift** I am to furnish you **exceedingly, and I will give in accordance with what you shall say to me.** I will agree to pay any amount you see fit, **and** I ask only that you **give me the young woman as a wife.**

[13]**The sons of Jacob answered Shekhem and Hamor his father with guile, and spoke** with cunning, **as he,** Shekhem, had **defiled Dina their sister.** [14]**They said to them: We cannot do this thing, to give our sister to a man who has a foreskin, as it is a disgrace for us.** [15]**Only with this will we accede to you: If you become like us, to have every male among you circumcised.** [16]**We will give our daughters to you, and we will take your daughters for us, and we will live with you, and we will become one people.** [17]**If you do not heed us, to be circumcised, we will take our daughter,** our sister, home, **and we will go.** [18]**Their statement was favorable,** acceptable, **in the eyes of Hamor, and in the eyes of Shekhem son of Hamor.** [19]**The lad did not tarry to perform the matter, because he de**sired Jacob's daughter. And he was more respected than anyone else in all the house of his father,** his family.

The Men of Shekhem Circumcise Themselves

Hamor and Shekhem approach the other city leaders, who generally sit at the city gates, and propose the agreement to them. They elide the fact of Shekhem's infatuation with Dina, and mention only the financial and political benefits that will accrue to the city from a union with the neighboring tribe, Jacob's clan.

[20]**Hamor and Shekhem his son came to the gate of their city, and** they **spoke with the men of their city, saying:** [21]**These men,** Jacob's family, **are** in **peaceful** relations **with us, and** we will benefit if **they will live in the land and trade in it; behold, the land is spacious before them;** there is

room for everybody. **Their daughters we will take as wives for us, and our daughters we will give to them.** ²²**But only with this condition will the men accede to us, to live with us, to become one people; with every male being circumcised, as they are circumcised.** ²³**Aren't their livestock and their property and all their animals ours?** We will absorb them economically and culturally, and we will thereby enrich ourselves. **We must only accede to them, and they will live with us.**

²⁴**All who emerged from the gate of his city,** all the residents, **heeded Hamor and Shekhem his son; every male, all who emerged from the gate of his city, was circumcised.**

Dina's Brothers Take Revenge

Shimon and Levi exploit the men of the city's post-circumcision weakness and kill them, in retaliation for their tacit support for Shekhem's defiling of Dina. Jacob becomes angry with his sons and expresses concern about the reaction of the other tribes nearby.

²⁵**It was on the third day, when they,** the men of Shekhem, **were in pain** from their circumcisions, **that the two sons of Jacob, Simeon and Levi, Dina's brothers, each** man **took his sword. And** they **came upon the city confidently,** as it was undefended, **and killed all the males.** ²⁶**And they killed Hamor and Shekhem his son by sword. And** then they **took Dina from the house of Shekhem and departed.** ²⁷**The** other **sons of Jacob beset the slain,** to take their valuables, **and looted the city,** with the justification **that** its residents had **defiled their sister.** ²⁸**They took their flocks, their cattle, and their donkeys, and that which was in the city and that which was in the field.** ²⁹**They took captive and looted all their wealth, all their children and wives, and everything that was in the house.**

³⁰**Jacob said to Simeon and Levi: You have sullied me, to render me loathsome to the inhabitants of the land, the Canaanites and the Perizites. I am few in number;** it is possible **they will mobilize against me and smite me, and I and my household shall be destroyed.** ³¹**They,** the two sons, **said: Shall he render,** treat, **our sister as a harlot?** It was unacceptable to allow Shekhem to treat Dina in this manner.

Jacob Fulfills His Vow

God fulfilled His promise to protect Jacob and assist him in returning to Canaan. Now it is Jacob's turn to fulfill his vow to serve God in Beit El. God continues to protect him as he makes his way there, and the neighboring peoples do not dare to attack him.

35 ¹God said to Jacob: Arise, ascend to Beit El, and settle there; and make there an altar to the God who appeared to you when you fled from Esau your brother. ²Jacob said to his household and to all who were with him, including his slaves, maidservants, and companions: **Remove the foreign gods that are in your midst,** in your possession, **and purify yourselves** in water, **and change your garments.** ³And we will arise and ascend to Beit El; and I will make there an altar to the God who answers me and assists me **on the day of my distress. He was with me on the path upon which I went.**

⁴They gave to Jacob all the foreign gods that were in their possession, and the rings that were in their ears, that were decorated with idolatrous images. **And Jacob interred them beneath the terebinth** tree **that is near Shekhem.** ⁵They traveled, and **the dread of** them, imposed by **God, was upon the cities that were surrounding them, and they did not pursue after the sons of Jacob.**

⁶Jacob came to Luz, which is in the land of Canaan, it is Beit El, he and all the people who were with him. ⁷He erected there an altar, and he called the place of the altar **El Beit El,** the God of Beit El, **because** it was there that **God was revealed to him when he fled from his brother.** ⁸The Torah relates, incidentally, that **Deborah, Rebecca's nurse, died, and she was buried below,** south of, **Beit El, beneath the oak** tree; **and he called its name Alon Bakhut,** Oak of Weeping, as a sign of mourning for her.

Another Revelation

On Jacob's way to Canaan he had been blessed by an angel, who also changed his name to Israel. Now God blesses him again and confirms his name change.

⁹God appeared to Jacob again, already upon his arrival from Padan Aram, and He blessed him. ¹⁰God said to him: Your name is currently Jacob. However, your name shall no longer be called Jacob, rather, Israel shall be your name; and He called his name Israel. ¹¹God said to him: I am God Almighty. Be fruitful and multiply; a nation and an assembly of nations shall be from you, and kings shall emerge from your *Sixth* loins. Your offspring will merit greatness. ¹²And the land that I gave in a *aliya* promise to Abraham and Isaac, I will give it to you, and to your descendants after you I will give the land. ¹³God ascended from upon him, parted from him, as it were, in the place that He spoke with him.

¹⁴Jacob established a monument in the place that He spoke with him, a monument of stone, and he poured out a libation of wine upon it, and poured oil upon it in commemoration of this further revelation. ¹⁵Jacob again called the name of the place where God had spoken with him Beit El, to reiterate that the place was a house [*beit*] of God [*El*] where the Divine Presence rested.

Rachel Dies

Rachel goes into labor while she and her family are traveling, far from any inhabited area. Her difficult childbirth causes her demise, and she is buried on the road, rather than in the family burial plot in Hebron.

¹⁶They traveled south from Beit El, and it was still some distance to when they would arrive at the city of Efrat; and Rachel was in childbirth, and she had exceptional difficulty in her childbirth. ¹⁷It was as she was having difficulty in her childbirth that the midwife said to her: Fear not, for this too is a son for you. ¹⁸It was with the departure of her soul, for she was dying in childbirth, that she called his name Ben Oni, son of my pain and anguish. And his father called him Benjamin, son [*ben*] of the right-hand [*yamin*]. ¹⁹Rachel died, and she was buried on the path to Efrat, it is Bethlehem. ²⁰Jacob established a monument upon her grave; it is the monument of Rachel's grave until today.

📖 **Further reading:** The Sages teach that Rachel's grave, on the road, takes on significance for the Jewish people many generations later. See *A Concise Guide to the Sages*, p. 54.

Reuben and Bilha

The following passage recounts Reuben's sin with Bilha, Jacob's concubine. It appears that Reuben consorts with her sexually, but the fact that no reaction by Jacob is recorded here calls that into question. Some argue that Reuben does not commit adultery, but merely interferes in his father's marital affairs by moving his father's bed from Bilha's tent to Leah's tent, perhaps to assert that his mother should be regarded as the chief wife. Jacob chooses not to react immediately.

²¹Israel, Jacob, traveled, and he pitched his tent southward, beyond Migdal Eder. ²²It was when Israel dwelled in that land, that Reuben went and lay with Bilha, his father's concubine, or, he moved Jacob's bed from Bilha's tent to Leah's. And Israel heard. The verse concludes: The sons of Jacob were twelve:

²³The sons of Leah were Reuben, Jacob's firstborn, and Simeon, Levi, Judah, Issachar, and Zebulun. ²⁴The sons of Rachel were Joseph and Benjamin. ²⁵The sons of Bilha, Rachel's maidservant, were Dan and Naftali. ²⁶And the sons of Zilpa, Leah's maidservant, were Gad and Asher. These are the sons of Jacob, who were born to him in Padan Aram, apart from Benjamin, who was born in the land of Canaan.

Isaac's Death

²⁷Jacob continued southward and came to Isaac his father at Mamre, Kiryat Ha'arba, which is Hebron, where Abraham and Isaac resided. ²⁸The days of Isaac were one hundred years and eighty years; he lived to one hundred and eighty. ²⁹Isaac expired, and he died, and he was gathered to his people; he joined the souls of his parents. He died old and full of days, content with his life, and Esau and Jacob his sons buried him.

Esau's Family

Esau married two Canaanite women, and another woman, who was his cousin. When Jacob returns to Canaan with numerous flocks, Esau decides to settle on Mount Se'ir, in the land of Edom, where his own livestock will have room to graze.

36 ¹These are the descendants of Esau, who is called Edom. ²Esau took his wives from the daughters of Canaan, as stated above (26:34–35): Ada, daughter of Eilon the Hitite, and Oholivama, daughter of Ana, daughter of Tzivon the Hivite. ³And he also married his cousin Basmat, daughter of Ishmael, sister of a man called Nevayot. ⁴Ada bore Elifaz to Esau, and Basmat bore Re'uel; ⁵and Oholivama bore Yeush, Ya'elam, and Korah; these are the sons of Esau who were born to him while he still lived in the land of Canaan.

⁶But Esau subsequently took his wives, his sons, his daughters, all the members of his household, his livestock, all his animals, and all his possessions that he had acquired in the land of Canaan; and he went to a different land, due to his brother Jacob, ⁷because their property was too great for living together, and the land of their residence could not support them due to their plentiful livestock. ⁸Esau settled on Mount Se'ir; Esau who is Edom.

⁹And this is the legacy of Esau, father of the nation of Edom on Mount Se'ir. ¹⁰These are the names of all of Esau's sons, including those born in Se'ir: Elifaz, son of Ada wife of Esau; Re'uel, son of Basmat wife of Esau. ¹¹The sons of Elifaz were Teman, Omar, Tzefo, Gatam, and

Kenaz. ¹²And Timna was a concubine of Elifaz son of Esau, and she bore Amalek to Elifaz. These are the sons of Ada, wife of Esau. ¹³And these are the sons of Re'uel: Naḥat, and Zeraḥ, Shama, and Miza; these were the sons of Basmat wife of Esau. ¹⁴And these were the sons of Oholivama, daughter of Ana, daughter of Tzivon, Esau's wife. She bore to Esau Ye'ush, Ya'elam, and Koraḥ.

Chieftains Descended from Esau

The term chieftain refers to petty rulers of the various tribes that descend from Esau.

¹⁵These are the chieftains of the sons of Esau. The chieftains of the sons of Elifaz, firstborn of Esau, were the chieftain of Teman, the chieftain of Omar, the chieftain of Tzefo, the chieftain of Kenaz, ¹⁶the chieftain of Koraḥ, the chieftain of Gatam, and the chieftain of Amalek. These are the chieftains of Elifaz in the land of Edom; these are the sons of Ada, wife of Esau. ¹⁷And these are the sons of Re'uel son of Esau: The chieftain of Naḥat, the chieftain of Zeraḥ, the chieftain of Shama, the chieftain of Miza. These are the chieftains of Re'uel in the land of Edom; these are the sons of Basmat wife of Esau. ¹⁸And these are the sons of Oholivama, wife of Esau: The chieftain of Ye'ush, the chieftain of Ya'elam, the chieftain of Koraḥ; these are the chieftains of Oholivama, daughter of Ana wife of Esau. ¹⁹These are the sons of Esau, and these are their chieftains; he is Edom.

Horite Chieftains

The Horites, who inhabited the land of Edom before Esau's invasion, ultimately assimilated into Esau's clans. Nevertheless, they retained a measure of autonomy, and their tribal leaders were called chieftains, like the Edomite rulers.

²⁰These are the sons of a man named Se'ir the Horite, from the original inhabitants of the land: Lotan, Shoval, Tzivon, Ana, ²¹Dishon, Ezer, and Dishan; these are the chieftains of the Horites, sons of Se'ir in the land of Edom. ²²The children of Lotan were Hori and Hemam, and Lotan's sister was Timna, the concubine of Elifaz, son of Esau. ²³And these are the children of Shoval: Alvan, and Manaḥat, and Eval, Shefo, and Onam. ²⁴And these are the children of Tzivon: Aya and Ana; he is Ana, who found the yemim in the wilderness, produced mules through crossbreeding, as he was herding the donkeys of Tzivon his father. ²⁵And these are the children of Ana: Dishon, and a girl, Oholivama, daughter of Ana, Esau's wife. ²⁶And these are the children of Dishon: Ḥemdan, Eshban,

enth
aliya

Yitran, and Keran. ²⁷These are the children of Ezer: Bilhan, Zaavan, and Akan. ²⁸These are the children of Dishan: Utz and Aran. ²⁹These are the chieftains of the Horites: the chieftain of Lotan, the chieftain of Shoval, the chieftain of Tzivon, the chieftain of Ana, ³⁰the chieftain of Dishon, the chieftain of Ezer, the chieftain of Dishan; these are the chieftains of the Horites, according to rank, of their chieftains in the land of Se'ir.

Edomite Kings

The Edomite tribes gradually unified under a centralized monarchy. However, this system of government was apparently unstable, as each successive king originated from a different city, and the Torah presents afterward another list of Edomite chieftains. That list concludes the story of Isaac, as it represents the fulfillment of the blessing he bestowed upon Esau; that his descendants would enjoy independence in their own apportioned land.

³¹And these are the kings who reigned in the land of Edom, before the reign of a king for the children of Israel. ³²Bela son of Beor reigned in Edom, and the name of his city was Dinhava. ³³Bela died, and Yovav son of Zerah, of Botzra, another city in Edom, reigned in his stead. ³⁴Yovav died, and Husham of the land of the Temanites reigned in his stead. ³⁵Husham died, and Hadad son of Bedad, who smote, defeated, the tribe of Midyan in the field of Moav, reigned in his stead. And the name of his city was Avit. ³⁶Hadad died, and Samla of Masreka reigned in his stead. ³⁷Samla died, and Shaul of Rehovot on the Euphrates river reigned in his stead. ³⁸Shaul died, and Baal Hanan son of Akhbor reigned in his stead. ³⁹And Baal Hanan son of Akhbor died, and Hadar reigned in his stead; and the name of the city was Pa'u. And his wife's name was Meheitavel, daughter of Matred, daughter of Mei Zahav.

Maftir ⁴⁰And these are the names of the chieftains of Esau, according to their families and according to their places, by their names: The chieftain of Timna, the chieftain of Alva, the chieftain of Yetet, ⁴¹the chieftain of Oholivama, the chieftain of Ela, the chieftain of Pinon, ⁴²the chieftain of Kenaz, the chieftain of Teman, the chieftain of Mivtzar, ⁴³the chieftain of Magdiel, and the chieftain of Iram. These are the chieftains of Edom, according to their settlements in their apportioned land. He is Esau, father of the nation of Edom.

Parashat Vayeshev

Jacob's clear preference for Rachel's son Joseph engenders hostility toward Joseph among his brothers. Their animosity develops into hatred when Joseph relates his dreams to them, which they interpret as indicating his desire to rule over them. When Joseph comes to where they are herding their father's flocks, they seize the opportunity to harm him and, after initially planning to kill him, they settle for selling him as a slave.

The Torah interrupts the narrative at this point to relate an ostensibly unrelated story about Judah and his daughter-in-law Tamar. After two of Judah's sons die during successive marriages to Tamar, Judah hesitates to marry his third son to her. But Tamar, determined to have children from Judah's line, dresses up as a harlot, convinces Judah to lie with her, and ultimately bears him twins.

Joseph, who has been sold as a slave in Egypt, makes himself indispensable to his master and quickly rises in his household. But when he refuses repeated attempts by his master's wife to seduce him, she publicly accuses him of rape, and he is incarcerated. While in prison, he interprets the mysterious dreams of two of Pharaoh's courtiers, who are jailed with him, and his predictions are fulfilled in all their particulars.

The Favored Son

From here on, the narrative shifts its primary focus to Jacob's favorite son, Joseph, who is a living reminder of Jacob's beloved wife Rachel.

37 **¹Jacob settled in the land of his father's residence, in the land of Canaan. ²This is the legacy of Jacob. Joseph, seventeen years old, was herding the flock** of his household **with his brothers. And he was a lad,** friendly, **with the sons of Bilha, and with the sons of Zilpa, his father's wives. Yet Joseph brought evil report of them to their father,** reporting their inappropriate behavior.

³Israel, Jacob, **loved Joseph more than all his sons, because he was a son of his old age. He,** Jacob, **made him a fine tunic,** a decorated and distinct garment. **⁴His brothers saw that their father loved him more than all his brothers, and they hated him, and could not speak peaceably to him.**

📖 Further reading: The Sages criticize favoritism on the part of parents. See *A Concise Guide to the Sages*, p. 55.

Joseph's Dreams

Since Joseph's brothers understand his dreams as underscoring his select status, their hatred of him intensifies. Nevertheless, Joseph persists in relating his dreams to them, judging the dreams to be prophetic rather than mere fancy.

⁵**Joseph dreamed a dream, and he told it to his brothers, and they hated him even more. ⁶He said to them: Please, hear this dream that I dreamed: ⁷Behold, we were binding sheaves in the field. And behold, my sheaf arose, and also stood upright; and behold, your sheaves gathered around, and prostrated themselves to my sheaf. ⁸His brothers said to him: Will you reign over us? Will you have dominion over us? They hated him even more,** both **for his dreams and for his** conveying of negative **words,** reports, about them to Jacob.

⁹**He dreamed yet another dream, and he related it to his brothers. He said: Behold, I dreamed another dream, and behold, the sun, the moon, and eleven stars prostrated themselves to me. ¹⁰He related it to his father and to his brothers. And his father rebuked him, and said to him: What is this dream that you dreamed?** If the sun and the moon are metaphors for one's parents, **will I and your mother and your brothers come to prostrate ourselves to you to the earth?** Surely we will not. Your mother is already dead. ¹¹**His brothers envied him. But his father kept the matter in mind.**

The Brothers' Plot

Jacob wishes to maintain contact with his sons, who had wandered with the flock all the way from Hebron to Shekhem, and he sends Joseph to inquire into their welfare. When the brothers see him approaching alone, they plot how they will exploit this opportunity to assault him.

Second aliya

¹²**His brothers went to herd their father's flock in Shekhem. ¹³Israel said to Joseph: Aren't your brothers herding in Shekhem? Go, and I will send you to them. He,** Joseph, **said to him: Here, I am** ready and willing. ¹⁴**He said to him: Go now, see the status of your brothers and the status of the flock and bring back word. He sent him from the Valley of Hebron, and he,** Joseph, **came to Shekhem.**

¹⁵**A man found him, and behold, he,** Joseph, **was wandering in the field. The man asked him, saying: What do you seek? ¹⁶He said: I seek my**

brothers. **Please tell me where they are herding.** [17]The man said: They traveled from here; for I heard them saying to each other: **We shall go to Dotan. Joseph went after his brothers, and he found them in Dotan.** [18]They saw him from afar, and before he approached them, they conspired against him to kill him. [19]They said one to another: **Here comes that dreamer.** [20]Now **let us go and kill him and cast him into one of the** nearby **pits, and we will say** to others: **A wild beast devoured him. And** then **we shall see what will become of his dreams.** [21]Reuben heard, and delivered him from their hand; and he said: **Let us not smite him mortally.** [22]Reuben said to them: **Do not** actively **shed blood; cast him into this pit that is in the wilderness,** where he will die on his own, **but do not lay a hand on him** yourselves to kill him. Reuben suggested this only **in order to deliver him from their hand, to restore him to his father.**

Joseph Is Sold

The brothers accept Reuben's proposal to cast Joseph into a pit, without deciding anything about how to dispose of him further. When Judah suggests selling him as a slave, they agree, as in this way he will be taken far away without their having to hurt him themselves.

Third aliya [23]**It was when Joseph came to his brothers that they stripped Joseph of his tunic, the fine tunic that was upon him.** [24]**They took him and cast him into the pit; and the pit was empty, there was no water in it.** [25]**They sat to eat bread. And they lifted their eyes and saw, and behold, a caravan of Ishmaelites was coming from Gilad,** on the eastern side of the Jordan River. **And their camels were bearing** bundles of **spices,** including **balm,** a very valuable spice, **and labdanum,** a plant used for manufacturing perfume. The caravan was **going to take them down,** these spices, **to** sell them in **Egypt.** [26]**Judah said to his brothers: What profit is it,** what will we gain, **if we kill our brother and conceal his blood?** [27]**Go and we will sell him** as a slave **to the** arriving **Ishmaelites, and let our hand not be** directly **upon him, as he is our brother, our flesh. His brothers heeded** Judah's suggestion.

[28]**Midyanite men, merchants, passed by, and they pulled and lifted Joseph from the pit,** with the brothers' assent. **They sold Joseph to the Ishmaelites for twenty silver pieces; and they brought Joseph to Egypt.** [29]**Reuben returned to the pit, and behold, Joseph was not in the pit; he rent his garments** in distress. [30]**He returned to his brothers, and said: The boy is not there; and I, where do I go?** What will I do now?

Genesis

Jacob's Reaction

Having sold Joseph, the brothers realize they need to explain his disappearance. They invent a cover story, using the tunic they stripped from him as a prop.

³¹They took Joseph's tunic, slaughtered a goat, and dipped the tunic in the blood. ³²They sent the fine tunic to Jacob; they brought it to their father and they said: We found this. Identify, please, whether it is your son's tunic or not? ³³He identified it, and said: This is my son's tunic; clearly an evil beast has devoured him; Joseph has been torn apart. ³⁴Jacob rent his garments in mourning, placed sackcloth on his loins, and mourned his son many days. ³⁵All his sons and all his daughters, including his daughters-in-law, arose to console him; but he refused to be consoled. He said: Nothing will change the present reality; for I will descend mourning to the grave, to my son. His father wept for him.

³⁶And the Midyanites sold him, Joseph, to Egypt, as a slave to Potifar, who was a courtier of Pharaoh and the chief executioner.

Tamar's Marriages to Judah's Sons

The story that follows illustrates the ancient custom of levirate marriage, in which the widow of a man who dies childless marries his brother. Any children born of that marriage are considered to be those of the deceased.

38 ¹It was at that time that Judah descended, parted, from his brothers, and he turned to befriend an Adulamite man, from the town of Adulam; and his name was Hira. ²Judah saw there, in Adulam, the daughter of a Canaanite man, and his name was Shua. He took her in marriage, and consorted with her. ³She conceived and she bore a son; he called his name Er. ⁴She conceived again and bore a son; she called his name Onan. ⁵She continued and bore a son again, and she called his name Shela. He, Judah, was at the place known as Keziv when she bore him.

Fourth aliya

⁶Judah took a wife for Er his firstborn, and her name was Tamar. ⁷Er, Judah's firstborn, was wicked in the eyes of the Lord, and the Lord put him to death. ⁸Judah said to Onan: Consort with your brother's wife, and consummate levirate marriage with her. Establish offspring for your brother. ⁹Onan knew that the offspring would not be his. It was, therefore, when he consorted with his brother's wife, that he would spill it on the ground; he practiced coitus interruptus, so as not to give offspring for his brother. ¹⁰That which he did was evil in the eyes of the Lord, and He put him to death too.

¹¹**Judah said to Tamar, his daughter-in-law:** This time, **remain a widow** and live alone **in your father's house, until Shela my** third **son matures; for he,** Judah, **said** to himself: **Lest he too die** in marriage to Tamar**, like his brothers. So Tamar went and lived in her father's house.**

Tamar Takes Action

Tamar is prohibited from remarrying while she is awaiting levirate marriage, but when Shela reaches adulthood and does not marry her, she suspects he never will. Unwilling to remain a childless widow forever, she decides to induce Judah to consummate levirate marriage with her. A union between a father-in-law and daughter-in-law is highly irregular, so she disguises herself in order to carry out her unconventional plan, with Judah none the wiser.

¹²**The days** and years **accumulated and the daughter of Shua, wife of Judah, died.** After the period of mourning, **Judah was comforted, and** he **went up to** visit **his sheepshearers** to participate in the shearing of his sheep. **He and Hira, his friend the Adulamite,** came **to** the place called Timna. ¹³**It was told to Tamar, saying: Behold, your father-in-law is going up to Timna to shear his sheep.** ¹⁴**She removed the garments of her widowhood from upon her, and she covered herself with a** large **veil and wrapped herself,** in the manner of harlots. **And she sat at the entrance of** a place called **Einayim,** or near a spring [*ma'ayan*]**, which is on the road to Timna; for she saw that Shela had matured, yet she had not been given to him as a wife.**

¹⁵**Judah saw her** on the road **and thought her to be a harlot, because she covered her face.** ¹⁶**He turned to her by the road, and he said: Please, let me consort with you; for he did not know that she was his daughter-in-law. She said: What** payment **will you give me for consorting with me?** ¹⁷**He said: I will send you a kid from the flock** as payment. **She said:** Yes, but only **if you give me collateral until your sending.** ¹⁸**He said: What is the collateral that I should give you? She said: Your signet, and your belt, and your staff that is in your hand,** your personal, identifiable objects. **He gave them to her, consorted with her, and she conceived by him.** ¹⁹After Judah left, **she arose, went, and removed her veil from upon her, and she donned the garments of her widowhood.**

²⁰Later, **Judah sent the kid** to Tamar **in the hand of his friend the Adulamite, to take the collateral** back **from the woman; but he,** Hira, **did not find her.** ²¹**He asked the men of her place, saying: Where is the harlot who was at Einayim on the way? They said: There was no harlot here.** ²²**He returned to Judah, and said: I did not find her. The men of**

the place also said: There was no harlot here. ²³Judah said: If so, let her take it, the collateral, for her, lest we become a laughingstock; behold, I sent this kid, and you did not find her.

Tamar's Pregnancy and Childbirth

Tamar had no qualms about her actions, as she felt that she had fulfilled the spirit of the law of levirate marriage. She therefore made no attempt to conceal her pregnancy. However, since she was tethered to Judah's family with a marriage-like bond, and it was assumed that she became pregnant through a man who was not from Judah's family, she was sentenced to be executed as an adulterous woman. When Judah learns the truth, he admits she behaved more righteously than he did, and takes responsibility for the children born to him from Tamar.

²⁴It was some three months later, after Judah's encounter with Tamar, that it was told to Judah, saying: Tamar, your daughter-in-law, acted licentiously; moreover, behold, she conceived through harlotry. Judah said: Take her out and she shall be burned, executed for adultery. ²⁵She was taken out to receive her punishment, and she sent to her father-in-law the items he had deposited with her, saying: By the man whose these are I am with child. She said: Identify, please, whose signet, belt, and staff are these. ²⁶Judah recognized them, his possessions, and said: She is more righteous than I, or she is innocent, as it was I who impregnated her; because indeed, I did not give her to Shela my son, as was my duty. And he was not intimate with her anymore.

²⁷It was at the time of her giving birth, and behold, twins were in her womb. ²⁸It was as she was giving birth that one of the twins extended a hand outside the womb. The midwife took and bound upon his hand a crimson thread, saying, indicating: This one emerged first and was the firstborn. ²⁹However, it was, as he retracted his hand back inside the womb, and behold, his brother emerged from the womb first. And she said to the child that emerged first: What breach [*paretz*] have you breached for yourself? Your brother was already poised to emerge first. Therefore, he, Judah, called his name Peretz. ³⁰Afterward his brother emerged, on whose hand was the crimson thread; he called his name Zerah.

Joseph in Slavery

The narrative returns to the primary story, that of Joseph, whose status has fallen from favored son in his father's household to lowly slave in Egypt. A countrified and inexperienced

youth, Joseph must also adapt to a metropolitan culture and a new language. Gradually, he begins to once again taste success.

39 ¹**Joseph was brought down to Egypt** as a slave. **Potifar, the court-**
Fifth
aliya **ier of Pharaoh, chief executioner, an Egyptian, bought him from the Ishmaelites, who had brought him down there.** ²**The Lord was with Joseph, and he was a successful man, and he was in the house of his master, the Egyptian.** ³After some time, **his master saw that the Lord was with him,** assisting him, **and** that **all that he did, the Lord made his undertaking successful.** ⁴**Joseph found favor in his eyes, and he served him** as his personal attendant. Following that, **he** promoted him and **appointed him overseer of his household, and everything that was his he placed in his charge.** ⁵**It was once he appointed him overseer of his household and over everything that was his, that the Lord blessed the Egyptian's house for Joseph's sake. The blessing of the Lord was in all that he had, in the house and in the field.** ⁶Therefore, **he left everything that he had in Joseph's charge; and he did not know anything about his doings except the bread that he would eat.** Potifar found it unnecessary to be involved in the household matters, as he trusted Joseph completely; he was therefore present only for his personal needs, such as eating. The Torah adds: **Joseph was of fine form, and handsome.**

Potifar's Wife

Joseph's attractiveness and success draw the attention of Potifar's wife. Willing to betray her husband to fulfill her desire, she exploits Joseph's status as a slave to proposition him crudely.

Sixth
aliya ⁷**It was after these matters that his master's wife cast her eyes upon Joseph;** she desired him. **And she said: Lie with me.** ⁸**He refused, and said to his master's wife: Behold, my master** Potifar **does not know anything about what is in the house.** He trusts me to such a degree that he has no idea what I do in this house, **and he has placed everything that he has in my charge.** ⁹**There is no one greater in this house than I, and he has not withheld anything from me but you, as you are his wife. How can I do this great wickedness, and sin to God?** ¹⁰**It was as she spoke to Joseph, day after day; and he did not heed her to lie with her, to be with her.**

¹¹**It was on a certain day** that she judged suitable for implementing her scheme; **he,** Joseph, **went into the house to perform his labor, and none of the people of the household were there in the house.** ¹²**She seized**

him by his garment, saying: Lie with me. He left his garment in her hand, fled, and went outside.

[13]It was when she saw that he had left his garment in her hand, and had fled outside; [14]she called to the people of her household, and spoke to them, saying: See, he, Potifar, **brought to us a Hebrew man to mock us,** or abuse us. He, Joseph, **came to me to lie with me, and I cried** out **with a loud voice.** [15]It was when he heard that I raised my voice and cried; he **left his garment with me, fled, and went outside.** [16]And she placed his garment beside her, until his master's arrival to his home.

Joseph in Prison

The fact that Joseph was not executed for the attempted rape of his master's wife suggests that Potifar might have had suspicions of his wife's version of the events. While he must nevertheless punish Joseph, his slave is not necessarily the object of his anger.

[17]**She spoke to him these words, saying: The Hebrew slave whom you brought to us came to me to mock me,** or abuse me sexually. [18]**It was as I raised my voice and cried that he left his garment with me and fled outside.** [19]**It was when his master heard the words of his wife that she spoke to him, saying: Your slave did to me in this manner,** he attempted to rape me, **that he,** Potifar, **was incensed.** [20]**Joseph's master took him and placed him in the prison, the place where the king's prisoners were incarcerated. And he was** imprisoned **there in the prison.**

[21]**The Lord was with Joseph, and endowed him with grace and disposed him favorably in the eyes of the commandant of the prison.** God gave Joseph charisma and he immediately won over the prison commandant. [22]**The commandant of the prison put in Joseph's charge all the prisoners that were in the prison. And everything that they did there, he,** Joseph, **would determine.** [23]**The commandant of the prison did not oversee anything in his charge,** or scrutinize Joseph's actions, as he trusted Joseph completely, **for** he could see that **the Lord was with him. That which he did, the Lord made successful.**

Pharaoh's Courtiers in Prison

The prison where Joseph was incarcerated held distinguished prisoners awaiting judgment. When two of Pharaoh's high-ranking courtiers are imprisoned there for an extended period, Joseph becomes their personal attendant.

40 [1]**It was after these matters that the butler of the king of Egypt,** who was responsible for providing the king with drink, **and the** chief **baker** of the

king, **sinned against their master, against the king of Egypt.** ²**Pharaoh became angry at his two courtiers, at the chief butler and at the chief baker.** ³**He placed them in custody in the household of the chief executioner, in the prison, the place where Joseph was incarcerated.** ⁴**The chief executioner,** Potifar, **assigned Joseph to them, and he served them; they had been in custody one year,**

⁵**and they,** the butler and the baker, **dreamed a dream, both of them – each man his dream during one night, each man in accordance with the interpretation of his dream.** The dreams of **the butler and the baker of the king of Egypt, who were incarcerated in the prison,** were meaningful, and demanded interpretation. ⁶**Joseph came to them in the morning and saw them, and behold, they were distressed.** ⁷**He asked Pharaoh's courtiers who were with him in the custody of his master's house, saying: Why are your faces wretched today?** ⁸**They said to him: We dreamed a dream, and there is no interpreter for it. Joseph said to them: Aren't interpretations** a matter **for God?** Only He can inform us of their meaning. Therefore, **please, tell me,** and perhaps I will succeed in interpreting it.

The Butler's Dream

One of the distinctive element of Joseph's interpretation of the dream is that he specifies that the time period in question will be three days. This makes it possible for Joseph's interpretation to be put to the test easily.

⁹**The chief butler told his dream to Joseph, and said to him: In my dream, behold, a vine was before me.** ¹⁰**On the vine were three tendrils** or branches, **and it was as though it,** the vine, **was budding. Its blossoms emerged, and its clusters produced ripe grapes.** ¹¹**Pharaoh's cup was in my hand; I took the grapes, pressed them into Pharaoh's cup, and I gave the cup into Pharaoh's hand.**

¹²**Joseph said to him: This is its interpretation: The three tendrils are three days;** ¹³**In three more days, Pharaoh shall raise your head,** your status, **and restore you to your position. You will put Pharaoh's cup into his hand, like the practice in the first place, when you would provide him with drink.** ¹⁴**If only you** will **remember me** then, **when it shall be well for you, and please, perform kindness with me and mention me to Pharaoh; and** you will thereby help **take me out of this house,** this prison. ¹⁵**For I was abducted from the land of the Hebrews. And here too I have**

done nothing wrong to justify the fact **that they placed me in the pit,** this prison.

The Baker's Dream

Joseph's interpretation of the butler's dream seems pleasing and persuasive to the baker. Therefore, the baker requests that Joseph interpret his dream as well.

[16]**The chief baker saw that he interpreted well. And he said to Joseph: I too, in my dream,** I dreamed that **behold, there were three wicker baskets** stacked **on my head.** Wicker baskets were typically used to hold baked goods, as the gaps in the weave allow for air to pass to the goods inside them. [17]**In the uppermost basket there was all manner of food for Pharaoh,** including **baked products, and the birds were eating them from the basket above my head.**

[18]**Joseph answered and said: This is its interpretation: The three baskets are three days.** [19]**In three more days Pharaoh shall raise,** remove, **your head from upon you, and shall hang you on a tree. The birds shall eat your flesh from upon you.**

The Dreams Are Fulfilled

During Pharaoh's birthday celebrations, he notices the absence of the butler and baker, and decides to issue their verdicts. The chief butler is reinstated to his position, but the hope that Joseph placed in him remains unfulfilled.

Maftir [20]**It was on the third day; for Pharaoh's birthday, he made a feast for all his servants, and** during that feast he **raised the head of the chief butler and the head of the chief baker,** he remembered them, **among his servants.** [21]**Accordingly, he,** Pharaoh, **restored the chief butler to his butlership, and he,** the butler, **gave the cup into Pharaoh's hand;** [22]**and he hanged the chief baker, as Joseph interpreted for them.** [23]**But the chief butler did not remember** the request that **Joseph** made of him; rather, **he forgot him.**

Further reading: For more on the significance of dreams, see *A Concise Guide to the Sages*, p. 415.

Parashat Miketz

Joseph's moment finally comes when the king of Egypt seeks someone with the understanding and courage to interpret his dreams. When Joseph is brought before Pharaoh, he not only explains his dreams, but suggests solutions to the problem presented in them. Pharaoh, impressed with Joseph's vision and bearing, appoints him as his second-in-command. Joseph will be responsible for collecting food during the years of abundance, and for distributing the food during the years of famine that will follow.

Like other residents of the lands near Egypt, Joseph's brothers come to Joseph to buy food. They do not recognize the governor of Egypt as their brother. He recognizes them but does not identify himself; instead, he accuses them of espionage and insists that they bring Benjamin, their youngest brother, to prove their claims of innocence. When they do, Joseph frames Benjamin for theft, to test his brothers' allegiance to Joseph's only full brother.

Pharaoh's Dreams

Joseph languishes in prison for two more years, forgotten by the chief butler, whom he had helped. But when Pharaoh has enigmatic dreams that his chief advisors are unable to interpret convincingly, the butler remembers the dream interpreter he met in prison, and suggests that Pharaoh utilize his services.

41 **¹It was at the conclusion of two years** since the butler had been restored to his post; **Pharaoh was dreaming: Behold,** in his dream **he stood at the Nile** River, upon which all life in Egypt depended. **²Behold, coming up from the Nile were seven cows, fair and fat fleshed, and they grazed in the pasture. ³Behold, seven other cows were coming up after them from the river, unsightly and lean fleshed, and they stood alongside the other cows on the bank of the Nile. ⁴The unsightly and lean-fleshed cows ate the seven fair and fat cows, and Pharaoh awoke.**

⁵He slept and dreamed a second time that night, **and behold, seven ears of grain were growing on one stalk.** These ears were **plump and good** and full of grain. **⁶And behold, seven ears, thin and blighted by the** dry **east wind, were growing after them. ⁷The thin ears swallowed the seven**

plump and full ears. And Pharaoh awoke, and behold, this too was only a dream.

⁸It was in the morning and his spirit was troubled. He sent and called for all the magicians of Egypt, its priests, who also engaged in science and medicine, and all its wise men; Pharaoh related his dream to them, but no one could interpret them satisfactorily for Pharaoh.

> Further reading: For more on the interpretations Pharaoh's advisors offered for his dreams, see *A Concise Guide to the Sages*, p. 60.

⁹The chief butler spoke to Pharaoh, saying: I must mention my sins to the king today. ¹⁰Pharaoh became angry with his servants, and he placed me in the custody of the house of the chief executioner, me and the chief baker. ¹¹We dreamed a dream one night, I and he; each of us dreamed in accordance with the interpretation of his dream; we both had dreams that demanded interpretation. ¹²There, with us, was a Hebrew lad, a slave of the chief executioner; we told him the dreams and he interpreted our dreams for us; for each of us in accordance with his own dream, he, the lad, interpreted. ¹³It was that as he interpreted to us, so it was; the dreams came true in accordance with his interpretation: Me, he, Pharaoh, restored to my position, and him, the chief baker, he, Pharaoh, hanged. ¹⁴Pharaoh sent and summoned Joseph, and they rushed him from the dungeon. He shaved, changed his garments, and came to Pharaoh.

Pharaoh Relates His Dreams to Joseph

Pharaoh describes his dreams to Joseph. He includes additional details and personal impressions that assist Joseph in divining the meaning of the dreams.

Second aliya

¹⁵Pharaoh said to Joseph: I dreamed a dream, and there is no satisfactory interpreter of it, and I heard about you, my butler mentioned you, saying: You will hear a dream and be able to interpret it. ¹⁶Joseph answered Pharaoh, saying: The wisdom to interpret is not possessed by me. Rather, God will respond for Pharaoh's peace; He will use me as an intermediary to assist you.

¹⁷Pharaoh spoke to Joseph: In my dream, behold, I am standing on the bank of the Nile. ¹⁸Behold, seven cows, fat fleshed and fair, were coming up from the Nile, and they grazed in the pasture. ¹⁹Behold, seven other cows were coming up after them, scrawny, very unsightly, and lean fleshed. I have not seen their like in all the land of Egypt for

deficiency; they seemed more unhealthy than any living cows I have ever seen. ²⁰**The lean and unsightly cows ate the first seven, fat cows.** ²¹**They were ingested by them, but it was not apparent that they were ingested by them,** as no change was discernible in the scrawny cows **and their appearance was** just as **unsightly as** it was **at first; and I awoke.**

²²**I saw in my** second **dream and behold, seven ears of grain growing on one stalk, plump and good.** ²³**Behold,** then I saw **seven ears of grain, parched, thin, and blighted by the east wind, growing after them.** ²⁴**The thin ears swallowed the seven good ears. I told it to the magicians, but no one could tell me** the interpretation.

Joseph Interprets Pharaoh's Dreams

Joseph demonstrates his ability to both recognize a prophetic dream as such, and to interpret it. Furthermore, since he, a lowly Hebrew slave, has been brought to Pharaoh to decipher his dreams, he understands this to indicate that God has designated him to assist Pharaoh even further. Therefore, he adds practical advice so that Pharaoh can solve the problem the dreams present.

²⁵**Joseph said to Pharaoh:** Although you saw two different dreams, in fact **the dream of Pharaoh is one; that which God does,** or plans to do, **He told Pharaoh.** ²⁶**The seven good cows are seven years, and the seven good ears are seven years: It is** as **one dream;** the two dreams are to be understood in conjunction. ²⁷**The seven scrawny and unsightly cows that come up after them are seven years, and the seven empty ears blighted by the east wind shall be seven years of famine.** ²⁸**That is the matter that I spoke to Pharaoh: That which God does, He showed Pharaoh** in advance.

²⁹**Behold, seven years are coming** in which there will be **great plenty,** abundant food **throughout the land of Egypt.** ³⁰However, **seven years of famine shall arise after them. And all the plenty in the land of Egypt shall be forgotten; the famine shall devastate the land.** ³¹**The plenty** of the past **shall not be known,** apparent, **in the land, due to that famine afterward, for it shall be very severe.** ³²**With regard to the repetition of the dream to Pharaoh,** as he dreamed a similar dream **twice, it is because the matter is determined by God, and God hastens to perform it.**

³³**Now, let Pharaoh look for an insightful and wise man, and install him over the land of Egypt.** ³⁴**Pharaoh should proceed and appoint officials over the land, and he shall supply the land of Egypt during the seven years of plenty.** ³⁵**They will gather all the food of these coming good**

years, and amass grain under the control of Pharaoh; in this way the **food in the cities** will be collected, **and they will preserve it.** [36]**The food shall be for a security for the land for the seven years of famine that shall be in the land of Egypt, and the land will not perish in the famine.**

Joseph's Rise

Like most people who have encountered Joseph, Pharaoh is deeply impressed by his character. He appreciates Joseph's suggested solution to the famine, as he readily discerns its advantages to the throne: It will concentrate power in Pharaoh's hands during the years of famine, without requiring great financial outlays.

[37]**The matter was worthy** and pleasing **in the eyes of Pharaoh and in the eyes of all his servants.** [38]**Pharaoh said to his servants: Can we find someone like this, a man in whom there is the spirit of God?** [39]**Pharaoh said to Joseph: Since God has disclosed all this to you, there is no one as insightful and wise as you.** [40]Therefore, **you will be in charge of my house,** my palace, **and all my people shall be sustained at your directive,** and subject to your authority. **Only the throne will I make too great for you;** only my status will exceed yours. [41]**Pharaoh said to Joseph: See, I have set you over the entire land of Egypt.**

Third aliya

[42]**Pharaoh removed his signet ring from upon his hand, and he placed it upon Joseph's hand; he dressed him in** official **garments, of linen, and he placed a** royal **gold chain,** or scarf, **on his neck.** [43]**He had him ride in the alternate chariot that he had,** the one alongside the king's chariot. **And they cried before him** to everyone: **Kneel. And he was set over the entire land of Egypt.** [44]**Pharaoh said to Joseph: I am Pharaoh, and** I declare that **without you no man shall lift his hand or his foot** to decide anything **in the entire land of Egypt.** [45]**Pharaoh called Joseph's name Tzafenat Paneah,** meaning, explainer of secrets, **and he gave him Asenat, daughter of Poti Fera, priest of On, as a wife. Joseph came out** to begin his rule **over the land of Egypt.** [46]**Joseph was thirty years old as he stood before Pharaoh king of Egypt. Joseph came out from before Pharaoh, and he passed through the entire land of Egypt** in order to put into practice his advice to Pharaoh.

Abundance Followed by Famine

Joseph gathers the excess food that is produced during the years of abundance into enormous storehouses, which are held by the king. When the famine begins, Joseph

receives sole authority over distributing the food in the storehouses to the Egyptians and the residents of the neighboring lands.

⁴⁷**The earth produced, during the seven years of plenty, in abundance.** ⁴⁸**He,** Joseph, **gathered all the** excess **food of the seven years that was in the land of Egypt, and placed food in the cities; he placed the food of the fields that were around the city within it.** ⁴⁹**Joseph amassed grain like the sand of the sea, very much, until one stopped counting, as it was without number.**

⁵⁰**Two sons were born to Joseph before the advent of the year of the famine, who were born to him by Asenat, daughter of Poti Fera, priest of On.** ⁵¹**Joseph called the name of the firstborn Manasseh, as** he felt: **God has made me forget** [*nashani*] **all my toil,** my suffering and hardship, and the trouble of **my father's entire house.** ⁵²**He called the name of the second** son **Efraim, as** he said: **God has made me fruitful** [*hifrani*]**,** in that I have become successful and risen to prominence **in the land of my affliction.**

ₐurth aliya ⁵³**The** period of **seven years of plenty that was in the land of Egypt concluded.** ⁵⁴**The seven years of famine ensued, as Joseph had said. There was famine in all the lands, but in all of the land of Egypt there was bread.** ⁵⁵**After** private **stores of food ran out, all of the land of Egypt was hungry, and the people cried to Pharaoh for bread. Pharaoh said to all the Egyptians: Go to Joseph; what he says to you, you shall do.** ⁵⁶**The famine was on the entire face of the earth; and Joseph opened all that was in them,** the storehouses, **and sold grain to the Egyptians. The famine was intensified in the land of Egypt.** ⁵⁷**All the land,** the neighboring territories, **came to Egypt to purchase grain from Joseph, for the famine was severe in all the land.**

Joseph's Brothers Come to Buy Food

As the famine has also afflicted the land of Canaan, Jacob seeks to purchase food from Egypt. He sends ten of his sons there, so they can bring back a large quantity of grain, but he keeps his youngest son, Benjamin, with him. Benjamin is Jacob's last connection to Rachel and to Joseph, and Jacob is unwilling to expose him to the risks involved in the journey.

42 ¹**Jacob saw that there was grain** for sale **in Egypt, and** therefore **Jacob said to his sons: Why are you putting on an act** as if the famine does not affect you? As shepherds, Jacob and his sons had more resources to survive the famine than neighboring farmers. Jacob says to his sons that they should not pretend that nothing is wrong. ²**He said: Behold, I have heard that**

there is grain in Egypt. Go down there and acquire grain for us from there, that we may live and not die. ³Ten of Joseph's brothers went down to acquire grain from Egypt. ⁴But Benjamin, Joseph's only full brother through both parents, Jacob did not send with his brothers, as he said to himself: Lest disaster befall him. ⁵The sons of Israel, Jacob, came to acquire grain among those others who came from Canaan to acquire grain in Egypt, as the famine was in the land of Canaan.

> 📖 **Further reading:** For more on the additional goals of this journey and the deeper meaning of the phrase "Joseph's brothers," see *A Concise Guide to the Sages*, p. 62.

Joseph Accuses His Brothers

Joseph does not handle the actual sale of food, but he is responsible for managing the overall process. When Joseph's brothers arrive in Egypt, as part of a larger group from a foreign land, they do not realize that the powerful viceroy before them is their brother. Joseph, who recognizes them immediately, asserts his authority and alleges that they came as spies.

⁶Joseph was the ruler over the land; he was the provider of grain to all the people of the land. Joseph's brothers came and prostrated themselves to him, faces to the earth. ⁷Joseph saw his brothers, and he recognized them. But he acted as though he were a stranger to them, and spoke harshly to them. He said to them: From where did you come? They said, From the land of Canaan, to acquire food. ⁸Joseph recognized his brothers, but they did not recognize him.

⁹Joseph remembered the dreams that he had dreamed about them, and he said to them: You are spies; to see the nakedness of the land you have come. You are foreign agents who have been sent to discover Egypt's weaknesses. ¹⁰They said to him: No, my lord, but your servants have come to acquire food. ¹¹We are all the sons of one man. We are sincere; your servants have not been spies. ¹²He said to them: No, that is your claim, but in truth it is the nakedness of the land, its weaknesses, that you came to see. ¹³They said: We, your servants, are twelve brothers, sons of one man in the land of Canaan; and behold, the youngest is with our father today, and one is absent. ¹⁴Joseph said to them: That is the truth, what I spoke to you, saying: You are spies. ¹⁵With this you shall be put to the test: By Pharaoh's life, you shall not depart from here unless your youngest brother comes here. ¹⁶Dispatch one of you, and he will take your brother from Canaan, and the rest of you shall be incarcerated. In that way your statements will be verified, whether there is truth with

you; and if not, by Pharaoh's life, you are spies. [17]He put them together under guard, where they remained for three days.

The Brothers' Remorse

With the viceroy indifferent to their protestations of innocence, the brothers' imprisonment prompts them to feel pangs of conscience for the similar experience they inflicted upon their brother years earlier. Joseph, who is already emotional from seeing his brothers after the long period of separation, is further moved by their expression of remorse.

[18]Joseph said to them on the third day: Do this and live, as I fear God; I *Fifth* am a fair man. [19]If you are sincere and honest, one of your brothers shall *aliya* be incarcerated as a guarantee in your place of custody, and the rest of you, go bring the grain you purchased for the hunger of your houses, for your hungry families. [20]Bring your youngest brother to me, and your statements will thereby be verified, and you shall not die. They did so; they were given their food and were permitted to leave.

[21]They said one to another: But we are indeed guilty with regard to what we did to our brother; that we saw the anguish of his soul as he pleaded with us and we did not heed. For that, this anguish has befallen us, as retribution. [22]Reuben responded to them, saying: Didn't I say this to you at the time, saying: Do not sin against the child; and you did not heed my words? Now, behold, there is a divine reckoning for his blood. [23]They did not know that Joseph understood their exchange, as the interpreter was between them, and had been interpreting all their conversations with Joseph. [24]He, Joseph, turned from them, walked away, and wept. And then he returned to them, and he spoke to them, took Simeon from them, and incarcerated him before their eyes.

[25]Joseph commanded his men that they fill their vessels, the brothers' sacks, with grain, and restore each man's silver to his sack. And he gave orders to give them provisions for the way, and he, his attendant, did so for them. [26]They loaded their grain that they had purchased onto their donkeys and went from there.

The Brothers Report Back to Jacob

When the brothers discover their silver in their sacks, it does not occur to them that the Egyptian ruler might have returned it as a kindly gesture. They recount their disturbing experiences to Jacob upon returning home, cataloging the false accusation, the presence of their silver, and the absence of Simeon. For his part, Jacob becomes gravely concerned and refuses to allow Benjamin to go to Egypt.

²⁷On their way back to Canaan, **one of them opened his sack to give feed to his donkey at the lodging place. He saw his silver, and behold, it was in the opening of his sack.** ²⁸He said to his brothers: My silver that I paid for the grain **was returned, and behold, it is in my sack. Their hearts sank, and they trembled** and spoke, **one with another, saying: What is this that God has done to us?**

²⁹**They came to their father Jacob, to the land of Canaan, and they told him all that had befallen them, saying:** ³⁰**The man, lord of the land, spoke harshly with us and accused us as spies of the land.** ³¹**We said to him: We are sincere; we have not** ever **been spies.** ³²And we explained that **we are twelve brothers, sons of our father; one is absent, and the youngest is today with our father in the land of Canaan.** ³³The man, **lord of the land, said to us: With this I shall know that you are sincere: One of your brothers** you will **leave with me, and** now **take** grain to assuage **the hunger of your households, and go.** ³⁴**Bring your youngest brother to me, and I shall** thereby **know that you are not spies, that you are sincere. I will** then **give you your** incarcerated **brother, and you shall trade in the land;** you will be permitted to buy more grain.

³⁵**It was as they were emptying their sacks, and behold,** they discovered that **each** and every **man's pouch of silver was in his sack.** They and their **father saw their pouches of silver** that had been returned to them, **and they were afraid.** ³⁶**Jacob their father said to them: You have bereaved me** of my sons. **Joseph is not, and Simeon is not, and you will take Benjamin? All of these** misfortunes **are upon me.**

³⁷**Reuben said to his father, saying:** You can **kill my two sons if I do not bring him,** Benjamin, back **to you; place him in my charge, and I will return him to you.** ³⁸**He,** Jacob, **said: My** youngest **son shall not go down with you, for,** as you know, **his brother is dead, and only he is left** from his mother; **and if disaster befalls him on the path on which you will go,** then **you will cause my old age to descend in sorrow to the grave.** I would die of grief.

Jacob Ponders His Course of Action

Although Judah is only Jacob's fourth son, his leadership qualities already came to the fore at the time of the sale of Joseph. When the family's food stores are nearly depleted, Judah confronts his father with the necessity of taking Benjamin with them to Egypt to purchase grain. He promises to protect Benjamin and to accept personal responsibility for his welfare.

43 ¹The famine was severe in the land. ²It was when they finished the grain that they had brought from Egypt that their father said to them: Return to Egypt and acquire a little more food for us. ³Judah said to him, saying: The man in charge of the land explicitly forewarned us, saying: You shall not see my face, and you will not be permitted to buy anything here, unless your youngest brother is with you. ⁴Consequently, if you send our brother with us, we will go down to Egypt and acquire food for you. ⁵But if you do not send him, we will not go down, for the man said to us: You shall not see my face unless your brother is with you.

⁶Israel, Jacob, said: Why have you harmed me, to tell the man that you have another brother? ⁷They said: The man asked with regard to us and with regard to our provenance. He interrogated us, saying: Is your father still alive? Do you have another brother? Therefore, we told him with regard to those matters. Could we know that he would say: Bring your brother down to Egypt?

⁸Judah said to Israel, his father: Send the lad with me, and we will arise and go; and if you do, we will live and not die of hunger, both we, and you, and our children. ⁹Finally, Judah promises his father: I will guarantee him and his safe return. From me you may solicit him; if I do not bring him to you and present him before you whole and sound, I will have sinned to you forever, a blot that will never be wiped clean, neither in my lifetime nor after my death. ¹⁰We will not be away long, but it is imperative that we leave immediately. For had we not tarried until this point, we would by now have traveled to Egypt and returned twice.

The Brothers Return to Egypt

With no viable alternative to sending Benjamin to Egypt, Jacob attempts to mitigate the risk. He advises his sons to bring gifts for the Egyptian ruler, especially items that are native to Canaan but not Egypt. He also instructs them to return the silver for their earlier purchase, surmising that its presence in their sacks was some kind of oversight.

¹¹Their father Israel, Jacob, said to them: If so, then since there is no other option, do this: Take of the choice produce of the land in your vessels, and take a gift down to the man: a little balm and a little honey, both used in medical treatments; spices and labdanum, for perfume; and pistachios and almonds. ¹²Take double the amount of silver in your hand, and the silver that was returned in the opening of your sacks return in your hand. Perhaps it was due to an oversight on their part that the silver was restored to you. ¹³And take your brother, Benjamin, and arise and

Genesis

return to the man, the Egyptian ruler. [14]**May God Almighty grant you mercy before the man,** may the ruler be merciful to you, **and he will send with you your other brother,** Simeon, **and Benjamin. And** as for **me, as I am bereaved, I am bereaved;** if I experience another tragedy, so be it; I am accustomed to tragedy. [15]**The men took that gift, and they took in their hand double the silver and** they took **Benjamin; they arose and went down to Egypt, and they stood before Joseph.**

The Brothers in Joseph's Mansion

Joseph instructs his men to bring the brothers to his home to dine with him. As his brothers do not understand his motive, they become frightened and attempt again to prove their honesty and integrity.

Sixth aliya [16]**Joseph saw Benjamin with them, and he said to the one in charge of his house: Bring the men** to me, **to the house, and slaughter** animals **and prepare** a meal, **as the men shall dine with me at noon.** [17]**The man did as Joseph said, and the man brought the men to Joseph's house.**

[18]**The men were afraid because they were brought to Joseph's house. They said: We have been brought on** account of **the matter of the silver that was restored to our sacks** last time we were here. The viceroy is certainly plotting **to falsely accuse us, attack us, and** eventually **take us as slaves, and** also take **our donkeys.** [19]**Therefore, they approached the man in charge of Joseph's house, and they spoke to him at the entrance of the house** before entering. [20]**They said: Please, my lord, we initially descended to acquire food.** [21]**It was when we came to the lodging place and we opened our sacks; behold, each man's silver was at the opening of his sack,** all of **our silver in its** exact **weight; and we returned it** now in **our hand.** [22]**Additionally, we brought down other silver in our hand to acquire food. We do not know who placed our silver in our sacks.**

[23]**He,** the steward, **said** to them: **Peace be with you, fear not; your God and the God of your father gave you hidden treasure in your sacks; your silver came to me.** The money you are obliged to pay has already reached me. **And he brought Simeon out to them.** [24]**The man brought the men to Joseph's house. He gave them water, and they washed their feet, and he gave feed to their donkeys.** [25]**They,** the brothers, **prepared the gift** and waited **until Joseph's arrival at noon, because they heard that they would eat bread there** with him.

Joseph's Encounter with Benjamin

This time Joseph acts in a friendly manner toward his brothers. They are bewildered by the change from his earlier demeanor, as well as by other unusual elements of the meal.

²⁶**Joseph came home, and they brought him the gift that was in their hand to the house, and they prostrated themselves to him, to the earth.** ²⁷**He asked them with regard to their well-being, and he** also said: **Is all well with your elderly father, whom you mentioned; is he still alive?** ²⁸**They said: All is well with your servant, with our father; he is still alive. They bowed, and they prostrated themselves.**

²⁹**He lifted his eyes and saw his brother Benjamin, his mother's son, and he said: Is this your youngest brother whom you mentioned to me? He,** Joseph, then **said: God be gracious to you, my son.** ³⁰**Joseph hurried, because his mercy was aroused toward his brother,** to whom he felt close, **and he sought to weep;** therefore, **he** quickly **entered the chamber,** his private room, **and wept there.**

nth
liya

📖 **Further reading:** For more on Joseph's tender meeting with Benjamin, see *A Concise Guide to the Sages*, p. 64.

³¹**He washed his face and emerged, and he restrained himself and said** to his attendants: **Serve bread;** serve the meal. ³²**They served** bread **for him by himself, and for them by themselves, and for the Egyptians who were eating with him by themselves.** The brothers were confused; although he was to all appearances Egyptian, the viceroy chose not to eat with the other Egyptians. The separation between the Egyptians and the Hebrews was **because the Egyptians may not eat bread with the Hebrews, as it is an abomination for the Egyptians.** ³³**They sat before him** in the places assigned by Joseph, **the firstborn according to his seniority and the younger according to his youth. And the men wondered to one another** how the ruler knew their birth order. ³⁴**He gave them gifts from before him, and Benjamin's gift was five times greater than the gifts of all of them,** the other brothers. **They drank and became inebriated with him.**

Joseph Frames Benjamin for Theft

Throughout these events, Joseph attempts to increase his brothers' confusion and distress. His goal is to test their behavior toward Benjamin in a situation that recreates the conditions of his own relationship with them in his youth, a test that will culminate with him accusing Benjamin of theft.

44 **¹He commanded the one in charge of his house, saying: Fill the men's sacks with food, as much as** the sacks **are able to carry, and place each man's silver at the opening of his sack,** as on the previous occasion. **²And place my** special **goblet, the silver goblet, at the opening of the sack of the youngest** brother, **and** also insert into the sacks **the silver of his purchase of the grain. He,** Joseph's steward, **did in accordance with the statement that Joseph had spoken.**

The Brothers Stand Accused of Theft

When Joseph's steward accuses the brothers of both ingratitude and stupidity in stealing his master's silver goblet, the brothers' bemusement reaches its peak. Certain that they are innocent of wrongdoing, they declare their willingness to suffer severe collective punishment if their guilt is proven. The steward, however, stresses that only the guilty man himself will be punished.

³The next **morning broke, and the men were dispatched, they and their donkeys. ⁴They left the city; they had not gone far, and Joseph said to the one in charge of his house: Arise** now and **pursue the men and overtake them, and say to them: Why have you repaid** with **evil for** the **good** treatment you received? **⁵Isn't this** goblet that you stole from Joseph's house, **that with which my lord drinks, and with which he divines,** performs divination? **You have done evil in what you did.**

📖 Further reading: For more about the importance of demonstrating gratitude, see *A Concise Guide to the Sages*, p. 89.

⁶He overtook them, and he spoke to them those words. ⁷They said to him: Why would my lord speak words like those? Far be it from your servants that they do such a thing. ⁸Behold, the silver that we found in the opening of our sacks we returned to you, or tried to return to you, **from the land of Canaan. How would we steal from the house of your lord silver or gold? ⁹With whomever of your servants it,** the goblet, **is found, he shall die, and we too,** all of us, **will be slaves to my lord.**

¹⁰He said: Now too, by rights, **it,** your punishment, **should be in accordance with your words,** but my master was lenient; he said: **He with whom it,** the goblet, **shall be found shall be a slave to me, and** the rest of **you shall be exonerated,** spared all punishment.

The Goblet Is Found

Their mysterious interactions with the Egyptian ruler, in which false accusations have been alternated with unexpected intimacy, have left the brothers bewildered. When the goblet is found in Benjamin's sack, Judah sees it as a divine punishment.

¹¹**Each man hurried and lowered his sack to the ground, and each man opened his sack.** ¹²**He,** the steward, **searched; he began with the eldest, and with the youngest he concluded. The goblet was found in Benjamin's sack.** ¹³**They rent their garments** in terror, shame, and mourning. **Each man loaded his donkey, and they returned to the city.**

📖 **Further reading:** The custom of rending garments as a sign of mourning and profound distress is still practiced today at funerals. See *A Concise Guide to Halakha*, p. 81.

Maftir ¹⁴**Judah and his brethren came to Joseph's house, and he,** Joseph, **was still there. They fell before him to the ground.** ¹⁵**Joseph said to them: What is this deed that you have done? Don't you know that a man who is** wise **like me will practice divination** and discover what happened to my goblet?

¹⁶**Judah said: What shall we say** in our defense **to my lord, what shall we speak, and how shall we justify ourselves? God has revealed the iniquity of your servants. Behold, we are my lord's slaves, both we and he in whose possession the goblet was found.**

¹⁷**He,** Joseph, **said: Heaven forfend that I should do so.** I will not act unjustly. **The man in whose hand the goblet was found, he shall be my slave; and** the rest of **you go up in peace to your father.**

Parashat Vayigash

The brothers' devotion to Benjamin touches Joseph's heart and prompts him to divulge his identity to them. He assuages their guilt and fear regarding their previous mistreatment of him, and encourages them to bring the entire extended family to Egypt. Eager to see Joseph, Jacob travels south, and he and his sons settle in the Goshen region of Egypt.

The protracted famine compels the Egyptians to deplete their savings and livestock to buy food from Joseph. With no alternative, they then sell their lands to Pharaoh, and even sell themselves as slaves to the king, who thus becomes an absolute ruler in the land.

Judah's Speech

Judah, whose influence over his brothers was established when they sold Joseph, now stands out as their leader, despite not being the oldest. As he has taken responsibility for Benjamin, he feels an obligation to try to save his younger brother from the fate that threatens him.

18Judah approached him, Joseph, **and said: Please, my lord, may your servant speak a word in my lord's ears? Do not become incensed with your servant, for you are** important **like Pharaoh. 19My lord** had previously **asked his servants, saying: Do you have a father or a brother? 20We said to my lord: We have an elderly father, and a young son of his old age; his brother,** the brother of this young son, **is dead, and he alone remains from** the children of **his mother, and his father loves him** above all. **21You said to your servants: Bring him down to me, and I will set my eye upon him.** I will treat him well and pay special attention to him. **22We said to my lord: The lad cannot leave his father,** for if he leaves his father, **then he,** the father, **would die** of sorrow. **23You said to your servants:** Nevertheless, **if your youngest brother does not come down with you, you shall not see my face again. 24It was when we went** back **up to your servant, my father, that we told him the words of my lord.**

25Eventually, **our father said: Return, acquire us a little food. 26We said: We cannot go down** to Egypt as we did before; **if our youngest brother**

is with us, we will go down, for we cannot see the face of the man who rules Egypt unless our youngest brother is with us. ²⁷Your servant, my father, said to us: You know that my wife Rachel bore me two sons; ²⁸the one departed from me, and I said to myself: Surely he was mauled. And I have not seen him since; ²⁹and if you will take this one too from my presence, and a disaster will befall him, you will thereby cause my old age to descend in woe to the grave; you will cause my anguished death.

³⁰Now, when I come home to your servant, my father, and the lad is not with us, and his, my father's, soul is bound with his son's soul; ³¹it will be, when he sees that the lad is not with us, he will die from excessive grief. Your servants will cause the old age of your servant, my father, to descend in sorrow to the grave. We will have caused our father's death. ³²I must speak out, for I, your servant, personally guaranteed the lad to my father, saying: If I do not bring him back to you, I will have sinned to my father forever, and my transgression will accompany me always. ³³Now, please, I suggest that your servant will remain in place of the lad as a slave to my lord, and the lad shall go up, return home, with his brothers. ³⁴For how will I go up to my father, and the lad is not with me? I cannot go, lest I see the woe that shall find my father and afflict him. I am unable to bear the sight of my father's reaction.

📖 **Further reading:** For more on Judah and Joseph's exchange, see *A Concise Guide to the Sages*, p. 65.

Joseph Reveals Himself to His Brothers

Step by step, Joseph had brought his brothers to a situation vis-a-vis Benjamin similar to the one he himself had been in with them. Judah's speech proves to Joseph that his brothers passed his test. Judah's willingness to exchange his own freedom for Benjamin's, even though Benjamin might be a thief, demonstrates his full repentance for having sold Joseph into slavery. Joseph cannot and need not continue to pretend.

45 ¹**Joseph could not restrain himself,** but he nevertheless held back **before all those standing before him,** whose presence he no longer desired. **And he called: Remove every man,** all my servants, **from before me. No** other **man stood with him when Joseph revealed himself to his brothers.** ²**He raised his voice in weeping. The Egyptians heard, and the house of Pharaoh,** the king's servants and attendants, **heard.** ³**Joseph said to his brothers: I am Joseph,** and then immediately asked: **Does my father still live? And his brothers could not answer him because they were alarmed before him.**

⁴Joseph said to his brothers: Please approach me, and they approached. He said again: I am Joseph your brother, whom you sold to Egypt. ⁵However, now all that is in the past; do not be sad about your actions, and do not become incensed with yourselves that you sold me here; it was for sustenance that God sent me before you, as I am now capable of supporting our family. ⁶For these past two years the famine is in the midst of the land, and there are an additional five years still to come during which there shall be neither plowing nor harvest. ⁷God sent me before you to establish for you a remnant in the land, to ensure your survival, and to sustain you for a great deliverance from these troubles. ⁸Now, it was not you who sent me here, but God. He made me into a father to Pharaoh, a guardian of his kingdom, and into a lord for all his house, and ruler over the entire land of Egypt.

Third aliya

⁹Hurry and go up to my father and say to him: So said your son Joseph: God has made me lord for all Egypt. Come down to me to Egypt now; do not tarry. ¹⁰You will live in the land of Goshen, and you will be near to me, you, and your children, and your children's children, and your flocks, and your cattle, and everything that you have. ¹¹I will sustain you there, for there are to be an additional five years of famine; come, lest you become impoverished, you, and your household, and everything that you have. ¹²Behold, your eyes see, and the eyes of my brother Benjamin, that it is my mouth that is speaking to you, in your language. ¹³You shall tell my father all my glory in Egypt, and all that you have seen; hurry and bring my father down here.

¹⁴He fell upon the neck of his brother Benjamin and wept, and Benjamin wept upon his neck. ¹⁵He then kissed all his brothers and wept upon them. And afterward, after they felt reassured, his brothers spoke with him.

Pharaoh's Advice and the Brothers' Provisions for the Journey

Having risen from slavery, Joseph had had no independent identity in Egypt. Pharaoh is pleased to discover that his second-in-command had originally been a free man, and that he occupied an honored place within a distinguished family. Magnanimously, he offers his full support to Joseph in his desire to relocate his family to Egypt.

¹⁶The news was heard in Pharaoh's house, saying: Joseph's brothers have come. And it was good in the eyes of Pharaoh and the eyes of his servants. ¹⁷Pharaoh said to Joseph: Say to your brothers: Do this: Load your animals, and go, and come to the land of Canaan. ¹⁸Take your

father and the members of **your households** from Canaan, **and come to me; I will give you the finest of the land of Egypt; eat of the fat of the** land. ¹⁹**You are commanded** to tell your brothers to **do this: Take wagons from the land of Egypt for your children and for your wives, and convey** them and **your father** in the wagons, **and come.** ²⁰**Your eye should not spare your vessels.** Do not be concerned about any possessions that might be damaged on your journey, **for the bounty of the entire land of Egypt is yours.**

²¹**The sons of Israel did so,** and prepared to return home. **Joseph gave them wagons by Pharaoh's order, and he gave them provisions for the journey.** ²²**To all of them he gave, each man, changes of garments** for the journey, **and to Benjamin he gave three hundred pieces of silver and five changes of garments.** ²³**To his father he sent** a gift, as follows: **Ten donkeys laden with the bounty of Egypt, and ten female donkeys laden with grain, and bread, and food for his father for the journey.** ²⁴**He sent his brothers** back to their home, **and** before **they went, he said to them: Do not quarrel on the way.**

Jacob Learns Joseph Is Alive

At first Jacob can hardly assimilate his sons' astonishing news, but once he hears about Joseph's proposal and sees the wagons, which the brothers would have been unable to acquire otherwise, he believes their account, and grows excited.

²⁵**They went up from Egypt, and they came to the land of Canaan, to Jacob their father.** ²⁶**They told him, saying: Joseph still lives, and he is ruler over the entire land of Egypt.** His, Jacob's, **heart faltered because he did not believe them.** ²⁷Due to Jacob's reaction, **they spoke to him** in more detail, sharing **all the words of Joseph that he had said to them, and he** also **saw the wagons that Joseph sent to convey him. And the spirit of Jacob their father was revived.**

²⁸**Israel said:** It is **enough** that **Joseph my son is still alive;** I need no more than this. **I will go and see him before I die.**

The Family's Journey to Egypt

Although Jacob has decided to travel to Egypt of his own accord, he still wishes to receive divine approval for his plan. God reveals Himself to Jacob, promising to protect him, and dispelling his concerns that his family might assimilate into Egyptian society.

46 ¹**Israel, and everything** and everyone **that he had, traveled, and came to Beersheba. And he slaughtered offerings** there **to the God of his father**

Genesis

Isaac. [2]God spoke to Israel in the visions of the night, either a dream-like vision or an actual dream, and said: Jacob, Jacob; and he said: Here I am; I am listening. [3]He said: I am the God, the God of your father; do not fear to go down to Egypt, as I will make you a great nation there. [4]I will go down with you to Egypt, and I will also take you up again from Egypt. And Joseph shall place his hand over your eyes; he will care for you when you die.

[5]Jacob arose from Beersheba, to travel. And the sons of Israel conveyed Jacob their father, and their children, and their wives, in the wagons that Pharaoh had sent to convey him. [6]They took their livestock and their movable property that they had acquired in the land of Canaan, and they came to Egypt: Jacob, and all his descendants with him. [7]His sons and his sons' sons came with him, his daughters and daughters-in-law, and his sons' daughters and daughters-in-law; and all his descendants he brought with him to Egypt.

Jacob's Descendants

This list of Jacob's descendants who went to Egypt is arranged according to the maternal line. Many of the people mentioned here later become heads of families of the Jewish people.

[8]And these are the names of the children of Israel who were coming to Egypt, Jacob and his sons: the firstborn of Jacob, Reuben. [9]And the sons of Reuben: Hanokh, Palu, Hetzron, and Karmi. [10]The sons of Simeon: Jemuel, Yamin, Ohad, Yakhin, Tzohar, and Shaul, son of the Canaanite woman. [11]The sons of Levi: Gershon, Kehat, and Merari. [12]The sons of Judah: Er, Onan, Shela, Peretz, and Zerah; Er and Onan died in the land of Canaan. And the sons of Peretz were Hetzron and Hamul. [13]The sons of Issachar: Tola, Puva, Yov, and Shimron. [14]The sons of Zebulun: Sered, Elon, and Yahle'el. [15]These are the sons of Leah, whom she bore to Jacob in Padan Aram, with his daughter Dina; all the people, his sons and his daughters, thirty-three.

[16]The sons of Gad: Ziphion, Hagi, Shuni, Etzbon, Eri, Arodi, and Areli. [17]The sons of Asher: Yimna, Yishva, Yishvi, Beria, and Serah their sister. And the sons of Beria: Hever and Malkiel. [18]These are the sons of Zilpa, whom Laban gave to Leah his daughter; she bore these to Jacob, sixteen souls.

[19]The sons of Rachel, Jacob's wife: Joseph and Benjamin. [20]To Joseph in the land of Egypt were born, whom Asenat, daughter of Poti Fera priest

of On, bore to him, Manasseh and Ephraim. ²¹The sons of Benjamin: Bela, Bekher, Ashbel, Gera, Naaman, Ehi, Rosh, Mupim, Hupim, and Ard. ²²These are the sons of Rachel, who were born to Jacob; all the people were fourteen.

²³The sons of Dan: Hushim. ²⁴The sons of Naphtali: Yahtze'el, Guni, Yetzer, and Shilem. ²⁵These are the sons of Bilha, whom Laban gave to Rachel his daughter, and these she bore to Jacob; all the people were seven. ²⁶All the people who were coming with Jacob to Egypt, the products of his loins aside from the wives of Jacob's sons, all the people were sixty-six. ²⁷The sons of Joseph, who were born to him in Egypt, were two people; all the people of the house of Jacob, all his family members who came to Egypt, were seventy.

Jacob and Joseph Reunite

As Judah had become the brothers' representative to Joseph, he goes to Egypt first to arrange the details of the journey and their settlement in Goshen.

Sixth aliya ²⁸He, Jacob, **sent Judah before him to Joseph, to guide him to Goshen. And they came to the land of Goshen.** ²⁹**Joseph harnessed his chariot and went up toward Israel his father, to Goshen, and he appeared to him, fell upon his neck** in an embrace, **and wept on his neck prodigiously.** ³⁰**Israel said to Joseph: I can die now** in peace **after my seeing your face, for you are still alive.**

Joseph Briefs His Family Before They Meet Pharaoh

Joseph exploits the fact that the Egyptians consider shepherding to be a despicable occupation to secure a separate area of Egypt for his family to settle in undisturbed, with official sanction.

³¹**Joseph said to his brothers and to his father's household: I will go up and tell Pharaoh, and I will say to him: My brothers, and my father's household who were in the land of Canaan, came to me.** ³²**The men are shepherds, as they are people of livestock** and always have been, **and they have brought their flocks, and their cattle, and everything that they have.** ³³**It shall be, when Pharaoh shall call you and say: What is your occupation?** ³⁴**You shall say: Your servants have been people of livestock from our youth until now, both we and our fathers; so that you may live in the land of Goshen, for every shepherd,** or the occupation itself, **is an abomination for the Egyptians.**

Joseph's Brothers Meet Pharaoh

Joseph does not present all of his brothers to Pharaoh. He selects five to serve as representatives, perhaps choosing the least impressive among them, so that Pharaoh does not seek to draft them into his army.

47 **¹Joseph went and told Pharaoh and said: My father and my brothers, and their flocks, and their cattle, and everything that they have, have come from the land of Canaan, and behold, they are in the land of Goshen. ²From among his brothers he took five men, and he presented them before Pharaoh. ³Pharaoh said to his brothers: What is your occupation? They said to Pharaoh: Your servants are shepherds, both we and our fathers. ⁴They said to Pharaoh: We have come to reside** temporarily **in the land,** not to settle permanently, **because there is no pasture** in Canaan **for your servants' flocks, as the famine is severe in the land of Canaan. Now, please, may your servants live in the land of Goshen?**

⁵Pharaoh spoke to Joseph, saying: Your father and your brothers have come to you. ⁶The land of Egypt is before you, at your disposal; **settle your father and your brothers in the best of the land; they shall live in the land of Goshen. And if you know any capable men among them, set them** as **chief herders over that** livestock **which is mine.**

> **Further reading:** The Sages advance a conjecture as to which brothers Joseph presented to Pharaoh. See *A Concise Guide to the Sages*, p. 68.

Jacob Meets Pharaoh

Due to Jacob's status, his meeting and exchange with Pharaoh differs from that of the brothers. Pharaoh is impressed with Jacob's longevity, but Jacob explains that he seems older than his true age because of the anguish he has suffered.

⁷Joseph brought Jacob his father, and stood him before Pharaoh. And Jacob blessed Pharaoh. ⁸Pharaoh said to Jacob: How many are the days of the years of your life? ⁹Jacob said to Pharaoh: The days of the years of my residing, the years of my wandering, **are one hundred and thirty years; few and unfavorable have been the days of the years of my life. And they,** my years, **have not reached the days of the years of the life of my fathers in the days of their residing;** Abraham and Isaac lived much longer than I have. **¹⁰Jacob blessed Pharaoh and departed from the presence of Pharaoh.**

Seventh aliya **¹¹Joseph settled his father and his brothers, and gave them a portion in the land of Egypt, in the best of the land, in the land of Rameses, in**

Goshen, as Pharaoh commanded. ¹²Joseph provided for his father, his brothers, and his father's entire household, with bread into the mouths of the children, allotments of food according to the number of children.

Reform of Egypt's Political Structure

The inhabitants of Egypt sell everything they have in order to buy provisions from Joseph, the exclusive supplier of food during the famine. Their money, animals, and land become royal property, and they themselves are transformed from Pharaoh's subjects to his serfs. Thus Joseph helps Pharaoh to accumulate unlimited power, while the Egyptians become completely dependent on their king.

¹³There was no bread in all the land, as the famine was very severe, and the land of Egypt and the land of Canaan languished due to the famine. ¹⁴Joseph collected all the silver that was found in the land of Egypt and in the land of Canaan in exchange for the grain which they, the people, were purchasing. Joseph brought the silver to Pharaoh's house. ¹⁵Once the silver was exhausted in the land of Egypt and in the land of Canaan, all the Egyptians came to Joseph, saying: Give us bread; why should we die in your presence because our silver has run out? ¹⁶Joseph said: Give your livestock, and I will give you food in exchange for your livestock, if silver has run out. ¹⁷They brought their livestock to Joseph; Joseph gave them bread in exchange for the horses, for the livestock of flocks, for the livestock of cattle, and for the donkeys; in exchange for all their livestock he provided them with bread during that year. ¹⁸That year concluded, and they came to him in the second year, the next year, and said to him: We will not conceal from my lord how our silver and the herds of cattle are spent to my lord; you have it all. Nothing remains before my lord to give you, except for our bodies and our lands. ¹⁹Why shall we die before your eyes, both we and our land? Purchase us and our land with bread, and we and our land will be slaves to Pharaoh, his property. Give us seed that we will live and will not die, and the land will not become desolate. ²⁰Joseph purchased all the land of Egypt for Pharaoh because each Egyptian sold his field, for the famine was severe upon them. All the land became Pharaoh's. ²¹As for the people, he, Joseph, transferred them to the cities, from one end of the Egyptian border to its other end. ²²Only the land of the priests he, Joseph, did not buy, for there was an allotment of food designated for the priests from Pharaoh, and they ate their allotment that Pharaoh gave them; therefore, they did not sell their land.

²³Joseph said to the people: Behold, I have purchased you today, and your land, for Pharaoh. Here is seed for you, and you shall sow the land. ²⁴It shall be, at the harvests of the crops, that you shall give one-fifth of the crop to Pharaoh, and the remaining four parts shall be yours, for seed of the field, and for your food, and for those in your house-

Maftir holds, and to be eaten by your children. ²⁵They said: You have saved our lives. Let us find favor in the eyes of my lord, and we will be slaves to Pharaoh. ²⁶Joseph instituted it, his condition, as a statute to this day with regard to the land of Egypt: One-fifth was to be for Pharaoh; only the land of the priests alone did not become Pharaoh's.

²⁷The nation of Israel lived in the land of Egypt, in the land of Goshen; they settled there, and they were fruitful and multiplied exceedingly.

Parashat Vayhi

Toward the end of his life, Jacob asks Joseph to see to his burial in Canaan. He bestows a special blessing upon his beloved son, and accords Joseph's sons, his grandsons, the same status as his own sons. He then delivers a personal message to each of his other sons, imparting blessings, reprimands, or his prophetic visions for their future.

Joseph arranges a stately funeral procession for Jacob, who is buried in the Land of Israel as he requested, in the burial plot of the patriarchs and matriarchs in Hebron. When the family returns to Egypt, Joseph reconciles with his brothers regarding the suffering they inflicted on him in his youth. Joseph is blessed with a relatively long life, and he lives to see great-grandchildren from both of his sons. Before he dies, he reminds his family of the divine promise that they will return to their land, and instructs them to bury him in Canaan at that time.

Jacob Is Buried in the Land of Israel

Joseph is the powerful ruler of Egypt, as well as Jacob's son. Therefore, Jacob speaks to him in a tone that reflects both his fatherly authority and his anxious desire for his son's assistance.

²⁸**Jacob lived in the land of Egypt seventeen years. The days of Jacob, the years of his life, were seven years and one hundred and forty years.** ²⁹**The time for Israel to die approached. And he called** for **his son Joseph, and he said to him: Please, if I have found favor in your eyes, please place your hand under my thigh and** swear to me (see 24:2) that you will **perform kindness and truth,** a pure favor, **with me; please do not bury me in Egypt.** ³⁰**Instead, I shall lie with my fathers** after my death, **and you will convey me from Egypt and bury me in their grave,** in my ancestors' burial plot. **He,** Joseph, **said: I will do in accordance with your words.** ³¹**He,** Jacob, **said: Take an oath to me** to that effect. **And he,** Joseph, **took an oath to him. Israel prostrated himself at the head of the bed** as a sign of gratitude to God.

📖 **Further reading:** For more on the importance of burial in Israel, see *A Concise Guide to the Sages*, p. 70; *A Concise Guide to Mahshava*, p. 132.

Jacob Transmits His Blessings to Joseph

Joseph visits Jacob shortly before his death, and Jacob tells him about the divine promises and blessings he received for the proliferation of his family and the inheritance of the Land of Israel. Jacob wishes to pass on these blessings to Joseph and to raise his standing among his brothers with regard to both blessings.

48 ¹**It was after these matters that one** person **said to Joseph: Behold, your father is ill. He took his two sons, Manasseh and Ephraim, with him,** to see Jacob. ²**One** person **told Jacob and said: Behold, your son Joseph is coming to you. Israel exerted himself, and he sat** up **upon the bed.**

³**Jacob said to Joseph: God Almighty appeared to me in Luz,** also known as Beit El, **in the land of Canaan, and He blessed me.** ⁴**He said to me: Behold, I will make you fruitful and multiply you** and your descendants, **and I will render you an assembly of peoples; and I will give this land to your descendants after you as an eternal portion.** ⁵**And now, your two sons, who were born to you in the land of Egypt before my coming to you to Egypt, they are** to be considered **like mine; Ephraim and Manasseh, like Reuben and Simeon they shall be for me.** ⁶**And your progeny that you beget after them,** after Manasseh and Ephraim, **they shall be** considered as **yours; they shall be called after the name of their brothers** Ephraim or Manasseh, as part of their tribes, **in their inheritance** of the Land of Israel. ⁷**And I, when coming** back **from Padan** Aram, your mother **Rachel died on me in the land of Canaan, on the way, while still some distance from arriving at Efrat,** not in an inhabited area. **And** therefore **I buried her there on the road to Efrat, which is** another name for **Bethlehem.**

> 📖 **Further reading:** For more on Rachel's burial on the road, see 35:16–20 and *A Concise Guide to the Sages*, p. 54.

Jacob Blesses Manasseh and Ephraim

Joseph brings his sons before his father to receive his blessings. As Jacob is a prophet, blessings he bestows are more than mere wishes; despite his illness and frailty, he retains the spiritual power to shape his grandsons' character and their status for generations to come.

⁸**Israel saw Joseph's sons, and he said: Who are these?** ⁹**Joseph said to his father: They are my sons,** Ephraim and Manasseh, **whom God has given me here** in Egypt. He, Jacob, **said: Please bring them to me, and I will bless them.** ¹⁰**And the eyes of Israel were heavy,** weakened, **with age;** he was unable to see clearly. He, Joseph, **had them approach him, and**

Second aliya

he, Jacob, **kissed them, and he embraced them.** **¹¹Israel said to Joseph: I did not expect to see** even **your face** after you were missing so long, **and behold, God has shown me your offspring as well.**

¹²Joseph took them, his sons, **out from between his knees, and he prostrated himself on his face to the earth,** bowing to God. **¹³**Then, while facing Jacob, **Joseph took the two of them: Ephraim,** his younger son, **in his right hand,** so that he would be **to the left of Israel,** which was the customary position for a younger son; **and** he took **Manasseh,** his older son, **in his left hand, to the right of Israel. And he had them approach him. ¹⁴But Israel extended his right hand,** which was opposite Manasseh, **and laid it upon the head of Ephraim, who was the younger** brother, **and his left hand** he laid **upon the head of Manasseh; he deliberately placed his hands** crosswise, **as Manasseh was the firstborn. ¹⁵He,** Jacob, **blessed Joseph** through his children, **and said: By the God before whom my fathers, Abraham and Isaac, walked,** and whom they served, **the God who shepherds,** directs, **me from my beginnings until this day, ¹⁶may the angel who delivers me from all evil,** and who has protected me until now, **bless the lads. And let my name and the name of my fathers, Abraham and Isaac, be called upon them;** may these two children continue my legacy. Additionally, **may they,** their descendants, **proliferate greatly in the midst of the earth.**

Third aliya **¹⁷Joseph saw that his father** had switched his hands, as he **would lay his right hand upon the head of Ephraim, and it displeased him. He** therefore **supported,** lifted, **his father's hand** from below, **to remove it from the head of Ephraim to the head of Manasseh. ¹⁸Joseph said to his father: Not so, my father, as this** one, Manasseh, **is the firstborn; place your right hand upon his head. ¹⁹His father refused and said: I know, my son; I know** he is the firstborn. **He too shall become a people,** a tribe, **and he too shall be great. However, his younger brother** Ephraim **shall be greater than he, and his descendants shall become a multitude of nations,** filling the world. **²⁰He blessed them that day, saying: By you shall** the nation of **Israel bless** their children throughout the generations, **saying: May God make you like Ephraim and like Manasseh; and he placed Ephraim before Manasseh** in the wording of this blessing.

²¹Israel said to Joseph: Behold, I am dying. Know that **God will be with you, and He will** eventually **restore you to the land of your fathers. ²²I have given to you one portion** of inheritance **beyond** that of **your**

brothers in the land **which I took from the hand of the Emorite with my sword and with my bow.**

Jacob Convenes His Sons

Jacob gives his final charge to his sons in lyric verse. He blesses some of his sons and reproves others, and only with regard to a few does he prophesy about the end of days, despite his opening declaration that that is his intent.

49 Fourth aliya **¹Jacob called to his sons, and he said: Gather and I will tell you that which shall befall you at the end of days. ²Assemble and hear, sons of Jacob, and heed Israel your father.**

Reuben

Addressing his oldest son, Jacob alludes to Reuben's episode with Bilha, explaining that this is the reason he has lost his status as firstborn.

³Reuben, you are my firstborn, my strength and the first of my potency. You should have merited **greater honor and greater power** and ruled over your brothers. **⁴However, since you were impetuous as water, you shall not excel;** you lost your precedence **because you mounted your father's bed,** the bed of your father' wife. **Then you desecrated he who ascended my couch,** yourself.

Simeon and Levi

Jacob reproves Simeon and Levi for massacring the men of Shekhem. He predicts that they will part ways and be dispersed, as together they are brutal and even dangerous.

⁵Simeon and Levi are brothers who act in concert. **Weapons of villainy are their heritage. ⁶My self shall not come in their company** or join in their covert plans. **With their assembly may my glory not be associated, for in their anger they killed men, and with their will they hamstrung** the legs of the **oxen** of Shekhem. **⁷Cursed be their anger, as it is** unacceptably **fierce, and their wrath, as it is** too **harsh; I will divide them in Jacob, and I will disperse them in Israel.**

Judah

In contrast to his statements to his first three sons, Jacob bestows a prophetic blessing on Judah, who is to be favored with a bountiful portion of the Land of Israel, and leadership throughout the generations.

⁸Judah, as for **you, your brothers shall acknowledge you** and give you honor. **Your hand shall be at the neck of your enemies;** you will subjugate

them. **Your father's sons shall prostrate themselves to you.** ⁹**Judah is a lion cub; from prey, my son, you rose up,** and you will emerge from each battle with the upper hand. **He crouched, lay like a lion, and like a great cat** at rest, **who shall dare rouse him?** ¹⁰**The scepter** of his reign **shall not depart from Judah, nor the ruler's staff from between his feet,** from among his descendants **until Shilo,** the redeemer, **arrives; to him,** to Judah, **nations shall assemble.** ¹¹**He shall bind his foal to the vine** without concern about its possible destruction, as grape vines will abound in his inheritance; **and to the branch of the vine** he shall bind **his donkey's foal. He launders his garments in wine;** the wine flowing from his grapes will be so abundant that he could use it even for laundering. **And in the blood of grapes,** wine, he shall cleanse **his clothes.** ¹²He will be **red-eyed from** drinking much **wine, and white-toothed from milk.**

Zebulun and Issachar

Jacob prophesies that Zebulun's descendants will be seafarers, whereas Issachar will live peacefully in his own land.

¹³**Zebulun shall dwell by the shore of seas; he,** his portion, **shall be on a shore for** merchant **ships,** as his inheritance will be on the shore of the Mediterranean Sea, **and his border will be upon Sidon,** in the north.

¹⁴**Issachar is a strong-boned donkey, lying** tranquilly **between the boundaries** of the pastures. ¹⁵**He saw rest, that it was good, and the land, that it was pleasant. He bowed his shoulder to bear** agricultural burdens **and he will be subjected to a tribute of labor.** Alternatively, tribute will be paid to him.

Dan, Gad, Asher, and Naphtali

Dan and Gad will be known for their military prowess. Asher will receive an especially fertile portion. Naphtali will excel in verbal expression.

¹⁶**Dan shall avenge his people, as one of the tribes of Israel.** ¹⁷**Dan shall be a serpent on the road, a viper on the path that bites a horse's heels and his rider falls backward.** ¹⁸**For your salvation I await, Lord.** *Fifth aliya* ¹⁹**Gad with a troop shall slash his enemies; and he shall slash their heel.** ²⁰**From Asher, his bread is fat, and he shall provide royal delicacies.** His fertile land will produce choice foods. ²¹**Naphtali is a doe let loose** to run freely; he is one **who provides pleasant sayings,** fine and praiseworthy statements.

Joseph and Benjamin

The special blessing Jacob gives Joseph alludes to the ordeals Joseph endured and overcame. He will be blessed with material abundance and divine assistance, and Jacob grants him leadership and preeminence among his brothers.

22The majority of descriptions in the blessings involve animals, but for Joseph, Jacob uses imagery of vegetation: **Joseph is a fruitful tree, a fruitful tree** growing tranquilly **alongside a spring; branches run over the wall.** Alternatively, Egyptian girls strolled upon the city wall to see him. 23Jacob describes Joseph's difficult experiences: **They embittered him,** afflicted him, **and shot him, and archers hated him.** 24But **his bow sat firm** in a powerful foundation, **and the arms of his hands were golden,** as dominant as gold. He is endowed with might **by the hands of the Mighty One of Jacob, from there, from** the strength of **the Shepherd of the stone of Israel;** or alternatively, by the Shepherd, the Rock of Israel. 25**From the God of your father** you shall receive assistance, **and He shall help you; and** support you through the name of **the Almighty, and He shall bless you:** With **blessings of heaven above,** rain, and **blessings of the depths lying beneath,** groundwater to moisten the land, as well as **blessings** of fertility, **of breasts and of womb.** 26**The blessings of your father** that I am bestowing upon you **surpass the blessings of my parents** to me, as I am blessing you with strength, courage, and constant support from Heaven, **until the edge of the eternal hills. They,** these blessings, **shall** all **be** like a crown **on the head of Joseph,** placed **on the head of** he who is **the elect among his brothers.**

Sixth aliya 27**Benjamin is a wolf that mauls; in the morning he devours prey, and in the evening he divides the spoils.**

> **Further reading:** For elaboration on the proceedings surrounding Jacob's blessing of his sons, see *A Concise Guide to the Sages,* p. 71.

Jacob's Legacy

Jacob already asked Joseph to swear to bury him in Canaan, as Joseph has the power to execute his wish. Now Jacob wants to apprise his other sons of his wishes.

28**All these are the tribes of Israel, twelve, and this is that which their father spoke to them, and he blessed them; each man in accordance with his blessing he blessed them.** 29**He instructed them and said to them: I am** about **to** die and **be gathered to my people; bury me with my ancestors in the cave that is in the**

field of Efron the Hitite, ³⁰in the cave that is in the field of Makhpela, that is opposite Mamre in the land of Canaan, which Abraham had bought with the field from Efron the Hitite as a burial portion. ³¹There they buried Abraham and Sarah, his wife; there they buried Isaac and Rebecca, his wife; and there I buried Leah. ³²The purchase of the field and the cave that is in it was effected by my grandfather; they were acquired from the children of Het.

³³Jacob concluded instructing his sons. He drew his feet to the bed, and he expired, and he was gathered to his people.

Jacob Is Embalmed

Joseph had physicians under his jurisdiction who were responsible for embalming deceased Egyptian notables, among their other duties. He instructs them to prepare and preserve his father's body.

50 ¹**Joseph fell upon his father's face, wept upon him, and kissed him.** ²**Joseph commanded his servants, the physicians, to embalm his father. The physicians then embalmed Israel.** ³**Forty days** following his death **were completed for him, as so are the days of embalming completed;** embalming typically took forty days. **Egypt wept for him seventy days,** in accordance with Egyptian mourning customs.

The Funeral Procession

Pharaoh sends an entourage with Joseph to bury Jacob. It is possible that the group of prominent Egyptians who accompany the brothers, presumably including troops, serves a dual purpose. It confers honor on Jacob, who was considered an important and holy personage, while at the same time it ensures that Joseph does not stay in his homeland of Canaan and establish an independent principality there.

⁴**The days of his weeping passed, and Joseph spoke to Pharaoh's household,** the king's associates, **saying: Please, if I have found favor in your eyes, please, speak** in my name **in the ears of Pharaoh, saying:** ⁵**My father administered an oath to me, saying: Behold, I am dying; in my grave that I dug for me in the land of Canaan, bury me there.** Joseph asks of Pharaoh: **I will go up** to the land of Canaan **now and bury my father** there, **and** afterward **I will return** to you. ⁶**Pharaoh said: Go up and bury your father, in accordance with the oath he administered to you.**

⁷**Joseph went up to bury his father, and all the servants of Pharaoh, the elders of his house, and all the elders of the land of Egypt went up with him,** ⁸**and all of Joseph's household,** his family, **and his brothers, and**

his father's household. They left only their children, their flocks, and their cattle in the land of Goshen. ⁹He took up with him both chariots and horsemen, and the camp was very substantial. ¹⁰They came to the threshing floor of Atad, which is beyond the Jordan. And they lamented a very great and intense lament, and Joseph observed mourning for his father seven days. ¹¹The inhabitants of the land, the Canaanites, saw the mourning at the threshing floor of Atad, and they said: This is intense mourning [*evel*] for Egypt [*mitzrayim*]. Therefore, it, this place, was called Avel Mitzrayim, which is beyond the Jordan.

¹²His, Jacob's, sons did for him just as he had commanded them. ¹³His sons conveyed him to the land of Canaan, and buried him in the cave of the field of Makhpela, which Abraham had bought with the field, as a burial portion, from Efron the Hitite, opposite Mamre. ¹⁴Joseph returned to Egypt, he, and his brothers, and all who went up with him to bury his father, after he had buried his father.

Reconciliation

Joseph's brothers become concerned that without their father's presence, Joseph will now exact retribution upon them for their past offenses. Therefore, they convey to him, in Jacob's name, an injunction to forgive them.

¹⁵Joseph's brothers saw that their father had died, and they said: Perhaps Joseph will hate us and will repay us for all the evil that we did to him. ¹⁶They instructed messengers to tell Joseph, saying: Your father instructed before his death, saying: ¹⁷So say to Joseph: Please, forgive the transgression of your brothers and their sin, as they did evil to you, or despite the evil they did to you. The brothers' message continues: And now, please fulfill your father's wishes and forgive the transgression of the servants of the God of your father. Joseph wept as they spoke to him. ¹⁸His brothers too, they themselves then went and fell, bowed, before him, Joseph, and they said: Behold, we are your slaves.

¹⁹Joseph said to them: Fear not, for am I in place of God, to punish or to grant atonement? ²⁰You intended me harm; God intended it for good, in order to make it, our situation, as it is today, to enable me to keep many *Seventh* people alive during the famine. ²¹And now, fear not; I will sustain you *aliya* and your children. He comforted them and spoke to their heart to assuage their fears.

Joseph's Last Wishes

Joseph lives many years after Jacob's death and is privileged to see his father's small clan grow to become a nation. Toward the end of Joseph's life, as the children of Israel become ensconced in Egypt, he reminds his brothers of the divine promise of redemption, and administers an oath to them that they bury him in his homeland, just as his father was.

²²**Joseph lived in Egypt, he and his father's household; Joseph lived** *Maftir* **one hundred and ten years.** ²³**Joseph saw great-grandchildren from Ephraim; also the children of Makhir son of Manasseh were born at Joseph's knees,** under his protection.

²⁴Before his death, **Joseph said to his brothers: I am dying, and God will remember you and bring you up from this land to the land about which He took an oath to Abraham, to Isaac, and to Jacob** to give to them. ²⁵**Joseph administered an oath to the children of Israel, saying: God will remember** [*pakod yifkod*] **you, and** when that occurs **you shall carry up my bones from there,** from Egypt.

²⁶**Joseph died at the age of one hundred and ten years. They embalmed him, and he was placed in a coffin in Egypt.**

📖 **Further reading:** Many years later, God repeats Joseph's expression, saying: I have remembered [*pakod pakadti*] you, and…I will take you up out of the affliction of Egypt, to the land of the Canaanites" (Exodus 3:16–17). When the children of Israel ultimately leave Egypt, they bring Joseph's bones with them in fulfillment of his last wishes (Exodus 13:19).

Exodus

Parashat Shemot

The children of Israel become a numerous, powerful nation in Egypt. Worried about the demographic threat they pose, Pharaoh attempts to suppress their strength, first by enslaving them and then by decreeing death upon their newborn boys. Moses, who is destined to lead the Jewish people, is born when conditions in this grim period reach their nadir. He grows up in the Egyptian royal palace but is eventually forced to flee to Midyan, where he marries and fathers children. While there, Moses also receives his first communication from God, the revelation near the bush, during which he is appointed to redeem the children of Israel from Egypt. When he returns to Egypt, he and Aaron approach Pharaoh, but Pharaoh refuses to free the Jews and even increases their workload.

Beginning of the Egyptian Enslavement

The children of Israel multiply rapidly in Egypt, causing Pharaoh concern that they will pose a threat. He imposes harsh decrees on them in order to halt their growth.

1 ¹**These are the names of the children of Israel, who came to Egypt with Jacob; each** man **came with his household.** ²**Reuben, Simeon, Levi, and Judah;** ³**Issachar, Zebulun, and Benjamin;** ⁴**Dan and Naphtali, Gad and Asher.** ⁵**All the people who emerged from Jacob's loins,** his descendants, **were seventy souls; and** this number includes **Joseph,** who **was** already **in Egypt.** ⁶**Joseph** died, **and** then **all of his brothers and all of that generation died.** ⁷**The children of Israel were fruitful and propagated and increased and grew exceedingly mighty,** becoming a powerful presence. **And the land** of Egypt **was filled with them.**

⁸**A new king arose over Egypt, one who did not know Joseph.** ⁹**He,** the king, **said to his people: Behold, the people of the children of Israel are more numerous and** are **mightier than we.** ¹⁰**Let us be cunning with it,** that nation; we must employ sophisticated methods to limit their growth. **Lest it increase, and it shall be that if a war will occur, it too will join our enemies and wage war against us, and go up from the land.** ¹¹**They,** the Egyptians, **appointed overseers over it,** conscripted the children of Israel into a labor force, **in order to afflict it with their burdens,**

to cause them misery and break their spirits. **It,** the Israelite nation, **built storehouse cities** for valuables **for Pharaoh: Pitom and Rameses.** [12]**But as they,** the Egyptians, **would afflict it,** the nation of Israel, **so it would increase and so it would proliferate** even more. And **they,** the Egyptians, **were revolted by the children of Israel.**

[13]**The Egyptians** consequently **coerced the children of Israel to work with travail,** hard physical labor. [14]**They embittered their lives with hard work, with mortar and with bricks,** construction work, **and with all work in the field; all their work with which they worked for them,** the Egyptians, **was with travail,** harsh servitude.

📖 **Further reading:** For more on Pharaoh's scheme for enslaving the children of Israel, see *A Concise Guide to the Sages,* p. 77.

Pharaoh's Decrees against the Hebrew Boys

Attempting to reverse the Israelite population surge, Pharaoh pronounces an appalling edict: He directs the two midwives, Shifra and Pua, to murder all Hebrew newborn boys at birth. When they fail to fulfill his instructions, he enlists the entire Egyptian people in drowning these babies in the Nile.

[15]**The king of Egypt spoke with the Hebrew midwives, of whom the name of one was Shifra, and the name of the other, Pua.** [16]**He said: When you deliver the Hebrew women, and you look upon the birthstool, if it is a son** that was born, **you shall kill him; but if it is a daughter, she shall live.**

[17]**The midwives feared God and** therefore they **did not do as the king of Egypt commanded them; they kept the children alive.**

Second aliya [18]**The king of Egypt summoned the midwives, and he said to them: Why did you do this thing, keeping the children alive?** [19]**The midwives said to Pharaoh:** We were unable to carry out your instructions **because the Hebrew women are not like the Egyptian women, as they are vigorous. Before the midwife comes to them, they have** already **given birth.**

[20]**God favored the midwives and the people** of Israel **increased and became very mighty.** [21]**It was, because the midwives feared God, He established households for them.** Their families grew and became honored and distinguished.

[22]**Pharaoh commanded all his people** directly, **saying: Every son who is born** to the Hebrews, **you shall cast him into the Nile, but every daughter you shall keep alive.**

Moses' Birth

The decree of infanticide is being fully enforced when Moses is born. At first his mother succeeds in concealing him at home, but once this becomes impossible, she places him in a waterproof basket near the bank of the Nile, under his older sister's watchful eyes.

2 ¹**A man from the house,** the tribe, **of Levi went and took a daughter** from the tribe **of Levi** as his wife. ²**The woman conceived and bore a son; she saw him, that he was good, and she concealed him for three months.** ³**Once she could no longer conceal him, she took a wicker basket** woven from reeds **for him, and** she **coated it with clay** on the inside **and with pitch** on the outside, to make it waterproof. **She placed the child in it and placed it among the reeds** growing **on the bank of the Nile.** ⁴**His sister stationed herself at a distance, to know what would be done to him.**

⁵**At that moment, Pharaoh's daughter went down to bathe in the Nile, and her maidens,** her servants, **walked alongside the Nile. She,** the princess, **saw the basket among the reeds, and** she **sent her maidservant and she took it.** ⁶**She opened it and she saw the child, and behold,** it was a **boy** and he **was crying. She had compassion for him, and she said: This** child **is from the children of the Hebrews.** ⁷**His sister said to Pharaoh's daughter: Shall I go and call a wet nurse for you from the Hebrews, and she will nurse the child for you?** ⁸**Pharaoh's daughter said to her: Go. The girl went, and summoned the child's mother.**

⁹**Pharaoh's daughter said to her: Take this child and nurse him for me, and I will pay your wages. The woman took the child and nursed him.** ¹⁰**The child grew, and she brought him to Pharaoh's daughter, and he was a son to her. She,** Pharaoh's daughter, **called his name Moses** [Moshe]**, and she said: I named him thus because I drew him from the water** [meshitihu]**.**

📖 **Further reading:** For more on Moses' childhood in the royal palace, see *A Concise Guide to the Sages,* p. 80.

Moses' Early Experiences in Egypt

Moses wanders about Egypt and discovers the suffering and torments of his Hebrew brethren. When he sees an Egyptian beating a Hebrew, he intervenes in favor of his fellow Hebrew. On another occasion he intercedes in a fight between two Hebrews.

Third aliya ¹¹**It was in those days, Moses grew, and he went out to his** Hebrew **brethren and he saw their burdens; and he saw an Egyptian man beating a Hebrew man, of his brethren.** ¹²**He,** Moses, **turned this way and that,**

Exodus

and he saw that there was no one in the vicinity. **He smote the Egyptian,** killing him, **and hid him** by burying the body **in the sand.**

¹³**He, Moses, emerged on the second day, and behold, two Hebrew men were fighting.** And he, Moses, **said to the wicked one,** the assailant: **Why do you strike your neighbor?** ¹⁴**He,** the assailant, **said: Who appointed you to be a leader and a judge over us,** that you see fit to judge me? **Do you propose to kill me, as you killed the Egyptian? Moses was frightened, and he said: Indeed,** apparently **the** earlier **matter is known.**

Moses Flees to Midyan
When Pharaoh hears that Moses killed the Egyptian, he seeks to kill him. Moses escapes to Midyan, where he is a complete stranger. He waits at an informal meeting place, beside a well.

¹⁵**Pharaoh heard this matter, and he sought to kill Moses. Moses fled from Pharaoh, and he settled in the land of Midyan, and he sat beside the well.**

¹⁶**The priest of Midyan had seven daughters** who shepherded his flock. **They came** to the well, **drew water, and filled the troughs** in order **to give their father's flock to drink.** ¹⁷**The** male **shepherds came and drove them away; Moses stood and rescued them, and he gave their flock to drink.** ¹⁸**They came to Re'uel, their father, and he said: Why were you so quick to come** back **today?** ¹⁹**They said: An Egyptian man rescued us from the shepherds, and he also drew water for us and gave the flock to drink.** ²⁰**He said to his daughters: And where is he? Why did you leave the man? Call him, and let him eat bread** with us. ²¹**Moses decided,** agreed, **to live with the man, and he,** Re'uel, **gave his daughter Tzipora to Moses** as a wife. ²²**She bore a son, and he called his name Gershom, as he said: I have been a stranger** [ger] **in a foreign land.**

Israel's Cry Prompts God's Redemption
The tribulations of the children of Israel lead them to sigh and cry out to God, who sets their redemption in motion.

²³**It was during those many days,** a long time later, **the king of Egypt died. The children of Israel sighed due to the work, and they cried out** to God, **and their plea rose to God due to the work.** ²⁴**God heard their groaning, and God remembered His covenant with Abraham, with Isaac, and with Jacob,** their forefathers. ²⁵**God saw the children of Israel, and God knew;** He acknowledged their plight, and He cared.

Revelation at the Bush

While herding sheep in the wilderness, Moses encounters a wondrous sight: A bush that is burning, but is not being consumed by the fire. Moses goes to investigate the phenomenon, and receives a revelation from God. This communication comprises a prophecy, a promise, and the assignment of a mission.

3 **¹Moses was herding the sheep of Yitro, his father-in-law, priest of** *urth* *aliya* **Midyan. He led the flock far into the wilderness, and** he **came to the mountain of God,** Mount Sinai, **to Horev. ²An angel of the Lord appeared to him in a flame of fire from inside the bush,** a prickly plant, **and he saw, and behold, the bush was burning in the fire, but the bush was not consumed. ³Moses said: I will turn** and approach **now, and see this great sight. Why does the bush not** completely **burn up? ⁴The Lord saw that he turned** and approached **to see, and God called to him from within the bush, and He said: Moses, Moses. He,** Moses, **said: Here I am. ⁵He said: Do not approach** near **here; remove your shoes from your feet, as the place upon which you are standing is sacred ground.**

⁶He said: I am the God of your father, the God of Abraham, the God of Isaac, and the God of Jacob. Moses hid his face, as he was afraid to look at God. ⁷The Lord said: I have seen the affliction of My people that is in Egypt, and I have heard their outcry because of its taskmasters, who abuse the people; **for I know its,** the people's, **pain. ⁸I have descended to rescue it,** the children of Israel, **from the hand of Egypt and to bring it up from that land to a good and expansive land, to a land flowing with milk and honey, to the place of the Canaanites and the Hitites and the Emorites and the Perizites and the Hivites and the Yevusites. ⁹And now, behold, the outcry of the children of Israel has come to Me, and I have also seen the oppression with which the Egyptians are oppressing them. ¹⁰Now go, and I will send you to Pharaoh; and take My people, the children of Israel, out of Egypt.**

¹¹Moses said to God: Who am I, that I should go to Pharaoh, and that I should take the children of Israel out of Egypt? ¹²He, God, **said:** You will manage, **because I will be with you. And this is your sign that I sent you: When you take the people out of Egypt, you** and the Israelites **will serve God upon this mountain,** and I will reveal Myself to you.

¹³Moses said to God: Behold, I am coming to the children of Israel, and I will say to them: The God of your fathers sent me to you, and they will say to me: What is His name? What shall I say to them? ¹⁴God said to Moses: I Will Be As I Will Be. I will always be with them. **And He**

Exodus

Exodus

said: So shall you say to the children of Israel: I Will Be sent me to you. Here it is clear that "I Will Be" is God's name.

¹⁵**God again said to Moses: So you shall say to the children of Israel: The Lord [*YHVH*], God of your fathers, God of Abraham, God of Isaac, and God of Jacob, sent me to you. This** special name, *YHVH*, is **My name** now and **forever; this is My appellation,** which you will use **for all generations.**

Fifth
aliya
¹⁶**Go and gather the elders of Israel and say to them: The Lord, God of your forefathers, God of Abraham, Isaac, and Jacob, appeared to me, saying: I have remembered you and what is being done to you,** the suffering being inflicted upon you, **in Egypt.** ¹⁷**I have said: I will take you up out of the affliction of Egypt, to the land of the Canaanites and the Hitites and the Emorites and the Perizites and the Hivites and the Yevusites,** all nations that inhabited Canaan, **to a land flowing with milk and honey.**

¹⁸**They,** the elders of Israel, **will heed your voice, and you shall go, you and the elders of Israel, to the king of Egypt, and you shall say to him: The Lord, God of the Hebrews, happened upon us;** He has revealed Himself to us and given us a message. **Now, please, let us go on a journey of three days in the wilderness, and we will sacrifice to the Lord our God.**

¹⁹**And I know that the king of Egypt will not allow you to go unless I** force him to do so **with a powerful hand.** ²⁰**I will send forth My hand; I** will descend and reveal Myself. **And I will smite Egypt with all My wonders that I will perform in its midst, and thereafter he will send you forth.** ²¹**I will grant this people favor in the eyes of Egypt and it shall be that when you go, you will not go empty-handed.** ²²**Each woman will borrow,** or take, **silver vessels and gold vessels and garments from her neighbor and from she who resides** with her **in her house. And you shall place them,** all the items that you take from the Egyptians, **upon your sons and upon your daughters, and you will** thereby **despoil the Egyptians.**

📖 **Further reading:** For more on why a bush was chosen as the site of Moses' first revelation, see *A Concise Guide to the Sages*, p. 82.

The Signs

Moses is given special signs from God that will prove to the children of Israel that he received a revelation. Even so, Moses is skeptical about his ability to be God's messenger.

4 ¹Moses answered and he said: But behold, they will neither believe me, nor will they heed my voice, as they will say: The Lord did not appear to you. ²The Lord said to him: What is that in your hand? And he said: A staff. ³He, God, said: Cast it on the ground. He cast it on the ground and it became a serpent. Moses fled from it. ⁴The Lord said to Moses: Send forth your arm and grasp its tail. He sent forth his arm and he seized it, and it became a staff in his hand. ⁵God explained: Show this sign to the people so that they will believe that the Lord, God of their fathers, God of Abraham, God of Isaac, and God of Jacob, appeared to you.

⁶The Lord said to him further: Bring your hand into your bosom, under your upper garment. He brought his hand into his bosom and then he withdrew it, and behold, his hand was leprous, like snow; covered with white sores and marks. ⁷He, God, said: Return your hand into your bosom. He returned his hand into his bosom and then he withdrew it from his bosom, and behold, it recovered, it was completely healthy, like his flesh had been previously. ⁸God said: It shall be, if they do not believe you, and do not heed the voice of the first sign, if the sign of the staff does not convince them, they will believe the voice of the latter sign, the leprous hand. ⁹And it shall be if they will not believe even these two signs, and they will not heed your voice, then you shall take water from the Nile and you shall pour it on the dry land, and the water that you take from the Nile will become blood on the dry land.

¹⁰Moses said to the Lord: Please, my Lord, I am not a man of words who can express himself eloquently, neither yesterday nor the day before, nor since You have spoken to Your servant, as I am cumbrous of speech and cumbrous of tongue. ¹¹The Lord said to him: Who gives a mouth to a person? Or who renders one mute or deaf, or sighted or blind? Is it not I, the Lord? ¹²Now, go, and I will be with your mouth, and I will instruct you in that which you shall say. I will guide you throughout your mission.

¹³He, Moses, said: Please, my Lord, please send help to the people by means of anyone else whom You will send. ¹⁴The wrath of the Lord was enflamed against Moses and He said: Is not Aaron the Levite your brother? I know that he can speak well, and also, behold, he is coming out to meet you; he will see you, and he will rejoice in his heart. ¹⁵You shall speak to him, and you shall place the words in his mouth; transmit

Exodus

to him the message I told you. **And I will be with your mouth and with his mouth, and I will instruct you** in **that which you shall do.** [16]**He shall speak to the people for you, and he shall be a mouth** to speak **for you, and you shall be a leader for him.** [17]**And this staff you shall take in your hand, with which you will perform the signs.**

Moses Returns to Egypt

Moses' wife and children accompany him as he returns to Egypt to meet Aaron and fulfill his mission. Along the way, a mysterious, dangerous event almost derails the mission before it begins.

Sixth aliya [18]**Moses went and returned to Yeter,** Yitro, **his father-in-law, and he said to him: Please, let me go and return to my brethren who are in Egypt and see if they are still alive. Yitro said to Moses: Go in peace.** [19]**The Lord said to Moses in Midyan: Go, return to Egypt, as all the men who were seeking your life** when you fled from Egypt as a fugitive accused of murder **have died.** [20]**Moses took his wife and his sons and mounted them on the donkey, and they returned to the land of Egypt. Moses took the staff of God in his hand.**

[21]**The Lord said to Moses: When you go to return to Egypt, see,** remember, **all the wonders that I have placed in your hand,** the signs I provided for you, **and perform them before Pharaoh. And I will harden his heart, and he will not send forth the people.** [22]**You shall say to Pharaoh: So said the Lord: My firstborn son is Israel,** most precious to Me. [23]**And I,** God, **say to you,** Pharaoh: **Send forth My son, and he will serve Me, and if you refuse to send him forth, behold, I will slay your firstborn son.**

[24]**It was on the way** to Egypt, **in the lodging** place, that an angel of **the Lord encountered him,** Moses, **and sought to kill him.** [25]**Tzipora took a flint and she cut her son's foreskin, and touched it to his feet,** placed the foreskin beside Moses' feet. **And she said: For you are a bridegroom of blood to me;** the merit of this circumcision has saved my husband from death. [26]**He,** the angel, **released him,** Moses. **Then she said: A bridegroom of blood because of circumcision.**

[27]**The Lord said to Aaron: Go toward Moses, to the wilderness. He went and he met him at the mountain of God,** Mount Sinai, **and he kissed him.** [28]**Moses told Aaron all the words of the Lord: That He sent him, and all the signs that He commanded him.** [29]**Moses and Aaron went, and they assembled all the elders of the children of Israel.** [30]**Aaron spoke all the words that the Lord spoke to Moses, and he performed**

the signs in the sight of the people. [31]The people trusted them, and heard that the Lord remembered the children of Israel and that He saw their affliction. And they bowed and prostrated themselves to God.

Moshe and Aaron Approach Pharaoh

Moses and Aaron go to Pharaoh and convey to him God's demand to free the children of Israel. Pharaoh refuses, as God had foretold, and instead increases their workload.

5 [1]Then Moses and Aaron came and said to Pharaoh: So says the Lord, God of Israel: Send forth and release My people, and they will celebrate for Me in the wilderness. [2]Pharaoh said: Who is the Lord, that I should heed His voice to send forth Israel? I do not know the Lord, and I also will not send forth Israel. [3]They said: The Lord, the God of the Hebrews, has called upon us, met us. Please, let us go on a three-day journey into the wilderness and there we will sacrifice to the Lord our God, lest He strike and punish us with pestilence or with the sword. [4]The king of Egypt said to them: Why, Moses and Aaron, do you disturb the people from its tasks? Go to your burdens, your own affairs. [5]Pharaoh said: Behold, the people of the land, the Hebrew slaves, are now many, and with this demand you will cause them to desist from their burdens. Egypt requires their constant labor.

[6]Pharaoh commanded the Egyptian taskmasters of the people that day, and their Hebrew foremen, saying: [7]You shall not continue to give straw to the people to produce bricks, as previously. They will be required to go and gather straw for themselves from the fields. [8]But you shall continue to impose upon them the quota of the bricks, the same quota that they produced previously; you shall not diminish from it. For they are indolent; therefore, they cry out, saying: We will go and we will sacrifice to our God. [9]In this manner, let the work become weighty upon the people, and they will engage in it and they will not have time to be occupied with false matters.

[10]The taskmasters of the people and their foremen went out, and they said to the people, saying: So said Pharaoh: I am not giving you straw. [11]You, go take straw for yourselves from what you find, wherever you can find straw, for nothing will be diminished from the number of bricks you have to provide for your work. [12]The people scattered throughout the entire land of Egypt to gather stalks to cut up for straw. [13]The taskmasters goaded them to work faster, saying: Complete your task, each

enth
aliya

day's portion on its day, just the same **as when there was straw** given to you.

The Hebrew Foremen

The first to bear the brunt of the new decree are the Hebrew foremen. They plead with Pharaoh to lighten his impossible demands, but he refuses and accuses them of laziness.

[14]**The foremen of the children of Israel, whom Pharaoh's taskmasters appointed over them, were beaten, saying: Why did you not complete your quota to produce bricks as previously, both yesterday and today?** [15]**The foremen of the children of Israel came and cried out to Pharaoh, saying: Why do you do this to your servants?** [16]**Straw is not given to your servants, and** despite this **they say to us: Produce bricks. And behold,** we **your servants are beaten, and it is the fault of your people.** [17]**He,** Pharaoh, **said: You are indolent, indolent; therefore you say: Let us go and sacrifice to the Lord.** [18]**Now, go work, and straw will not be given to you; and the** usual required **total of bricks, you will** continue to **provide.**

[19]**The foremen of the children of Israel saw them in distress, saying: Do not diminish from your** quota of **bricks, each day's portion on its day.** [20]**They,** the foremen, **encountered Moses and Aaron standing facing them as they came out from before Pharaoh.** [21]**They,** the foremen, **said to them: May the Lord look upon you and judge** you, **because you have rendered us putrid in the eyes of Pharaoh and in the eyes of his servants;** now they have an excuse **to put a sword in their hand to kill us,** to oppress us and increase our burdens.

📖 **Further reading:** The Hebrew foremen are credited with devotion to their people, and were later accorded honor and stature for their efforts on behalf of the children of Israel. See *A Concise Guide to the Sages*, p. 83.

Moses Laments to God

The foremen's complaints to Moses prompt him in turn to protest to God. Moses claims that instead of redeeming the children of Israel, he has only brought more suffering upon them.

Maftir [22]**Moses returned to the Lord and he said: My Lord, why did You harm this people? Why did You send me?** [23]**Since I came to Pharaoh to speak in Your name, he has harmed this people, and You did not save Your**

6 **people.** [1]**The Lord said to Moses: Now you will see what I will do to Pharaoh, for with a powerful hand he will send them forth, and with a powerful hand he will drive them from his land.**

Parashat Va'era

Exodus

Moses and Aaron's first attempt to petition the king for freedom for their people only resulted in an exacerbation of their enslavement. Now God promises that he will redeem the children of Israel "with an outstretched arm," afflicting Egypt with severe plagues. Moses and Aaron return repeatedly to Pharaoh to demand that he release their people, and each time that Pharaoh refuses, Egypt suffers from a new plague. While at times Pharaoh relents, his change of heart is always temporary, and he returns to his intransigence.

Renewal of Moses' Mission

Moses receives another revelation from God, who reiterates His previous message: He remembers His covenant with the patriarchs, and He promises to redeem the children of Israel from Egypt and give them the land of Canaan. Moses conveys God's statement to the people.

²**God spoke to Moses, and He said to him: I am the Lord,** who appeared to you at the burning bush. ³**I appeared to Abraham, to Isaac, and to Jacob,** making Myself known **as God Almighty; but with My name, the Lord,** the Tetragrammaton, **I was not known to them.** ⁴**I also established My covenant with them, to give them the land of Canaan, the land of their residence, in which they resided.** ⁵**And I have also heard the groans of the children of Israel, whom the Egyptians are coercing to work, and I have remembered My covenant** with the patriarchs.

⁶**Therefore, say to the children of Israel: I am the Lord,** who made this promise to your fathers. **And I will take you out from under the burdens of Egypt; and I will deliver you from their work,** so that you will no longer be slaves; **and I will redeem you** from Egypt **with an outstretched arm,** with great strength, **and with great punishments** that will be exacted upon the Egyptians; ⁷**and I will take you for Me as** My **people; and I will be God for you. And you will know that I am the Lord your God, who takes you out from under the burdens of Egypt.** ⁸Finally, **I will bring you to the land with regard to which I raised My hand** as a sign of My oath **to give it to Abraham, to Isaac, and to Jacob, and I will give it you**

145

as an eternal **heritage: I am the Lord.** [9]**Moses spoke so to the children of Israel. But they did not heed Moses,** they remained unaffected by his statements, **because of** their **lack of patience and because of** the **hard work** they were forced to do.

> 📖 **Further reading:** The Sages read a trace of criticism of Moses in the mention of the patriarchs in God's response. See *A Concise Guide to the Sages,* p. 84.

God Sends Moses to Pharaoh

God instructs Moses to return to Pharaoh and demand freedom for the children of Israel, but Moses expresses uncertainty about Pharaoh's anticipated reaction, as even the children of Israel had been skeptical when Moses spoke to them.

[10]**The Lord spoke to Moses, saying:** [11]**Come** and **speak** again **to Pharaoh king of Egypt, and he will send forth the children of Israel from his land.** [12]**Moses spoke before the Lord, saying: Behold, the children of Israel did not heed me, and how,** then, **will Pharaoh heed me? And** moreover, **I am one whose lips are obstructed;** I do not even speak well (see 4:10).

[13]**The Lord spoke to Moses and to Aaron, and He commanded them** to speak **to the children of Israel and to Pharaoh king of Egypt,** as part of his mission **to take the children of Israel out of the land of Egypt.**

Moses and Aaron's Extended Family

The Torah presents the heads of the clans of the tribes of Reuven and Simeon, and then a fuller genealogy of the tribe of Levi, including Moses and Aaron, and Aaron's sons, concluding with Pinhas, Aaron's grandson.

Second aliya [14]**These are the heads of their patrilineal houses. The sons of Reuben, firstborn of Israel,** Jacob: **Hanokh and Palu, Hetzron and Karmi; these are the families of Reuben.** [15]**The sons of Simeon: Yemuel, Yamin, Ohad, Yakhin, Tzohar, and Shaul,** who was **the son of a Canaanite woman; these are the families of Simeon.** [16]**These are the names of the sons of Levi by their descendants,** in birth order: **Gershon, Kehat, and Merari. And the years of the life of Levi were one hundred and thirty-seven years.** [17]**The sons of Gershon: Livni and Shimi, according to their families.** [18]**The sons of Kehat: Amram, Yitzhar, Hevron, and Uziel; and the years of the life of Kehat were one hundred and thirty-three years.** [19]**The sons of Merari: Mahli and Mushi; these are the families of the Levites by their descendants.**

²⁰**Amram took Yokheved his aunt as his wife, and she bore him Aaron and Moses. And the years of the life of Amram were one hundred and thirty-seven years.** ²¹**The sons of Yitzhar** son of Kehat: **Korah, Nefeg, and Zikhri.** ²²**The sons of Uziel** son of Kehat: **Mishael, Eltzafan, and Sitri.**

²³**Aaron took Elisheva, daughter of Aminadav** and **sister of Nahshon, for his wife. And she bore him Nadav and Avihu, Elazar and Itamar.** ²⁴**The sons of Korah: Asir, Elkana, and Aviasaf; these are the families of the Korahites.** ²⁵**Elazar son of Aaron took from the daughters of Putiel for his wife, and she bore him Pinhas. These are the heads of the house of the fathers of the Levites by their families.** ²⁶**These were that** same **Aaron and Moses to whom the Lord said: Take out the children of Israel from the land of Egypt with their hosts,** the entire nation; ²⁷**it is they who speak to Pharaoh king of Egypt to take the children of Israel out from Egypt: that Moses and Aaron.**

God Addresses Moses' Concerns

After interrupting the narrative to present Moses' genealogy, the Torah returns to the earlier dialogue between God and Moses. Responding to Moses' concern that his lack of speaking expertise will prevent him from persuading Pharaoh, God reassures him, and tells him how Pharaoh will react, and how events will play out.

²⁸**It was on the day that the Lord spoke to Moses in the land of Egypt.**

Third *aliya* ²⁹**The Lord spoke to Moses, saying: I am the Lord; speak to Pharaoh king of Egypt everything that I speak to you.** ³⁰**Moses said before the Lord: Behold, I am one whose lips are obstructed,** who speaks poorly; **how will Pharaoh heed me?** **7** ¹**The Lord said to Moses: See, I have set you as a god for Pharaoh,** I have given you the power to judge and punish him, **and Aaron your brother will be your prophet,** he will serve as your agent. ²**You shall speak all that I will command you, and Aaron your brother will speak to Pharaoh, and** ultimately **he will send forth the children of Israel from his land.**

³**But** beforehand, **I will harden Pharaoh's heart** so he will refuse to surrender, **and I will increase My signs and My wonders in the land of Egypt.** ⁴**Pharaoh will not heed you, and** therefore **I will put My hand upon Egypt** to punish it, **and I will take out My hosts, My people, the children of Israel, from the land of Egypt, with great punishments** upon Egypt. ⁵**The Egyptians will know that I am the Lord when I extend My hand over Egypt** to strike it, **and I will take out the children of Israel from**

their midst. ⁶Moses and Aaron did as the Lord had commanded them; so they did. ⁷Moses was eighty years old and Aaron was eighty-three years old when they spoke to Pharaoh.

> 📖 **Further reading:** For more on the origins of Moses' difficulty in speaking, see *A Concise Guide to the Sages,* p. 80.

A Wonder before the Plagues Begin

God instructs Moses and Aaron to perform a wonder in order to prove to Pharaoh that they are indeed His messengers. Although the Egyptian magicians attempt to demonstrate their power though performing a similar trick, Moses and Aaron's wonder overcomes theirs.

Fourth aliya ⁸The Lord spoke to Moses and to Aaron, saying: ⁹When Pharaoh will speak to you, saying: Provide you a wonder to prove what you say, **you shall say to Aaron: Take your staff and cast it before Pharaoh,** and it will become a crocodile. ¹⁰Moses and Aaron came to Pharaoh and they did so, as the Lord had commanded; Aaron cast his staff before Pharaoh and before his servants, and it became a crocodile. ¹¹Pharaoh also summoned the wise men and the sorcerers of his court, and they, the magicians of Egypt, also did so with their artifices, by sleight of hand. ¹²Each man cast his staff, and they became crocodiles, and Aaron's staff swallowed their staffs. ¹³But Pharaoh's heart hardened; he was obstinate and he did not heed them, just as the Lord had spoken.

Announcement of the First Plague: Blood

God instructs Moses and Aaron to tell Pharaoh that his obstinacy will bring a severe plague upon his land; all the water in the Nile will be transformed into blood. The plague will serve not only to punish Egypt, but also to demonstrate God's power to Pharaoh.

¹⁴The Lord said to Moses: Pharaoh's heart is stubborn and he is not capitulating; he has refused to send forth the people. ¹⁵Therefore, go to Pharaoh in the morning: Behold, he goes out to the water of the Nile, and you shall stand facing him on the bank of the Nile, and the staff that was transformed into a serpent, take in your hand. ¹⁶You shall say to him: The Lord, God of the Hebrews, sent me to you, saying: Send forth My people and they will serve Me in the wilderness, and behold, you have not heeded until now. ¹⁷So says the Lord: With this phenomenon you will know that I am the Lord: Behold, I will strike with the staff that is in my hand on the water that is in the Nile, and it will be transformed into blood. ¹⁸Consequently, the fish that are in the Nile

will die, and the Nile will reek from the many dead fish, **and Egypt will be unable to drink water from the Nile.**

Implementation of the First Plague: Blood

The plague afflicts all sources of water in Egypt, not just the Nile. Although the Egyptian magicians show that they too can turn water to blood, they are unable to mitigate the severity of the plague's effects on the land.

[19] **The Lord said to Moses: Say to Aaron: Take your staff and extend your hand over the waters of Egypt: Over their rivers, over their** Nile and its **canals, over their lakes, and over all their pools of water, and they will** all **become blood; and there will be blood in the entire land of Egypt,** even **in the wooden** vessels **and in the stone** vessels.

[20] **Moses and Aaron did so, as the Lord had commanded; and he,** Aaron, **raised the staff and struck the water that was in the Nile, before the eyes of Pharaoh and before the eyes of his servants, and all the water that was in the Nile was transformed into blood.** [21] **The fish that were in the Nile died, and the Nile reeked; the Egyptians were unable to drink water from the Nile; the blood was in the entire land of Egypt.** [22] **The magicians of Egypt** in Pharaoh's court **did so;** they turned water to blood **with their artifices and Pharaoh's heart hardened and he did not heed them,** just **as the Lord had spoken.** [23] **Pharaoh turned** from the Nile **and came to his house and he did not pay attention to this either.** [24] **All of Egypt dug around the Nile for** potable **water to drink, as they were unable to drink from the water of the Nile.**

The Second Plague: Frogs

Moses returns to Pharaoh and demands that he free the children of Israel; otherwise God will inflict an additional plague on Egypt. Pharaoh refuses, and hordes of frogs overrun the land, infesting every nook and cranny. In response, the Egyptian magicians again attempt to demonstrate that they are as powerful as Moses and Aaron.

[25] **Seven days were completed,** passed, **after the Lord struck the Nile.**

[26] **The Lord said to Moses: Go to Pharaoh and say to him: So said the Lord: Send forth My people and they will serve Me.** [27] **If you refuse to send them forth, behold, I will afflict all** the land within **your borders with frogs.** [28] **The Nile will swarm with frogs. And they will arise and come into your house and into your bedroom, and upon your bed, and into the house of your servants and your people, and into your ovens**

Exodus

Exodus

and into your kneading bowls. ²⁹And even **upon you, upon your people, and upon all your servants, the frogs will rise.**

8 ¹**The Lord said to Moses: Say to Aaron: Extend your hand with your staff over the rivers, over the canals, and over the lakes, and raise the frogs upon the land of Egypt. ²Aaron extended his hand over the wa-ter of Egypt, and the frogs arose and covered the** entire **land of Egypt. ³The magicians did the same with their artifices, and they** too **raised the frogs upon the land of Egypt.**

Pharaoh Requests an End to the Frogs

Pharaoh shows the first signs of yielding, asking Moses and Aaron to appeal to God to stop the plague of frogs and promising to free the children of Israel. But when Moses fulfills his request, Pharaoh has a change of heart.

⁴**Pharaoh summoned Moses and Aaron, and he said: Plead with the Lord that He remove the frogs from me and from my people, and I will send forth the people, and they will sacrifice to the Lord. ⁵Moses said to Pharaoh: Test me: For what time shall I plead, for you and for your servants and for your people, that the frogs be eliminated from you and from your houses?** From that time, **only in the Nile will they remain. ⁶He,** Pharaoh, **said: Tomorrow, and he,** Moses, **said:** It shall be as your word, so that you will know that there is none like the Lord our

Fifth aliya **God. ⁷Tomorrow the frogs will depart from you and from your houses, and from your servants and from your people; only in the Nile will they remain. ⁸Moses and Aaron left Pharaoh's presence, and Moses cried out to the Lord over the matter of the frogs that He had inflicted upon Pharaoh.**

⁹**The Lord did in accordance with the word,** the request, **of Moses, and the frogs died from the houses, from the courtyards, and from the fields. ¹⁰They piled them into heaps, and the land reeked** from the dead frogs. ¹¹**Pharaoh saw that there was respite,** as the frogs had gone, **and he made his heart stubborn and he did not heed them,** just **as the Lord had spoken.**

The Third Plague: Lice

A third plague strikes the land, in the form of lice that infest the bodies of the Egyptian animals and people. When the Egyptian magicians are unable to mimic the plague, they admit that it is the work of God. Pharaoh, however, steadfastly refuses to release the children of Israel.

¹²The Lord said to Moses: Say to Aaron: Extend your staff and strike the dust of the earth, and it will become lice in the entire land of Egypt. ¹³They, Moses and Aaron, did so. Aaron extended his hand with his staff and struck the dust of the earth, and the lice were upon man and upon animal; all the dust of the earth was lice, became lice, in the entire land of Egypt. ¹⁴The magicians in Pharaoh's court did so with their artifices: They attempted to draw out the lice, to produce lice too, but they could not. And the lice that God made infested man and animal. ¹⁵The magicians said to Pharaoh: It is the finger of God. Pharaoh's heart hardened and he did not heed them, just as the Lord had spoken.

The Fourth Plague: A Horde of Wild Beasts

Moses again returns to Pharaoh, demands the release of his people, and warns him that another plague will afflict Egypt if he fails to cooperate: Wild beasts will descend upon the land, causing damage, injury, and death. Only the land of Goshen, where the children of Israel live, will be spared.

¹⁶The Lord said to Moses: Arise early in the morning and stand before Pharaoh when, behold, he goes out to the water. And you shall say to him: So said the Lord: Send forth My people and they will serve Me. ¹⁷For if you do not send forth My people, I will cast the horde of various wild beasts among you, among your servants, among your people, and in your houses; the houses of Egyptians will be filled with the horde, as well as the ground on which they are. ¹⁸I will distinguish on that day the land of Goshen, upon which My people stands, so that a horde will not be there. This will occur so that you will know that I am the Lord in the midst of the land, watching over and controlling it at all times. ¹⁹I will set a division between My people and your people; tomorrow this sign will come to be.

Pharaoh Requests an End to the Horde

The horde of wild beasts causes Pharaoh to offer a compromise, to have the Israelites offer sacrifices in Egypt. Moses rejects the compromise, arguing that the Israelites' slaughtering animals that are sacred to the Egyptians will cause outrage. The Torah's report of this conversation replaces whatever words Moses used to describe the sacred animals with the expression "the abomination of Egypt," as an indication to the reader of what the correct attitude should be to Egyptian idolatry.

²⁰The Lord did as He had so spoken, and a heavy horde of wild beasts came upon the house of Pharaoh and the house of his servants; in the entire land of Egypt the land was destroyed because of the horde.

²¹Pharaoh summoned Moses and Aaron, and he said: Go, sacrifice to your God in the land, in Egypt. ²²Moses said to Pharaoh: It is not proper to do so, as we will be sacrificing the abomination of Egypt, animals sacred according to Egyptian religion, to the Lord our God. Behold, will we sacrifice the abomination of Egypt before their eyes, and they not stone us? ²³Rather, we will go on a three-day journey into the wilderness and we will sacrifice to the Lord our God, as He will tell us.

Pharaoh Initially Capitulates and Then Reneges

The horde of wild beasts causes Pharaoh to capitulate, and Moses asks God to remove the horde, which He does. Pharaoh then reneges.

²⁴Pharaoh said: I will send you forth, and you will sacrifice to the Lord your God in the wilderness, just do not go very far; plead for me that the wild beasts will be removed from the land.

²⁵Moses said: Behold, I am departing from your presence and I will plead with the Lord, and the horde will depart from Pharaoh, from his servants, and from his people tomorrow. Only, Pharaoh must not continue provoking by not sending forth the people to sacrifice to the Lord.

²⁶Moses departed from Pharaoh's presence and he pleaded with the Lord. ²⁷The Lord did in accordance with the word of Moses and the horde departed from Pharaoh, from his servants, and from his people; not one wild beast remained. ²⁸But Pharaoh made his heart stubborn this time as well, and he did not send forth the people.

The Fifth Plague: Pestilence

God again sends Moses to Pharaoh to alert him to the coming of the next plague. The next day a pestilence afflicts all the Egyptians' animals, but bypasses the animals belonging to the children of Israel.

9 ¹The Lord said to Moses: Go to Pharaoh and speak to him: So said the Lord, God of the Hebrews: Send forth My people and they will serve Me. ²For if you refuse to send them forth, and continue to hold them, ³behold, the hand of the Lord is upon your livestock that is in the field: On the horses, on the donkeys, on the camels, on the cattle, and on the flocks; it will be a very severe pestilence. ⁴And the Lord will distinguish between the livestock of Israel and the livestock of Egypt, and nothing of all the livestock that belongs to the children of Israel will die.

⁵The Lord set an appointed time, saying: Tomorrow the Lord will perform this matter in the land. ⁶The Lord did this thing on the next day, and all the livestock of Egypt died, but from the livestock of the children of Israel not one died. ⁷Pharaoh sent inspectors and, behold, from the livestock of Israel not even one died. But Pharaoh's heart became stubborn and he did not send forth the people.

The Sixth Plague: A Blistering Rash

God commands Moses and Aaron to initiate another plague on Egypt by throwing soot in the air. The dust is transformed into a painful and debilitating skin disease that affects the Egyptians and the few animals they owned that survived the pestilence.

⁸The Lord said to Moses and Aaron: Take for yourselves two handfuls of furnace soot, and Moses shall throw it heavenward before the eyes of Pharaoh. ⁹It will become fine dust over the entire land of Egypt, and it will become a rash on the skin, erupting in blisters on man and on animal in the entire land of Egypt. ¹⁰They took the furnace soot and stood before Pharaoh, and Moses threw it heavenward; it became a rash erupting in blisters on man and on animal. ¹¹The magicians could not stand before Moses because of the rash, as the rash was on the magicians and on all the Egyptians. ¹²The Lord hardened Pharaoh's heart and he did not heed them, just as the Lord had spoken to Moses.

Announcement of the Seventh Plague: Hail

Moses forewarns Pharaoh and his servants of the plague of hail that God will visit upon them and emphasizes that the purpose of this plague extends beyond the applying of pressure on Pharaoh so he will yield. This plague is also meant to make Pharaoh and his servants internalize the reality of God's supremacy and singularity.

¹³The Lord said to Moses: Arise early in the morning, stand before Pharaoh, and say to him: So said the Lord, God of the Hebrews: Send forth My people and they will serve Me. ¹⁴For this time, I will send all My plagues upon your heart and against your servants and against your people, so that you will know that there is none like Me on the entire earth. ¹⁵For I could have sent My hand now and smitten you and your people with pestilence, and you would have been eradicated from the earth. ¹⁶However, for this I have sustained you and kept you alive: In order to show you My power and in order to promulgate My name, My kingship, throughout the entire earth.

Exodus

Seventh
aliya

¹⁷You continue to abuse My people, in not sending them forth. ¹⁸Behold, at this time tomorrow I will rain down a very heavy hail, the like of which has not been in Egypt from the day of its founding until now. ¹⁹And now, send and collect your livestock and everything that is yours in the field; every man and animal that will be found in the field and will not be gathered into the house, the hail will fall upon them and they will die. ²⁰He who feared, believed, the word of the Lord among the servants of Pharaoh drove his servants and his livestock into the houses. ²¹But he who did not pay attention to the word of the Lord, he left his servants and his livestock in the field.

Implementation of the Seventh Plague: Hail and Fire

Preternatural hail mixed with fire batters Egypt, causing heavy losses everywhere in the land, to crops, animals, and people. Only the land of Goshen remains free of the hail.

²²The Lord said to Moses: Extend your hand upon the heavens and there will be hail in the entire land of Egypt, on man and on animals and on all the vegetation of the field in the land of Egypt. ²³Moses extended his staff upon the heavens, and the Lord provided thunder and hail, and fire descended to the earth; the Lord rained hail on the land of Egypt. ²⁴There was hail, and fire igniting, burning, amid the hail: Very heavy, that there had not been the like in the entire land of Egypt since it became a nation. ²⁵The hail struck in the entire land of Egypt, everything that was in the field, from man to animal, and the hail struck all the vegetation of the field and broke every tree of the field. ²⁶Only in the land of Goshen, where the children of Israel were, was there no hail.

Further reading: For more on the synergy between the fire and the hail, see *A Concise Guide to the Sages,* p. 90.

Pharaoh Admits His Guilt

Again Pharaoh summons Moses and Aaron, promises to release the children of Israel, and asks them to pray for him. He even admits that he sinned against God, although Moses retorts that he puts little stock in Pharaoh's confession. Nevertheless, Moses prays for him.

²⁷Pharaoh sent and summoned Moses and Aaron, and he said to them: I sinned this time; the Lord is the righteous and I and my people are the wicked. ²⁸Plead with the Lord; there has been too much thunder of God and hail. I will send you forth and you will not continue to abide. ²⁹Moses said to him: Upon my leaving the city, I will spread my hands

Exodus

in prayer **to the Lord. The thunder will cease and the hail will be no longer, so that you will know that the earth is the Lord's.** ³⁰**And as for you and your servants, I know that you do not yet** truly **fear the Lord God.** ³¹**The flax and the barley** in the fields **were struck** by the hail, **as the barley was just ripened and the flax had seedpods.** ³²**But the wheat and the spelt were not struck, as they are late ripening,** and were therefore still soft and less fragile.

Maftir ³³**Moses emerged from Pharaoh's presence, from the city, and spread his hands to the Lord** in prayer; **the thunders and hail ceased and rain did not pour onto the earth.** ³⁴**Pharaoh saw that the rain, the hail, and the thunders ceased, and he continued to sin; he made his heart stubborn, he and his servants.** ³⁵**Pharaoh's heart was hardened and he did not send forth the children of Israel,** just **as the Lord had spoken at the hand of Moses.**

Exodus

Parashat Bo

More plagues strike Egypt. An enormous swarm of locusts ravages the land, followed by three days of absolute darkness. While at times Pharaoh claims to be amenable to Moses' demands, he always reverts to form and refuses to let the people of Israel go. With the tenth plague, God slays all the firstborn sons in Egypt, which leads Pharaoh to press the children of Israel to leave immediately, in the middle of the night. They leave, taking considerable wealth, and God commands them to memorialize this great event in every generation, detailing a series of commandments associated with the redemption: the paschal offering; the Passover festival, during which they are to eat matza and refrain from eating leaven; phylacteries (*tefillin*); and redemption of the male firstborn offspring of both humans and animals.

Announcement of the Eighth Plague: Locusts

Having already struck Egypt with seven plagues, God instructs Moses to again go to Pharaoh and warn him of the consequences if he persists in his intransigence: An enormous swarm of locusts will consume all vegetation.

10 **¹The Lord said to Moses: Come to Pharaoh, for I made his heart and the heart of his servants stubborn so that I might place these signs of Mine in his midst. ²And** I have inflicted these plagues on his person and on his land **so that you may** also **relate, in the ears of your son and the son of your son,** your descendants, **how I have harried Egypt, and** relate the power of **My signs that I placed among them; and you will know that I am the Lord,** who has done this. **³Moses and Aaron came to Pharaoh and said to him: So said the Lord, God of the Hebrews: How long will you refuse to submit before Me** and refuse to obey Me? **Send forth My people, and they will** be free to **serve Me.**

⁴For if you refuse to send forth My people, behold, tomorrow I will bring swarms of **locusts into your border,** into your land. **⁵They,** the great swarms of locusts, **will cover the face of the earth,** so that one will be unable to see the earth, and they will devour the rest of that which was saved, the vegetation **that remains for you from the hail, and they will devour all** the leaves on **the trees that grow for you from the field. ⁶They**

will fill your houses and the houses of all your servants and the houses of all Egypt, an infestation **as your fathers and the fathers of your fathers did not see from the day that they were** born **upon the earth until this day. He,** Moses, **turned** away **and departed from Pharaoh's presence.**

📖 **Further reading:** For more on the significance of the order and content of the plagues, see *A Concise Guide to the Sages*, p. 86.

Pharaoh Again Attempts to Negotiate

After Pharaoh's servants implore him to free the children of Israel, he summons Moses and Aaron and negotiates with them over who will leave Egypt to serve God in the wilderness. Moses insists that all the people and livestock must participate, but Pharaoh agrees to release only the men.

[7]**Pharaoh's servants said to him: Until when will this** man, Moses, **be a snare for us,** constantly bringing troubles? **Send forth the people that they may serve the Lord their God; do you not yet know that Egypt is** about to be **lost?** [8]**Moses and Aaron were returned to Pharaoh, and he said to them: Go, serve the Lord your God. Who are those who are going?** [9]**Moses said: With our youth and with our elders we will go; with our sons and with our daughters, with our flocks and with our cattle we will go, because it is a festival of the Lord for us.** Moses is alluding to the fact that Israel's exit will signal its independence, and he does not promise their return. [10]**He,** Pharaoh, **said to them** derisively: **If so, may the Lord be with you when I will send forth you and your children.** You will **see that evil faces you,** and you will experience tribulation. [11]Therefore, the entire nation will **not** leave **so. Rather, let the men go now and serve the Lord, as that is what you seek;** no one else needs to go. **He banished them from Pharaoh's presence.**

Implementation of the Eighth Plague: Locusts

An immense swarm of locusts spreads across Egypt. The locusts are so numerous it becomes impossible to even see the ground; they consume all vegetation that survived the hail. Pharaoh again asks Moses to pray for the plague to cease, and Moses fulfills his request.

[12]**The Lord said to Moses: Extend your hand over the land of Egypt for the** plague of **locusts** to begin. **And they shall go up upon the land of Egypt and eat all the vegetation of the land, everything that the hail left.**

cond aliya

¹³Moses extended his staff over the land of Egypt and the Lord directed an east wind in the land all that day and all the night; it was morning, and the east wind carried the locusts. ¹⁴The locusts went up upon the entire land of Egypt and settled everywhere within the entire border of Egypt. It was very severe; before them there were no locusts like them, and there will never be so again after them. ¹⁵They covered the face of the entire land, and the land was darkened. And they consumed all the vegetation of the land and all the fruit of the trees that the hail left, and no greenery remained, on tree or on vegetation of the field, in the entire land of Egypt.

¹⁶Pharaoh hastened to summon Moses and Aaron, and he said: I have sinned to the Lord your God, and to you. ¹⁷Now, please pardon my sin just this time, and plead with the Lord your God that He will remove from me just this plague of locusts that brings death. ¹⁸He, Moses, departed from Pharaoh's presence, and pleaded with the Lord. ¹⁹The Lord changed the wind's direction to a very powerful west wind, and it carried the locusts and cast them into the Red Sea; not one locust remained within the entire border of Egypt. ²⁰The Lord hardened Pharaoh's heart and he did not send forth the children of Israel.

The Ninth Plague: Darkness

Egypt becomes pitch dark for three days. Pharaoh summons Moses and agrees to allow the entire people to leave, but not their animals. When Moses declares this condition unacceptable, Pharaoh warns him that he will kill him if he appears before him again.

²¹The Lord said to Moses: Extend your hand upon the heavens, and let there be darkness over the land of Egypt; and the darkness will be palpable. ²²Moses extended his hand upon the heavens, and there was pitch darkness in the entire land of Egypt for three days. ²³They did not see one another, nor did anyone rise from his place, for three days. But all the children of Israel had light in their dwellings.

Third aliya ²⁴Pharaoh summoned Moses and he said: All of you, go, serve the Lord; only your flocks and your cattle will remain. Even your children will go with you. ²⁵Moses said: No, you too will put animals in our hand for peace offerings and burnt offerings, and we will sacrifice to the Lord our God. ²⁶Our livestock and all of our property will also go with us; a hoof from our animals shall not remain, as we will take from it, our herds and flocks, to serve the Lord our God, and we will not know with what animals we will serve the Lord until we come there. ²⁷The Lord

hardened Pharaoh's heart, and he did not assent to send them forth. [28]Pharaoh said to him, Moses: Go from my presence; beware, do not continue to see my face, because on the day that you see my face again you shall die. [29]And Moses said: You have spoken truly; I will not continue to see your face anymore.

Announcement of the Tenth Plague: Smiting of the Firstborn

God instructs Moses how the children of Israel should prepare for the last plague and for the redemption. Moses announces to Pharaoh that a plague of death will engulf Egypt, and he leaves the king's presence in fury.

11 [1]The Lord said to Moses: One more blow I will bring upon Pharaoh and upon Egypt. Afterward, he will send you forth from here; when he sends you forth, he will completely expel you from here. [2]Speak now in the ears of the people, and they shall borrow, each man from his Egyptian neighbor, and each woman from her Egyptian neighbor, silver vessels and gold vessels. [3]The Lord granted the people favor in the eyes of Egypt so that the Egyptians would relate positively toward them, while the man Moses was of very great stature in the land of Egypt, in the eyes of Pharaoh's servants, and in the eyes of the people.

ourth aliya [4]Moses said: So said the Lord: At midnight, I will emerge and reveal Myself in the midst of Egypt. [5]Every firstborn in the land of Egypt will die, from the firstborn of Pharaoh, who sits on his throne, to the firstborn of the maidservant, a slave who is standing behind the mill grinding grain, and all firstborn animals. [6]There will be a great outcry in the entire land of Egypt, such that there has not been the like of it, nor will there be the like of it again. [7]But for all the children of Israel, a dog will not extend his tongue to bark at anyone, from man to beast, so that you will know that the Lord distinguishes between Egypt and Israel. [8]All these servants of yours, Pharaoh, will descend to me, Moses, and prostrate themselves to me, saying: Leave, you and all the people that follow you; and thereafter I will leave Egypt. He departed from Pharaoh's presence in enflamed wrath, visibly angry.

[9]The Lord had said to Moses already: Pharaoh will not heed you, in order to increase My wonders in the land of Egypt. [10]Moses and Aaron performed all these wonders before Pharaoh, and the Lord hardened Pharaoh's heart, and he did not send forth the children of Israel from his land.

Exodus

The Paschal Offering in Egypt

God commands the children of Israel to sacrifice the paschal offering. While the commandment applies to future generations as well, some details are particular only to this initial performance of the sacrifice, at the time of the redemption from Egypt.

12 ¹**The Lord spoke to Moses and Aaron in the land of Egypt, saying:** ²**This current** month, Nisan, **is for you the beginning of months; it is first for you of the months of the year.** ³**Speak to the entire congregation of Israel, saying: On the tenth** day **of this month they shall take for themselves, each one, a lamb** or kid **for each house of the fathers, a lamb** or kid **for the household,** one per family. ⁴**If the** members of the **household will be too few for** eating **an** entire **lamb, then he and his neighbor who is near his house shall take** one lamb together, **according to the number of people; each** person **according to his** capacity for **eating you shall account for** in the tally for eating **the lamb.** ⁵**An unblemished lamb, a male in the first year** of its life **it shall be for you; you shall take it from the sheep or from the goats.**

⁶**It shall be for you for safekeeping** against blemishes **until the fourteenth day of this month, and the entire assembly of the congregation of Israel shall slaughter it in the afternoon.** ⁷**They shall take from the blood and put it on the two doorposts and on the lintel, on the houses in which they will eat it.** ⁸**They shall eat the meat on that night, roasted over fire, and they shall eat it with unleavened bread** and **with bitter herbs.** ⁹**You shall not eat** meat **from it** raw or **half cooked, nor cooked in water; only** prepare it **roasted over fire, its head with its legs and with its innards,** as a single unit. ¹⁰**You shall not leave anything from it until morning. And** if this nevertheless occurs, **that which remains until morning you shall burn with fire.**

The Paschal Lamb

The children of Israel are to eat this paschal offering during the night before they depart Egypt, while God is slaying the Egyptian firstborns. God instructs them to eat hastily, when they are already dressed and ready to leave.

¹¹**So you shall eat it: Your loins girded,** completely dressed to leave, with **your shoes on your feet, and your** walking **staff in your hand; you shall eat it in haste, it is the paschal lamb** offering **to the Lord.** ¹²**I will pass through the land of Egypt on that night and I will smite all the firstborn in the land of Egypt, from man to animal; and against all the gods of Egypt I will administer** great **punishments: I am the Lord;** rely on me

to fulfill this. ¹³**The blood** that you will place on the doorways **shall be a sign for you on the houses where you are, and I will see the blood; I will pass over you.** And there shall not be a stroke against you to destroy you when I smite the land of Egypt.

The Passover Festival

Future generations are to commemorate the redemption from Egypt on the date on which the children of Israel departed that land. The annual observance will perpetuate the memory of this great event through the eating of matza, the prohibition against eating leaven, and the celebration of the festival.

¹⁴**This day shall be a remembrance for you,** so you will remember it, **and you shall celebrate it as a festival to the Lord; for** all **your** future **generations, you shall celebrate it as an eternal statute.** ¹⁵**Seven days you shall eat unleavened bread. However, on the first day you shall eliminate leaven from your houses. For anyone who eats leavened bread from the first day until the seventh day, that person shall be excised from Israel.** ¹⁶**It shall be for you a** day of **holy convocation on the first day** of the festival, **and a holy convocation on the seventh day. No labor shall be performed on them, except** preparation **for that which shall be eaten for each person; it alone,** the labor of food preparation, **may be performed for you.**

¹⁷**You shall watch over the unleavened bread** that it not become leavened **because on this very day I brought your hosts out of the land of Egypt, and you shall** continue to **observe this day for your** future **generations, an eternal statute.** ¹⁸**In the first** month, Nisan, **on the fourteenth day of the month, in the evening, you shall eat unleavened bread, until the twenty-first day of the month in the evening.** ¹⁹**For** these **seven days, leaven,** the sourdough used to leaven other dough, **shall not be found in your houses; as anyone who eats** food with **leavening, that person shall be excised from the congregation of Israel, whether he is a stranger or a native of the land.** ²⁰**You shall not eat anything leavened,** or containing leavening; **in all your dwellings you shall eat unleavened bread** during the festival of Passover.

📖 **Further reading:** For more on the Passover festival, see *A Concise Guide to the Sages,* p. 306; *A Concise Guide to Mahshava,* p. 93; *A Concise Guide to Halakha,* p. 274.

Exodus

Preparations for Protection from the Plague of Firstborns

Moses directs the children of Israel to prepare for the plague of the firstborns that will soon strike Egypt. He explains in detail how they are to mark the entrances of their houses, and enjoins them from leaving their homes until morning.

Fifth aliya **²¹Moses summoned all the elders of Israel and said to them: Select and take for yourselves lambs for** each of **your families and slaughter the paschal lamb** as an offering. **²²You shall take a bunch of hyssop and dip it in the blood that is in the basin** containing the blood of the lamb, **and you shall touch** or smear **the lintel and the two doorposts with the blood that is in the basin, and no man shall emerge from the entrance of his house until morning. ²³The Lord will pass through** the land **to strike the Egyptians, and when He sees the blood on the lintel and on the two doorposts, the Lord will pass over the entrance, and He will not allow the destroyer,** the destroying angel, **to come to your houses to strike. ²⁴You shall observe this matter** of the festival of Passover and its commemorative activities **as a statute for you and for your children forever.**

²⁵It shall be when you come to the land that the Lord will give you, as He spoke and promised, **you shall observe this service;** the laws of Passover He has given you. **²⁶It shall be when,** or if, **your children will say to you: What is this service to you?** Why are you performing it? **²⁷You shall say: It is the paschal offering to the Lord, who passed over the houses of the children of Israel in Egypt when He struck Egypt, and our households He saved. The people bowed their heads and prostrated themselves** to indicate their consent. **²⁸The children of Israel went and did; as the Lord had commanded Moses and Aaron, so they did.**

Implementation of the Tenth Plague: Smiting of the Firstborns

All the firstborns in Egypt are struck dead precisely at midnight. The plague creates terror throughout the land, and Pharaoh rises immediately to free the children of Israel.

Sixth aliya **²⁹It was at midnight, and the Lord smote every firstborn in the land of Egypt, from the firstborn** son **of Pharaoh,** the prince, **who was sitting on his throne, to the firstborn of the captive who was in the dungeon, and every firstborn animal. ³⁰Pharaoh arose during** the middle of the **night, he, and all his servants, and all Egypt; and there was a great outcry** everywhere **in Egypt, because there was no house in which there were no dead. ³¹He summoned Moses and Aaron at night and said: Rise and go**

out from among my people, both you and the children of Israel, and go serve the Lord as you have spoken. ³²Take both your flocks and your cattle, as you have spoken, and go, and bless me too; please pray for me. ³³The Egyptians urged the people, to hasten to send them forth from the land, as they said: We are all dying, or, about to die. ³⁴The people carried their dough with them before it became leavened, their kneading bowls containing the dough bound in their garments on their shoulders. ³⁵The children of Israel acted in accordance with the word of Moses, and they borrowed silver vessels, gold vessels, and garments from Egypt. ³⁶The Lord granted the people favor in the eyes of Egypt, and they lent them, and they stripped Egypt, taking everything they could.

³⁷The children of Israel traveled from the city of Rameses to a place called Sukot. The Israelites numbered some six hundred thousand men on foot, besides children, women, and the elderly. ³⁸A mixed multitude of other peoples came up with them, and also flocks and cattle, very considerable livestock. ³⁹They baked the dough that they took out from Egypt into unleavened cakes, matzot, as it was not leavened because they were banished from Egypt and could not linger and wait for the dough to rise. And they also did not have time to prepare provisions for themselves for a long journey. ⁴⁰The period of dwelling of the children of Israel that they dwelled in Egypt was thirty years and four hundred years. ⁴¹It was at the end of thirty years and four hundred years; it was on that very day, the fifteenth of Nisan, that all the hosts of the Lord, God's nation, departed from the land of Egypt. ⁴²It is a night of vigilance of the Lord. God had waited with anticipation for this night, to bring them out of the land of Egypt; it is this night for the Lord. This night will become one of vigilance for all the children of Israel, to celebrate and commemorate for all their future generations.

The Statute of the Paschal Lamb

⁴³The Lord said to Moses and Aaron: This is the statute of the paschal lamb. No foreigner from another nation shall eat from it. ⁴⁴Any man's slave, purchased with silver: You shall circumcise him, and only then he shall eat from it. ⁴⁵A gentile resident alien in the Land of Israel and a gentile hired laborer shall not eat from it. ⁴⁶It shall be eaten in one house; you shall not remove any of the meat from the house where it is eaten to the outside. It is consecrated as an offering in its entirety and must be eaten

Exodus

in a designated space. **And you shall not break a bone of it.** ⁴⁷The entire congregation of Israel shall do it.

⁴⁸**When a stranger resides with you, and** he **performs the** commandment of the **paschal offering to the Lord,** one must first **circumcise every male of his.** And only **then shall he** be allowed to **approach to perform it, and he shall be** considered **like a native of the land; but all uncircumcised persons shall not eat from it.** ⁴⁹**There shall be one,** the same, **law for the native and for the stranger who resides among you.** ⁵⁰The children of Israel did as the Lord had commanded Moses and Aaron; so they did.

⁵¹**It was on that very day,** the fifteenth of Nisan, that **the Lord brought the children of Israel out of the land of Egypt by their hosts,** with every tribe.

Illustrations: See p. 523 for a map of the route of the children of Israel as they left Egypt.

Commandments to Commemorate the Exodus
The children of Israel are commanded to remember their redemption from Egypt though several new commemorative activities: sanctifying Jewish firstborns, donning *tefillin*, and retelling the story of the exodus.

13 ¹**The Lord spoke to Moses, saying:** ²**Sanctify to Me every firstborn; the**
Seventh **first issue of any womb among the children of Israel, from man and an-**
aliya **imal, is Mine.** ³**Moses said to the people: Remember this day on which you departed from Egypt, from the house of bondage,** the place where you were slaves. **For with strength of hand,** by force, **the Lord took you out from this** land, **and leavened bread may not be eaten** at this time of year, even in the future. ⁴**This day you depart, in the month of the ripening,** the month of Nisan, which falls in the spring.

⁵**It shall be, when the Lord shall bring you to the land of the Canaanites, the Hitites, the Emorites, the Hivites, and the Yevusites;** which is the land **that He took an oath to your forefathers to give to you, a land flowing with milk and honey, you shall perform this service** of the paschal offering **in this month.** ⁶**During the seven days** of the Passover festival **you shall eat unleavened bread; and on the seventh day is a festival to the Lord.** ⁷**Only unleavened bread shall be eaten for the seven days. Neither leavened bread shall be seen with you, nor shall leaven be seen with you;** these may not be in your possession anywhere **within your entire border.**

⁸You shall tell your son on that day, on the Passover festival, **saying: It is because of this,** so that I will preserve the memory of these events and perform the commandments, **that the Lord did this for me,** the redemption with its signs and wonders, **upon my exodus from Egypt.** ⁹**It,** the story of the exodus, **shall be a sign for you on your hand, and a remembrance between your eyes.** Write a reference to this story on an object that you will attach to your arm and between your eyes, **so that the law of the Lord will be** constantly **in your mouth, because with a powerful hand the Lord took you out of Egypt.** ¹⁰**You shall observe this statute,** these laws, **at its appointed time, from year to year,** annually.

Details of the Sanctification of Israelite Firstborns

In commemoration of God's protection during the plague of the firstborns, the Israelite firstborns are to be sanctified to God. This additional measure of holiness is to apply to all present and future Israelite firstborns, whether human or animal.

¹¹**It shall be, when the Lord will take you to the land of the Canaanites, as He took an oath to you and to your forefathers, and He gives it to you,** ¹²**you shall** separate and **transfer to the Lord each first issue of the womb, and of each first issue discharged** from the body **of an animal that you will have, the males** are sanctified and **are the Lord's.** ¹³**Every first issue of a donkey you** shall not sacrifice, but **shall redeem with a lamb** or young goat. **And if you do not redeem it,** the firstborn donkey, **then you shall behead it. And every human firstborn, among your sons, you shall redeem** with money.

Maftir ¹⁴**It shall be, when your son asks you tomorrow,** in the future, **saying: What is** the reason you do **this** to the human and animal firstborns? **You shall say to him: With strength of hand,** power and force, **the Lord took us out from Egypt, from the house of bondage,** where we were enslaved. ¹⁵**It was when Pharaoh hesitated,** and stubbornly refused **to send us forth,** that **the Lord killed all the firstborn in the land of Egypt, from the firstborn man to the firstborn animal. Therefore, I sacrifice to the Lord every first issue of the womb** of an animal, **the males** that are their mothers' firstborns; **and all the firstborn of my sons I will redeem** with money.

¹⁶**It shall be a sign upon your arm and an ornament between your eyes,** in the form of *tefillin;* **for with strength of hand the Lord took us out of Egypt.**

Exodus

📖 **Further reading:** For more on the commandment and ceremony of redeeming Jewish firstborns, see *A Concise Guide to Halakha*, p. 17. For more on the commandment of *tefillin* and the methods of donning them, see *A Concise Guide to Halakha*, p. 589.

Parashat Beshalah

Once the children of Israel leave Egypt and embark on their journey through the wilderness, they are completely dependent on God, who chooses their route, their resting points, and when they are to encamp and travel. The Egyptians pursue them, and the people's situation looks hopeless, but then the great miracle of the splitting of the sea occurs: The children of Israel walk through safely and the Egyptians drown. In the wake of this miracle, the people sing the Song at the Sea, a poem of gratitude and praise highlighting God's triumph over the Egyptians. Nevertheless, they repeatedly complain to Moses on their journey as they encounter tribulations: thirst, hunger, and war. They continue to benefit from divine assistance, receiving water from a rock, food from the heavens, and God's help in the battle with the Amalekite enemy.

The People Begin Their Journey through the Wilderness

As the children of Israel set off into the wilderness, they are given divine assistance: They are accompanied by a pillar of cloud to guide them on their route, and a pillar of fire to illuminate the darkness of night.

¹⁷**It was, in Pharaoh's sending forth the people, that God did not guide them** to go **via the land of the Philistines,** along the Mediterranean coast, **although it was near, for God said: Lest the people reconsider when they see war** with the Philistines, **and** they will then **return to Egypt.** ¹⁸**God led the people circuitously, via the wilderness of the Red Sea. And the children of Israel came up armed from the land of Egypt** in preparation for eventual battle. ¹⁹**Moses took the bones of Joseph with him, for he,** Joseph, **had administered an oath to the children of Israel,** the children of Jacob, **saying: God will remember** and redeem **you, and** I ask that at that time **you shall bring my bones up from here,** from Egypt, **with you.**

²⁰**They,** the Israelites, **traveled from** a place called **Sukot, and they encamped in Etam, at the edge of the wilderness.** ²¹**The Lord was going before them, by day in a pillar of cloud to guide them on the way, and by night in a pillar of fire to illuminate for them, to go day and night.**

²²**The pillar of cloud by day and the pillar of fire by night would not move from before the people.**

Pharaoh Pursues the Children of Israel
When Pharaoh sees that the people do not return on schedule, he gathers an enormous army and chases after them.

14 ¹**The Lord spoke to Moses, saying:** ²**Speak to the children of Israel, that they return** in the direction of Egypt **and encamp before Pi HaHirot, between Migdol and the Red Sea, before Baal Tzefon,** all names of places. **Opposite it you shall encamp, by the sea.** ³**Pharaoh will** then **say of the children of Israel: They are astray in the land.** They have lost their way, and are doubling back. **The wilderness has closed in on them,** with no way out. ⁴**I will harden Pharaoh's heart, and he will pursue them, and I will be exalted through Pharaoh and through his entire army** by wreaking vengeance on them, **and the Egyptians will know that I am the Lord. And they,** the Israelites, **did so.**

⁵Meanwhile, **it was told to the king of Egypt that the people had fled,** as they had not returned after three days. **The heart of Pharaoh and his servants was transformed with regard to the people** since the moment they had let them go, **and they said: What is this that we have done, that we have sent Israel from our servitude?** ⁶**He harnessed his chariot. And** he **took his people,** his soldiers, **with him.** ⁷**He took six hundred select** war **chariots, and** he took **all the** other **chariots of Egypt. And there were auxiliaries,** or officers, **with all of them.** ⁸**The Lord hardened the heart of Pharaoh, king of Egypt, and he pursued the children of Israel; the children of Israel went out with a high hand,** boldly.

Pharaoh Reaches the Israelite Encampment
Pharaoh and his forces advance until they are within eyeshot of the children of Israel. The people become frightened at the sight of the colossal army and cry out to Moses and to God. Moses reassures them that they can trust God to save them.

Second
aliya
⁹**Egypt pursued them; all the horses and chariots of Pharaoh and his horsemen and his army caught up with them** as they were **encamped by the sea, by Pi HaHirot, before Baal Tzefon.** ¹⁰**Pharaoh approached the Israelite encampment; the children of Israel lifted their eyes and behold,** the forces of **the Egyptians were traveling after them, and they were very frightened. The children of Israel cried out to the Lord.** ¹¹**The people complained to Moses. They said to Moses: Is it due to the lack**

of graves in Egypt that you took us to die in the wilderness? What is this that you have done to us, to take us out of Egypt? [12]Is this not the matter of which we spoke to you in Egypt, saying: Let us be, and we will serve Egypt? For serving Egypt is preferable to us than dying in the wilderness. [13]Moses said to the people: Fear not; stand and see the salvation of the Lord that He will perform for you today; for as you saw the Egyptians today, you shall not see them ever again. [14]The Lord will make war for you, and you will be silent.

Splitting of the Red Sea

God instructs Moses on how to initiate the splitting of the sea. The pillar of cloud stands between the Egyptians and the children of Israel, preventing the Egyptians from advancing further toward them. Through the course of the night, a strong wind splits the Red Sea.

Third aliya [15]The Lord said to Moses: For what reason are you crying out to Me? Speak to the children of Israel, that they will begin to travel forward. [16]And you, raise your staff, and extend your hand over the sea, and split it, and the children of Israel will go into the sea on dry land; the sea will turn into dry land. [17]As for me, behold, I am hardening the heart of Egypt, and they, the Egyptians, will come after them, the children of Israel. And I will be exalted through Pharaoh and through his entire army, through his chariots and through his horsemen. [18]Egypt will know that I am the Lord when I am exalted through the downfall of Pharaoh, through the loss of his chariots, and through the loss of his horsemen.

[19]The angel of God, who was going before the camp of Israel, traveled and went behind them; and the pillar of cloud traveled from before them and stood behind them. [20]It, the cloud, came between the camp of Egypt and the camp of Israel, and there was the cloud and the darkness between the camps, and it illuminated the night for the Israelites. And one camp did not approach the other camp the entire night. [21]Moses extended his hand over the sea, and the Lord moved the waters of the sea with a powerful east wind the entire night, and it rendered the sea dry land, and the water split in two. [22]The children of Israel came into the sea, on the area where it had become dry land; and the water was like a wall for them on their right and on their left.

Illustrations: See map indicating the main opinions as to where the children of Israel crossed the sea, indicated there by arrows, p. 523.

Exodus

The Egyptians Become Alarmed

When the Egyptians follow the children of Israel into the sea, God sows confusion in their midst. He strikes them with the pillars of cloud and fire, badly damaging their chariots, which become mired in the ground. Panic spreads throughout their ranks.

²³**Egypt pursued and came after them, all Pharaoh's horses, his chariots, and his horsemen, into the sea.** ²⁴**It was at the morning watch,** before dawn, **and the Lord looked down at the camp of Egypt and** struck at them **with a pillar of fire and cloud and confounded the camp of Egypt.** ²⁵**He removed the wheels of its chariots and caused them to drive with difficulty. Egypt said: I will flee from before Israel, as the Lord is making war for them against Egypt.**

The Egyptians Drown in the Sea

God tells Moses to reach his arm out again, and the sea reverts to its normal state, while the Egyptians are in its midst. The immense Egyptian army drowns in the sea, and the children of Israel are infused with faith in God.

Fourth aliya ²⁶**The Lord said to Moses: Extend your hand over the sea, so that the water will return** to its place, **upon Egypt, upon its chariots, and upon its horsemen.** ²⁷**Moses extended his hand over the sea, and the sea returned to its** original **vigor before morning. And Egypt was fleeing toward it,** into the water, **and the Lord shook up the Egyptians in the sea.** ²⁸**The water returned** to its normal state, **and it covered the chariots and the horsemen, all the army of Pharaoh that came after them into the sea; not one of them remained** alive.

²⁹**The children of Israel walked on the dry land** that had been created **in the sea, and the water was** like **a wall for them on their right and on their left.** ³⁰**The Lord saved Israel on that day from the hand of Egypt, and Israel saw the Egyptians dead on the seashore.** ³¹**Israel saw the great power that the Lord wielded against Egypt. And the people feared the Lord and believed in the Lord and in Moses, His servant.**

The Song at the Sea

The great miracle of the splitting of the sea prompts the children of Israel to sing a song of praise and glory to God. They describe the Egyptians' defeat and their own hope of entering the Land of Israel.

15 ¹**Then,** immediately thereafter, **Moses and the children of Israel sang this song to the Lord. And they said, saying: I will sing to the** honor of the **Lord, as He is** highly **exalted;** both **the horse and its rider He cast into**

Exodus

the sea. [2]The Lord is my strength and song, and He has become my salvation; this is my God, and I will glorify Him, my father's God, and I will exalt Him. [3]The Lord is a warrior; the Lord is His name. [4]Pharaoh's chariots and his army He cast in the sea, and the elite of his officers were drowned in the Red Sea. [5]The deep covers them; they descended and sank into the depths of the sea like a stone. [6]Your right hand, Lord, is glorious in its enormous power; Your right hand, Lord, shatters an enemy. [7]In the abundance of Your majesty You overthrow those who rise against You; You send forth Your wrath, and it consumes them like straw consumed in fire. [8]With the blast of wind from Your nostrils, the water was piled up, stream stood like a stack; the deep was congealed in the heart of the sea. [9]The enemy said: I will pursue, I will overtake the Israelites, and I will divide the spoils of victory. My desire shall be sated upon them; I will devour them, I will draw my sword and my hand will dispossess them. [10]But You blew with Your wind, and the sea covered them; they sank like lead in the mighty water. [11]Who is mighty like You among the powers, Lord? Who is like You, mighty in sanctity, awesome in praise, with praise that inspires awe, performer of wonders? [12]You extended Your right hand against the enemy, and the earth swallowed them. [13]You guided with Your kindness this people that You redeemed; You directed them with Your strength to their ultimate goal, Your holy abode. [14]When nations heard this, they were agitated; trembling has gripped the inhabitants of Philistia. [15]Then the army chieftains of Edom were alarmed, and trembling gripped the powers, the leaders, of Moav; all the inhabitants of Canaan have dissipated, melted away in fear. [16]May dread and fear fall over them; with the display of the greatness of Your arm may they be stilled and silent as a stone until Your people will pass to their destination, Lord, until this people whom You have acquired will pass. [17]You will bring them, the Israelites, and plant them in the mountain of Your inheritance, the place You fashioned and set aside for Your dwelling, Lord, the Sanctuary, my Lord, that Your hands have already established. [18]The Lord shall reign forever and ever. [19]In summary: For the horses of Pharaoh came with his chariots and with his horsemen into the sea, expecting to traverse the divided sea, and the Lord returned the water of the sea upon them to drown them; and the children of Israel walked on dry land in the sea.

Exodus

📖 **Further reading:** For more on the splitting of the sea and on the song, see *A Concise Guide to the Sages*, p. 98. This event is commemorated to this day through various celebratory practices; see *A Concise Guide to Halakha*, p. 327.

Miriam's Song

Miriam leads the women in their own singing and dancing.

²⁰**Miriam the prophetess, sister of Aaron, took the drum in her hand, and all the women came out after her with drums, and in dance.** ²¹**Miriam called to them** and led them in responsive singing: **Sing to the Lord, as He is** highly **exalted,** both **the horse and its rider He cast into the sea.**

📖 **Further reading:** For more on the women's instruments, see *A Concise Guide to the Sages*, p. 99.

Bitter Waters at Mara

The children of Israel travel to Mara and discover that the water is not fit for drinking. When they complain to Moses, he follows God's instructions for purifying the water. Moses also teaches them several new commandments.

²²**Moses led Israel from the Red Sea, and they went out to the wilderness of Shur. They walked three days in the wilderness, and did not find water.** ²³**They came to Mara, and they could not drink** the **water from Mara, as it is bitter. Therefore, its name is called Mara,** meaning bitter. ²⁴**The people complained against Moses, saying: What will we drink?** ²⁵**He,** Moses, **cried out to the Lord, and the Lord indicated a** certain **tree to him, and he cast it into the waters, and the waters** were **sweetened. There He,** God, **instituted for it,** Israel, **statutes and ordinances,** teaching them some new commandments. **And there He tested it,** the nation, in that they initially did not have potable water. ²⁶**God said: If you heed the voice of the Lord your God, and will perform that which is right in His eyes** by doing His will, **and listen to** the details of **His commandments and observe all His statutes, all of the diseases that I placed on Egypt I will not place upon you, as I am the Lord your healer.**

The Children of Israel Complain

As the children of Israel continue traveling through the wilderness, they complain to Moses and Aaron about the lack of food. God tells Moses that He will sustain them from the sky, in a manner that will be both miracle and trial.

16 ¹They traveled from Eilim, and the entire congregation of the children *Fifth* *aliya* of Israel came to the wilderness of Sin, which is between Eilim and Sinai, on the fifteenth day of the second month since their exodus from the land of Egypt. ²The entire congregation of the children of Israel complained against Moses and against Aaron in the wilderness. ³The children of Israel said to them: If only our death had been at the hand of the Lord in the land of Egypt, when we sat by the fleshpots, when we ate bread until satiation. For you have taken us out into this wilderness to kill this entire assembly through famine.

⁴The Lord said to Moses: Behold, I am raining food for you from the heavens, and the people shall go out and gather each day's portion on its day, so that I may test them, to see whether they will follow My law, and gather only one portion each day, or not. ⁵It shall be on the sixth day that they will prepare that which they will bring, and it will be twice what they gather each day.

⁶Moses and Aaron said to all the children of Israel: In the evening you will know that it was the Lord, who took you out of the land of Egypt. ⁷And in the morning you will see the glory of the Lord, because He has heard your complaints against the Lord and will attend to your needs. And what are we that you bring complaints against us? We are only God's messengers. ⁸Moses said: You will be convinced of God's providence, with the Lord giving you meat to eat in the evening and bread in the morning to be satiated, with the Lord hearing your complaints that you bring against Him; and what are we? Your complaints are not against us, but against the Lord.

⁹Moses said to Aaron: Say to the entire congregation of the children of Israel: Approach before the Lord, to the location where the cloud will descend, as He has heard your complaints. ¹⁰And it was, as Aaron spoke to the entire congregation of the children of Israel, that they turned toward the wilderness, and behold, the glory of the Lord appeared in a cloud.

Manna from Heaven

The promise that the children of Israel would receive their sustenance from the heavens is fulfilled. In the evening quail fly down to the ground, and in the morning the people discover the manna. The people are commanded to collect a specified amount of manna per individual. Despite some collecting more, and some less, miraculously, when they come to weigh their portions, they are all exactly the same.

Sixth
aliya
¹¹The Lord spoke to Moses, saying: ¹²I have heard the complaints of the children of Israel. Speak to them, saying: In the afternoon you shall eat meat, and in the morning you shall be sated with bread, and you shall thereby **know that I am the Lord your God.** ¹³Indeed, it was in the evening that the quail came up and covered the camp, and in the morning there was a layer of dew around the camp. ¹⁴The layer of dew evaporated and **lifted, and behold, on the surface of the wilderness** there lay **a fine, grainy substance, fine as the frost on the earth.**

¹⁵The children of Israel saw it, and they said one to another: What [man] is it? As they did not know what it was, Moses said to them: It is the bread that the Lord has given you for eating. ¹⁶This is the matter that the Lord has commanded: Gather from it, each man according to his eating. Take **an omer,** a dry measure greater than two liters, **for a person; according to the number of your people you shall each take for whoever is in his tent,** his family. ¹⁷The children of Israel did so; they gathered manna, and **some** took **more, and some** took **less.** ¹⁸But then **they measured it with an omer** measure, **and** they found that **he who took more did not have excess, and he who took less did not lack;** rather, **each** had **gathered according to his eating,** exactly one omer.

Manna and Shabbat

The provision of the manna is accompanied by the first instruction to observe Shabbat. The people discover that on Friday they receive a double portion of manna, to enable them to prepare food for Shabbat. No manna falls on Shabbat; instead, the children of Israel are commanded to rest.

¹⁹Moses said to them: No man may leave leftovers **from it,** the manna, until morning. ²⁰But they did not heed Moses; people left from it until the morning. And it, the manna, **became infested with worms, and reeked; and Moses became angry with them.** ²¹They gathered it each morning, each man **according to his eating,** his needs, **and** then **the sun grew hot and it melted.** ²²It was on the sixth day that they gathered **double the bread, two omer for each one. And all the princes,** leaders, **of the congregation came and told Moses** about this anomaly. ²³He said to them: It is what the Lord said: Tomorrow is a day of rest, a holy Sabbath to the Lord. That which you would bake, bake today, and that which you would cook, cook today; and all that remains after you have eaten for the day, set aside for safekeeping until morning. ²⁴They set it

aside until the morning, as Moses had commanded; and it did not reek the next day, **and there were no maggots in it.**

[25]**Moses said: Eat it today, for today is a Sabbath of the Lord; today you will not find it in the field.** [26]**Henceforth, six days you shall gather it, and on the seventh day it is Sabbath; on it, there will be none,** no manna. [27]**It was on the seventh day, and some of the people went out to gather, and they did not find** any manna. [28]**The Lord said to Moses: Until when do you** continue to **refuse to observe My commandments and My laws?** [29]**See that the Lord has given you the Sabbath; therefore, He gives you on the sixth day bread for two days. Remain each man where he is; no man shall leave his place on the seventh day.** [30]The majority of the people rested on the seventh day. [31]**The house of Israel called it manna. And it was** round, **like a white coriander seed, and its taste was like a cake,** or fried bread **with honey.**

[32]**Moses** later **said: This is the matter that the Lord has commanded: An omerful from it,** the manna, **is to be a keepsake for your generations, so that they,** your descendants, **will see the bread that I fed you in the wilderness when I took you out of the land of Egypt,** and will remember these events. [33]**Moses said to Aaron: Take one jar and put there an omerful of manna, and set it before the Lord as a keepsake for your** future **generations.** [34]**As the Lord had commanded Moses** to place the manna before the Lord, **Aaron set it before** the Ark of **the Testimony** in the Tabernacle, **as a keepsake.** [35]**The children of Israel ate the manna** for **forty years, until they came to an inhabited land; they ate the manna until they came to the border of the land of Canaan,** and stopped when they crossed the Jordan River. [36]**And the omer is one-tenth of an ephah,** another dry measure.

> Further reading: For more on the manna's wondrous qualities, see *A Concise Guide to the Sages*, p. 99.

A New Demand for Water

Again the children of Israel complain of thirst and lament their departure from Egypt. When Moses asks God what to do, God instructs him to strike a rock in order to extract a flow of water from it.

17 [1]**The entire congregation of the children of Israel traveled from the wilderness of Sin on their travels, at the word of the Lord,** with the guidance of the pillar of cloud; **they encamped in Refidim, and there was no water**

there **for the people to drink. ²The people quarreled with Moses and said: Give us water that we may drink.** Moses said to them: **Why do you quarrel with me,** and **why do you try the Lord,** testing Him? **³The people thirsted there for water, and the people complained against Moses and said: Why did you bring us up from Egypt, to kill me and my children and my livestock with thirst?**

⁴Moses cried out to the Lord, saying: What shall I do for this people? A moment more of their clamor **and they will stone me. ⁵The Lord said to Moses: Pass before the people, and take with you some of the elders of Israel, and take in your hand your staff with which you struck the Nile, and go. ⁶Behold, I am standing before you, there upon the rock at Horev,** Mount Sinai; you will feel My presence there. **You shall strike the rock, and water will emerge from it, and the people will drink.** Moses did so before the eyes of the elders of Israel. **⁷He called the place Masa and Meriva,** meaning trial and quarrel, **due to the quarrel of the children of Israel, and due to their trying of the Lord, saying: Is the Lord among us, or not?**

War with Amalek

When the Amalekite nation attacks the children of Israel, Moses appoints Joshua to lead the battle against the aggressors. Moses himself ascends a hill with Aaron and Hur, and raises his hands, which helps Joshua and the people defeat the Amalekites. God then commands Moses to record the details of the battle so that future generations can remember it.

⁸The nation of Amalek came and waged war against Israel in Refidim. ⁹Moses said to Joshua: Choose men for us who are capable of fighting, **and go out and wage war against Amalek; tomorrow,** during the battle, **I will be standing on top of the hill, and the staff of God will be in my hand. ¹⁰Joshua did as Moses said to him, to wage war against Amalek, and Moses, Aaron** his brother, **and Hur,** Miriam's son, **ascended to the top of the hill. ¹¹So it was** that **when Moses raised his hand, Israel prevailed** in battle; **and when he** tired and **lowered his hand, Amalek prevailed. ¹²Moses' hands were heavy;** he wearied of raising them. **And they took a stone and they placed it beneath him, and he sat on it; and Aaron and Hur supported his hands, one** of them **on this side, and the other on that side, and his hands were steady until the setting of the sun.**

📖 **Further reading:** How did Moses' raising of his hand aid the children of Israel in their battle with Amalek? See *A Concise Guide to the Sages*, p. 101. For more on the spiritual implications of Amalek, see *A Concise Guide to Mahshava*, p. 289.

Maftir ¹³**Joshua defeated** and weakened **Amalek and** killed **its people by sword.** ¹⁴**The Lord said to Moses: Write** down **this** episode **as a remembrance in the book, and set it in the ears of Joshua** to teach him, **for** I promise that **I will expunge the memory of Amalek from under the heavens.** ¹⁵**Moses built an altar** out of gratitude to God, **and** he **called it: The Lord is my standard.** ¹⁶**He said: For a hand is** raised **on the throne of the Lord,** to express the taking of an oath: **The Lord's war with Amalek is from generation to generation,** until all descendants of Amalek have been wiped out.

Exodus

Parashat
Yitro

Yitro, Moses' father-in-law, comes to visit following the great miracles that God performed for the children of Israel, and he offers advice to Moses on how to establish an administrative and judicial system for the people. Later in the *parasha*, the children of Israel arrive at Mount Sinai and undergo one of the nation's formative experiences: God's revelation and the giving of the Torah. They establish a covenant with God and witness a unique and wondrous revelation in which they hear the divine voice and receive the Ten Commandments.

Yitro's Visit

Having heard about the extraordinary wonders God performed for the children of Israel when they left Egypt, Yitro comes to the wilderness to visit Moses. He brings Moses' family: his wife Tzipora, and his sons, who had stayed in Midyan during the exodus.

18 **¹Yitro, priest of Midyan** and **father-in-law of Moses, heard all that God had done for Moses, and for Israel His people, that the Lord took Israel out of Egypt. ²Yitro, father-in-law of Moses, took Tzipora, wife of Moses, after she had been sent away** by Moses to her father. **³And her two sons, one of whom was named Gershom, as he,** Moses, **said: I was a stranger** [*ger*] **in a foreign land** there [*sham*]. **⁴And the name of the other was Eliezer,** as Moses had said: **For the God** [*Elohei*] **of my father was my assistance** [*ezri*]**, and He delivered me from the sword of Pharaoh.**

⁵Yitro, father-in-law of Moses, came with his sons and his wife, Moses' family, **to Moses, to the wilderness where he was encamped,** at **the mountain of** the revelation of **God,** Mount Sinai. **⁶He,** Yitro, **said to Moses: I, your father-in-law Yitro, am coming to you, and** I bring **your wife and her two sons with her. ⁷Moses went out toward his father-in-law, and prostrated himself** deferentially, **and kissed him. And each** man **greeted the other, and they came into the tent** of Moses. **⁸Moses related to his father-in-law everything that the Lord had done to Pharaoh and to the Egyptians on behalf of Israel.** Moses also described to him **all the**

adversity that encountered them on the way, and how **the Lord had delivered them.**

⁹**Yitro rejoiced over all the good that the Lord had done for Israel, that He had delivered it from the hand of Egypt.** ¹⁰**Yitro said: Blessed is the Lord, who delivered you from the hand of Egypt and from the hand of Pharaoh, and who delivered** the entire **people from under the hand of Egypt.** ¹¹**Now I know** and understand **that the Lord is greater than all the gods, as** God punished the Egyptians **in,** through, **the** very **matter that they,** the Egyptians, **conspired against them,** the people. Since the Egyptians drowned Israelite children in the Nile, they themselves were drowned in the Red Sea. ¹²**Yitro, father-in-law of Moses, took a burnt offering and feast offerings to God. Aaron and all the elders of Israel came to break bread** in the ritual consumption of the offerings **with the father-in-law of Moses before God,** in His honor.

Yitro Advises Moses

Yitro sees that Moses is constantly occupied with administering the communal affairs of the children of Israel. As the people all come to Moses to learn, to inquire, and to receive counsel, they must often wait a lengthy period before they can speak with him. Yitro suggests that Moses lighten his burden and relieve the bottleneck by delegating responsibility to others.

ond
aliya ¹³**It was the next day that Moses sat to judge** and instruct **the people, and the people stood over Moses,** waiting for him, **from the morning until the evening.** ¹⁴**The father-in-law of Moses saw everything that** he, Moses, **was doing with the people. And he said: What is it that you are doing with the people? Why are you sitting by yourself and all the people stand over you,** waiting for you **from morning until evening?** ¹⁵**Moses said to his father-in-law: Because the people come to me to seek God,** to learn His laws. ¹⁶**When they have a matter** that requires judgment, **it comes before me, and I adjudicate between one man and another** to resolve disputes, **and I communicate** and teach **the statutes of God and His laws.**

¹⁷**The father-in-law of Moses said to him: It is not a good thing that you are doing.** ¹⁸**You will wither away** like a wilted plant, **both you and this people that is with you, as the matter is too arduous for you; you cannot do it by yourself.** ¹⁹**Now heed my voice, let me advise you, and may God be with you. You will be** the representative **for the people before God, and you will bring the matters to God.** ²⁰**You shall caution them of the statutes and the laws** that you receive from God, **and shall**

communicate and teach **to them the path in which they should walk and the actions that they should perform.**

[21]In addition **you shall identify,** through divine inspiration, **from** among **all the people, capable men** who are **fearers of God, men of truth,** and **haters of ill-gotten gain.** Set these as judges **over them,** the people, in a hierarchy, as **leaders of thousands, leaders of hundreds, leaders of fifties, and leaders of tens.** There will be a judge over each group of ten, fifty, one hundred, and one thousand people. [22]**They shall judge the people at all times; it shall be that every major** and complex **matter they shall bring to you** for a decision, **and every minor,** simple, **matter they shall adjudicate themselves. It will ease the burden** of leadership **from upon you, and they will bear** it together **with you.** [23]**If you do this thing, and God commands you** to do this by confirming this plan, then **you will be able to endure, and also this entire people will come to their place in peace.**

Third aliya [24]**Moses heeded the voice of his father-in-law and did everything that he said.** [25]**Moses selected capable men from all Israel and set them to be heads over the people; leaders of thousands, leaders of hundreds, leaders of fifties, and leaders of tens.** [26]**They would judge the people at all times; the difficult matter they would bring to Moses, and any minor matter they would adjudicate themselves.** [27]**Moses sent forth his father-in-law,** parting from him in peace, **and he went to his land.**

The Covenant at Mount Sinai

The people encamp at Mount Sinai. There, God informs Moses that He wishes to establish a covenant with the children of Israel: They must obey His commands, and He will protect them as His own people. When Moses conveys God's charge to the people, their answer is unanimous and unequivocal.

19 Fourth aliya [1]**In the third month from the exodus of the children of Israel from the land of Egypt,** the month of Sivan, **on that day,** the first of the month, **they came to the wilderness of Sinai.** [2]**They traveled from Refidim and came to the wilderness of Sinai and encamped in the wilderness; Israel encamped there next to the mountain.** [3]**Moses ascended** the mountain **to God; the Lord summoned him from the mountain, saying: So you shall say to the house of Jacob, and tell to the children of Israel:** [4]**You saw what I did to Egypt, and I bore you on the wings of eagles,** as an eagle carries its young. **And I brought you** here **to Me.** [5]**Now, if you will heed My voice, and observe My covenant,** then **you shall be distinguished,** a special treasure **for Me from among all the peoples, as all the earth is**

Mine. **⁶You shall be for Me a kingdom of priests,** a people who serve as priests for all humanity, **and a holy nation. These are the words that you shall speak to the children of Israel.**

Fifth aliya **⁷Moses came and summoned the elders of the people, and he set before them,** told them, **all these matters that the Lord had commanded him** to say. **⁸All the people answered together and said: Everything that the Lord has spoken we will perform.** Moses returned, relayed, **the statement of the people to the Lord. ⁹The Lord said to Moses: Behold, I am coming** to reveal Myself **to you in a thickness of the cloud,** in fog, **so that the people will hear while I speak with you. And they will believe also in you, forever.** Moses related the statement of the people to the Lord.

Preparations for Revelation at Mount Sinai

God instructs Moses to tell the children of Israel to prepare for their encounter with Him at Mount Sinai. For two days the people purify and sanctify themselves through washing their garments and refraining from sexual relations. No one may pass the boundary marked all around the mountain. On the morning of the third day, they hear loud shofar blasts and witness wondrous and awe-inspiring events.

¹⁰The Lord said to Moses: Go to the people and sanctify them, prepare them **today and tomorrow** for the revelation; **and they shall wash their garments** and purify themselves. **¹¹They shall be ready for the third day, as on the third day the Lord will descend** and reveal Himself **before the eyes of all the people on Mount Sinai. ¹²And you shall restrict the people** by establishing a boundary **all around** the mountain, **saying: Beware of ascending the mountain or** even **touching its edge, as anyone who touches the mountain shall be put to death. ¹³No hand shall** enter to **touch him,** one who touches the mountain, **for** instead **he shall be stoned** from afar **or shot** with arrows; **whether** the offender is **animal or man, it will not live.** Only later, **with the extended blast of the shofar, they shall ascend the mountain.**

¹⁴Moses descended from the mountain to the people. He sanctified and prepared **the people, and they washed their garments. ¹⁵He said to the people: Be prepared** for this revelation **in three days. Do not approach a woman;** separate temporarily from your wives. **¹⁶It was on the third day, when it was morning, and there was thunder and lightning and a thick cloud on the mountain, and the blast of a shofar** was **extremely powerful, and all the people who were in the camp trembled** in fear. **¹⁷Moses took the people out of the camp toward God, and they stood at the foot**

Exodus

of the mountain, outside the boundary. ¹⁸Mount Sinai was all covered in smoke, because the Lord descended upon it, revealing Himself in fire. Its thick, concentrated smoke ascended like the smoke of a furnace, and the entire mountain trembled greatly. ¹⁹The loud blast of the shofar grew continuously stronger. As this occurred, Moses would speak, and God would answer him with a voice that was audible to the entire people.

Sixth aliya ²⁰The Lord descended upon Mount Sinai to the top of the mountain in a revelation; the Lord summoned Moses to the top of the mountain, and Moses ascended. ²¹The Lord said to Moses: Descend, and again warn the people, lest they break through to the Lord to see, and many of them fall. ²²Also the priests, who approach the Lord and stand in front of the people, shall sanctify themselves and beware, lest the Lord burst out against them and hurt them. ²³Moses said to the Lord: In any event the people will not be able to ascend Mount Sinai, as you have already warned us, saying: Demarcate the mountain, and sanctify it by not crossing the boundary around it. ²⁴The Lord said to him: Go, descend, and then you shall ascend, and Aaron with you. But the priests and the people shall not advance and break through to ascend to the Lord, lest He burst out against them and hurt them. ²⁵Moses descended to the people, and said God's repeated warning to them.

The Ten Commandments

In the wondrous encounter at Mount Sinai, God issues the Ten Commandments. These statements, which encompass both action and attitude, form the foundation of Jewish life. Some address interpersonal conduct, whereas others govern one's relation to God.

20 ¹God spoke all these matters, saying: ²I am the Lord your God, who took you out of the land of Egypt, from the house of bondage. ³You shall have no other gods before Me, instead of me; do not accept gods that other people establish. ⁴You shall not make for you an idol to worship, nor any item that is an image of that which is in the heavens above, or that which is on the earth below, or that which is in the water beneath the earth. ⁵You shall not prostrate yourselves to them, and you shall not worship them, because I am the Lord your God, a zealous God, and will not abide it. I am He who reckons the iniquity of the fathers against the children, against the third generation, grandchildren, and against the fourth generation, great-grandchildren, to My enemies, those who continue sinning like their forebears. ⁶And conversely, I am also

a God **who engages in kindness for the thousands** of generations **for those who love Me and observe My commandments.**

[7]**You shall not take the name of the Lord your God in vain,** by swearing falsely or mentioning it for no reason, **as the Lord will not absolve one who takes His name in vain.**

[8]**Remember the Sabbath day, to keep it holy.** [9]**Six days you shall work and perform all your** necessary **labor.** [10]**The seventh day is** the Sabbath **for the Lord your God,** in His honor. **You shall not perform any labor; you, and your son, and your daughter, your slave and your maidservant, and your animal, and your stranger who is within your gates,** living in your land. [11]**Because in six days the Lord made the heavens and the earth, the sea, and everything that is in them, and He rested on the seventh day; therefore, the Lord blessed the Sabbath day,** as the day on which the labor of creation was completed, **and He sanctified it.**

[12]**Honor your father and your mother, so that your days will be extended** and you will live long **on the land that the Lord your God gives you.** [13]**You shall not murder. You shall not commit adultery,** which is defined as a relationship between a married woman and a man other than her husband. **You shall not steal. You shall not bear false witness against your neighbor** by testifying dishonestly. [14]**You shall not covet,** envy, **your neighbor's house; you shall not covet your neighbor's wife, or his slave, or his maidservant, or his ox, or his ass, or anything that is your neighbor's.**

📖 **Further reading:** For more on the revelation at Sinai and the giving of the Torah and the Ten Commandments, see *A Concise Guide to the Sages*, pp. 103, 309; *A Concise Guide to Mahshava*, p. 103.

Fear of God

The visions and sounds coming from the mountain terrify the people. Fearing for their lives, they appeal to Moses to act as their intermediary with God. Moses explains to them that, indeed, the purpose of this wondrous encounter was to engender their fear of God.

[15]**All the people were seeing the thunder, and the flames, and the blast of the shofar, and the mountain smoking; the people saw** these phenomena **and trembled, and stood at a distance.** [16]**They said to Moses: You speak with us, and we will hear** you; **and God should not speak with us, lest we die.** [17]**Moses said to the people: Do not fear, as it is in order to test** [*nasot*] **you that God has come, and so that His fear will**

be on your faces, that you will fear Him, so **that you will not sin. ¹⁸The people stood at a distance, and Moses approached,** going **into the fog** on the mountain **where God was** revealing Himself.

📖 **Further reading:** For more on the meaning of the phrase "were seeing the thunder," see *A Concise Guide to the Sages,* p. 106.

Additional Commands

God issues additional restrictions on the form the people's worship may take. He connects these to the revelation at Mount Sinai, which occurred without a physical representation of God.

Maftir ¹⁹**The Lord said to Moses: So you shall say to the children of Israel: You saw that from the heavens I spoke with you,** in an incorporeal manner. ²⁰Therefore, **You shall not make with Me,** or for Me, any physical image or bodily form; **gods of silver or gods of gold,** idols made of silver or gold, **you shall not make for yourselves. ²¹You shall make for Me an altar of earth,** attached to the ground, **and shall slaughter upon it your burnt offerings and your peace offerings, your sheep and your oxen; in every place where I mention My name,** in every place where I choose to rest My Presence, **I will come to you and I will bless you. ²²If you make Me an altar of stone, you shall not build it of hewn stones, for you wielded your sword upon it,** you used a destructive iron tool to cut the stone, **and** you thereby **profaned it. ²³You shall not ascend on stairs to My altar, so that your nakedness will not be exposed upon it.**

Parashat Mishpatim

This *parasha* enumerates many commandments. Some relate to the establishment of a properly functioning society, and address capital crimes, torts, and commerce. Others are concerned with the suitable treatment of various classes of people, such as slaves, orphans, foreigners, and the poor. There are also many laws that do not fit into either category. Toward the end of the *parasha*, God instructs the people in preparation for the journey to Canaan and the entry into the land, and the narrative returns to the story of the covenant established at Mount Sinai.

The Hebrew Slave and Maidservant
God imparts laws to Moses concerning Hebrew slaves and maidservants: marriage, rights, and emancipation.

21 ¹**These are the ordinances that you shall place before them,** to teach the people. ²**If you acquire a Hebrew slave, six years he shall work. And in the seventh** year **he shall go free, without** paying a **charge** to redeem himself. ³**If he shall come,** be bought, **by himself,** without a wife and children, **he shall leave** his servitude **by himself. If he is the husband of a wife** when he becomes a slave, then **his wife shall leave with him,** when he does. ⁴**If his master shall give him a wife, and she bears him sons or daughters, the wife and her children shall belong to her master** as maidservant and slaves, **and he,** the Hebrew slave, **shall leave by himself.**

⁵**But if the slave shall say: I love my master, my wife, and my children,** and therefore **I will not go free,** I wish to remain a slave; ⁶**then his master shall** ceremoniously **bring him to the judges; he shall bring him to the door or to the doorpost. And his master shall perforate his ear with an awl, and he shall serve him forever.**

⁷**If** an Israelite **man sells his** minor **daughter as a maidservant, she shall not leave like** gentile **slaves' leaving. ⁸If she is displeasing in the eyes of her master, to whom she was designated,** and he does not wish to marry her off to his son or to marry her himself, **he shall facilitate her redemption. He shall not presume to sell her to a foreign people,** another family,

in what would constitute **his betrayal of her.** ⁹**If he designates her for his son** in marriage, **he shall treat her as is the practice of the daughters,** like a full-fledged daughter-in-law. ¹⁰Consequently, **if he,** the son, **takes another** wife **for himself, he shall not diminish** the rights of the former maidservant to **her food, her garments, or her conjugal rights.** ¹¹**If he,** the son, **does not perform these three** obligations **for her, she shall leave without charge; there is no payment,** and all her obligations to the master are canceled.

Laws Concerning Injury and Death

The following laws address cases in which one person strikes another, whether intentionally or unwittingly. They include situations where the victim is injured, as well as those where he dies. They also include special categories of victims, such as a parent, a slave, or a pregnant woman.

¹²In the case of **one who strikes a man, and he dies** as a result of his wounds, he **shall be put to death.** ¹³**But for one who did not have intent to kill him, and God caused it to come to his hand** through some accident, **I will** instead **provide you a place where he shall flee.**

¹⁴**If a man shall act intentionally against his neighbor to kill him cunningly, you shall take him** even **from My altar to die,** to be executed.

¹⁵**One who strikes his father or his mother shall be put to death.**

¹⁶In the case of **one who abducts a man, and he sells him** as a slave, **or he is found in his possession** before he could be sold, **he,** the kidnapper, **shall be put to death.** ¹⁷**One who curses his father or his mother shall be put to death.**

¹⁸**If men quarrel, and one strikes the other with a stone or with a fist, and he does not die but collapses into bed** due to his injuries, ¹⁹**if he,** the injured person, **arises and walks outside on his** walking **cane** as he is recuperating, then **the assailant shall be absolved** of the death penalty. **He shall give only his loss of livelihood, and he shall provide healing;** he must compensate the victim for his lost wages and pay for his medical treatment.

Second aliya ²⁰**If a man strikes his** gentile **slave or his** gentile **maidservant with a staff** or whip, **and he dies under his hand,** from the master's blows, **he shall be avenged;** the master is liable to receive the death penalty. ²¹**However, if he shall survive a day or two days, he shall not be avenged.** The master is not liable to receive the death penalty, **as he,** the slave, **is his property.**

²²**If men fight, and they** accidentally **strike** a bystander who is **a pregnant woman and her children are miscarried, but there is no fatality** of the woman herself; **he,** the individual who struck the woman, **shall be fined, as the husband of the woman shall impose upon him,** will sue him, **and he shall give** the compensation **in court,** in accordance with the determination of the judges. ²³**But if there will be a fatality,** if the woman dies, then **you shall give a life for a life,** a monetary payment for accidentally killing her. ²⁴Similarly, one must give a monetary payment if she was injured but did not die: The amount of **an eye for an eye; a tooth for a tooth; a hand for a hand; a foot for a foot;** ²⁵**a burn for a burn;** an open **wound for a wound; an injury,** without breaking the skin, **for an injury.**

> 📖 **Further reading:** The Sages do not interpret the expression "an eye for an eye" literally; see *A Concise Guide to the Sages*, p. 113.

²⁶**If a man shall strike the eye of his** gentile **slave, or the eye of his** gentile **maidservant, and he** thereby **destroys it, he shall send him to freedom** in compensation **for his eye.** ²⁷And even **if he shall dislodge the tooth of his slave or the tooth of his maidservant, he shall send him to freedom for his tooth.**

Injury and Damage from Goring and an Open Pit

These laws deal with damage or injury caused by one's property. The types of damage listed here serve as the basis for the primary categories of damage in Jewish law.

²⁸**If an ox** belonging to someone **gores a man or a woman and he shall die, the ox shall be stoned, and its meat shall not be eaten. And the owner of the ox is absolved** from any further punishment. ²⁹**But if the ox was wont to gore** people **previously, and its owner was warned** after such events that this is a dangerous ox **but** he nevertheless **did not guard it, and it killed a man or a woman,** then **the ox shall be stoned, and** it is fitting that **its owner too shall die,** although he is not punished with execution; ³⁰instead, **when** a monetary **ransom is imposed upon him,** when charges are brought against him, then **he shall give ransom of** the value of **his life, in accordance with all that will be imposed upon him** by the court. ³¹**Whether it shall gore a son or it shall gore a daughter, in accordance with this ordinance shall be done to him.** ³²**If the ox shall gore a** gentile **slave or a** gentile **maidservant, he,** the owner of the ox, **shall give thirty silver shekels to his,** the slave's, **master, and the ox shall be stoned.**

³³**If a man shall uncover a pit** that had previously been covered up properly, **or if a man shall dig a pit** himself **and he does not cover it, and an ox or a donkey** or any other living creature **falls there,** ³⁴**the owner of the pit,** the one who dug or uncovered it, **shall pay** the animal's owner. **He shall compensate its owner with silver, and the carcass shall be his.**

³⁵**If the ox of a man shall strike** and injure **the ox of his neighbor, and it dies, they shall sell the living ox and divide its value, and they shall divide** the value of **the carcass too.** ³⁶**Or if it became known** to the court **that it is an ox wont to gore previously,** on at least two past occasions, **and** yet **its owner would not guard it, he shall pay** a live **ox in exchange for** the dead **ox, and the carcass shall** then **be his.**

Theft

The Torah sets forth the punishments and fines imposed upon a thief in various circumstances, and establishes the law applying to one who defends himself against a thief.

³⁷**If a man steals an ox or a sheep, and slaughters it or sells it, he shall**
22 **pay five oxen for the ox, and four sheep for the sheep.** ¹**If the thief is found while excavating** in order to break in through a tunnel, or while he is sneaking into a house another way, **and he is struck** by the homeowner or someone else **and** he **dies, there is no bloodguilt for him.** The person who kills him is not liable for his death. ²**If the sun shone upon him,** if he came openly, **there is bloodguilt for him;** his killer is punished. If a thief steals property, **he shall pay; if he has nothing** with which to pay, then **he shall be sold** as a Hebrew slave to pay **for his theft.** ³**If the stolen object shall be found alive in his possession, whether an ox, or a donkey, or a sheep, he shall pay double** its value.

📖 **Further reading:** The Sages explain why a thief must provide different restitution for an ox than for a sheep; see *A Concise Guide to the Sages*, p. 110.

Damage from Grazing and Fire

The Torah returns to laws of damages, and covers other causes of property damage. First it addresses the case of an animal that grazes in another's field and causes him a monetary loss through eating or trampling there. Afterward it establishes the law regarding when a fire spreads to another person's field.

Third aliya ⁴**If a man grazes an animal in a field or a vineyard, and dispatched his animal** or allowed it leave, **and it grazes in another's field, he,** the animal's owner, **shall pay** compensation from **the best of his field and** from **the best of his vineyard.**

⁵**If a fire spreads and encounters thorns,** which amplify the flames, **and** as a result **a grain pile or standing grain or a field is consumed, the one who ignited the fire shall pay** for the damage.

Bailees

These laws outline one's obligation if he has assumed responsibility for another person's object or animal, and that item is stolen or damaged. The laws differentiate between different situations and also address the possibility that the bailee is trying to steal the item for himself. At the end of the section, the Torah relates to a different kind of theft, in which a man seduces a young virgin, and must either pay compensation or marry her himself.

⁶**If a man gives silver or vessels to his neighbor to safeguard** as an unpaid bailee, **and it is stolen from the man's house,** the neighbor's house, **if the thief is found, he shall pay double** the value of the item. ⁷**If the thief is not found, the householder,** meaning the bailee, **shall be brought to the judges** to swear **that he did not extend his hand to** steal **the property of his neighbor** himself. ⁸**For every matter of transgression** of someone suspected of making a false claim, **whether for an ox, for a donkey, for a sheep, for a garment, or for any lost item, with regard to which he shall say: This is it,** it can be identified in the possession of the person who does not own it, **the statement of both parties** to the dispute **shall come to the judges** for a ruling. **Whomever the judges shall condemn shall pay double to his neighbor,** the item's owner.

📖 Further reading: For more on the criteria for selecting judges, and the moral standards they are expected to uphold, see *A Concise Guide to the Sages*, pp. 103, 225, 243.

⁹**If a man shall give his neighbor a donkey, or an ox, or a sheep, or any animal to safeguard** as a paid bailee, **and it dies, or is injured, or** is captured, **and there is no onlooker** who witnessed the event, ¹⁰**the oath of the Lord shall be between the two of them** to resolve the potential dispute. The bailee must swear **that he** has taken proper care of the item and **has not extended his hand to the property of his neighbor; and its owner shall accept it,** the oath, **and he,** the bailee **shall not pay.**

¹¹**But if it,** the animal, **is stolen from him,** from the bailee, who was charged with preventing its theft, **he shall pay** compensation **to its owner.** ¹²**If it is mauled** by a wild animal, **he shall bring** what remains of **it as evidence** that it was mauled, and **he shall not pay for the mauled animal.**

¹³**If a man borrows** an animal or item **from his neighbor, and it,** a borrowed animal, **is injured or dies,** or an object breaks, and **its owner is not**

with it at the time, **he,** the borrower, **shall pay.** ¹⁴**If its owner is with it, he,** the borrower, **shall not pay,** as the owner's presence indicates that the borrower did not use the item in an inappropriate manner. **If he is a renter,** and the item was not lent as a favor but in exchange for a rental fee, then **it,** the loss incurred by the owner, **goes for his rent,** and he is not entitled to further restitution. ¹⁵**If a man seduces a virgin who was not betrothed and lies with her, he shall pay the bride price, for her to be a wife for him;** he is required to marry her and pay her dowry. ¹⁶**If her father shall refuse to give her** in marriage **to him,** then **he,** the seducer, **shall weigh out** and pay **silver according to the bride price of virgins,** the dowry one would pay when marrying a virgin.

Religious Corruption

The style in which the laws are stated changes at this point. Until now the Torah described situations and stated the law in the various cases. From this point forward the laws are stated mostly as statutes, as positive or negative commands. The first laws address fundamentals of a good society – banning witchcraft, bestiality, and idolatry.

¹⁷**You shall not keep a witch alive.** ¹⁸**Anyone who lies with an animal shall be put to death.**

¹⁹**One who sacrifices to gods** as part of idol worship **shall be destroyed;** he is liable to receive the death penalty for bringing offerings, **except** offerings **to the Lord alone.**

Vulnerable Members of Society

The Torah charges everyone to demonstrate sensitivity toward foreigners, orphans, widows, and the poor, and outlines proper behavior toward these vulnerable members of society.

²⁰**You shall not mistreat** or deceive **a stranger, and you shall not oppress him. For you** too **were strangers, in the land of Egypt.** ²¹**You shall not afflict any widow or orphan.** ²²**If you afflict him, then when he cries out to Me, I will hear his cry.** ²³Then **My wrath will be enflamed, and I will kill you with the sword; and your** own **wives will be widows, and your** own **children orphans.**

> 📖 **Further reading:** For more on proper treatment of the stranger, see *A Concise Guide to the Sages,* pp. 112, 162.

²⁴**If you shall lend silver to** any of **My people,** especially **to the poor who is with you, you shall not be as a creditor to him,** pressuring him to repay his loan. And **you shall not impose upon him interest.** ²⁵**If you take your**

neighbor's garment as collateral, you shall return it to him by the time of the setting of the sun. ²⁶For that alone is his covering; it is his only garment for his skin; in what shall he lie? It shall be that when he cries out to Me in distress, I will hear, as I am gracious and compassionate.

Miscellaneous Laws
The following compilation of laws addresses various topics, from proper conduct toward judges and leaders, to the handling of nonkosher meat.

Fourth
aliya

²⁷You shall not curse judges, and a prince among your people you shall not imprecate. ²⁸The surfeit of your crops and the outpouring of your juices you shall not delay. You must promptly separate teruma and tithes from your agricultural produce, and give the resulting food or beverage to the priests. The firstborn of your sons you shall give to Me, in that you must redeem him for money. ²⁹So shall you do to your cattle and to your flock: During the firstborn animal's first seven days it shall be with its mother; on the eighth day, you shall give it to Me as an offering. ³⁰You shall be holy people to Me, and avoid transgression. You shall not eat meat of a mauled animal in the field; instead, you shall cast it to be eaten by the dog.

Laws Governing Judges and Court Proceedings
The Torah presents a collection of laws that are essential for proper functioning of the justice system. While most of these laws seem to be directed toward judges, they apply to private citizens as well.

23 ¹You shall not accept a false report, untruthful testimony. Do not place your hand in participation with the wicked, to be a corrupt witness, a dishonest witness. ²You shall not follow the majority of judges for evil. And you shall not respond in a dispute to distort justice by inclining after the majority against your better judgment. ³You shall not favor even a poor man in his legal dispute.

⁴If you encounter the ox of your enemy or his donkey lost and wandering, you shall return it to him. ⁵If you see the donkey of your enemy crouching under its overly heavy burden, shall you refrain from assisting him, its owner? Not so; rather, you shall assist him by lightening the donkey's load with him.

Further reading: Assisting one's enemy in his time of need can lead to reconciliation and harmony; see A Concise Guide to the Sages, p. 111.

Fifth aliya **⁶You shall not distort the judgment of,** upon, **your poor in his dispute** to favor the wealthy litigant; you must uphold justice. **⁷You shall distance yourself from falsehood. And you shall not kill the innocent and the righteous** by convicting them of a capital crime, **as I will not vindicate the wicked** who do so. **⁸You shall not take a bribe, as a bribe will blind** even **the perceptive** from recognizing the truth, **and** will **corrupt the words of the righteous. ⁹You shall not oppress a stranger, for you** Israelites **know the soul of a stranger, as you were strangers in the land of Egypt.**

The Sabbatical Year and Shabbat

The Torah introduces the obligation of refraining from agricultural labor during the Sabbatical Year, and follows this law with a reminder to refrain from labor on Shabbat.

¹⁰For six years you shall sow your land, perform agricultural labors, **and gather its produce. ¹¹But** in **the seventh year you shall leave it fallow and relinquish it.** You must cease your agricultural activities and abandon ownership of the field, so **that the poor of your people may eat** its produce and its grain yield; **and** with regard to **their leftovers, the beast of the field shall eat** them. **So shall you do to your vineyard** and **to your olive grove.**

¹²Similarly, for six days you shall perform your activities, and on the seventh day you shall rest, so that your ox and your donkey will also **rest, and the son of your maidservant and the stranger** who works as a hired laborer **will** rest and **be invigorated. ¹³You shall observe everything that I have said to you. You shall not mention the name of other gods; they shall not be heard from your mouth.**

The Three Pilgrimage Festivals

The children of Israel are to celebrate three festivals during the year. At these times they are obligated to travel to the Temple in Jerusalem and sacrifice offerings there.

¹⁴Three times in the year you shall hold, celebrate, **a festival to Me. ¹⁵You shall observe the Festival of Unleavened Bread; seven days you shall eat unleavened bread as I commanded you, at the appointed time, in** the period of **the month of the ripening,** Nisan, **for during it you came out from Egypt; they shall not appear before Me empty-handed,** but shall bring offerings to the Temple. **¹⁶And** observe **the festival of the** wheat **harvest,** *Shavuot,* at the time of the harvest of **the first fruits of your handiwork that you sow in the field; and the festival of the ingathering,**

Sukkot, **at the end of the year, when you gather** and store **your handi-work,** the produce and grain **from the field.** [17]**Three times during the year,** on Passover, *Shavuot,* and *Sukkot,* **all your males shall appear before the Master, the Lord,** in the Temple. [18]**You shall not slaughter the blood of My offering,** the paschal lamb, **with leavened bread** still in your possession. **And the fat of My** festival peace **offering,** which must be burned on the altar, **shall not remain overnight until morning.** [19]**You shall bring the choicest of the first fruits of your land to the House of the Lord your God,** the Temple. **You shall not cook a kid in its mother's milk,** or in the milk of any animal.

📖 **Further reading:** For more on the three pilgrimage festivals, namely Passover, *Shavuot,* and *Sukkot,* see *A Concise Guide to the Sages,* pp. 290, 306, 309; *A Concise Guide to Mahshava,* pp. 72, 93, 99; *A Concise Guide to Halakha,* pp. 176, 274, 340.

God Encourages and Exhorts the People about the Conquest of the Land
In preparation for the people's entry into Canaan and their settlement of the land, God warns them expressly against emulating the culture and behavior of the inhabitants of the land. Conversely, if the children of Israel guard themselves from those spiritual threats, they are promised great rewards.

ixth
aliya [20]**Behold, I am sending an angel before you to protect you along the way, and to take you to the place that I have prepared.** [21]**Beware of him and heed his voice; do not defy him, for he will not forgive your transgression. For My name,** God's manifestation in the world, **is in him.** [22]**For if you heed his voice and perform all that I say, then I will be an enemy to your enemies, and I will be hostile to those who are hostile to you.** [23]**For My angel shall go before you, and he will take you to** the land of Canaan, currently inhabited by **the Emorites, the Hitites, the Perizites, the Canaanites, the Hivites, and the Yevusites, and I will annihilate them.** [24]**You shall not prostrate yourselves to their gods, you shall not serve them, and you shall not act in accordance with their actions;** rather, **you shall** actively **destroy them and smash their monuments** and all their places of religious worship. [25]**You shall serve the Lord your God, and He will bless your bread,** your food, **and your water; and I will remove illness from your midst.**

venth
aliya [26]**There shall be no woman who miscarries or is barren in your land. I will fill the number of your days;** you will merit long lives. [27]**I will send My fear,** fear of Me, **before you, and I will stun,** disorient and disorder, **all the people into whose midst you shall come** for war; **and I will cause all**

Exodus

your enemies to turn their backs to you and flee from you. ²⁸I will send the hornet before you to join the attack, and it shall expel the Hivites, the Canaanites, and the Hitites from before you.

²⁹I will not expel them from before you in one year, lest the land become desolate and the beasts of the field multiply against you. ³⁰Rather, I will expel them from before you little by little, until you increase and inherit the entire land. ³¹I will set your border from the Red Sea to the sea of the Philistines, the part of the Mediterranean Sea adjacent to the Philistine settlements, and from the wilderness of the Arabian Desert in the east to the Euphrates River in the north, for I will deliver into your hand the inhabitants of the land and you shall expel them from before you.

³²You shall not establish a covenant of peace with them or with their gods. ³³They shall not live in your land lest they cause you to sin against Me. For if they remain, you will serve their gods, for they will be a snare for you, entrapping you in idolatry.

Covenant at Sinai

The narrative returns to Mount Sinai to provide additional details about the covenant that was established between God and the children of Israel, before the giving of the Ten Commandments. It was accompanied by dramatic pageantry, the building of a memorial, the sacrifice of offerings and the sprinkling of their blood, and a prophetic revelation to the elders of Israel.

24 ¹To Moses, He said: Ascend to the Lord, to Mount Sinai, you and Aaron, Nadav and Avihu, and seventy of the elders of Israel, and prostrate yourselves from a distance. ²Moses alone shall approach the Lord at the top of the mountain, and they shall not approach; and the people shall not ascend with him either. ³Moses came and related to the people all the words of the Lord, and all the ordinances. All the people answered in one voice, in unanimous agreement, and said: Everything that the Lord has spoken, we will do. ⁴Moses wrote all the words of the Lord, and he arose early in the morning and built an altar at the foot of the mountain, and he erected twelve commemorative stones as pillars for the twelve tribes of Israel, one for each tribe.

⁵He sent the young men of the children of Israel. And they offered up burnt offerings, and they slaughtered feast offerings of bulls to the Lord. Burnt offerings are burnt in their entirety upon the altar, whereas peace offerings are eaten mostly by those who brought them. ⁶Moses took

half the blood of the bulls, and he placed it in the basins, and half the blood he sprinkled upon the altar in an atonement rite. ⁷He, Moses, took the Book of the Covenant containing the words of God, which he had already written, and he read it in the ears of the people. And they said: Everything that the Lord has spoken we will do and we will heed. They declared their commitment to first obey God's commands and only afterward to seek to understand them. ⁸Moses took the blood that was in the basins and sprinkled it on the people for atonement, and he said: This is the blood that is a symbol of the covenant that the Lord has established with you with regard to everything that you have accepted upon yourselves. ⁹Moses and Aaron, Nadav, and Avihu, and seventy of the elders of Israel went up. ¹⁰They saw the God of Israel in a prophetic vision, and under His feet was like a configuration of sapphire brick, a square blue gemstone. And it was like the very heavens in its clarity and purity. ¹¹Against the noblemen of the children of Israel, Aaron, Nadav, Avihu, and the elders, He did not extend His hand to strike them down, despite the fact that they had approached the Divine Presence. And they beheld God, in the sense of seeing this vision, and ate the peace offerings and drank, as though sharing a meal with God.

¹²The Lord said to Moses: Ascend higher to Me, to the mountaintop, and be there for some time; and there I will give you the stone tablets of the covenant, and the law and the commandment that I have written, to teach them. ¹³Moses and his servant Joshua rose. And Moses ascended the mountain of God. ¹⁴To the elders, he, Moses, had said before ascending: Remain here for us until we will return to you; behold, Aaron and Hur are with you; whoever has a matter, a dispute with someone, shall approach them for mediation.

Maftir ¹⁵Moses ascended to the mountaintop, and the cloud covered the mountain. ¹⁶The glory of the Lord rested upon Mount Sinai, and the cloud covered it for six days. Then He, God, called to Moses on the seventh day from the midst of the cloud. ¹⁷The appearance of the glory of the Lord was like devouring fire on the top of the mountain in the eyes of the children of Israel. ¹⁸Moses entered into the midst of the cloud, and went up to the mountaintop. Moses was on the mountaintop for forty days and forty nights.

Further reading: For more on the revelation at Mount Sinai, the giving of the Ten Commandments, and Moses' stay on the mountaintop, see pp. 180, 218.

Parashat
Teruma

God commands the children of Israel to construct the Tabernacle, which will serve as the focal point for His contact with Moses and the people through revelation. The Israelites are asked to donate the many different types of materials necessary for the project. While Moses is on Mount Sinai, God instructs him in great detail as to how to build the Tabernacle and its vessels, and even imparts a vision of the precise configuration of each item.

These instructions progress from the interior outward. First is the Ark of the Testimony, located in the innermost area of the Tabernacle, the Holy of Holies. Next is the command to fashion the table and candelabrum, in the outer portion of the Tent of Meeting. These are followed by the particulars of erecting the Tabernacle itself, with its roof and walls. The sacrificial altar, which is in the courtyard outside the Tabernacle, is last.

Call for Donations

The construction of the Tabernacle requires a wide range of both expensive and inexpensive materials. The Israelites are asked to donate material in accordance with their individual means and levels of generosity.

25 ¹**The Lord spoke to Moses, saying:** ²**Speak to the children of Israel and** command them that **they shall collect a gift for Me, from every man whose heart pledges,** who wishes to donate, **you shall collect My gift.** ³**This is the gift that you shall collect from them:** The metals **gold, sil-ver, and bronze;** ⁴**and** textiles: **sky-blue** wool, **purple and scarlet wool,** as well as **linen and** woven **goat hair;** ⁵**and** materials for the roofs and the walls: processed **rams' hides dyed red,** taḥash **hides, and** boards of **acacia wood;** ⁶**and** materials produced from plants: **oil** suitable **for the lighting** of the candelabrum, and **spices** used **for the anointing oil and for the in-cense of the spices;** ⁷**and** precious stones: **Onyx stones, and stones for setting,** the former **for the ephod,** which was a type of apron worn by the High Priest, **and** the latter **for** affixing on **the** square cloth **breast piece.** ⁸**They shall make for Me a sanctuary, and** through it **I will dwell among them.** ⁹**In accordance with everything that I show you,** Moses, **the**

configuration of the Tabernacle and the configuration of all its vessels, so you shall make it.

📖 **Further reading:** In the Land of Israel, the Temple ultimately replaced the Tabernacle. For more on both the Tabernacle and the Temple, see *A Concise Guide to the Sages*, p. 114; *A Concise Guide to Mahshava*, p. 160.

The Ark of the Testimony

God provides the children of Israel with detailed instructions for building the ark, which will hold the Tablets of the Covenant, the physical symbol of the connection between God and His people. The ark will be located in the holiest portion of the Tabernacle, the place where Moses will receive God's revelation.

¹⁰**They shall make an ark of acacia wood: Its length shall be two and a half cubits, its width a cubit and a half, and its height a cubit and a half.** A cubit is the distance between a man's elbow and the end of his fingers, about 50 cm. ¹¹**You shall plate it,** the acacia wood, **with pure gold; within and without you shall plate it,** on its inner and outer surfaces. **And you shall make a** decorative **gold rim** like a crown **upon** the top of **it, all around.** ¹²**You shall cast four rings of gold for it,** the ark, **and place them on its four corners, two rings on its one side and two rings on its second side.** ¹³**You shall make staves of acacia wood and plate them** too **with gold.** ¹⁴**You shall insert the staves into the rings on the sides of the ark, to lift and carry the ark with them.** ¹⁵**The staves shall be in the rings of the ark** at all times; **they shall not be removed from it.** ¹⁶**You shall place in the ark** the Tablets of **the Testimony that I will give you,** the two Tablets of the Covenant.

cond *aliya* ¹⁷**You shall make an ark cover of pure gold. Its length shall be two and a half cubits and its width a cubit and a half.** ¹⁸**You shall make two cherubs of gold,** angelic figures. **Hammered you shall make them,** from one contiguous piece of solid gold, **at the two ends of the ark cover.** ¹⁹**And make one cherub from this end** of the ark cover **and one cherub from that end; from the ark cover you shall make the cherubs from its two ends.** ²⁰**The cherubs shall have wings spread from above, shielding with their wings over the ark cover, and their faces one to another; toward the ark cover the faces of the cherubs shall be** directed. ²¹**You shall place the ark cover upon the ark from above; and in the ark you shall place** the Tablets of **the Testimony that I shall give you.** ²²**I will meet with you there, and I will tell you,** when My voice will issue **from upon the ark cover, from between the two cherubs that are upon the**

Exodus

Ark of the Testimony, saying **everything that I will command you to the children of Israel.**

Illustrations: See image of the Ark of the Testimony, p. 523.

The Table
The showbread, one of the gifts given to priests serving in the Tabernacle, will rest on a unique table. God apprises Moses of the specifications for this table and its accessories.

²³**You shall make a table of acacia wood: Its length shall be two cubits, and its width a cubit, and its height a cubit and a half.** ²⁴**You shall plate it with pure gold, and you shall make for it a** decorative **rim of gold,** like a crown, **all around.** ²⁵**You shall make for it a border of one handbreadth all around, and you shall make** the aforementioned **rim of gold for its border all around.** A handbreadth is the width of a fist, around 8 cm. ²⁶**You shall make for it four rings of gold, and you shall place the rings on the four corners that are on its,** the table's, **four legs.** ²⁷**Adjacent to,** or opposite, **the border the rings shall be, as housings for the staves** used to carry the table. ²⁸**You shall make the staves of acacia wood and you shall plate them with gold; and the table will be carried with them,** by its staves. ²⁹**You shall make** for the table **its bowls, and its spoons, and its tubes,** which formed a layered frame above the table on which to place the bread, **and its supports,** posts to hold the frame. These are the accoutrements **with which it,** the table, **shall be covered. From pure gold you shall make** all of **them.** ³⁰**You shall place showbread** [*lehem panim*], literally "bread [*lehem*] with a front [*panim*]," **upon the table, before Me always.**

The Candelabrum
Like the ark cover and its cherubs, the candelabrum with its elaborate ornamentation was fashioned not by casting a mold or by joining separate pieces, but by beating, chiseling, and shaping a single block of gold.

³¹**You shall make a candelabrum of pure gold; the candelabrum shall be made hammered** from one piece of gold. **Its base and its** main, central **shaft,** and even the decorative elements, namely **its cups, its knobs, and its flowers, shall** all **be** fashioned **from it,** the same block of gold. ³²**Six branches shall emerge from its sides,** from the central shaft: **Three branches of the candelabrum from its one side and three branches of the candelabrum from its second side.** ³³These are the decorations

on the branches: **Three finely crafted cups on the one branch,** with a **knob and a flower. And three finely crafted cups on the next branch, a knob and a flower;** do **so for** all **of the six branches that emerge from the candelabrum.** ³⁴**On** the central shaft of **the candelabrum, four finely crafted cups, with its knobs and its flowers.** ³⁵There shall be **a knob under the** first set of **two branches extending from it,** from the central shaft, **and a knob under the** second set of **two branches extending from it, and a knob under the** third set of **two branches extending from it;** so it shall be **for the six branches emerging from the candelabrum.** ³⁶The Torah reiterates: **Their knobs and their branches,** all the knobs and branches, **shall be** made **from it,** as an integral part of the candelabrum itself, **all of it hammered** from one slab **of pure gold.**

³⁷**You shall make its lamps,** receptacles for the oil, **seven. And he shall kindle** the wicks in **its lamps so that it will illuminate toward its front.** All the flames were turned toward the central shaft. ³⁸**Its tongs,** used for handling the wicks, **and its** raking **pans,** for holding the ash removed from the lamps; these **shall be** fashioned **of pure gold.** ³⁹**He shall make it,** the candelabrum, **of a talent of pure gold, with all these vessels** included in the total weight. A talent is equivalent to about 50 kg. ⁴⁰**See and craft** the candelabrum and the other vessels **in their form, as you are shown on the mountain.** God showed Moses an image of the vessels to enable him to guide the craftsmen in constructing them properly.

Illustrations: See image of the candelabrum as well as a detailed sketch of its central shaft, p. 523.

The Sheets for the Roof of the Tabernacle

Special arrangements of sheets will constitute the roof of the Tabernacle. Some of the sheets are to be woven of twined linen and wool threads, and others will be made of rams' hides and taḥash hides. Different opinions exist with regard to the identity of the taḥash. Some think it is a species of animal and others a kind of dyed hide.

26 ¹**You shall make the Tabernacle of ten sheets** made **of twined linen,** *Third* threads twisted together, **and** dyed threads of **sky-blue, purple, and scar-** *aliya* **let wool** shall be spun into it. **With artfully worked** likenesses of **cherubs shall you make them,** the sheets. ²**The length of each sheet shall be twenty-eight cubits, and the width** shall be **four cubits for each sheet; there shall be one** uniform **measure for all the sheets.** ³**Five of the** ten **sheets shall be attached,** stitched, **one to another, and** the other **five sheets shall be attached one to another** in the same fashion.

⁴**You shall make loops of sky-blue wool,** and attach them **on the edge of the** outermost **sheet, at the extremity,** at the edge **of the first array** of five sheets, and **you shall do likewise at the edge of the outermost sheet of the second array** of five sheets. ⁵**Fifty loops shall you make in the one sheet, and fifty loops you shall make at the extremity of the sheet that is in the second array; the loops shall correspond one to another,** fifty loops facing fifty loops.

⁶**You shall make fifty hooks of gold and attach the sheets one to another with the hooks. And the Tabernacle shall be one,** a single unit.

⁷**You shall make sheets of goats' hair as a tent over the Tabernacle,** a second layer over the aforementioned cover; **you shall make them eleven sheets.** ⁸**The length of each sheet shall be thirty cubits, and the width of each sheet four cubits;** there shall be **one** uniform **measure for** all **eleven sheets.** ⁹**You shall attach five sheets alone,** in one unit, **and six sheets alone,** in a separate unit. **And you shall fold** down half of the width of **the sixth sheet** to hang over the roof's edge **at the front of the tent.**

¹⁰**You shall make fifty loops on the edge of the one sheet, the outermost of the first array, and fifty loops on the edge of the** outermost **sheet of the second array.**

¹¹**You shall make fifty hooks of bronze, and you shall place the hooks into the loops and attach the tent, and it shall be one,** a single unit. ¹²**As** for **the overhang that remains of the sheets of the tent, the half-sheet that remains shall** be folded down and shall **hang over** the ground at **the back of the Tabernacle,** where there is no entrance. ¹³With regard to the breadth of the cover, **the** excess **cubit on this side and the** excess **cubit on that side, from that which remains of the length of the sheets of the tent, shall hang over the sides of the Tabernacle on this side and on that side, to cover it.** ¹⁴**You shall** also **make a cover for the tent.** This covering shall be made **of rams' hides dyed red, and** then there will be a fourth layer, **a cover of** taḥash **hides over the top.** The taḥash was an animal that has since become extinct.

The Walls of the Tabernacle
The walls of the Tabernacle are to be made from interlocking panels connected by means of pegs and sockets.

Fourth aliya ¹⁵**You shall make the boards for the Tabernacle of acacia wood,** sanded and **standing upright.** ¹⁶**Ten cubits shall be the length of a board, and**

a cubit and a half shall be the width of each board. [17]Two tenons, pegs, for each board will protrude from the edges, parallel one to another, and will fit into corresponding sockets in the next board. So you shall make for all the boards of the Tabernacle. [18]You shall make the boards for the Tabernacle: Twenty boards for the southern side. [19]You shall make forty silver sockets under the twenty boards: Two sockets under the one board for its two tenons protruding from the bottom of the boards, and two sockets under the one board for its two tenons. These tenons were inserted into the corresponding sockets below them. [20]For the second side of the Tabernacle, for the north side: twenty boards, [21]and their forty sockets of silver: two sockets under the one board and two sockets under the one board.

[22]For the side, the back, of the Tabernacle, on the west, you shall make six boards. [23]And you shall make two boards for the southwest and northwest corners of the Tabernacle on the sides, in the back. [24]They, the boards, shall be even at the bottom. And they shall meet together at its top, at its one ring, a ring at the top of each pair of boards which will bind them together. So it shall also be for two of them, the two extra planks mentioned above; they shall be for the two corners. [25]There shall be on the west side a total of eight boards, and their silver sockets: Sixteen sockets, two sockets under the one board and two sockets under the one board, two sockets under each of the eight boards.

[26]You shall make bars of acacia wood to support the boards and lock them in place: Five for the boards of the one side of the Tabernacle, [27]and five bars for the boards of the second side of the Tabernacle, and five bars for the boards of the side of the Tabernacle, for the side to the west, in back. [28]And the fifth bar in each set will function as the central bar and shall be inside the boards, running through a hole through the width of the boards, connecting all the boards into one wall, from the end to the end. [29]You shall plate the boards with gold, and their rings, which join them together, you shall make of gold. These rings shall be housings for the bars. And you shall plate the bars with gold. [30]You shall establish the Tabernacle in accordance with its proper design, the details of which you were shown on the mountain.

Illustrations: See images of the boards and the bars, as well as the overall appearance of the Tabernacle, p. 524.

Exodus

The Curtain and the Screen

The Holy of Holies, which contains the Ark of the Testimony, is the area of the Tabernacle with the highest level of sanctity. The curtain divides it from the Sanctuary. The screen at the entrance to the Tent of Meeting separates the Sanctuary from the Tabernacle courtyard.

Fifth aliya **³¹You shall make a curtain of sky-blue, purple, and scarlet wool and twined linen; it shall be artfully made,** woven **with** decorative **cherubs. ³²You shall place it on four acacia pillars plated with gold,** with **their hooks of gold,** used for hanging the curtain, **upon four silver sockets. ³³You shall place the curtain under the** gold **hooks** which connect the sets of overhanging sheets (see verse 6), **and you shall bring there the Ark of the Testimony, behind the curtain, and the curtain shall partition for you between the Sanctuary and the Holy of Holies. ³⁴You shall place the** golden **ark cover upon the Ark of the Testimony in the Holy of Holies. ³⁵You shall place the table outside the curtain,** in the Sanctuary, **and the candelabrum opposite the table, on the side of the Tabernacle to the south, and the table you shall place on the north side. ³⁶At the** eastern end of the Tent of Meeting, **you shall make a screen for the entrance of the tent, of sky-blue, purple, and scarlet wool, and twined linen, the work of an embroiderer. ³⁷You shall make five acacia pillars for the screen, and you shall plate them with gold; their hooks,** upon which the screen is to be hung, **shall be of gold. You shall cast for them five bronze sockets.** The screen of the Tabernacle, which served as the fourth wall of the Tent of Meeting, was hung on the five pillars inserted into bronze sockets.

The Altar

God instructs Moses to build the altar for sacrificial offerings and to place it in the Tabernacle courtyard. The detailed instructions extend to the rest of the equipment required for sacrificing offerings: the shovels, for clearing away ashes; the basins, for collecting blood from the slaughtered offering; and the fork, for handling the flesh of the offering.

Illustrations: See images of the curtain, the screen, the altar, and the altar vessels, p. 524.

27 *Sixth aliya* **¹You shall make the altar,** where most offerings will be brought, **of acacia wood, five cubits' length and five cubits' width; the altar shall be square. And three cubits shall be its height. ²You shall make its horns,** which were square protrusions, **on its four corners. Its horns shall be from it,** the altar, rather than from separate material joined to the altar. **And you shall plate it,** the entire altar, **with bronze. ³You shall make its pots**

to clear its ashes, the soot and waste left from the offerings, **and its shovels,** for sweeping away the ashes, **and its basins,** for collecting the blood of offerings and sprinkling it upon the altar; **and its** large **forks,** for handling pieces of meat upon the altar and turning them over; **and its pans,** for raking the coals and moving them around. **All its vessels you shall make of bronze.** [4]**You shall make for it a grate, a work of bronze mesh. And you shall make on the mesh four bronze rings on its,** the altar's, **four corners.** [5]**You shall place it,** this grate, **under the surrounding ledge of the altar from below. And the mesh shall be up to the middle** of the height of the altar. [6]**You shall make staves for the altar, staves of acacia wood, and you shall plate them with bronze.** [7]**Its staves shall be inserted into the rings** which are on the grate, **and the staves shall be on the two sides of the altar when carrying it** from place to place. [8]**You shall make it,** the altar, **hollow,** forming a framework **out of planks,** with no bottom part closing it. **As He showed you on the mountain, so shall they,** the children of Israel, **make it.**

The Tabernacle Courtyard

The courtyard outside the Tent of Meeting is delimited by a fence constructed of hangings draped on bronze pillars. These hangings are woven from linen threads spun into perforated curtains, which are then attached by silver hooks to silver bands around the pillars.

[9]**You shall make the courtyard of the Tabernacle: On the south side there shall be hangings,** perforated curtains, **for the courtyard.** The hangings shall be woven **of twined linen** threads, and shall be **one hundred cubits long for the one side.** [10]**Its pillars** for supporting the hangings demarcating the courtyard **shall be twenty** in number. **And their sockets** for holding them shall be **twenty** in number and made **of bronze. But the hooks of the pillars,** for attaching the hangings to the pillars, **and their bands, shall** all **be of silver.** [11]**Likewise, on the north side, in length, there shall be hangings one hundred cubits long, their pillars twenty** in number **and their sockets twenty** in number, **of bronze. The hooks of the pillars and their bands shall be of silver.** [12]**The width of the courtyard on the west side shall be** enclosed by **hangings of fifty cubits, their pillars ten** in number **and their sockets ten** in number.

[13]**The width of the courtyard on the east side shall** also **be fifty cubits.** [14]**Fifteen cubits of hangings** shall be allocated **for the** one **side of the entrance, their pillars three** in number **and their sockets three** in number, [15]**and on the second side of the entrance** shall also be **fifteen** cubits'

length of **hangings, their pillars three** in number **and their sockets three** in number. ¹⁶In the middle, **for the gate of the courtyard,** there shall be **a screen of twenty cubits,** which will be a curtain made **of sky-blue, purple, and scarlet wool, and twined linen, the work of an embroiderer. Their pillars** for holding the screen shall be **four** in number, **and their sockets** shall be **four** in number. ¹⁷**All the pillars of the courtyard all around shall be banded with silver. Their hooks shall be of silver, and their sockets** shall be **of bronze.** ¹⁸**The length of the courtyard shall be one hundred cubits, and the width shall be fifty on each side,** a rectangle. **And the height** of the hangings of the courtyard **shall be five cubits,** and they shall be **of twined linen, and their sockets** shall be **of bronze.** ¹⁹**All the vessels of the Tabernacle, for all its craftsmanship,** all the instruments required for its assembly, **and all its pegs, and all the pegs of the courtyard, shall be** made of **bronze.**

Illustrations: For a bird's-eye view of the Tabernacle courtyard, see p. 525.

Maftir

Parashat Tetzaveh

Following the commands related to the building of the Tabernacle and its vessels in the previous *parasha*, this *parasha* covers the instructions for the consecration of the Tabernacle and the service there. God tells Moses how to prepare the priestly vestments and how to conduct the seven-day investiture ceremony. During that week, Moses is to sanctify the Tabernacle by sacrificing offerings and performing other rites. He is also to consecrate the priests by immersing them, robing them, and anointing them. The daily service in the Tabernacle will include the kindling of the eternal flame in the candelabrum and the sacrifice of the daily offerings, commands that are given to the children of Israel as well as the priests.

The Eternal Flame
The children of Israel are commanded to provide choice olive oil for the candelabrum in the Tabernacle. The priests will forever more perform the rite of kindling the lamps of the candelabrum, beginning now with Aaron and his sons.

²⁰**You, Moses, shall command the children of Israel, and they shall take for you pure, virgin olive oil.** This oil shall be **for the light, to kindle a lamp continually.** ²¹**In the Tent of Meeting, outside the curtain which is before the** Ark of the **Testimony, Aaron and his sons shall arrange it,** to burn **from evening to morning before the Lord. It is an eternal statute for** all **their generations,** that the priests will receive the oil **from the children of Israel,** who are commanded to provide it.

The Priestly Vestments
Aaron and his sons are to be robed in their priestly vestments as part of their investiture ceremony. Afterward, they will wear them whenever they serve in the Tabernacle. These are ornate, unique garments that are to be fashioned according to precise instructions.

28 ¹**And you, have Aaron your brother approach you, and his sons with him, from among the children of Israel, to serve as priests to Me: Aaron,** and **Nadav and Avihu, Elazar and Itamar, Aaron's sons.** ²**You shall make holy vestments** to be worn while performing the sacred service **for Aaron your brother, for glory and for splendor.** ³**You shall speak**

to all the wisehearted in these crafts, **whom I have filled with a spirit of wisdom, and they shall make Aaron's vestments to sanctify him,** to invest him **to serve as a priest to Me. ⁴These are the vestments that they shall make: a breast piece,** a gem-studded ornament; **and an ephod,** an apron-like cloak; **and a robe; and a quilted tunic; a mitre; and a sash. And they shall make holy vestments for Aaron your brother and for his sons to serve as priests to Me. ⁵They,** the craftsmen, **shall take the gold and the sky-blue and purple and scarlet wool and the linen,** to fashion the priestly vestments.

📖 **Further reading:** For more on why Aaron and his descendants were selected for the priesthood, see *A Concise Guide to the Sages*, p. 117.

The Ephod

The ephod is one of the vestments unique to the High Priest of every generation, starting with Aaron. The craftsmen are to engrave the names of the tribes of Israel upon two precious stones and attach the stones to the ephod.

⁶They shall make the cloth of the **ephod of gold, sky-blue, purple, and scarlet wool, and twined linen, artfully crafted. ⁷It shall have two shoulder pieces attached to its two ends, and it will be attached.** That is, they must attach the shoulder pieces to the ephod. **⁸The belt of his ephod, which is on it, shall be of similar craftsmanship; it shall be from it.** The belt is to be woven as an inseparable part of the apron, and from the same materials: **gold, sky-blue, purple, and scarlet wool, and twined linen.**

⁹You shall take two onyx stones, and engrave on them the names of the twelve tribes **of the children of Israel. ¹⁰Six of their names shall be** engraved **on the one stone, and** engrave **the names of the six that remain on the second stone, according to** the order of **their birth. ¹¹The** engraving shall be done with **the craftsmanship of an engraver in stone,** like **the engravings of a signet,** a delicate and exact procedure. **You shall engrave the two stones with the names of the children of Israel; you shall make them surrounded with settings of gold. ¹²You shall place the two stones on the shoulder pieces of the ephod; they are stones of remembrance for the children of Israel. Aaron shall carry their names before the Lord on his two shoulders as a remembrance.**

Second aliya **¹³You shall make settings of gold, ¹⁴and two chains of pure gold: You shall make them at the edges** of the settings; **they shall be braided**

craftsmanship, rather than clipped. And **you shall set the braided chains in the settings.**

The Breast Piece

Like the ephod, the breast piece is a vestment unique to the High Priest. It is worn attached to the ephod and has twelve different precious stones mounted on it, arranged in three columns. The name of a different tribe is engraved on each gem.

[15]**You shall make a breast piece,** which will be utilized in the administration **of judgment.** It shall be **artfully crafted; you shall make it like the craftsmanship of the ephod;** from **gold, sky-blue, purple, and scarlet wool, and twined linen you shall make it.** [16]**It shall be square,** made from a rectangular cloth that has been **folded** over. **Its length** shall be **a span** [*zeret*]**, and its width a span,** the distance from the tip of one's little finger [*zeret*] and the tip of one's thumb, approximately 25 cm. [17]**You shall set in it,** the breast piece, **a mounting of stone, four rows of stone. A row of a ruby, a peridot, and an emerald;** this shall be **the first row.** [18]**And the second row: a turquoise, a sapphire, and a clear quartz.** [19]**And the third row: a jacinth, an agate, and an amethyst.** [20]**And the fourth row: a beryl, and an onyx, and a chalcedony; they shall be set in gold in their mountings,** each according to its size. [21]**The stones shall correspond to the names** of the tribes **of the children of Israel: Twelve, according to their names,** engraved like the **engravings of a signet, each according to its name, for the twelve tribes.**

Illustrations: See image of the High Priest's vestments, p. 525.

[22]**You shall fix bordering chains of braided craftsmanship on** the edges of **the breast piece, of pure gold.** [23]**You shall fix two rings of gold upon the breast piece, and you shall put the two rings on the two ends of the breast piece,** the two upper corners. [24]**You shall put the two braids of gold on the two rings at the ends of the breast piece.** [25]**The** other **two ends of the two braids you shall put on the two** gold **settings** of the ephod, **and you shall place them,** the settings, **on the shoulder pieces of the ephod, on its front** side, near the neck. [26]**You shall make two** additional **rings of gold, and you shall place them on the two ends of the breast piece, on its edge that is toward the ephod on the inner side** of the folded breast piece, which faces the ephod.

Exodus

²⁷You shall make two additional rings of gold, and you shall put them on the two shoulder pieces of the ephod, at the bottom end of the shoulder pieces, on its front side, adjacent to its seam, that is, near where the shoulder pieces are sewn to the ephod, above the belt of the ephod. ²⁸They shall lace the breast piece, from its rings to the rings of the ephod, with a thread of sky-blue wool, to be on the belt of the ephod; and the breast piece shall not be detached from upon the ephod. ²⁹Aaron shall bear the names of the children of Israel on the breast piece of judgment upon his heart upon his entry into the Sanctuary, as a constant remembrance before the Lord. ³⁰You shall place the Urim and the Tumim, bearing the Tetragrammaton, in the pouch between the folds of the breast piece of judgment. And they shall be upon Aaron's heart upon his entry before the Lord, and Aaron shall constantly bear the judgment, meaning the ways and practices, of the children of Israel on his heart, inside the breast piece, before the Lord.

The Robe

The robe, another vestment unique to the High Priest, is to be worn under the ephod. The craftsmen are to make it from sky-blue wool and trim the hem with decorations shaped like pomegranates and bells.

Third aliya ³¹You shall make the robe of the ephod, to be worn under the ephod, entirely of sky-blue wool. ³²The opening for his, the High Priest's, head shall be within it, in its center. There shall be a hem, the craftsmanship of a weaver rather than a tailor, around its opening; like the opening of a coat of mail it shall be for it, so that it, the robe, shall not rip. ³³You shall fix ornaments on its hem in the shape of pomegranates, made of sky-blue, purple, and scarlet wool, all around its hem; there shall be bells of gold among them, all around: ³⁴A golden bell and then a pomegranate, a golden bell and then a pomegranate, on the hem of the robe, all around. ³⁵It, the robe, shall be on Aaron when he comes to serve, and its sound shall be heard upon his entry into the Sanctuary before the Lord and upon his emergence, and he will not die, meaning that he must wear these garments.

The Diadem, Mitre, Tunic, and Sash

The diadem is a golden crown-like ornament with the words "Holy to the Lord" engraved upon it. The High Priest is to wear it over the mitre, on his forehead.

³⁶**You shall make a diadem of pure gold,** also called "the crown of sanctity" (29:6), **and you shall engrave upon it the engravings of a signet,** in decorative and elegant writing, the phrase **Holy to the Lord.** ³⁷**You shall place on it a thread of sky blue,** in order to tie the diadem, **and it shall be upon the mitre; it shall be toward the forefront of the mitre.** ³⁸**It shall be on Aaron's forehead, and Aaron shall bear,** atone for, by means of the diadem, **the iniquity of the sacraments,** any ritually impure sacred gifts brought into the Sanctuary, **that the children of Israel shall consecrate, for all their sacraments. It shall be on his forehead always, for propitiation for them,** the Israelites, **before the Lord.** ³⁹**You shall quilt the linen tunic,** which is worn against the body and woven with quilted patterns. **And you shall make a mitre of linen,** a long piece of linen cloth to be wrapped around the head. **And you shall make a sash, the craftsmanship of an embroiderer.**

Exodus

Vestments for the Ordinary Priests

The vestments of the ordinary priests are fewer and simpler than those of the High Priest, but will nevertheless distinguish the priests from the rest of the people. The four vestments correspond to four of the eight vestments worn by the High Priest. Like the High Priest, they wear tunics, sashes, and trousers. Instead of a mitre, they wear simpler headdresses. These garments will be worn by all priests when they serve in the Temple in future generations.

⁴⁰**You shall make tunics for the sons of Aaron,** the other priests, **and you shall make for them sashes, and** tall, brimless **headdresses you shall make for them, for glory and for splendor.** ⁴¹**You shall dress them** with these garments, **Aaron your brother and his sons with him; you shall anoint them** with the anointing oil, **and you shall invest them, and you shall sanctify them, and they shall serve as priests for Me.** ⁴²**Make them linen trousers,** which will serve as an undergarment **to cover the flesh of their nakedness. They shall be** worn **from waist to thighs.** ⁴³**They,** all the priestly vestments, **shall be on Aaron and on his sons, upon their entry into the Tent of Meeting, or upon their approach to the altar to serve in sanctity, that they will not bear iniquity,** perform transgression, **and die. It is an eternal statute for him and for his descendants after him** to don these garments while serving in the Sanctuary.

Illustrations: For images of the High Priest's diadem and the hem of his robe, as well as the vestments of the ordinary priests, see p. 525.

The Seven Days of Investiture

In the seven-day investiture ceremony, Moses will dedicate the Tabernacle through sacrificing special offerings, and will inaugurate the priests through robing them, immersing them, and anointing them. To complete the ceremony, he will perform initiatory rites with the blood of the offerings. The details of this ceremony are specific to the dedication of the Tabernacle, and they will not be repeated in the regular service of the Tabernacle or the Temple.

29 **¹This is the thing that you shall do to them,** Aaron and his sons, **to sanc-** *Fourth aliya* **tify them to serve as priests to Me: Take one young bull** in its third year **and two** adult **rams,** all of which must be **unblemished. ²And** you shall bring **unleavened bread** cakes fried in oil; **and** baked **unleavened loaves** with a particular shape, in which the flour was **mixed with oil; and unleavened wafers anointed,** smeared, **with oil. You shall make them of choice wheat flour. ³You shall place them,** these meal offerings, **in one basket, and bring them near,** to the Tabernacle courtyard, **in the basket, with the bull and the two rams.**

⁴You shall have Aaron and his sons approach the entrance of the Tent of Meeting, and you shall wash them in water, immerse them. **⁵You shall take the vestments and dress Aaron in the tunic, and** above it **the robe of the ephod, and the ephod,** tied around the robe, **and the breast piece, and gird him with the belt of the ephod. ⁶You shall place the mitre on his head, and you shall place the crown of sanctity,** the diadem, **on the mitre. ⁷**Before placing the mitre on his head, **you shall take the anointing oil, and you shall pour it** directly **on his head and anoint him,** smear it on.

The Bull for the Sin Offering

A bull is brought as a sin offering during the days of investiture. This offering, which is brought to atone for transgressions, may not be eaten.

⁸And his sons you shall bring near and you shall dress them in tunics. ⁹You shall gird them with a sash, Aaron and his sons. Aaron was not yet girded with a sash, but with the belt of the ephod (verse 5). **And you shall wrap the headdresses on them,** Aaron's sons, **and the priesthood shall be for them as an eternal statute,** an obligation for all generations. **And, in this manner, you shall invest Aaron and his sons** for the priesthood. **¹⁰You shall bring the bull before the Tent of Meeting, and Aaron and his sons shall place their hands** forcefully **on the head of the bull. ¹¹You shall slaughter the bull before the Lord, at the entrance of the Tent of**

Meeting. ¹²**You shall take from the blood of the bull, and you shall place it on the horns,** the corners, **of the altar with your finger, and you shall pour all the** remaining **blood at the base of the altar.** ¹³**You shall take all the fat that covers the innards,** the inner organs of the bull, **and the diaphragm above the liver, and the two kidneys and the fat that is on them, and burn them on the altar.** ¹⁴**You shall burn the flesh of the bull, its hide, and its dung** found in the intestines, **in fire outside the camp; it is a sin offering** for atonement, and its flesh is not to be consumed.

The Ram for the Burnt Offering

One of the two rams is to be brought as a burnt offering and entirely consumed by fire. No one may partake of its flesh.

¹⁵**You shall take the one ram, and Aaron and his sons shall place their hands on the head of the ram.** ¹⁶**You shall slaughter the ram and you shall take its blood and you shall cast it around the altar,** on the horns of the altar, which are in the corners. ¹⁷**You shall cut the ram into its pieces, and you shall wash its innards,** its inner organs, **and its legs, and you shall put them with its pieces and with its head,** which was previously severed from the body. ¹⁸**You shall burn the entire ram on the altar; it is a burnt offering to the Lord, a pleasing aroma, a fire offering to the Lord.**

Illustrations: See drawing of the parts of a ram that are sacrificed upon the altar, p. 527.

The Ram of Investiture

As the second ram is an offering that is specific to the dedication ceremony, it is called the ram of investiture. Its sacrifice involves special rites tied to the investiture of the priests. Some parts of the ram are brought to the altar, whereas others are given to Aaron and his sons to eat.

Fifth
aliya ¹⁹**You shall take the second ram, and Aaron and his sons shall place their hands on the head of the ram.** ²⁰**You shall slaughter the ram** and take up **its blood** in a vessel, **and you shall place it,** some of the blood, **on the tip of Aaron's right ear, and on the tip of the right ear of his sons, and on the thumb of their right hand, and on the big toe of their right foot, and you shall** then **cast the** remaining **blood around the altar,** on the horns of the altar, which are in the corners. ²¹**You shall take from the blood that is on the altar, and from the anointing oil, and you shall sprinkle it on Aaron and on his vestments, and on his sons and on the**

vestments of his sons with him; and he and his vestments shall be sanctified, and his sons and the vestments of his sons with him.

²²You shall take the fat from the ram, and the fat tail, and the fat that covers the innards, and the diaphragm above the liver, and the two kidneys and the fat that is on them, and the right haunch, as it is a ram of investiture, sacrificed in honor of the appointment of the priests. ²³And take one cake of unleavened bread, and one loaf of oil bread, and one wafer, from the aforementioned basket of unleavened bread that is before the Lord. ²⁴You shall place everything on the palms of Aaron and on the palms of his sons, and you shall wave them, that is, lift up their full hands, as a wave offering before the Lord. ²⁵You shall take them, the parts of the ram and the unleavened breads, from their hands, and you shall burn them on the altar with, in addition to, the burnt offering, the first ram, for a pleasing aroma before the Lord; it is a fire offering to the Lord.

²⁶You shall take the breast from the ram of investiture that is Aaron's, and you shall wave it, lift it, as a wave offering before the Lord, and it, the breast, shall be a portion for you, Moses, to eat. This ram is a type of peace offering. ²⁷You shall sanctify, set aside, the breast of the wave offering and the gift haunch that was waved and that was lifted, from the ram of investiture, from that of Aaron and from that of his sons. ²⁸From this point forward, it, the breast and haunch, shall be for Aaron and for his sons as an eternal portion from the children of Israel. For it is a gift, and as it shall be a gift from the children of Israel set aside from their peace offerings and given to the priests for consumption, it is considered their gift to the Lord.

²⁹The holy vestments of Aaron shall be for his sons and later descendants after him, for prominence through them, and with them to invest them. That is, one becomes High Priest by donning the priestly vestments. ³⁰For seven days the priest from among his, Aaron's, sons who will be serving in his stead, after the High Priest dies or retires, who will come into the Tent of Meeting to serve in the Sanctuary, shall first don them, the vestments of the High Priest.

³¹You shall take the ram of investiture and you shall cook its meat in a holy place, in the courtyard of the Tent of Meeting. ³²Aaron and his sons shall eat the meat of the ram, and also the bread that is left in the basket at the entrance of the Tent of Meeting. ³³They who have received

atonement through them, these portions, shall eat them, to invest them for their office and to sanctify them for the priesthood. But a stranger shall not eat from these portions, because they are sacred. ³⁴If there remains anything from the meat of the investiture, or from the bread for the priests, and it is left over until the morning, then you shall burn the leftover in the fire; it shall not be eaten, as it is sacred. ³⁵You shall do so to Aaron and to his sons, in accordance with everything that I commanded you; seven days you shall invest them with these offerings. ³⁶You shall sacrifice a bull for a sin offering each day of investiture, for atonement; and you shall cleanse and purify the altar by your act of atoning for it, by placing the blood of the bull upon it; and you shall anoint it in order to sanctify it. ³⁷Seven days you shall atone for the altar and sanctify it; therefore, from then on, the altar shall be a sacred sacrament. Anything that is fit to be sacrificed as an offering and which touches the altar by ascending upon it shall be holy, and must be burned there.

The Daily Offering

Alongside the offerings that are specific to the investiture ceremony, Moses is commanded to sacrifice two daily offerings. From this point forward, they will be part of the daily routine in the Tabernacle and the Temple.

ixth
aliya
³⁸This is that which you shall offer upon the altar every day: Two lambs in the first year of their lives, for each day continually. ³⁹The one lamb you shall offer in the morning, and the second lamb you shall offer in the afternoon, ⁴⁰and each time bring a meal offering: One-tenth of an ephah, slightly larger than 2L, of choice flour mixed with one-fourth of a hin of virgin olive oil (see 27:20), approximately 1L. And you shall also bring a libation of one-fourth of a hin of wine for the one lamb. ⁴¹The second lamb you shall sacrifice in the afternoon, with a meal offering like the meal offering of the morning, and with a libation like its libation, for a pleasing aroma, to be accepted, a fire offering to the Lord. ⁴²It is a continual burnt offering for your generations, which you shall sacrifice at the entrance of the Tent of Meeting before the Lord, where I will meet with you to speak to you there.

⁴³I will meet there with the children of Israel, and it, the Tent, shall be sanctified with My glory. ⁴⁴I will sanctify the Tent of Meeting and the altar, and Aaron and his sons I will sanctify, to serve as priests to Me. ⁴⁵I will dwell among the children of Israel, and I will be their God. ⁴⁶They

Exodus

will know that I am the Lord their God who brought them out from the land of Egypt to dwell among them; I am the Lord their God.

The Altar of Incense

The Torah returns to the commands to fashion the vessels of the Tabernacle. Here Moses is instructed to build the incense altar, which will stand in the Sanctuary of the Tent of Meeting, with the candelabrum and the table.

30 ¹**You shall make** a separate **altar for burning incense; of acacia wood you**
Seventh **shall make it.** ²**A cubit shall be its length and a cubit its width; it,** the
aliya altar, **shall be square, and two cubits shall be its height. From it,** from the same substance as the altar, **shall be its horns,** in each corner of the top. ³**You shall plate it with pure gold, its top and its sides all around and its horns, and you shall make for it** an ornamental **rim of gold all around.** ⁴**You shall make two gold rings for it under its rim; on its two corners you shall make them, on its two sides,** at opposing corners; **and they,** the rings, **shall be as housings for staves with which to carry it,** the altar. ⁵**You shall make the staves of acacia wood, and you shall plate them with gold.**

Illustrations: See image of the incense altar, p. 526.

⁶**You shall put it before,** outside, **the curtain that is upon the Ark of the Testimony** at the entrance to the Holy of Holies, **before,** opposite, **the ark cover that is over** the Ark of **the Testimony, where I will meet with you.** ⁷**Aaron shall burn on it incense of spices; every morning when he**
Maftir **cleans the lamps** that burned during the night **he shall burn it.** ⁸**Likewise, when Aaron kindles the lamps in the afternoon, he shall burn it, daily incense before the Lord for your generations.**

⁹**You shall not offer up on it strange incense,** incense not commanded by the Torah, **or** an animal offering such as **a burnt offering, or a meal offering** of produce, **and you shall not pour a libation** of wine **on it.** ¹⁰Notwithstanding these restrictions, **Aaron shall** ritually **atone on its horns, with** some of **the blood of the sin offering of atonement, once in the year,** on Yom Kippur; **once in the year he shall atone for it for your generations; it is a sacred sacrament to the Lord.** Placing some of the blood of the sin offering of atonement on the horns of the altar purifies it from the contamination it symbolically acquires from the sins of Israel.

Further reading: The word *mizbe'ah*, meaning altar, alludes to a great blessing. See *A Concise Guide to the Sages*, p. 119.

Parashat Ki Tisa

The *parasha* opens with the commands to give half a shekel and to prepare the oil of anointment and the incense. It also briefly addresses other matters related to the Tabernacle, its vessels, and its service. However, most of the *parasha* recounts the incident of the Golden Calf and the severe consequences of this grave transgression, which the people committed shortly after they received the Torah.

The Half Shekel

Every man must donate a half shekel of silver to the Tabernacle as a ransom that will prevent a plague from afflicting the people during the national census.

¹¹The Lord spoke to Moses, saying: ¹²When you take a census of the children of Israel, according to their count of adult men, then each man shall give a ransom payment for himself to the Lord upon their counting, and there will not be a plague against them upon their counting. ¹³This is what everyone who passes among the counted, all those who are counted, shall give: One half shekel in the sacred shekel, the unit of monetary weight used in sacred contexts. Twenty gera is equivalent to the shekel; one half shekel shall be given as a gift to the Lord. ¹⁴Everyone who passes among the counted, from twenty years old and above, shall give the gift of the Lord. ¹⁵The wealthy shall not add and the poor shall not subtract from the half shekel, to give the gift of the Lord, to atone for your souls. ¹⁶You shall take the silver of the atonement from the children of Israel, and you shall allocate it for the service of the Tent of Meeting, for the needs of the Tabernacle. And it, the silver, shall be for the children of Israel as a remembrance before the Lord, to prompt Him to remember you and to atone for your souls.

The Laver, Oil of Anointment, and Incense Spices

¹⁷The Lord spoke to Moses, saying: ¹⁸You shall make a laver of bronze, and its base also of bronze, for washing; you shall place it in the Tabernacle courtyard between the Tent of Meeting and the altar, and

you shall put water there, in the laver. ¹⁹Aaron and his sons shall wash their hands and their feet from it. ²⁰Before their entry into the Tent of Meeting they shall wash with water, and they will not die, or before their approach to the altar to serve, to burn a fire offering to the Lord; ²¹they shall wash their hands and their feet and not die, and it shall be for them an eternal statute, for him and for his descendants for their generations, applying forever.

Illustrations: See image of the bronze laver, p. 526.

²²The Lord spoke to Moses, saying: ²³You, Moses, shall take for yourself, personally take, choice spices: Pure, unadulterated myrrh weighing five hundred shekels; and fragrant cinnamon, where each half of it, weighed separately, weighs two hundred and fifty shekels; and fragrant cane, a type of aromatic grain, weighing two hundred and fifty shekels; ²⁴and cassia [kidda] weighing five hundred shekels in the sacred shekel; and olive oil measuring one hin, a liquid measure. ²⁵You shall make it oil of sacred anointment, for sanctification through anointment. It shall be a blended mixture using the craftsmanship of a blender, someone who prepares mixtures of spices; oil of sacred anointment it shall be. ²⁶You shall anoint with it the Tent of Meeting, the Ark of the Testimony, ²⁷the table and all its vessels, the candelabrum and its vessels, the altar of incense, ²⁸the altar of the burnt offering and all its vessels, and the laver and its base. ²⁹You shall sanctify them, all of these vessels, and they shall be a sacred sacrament; anything or anyone that touches them shall first become sanctified; one must purify himself before touching these vessels. ³⁰You shall also anoint Aaron and his sons with the anointing oil, and you shall sanctify them to serve as priests to Me. ³¹You shall speak to the children of Israel, saying: This shall be oil of sacred anointment for Me, for your generations. ³²It shall not be poured on a person's flesh unless he is a priest, and you shall not make any substance like it, according to its formula, for any other purpose; it is sacred, and it shall be sacred to you. ³³Anyone who shall blend any oil like it for use outside the Temple, or who shall put of it on a non-priest, shall be excised from his people.

³⁴The Lord said to Moses: Take for yourself spices: stacte, oil produced from tree resin; onycha, perhaps cloves; and galbanum, a plant with a strong odor; other, unspecified spices; and pure frankincense; each part

shall be equal. ³⁵You shall make incense of it, with the aforementioned components blended, the craftsmanship of a blender. It must be well mixed, pure, and sacred. ³⁶You shall grind some of it finely to powder, and you shall put some of it before the Ark of the Testimony in the Tent of Meeting, where I shall meet with you, and you shall burn it there. It shall be a sacred sacrament for you. ³⁷The incense that you shall make, you shall not make for yourselves according to its formula; it shall be sacred for you to the Lord. ³⁸Anyone who makes incense like it, even for it to serve as perfume and not for burning, shall be excised from his people.

31 ¹The Lord spoke to Moses, saying: ²See, I have called by name, appointed, **Betzalel, son of Uri, son of Hur, of the tribe of Judah.** ³I have filled him with a divine spirit; with wisdom, with understanding, with knowledge, and with familiarity with all craftsmanship. ⁴He is able to implement complex designs and to work with gold, with silver, and with bronze, as an expert in metalwork. ⁵He is also skilled in the cutting of precious stone for setting, and in the carving of wood; he has the ability to perform all types of craftsmanship. ⁶And I, behold, have appointed with him, as his deputy, **Oholiav son of Ahisamakh of the tribe of Dan. And in the hearts of all the wise-hearted** men, the craftsmen, **I have put** additional **wisdom, and they shall make everything that I have commanded you:** ⁷The Tent of Meeting, and the Ark for the Testimony, and the Ark cover that is upon it, and all the other vessels of the Tent; ⁸the table and its vessels, the pure candelabrum and all its vessels, the altar of incense, ⁹the altar of the burnt offering and all its vessels, the laver and its base, ¹⁰and the woven fabrics used to cover the service vessels when the people traveled. And they shall make the sacred vestments for Aaron the priest, and the vestments of his sons, to serve as priests. ¹¹And they shall prepare the anointing oil and the incense of the spices for the Sanctuary; in accordance with everything that I commanded you, they shall do.

¹²The Lord spoke to Moses, saying: ¹³And you, speak to the children of Israel, saying: However, you shall observe My Sabbaths and refrain from building the Tabernacle on that day, as it is a sign between Me and you for your generations, to lead you to know through observing the Sabbath that I am the Lord, your Sanctifier. ¹⁴You shall observe the Sabbath, as it is sacred for you; its desecrators shall be put to death. For anyone who performs labor on it, that person shall be excised from

Exodus

among his people. ¹⁵**Six days labor shall be performed, and on the seventh day shall be a sabbatical rest, sacred to the Lord.** Anyone who performs creative **labor on the Sabbath day shall be put to death.** ¹⁶**The children of Israel shall keep the Sabbath, to observe the Sabbath for their generations, an eternal covenant.** ¹⁷**Between Me and the children of Israel, it is a sign forever. For in six days the Lord made the heaven and the earth, and on the seventh day He rested** from His creative labor **and was invigorated.**

> **Further reading:** For more on Shabbat and its significance, see *A Concise Guide to the Sages*, p. 275; *A Concise Guide to Mahshava*, p. 33; *A Concise Guide to Halakha*, p. 379.

Second aliya ¹⁸**At the conclusion of His speaking with him on Mount Sinai, He gave to Moses the two Tablets of Testimony** engraved with the Ten Commandments. They were **tablets of stone,** created by God and **written with the finger of God.**

The Sin of the Golden Calf

The sin of the Golden Calf is the nation's most severe and well-known transgression. The Torah details the elements of this spiritual collapse, and its aftermath: Aaron's fashioning of the calf, the nation's worship of it, God and Moses' wrath, and the shattering of the Tablets of Testimony.

32 ¹**The people saw that Moses tarried in descending from the mountain, and the people assembled around Aaron and said to him: Rise, make us a god that will go before us** and lead us, **because this man, Moses, who brought us up from the land of Egypt, we do not know what became of him.** ²**Aaron said to them: Remove the gold rings that are in the ears of your wives, your sons, and your daughters, and bring them to me.** ³**All the people removed the gold rings that were in their ears, and they brought them to Aaron.** ⁴**He took them from their hands, and, fashioning it with a graving tool** used by goldsmiths, **he made a cast figure of a calf. They said: This is your god, Israel, who brought you up from the land of Egypt.** ⁵**Aaron saw** the people's attitude toward the calf, **and he built an altar before it; and Aaron proclaimed and said: A festival for the Lord tomorrow.** ⁶**They arose early the next day, and they offered up burnt offerings,** which are entirely consumed upon the altar, **and brought peace offerings,** most parts of which are eaten by the one who brings the offering; **and the people sat to eat and drink, and they** also **rose to frolic.**

📖 **Further reading:** For more on the circumstances that led to the sin of the Golden Calf, and for details of the episode that are not recounted in the Torah, see *A Concise Guide to the Sages*, from p. 120.

⁷**The Lord spoke to Moses: Go, descend** from the mountaintop, **for your people whom you brought up from the land of Egypt have acted corruptly.** ⁸**They quickly deviated from the path that I have commanded them; they made for themselves a cast figure of a calf, they prostrated themselves before it and slaughtered** animals **to it, and said: This is your god, Israel, who brought you up from the land of Egypt.** ⁹**The Lord said to Moses: I have seen this people, and behold, it is a stiff-necked,** stubborn, **people.** ¹⁰**Now allow Me, and My wrath will be enflamed against them, and I will destroy them; and I will make you** and your own descendants **into a great nation.** ¹¹**Moses implored the Lord his God, and he said: Lord, why shall Your wrath be enflamed against Your people that You took out of the land of Egypt with great power,** glory, **and with a mighty hand,** determination? ¹²**Why shall the Egyptians say,** why give them cause to think, **saying: He took them out for evil, to kill them in the mountains and to destroy them from upon the face of the earth? Relent from Your enflamed wrath and reconsider with regard to the evil for Your people.** ¹³**Remember Abraham, Isaac, and Israel, Your servants, to whom You swore by** Your own Name, **Yourself. And** You **spoke to them** and promised: **I will multiply your offspring like the stars of the heavens, and this entire land that I said I will give to your descendants, they shall inherit it** and settle there **forever.** ¹⁴**The Lord reconsidered the evil that He had spoken of doing to His people.**

¹⁵**Moses turned and descended from the mountaintop, and the two Tablets of Testimony were in his hand, the tablets inscribed on both their sides; from this side and from that side they were inscribed.** ¹⁶**The tablets were the work of God, and the writing was the writing of God, engraved** by Him **on the tablets.** ¹⁷**Joshua heard the sound of the people in its uproar, and he said to Moses: There is the sound of battle in the camp.** ¹⁸**He,** Moses, **said** to Joshua: **There is not the sound of a cry of valor,** of triumph in battle, **and there is not the sound of a cry of weakness,** the wail of the defeated. It is merely **the** indistinct **sound of a cry I hear.** ¹⁹**It was when he approached the camp; he saw the calf and** the **dancing** around it, **and Moses' wrath was enflamed, and he cast the tablets from his hands, and he shattered them at the foot of the mountain.** ²⁰**He took the calf that they** had **made, and he burned it in the fire and ground it**

Exodus

into powder. And he scattered it, the powder, on the surface of the water and gave the solution to the children of Israel to drink. [21]Moses said to Aaron: What did this people do to you that you brought great sin upon them? [22]Aaron said: Let the wrath of my lord not be enflamed; you have known the character of the people, that it is in an evil state. [23]They said to me: Make us a god that will go before us, because this man, Moses, who brought us up from the land of Egypt, we do not know what became of him. [24]I said to them: Who has any gold? If you do, remove it. They gave it to me, and I cast it into the fire, and without any further intervention on my part, this calf emerged.

[25]Moses saw the people, that it was unsettled. For Aaron had exposed them to ignominy on the part of those who would rise against them. [26]Moses stood at the gate of the camp and said: Whoever is for the Lord, still faithful to Him, come to me. And all the sons of Levi gathered to him. [27]He said to them: So said the Lord, God of Israel: Each man, place his sword upon his thigh, in his belt. Pass to and fro from gate to gate in the camp, and slay anyone who worships the calf; each may need to kill his brother, and each his neighbor, and each his relative. [28]The sons of Levi acted in accordance with the word of Moses, and some three thousand men fell from the people on that day. [29]Moses said: Dedicate yourselves today to the Lord, as each man of you is one who did his duty, even against his son and against his brother, disregarding considerations of sentiment. And so He may bestow upon you a blessing this day; you will receive a blessing for your deeds.

Repercussions of the Sin of the Golden Calf

Moses again implores God to forgive the people and not destroy them entirely. God agrees and puts only the worst transgressors to death by afflicting them with a plague. As an additional consequence, He announces that instead of leading the people to Canaan Himself, He will send an angel to do so.

[30]It was on the next day, Moses said to the people: You have sinned a great sin, and now I will again ascend the mountain to the Lord; perhaps I will succeed in pleading on your behalf and will be able to atone for your sin. [31]Moses returned to the Lord, and he said: Please, this people has sinned a great sin, and they made themselves a god of gold. [32]Now, I implore You to forgive them: If You will bear their sin…; Moses does not even suggest to God how He can tolerate this sin, he just insists upon it; and if not, erase me, now, from Your book of life that You have written.

³³The Lord said to Moses: Whoever sinned against Me, I shall erase him alone from My book of life. ³⁴Now go, lead the people to where I have spoken to you, to the land of Canaan. But behold, henceforth My angel will go before you, and I will not. And on the day of My reckoning, when judgment will be meted out, I will reckon their sin of the Golden Calf upon them. ³⁵The Lord afflicted the people with a plague because they made the calf that Aaron had made.

33 ¹The Lord spoke to Moses: Set out and go up from here, you and the people whom you brought up from the land of Egypt, to the land about which I took an oath to Abraham, to Isaac, and to Jacob, saying: I will give it to your descendants. ²I will send an angel before you, and by means of this angel I will expel the Canaanites, the Emorites, the Hitites, the Perizites, the Hivites, and the Yevusites. ³The angel will bring you to a land flowing with milk and honey; I will not go up in your midst Myself since you are a stiff-necked people, lest I destroy you on the way. ⁴The people heard these evil tidings, and they mourned, and no man put on his adornment.

⁵The Lord said to Moses: Say to the children of Israel: You are a stiff-necked people; if for one moment I would go up in your midst, I would destroy you. Now, remove your adornment from yourselves, as you are no longer fit to wear it, and I will know, decide, what I will do to you as you progress from here. ⁶The children of Israel were stripped of their adornment, or removed it themselves. They had received it from Mount Horev, with the giving of the Torah. ⁷Moses would take the tent, his tent, and pitch it outside the camp, far from the camp. And he called it the Tent of Meeting. It was the practice that anyone who sought the Lord and wanted to ask a question would go out to the Tent of Meeting, which was outside the camp. ⁸It would be, upon Moses' going out to the Tent, that all the people would rise, and each would stand at his tent's entrance; they would gaze after Moses until he went into the Tent. ⁹It would be upon Moses' entry into the Tent of Meeting, that the pillar of cloud would descend and stand at the entrance of the Tent; and He, God, would speak with Moses. ¹⁰The entire people would see the pillar of cloud standing at the entrance of the Tent, and the entire people would rise and prostrate themselves, each man at the entrance of his tent. ¹¹The Lord would speak to Moses face-to-face, as a man speaks intimately to his neighbor. And after God spoke to him, he would return to

Exodus

his personal tent in **the camp. But his servant Joshua son of Nun, a lad, would not move from within the Tent** of Meeting.

Third aliya ¹²**Moses said to the Lord: See, You say to me: Take this people up,** lead them, **but You did not inform me whom You will send with me,** how you will send the angel. **And You said** to me, about me: **I know you by name;** I have chosen you for a uniquely close relationship with Me, **and you have also found favor in My eyes.** ¹³**Now, if I have indeed found favor in Your eyes, inform me, please, of Your ways,** allow me greater knowledge of the Divine, **and I will know You** more intimately, **so that I will find** even greater **favor in Your eyes. And see that this nation is Your people;** do not repudiate them. ¹⁴**He,** God, **said:** Instead of an angel, **My presence will go** with you, **and I will give you rest.** ¹⁵**He,** Moses, **said to Him: If Your presence does not go** with us, please **do not bring us up from here.** ¹⁶**How then will it be known that I have found favor in Your eyes, I and Your people? Is it not by Your going with us** in our midst? Furthermore, **we will be distinct, I and Your people, from every people that is on the face of the earth,** as Your chosen nation.

Fourth aliya ¹⁷**The Lord said to Moses: This matter that you have spoken,** requested, **I will do as well, as you have found favor in My eyes, and I have known you by name.** ¹⁸**He,** Moses, **said: Please show me Your glory,** your essence. ¹⁹**He,** God, **said: I Myself will pass** with **all My goodness before you,** and furthermore **I will call with the name of the Lord before you. And I will favor whom I will favor and I will have mercy on whom I will have mercy.** ²⁰**He** further **said:** Nevertheless, **you will not be able to see My face,** as man shall not see Me and still **live.** ²¹**The Lord** therefore **said: Behold, there is a place with Me** where you can safely see a part of My presence. **And you shall stand on the rock.** ²²**It shall be with the passage of My glory** that I will place you, shelter you, **in the crevice of the rock, and I will cover My hand upon you** and protect you **until My passage** has been completed. ²³Then **I will remove My hand, and you will see My back,** the external aspects of My presence. **But My face,** the essence of My being, **will not be seen.**

The Second Set of Tablets

Moses ascends the mountain to receive the second set of Tablets of the Testimony.

34 ¹**The Lord said to Moses: Carve for yourself two tablets of stone like the** *Fifth aliya* **first** set. **And I will write on the tablets the words that were on the first tablets, which you shattered.** ²**Be prepared for the morning; you shall**

ascend in the morning to Mount Sinai, and you shall stand there and wait for Me on top of the mountain. ³No man shall ascend with you, and no man shall be seen on the entire mountain; the flocks and the cattle shall not graze before that mountain. ⁴He carved two tablets of stone like the first tablets; Moses arose early in the morning and ascended to the top of Mount Sinai, as the Lord had commanded him, and he took in his hand the two tablets of stone. ⁵The Lord descended in the cloud and stood with him there, and He called with the name of the Lord. ⁶The Lord passed before him, and God called: The Lord, the Lord, God, merciful and gracious, slow to anger, and abounding in kindness and truth. ⁷He remembers and maintains kindness to the thousands of generations, bearing, tolerating, their iniquity and transgression and sin. And yet He will not immediately and completely exonerate, instead reckoning the iniquity of the fathers upon the children and upon the children's children, upon the third and upon the fourth generation. ⁸Moses hastened and bowed to the ground and prostrated himself.

Cornerstones of the Covenant

Moses again requests that God Himself, and not an angel, go with the people. God assents, but He reiterates the terms of the covenant and warns that the people must fulfill their part.

⁹He, Moses, said: If I have indeed found favor in Your eyes, my Lord, may my Lord please go in our midst; for it is a stiff-necked people; may You in your mercy and graciousness forgive our iniquity and our sin and be our inheritance. ¹⁰He, God, said to Moses: Behold, I am establishing a covenant. When you conquer the land of Canaan, before your entire people I will perform wonders that have not been wrought until now in the entire earth and in all the nations; the entire people, with you in their midst, will see the work of the Lord, that it is awesome what I am doing with you.

Sixth aliya

¹¹Mark for yourself that which I am commanding you today; behold, for My part, I promise you that I am expelling from before you the current inhabitants of the Land of Israel: the Emorites, the Canaanites, the Hitites, the Perizites, the Hivites, and the Yevusites. ¹²And you, for your part, beware, lest you establish a covenant with the inhabitant of the land into which you are entering, to not expel him, lest he be a snare in your midst and corrupt your behavior. ¹³Rather, you shall smash their altars, and shatter their monuments to false gods, and chop down their sacred trees used as part of idolatrous rites. ¹⁴For you shall not prostrate

yourself to another god, as the Lord, His name is Zealous, He is a zealous God. ¹⁵Pay heed **lest you establish a covenant with the inhabitants of the land, and they,** those inhabitants, continue to **stray after their gods and slaughter to their gods. And they will call** to you, **and you will eat from their slaughter.** ¹⁶That will lead to closer relationships: **You will take from their daughters** as brides **for your sons. And their daughters will stray after their gods, and they will cause your sons to stray after their gods.** ¹⁷**You shall not make for yourself gods of cast figures.**

¹⁸**You shall observe the Festival of Unleavened Bread,** Passover. For **seven days you shall eat unleavened bread, as I commanded you, at the appointed time of the month of ripening,** the month of Nisan, **as in the month of ripening you emerged from Egypt.** ¹⁹**Every first issue of the womb,** the firstborn animal, **is Mine; from all your livestock you shall take the males** that are **the first issue of a bull and a sheep.** You shall sacrifice the firstborn male animals as offerings, as you were commanded at the time of the exodus from Egypt. ²⁰**The first issue of a donkey you shall redeem with a lamb,** which will be sacrificed in its place; **and if you do not redeem it, you shall behead it,** as it is forbidden for use. **Every firstborn of your sons you shall redeem** as well. **And they,** people who ascend to the Temple, **shall not appear** there **before Me empty-handed,** but should bring a gift, an offering. ²¹**Six days you shall perform labor, and on the seventh day you shall rest;** even **from plowing and from harvest,** even during these busy periods, **you shall rest.** ²²**You shall hold the Festival of Weeks,** *Shavuot,* **with the** ripening of the **first fruits of the wheat harvest, and** observe **the Festival of the Ingathering of the Crops,** *Sukkot,* **at the turn of the year,** when the new year commences, in the autumn. ²³**Three times in the year,** on Passover, *Shavuot,* and *Sukkot,* **all your males shall appear before the Master, the Lord, God of Israel.** ²⁴**For I will expel nations before you, and I will expand your borders.** Since your borders will expand, it will take a long time for some of you to make the pilgrimage to the Temple. **And** yet you will not need to worry that your land will be stolen during your lengthy absence; **no man will covet your land when you go up to appear before the Lord your God three times in the year.** ²⁵**You shall not slaughter with,** while, **leavened bread** is in your possession, to offer **the blood of My offering;** you may own no leavened bread when your paschal lamb is slaughtered. **And the feast of the Paschal Festival,** the meat of the paschal lamb, **shall not lie until the morning,** but must be eaten on the first night of Passover. ²⁶**You shall bring the choicest** of the

first fruits of your land to the house of the Lord your God. You shall not cook a kid in its mother's milk.

> **Further reading:** For more on the ceremony of bringing the first fruits, see *A Concise Guide to the Sages*, p. 253. For the laws detailing the prohibition against mixing milk and meat, see *A Concise Guide to Halakha*, p. 553.

venth
aliya
²⁷The Lord said to Moses: Write for yourself these matters, as according to these matters I established a covenant with you and with Israel.

Moses' Face Is Radiant

Moses spends another forty days on the mountaintop. When he descends with the second set of tablets, the Israelites see that his face is radiant, and they become frightened. He therefore dons a mask whenever he is not speaking with God.

²⁸He, Moses, was again **there** on the mountaintop **with the Lord forty days and forty nights; he did not eat bread, and he did not drink water. He, God, wrote upon the tablets the words of the covenant, the Ten Commandments. ²⁹It was upon Moses' descent from Mount Sinai; the two Tablets of the Testimony were in the hand of Moses upon his descent from the mountain, and Moses did not know that the skin of his face was radiant upon His speaking with him,** as a result of God speaking to him face-to-face. **³⁰Aaron and all the children of Israel saw Moses, and behold, the skin of his face was radiant; and they feared approaching him. ³¹Moses called to them, and Aaron and all the princes in the congregation returned to him, and Moses spoke to them. ³²Thereafter, all the children of Israel approached** Moses. **And he commanded them**

Maftir **everything that the Lord spoke with him on Mount Sinai. ³³Moses concluded speaking with them, and put a mask on his face. ³⁴Upon the coming of Moses before the Lord to speak with Him, he would remove the mask until his emergence** from God's presence. **He would emerge and speak to the children of Israel that which he would be commanded. ³⁵When** Moses exited the Tent of Meeting, **the children of Israel saw the face of Moses** and saw **that the skin of Moses' face was radiant. And Moses replaced the mask on his face, until his entering to speak with Him** again.

> **Further reading:** Moses our teacher was the Jewish people's greatest prophet. For more on prophecy, see *A Concise Guide to Mahshava*, p. 203.

Exodus

Parashat Vayak'hel

This *parasha* describes the construction of the Tabernacle in great detail. Before the Israelites begin the project, Moses alerts them that the commandments of Shabbat override the building of the Tabernacle. He then requests the people's financial and professional involvement in this awesome task. His appeal is intended to enlist all of Israel, and indeed they respond with enthusiasm, offering more than expected; ultimately Moses is even obliged to tell the people to cease bringing contributions.

The people first prepare the Tabernacle itself, including its boards and sheets. Afterward they fashion the vessels that will be used there, and finally they prepare the materials for the barrier that will enclose the courtyard surrounding the Tent of Meeting.

The Primacy of Shabbat

Notwithstanding the importance of building the Tabernacle, Moses initiates the project by emphasizing to the people that on Shabbat it is prohibited to engage in creative labor. Shabbat overrides even labor performed for the Tabernacle.

35 **¹Moses assembled the entire congregation of the children of Israel and said to them: These are the matters that the Lord commanded to perform them.**

²Six days shall labor be performed, and on the seventh day there shall be a sacrament for you, a day of sabbatical rest, a full rest day on which all labor is prohibited, **to the Lord; anyone who performs any** materially creative **labor on it shall be put to death. ³You shall not kindle fire in all your dwellings on the Sabbath day.**

📖 **Further reading:** For the labors prohibited on Shabbat, see *A Concise Guide to Halakha*, p. 405.

Moses Calls for Donations

Moses asks the Israelites to contribute the human and material resources required for the Tabernacle and the service there. He first specifies all the raw materials that are needed, and then calls for volunteers among those skilled in various crafts. Afterward he details how all the raw materials will be used.

⁴Moses said to the entire congregation of the children of Israel, saying: This is the matter that the Lord commanded, saying: ⁵**Take,** collect, from among you a voluntary **gift to the Lord; anyone who is generous of heart shall bring it. The gift of the Lord,** materials required for the Tabernacle, included the metals **gold, silver, and bronze;** ⁶the textiles **sky-blue** wool, **purple** or reddish wool, **and scarlet wool,** and **linen and** woven **goats' hair;** ⁷**rams' hides dyed red,** taḥash **hides** from this extinct species which had a valuable hide, **and** beams of **acacia wood;** ⁸**oil for the lighting, and spices for the anointing oil and for the incense of the spices;** ⁹**and onyx stones, and stones for setting, for the ephod and for the breast piece,** respectively.

¹⁰**Every wise-hearted man among you shall come and make everything that the Lord commanded:** ¹¹**The** linen and wool sheets of the ceiling of the **Tabernacle, its tent** of goats' hides on top of that layer, **and its covering** of hides as the ceiling's top layer; **its hooks** for connecting the sheets **and its boards, its bars** for bracing the boards, **its pillars, and its sockets;** ¹²**the ark and its** carrying **staves** and **the ark cover** with its cherubs, **and the curtain for the screen** separating the Holy of Holies from the Sanctuary; ¹³**the table** for the showbread, **and its staves, all its vessels, and the showbread;** ¹⁴**the candelabrum of the light, and its vessels, and its lamps, and the lighting oil;** ¹⁵**the altar of incense and its staves, the anointing oil,** and **the incense of the spices; and the screen of the entrance for the entrance of the Tabernacle;** ¹⁶**the altar of the burnt offering, its bronze grate, its staves and all its vessels,** and **the laver and its base;** ¹⁷**the hangings of the courtyard,** which were stretched around it, **its pillars and its sockets, and the screen of the gate of the courtyard;** ¹⁸**the pegs of the Tabernacle,** by which the sheets are tied, **the pegs of the courtyard, and their cords** that bind them; ¹⁹**the woven fabrics to serve in the Sanctuary,** used for covering the vessels while traveling, and **the sacred vestments for Aaron the priest and the vestments of his sons, to serve as priests.**

²⁰**The entire congregation of the children of Israel departed from the presence of Moses.**

The People's Response

The entire people answers Moses' call for donations. Women and men, the wealthy leaders and the simple people – all contribute the necessary materials.

Second aliya ²¹**Every man whose heart inspired him** to participate in the building of the Tabernacle **came, and everyone whose spirit was generous brought the gift of the Lord for the labor of the Tent of Meeting, for all its service,** its requirements, **and for the sacred vestments.** ²²**The men came along with the women: Everyone generous of heart brought a bracelet** or nose ring, **an earring, ring, or girdle,** or **any gold vessel, and** besides these donations of valuable adornments, there was **every man who made a donation of gold** of any sort **to the Lord.** ²³**And every man with whom was found sky-blue, purple, and scarlet wool, linen, goats' hair, rams' hides dyed red, and** taḥash **hides, brought them.** ²⁴**Everyone who raised a gift of silver and bronze brought the gift of the Lord, and everyone with whom was found acacia wood for any labor of the service brought it.** ²⁵**Every woman who was wise-hearted,** skilled in crafts, **spun with her hands, and they brought yarn: the sky-blue and the purple wool, the scarlet wool and the linen;** that is, the spun threads of dyed wool and linen. ²⁶**All the women whose hearts inspired them in wisdom,** the most talented craftswomen, **spun the goats' hair.**

²⁷**The princes,** who were wealthiest, **brought the onyx stones and the stones for setting, for the ephod and for the breast piece** respectively; ²⁸**and the spice and the oil, for the light, for the anointing oil, and for the incense of the spices.**

²⁹In sum, **every man or woman whose heart was generous for them to bring** materials and skills **for all the labor that the Lord commanded to perform at the hand of Moses – the children of Israel brought** these **as a pledge to the Lord.**

The Craftsmen and the Contributions

The highly skilled craftsman Betzalel, from the tribe of Judah, is appointed to oversee the planning and construction of the Tabernacle. He manages a large staff of craftsmen divided into teams according to their area of expertise. As they begin work, it becomes apparent that more materials were donated than are needed; therefore, the people are told to cease bringing these contributions.

Third aliya (Second aliya) ³⁰**Moses said to the children of Israel: See, the Lord has called by name,** appointed, **Betzalel, son of Uri, son of Hur, of the tribe of Judah.** ³¹**He has filled him with the spirit of God, in wisdom, in understanding, and in knowledge, and in all craftsmanship:** ³²**to devise designs** and prepare plans; **to work with gold, with silver, and with bronze;** ³³**and in stone-cutting for setting,** polishing the precious stones and inserting

them into the breast piece; **and in wood-carving** and carpentry – **to perform all artful craftsmanship.** [34]**He,** God, **has put in his,** Betzalel's, **heart to teach, he and Oholiav, son of Ahisamakh, of the tribe of Dan.** [35]**He filled them with wisdom of heart, to perform all craft, of the carver, and of the artisan, and of the embroiderer in sky-blue** wool, **and purple wool,** and **scarlet wool, and in linen, and of the weaver; performers**

36 **of craftsmanship and devisers of designs.** [1]**Betzalel and Oholiav, and every wise-hearted man in whom the Lord has put wisdom and understanding to know** how **to perform all the labor of the service of the Sanctuary, shall perform everything that the Lord commanded.**

[2]**Moses summoned Betzalel and Oholiav and every wise-hearted man in whose heart the Lord put wisdom, everyone whose heart inspired him to approach the work** and volunteer **to perform it.**

⌂ Further reading: For more on the selection of Betzalel and Oholiav and what it symbolizes, see *A Concise Guide to the Sages*, p. 126.

[3]**They,** the craftsmen, **took from before Moses all the gifts that the children of Israel brought for the labor of the service of the Sanctuary, to perform it.** They, the Israelites, **brought him,** Moses, **more pledges morning after morning.**

[4]**All the wise men,** the craftsmen **who performed all the craftsmanship of the Sanctuary, each one came from his craft that they were performing.** [5]**They said to Moses, saying: The people are bringing more than enough for the service of the labor that the Lord commanded** us **to perform.**

[6]**Moses commanded, and they circulated a proclamation in the camp, saying: Man or woman shall not perform any more labor for the gifts of the Sanctuary; and the people ceased bringing** materials.

[7]**And the labor,** the bringing of the donations, **was sufficient for all the labor to perform it, and beyond.** There was leftover material, which was not used.

Manufacture of the Materials for the Roof of the Tabernacle

The roof of the Tent of Meeting was composed of four layers. The bottom layer, which could be seen from inside the tent, is intricately decorated. By contrast, the other layers were simpler, as they functioned merely to cover the tent and protect it.

Fourth aliya ⁸**All the wise-hearted among the performers of the labor made** the ceiling of **the Tabernacle,** consisting of **ten** fabric **sheets** made **of twined** white **linen and sky-blue, purple, and scarlet wool; with artfully craft**ed forms of **cherubs** on them **they made them.** ⁹**The length of one sheet was twenty-eight cubits,** one cubit is approximately half a meter, **and the width** was **four cubits for each sheet; there was one** uniform **measure for all the sheets.** ¹⁰**He attached five sheets** by sewing them **one to anoth**er into a single unit, **and** the other **five sheets he attached one to another.**

¹¹**He made loops of sky-blue wool at the edge of the one sheet** located **at the extremity of the array** of five sheets sewn together, **and he did likewise at the edge of the outermost sheet in the second array** of five sheets. ¹²**Fifty loops he made in the one sheet, and fifty loops he made at the extremity of the sheet that was in the second array,** along the entire length; **the loops corresponded one to another.** ¹³**He made fifty hooks of gold and attached the sheets one to another with the hooks** and loops, **and the Tabernacle was one;** a single, connected structure.

¹⁴**He made sheets of goats' hair as a tent over the Tabernacle,** to cover it; **eleven sheets he made them.** ¹⁵**The length of the one sheet was thirty cubits, and four cubits the width of the one sheet; there was one** uniform **measure for eleven sheets.** ¹⁶**He attached,** sewed, **five sheets by themselves and six sheets by themselves.** ¹⁷**He made fifty loops at the edge of the outermost sheet in the array, and he made fifty loops at the edge of the sheet in the second array.** ¹⁸**He made fifty hooks of bronze to attach the tent, to be one** connected unit.

¹⁹**He made a cover for the tent of rams' hides dyed red, and a cover of** taḥash **hides above** it.

Construction of the Tabernacle Walls, Curtain, and Screen

The Tabernacle walls were constructed from adjoining wooden boards, a specified number for each side. They rested upon silver sockets for stability, and were girded together by means of interior and exterior wooden bars. Two fabric partitions, the curtain and the screen, separated the main areas of the Tabernacle tent and enclosure.

Fifth aliya ²⁰**He made the** smoothed **boards for** the walls of **the Tabernacle of acacia wood, standing.** ²¹**Ten cubits was the length of a board, and a cubit and a half** was **the width of each board.** ²²**Two tenons,** protrusions at their sides **were for one board, parallel one to another,** and were placed into corresponding indentations in the adjacent board, to join them. **So he did for all the boards of the Tabernacle.**

📖 **Further reading:** What is a taḥash? And how did the children of Israel obtain acacia wood in the wilderness? See *A Concise Guide to the Sages*, p. 116.

[23]He made the boards for the Tabernacle; twenty boards were used for the southern side. [24]He made forty silver sockets placed under the twenty boards, as a base for the boards: Two sockets under the one board for its two tenons at the bottom of it, and two sockets under the one board for its two tenons.

[25]For the second side of the Tabernacle, for the north side, he made twenty boards. [26]Their forty sockets were of silver: Two sockets under the one board and two sockets under the one board.

[27]For the side of the Tabernacle that faced to the west, in the back, he made six boards. [28]He made two additional boards for the corners of the Tabernacle on the sides of the back wall. [29]They, all the boards, were even and adjacent to one another at the bottom, with no space between them, and they each met the adjacent board at its top for the one ring, which was itself inserted into grooves in the top of each pair of boards, holding the ends together. So he did for the two of them, for the boards in the two corners. [30]There were on the west side a total of eight boards and their silver sockets: Sixteen sockets, two sockets under the one board.

[31]He made bars of acacia wood for holding the boards together: Five for the boards of the one side of the Tabernacle, [32]and five bars for the boards of the second side of the Tabernacle, and five bars for the boards of the Tabernacle for the side to the west. [33]He made the central bar of the five to run inside the boards from end to end, to connect them. [34]He plated the boards with gold, and their rings, for joining them, he made of gold. The rings were made as housings, receptacles, for the bars. He also plated the bars themselves with gold.

[35]He made the curtain, which separated the Holy of Holies from the Sanctuary, of sky-blue, purple, and scarlet wool, and twined linen; he made it artfully crafted with cherubs so that the design could be seen on each side. [36]He made for it four acacia pillars and plated them with gold; their hooks for hanging the curtain were of gold. He cast for them four silver sockets.

[37]Instead of a fourth wall on the eastern side, he made a screen for the entrance of the Tent, of sky-blue, purple, and scarlet wool, and twined linen, the work of an embroiderer. [38]And he made its five pillars and

their hooks, for hanging the screen; **he plated their tops and their bands with gold. And their sockets were five,** made **of bronze.**

Fashioning the Tabernacle Vessels

The description of the vessels begins with the innermost ones: the ark and ark cover in the Holy of Holies. Next the Torah describes the vessels in the Sanctuary: the table, the candelabrum, and the incense altar. The focus then moves outward again, to the Tabernacle courtyard, and the altar of burnt offerings and the laver are described.

37 **¹Betzalel made the ark of acacia wood; its length was two and a half cubits, and its width a cubit and a half, and its height a cubit and a half. ²He plated it with pure gold within and without. And he made a** decorative **rim of gold upon it, all around. ³He cast for it four rings of gold, on its four corners: Two rings on its one side, and two rings on its second side. ⁴He made staves of acacia wood, and he plated them with gold. ⁵He brought the staves into the rings on the sides of the ark, to** lift and carry the ark. **⁶He made an ark cover of pure gold; its length was two and a half cubits, and its width a cubit and a half.**

⁷He made two cherubs of gold, hammered out of the same gold block as the ark cover. **He made them hammered, at the two ends of the ark cover: ⁸One cherub from this end** of the ark cover **and one cherub from that end; he made the cherubs** extend **from the ark cover at its two ends. ⁹The cherubs had wings spread from above, shielding with their wings over the ark cover and their faces one to another; the faces of the cherubs were toward the ark cover,** facing each other and directed downward.

¹⁰He made the table for the showbread **of acacia wood; its length was two cubits, its width a cubit, and its height a cubit and a half. ¹¹He plated it with pure gold, and he made for it a rim of gold all around. ¹²He made for it a border** the height **of one handbreadth all around, and he made** the aforementioned **rim of gold for its border all around. ¹³He** also **cast for it four gold rings, and he put the rings on the four corners that were on its,** the table's, **four legs. ¹⁴The rings were adjacent to the border** and beneath it, and functioned as **housings for the staves,** the poles used to carry the table. **¹⁵He made the staves of acacia wood, and he plated them with gold, to carry the table. ¹⁶He made the vessels that were on the table: its bowls,** for flour or dough; **its spoons,** for the frankincense; **its supports,** posts to hold the frame; **and the tubes,** the lattice frame above the table, composed of metal tubes that held the bread, **with which it,** the table, **was to be covered.** All these he made **of pure gold.**

¹⁷He made the candelabrum of pure gold; hammered he made the candelabrum, not by casting or by joining separate pieces, but by beating a single block of gold. And he made **its base and its** central **shaft,** or all its shafts, and **its cups, its knobs, and its flowers,** various decorations. All of these **were from it;** they were all fashioned from the same block of gold as the candelabrum itself. **¹⁸Six branches emerged from its sides,** from the central shaft: **Three branches of the candelabrum from its one side and three branches of the candelabrum from its second side; ¹⁹three finely crafted** ornamental **cups were on the one branch,** along with **a** decorative **knob and a flower** on each branch. **And** there were likewise **three finely crafted cups on the other branch, with a knob and a flower.** So it was for each of **the six branches that emerged from the candelabrum.**

Illustrations: See images of the table and candelabrum, p. 523.

²⁰On the body of **the candelabrum,** its central shaft, **were four finely crafted cups,** with **its knobs and its flowers, ²¹and** there was **a** decorative **knob under two of the branches from it,** where they met the central shaft, **a knob under two of the branches from it, and a knob under two of the branches from it, for the six branches emerging from it.** There were ornamental knobs where each pair of branches met the central shaft. **²²Their knobs and their branches,** the branches of the candelabrum, **were from it,** of the same block of gold as the candelabrum, **all of it hammered of pure gold. ²³He made its seven lamps,** receptacles atop the branches for the oil and the wicks; **and its tongs,** for handling the wicks; **and its firepans,** spoon-like receptacles for removing the burnt wicks, **of pure gold. ²⁴He made it and all its vessels of a talent of pure gold,** approximately 50 kg total.

²⁵He made the incense altar of acacia wood; its length was a cubit and its width a cubit, i.e., it was **square, its height was two cubits, and its horns were from it,** protruding up from each corner. **²⁶He plated it with pure gold, its top, its sides all around, and its horns; and he made a rim of gold upon it around. ²⁷He made two gold rings for it under its rim, on two of its corners and on two of its sides,** on diagonally opposite corners, **as housings for** inserting **staves,** the poles **with which to** lift and carry it. **²⁸He made the staves of acacia wood, and he plated them with gold.**

Illustrations: See image of the incense altar, p. 526.

²⁹**He made the anointing oil in sanctity, and the incense of the spices pure** of all waste and impurity. Both were prepared with **the craftsmanship of a blender,** someone who prepares mixtures of spices.

38 ¹**He made the altar of the burnt offering** out of acacia wood: **Its length** _{Seventh}**was five cubits and its width five cubits,** i.e., it was **square, and its height** *aliya* **was three cubits** (see 27:1). ²**He made its horns,** square protrusions, **on** *(Fourth* *aliya)* its four corners: Its horns were from it,** not made from additional material joined to the altar, **and he plated it with bronze.** ³**He made all the vessels of the altar: the pots** for removing the waste; **the shovels** for gathering the ashes; **the basins** for collecting the blood of offerings; **the forks** for handling the meat on the altar; **and the pans** for raking the coals. **He made all its vessels of bronze.**

⁴**He made a grate for the altar, a work** made **of bronze mesh. It was** placed **under its,** the altar's, **surrounding ledge from below, until its middle,** half its height. ⁵**He cast four rings on the four ends,** or corners, **for the bronze grate, as housings for the staves** for carrying the altar. ⁶**He made the staves of acacia wood, and he plated them with bronze.** ⁷**He brought the staves into the rings on the sides of the altar** in order **to carry it with them; he made it,** the altar, **hollow, out of planks.**

⁸**He made the laver of bronze and its base of bronze,** both parts made **with the mirrors of the assembled women who assembled at the entrance of the Tent of Meeting.**

Preparing the Tabernacle Courtyard

The Tabernacle courtyard is demarcated by draperies that hang from wooden pillars arranged around it set five cubits apart. At the entrance, on the east side, is a decorated cloth screen that can be moved aside to allow people to enter.

⁹**He made the courtyard; on the south side, the hangings of the courtyard were of twined linen,** and they were **one hundred cubits** in length. ¹⁰**Their pillars** supporting the hangings **were twenty, and their sockets twenty,** made **of bronze. The hooks of the pillars,** to which the hangings were fastened, **and their bands,** surrounding the pillars, **were** made of **silver.** ¹¹**On the north side, they,** the hangings, **were one hundred cubits,** and their pillars were **twenty and their sockets twenty, of bronze; the hooks of the pillars and their bands were silver.** ¹²**On the west side there were hangings of fifty cubits,** and **their pillars** were **ten and their**

sockets ten; the hooks of the pillars and their bands were made of silver. [13]On the east side, the total width of the Tabernacle was fifty cubits. [14]It had hangings fifteen cubits long on the one side of the entrance; their pillars were three and their sockets three. [15]It was the same on the second side of the entrance; from this side and from that side of the gate of the courtyard, the hangings were fifteen cubits, their pillars were three, and their sockets were three.

Illustrations: See illustrations of the incense altar, p. 526, and the Tabernacle courtyard, pp. 524–525.

[16]All the hangings of the courtyard all around were of twined linen. [17]The sockets for the pillars were bronze, the hooks of the pillars and their bands were silver, the plating of their tops was silver, and all the pillars of the courtyard were banded with silver.

aftir [18]The screen of the gate of the courtyard, a curtain, was made using the craftsmanship of an embroiderer, of sky-blue, purple, and scarlet wool, and twined linen. It was twenty cubits in length, and its height, in the width of the cloth, was five cubits, corresponding to the hangings of the courtyard; the screen was between the hangings, on the same plane as them. [19]Their pillars, the pillars for the screen, were four, and their sockets four, of bronze; their hooks were silver, and the plating of their tops and their bands were silver. [20]All the pegs of the Tabernacle and of the courtyard around, with which the hangings were fixed in place, were made of bronze.

Exodus

Parashat
Pekudei

The Torah records the amounts of the various raw materials used for the Tabernacle project, including for the vestments of the priests. Afterward it describes the crafting of the vestments worn by the High Priest and the ordinary priests. Once all the parts have been prepared in precise accordance with God's detailed instructions, God commands Moses to assemble the Tabernacle and to sanctify both it and the priests by anointing them with the anointing oil. This lays the groundwork for the Divine Presence to descend and rest in the Israelite camp, enabling an intimate connection between the children of Israel and their Creator.

Resource Inventory

The Torah presents an accounting of each type of raw material used in building the Tabernacle, its vessels, and their accompanying implements: amounts, sources, and uses. While most of these materials were freely donated, the silver sockets were made from the silver half shekels that every adult male Israelite was required to give.

²¹**These are the** detailed **reckonings** of the materials used in the construction **of the Tabernacle,** also called **the Tabernacle of the Testimony, as they were reckoned at the directive of Moses: The service of the Levites was in the hand of,** headed by, **Itamar, son of Aaron the priest.** ²²**Betzalel, son of Uri, son of Hur, of the tribe of Judah made everything that the Lord had commanded Moses.** ²³**With him was Oholiav son of Ahisamakh of the tribe of Dan,** who was **a carpenter,** or a skilled metalworker, **and a craftsman,** a designer, **and an embroiderer in the sky-blue, purple, and scarlet wool, and in the linen.** ²⁴**All the gold that was used for the work, in all the sacred work, the gold of the donation was twenty-nine talents and seven hundred and thirty shekels in the sacred shekel.** A talent is 30–50 kg.

Further reading: For more on the collections of the half shekels, see p. 215. For more on the importance of transparency and detailed reporting, see *A Concise Guide to the Sages,* p. 128.

236

²⁵The silver of those who were counted of the congregation via the compulsory half-shekel contributions **was one hundred talents and one thousand seven hundred and seventy-five shekels, in the sacred shekel.** ²⁶**One** beka weight **was** donated **per head,** by each person; one *beka* is equal to **half** of a shekel in the sacred shekel. A *beka* was given **for everyone who passed among the counted,** who was included in the census, **from twenty years old and above, for six hundred thousand three thousand five hundred and fifty.** ²⁷**The one hundred talents of silver were** utilized **to cast the sockets of the Sanctuary and the sockets of the curtain, one hundred sockets for one hundred talents,** or **one talent for a socket.** ²⁸**Of the** remaining **one thousand seven hundred and seventy-five** silver shekels, **he made hooks for the pillars and plated their tops and banded them.**

²⁹**The donated bronze was seventy talents and two thousand four hundred shekels.** ³⁰**He made with it,** the bronze, **the sockets of the entrance of the Tent of Meeting, the bronze altar** of the offerings, **its bronze grate, all the vessels of the altar,** ³¹**the sockets of the courtyard around, the sockets of the gate of the courtyard, all the pegs of the Tabernacle, and all the pegs of the courtyard around.**

39 ¹**From the sky-blue, purple, and scarlet wool they made woven** or mesh **fabrics for service in the Sanctuary.** This refers to the coverings of the Tabernacle, the screen of the gate of the Tabernacle, and the cloths that covered the vessels during the Israelites' travels. **They** also **made the sacred vestments for Aaron, as the Lord commanded Moses.**

Fabrication of the Priestly Vestments

The Torah describes the process of preparing the priestly garments. The High Priest's vestments are more elaborate than those of ordinary priests, and incorporate precious metals and stones.

ond ²**He made the ephod of gold, and of sky-blue, purple,** and scarlet wool, *liya* *ifth* **and twined linen.** ³**They hammered out the sheets of gold, and** then **cut** *ya)* **wires to work in,** to weave **with the sky-blue wool, with the purple wool, with the scarlet wool, and with the linen.** This was **artfully** and specially crafted. ⁴**They made shoulder pieces for it,** the ephod, **and attached** it; **it was attached at the two ends.** ⁵**The belt of his ephod that is upon it,** the ephod, **is from it,** part of the woven fabric of the ephod, **like its work:** Of **gold,** and of **sky-blue, purple, and scarlet wool, and twined linen as the Lord had commanded Moses.** ⁶**They made the onyx stones surrounded**

with settings of gold and engraved with the engravings of a signet, with the names of the children of Israel. [7]He placed them on the shoulder pieces of the ephod as stones of remembrance for the children of Israel, as the Lord had commanded Moses.

Illustrations: For images of the priestly vestments, see p. 525.

[8]He made the breast piece artfully crafted, like the work of the ephod, with gold, and sky-blue, purple, and scarlet wool, and twined linen. [9]It was square; they made the breast piece folded, so that it formed a pouch; its length was a span, approximately 25 cm, and its width a span, folded. [10]They mounted in it, the breast piece, four rows of stones: A row of a ruby, a peridot, and an emerald, the first row; [11]and the second row: a turquoise, a sapphire, and a clear quartz; [12]and the third row: a jacinth, an agate and an amethyst; [13]and the fourth row: a beryl, an onyx, and a chalcedony; surrounded in settings of gold in their mountings. [14]The stones were according to the names of the children of Israel; they were twelve, according to their names, the engravings of a signet, each man according to his name, for the twelve tribes.

[15]They crafted bordering chains on the breast piece of braided craftsmanship, like twined cords, of pure gold. [16]They crafted two settings of gold and two gold rings, and they put the two rings at the two ends of the breast piece, at the corners. [17]They put the two braids of gold on the two rings at the ends of the breast piece. [18]The two ends of the two braids they put on the two settings, and they put them, the settings, on the shoulder pieces of the ephod, on its front. [19]They made two gold rings, and they put them on the two ends of the breast piece, on its edge that was toward the ephod, on the inner side. [20]They made another two gold rings and they put them on the two shoulder pieces of the ephod from below, on its front, on the front side of the ephod adjacent to its seam, above the belt of the ephod. [21]They attached the breast piece with its rings to the rings of the ephod with a thread of sky-blue wool, to be on the belt of the ephod. This ensured that the breast piece would not be detached from the ephod, as the Lord had commanded Moses.

Third aliya (Sixth aliya) [22]He made the robe of the ephod, the robe upon which the ephod is bound, of woven work, entirely of sky-blue wool. [23]The opening of the robe at the neck was made within it; the edge of the robe was folded over into the garment and hemmed, like the opening of a coat of mail, which

is folded inward. There was a stitched **hem for its opening around,** so that **it would not rip.** [24]**They made** ornaments **on the** bottom **hem of the robe** in the shape of **pomegranates, of sky-blue, purple, and scarlet wool,** all **twined together.** [25]**They made bells of pure gold, and they put the bells among the pomegranates on the hem of the robe around, among the pomegranates,** alternating bells and pomegranates. [26]**A bell and a pomegranate, a bell and a pomegranate were on the hem of the robe around, to serve, as the Lord commanded Moses.**

[27]**They made the tunics of linen, woven work for Aaron and for his sons, for all** of the priests, [28]**and the mitre,** similar to a turban, for the High Priest, **of linen, and the headdresses of linen** for the other priests, **and the linen trousers of twined linen** for all the priests, [29]**and the sash** worn by all the priests **of twined linen, and sky-blue, purple, and scarlet wool, the work of an embroiderer, as the Lord had commanded Moses.**

[30]**They made the diadem of the crown of sanctity,** a gold ornament positioned on the High Priest's forehead, **of pure gold, and they wrote upon it in the writing of the engraving of a signet: Holy to the Lord.** [31]**They put upon it a thread of sky-blue wool, to put it,** tie it, **on the mitre from above, as the Lord had commanded Moses.**

The Tabernacle Pieces Are Brought to Moses

The children of Israel finish manufacturing everything necessary for the divine service. This includes the parts of the Tabernacle itself, its vessels and their appurtenances, the priestly vestments, and even the goods such as the showbread, the oil for illumination, and the incense of the spices. They bring all these items to Moses so he can examine them.

[32]**All the work of the Tabernacle of the Tent of Meeting was completed, and the children of Israel did in accordance with all that the Lord had commanded Moses; so they did.**

Illustrations: For images of the Tabernacle and its parts, the service vessels, and the priestly vestments, see p. 524.

[33]**They brought the Tabernacle to Moses, with the** sheets covering the **tent, and all its vessels: its hooks** for connecting the sheets, **its boards, its bars** for girding the boards together, **and its pillars, and its sockets,** [34]**and the covering of rams' hides dyed red, and the covering of** taḥash **hides, and the curtain of the screen,**

³⁵**the Ark of the Testimony, and its staves** for carrying it, **and the ark cover** with its cherubs; ³⁶**the table, all its vessels, and the showbread;** ³⁷**the pure candelabrum, its lamps,** that is **the lamps of the arrangement** on the candelabrum, **and all its vessels, and the lighting oil,** ³⁸**and the golden altar, and the anointing oil, and the incense of the spices, and the screen of the entrance of the tent,** ³⁹**the bronze altar** of the burnt offerings, **and its grate of bronze, its staves and all its vessels; the laver and its base,**

⁴⁰**the hangings of the courtyard, its pillars, and its sockets, and the screen for the entrance of the courtyard, its,** the courtyard's, **cords, and its pegs, and all the vessels of the service of the Tabernacle for the Tent of Meeting;**

⁴¹**the woven fabrics to serve in the holy place,** which were used to cover the Tabernacle vessels when it was dismantled for travel, and **the sacred vestments for Aaron the priest and the vestments of his sons to serve as priests.**

⁴²**In accordance with everything that the Lord had commanded Moses, so did the children of Israel perform all the work.** ⁴³**Moses saw all the** products of the **labor** that were brought before him for inspection, **and behold, they had performed it,** the labor; **as the Lord had commanded, so had they performed; and Moses blessed them.**

Assembly of the Tabernacle and Sanctification of the Priests

Moses himself assembles the Tabernacle for the first time. The placement of its vessels begins with the ark, the focal point of its holiness. Once everything is in place, the Tabernacle is sanctified by being anointed with the anointing oil, as are the people and the vessels that will serve there.

40 ¹**The Lord spoke to Moses, saying:** ²**On the day of the first month, on**
Fifth **the first of the month** of Nisan, **you shall erect the Tabernacle of the**
aliya **Tent of Meeting.** ³**You shall place there the Ark of the Testimony, and**
(Seventh **you shall screen the ark with the curtain,** to separate and conceal the
aliya) Holy of Holies. ⁴**You shall bring the table, and you shall arrange its arrangement** of the showbread; **you shall bring the candelabrum, and you shall kindle its lamps.** ⁵**You shall put the golden altar for incense before the Ark of the Testimony. And you shall set in place the screen of the entrance of the Tabernacle,** the entrance to the Sanctuary, the structure in the center of the courtyard. ⁶**You shall put the altar of the burnt offering before the entrance of the Tabernacle of the Tent of Meeting,** in the

courtyard. ⁷**You shall put the laver between the Tent of Meeting and the altar, and you shall put water there,** in the laver. ⁸**You shall place** the pillars, sockets, and hangings, which together demarcate **the courtyard, all around** the Tabernacle, **and you shall put the screen of the gate of the courtyard** in its appropriate place.

⁹**You shall take the anointing oil,** which is meant for sanctifying the vessels, **and anoint the Tabernacle and all that is in it; you shall sanctify it and all its vessels; it shall be holy.** ¹⁰**You shall anoint the altar of the burnt offering and all its vessels; you shall sanctify the altar, and the altar shall be a sacred sacrament.** ¹¹**You shall anoint the laver and its base, and you shall sanctify it.**

¹²**You shall bring Aaron and his sons near to the entrance of the Tent of Meeting, and you shall wash them with water.** ¹³**You shall clothe Aaron with the sacred vestments; you shall anoint him** and **you shall** thereby **sanctify him, that he will serve as priest to Me.** From this point onward he shall be fit for the priesthood. ¹⁴**You shall bring near his sons, and you shall clothe them in tunics.** ¹⁵**You shall anoint them as you anointed their father, that they may serve as priests to Me. And their anointment shall be to them for an eternal priesthood, for their generations.** Their sons will be priests automatically, and will not need to be anointed.

¹⁶**Moses did in accordance with everything that the Lord had commanded him** with regard to erecting the Tabernacle; **so he did.**

Sixth aliya ¹⁷**It was in the first month,** Nisan, **during** the beginning of **the second year** following the exodus from Egypt, **on the first of the month; the Tabernacle was erected.** ¹⁸**Moses** himself **erected the Tabernacle; he put down its sockets,** the bases for the boards, **he placed its boards** by inserting the bottom tenons into the sockets that served as the base, **he put in its bars** to hold up the walls, **and he erected its pillars** at the entrance to the Tabernacle.

📖 **Further reading:** For more on the erection of the Tabernacle by Moses, see *A Concise Guide to the Sages,* p. 129.

¹⁹**He spread the tent,** the tapestry of goat hair, **over the** decorated cloth covering of the **Tabernacle, and he placed the covering of the tent,** made of rams' skins dyed red and taḥash skins, **over it from above, as the Lord had commanded Moses.**

Exodus

²⁰**He took the Testimony,** the Tablets of the Covenant, **and put it into the ark. And he placed the staves on the ark, and he put the ark cover on the ark from above.** ²¹**He brought the ark into the Tabernacle, and he placed the curtain of the screen,** which separated the Holy of Holies from the Sanctuary, **and he screened,** or concealed, **the Ark of the Testimony, as the Lord had commanded Moses.**

²²**He put the table in the Tent of Meeting, on the side of the Tabernacle to the north, outside the curtain,** in the Sanctuary. ²³**He arranged upon it an arrangement of bread before the Lord, as the Lord had commanded Moses.**

²⁴**He put the candelabrum in the Tent of Meeting, opposite the table, on the side of the Tabernacle to the south.** ²⁵**He kindled the lamps before the Lord, as the Lord had commanded Moses.**

²⁶**He placed the golden altar in the Tent of Meeting before the curtain,** opposite it. ²⁷**He burned on it incense of the spices, as the Lord had commanded Moses.**

Seventh aliya ²⁸**He placed the screen of the entrance to the Tabernacle.**

²⁹**The altar of the burnt offering he placed at the entrance of the Tabernacle of the Tent of Meeting,** in the courtyard, **and he offered up on it the burnt offering and the meal offering, as the Lord had commanded Moses.**

³⁰**He placed the laver between the Tent of Meeting and the altar, and he put water there for washing.** ³¹**Moses and Aaron and his sons shall wash their hands and their feet from it;** ³²**upon their entry into the Tent of Meeting and upon their approach to the altar, they shall wash, as the Lord had commanded Moses.**

³³**He erected the courtyard around the Tabernacle and the altar, and he put up the screen of the gate of the courtyard; Moses concluded the labor.**

The Divine Presence Rests upon the Tent of Meeting

The children of Israel began the Tabernacle project with an enthusiastic outpouring of donations, and executed the instructions with precise attention to every detail. Now their devotion and obedience is affirmed as the cloud of the Divine Presence descends and rests upon the Tent of Meeting. Made by human hands, the Tabernacle becomes the point of contact between God and the children of Israel.

aftir [34]The cloud covered the Tent of Meeting, and the glory of the Lord filled the Tabernacle.

[35]Moses was unable to enter the Tent of Meeting because the cloud rested upon it and covered it, and the glory of the Lord filled the Tabernacle.

[36]Upon the ascent of the cloud higher over the Tabernacle, the children of Israel would travel on all their journeys. [37]But if the cloud would not ascend from atop the Tabernacle, they would not travel until the day of its ascent.

[38]For the cloud of the Lord was on the Tabernacle by day, and fire would be in it by night, before the eyes of the entire house of Israel, on all their journeys.

📖 **Further reading:** For more on the significance of the Divine Presence resting upon the Tabernacle and, later, upon the Temple, see *A Concise Guide to Mahshava*, p. 160.

Exodus

Leviticus

Parashat Vayikra

The book of Leviticus opens with the laws governing the sacrificial service. The Torah explains in detail how the various offerings are brought and what must be done with each of them. The sacrifices are divided into two principal categories: free-will offerings, which are voluntarily brought, a gift, as it were, that the individual presents to God; and obligatory offerings, which a sinner must offer in order to atone for his or her transgression.

The *parasha* begins with the laws governing the free-will offerings: the burnt offering, the meal offering, and the peace offering. It then continues with the obligatory offerings: the sin offering and the guilt offering, which are brought to atone for a person's transgressions.

The Burnt Offering

The first offering whose rite is spelled out in this *parasha* is the burnt offering. The Hebrew term for a burnt offering is *ola*, which means "that which goes up." This name presumably is derived from the fact that this offering is burned in its entirety on the altar. This offering may be brought from cattle, sheep, goats, or birds. The Torah explains in detail each type of offering.

1 **¹The Lord called to Moses, and spoke to him from the Tent of Meeting, saying: ²Speak to the children of Israel, and say to them: When any man of you brings an offering to the Lord,** if **you shall bring your offering from animals,** then **from the cattle or from the flock you shall bring your offering.**

📖 **Further reading:** For more on the inner significance of offering sacrifices, see *A Concise Guide to Mahshava*, p. 163. There is a wondrous quality to the study of these laws; see *A Concise Guide to the Sages*, p. 133.

³If his offering is a burnt offering from the cattle, an unblemished male he shall present it. To the entrance of the Tent of Meeting he shall present it, as the burnt offering is offered upon the outer altar, i.e., the large altar in the courtyard, **for his propitiation before the Lord,** in order to find favor in His eyes, and of his own free will, as a gift offering rather than in fulfillment of an obligation. **⁴He shall lay his hand upon the head of**

the burnt offering, and it shall be accepted for him, causing him to be accepted and to find favor in God's eyes, **to atone for him.** ⁵**He, the owner or any other Jew, shall slaughter the young bull before the Lord. And Aaron's sons, the priests, shall present the blood,** collect the blood that flows out of the neck of the animal in a bowl, convey it to the altar, **and cast the blood** on all sides **around the** outer **altar that is at the entrance of the Tent of Meeting.** ⁶**He shall** subsequently **flay the burnt offering,** remove its hide, **and cut it,** the animal, **into its pieces.** ⁷**The sons of Aaron the priest shall place,** light, **fire upon the altar and arrange wood upon the fire.** ⁸**Aaron's sons, the priests, shall arrange the pieces, the head, and the fats** surrounding the inner organs **on the wood that is on the fire that is on the altar.** ⁹**Its innards,** including the stomach and intestines, **and its legs, he shall wash with water. The priest shall burn everything on the altar,** the head, the fats, the inner organs, and the rest of the flesh, **as a burnt offering, a fire offering of a pleasing aroma to the Lord.**

¹⁰**If his offering is from the flock, from the sheep or from the goats, as a burnt offering; an unblemished male he shall present it.** ¹¹**He shall slaughter it on the north side of the altar before the Lord; and Aaron's sons, the priests, shall cast its blood around the altar.** ¹²**He shall cut it,** the body of the animal, **into its pieces, and** sever **its head, and** separate **its fats** from the rest of the flesh. **And the priest shall arrange them,** the pieces of the animal, **on the wood that is on the fire that is upon the altar.** ¹³**The innards and the legs he shall wash with water** before arranging them on the altar. **And the priest shall present everything, and burn it on the altar. It is a burnt offering, a fire offering of a pleasing aroma to the Lord.**

Second aliya ¹⁴**If his offering is from the birds, a burnt offering to the Lord, from turtledoves,** a type of wild bird, **or from young pigeons, he shall bring** one as **his offering.** ¹⁵**The priest shall bring it to the altar, shall pinch its head,** severing its neck with his thumbnail, **and shall burn it,** the severed head, **on the altar,** separately from the body. Prior to burning the bird's head, **its blood shall** forcibly **be squeezed out onto the wall of the altar.** ¹⁶Before burning the bird on the altar **he shall remove its crop,** the wide section of the gullet, **with its feathers, and cast it beside the altar to the east, to the place of the ashes,** where a portion of the ashes removed from the altar was placed (see 6:3). ¹⁷After removing the crop, **he,** the priest, **shall split it,** the bird's body, **by its wings, but shall not separate** it into two completely detached parts. **The priest shall burn it on the altar, on**

the wood that is on the fire; it is a burnt offering, a fire offering of a pleasing aroma to the Lord.

Illustrations: For a drawing illustrating the digestive tract of a bird, see p. 528.

The Meal Offering

The meal offering does not involve animal sacrifice; it is made of flour and oil. The priest takes a handful of the offering and burns it on the altar, and the rest of the offering is eaten by the priests. The basic method of preparing the offering involves simply mixing the ingredients, but some meal offerings are also baked or fried.

2 ¹When a person brings a meal offering to the Lord, his offering shall be of choice flour. He shall pour oil upon it and place frankincense, a type of spice, on it. ²He shall bring it to Aaron's sons, the priests, and he, the priest, shall take from there his handful, from its choice flour and from its oil, with all its frankincense that is on it. The priest shall burn its memorial portion, the handful of flour and oil, and all of the frankincense, which serve as a remembrance before God, on the altar, as a fire offering of a pleasing aroma to the Lord. ³The remnant of the meal offering, everything apart from the small portion that was burned on the altar, shall be for Aaron and for his sons; it is a sacred sacrament from the fire offerings of the Lord.

⁴There are additional types of meal offerings: When you bring a meal offering baked in the oven, it shall be unleavened loaves of choice flour mixed with oil, or thin unleavened wafers smeared with oil.

⁵If your offering is a meal offering fried on a flat pan, it shall also be made of choice flour, mixed with oil, and it shall also be unleavened bread. ⁶Break it into small pieces, and pour oil on it a second time. It is a meal offering.

Third aliya ⁷If your offering is a meal offering fried in a deep pan, it shall also be prepared of choice flour with oil.

⁸You shall bring the meal offering that is prepared of these, in these various ways, to the Lord. He, the individual bringing the offering, shall bring it to the priest, and he, the priest, shall bring it to the altar. ⁹The priest shall separate from the meal offering its memorial portion, the handful and the frankincense, and he shall burn it upon the altar, a fire offering of a pleasing aroma to the Lord. ¹⁰The remnant of the meal offering shall be for Aaron and for his sons; it is considered a sacred sacrament from the fire offerings of the Lord.

Leviticus

Leavened Meal Offerings

The meal offerings that are burned on the altar must be plain and simple; leaven and honey, which change the form and the taste of the offering, may not be added. Almost all of the meal offerings are prepared as unleavened bread, with the exception of the two loaves that are brought from the new crop of wheat on the festival of *Shavuot*.

¹¹**All meal offerings that you shall bring to the Lord shall not be pre-pared as leavened bread, for all leaven,** sourdough, **and all honey,** the sweet liquid that seeps out of various fruits, **you shall not burn as a fire of-fering to the Lord.** ¹²**Nevertheless, as an offering of first fruits you shall bring them,** leaven and honey, **to the Lord.** The two loaves brought on *Shavuot* from the new crop of wheat were baked as leavened bread (23:17), and the first fruits were brought near to the altar despite the fact that they contained fruit juice. These offerings shall be brought to the Temple, **but on the altar they shall not ascend for a pleasing aroma;** they are not burned on the altar. ¹³**All your meal offerings you shall salt with salt; you shall not withhold the salt** which is a symbol **of the covenant of your God from upon your meal offering.** Moreover, **on all your offerings you shall bring salt,** not just on meal offerings.

¹⁴**If,** or when, **you bring a meal offering of first fruits to the Lord,** i.e., the omer offering, the meal offering of barley brought on the sixteenth of Nisan as the first meal offering of the new crop, it shall be made of **just-ripened** grain, **roasted in fire, ground from a moist,** soft **kernel.** In this manner **you shall bring the meal offering of your first fruits.** ¹⁵**You shall put oil on it, and place frankincense on it. It is a meal offering.** ¹⁶**The priest shall burn its memorial portion,** consisting of a handful **from its flour and from its oil, with all its frankincense; it is a fire offering to the Lord.**

The Peace Offering

The peace offering is consumed by all the parties who have a share in it; some is offered to God and is burned on the altar, some is given to the priests, and the rest is eaten, in sanctity, by the owner. The name of the offering, *shelamim*, gives expression to the perfection (*sheleimut*) and the peace (*shalom*) that follow from this sharing.

3 ¹**If his offering is a peace offering: If he brings it from cattle, wheth-**

Fourth aliya **er male or female,** a bull or a cow, **he shall offer it unblemished before the Lord.** ²**He,** the owner, **shall lay his hand on the head of his offer-ing. And** he shall **slaughter it at the entrance of the Tent of Meeting** in the Tabernacle courtyard. **Aaron's sons, the priests, shall cast the blood**

around the altar. ³The peace offering is not burned in its entirety. Rather, he shall present from the peace offering a portion that will be burned on the altar as a fire offering to the Lord: The layer of fat that covers the innards, and all the fat that is on the innards. ⁴Also included in the portion of the offering burned on the altar are the two kidneys, and the fat that is on them, that is on the animal's flanks. And the diaphragm above the liver, together with the kidneys, he shall remove it. ⁵Aaron's sons shall burn it, the above sections of the animal, on the altar, on the burnt offering, i.e., together with it, on the wood that is on the fire; it is a fire offering of a pleasing aroma to the Lord.

⁶If his offering is from the flock as a peace offering to the Lord, it may also be male or female; unblemished he shall present it. ⁷If he brings a lamb as his offering, he shall bring it before the Lord to the Tabernacle's entrance. ⁸He shall lay his hand on the head of his offering, and slaughter it before the Tent of Meeting. Aaron's sons shall cast its blood around the altar. ⁹He shall present from the peace offering a fire offering, the part burned by fire, to the Lord. Its fats include the long, thick, fatty tail in its entirety; opposite the last vertebrae of the backbone, at the lower end of the spine, he shall remove it. Also to be burned is the fat that covers the innards, all the fat that is on the innards, ¹⁰the two kidneys, the fat that is on them, that is on the flanks, and the diaphragm above the liver, with the kidneys he shall remove it. ¹¹The priest shall burn it, the aforementioned part of the offering, on the altar; it is the food of the fire offering to the Lord.

¹²If his offering is a goat, he shall bring it before the Lord. ¹³He shall lay his hand upon its head, and slaughter it before the Tent of Meeting; the sons of Aaron shall cast its blood around the altar. ¹⁴He shall present from it his offering, a fire offering to the Lord: The fat that covers the innards, all the fat that is on the innards, ¹⁵the two kidneys, the fat that is on them that is on the flanks, and the diaphragm above the liver, with the kidneys he shall remove it. ¹⁶The priest shall burn them on the altar; it is the food of the fire offering, for a pleasing aroma. All the fat of the animal is burned on the altar as an offering for the Lord. ¹⁷It shall be an eternal statute for your generations, at all times and in all your dwellings, both inside and outside the Land of Israel: All fat, i.e., all the fat that is burned on the altar in an offering, and all blood you shall not eat.

Illustrations: See drawing of bull and its sacrificial parts, p. 527.

Leviticus

The Sin Offering – the Sin Offerings Whose Blood Is Sprinkled inside the Sanctuary

After describing the free will offerings, the Torah explains in detail the laws of the obligatory offerings, beginning with the sin offering. A sin offering is brought to atone for sins committed unwittingly, due to forgetfulness, or by confusing a prohibited matter with a permitted matter. The Torah first explicates the sin offerings brought by the High Priest and the High Court, the spiritual authorities of the people of Israel, which are different from other sin offerings in that the blood of the offering is sprinkled inside the Sanctuary before the curtain and placed on the incense altar. The fats of these offerings are offered on the altar in the courtyard, and the flesh is not offered at all, but burned outside the courtyard.

4 ¹**The Lord spoke to Moses, saying:** ²**Speak to the children of Israel, say-**
Fifth
aliya
ing: When a person sins unwittingly, out of forgetfulness or by mistake, **with regard to any of the commandments of the Lord that may not be performed,** the negative precepts, **and he performs one of them,** violating one of the prohibitions, the laws of the sin offering vary depending on the identity of the transgressor:

³**If the anointed priest,** the High Priest, erroneously rules that a forbidden matter is permitted and subsequently follows that ruling, he thereby **sins to bring guilt on the** entire **people. He shall present,** as atonement **for his sin that he sinned, an unblemished young bull to the Lord, as a sin offering.** ⁴**He shall bring the bull to the entrance of the Tent of Meeting before the Lord; he shall lay his hand on the head of the bull, and slaughter the bull before the Lord.** ⁵**The anointed priest shall take from the blood of the bull, and bring it to the Tent of Meeting.** ⁶**The priest shall dip his finger in the blood, and sprinkle from the blood seven times before the Lord, before the curtain of the Sanctuary.** ⁷**The priest shall place from the blood on the horns,** the corners, **of the altar of the incense of the spices, before the Lord, which is in the Tent of Meeting. All the** remaining **blood of the bull, he shall pour at the base of the altar of the burnt offering, which is at the entrance of the Tent of Meeting.** ⁸**All the fat of the bull of the sin offering he shall remove from it;** ⁹**and the two kidneys, and the fat that is on them that is on the flanks,** extending to the hindquarters; **and the diaphragm above the liver with the kidneys, he shall remove them,** ¹⁰**as it,** the sacrificial portion consisting of the fat and internal organs, **is separated from the bull of the peace offering** to be burned on the altar (see 3:3); **the priest shall burn them on the altar of the burnt offering.** ¹¹**As for the bulk of the animal** that remains, **and** this includes **the hide of the bull, and all its flesh, with**

its head, and with its legs, and its innards, and its dung, **¹²he shall take the entire** remainder of the **bull outside the camp to a pure place, to the place where the ashes** of all the offerings burned on the altar **are poured** (see 6:1–4). He shall **burn it on wood in the fire; on the place where the ashes are poured it shall be burned,** not as an offering.

Illustrations: See images of the altar of the burnt offering and the altar of the incense of the spices, pp. 525–6.

¹³The Torah now presents the second type of sin offering: **If the entire congregation of Israel errs unwittingly,** that is, if the High Court unwittingly issued an erroneous ruling permitting a severe transgression, and as a result **the matter is concealed from the eyes of the assembly,** the people having been led astray, **and they,** the community as a whole, **perform one of all the commandments of the Lord that may not be performed,** the entire community erred, **and they,** the court, **are guilty. ¹⁴When the sin in which they sinned** subsequently **becomes known, the assembly shall present a young bull as a sin offering, and bring it before the Tent of Meeting. ¹⁵The elders of the congregation shall lay their hands on the head of the bull before the Lord; and one shall slaughter the bull before the Lord. ¹⁶The anointed priest shall bring from the blood of the bull to the Tent of Meeting. ¹⁷The priest shall dip his finger in the blood, and sprinkle it seven times before the Lord, before the curtain. ¹⁸From the blood, he shall** also **place** some **on the horns of the** incense **altar that is before the Lord, that is in the Tent of Meeting, and all the** remaining **blood he shall pour at the base of the altar of the burnt offering, which is at the entrance of the Tent of Meeting. ¹⁹All its fat he shall separate from it,** as explained above (verses 8–10), **and burn it on the altar. ²⁰He shall do to the bull as he did to the bull of the** High Priest's **sin offering; so shall he do to it; and the priest shall atone for them,** for the entire community, **and it shall be forgiven for them. ²¹He shall take the bull outside the camp, and burn it** in the same place and in the same manner **as he burned the first bull,** the bull of the anointed priest; **it is the sin offering of the assembly.**

The Sin Offering – the Sin Offerings Whose Blood Is Sprinkled on the Altar in the Courtyard

The sin offerings of the king and of an ordinary person are similar in character: The blood of the offering is sprinkled on the the large altar in the courtyard, and the flesh is burned there

as well. The similarity of the offering brought by the highest civil authority to that brought by an ordinary person teaches that all members of the nation are equally subject to the Torah's commandments.

²²The Torah describes the third type of sin offering: **When a ruler,** the king, **sins, and unwittingly performs one of all the commandments of the Lord his God that may not be performed, and he** subsequently recognizes that he **is guilty,** ²³**or if his sin that he sinned becomes known to him** because he is informed of it by others, **he shall bring his offering, an unblemished male goat.** ²⁴**He shall lay his hand on the head of the goat, and slaughter it in the place where he shall slaughter the burnt offering,** to the north of the altar (1:11), **before the Lord; it is a sin offering.** ²⁵**The priest shall take from the blood of the sin offering with his finger, and place it on the horns of the altar of the burnt offering, and the** remainder of the **blood he shall pour at the base of the altar of the burnt offering.** ²⁶**All its fat he shall burn on the altar, like the fat of the peace offering. The priest shall atone for him for his sin, and it shall be forgiven for him.**

²⁷The Torah describes the fourth type of sin offering, the sin offering of an ordinary person: **If one person from the common people sins unwittingly, in his performance of any of the commandments of the Lord that may not be performed, and** he subsequently realizes that he **is guilty,** he shall bring a sin offering. ²⁸**Or if his sin that he sinned becomes known to him** because he is informed of it by others (see verse 23), **he shall bring his offering, an unblemished female goat for his sin that he sinned.** ²⁹**He shall lay his hand upon the head of the sin offering, and slaughter the sin offering in the place of the burnt offering.** ³⁰**The priest shall take from its blood with his finger, and place it on the horns of the altar of the burnt offering, and all** of the remainder of **its blood he shall pour at the base of the altar.** ³¹**All its fat he shall remove, as the fat was removed from the peace offering, and the priest shall burn it upon the altar for a pleasing aroma to the Lord; and the priest shall atone for him, and it shall be forgiven for him.**

³²**And if he brings a lamb** rather than a goat **as his offering for a sin offering, an unblemished female he shall bring it.** ³³**He shall lay his hand on the head of the sin offering, and slaughter it as a sin offering in the place where he shall slaughter the burnt offering.** ³⁴**The priest shall take from the blood of the sin offering with his finger, and place it on the horns of the altar of the burnt offering, and all** the remainder of **its**

Sixth aliya

blood he shall pour at the base of the altar. ³⁵He shall remove all its fat, just as the fat of the lamb is removed from the peace offering, including the sheep's fatty tail. The priest shall burn them on the altar, on the fire offerings of the Lord, or, alternatively, on the fire that burns for the Lord on the altar; and the priest shall atone for his sin that he sinned, and it shall be forgiven for him.

The Sliding-Scale Offering

In special cases, the type of sin offering that must be brought varies in accordance with the financial situation of the sinner. One who evades giving testimony on behalf of another person by taking an oath that he does not know anything, or one who enters the Temple or partakes of sacrifices while ritually impure, or one who takes an oath and violates it – in all of these cases the sinner brings a sin offering in accordance with his means. An affluent person brings a female lamb or goat, and a poor person brings a pair of doves; and if he cannot afford even that, he brings a meal offering. This sin offering is called in the Talmud a "sliding-scale offering," as its value fluctuates in accordance with the sinner's financial means.

5 ¹If a person sins in that he hears the voice of an oath administered to him to speak the truth, and he is a witness who either saw a certain occurrence or knew of a certain matter; if he does not tell whatever he knows, but rather takes an oath denying knowledge of the matter, he shall bear his iniquity and receive his punishment. ²Or a person who touches any impure thing: The carcass of a non-pure beast, i.e., an undomesticated animal, the carcass of a non-pure domesticated animal, or the carcass of an impure swarming animal, and it is hidden from him, that is, he forgets that he is impure, and he is impure, and he is guilty, because he entered the Temple or partook of sacrificial food in his ritually impure state, ³or if he touches human impurity, in any type of impurity with which he will become impure, and then forgets, so that it is hidden from him; and subsequently he remembers and knew that he was impure, and he is guilty, ⁴or, lastly, a person who takes an oath, to express with lips an undertaking to do harm to himself by abstaining from a certain matter, or to do good to himself by performing a certain matter, for everything that a person shall express in an oath, and it was subsequently hidden from him, as he forgot his oath, and he violated it, and he subsequently knew and he is guilty of violating one of these oaths.

⁵It shall be, when he is guilty of one of these transgressions, he shall verbally confess with regard to that which he sinned. ⁶He shall then bring his restitution to the Lord for his sin that he sinned, an offering, a

Leviticus

female from the flock, a lamb or a goat, as a sin offering; and the priest shall atone for him for his sin, performing the rites of the sin offering as described above (4:27–35).

⁷**If his means do not suffice for** the purchase of **a lamb, he shall bring his restitution,** his offering **for that which he sinned, two turtledoves or two young pigeons, to the Lord: One as a sin offering and one as a burnt offering.** ⁸**He shall bring them to the priest, and** the priest **shall offer that** bird **which is** intended **for the sin offering first. He shall pinch its head adjacent to its nape** with his thumbnail, severing its spine, **but shall not separate** the head from the body. ⁹**He shall sprinkle from the blood of the sin offering on the wall of the altar, and the remainder of the blood shall be squeezed at the base of the altar; it is a sin offering.** ¹⁰**And the second** bird **he shall prepare as a burnt offering, in accordance with the procedure** stated above (1:14–17), and then burn the bird in its entirety on the altar. **And the priest shall atone for him** with the two bird offerings **for his sin that he sinned, and it shall be forgiven for him.**

Seventh aliya ¹¹**If** he is so poor that **his means do not suffice** even **for two turtledoves or two young pigeons, he shall bring his offering for that which he sinned, one-tenth of an ephah of choice flour as a sin offering.** However, **he shall not place oil on it, nor shall he place frankincense on it, as it is a sin offering.** ¹²**He shall bring it to the priest, and the priest shall take his handful from it, his full handful, its memorial portion, and** he shall **burn it on the altar, on the fire offerings of the Lord; it is a sin offering.** ¹³**The priest shall atone for his sin that he sinned for one of these, and it shall be forgiven for him; and it,** the remainder of the sinner's meal offering that is not burned, **shall be for the priest like the meal offering,** and he is commanded to eat it.

The Guilt Offering

Guilt offerings are brought to atone for certain transgressions: a guilt offering for misuse of sacred articles, for the unwitting misuse of consecrated property; a guilt offering brought in a state of uncertainty, for the performance of an action the prohibition of which is in doubt; and a guilt offering for robbery, for denying owing money to another person and taking a false oath to that effect. As opposed to a sin offering, which can be a female goat or lamb, the only animal used for a guilt offering is a ram (a mature male sheep) with a minimal value of two silver shekels.

¹⁴**The Lord spoke to Moses, saying:** ¹⁵**A person who commits a trespass, and sins unwittingly with regard to the sacred items of the Lord,**

taking or deriving benefit from consecrated property, **he shall bring his restitution,** his offering, **to the Lord, an unblemished ram from the flock, according to the valuation of** at least two **silver shekels, according to the sacred shekel, as a guilt offering.** [16]In addition to bringing this guilt offering, **that which he sinned** by taking or benefiting **from the sacred** property **he shall pay,** repay, **and one-fifth of it,** its value, **he shall add to it,** the repayment, **and he shall give it to the priest; the priest shall atone for him with the ram of the guilt offering, and it shall be forgiven for him.**

[17]The Torah discusses a second type of guilt offering: **And if a person sins, and performs one of all the commandments of the Lord that shall not be performed, and he did not know** whether or not he committed a sin, **and he is guilty, and he shall bear his iniquity,** receive his punishment. [18]**He shall bring an unblemished ram from the flock, according to the valuation** of at least two silver shekels (see verse 15), **as a guilt offering to the priest. The priest shall atone for him for the unwitting sin that he performed unwittingly, and he did not know,** at the time that he presented the offering, whether or not he had committed a sin, **and it shall be forgiven for him.** [19]**It is a guilt offering; he is guilty to the Lord.**

Illustrations: For drawings illustrating the sacrificial parts of the ram, see p. 528.

[20]The Torah introduces the third type of guilt offering. **The Lord spoke to Moses, saying:** [21]**A person who sins and commits a trespass against the Lord, and lies to his counterpart with regard to a deposit,** denying that he had received the deposit from the other person; **or with regard to** returning money received as **a loan, or with regard to** open **robbery** that he denies having perpetrated; **or** he **exploited his counterpart,** e.g., by refusing to pay the wages due to him; [22]**or** the trespass occurs when he **finds a lost item and lies with regard to it,** telling the owner that he does not have it. **And** if, after taking someone's property in one of these ways, he **takes a false oath about anything that a person does to sin with regard to these** situations listed above, [23]**it shall be, when he sins and is guilty, he shall restore** to its owner **the stolen item that he stole, or the proceeds of his exploitation, or the deposit that was deposited with him,** *Maftir* **or the lost item that he found,** whether it was money or other items, [24]**or** in **any** similar case concerning an **item with regard to which he has taken a false oath, he shall repay its principal,** the value of whatever he stole

Leviticus

257

or withheld, **and one-fifth of it he shall add to it** as a penalty. **To him to whom it belongs, he shall give it,** the total sum, **on the day** on which he recognizes the fact **of his guilt.** [25]After he returns the money, **his restitution,** his offering **he shall bring to the Lord; an unblemished ram from the flock, according to the valuation** of at least two silver shekels (see verse 15), **as a guilt offering, to the priest.** [26]**The priest shall atone for him before the Lord,** performing the rites of the guilt offering as described below (7:1–5), **and he shall be forgiven for anything that he may have done to incur guilt.**

Parashat Tzav

Parashat Tzav relates to the practical side of the sacrificial service. It is addressed to the priests, instructing them with regard to their role in the service in the Tabernacle. The order of the offerings presented in this *parasha* differs from the order in which they were presented in *Parashat Vayikra*. This *parasha* opens with the holiest sacrifices – the burnt offerings, meal offerings, sin offerings, and guilt offerings, and then explains the peace offerings, which are sacrifices of lesser holiness. In most cases, parts of the holiest sacrifices are eaten by priests in the Temple courtyard, whereas sacrifices of lesser holiness may be eaten also by the people bringing the offerings, and generally for a longer period of time than that allotted to the eating of the holiest sacrifices.

The second half of the *parasha* describes the days of consecration, the seven days during which the Tabernacle was sanctified and Aaron and his sons were consecrated, in anticipation of the beginning of their service in the Tent of Meeting.

The Burnt Offering

The offerings that were sacrificed over the course of the day would burn on the altar throughout the night. It was therefore necessary to keep a fire burning on the altar all night, and in the morning, to remove the ashes and build up the pyre. The Torah spells out these procedures in the context of the burnt offering because that sacrifice is burned in its entirety on the altar over the course of many hours.

6 ¹**The Lord spoke to Moses, saying:** ²**Command Aaron and his sons, saying: This is the law of the burnt offering. It is the burnt offering** that burns **on the pyre on the altar all night until the morning, and the fire of the altar shall be kept burning on it.** ³At the end of the night, **the priest shall don his linen vestment** [*middo*], which is precisely fitted to his size [*midda*], **and his linen trousers he shall don on his flesh, and he shall separate** from the altar **the ashes of the burnt offering that the fire consumes on the altar, and he shall place it beside the altar.** ⁴He, the priest, **shall then remove his vestments and don other** priestly **vestments** of lesser quality, to perform this next rite, in which he was likely to get dirty; **and he shall take the ashes outside the camp, to a pure place.** ⁵**The fire on the altar shall be kept burning on it; it shall not**

be extinguished and, to that end, **the priest shall kindle** a new pyre of **wood on it every morning.** In addition, **he shall arrange on it** the pieces of **the burnt offering so that they will burn, and** also **burn on it the fats of the peace offering.** ⁶**A perpetual fire shall be kept burning upon the altar; it shall not be extinguished.**

📖 **Further reading:** For more on the fire that burned upon the altar, see *A Concise Guide to the Sages*, p. 137.

The Meal Offerings

In the case of a meal offering by a non-priest, a handful of the offering is burned on the altar, while the rest of the offering is eaten by the priests. This consumption of the remnant is itself a sacrificial rite, paralleling to a certain degree the consumption of the handful by the fire on the altar. Certain meal offerings are brought only by priests: the griddle-cake offering brought every day by the High Priest and the priestly meal offering of inauguration brought by every priest on the first day that he performs the Temple service. These meal offerings, as well as every other meal offering brought by a priest, are burned in their entirety on the altar.

⁷**This is the law of the meal offering: The sons of Aaron shall present it before the Lord at the front of the altar.** ⁸**He,** the priest, **shall** then **separate from it,** from the meal offering, **his handful from the choice flour of the meal offering and from its oil. And** he shall also remove **all the frankincense that is on the meal offering. He shall burn its memorial portion,** both the handful of flour and all the frankincense, **on the altar,** as **a pleasing aroma to the Lord.** ⁹**The remnant of it** that was not offered on the altar **Aaron and his sons shall eat; as unleavened bread it shall be eaten, in a holy place; in the courtyard of the Tent of Meeting they shall eat it.** ¹⁰**It,** the meal offering, **shall not be baked leavened. I have given it as their,** that is, the priests', **portion from My fire offerings; it,** the entire meal offering, **is a sacred sacrament like the sin offering and like the guilt offering.** ¹¹**Every male among the children of Aaron shall eat it.** It is **an eternal statute for your generations from the fire offerings of the Lord. Anything,** any food, **that touches them,** the meal offerings, **shall become sacred** with their sanctity.

Second aliya ¹²**The Lord spoke to Moses, saying:** ¹³**This is the offering of Aaron** the High Priest **and of his sons that they shall present to the Lord on the day he is anointed.** This offering is to be brought every day by the High Priest, and is known as the griddle-cake offering of the High Priest. A similar offering is to be brought by any priest on the first day that he performs the

Temple service. This is known as the priestly meal offering of inauguration: **One-tenth of an ephah of choice flour as a perpetual meal offering, half of it in the morning, and half of it in the evening.** [14]**On a pan, it,** the meal offering, **shall be prepared with oil, you shall bring it boiled. You shall present the baked meal offering in** small **pieces;** that is, it is boiled, then baked, and then fried and broken into pieces. All of it was burned on the altar as **a pleasing aroma to the Lord.** [15]**The priest who is anointed in his stead from his sons,** the High Priest, who is descended from Aaron, **shall prepare it** every day as a fixed offering. **It is an eternal statute to the Lord; it shall be burned in its entirety** upon the altar. [16]**Likewise, every meal offering of the priest shall be offered** to God **in its entirety,** completely burned on the altar; **it shall not be eaten.**

The Laws Pertaining to the Priests – Other Offerings

The Torah spells out the laws governing the sin offering and the guilt offering. The meat of both of these offerings is eaten by priests in a state of sanctity. The priest who engages in the sacrificial rites of the offering enjoys the first right to its consumption.

[17]**The Lord spoke to Moses, saying:** [18]**Speak to Aaron and to his sons, saying: This is the law of the sin offering. In the place where the burnt offering is slaughtered,** on the north side of the altar (see 1:11), **the sin offering shall be slaughtered before the Lord; it is a sacred sacrament.** [19]Furthermore, **the priest who presents it as a sin offering** [*hamehatei*], i.e., who engages in the sacrificial rite of the sin offering, **shall eat it. In a holy place it shall be eaten, in the courtyard of the Tent of Meeting.** [20]**Whatever shall touch its flesh,** the flesh of the sin offering, **shall become holy,** and must be treated with sanctity. **And if some of its blood is** accidentally **sprinkled on a garment,** rather than the altar, then **that upon which it is sprinkled you shall wash in a holy place,** as it may not be removed from the holy place. [21]**An earthenware implement in which it,** the sin offering, **shall be cooked shall** subsequently **be broken. If it is cooked in a bronze implement, it shall be scoured,** scrubbed clean, then placed in boiling water, **and rinsed in** cold **water,** after which it may be used again. [22]**Every male among the priests shall eat it,** that is, may partake of it. **It,** the entire sin offering, **is a sacred sacrament.** [23]As mentioned earlier (chap. 4), the blood of certain sin offerings is not sprinkled on the outer altar, but inside the Sanctuary itself. These offerings are referred to by the Sages as the inner sin offerings. **Any sin offering from which blood shall be brought to the Tent of Meeting** to sprinkle opposite the curtain and

on the incense altar, **to atone in the holy place, shall not be eaten** at all; rather, **it shall be burned in fire.**

7 ¹**This is the law of the guilt offering; it is a sacred sacrament.** ²**In the place where the burnt offering is slaughtered,** on the north side of the altar (see 1:11), **they shall** also **slaughter the guilt offering. And its blood, he,** the priest, **shall cast around the altar** on all sides. ³**All of its fat he shall offer from it: The fat tail** of the guilt offering, which may be either a ram or a lamb, **and the** large layer of **fat that covers the innards,** ⁴**and the two kidneys and the fat that is on them, which is on the flanks, and the diaphragm above the liver; he shall remove it with the kidneys.** ⁵**The priest shall burn them on the altar as a fire offering to the Lord; it is a guilt offering.** ⁶**Every male among the priests may eat it,** the flesh that is not burned on the altar; **in a holy place,** the courtyard of the Tabernacle or Temple, **it shall be eaten: It is a sacred sacrament.**

⁷**Like the sin offering, so is the guilt offering; there is one law for them.** In both cases, **the priest that atones with it,** performing the sacrificial rites, **it,** the flesh of the offering, **shall be his.** ⁸Similarly, in the case of **the priest who presents the burnt offering of a man, the hide of the burnt offering that he presents,** which is not burned on the altar, **it shall be for the priest,** and not for the individual bringing the offering. ⁹**Every meal offering that is baked in the oven, and any prepared** by frying **in a deep pan, or on a** shallow **pan, it shall be for the priest who presents it.** ¹⁰**Every meal offering,** either **mixed with oil,** e.g., the voluntary meal offering of flour mixed with oil (see 2:1), **or dry,** e.g., the meal offering of a sinner, which does not contain any oil (see 5:11), **shall be for all the sons of Aaron, one like another,** divided equally among them.

The Thanks Offering and the Peace Offering

In the case of a peace offering, the owner of the animal plays an active role in its sacrifice. He waves certain parts of the offering, and eats most of the flesh, in a sanctified area. In the case of a thanks offering, which a person offers as an expression of gratitude for a miracle performed on his or her behalf, the person bringing the offering organizes a meal with many diners so that they are able to consume the entire offering, and also the breads that accompany it. In this way the miracle is publicized. The Torah spells out the prohibition to eat of the offering in a state of ritual impurity or beyond the permitted time, as well as the prohibition to eat of the fats of an animal that are to be burned on the altar.

Third
aliya
¹¹**This is the law of the peace offering that one presents to the Lord.** ¹²**If he presents it for thanksgiving,** in gratitude for a miracle that had been

performed on his behalf, then **he shall present with the thanks offering unleavened loaves mixed with oil, and unleavened wafers,** similar to pitas, **smeared with oil, and loaves of boiled choice flour,** flour that is first boiled and then baked into loaves, **mixed with oil.** [13]**With loaves of leavened bread he shall present his offering with the thanks offering of his peace offerings.** [14]**He shall present from it,** the loaves, **one of each offering,** i.e., one of each type of loaf, **as a gift to the Lord; it shall be for the priest who sprinkles the blood of the peace offering.** The remaining loaves belong to the owner of the thanks offering. [15]**The flesh** that remains **of the thanks offering of his peace offerings shall be eaten** only **on the day of its offering; he shall not leave any of it until the** next **morning.**

[16]**If his** peace **offering is** brought not as a thanks offering, but rather in fulfillment of **a vow** to bring an offering, **or a pledge** to offer a specific animal, **on the day that he presents his offering it shall be eaten and** also **on the morrow, and that which remains of it** on the first day **may be eaten on the morrow** as well. [17]**That which remains of the flesh of the offering on** the morning of **the third day shall be burned in fire.**

[18]**If,** at the time of the animal's sacrifice, his intention is that some of **the flesh of his peace offerings shall be eaten on the third day,** past the time that it is permitted to be eaten, the offering is disqualified. **It shall not be accepted, nor shall it be credited to him that presents it;** rather, **it shall be a detestable thing, and the person who eats from it shall bear his iniquity** and be punished.

[19]**The flesh** of an offering **that shall touch any impure item shall not be eaten;** rather, **it shall be burned in fire. And with regard to the** ritually pure **flesh** of a peace offering, **every pure person may eat the flesh,** not only the owner of the offering. [20]**The person who eats flesh of the peace offering that is to the Lord while his ritual impurity is upon him** is liable to severe punishment; **that person shall be excised from his people.** [21]**When a person touches anything impure: the impurity of man,** that is, a person who contracted any of the types of impurities that a person may contract, **or a non-pure animal,** that is, the carcass of a non-kosher animal, **or any impure, detestable thing,** a dead creeping animal (see 11:20–43), he is rendered impure, **and** consequently, **if he shall eat of the flesh of the peace offering that is to the Lord, that person shall be excised from his people.** [22]**The Lord spoke to Moses, saying:** [23]**Speak to the children of Israel, saying: Any** of the **fat of a bull or a sheep or a goat** that is meant to be offered on the altar, **you shall not eat.** [24]**The** same type of **fat of an**

unslaughtered carcass of a pure animal that died naturally, **and the fat of a mauled animal** or an animal that died with a severe injury **may be used for all labor, but you shall not eat it.** ²⁵**For anyone who eats fat from an animal that one could offer from it a fire offering to the Lord, the person eating shall be excised from his people.** ²⁶Likewise, **all blood you shall not eat in any of your dwellings, of bird or of animal.** ²⁷Moreover, **any person who eats any blood,** even the blood of an animal that may not be sacrificed as an offering, **that person shall be excised from his people.**

📖 **Further reading:** For the practical implications of the prohibition against eating blood or forbidden fat, see *A Concise Guide to Halakha*, p. 550.

²⁸**The Lord spoke to Moses, saying:** ²⁹**Speak to the children of Israel, saying: He who presents his peace offering to the Lord shall** himself **bring his offering to the Lord; it shall be from his peace offerings.** ³⁰**His own hands shall bring the fire offerings of the Lord; the fat on the breast he shall bring it** to be burned on the altar; while, with regard to **the breast,** he is **to wave it** upward **as a wave offering** to display it **before the Lord,** but it is not offered on the altar. ³¹**The priest shall burn the fat on the altar, and the breast shall be for Aaron and for his sons,** the priestly portion of the peace offering. ³²In addition to the breast, **the right haunch** of the offering **you shall give to the priest as a gift from your peace offerings.** ³³**The one who presents the blood of the peace offering and the fat from the sons of Aaron,** i.e., the priest who sacrifices the peace offering, **for him shall be the right haunch as a portion.** ³⁴**For I have taken the breast of waving and the haunch of lifting from the children of Israel, from their peace offerings, and have given them to Aaron the priest and to his sons as an eternal allotment from the children of Israel.**

Illustrations: See drawing of bull illustrating the breast of waving and the haunch of lifting, p. 527.

³⁵**This is the portion** [*mishhat*], or, alternatively, the gift of splendor or greatness, **of Aaron, and the portion of his sons, from the fire offerings of the Lord, on the day that He brought them near to serve as priests to the Lord,** ³⁶**that the Lord commanded to give to them on the day He anointed them, from the children of Israel.** The gifts of the priesthood shall be **an eternal statute for their generations.** ³⁷**This is the law,** the statutes and ordinances, **for the burnt offering, for the meal offering, for the sin offering, for the guilt offering, for the investiture offering,**

and for the peace offering [38]that the Lord commanded Moses at Mount Sinai, on the day of His commanding the children of Israel to present their offerings to the Lord in the Tabernacle, in the wilderness of Sinai.

The Consecration of the Priests and the Tabernacle

During the "seven days of investiture," the days during which the Tabernacle is consecrated for service and Aaron and his sons are dedicated as priests, Moses serves in the role of priest. He anoints and sanctifies the Tabernacle, Aaron and his sons, and the priestly vestments. He also offers the special investiture offerings that are to be brought during this period. The consecration ceremony is repeated until the eighth day, at which time the priests themselves begin to conduct the holy service.

8 [1]**The Lord spoke to Moses, saying:** [2]**Take Aaron and his sons with him,** the priestly **vestments, the anointing oil, the bull of the sin offering, the two rams, and the basket of unleavened bread.** [3]**Assemble the entire congregation at the entrance of the Tent of Meeting,** so that they may witness these events. [4]**Moses did as the Lord had commanded him, and the congregation was assembled at the entrance of the Tent of Meeting.** [5]**Moses said to the congregation: This is the matter that the Lord commanded to be done.**

urth
liya

📖 **Further reading:** For more on the selection of Aaron and his sons as priests, see *A Concise Guide to the Sages*, p. 139.

[6]**Moses brought Aaron and his sons near, and he washed them with water,** that is, he commanded them to immerse. [7]**He placed upon him, Aaron, the tunic,** a simple garment worn next to the skin, **and girded him with the belt, and clothed him with the robe, and placed the ephod on him, and he girded him with the belt of the ephod and adorned him with it,** the ephod, which was placed, apron-like, over the other vestments. [8]**He placed the breast piece on him, and in the breast piece he placed the Urim and the Tumim,** which contained the special name of God. [9]**He placed the mitre,** a long band of cloth, **on his,** Aaron's, **head; and he placed on the mitre, toward** the fore of **his head, the golden frontplate, the sacred diadem,** the crown of the High Priest, **as the Lord had commanded Moses.** [10]**Moses took the anointing oil and anointed the Tabernacle and all that was in it, and he consecrated them** through this anointing. [11]**He sprinkled from it,** the anointing oil, **on the altar seven times, and he anointed the altar and all its vessels,** the vessels used in the service of the altar, **and**

the laver and its base, to consecrate them. ¹²He poured from the anointing oil on Aaron's head and anointed him to consecrate him. ¹³Moses brought Aaron's sons near, clothed them in tunics, girded them with a belt, and wrapped headdresses on them, different from the mitre worn by the High Priest, as the Lord had commanded Moses.

Fifth aliya ¹⁴He, Moses, brought forward the bull of the sin offering, and Aaron and his sons laid their hands on the head of the bull of the sin offering. ¹⁵He, Moses, slaughtered the bull of the sin offering, and Moses took the blood, placed it all around on the horns of the outer altar with his finger, and purified the altar. He poured the blood at the base of the altar, and he consecrated it to atone for it. ¹⁶He took all the fat that was on the innards, the diaphragm of, above, the liver, and the two kidneys, and their fat, and Moses burned it on the altar. ¹⁷The bull, its hide, its flesh, and its dung that remained in its intestines, he burned in fire outside the camp, as the Lord had commanded Moses.

¹⁸He brought the ram of the burnt offering near, and Aaron and his sons laid their hands on the head of the ram, as it was their offering. ¹⁹He slaughtered it, and Moses cast the blood around the altar. ²⁰He cut the ram into its pieces, and Moses burned the head, the pieces, and the fats. ²¹The innards and the legs he washed with water, and Moses burned the entire ram on the altar. It is a burnt offering for a pleasing aroma; it is a fire offering to the Lord as the Lord had commanded Moses.

Sixth aliya ²²He brought near the second ram, the ram of investiture, the ram brought as part of the investiture ceremony in which the priests would be officially appointed to their position, and Aaron and his sons laid their hands on the head of the ram. ²³He slaughtered it, and Moses took from its blood and placed it on the tip of Aaron's right ear, and upon the thumb of his right hand, and upon the big toe of his right foot. ²⁴He brought Aaron's sons near, and Moses placed the blood on the tip of their right ear, and on the thumb of their right hand, and on the big toe of their right foot; and Moses cast the remaining blood around the altar. ²⁵He took the fat, the fat tail, and all the fat that was upon the innards, and the diaphragm of, above, the liver, and the two kidneys, and their fat, and the right haunch, and brought all of this to the altar. ²⁶From the basket of unleavened bread that was before the Lord, he took one unleavened loaf, one loaf of oil bread, and one wafer, and he placed them on the fat and on the right haunch. ²⁷He placed it all, the loaves and the sacrificial portions, on the palms of Aaron and on the palms of his sons,

and Moses **waved them,** i.e., Aaron and his sons' hands, which held the sacrificial portions, **as a wave offering before the Lord.** [28]**Moses took them,** the loaves and sacrificial portions, **from on their palms, and burned them on the altar, on,** after, the ram **burnt offering. They are an investiture offering for a pleasing aroma; it is a fire offering to the Lord.** [29]**Moses took the breast** as well **and waved it as a wave offering before the Lord;** it, the breast, **was the portion for Moses from the ram of investiture, as the Lord had commanded Moses.**

nth
liya [30]**Moses took from the anointing oil and from the blood that was** placed **on the altar, and he sprinkled it on Aaron, on his vestments, and on his sons, and on the vestments of his sons with him, and he** again **consecrated Aaron and his vestments, and his sons and the vestments of his sons with him.**

[31]**Moses said to Aaron and to his sons: Cook the flesh** that remains of the ram of investiture **at the entrance of the Tent of Meeting, and there you shall eat it and the bread that is in the basket of investiture, as I commanded, saying: Aaron and his sons shall eat it.** [32]If the flesh and the bread are not entirely consumed by the next morning, **that which remains of the flesh and of the bread you shall burn in fire.**

ftir [33]**From the entrance of the Tent of Meeting you shall not emerge seven days, until the day of completion of the days of your investiture** as priests, **as for seven days He shall invest you.** [34]**As he did on this day,** referring to all the sprinkling of blood and offerings, **the Lord commanded to do, to atone for you.** [35]**At the entrance of the Tent of Meeting you shall remain day and night,** for all **seven days** of the investiture, **and** you shall serve as an honorary guard, and **keep the commission of the Lord, that you shall not die, for so I was commanded.** [36]**Aaron and his sons did all the things that the Lord commanded at the hand of Moses.**

Leviticus

Parashat Shemini

The *parasha* opens with an account of the dedication of the Tabernacle, which took place on the eighth day of the days of investiture, the days of initiation and practice of the Tabernacle service. In the midst of the festivities, two of the priests, Nadav and Avihu, died, because they burned incense not in accordance with God's command, breaching thereby the severe fences that had been erected around the sanctity of the Tabernacle. In the wake of this event, the *parasha* deals at length with commands related to the guarding of sanctity, and to distinguishing between the pure and the impure, and with prohibitions against the external manifestation of mourning and against drunkenness. The *parasha* proceeds from the prohibition against entering the Tabernacle in a state of ritual impurity to an extensive discussion about which living creatures are permitted as food and which are prohibited, and about the ritual impurity that is imparted from living creatures to man.

The Eighth Day – the Dedication of the Tabernacle
On the eighth day of the days of investiture, Aaron and his sons themselves begin to serve in the Temple. Special offerings are brought in honor of the dedication of the Tabernacle: Aaron first sacrifices his personal offerings, and afterward the offerings of the people. The event reaches its climax when, after the people are blessed and Moses and Aaron offer a prayer, a fire descends from heaven and burns the offerings on the altar.

9 ¹**It was on the eighth day** of the days of investiture that **Moses summoned Aaron and his sons and the elders of Israel.** ²**He,** Moses, **said to Aaron: Take for yourself a young calf as a sin offering and a ram as a burnt offering, unblemished, and present them,** you yourself, **before the Lord.** ³**Speak to the children of Israel, saying: Take a goat as a sin offering, and a calf and a lamb, one year old, unblemished, as a burnt offering,** ⁴**and a bull and a ram as peace offerings, to slaughter before the Lord, and a meal offering** of flour **mixed with oil. For today the Lord appears to you** to rest His Presence in the Tabernacle.

⁵**They took that which Moses commanded before the Tent of Meeting, and the entire congregation approached and stood before the Lord.** ⁶**Moses said: This is the matter that the Lord commanded that you shall**

do, and, if you obey, **the glory of the Lord will appear to you;** God will reveal Himself to you.

[7]**Moses said to Aaron: Approach the altar and perform your sin offering and your burnt offering, and atone for yourself and** afterward **for the people; perform the offering of the people and atone for them, as the Lord commanded.**

[8]**Aaron approached the altar** in the courtyard of the Tabernacle, **and he slaughtered the calf of the sin offering that was** to atone **for him.** [9]**The sons of Aaron presented the blood** in a vessel **to him,** their father. Aaron **dipped his finger in the blood, and he placed it on the horns of the altar, and he poured** out the remainder of **the blood at the base of the altar.** [10]**The fat, the kidneys, and the diaphragm above the liver of the sin offering he burned on the altar, as the Lord had commanded Moses.** [11]**The flesh and the skin** he did not offer on the altar, but rather **he burned in fire outside the camp.**

[12]**After the sin offering, he slaughtered the burnt offering, and Aaron's sons** stretched out their hands and **passed the blood to him, and he cast it around the altar.** [13]**They passed the burnt offering to him** cut up **in its pieces, and the head, and he burned them,** the pieces and the head, **on the altar.** [14]**He washed the innards and the legs and burned them on,** after, the pieces of **the burnt offering** that he had placed **on the altar.**

[15]**After** sacrificing his own sin offering and burnt offering, **he,** Aaron, **brought the people's offering near. He took the goat of the sin offering that was for the people, and slaughtered it and presented it as a sin offering like the first,** like Aaron's calf of the sin offering. [16]**He brought the burnt offering near, and he performed it in accordance with the**

cond
aliya

procedure stated with regard to the burnt offering (see chap. 1). [17]**He brought the meal offering near, and he filled his palm from it,** removing a handful, **and burned it on the altar, in addition to the morning burnt offering.** All of these offerings were brought after the mourning burnt offering which is part of the regular daily service.

[18]**He slaughtered the bull and the ram, the peace offerings that were for the people, and Aaron's sons passed the blood to him, and he cast it around the altar.** [19]They passed him **the fats from the bull and from the ram, the fat tail** of the ram, **and those that cover,** the fats of the bull and the ram that cover various parts of the animal, **and the kidneys, and the diaphragm above the liver.** [20]**They placed the fats upon the breasts**

in order to wave them before God, **and he burned the fats on the altar.** **²¹Aaron waved the breasts and the right haunch as a wave offering before the Lord,** but did not burn them on the altar, **as Moses had commanded.**

²²Aaron raised his hands toward the people and blessed them with the priestly blessing. **And** before that **he descended from** the altar after **performing the sin offering, the burnt offering, and the peace offerings.** **²³Moses and Aaron came into the Tent of Meeting** in order to pray. **And** they **emerged and blessed the people, and** then **the glory of the Lord**

Third **appeared to the entire people.** **²⁴Fire emerged from before the Lord,**
aliya from the Holy of Holies, **and consumed upon the altar the burnt offering and the fats; all the people saw it, and sang praise,** or shouted, **and fell upon their faces** due to this revelation.

The Death of Nadav and Avihu

At the height of this joyful day, two sons of Aaron burn incense in the Tabernacle on their own, not on God's command.

Despite their good intentions, the Tabernacle leaves no room for spontaneity; the service must be executed precisely in accordance with God's will. Aaron's two sons die, and their deaths cast a shadow over the celebration.

10 **¹Each of the** two eldest **sons of Aaron, Nadav and Avihu, took his firepan and placed in it** coals **of fire, and placed incense upon it,** the fire, **and they offered before the Lord strange fire that He had not commanded them** to bring as an offering on that day. **²Fire emerged from before the Lord and consumed them, and they died before the Lord,** inside the Sanctuary. The fire killed them though their bodies remained intact.

³Moses said to Aaron: This is that about **which the Lord spoke, saying: Through those who are near Me I will be sanctified and before all the people I will be glorified.** God's sanctity is made known by the death of anyone, even Aaron's sons, who encroaches upon it without permission. **And Aaron was silent.** **⁴Moses called Mishael and Eltzafan, the sons of Uzziel,** an **uncle of Aaron. And Moses said to them: Approach, carry your brethren,** your cousins, **from inside the Sanctuary to outside the camp.** **⁵They approached and carried them by their tunics to outside the camp,** for the dead were not left inside the camp, **as Moses had spoken.**

The Commandments in the Wake of the Deaths of Nadav and Avihu

Despite the great sadness in the wake of the deaths of Nadav and Avihu, the priests must continue with their service in the Tabernacle, and may not stop and mourn. The importance of the priests' mission also finds expression in the prohibition to be drunk while engaged in the Tabernacle service or while occupied in teaching God's Torah to the people of Israel.

⁶Moses said to Aaron, and to Elazar and to Itamar, his, Aaron's, **other sons: You shall not grow out the hair of your heads,** letting it grow wild, **and you shall not rend your garments** in the manner of mourners, so **that you will not die.** If you observe the usual customs of mourning, not only will you be liable to death, but **He,** God, **will rage against all the congregation. And your brethren, the entire house of Israel, shall weep** over **the burning that the Lord has burned. ⁷From the entrance of the Tent of Meeting you shall not emerge** for as long as you are obligated to perform the service, so **that you not die, as the anointing oil of the Lord is upon you,** and you have been consecrated for this lofty mission. **They,** Aaron and his surviving sons, **acted in accordance with the word of Moses,** and remained in the Tabernacle.

⁸The Lord spoke to Aaron, saying: ⁹You shall not drink wine or any **intoxicating drink, neither you nor your sons with you, upon your entry into the Tent of Meeting, that you not die;** this is **an eternal statute for your generations.** ¹⁰You shall refrain from intoxicating drinks, so that you will be able to **distinguish** for the people **between the sacred and the profane, and between the impure and the pure,** ¹¹**and** in order **to teach the children of Israel all the statutes that the Lord spoke to them at the hand of Moses.** The priests' role in instructing the people demands that they avoid drunkenness, which can lead to error and confusion.

urth
liya
¹²Moses spoke to Aaron, and to Elazar and to Itamar, his surviving sons: Take the meal offering that remains from the fire offerings of the Lord, after its handful has been sacrificed, **and eat it unleavened beside the altar,** in the Tabernacle courtyard, **as it is a sacred sacrament. ¹³You shall eat it in a holy place, as it is your allotment,** Aaron, **and the allotment of your sons, from the fire offerings of the Lord,** and it is their sustenance. **For so I was commanded** that you must eat the meal offering. **¹⁴You shall eat the breast of waving and the haunch of lifting in a pure place,** not necessarily inside the Sanctuary, **you and your sons and your daughters with you, as they are given as your allotment and the allotments of your sons from the peace offerings of the children of Israel. ¹⁵The haunch of lifting and the breast of waving they shall bring** to the

Leviticus

altar **with the fire offerings of the fats,** not for burning, but **to wave it for a wave offering before the Lord, and it shall be for you and for your sons with you,** a gift from the altar, **as an eternal allotment, as the Lord commanded.**

The Goat of the Sin Offering

Moses learns that the priests did not eat the meat of the sin offering of the people, but rather took it to be burned outside the camp. While Moses expresses his anger, Aaron rises to the priests' defense and explains that, the need to continue the Tabernacle service notwithstanding, the priests' hearts are filled with pain and sorrow. Such feelings are inappropriate for the eating of sacrificial meat, which must be done with joy. Moses accepts Aaron's explanation.

Fifth aliya ¹⁶**Moses inquired about the goat of the sin offering, and** discovered that **behold, it was burned,** and not eaten, **and he was angry with Elazar and with Itamar, the surviving sons of Aaron, saying:** ¹⁷**Why didn't you eat the sin offering in the holy place, as it is a sacred sacrament,** and it should have been eaten there? **He,** God, **gave it to you** and commanded you to eat the sacrificial meat in order **to bear the iniquity of the congregation, to atone for them before the Lord,** the consumption of the sin offering by the priests being part of the atonement process. ¹⁸**Behold, its blood was not brought to the Sanctuary within** to be sprinkled inside the Sanctuary, like the inner sin offerings, the meat of which is burned and not eaten (6:23). Therefore, **you should have eaten it in the holy place, as I commanded.** ¹⁹**Aaron spoke to Moses: Indeed, today they,** my sons, **offered their sin offering and their burnt offering before the Lord and these** tragedies **have befallen me; had I eaten the sin offering today, would it have been satisfactory in the eyes of the Lord?** ²⁰**Moses heard and it was satisfactory in his eyes.**

Living Creatures That Are Permitted or Prohibited for Consumption

The Torah describes the characteristics that determine whether animals, birds, fish, and locusts are permitted for consumption. Mammals, domesticated or not, must chew their cud and have cloven hooves; fish must have fins and scales; kosher locusts are those that have two upper legs with joints for leaping; as for birds, the Torah lists those that are prohibited, all others being permitted.

11 ¹**The Lord spoke to Moses and to Aaron, saying to them:** ²**Speak to** *Sixth aliya* **the children of Israel, saying: These are the living creatures that you may eat from all the animals that are on the earth,** i.e., land animals: ³**Anything that has hooves,** as opposed to paws, **and the hooves are split,**

like those of sheep, goats, and cows, **and** it **brings up the cud,** it regurgitates its food and chews it a second time, **among the animals, that you may eat.**

⁴However, these you shall not eat from those that bring up the cud and have hooves, for they have only one of the two necessary characteristics: **the camel, because it brings up the cud but it does not have hooves,** and it is therefore **impure to you. ⁵The hyrax, because** it appears as if **it brings up the cud but it does not have hooves,** and consequently **it is impure to you. ⁶The hare, because** it appears as if **it brings up the cud but it does not have hooves,** and **it is** therefore **impure to you. ⁷And the pig, because it has hooves, and its hoof is split,** like those of kosher animals, **but it does not chew the cud** at all. Consequently, **it is impure to you. ⁸From their flesh you shall not eat, and their carcasses you shall not touch** if you wish to enter the Tabernacle or partake of consecrated foods; **they are impure to you.**

⁹This you may eat from everything that is in the water: All things that have fins and scales in the water, whether they live **in the seas, or in the rivers, those you may eat. ¹⁰And all things that do not have fins and scales in the seas and in the rivers, of all** small **creatures that swarm in the waters, and of all the living creatures that are in the water, they are a detestable thing to you. ¹¹They shall be a detestable thing to you; you shall not eat from their flesh, and their carcasses you shall detest,** distancing yourself from eating them. **¹²Anything that does not have fins and scales in the water, is a detestable thing to you.**

¹³And these you shall detest and distance yourselves from, **among the fowls; they shall not be eaten, they are a detestable thing: the griffon vulture, the bearded vulture, and the lappet-faced vulture. ¹⁴And the kite, and the buzzard,** middle-sized birds of prey, **after its kind,** all the birds of similar or identical species. **¹⁵Every raven after its kind. ¹⁶And the ostrich, and the swift, the seagull, ¹⁷the little owl, the fish owl,** a coastal bird that snatches fish from the sea, **and the short-eared owl. ¹⁸The barn owl, the eagle-owl, and the roller. ¹⁹The stork, and the heron, after its kind, the hoopoe, and the bat.**

²⁰Every flying swarming creature that walks on all fours, flying insects that have four legs, **is a detestable thing to you. ²¹However, this you may eat from all flying swarming creatures that walk on all fours: Those that have jointed legs above their feet, to leap with them upon the earth.**

Leviticus

²²These of them you may eat: the locust after its kind, the bald locust after its kind, the cricket after its kind, and the grasshopper after its kind. ²³But all flying swarming creatures that have only four feet are a detestable thing to you.

Illustrations: See image of grasshopper with jointed leg, p. 528.

The Ritual Impurity of Animal Carcasses

The carcasses of unkosher animals impart ritual impurity to humans, objects, and foods. Here the Torah spells out the details of the laws governing this type of impurity. The carcass of a mammal imparts impurity to a person who touches or lifts it. As for other animals, the Torah lists eight creatures that impart impurity; all others are forbidden for consumption, but do not impart impurity. The purification process after contracting such impurity involves immersion in a ritual bath.

²⁴By these creatures you shall become impure; anyone who touches their carcasses shall be impure until the evening. ²⁵And furthermore, anyone who carries some of their carcasses, even without touching them directly, shall wash his garments, and be impure until the evening. ²⁶In addition, with regard to any animal that has hooves, but they are not split, e.g., a horse, or it does not bring up the cud, it is impure to you; anyone who touches their carcasses shall become impure. ²⁷And likewise, anything that walks on its paws, that does not have hooves, among all beasts that walk on all fours, i.e., most mammals, they are impure to you; anyone who touches their carcasses shall be impure until the evening. ²⁸And one who carries their carcasses shall wash his garments and shall be impure until the evening; they are impure to you.

²⁹And this is impure to you among the small swarming creatures that teem upon the earth: the marten, the mouse, and the spiny-tailed lizard after its kind, ³⁰the shrew, the monitor, the lizard, the skink, and the chameleon. ³¹These are those that are impure to you among all the swarming creatures; anyone who touches them when they are dead shall be impure until the evening.

³²And anything upon which some of these swarming creatures may fall when they are dead shall become impure; any wooden implement, or garment, or leather, or sackcloth, any fashioned item with which work is done, it shall be brought into water, immersed, and it shall be impure until the evening; and then it will be purified. ³³And any earthenware vessel into which any of them falls, anything that is found in it shall

Seventh aliya

become impure, even if the dead swarming creature did not come into contact with it; and it, the earthenware vessel, you shall break, as it cannot be purified. ³⁴Any food that may be eaten upon which water has come, which came into contact with water, shall become impure, shall become susceptible to contracting ritual impurity. And any liquid that may be drunk, that is fit for drinking, in any vessel shall become impure, i.e., susceptible to ritual impurity. Only food that has come into contact with water and liquids that are detached from the ground is susceptible to impurity. ³⁵And anything upon which shall fall some of their carcasses, of swarming creatures, shall become impure. For example, an oven or stove, which are earthenware vessels, shall be shattered, as they are impure, and shall be impure to you, as there is no way to purify them. ³⁶However, a spring or cistern, a gathering of natural water, shall be pure, if a swarming creature falls into it. But even so, one who touches their carcasses in the water shall become impure. ³⁷And if some of their carcasses, of the swarming creatures, shall fall upon any sown seed that shall be sown, that has not been processed as food, it is pure. ³⁸But if water shall intentionally be placed on the seed, if it was washed with water to prepare it for eating, and some of their carcasses, of these swarming creatures, shall fall on it, it is impure to you.

³⁹And if any animal that is for your consumption, that comes from a species whose consumption is permitted, shall die not by way of ritual slaughter, one who touches its carcass shall be impure until the evening. ⁴⁰One who eats of its carcass shall wash his garments and be impure until the evening; and one who carries its carcass, even without touching it, shall wash his garments and be impure until the evening.

⁴¹And any other swarming creature that swarms upon the earth, but is not included in the list of swarming creatures whose carcasses impart impurity (11:29–30), is a detestable thing; it shall not be eaten, but it does not impart impurity. ⁴²Consequently, any creature that crawls upon the belly, e.g., snakes and worms, and any creature that walks on four legs, up to any creature that has numerous feet among all swarming creatures that swarm on the earth, you shall not eat them, as they are a detestable thing. ⁴³You shall not render yourselves detestable with any swarming creature that swarms by eating them, and you shall not be rendered impure by them, and become impure through them.

⁴⁴For I am the Lord your God; you shall sanctify yourselves and be holy, set apart, for I am holy. And, therefore, you shall not render yourselves

Leviticus

Maftir **impure with any swarming creature that creeps upon the earth.** [45]**For I am the Lord who brought you up from the land of Egypt to be your God; you shall be holy, as I am holy.** [46]In summation: **This is the law of the animals, and of the birds, and of every living creature that creeps in the water, and of every creature that swarms on the earth.** [47]With regard to all of these, it is necessary **to distinguish between the impure and the pure, and between the living creature that may be eaten and the living creature that may not be eaten.**

📖 **Further reading:** For more on keeping kosher, see *A Concise Guide to the Sages*, p. 142; *A Concise Guide to Halakha*, p. 545.

Parashat Tazria

In this *parasha* the Torah continues to relate the laws of impurity and the rites of purification. The concept of impurity in the Torah does not correspond to anything physical. These laws and rites are decrees for which no rational explanation is provided.

The birthing process causes a woman to become ritually impure, and the Torah spells out the manner by way of which she can return to a state of purity. Leprous spots that appear on a person's body or on his garments give rise to a severe form of ritual impurity; a person who is possibly affected must turn to a priest to determine whether the affliction is leprosy[1] or not.

The Ritual Impurity of a Birthing Mother and the Rites of Her Purification

The birth of a male child renders a woman ritually impure for seven days, after which she must wait thirty-three days and then bring an offering. These times are doubled in the case of the birth of a female child; two weeks of impurity and sixty-six days before the mother brings an offering.

12 **¹The Lord spoke to Moses, saying: ²Speak to the children of Israel, saying: If a woman conceives and bears a male child, she shall be impure seven days; like the days,** the duration, **of her menstrual** [*niddat*] **suffering,** that is, for seven days, **she shall be impure. ³On the eighth day, the flesh of his foreskin shall be circumcised. ⁴After the seven days of impurity, for thirty days and three days she shall abide in the** state of **blood of purity;** even if she continues to bleed, she will not have to distance herself from her husband. Nevertheless, **she shall not touch any consecrated item, and she shall not enter the Sanctuary until the completion of the days of her purity.** Only after forty days from the birth will she become fully purified from her impurity.

Leviticus

---

1. The terms 'leprosy', 'leprous', etc. as used here do not refer to the disease known today as leprosy. The symptoms described in the Torah do not correspond to any known disease.

📖 **Further reading:** For the inner significance of the covenant of circumcision, see *A Concise Guide to the Sages*, p. 144; *A Concise Guide to Mahshava*, p. 9. The circumcision ceremony itself is described in *A Concise Guide to Halakha*, p. 5.

⁵**If she bears a female child, then she shall be impure two weeks as during her menstruation,** when she must separate herself from her husband. **And sixty days and six days she shall abide in the** state of **blood of purity.**

⁶**With the completion of the days of her purity,** the end of the forty-day period **for a son or** the eighty-day period **for a daughter, she shall bring a lamb in its first year as a burnt offering, and** either **a young pigeon or a turtledove as a sin offering, to the entrance of the Tent of Meeting, to the priest.** ⁷**He,** the priest, **shall offer it,** the pair of offerings, **before the Lord, and** thereby **atone for her; and she shall be purified from the source of her blood,** from the bleeding from her womb. **This is the law of the woman after childbirth of a male child or of a female child.**

⁸**If her means do not suffice for** buying **a lamb** for her burnt offering, **she shall take two turtledoves, or two young pigeons, one** bird **as a burnt offering** in place of the lamb, **and one as a sin offering,** which all such women must bring (see verse 6); **and the priest shall atone for her, and she shall be purified.**

Leprosy of the Body

The appearance of a lesion on a person's skin requires that it be examined by a priest. If at least two white hairs or healthy flesh appear within the confines of the lesion, it is confirmed as leprosy. In a case of doubt, the individual is confined to his house for seven days, after which he is reexamined. If at the end of the week the lesion has spread, it is confirmed as leprosy.

13 ¹**The Lord spoke to Moses and to Aaron, saying:** ²**A man** or a woman, **when he shall have on the skin of his flesh a spot, or a scab, or a pale spot,** which are various types of skin discolorations, **and it shall become in the skin of his flesh a mark of leprosy, he shall be brought to Aaron the priest, or to one of his sons the priests,** who are the exclusive authorities on matters of leprosy. ³**The priest shall examine the mark on the skin of the flesh. If hair in,** within the area of, **the mark turned white, and** in addition **the appearance of the mark is deeper than the skin of his flesh,** the mark's pale color causing it to appear as though it were sunken, **it is the mark of leprosy** in all aspects. Therefore, **the priest shall see it and pronounce it impure,** thereby establishing the person as a leper.

📖 **Further reading:** Learn the reason this type of leprosy would appear; see *A Concise Guide to the Sages*, p. 147.

⁴On the other hand, **if it is a pale white spot on the skin of his flesh** but there are no other symptoms, **and its appearance is not deeper than the skin,** because it is not that pale, **and its hair did not turn white, the priest shall quarantine** the person with **the mark** for **seven days** and then perform a follow-up examination. ⁵**The priest shall examine it,** the mark, once again **on the seventh day** of the quarantine, **and behold,** if **the mark maintained its** previous **appearance, and the mark did not spread on the skin** and grow beyond its original size, then **the priest shall quarantine** the person with **it seven days again,** as the mark can still turn into leprosy. ⁶**The priest shall examine it on the seventh day again,** for the third time; **and behold, if the mark** has **darkened, or** at least **the mark did not spread on the skin, the priest shall pronounce it pure: It is a scab,** a mere skin disease that does not entail ritual impurity; **and he,** the person who had been quarantined, **shall wash his garments, and he shall be purified.** ⁷**But if the scab spread on the skin,** the affected area grew **after he was shown to the priest for** the sake of **his purification, he shall be examined again by the priest.** ⁸**The priest shall examine; and behold, if the scab spread on the skin, the priest shall pronounce him impure: It is leprosy.**

⁹**A mark of leprosy, when it is on a person, he shall be brought to the priest.** ¹⁰**The priest shall examine; and behold, if there be a white spot on the skin, and it turned** the **hair** found within it **white, or there is a growth of raw flesh in the spot,** meaning that in the affected area there appears tissue that looks healthy, ¹¹**it is an old,** extended **leprosy in the skin of his flesh; the priest shall pronounce him impure.** The growth of healthy flesh indicates that it is old leprosy. **He,** the priest, **shall not quarantine him,** since this is unnecessary, **as he,** the afflicted individual, **is** immediately declared **impure.**

¹²**And if the leprosy shall erupt** and keep growing larger **on the skin, and the leprosy shall cover all the skin of** the individual with **the mark, from his head to his feet, for the entire view of the eyes of the priest,** all of the skin exposed to the priest becoming lighter in color, ¹³**the priest shall examine; and behold, the leprosy covered all his flesh; he shall pronounce the mark pure.** Since **it turned white in its entirety,** therefore **it is pure.** ¹⁴**But on the day that raw flesh appears on him,** and some of his flesh regains its natural appearance, only then **he shall be impure.** ¹⁵**The priest shall examine the raw flesh and pronounce it impure;** because

of the raw flesh he is impure: It is leprosy. [16]Or if, but if, afterward, the raw flesh because of which he was rendered impure is restored and turns white, he shall come to the priest. [17]The priest shall examine him; and behold, the skin affected by the mark turned white, the priest shall pronounce the mark to be pure: It is once again pure.

Rashes and Burns

Leprosy can occur also in the wake of a rash or burn. As in prior examples, in such cases the leprosy is confirmed if at least two hairs within the confines of the mark turn white, or if the mark spreads during the course of the afflicted individual's confinement. In contrast to the regular form of skin leprosy, if signs of impurity do not appear after a week of confinement, the individual is pronounced pure.

Third aliya [18]Flesh, when there is in its skin a rash, some sort of skin disease, that is healed, [19]and on the place of the rash, where the skin has not yet fully mended, there is a white spot, or a white-red pale spot, it shall be shown to the priest. [20]The priest shall examine; and behold, if its appearance, the appearance of the pale spot, is lower than the skin, and its hair turned white, the priest shall pronounce it impure: It is a mark of leprosy, as it erupted in the place where there had earlier been a rash. [21]But if the priest shall examine it, and behold, there is no white hair in it, and it is not lower than the skin, and it has darkened, then the priest shall quarantine him for seven days. [22]And if after a week it shall spread on the skin, the priest shall pronounce him impure: It is a mark. [23]But if the pale spot shall remain in place, and it did not spread, it is a natural scar of the rash. The priest shall pronounce him pure.

Fourth aliya (Second aliya) [24]Or flesh, when there is on its skin a burn by fire, and the healed flesh of the burn became a pale spot, reddish white, or white, [25]the priest shall examine it; and behold, hair in the pale spot turned white, and its appearance is deeper than the skin, it is leprosy that erupted in the spot of the burn; the priest shall pronounce him impure: It is a mark of leprosy. [26]But if the priest shall examine it, and behold, there is no white hair in the pale spot, and it is no lower than the skin, and it has darkened, the priest shall quarantine him seven days. [27]The priest shall examine him on the seventh day; if the pale spot has spread on the skin, the priest shall pronounce him impure, because it is a mark of leprosy. [28]But if the pale spot remains in its place and has not spread on the skin, and it has darkened, it is the spot of the burn; the priest shall pronounce him pure, as it is the scar of the burn.

Leprosy of the Head and the Beard

A scall is a lesion of the scalp or beard, with yellow hair growing from it attesting to its impurity. Here, too, in cases of uncertainty the individual presenting with the scall is put into quarantine for up to two weeks, and if the scall spreads or the hair turns yellow, he is declared impure. If a person is bald, a lesion that developed on the bald spot is governed by the laws of leprosy of the skin.

Fifth aliya 29A man or woman, when there shall be a mark on a head or on a beard, 30the priest shall examine the mark, and behold, its appearance is deeper than the skin, and if there is yellow, thin hair in it, thinner than the rest of his hair, the priest shall pronounce it impure: It is a scall; it is leprosy of the head or of the beard. 31When the priest examines the mark of the scall, and behold, its appearance is not deeper than the skin, and yet there is no ordinary black hair in it, the priest shall quarantine the individual with the mark of the scall seven days. 32The priest shall examine the mark on the seventh day; and behold, if the scall did not spread, and there is no yellow hair in it, and the appearance of the scall is not deeper than the skin, 33he, the quarantined leper, shall be shaved, the hair surrounding the mark must be shaved, but the hair growing in the scall itself or along its edges he shall not shave. And the priest shall quarantine the scall seven days again. 34The priest shall examine the scall once again on the seventh day; and behold, if the scall did not spread in the skin, and its appearance is not deeper than the skin, the priest shall pronounce it pure; and he shall wash his garments and be purified. 35But if the scall did not spread during the quarantine period, and yet it shall spread on the skin after his purification, 36the priest shall examine him; and behold, the scall spread on the skin, and therefore the priest shall not have to inspect for the yellow hair and see whether or not there is any yellow hair in it, as in any case it is impure. 37But if after the priest pronounced him impure the scall maintained its appearance, and black hair grew in it, it is a sign that the scall has healed, it is pure. The priest shall pronounce it pure.

38A man or a woman, if there will be in the skin of their flesh pale spots, pale white spots, 39the priest shall examine; and behold, the pale spots in the skin of their flesh are dull white, whitish but not pure white, it is a tetter, a certain skin disease, that erupted on the skin, and therefore it is pure.

Sixth aliya *Third (iya)* 40A man, if the hair of his head falls out for any reason, he is merely bald; he is pure, as baldness in itself is not a sign of ritual impurity. 41And

likewise, **if on the front of his face the hair of his head falls out, he is frontally bald; he is pure.** [42]**But when there is on the bald head, or the bald forehead, a reddish-white mark,** a white mark with a reddish hue, **it is leprosy erupting on his bald head or on his bald forehead.** [43]**The priest shall examine it; and behold, if the spot of the mark is reddish white on his bald head, or on his bald forehead,** and it is **like the appearance of** ordinary **leprosy in the skin of the flesh,** [44]**he is a leprous man, he is impure; the priest shall pronounce him impure: His mark is on his head.**

[45]**And the leper in whom the mark is,** and whom the priest has formally pronounced as a leper, **his garments shall be rent;** he must tear his garments. **And the hair of his head shall be grown out, and he shall cover** his mouth and **his upper lip** with his outer garment **and shall cry: Impure, impure,** thereby informing others of his ritually impure status. [46]**All the days that the mark is on him he shall be impure; he is impure, he shall live alone, outside the camp is his dwelling,** where he is cut off almost entirely from human society.

Leprosy of Garments

Leprosy of garments, which involves red and green spots found on clothing, is a miraculous phenomenon that is not part of the natural order. In contrast to leprosy of the skin, garments afflicted with leprosy are not immediately declared impure, but only after a week-long period of quarantine. After the time has passed, the garment is declared impure even if it has not changed in any way.

[47]**The garment, if there shall be in it a mark of leprosy,** an abnormal mark growing on the garment through no apparent cause, **whether in a woolen garment, or in a linen garment,** [48]**if it is either in the warp,** the threads that run lengthwise in a woven fabric, **or in the woof,** the threads that run crosswise in such a fabric, at right angles to the warp threads, **for linen or for wool, or in leather, or in anything made of leather;** [49]**if the mark was deep green or deep red, in the garment, or in the leather, or in the warp, or in the woof, or in any implement of leather, it is a mark of leprosy and shall be shown to the priest.** [50]**The priest shall examine the mark, and he shall quarantine the mark seven days** for observation.

[51]**He shall examine the mark on the seventh day: If the mark spread in the garment, or in the warp, or in the woof, or in the leather, for any labor that leather is utilized, the mark is a malignant leprosy** that impairs the item and has no remedy; **it is impure.** [52]Therefore, **he shall burn the**

garment, or the warp, or the woof, of wool or of linen, or any leather implement in which there is a mark, as it is a malignant leprosy; it shall be burned in fire.

⁵³If the priest shall examine the garment or implement at the end of the seven days, and behold, the mark did not spread in the garment, or in the warp, or in the woof, or in any implement of leather, ⁵⁴the priest shall command, and they shall wash that in which there is a mark with certain cleansing agents, and he shall quarantine it seven days again.

⁵⁵The priest shall examine after the mark has been washed, and behold, if the mark has not changed its appearance, and the mark did not spread, it is impure. Therefore, you shall burn it in fire; it is a depression, a deficiency, or a loss, whether it is in its back or its front. ⁵⁶And if the priest examines, and behold, the color of the mark has faded after it has been washed, he shall rip it, the affected area, from the garment, or from the leather, or from the warp, or from the woof. ⁵⁷If it, the mark, shall be seen again in the garment, or in the warp, or in the woof, or any leather implement, after the affected area was cut off and removed, it is erupting leprosy, and therefore you shall burn in fire that in which the mark is.

⁵⁸The garment, or the warp, or the woof, or any leather implement that you shall wash and the mark leaves them, that is, it disappears through the laundering, it shall be washed again, this time by immersion in a ritual bath, and it shall be purified from its impurity. ⁵⁹This is the law of the mark of leprosy of the woolen or the linen garment, or the warp, the woof, or any leather implement, to pronounce it pure or to pronounce it impure.

📖 Further reading: The following *parasha* covers the process of the leper's purification and the phenomenon of leprosy of the house.

Parashat Metzora

In the previous sections the Torah clarified the laws governing leprosy of the body and leprosy of garments. In this section it describes the process of purification that the leper must undergo after the lesions on his body have healed. The Torah also introduces another type of leprosy, leprosy of the house, which involves the appearance of spots on the walls of a person's house. The complicated purification process and the appearance of leprous spots on the walls of a house attest to the fact that leprosy is not a natural phenomenon, but rather a sign through which God communicates to man that his actions require correction.

Later in the *parasha* the Torah elucidates other types of ritual impurity stemming from illnesses or from natural processes in the human body, e.g., gonorrhea in men and the menstrual cycle in women.

A Leper's Purification Process

The Torah explicates the leper's process of purification, which is divided into several stages. First the leper re-enters the camp; afterward he returns to his tent and his family; and only at the end, with the offering of his sacrifices, is he permitted to enter the Tabernacle. No other process in the Torah has as many stages and details as does the leper's process of purification.

14 **¹The Lord spoke to Moses, saying: ²This shall be the law of the leper on the day,** at the time, **of his purification,** when he heals from his leprosy. **He shall be brought to the priest,** who has the exclusive authority to deal with leprosy. **³The priest shall go outside the camp,** where the leper had spent the period of his impurity. **And the priest shall examine, and behold, the mark of leprosy has been healed from the leper.**

> **Further reading:** For more on the significance of the elements of the leper's purification rites, see *A Concise Guide to the Sages*, p. 148.

⁴The priest shall command, and one, that is, any person, **shall take for the one being purified** from his leprosy **two living, pure birds, and** a piece of **cedar wood, and scarlet wool, and hyssop. ⁵The priest shall command, and one shall slaughter the one bird** of the two, so that its blood shall fall

in an earthenware vessel, over spring water that is already in the vessel. [6]The living bird, he shall take it, and the cedar wood, and the scarlet wool, and the hyssop, and he shall dip them and the living bird in the blood of the slaughtered bird that is over the spring water. [7]Using these dipped items, he shall sprinkle this mixture of blood and spring water on the one being purified from the leprosy, seven times, and he shall then be able to pronounce him pure, and shall dispatch the living bird over the field, setting it free.

[8]The one being purified shall wash, immerse, his garments, shave all his hair, bathe, immerse, in water, and be purified; and then he shall enter the camp, and shall dwell outside his tent seven days. Though now inside the Israelite camp, he may not yet enter his house and return to his wife.

[9]It shall be on the seventh day; he shall again shave all his hair, his head and his beard and his eyebrows; all his hair he shall shave from his entire body. And he shall wash his garments a second time, bathe his flesh in water, and be purified.

[10]Though ritually purified, the leper must still bring certain offerings in order to be rendered fit to enter the Temple and partake of consecrated food. Therefore, on the eighth day he shall take two unblemished male lambs, and one unblemished ewe in its first year, and three-tenths of an ephah, which is more than 7 liters, of choice flour mixed with oil as a meal offering, and one log of oil, which is about a third of a liter. [11]The priest who purifies shall position the man who is being purified and them, the lambs, before the Lord, at the entrance of the Tent of Meeting; he is not fit to enter the Tabernacle until he completes his atonement. [12]The priest shall take one of the lambs and present it as a guilt offering, and likewise he shall present the log of oil, and wave them, the live sheep with the log of oil, as a wave offering before the Lord. [13]He shall slaughter the lamb in the same place where one slaughters the sin offering and the burnt offering, in the holy place, on the north side of the altar (1:11, 6:18) since, like the sin offering, so too the guilt offering is for the priest, they are similar with regard to all matters involving the service of the priest; it is a sacred sacrament, an offering of the most sacred order.

[14]The priest shall take from the blood of the slaughtered guilt offering, and the priest shall place some of the blood on the tip of the right ear of the one being purified, and on the thumb of his right hand, and on the

big toe of his right foot. ¹⁵**The priest shall take** with his right hand **from the log of oil** brought by the one undergoing purification, **and pour it on** the cupped **left palm of the priest.** ¹⁶**The priest shall dip his right finger from,** into, **the oil that is** accumulated **on his left palm, and he shall sprinkle from the oil with his finger seven times before the Lord,** toward the Sanctuary. ¹⁷**And from the rest of the oil that is** left **on his palm, the priest shall place** some **on the tip of the right ear of the one being purified, and on the thumb of his right hand, and on the big toe of his right foot, on the blood of the guilt offering,** which he had previously placed on those spots. ¹⁸**The remainder of the oil that is on the priest's palm, he,** the priest, **shall place on the head of the one being purified; and the priest shall** thereby **atone for him before the Lord.**

¹⁹**The priest shall perform** the service of **the sin offering** that was brought by the one undergoing purification, **and atone for the one being purified from his impurity; and then he shall slaughter** the lamb of **the burnt offering.** ²⁰**The priest shall offer up the burnt offering and the meal offering,** consisting of the three-tenths of an ephah of fine flour that was brought by the leper being purified, **on the altar; and the priest shall atone for him** through these rites, **and he shall become pure.**

📖 **Further reading:** For more on guilt offerings, see p. 256.

The Offerings Brought by a Poor Leper

A poor leper, who lacks the means to bring the purification offerings described above, may offer birds for his sin offering and burnt offering rather than animals, which are more expensive. He still must offer a lamb as a guilt offering. His meal offering is also reduced to only one-tenth of an ephah of choice flour. Even though the offering brought by a poor leper appears inferior, the Torah repeats the entire process of purification using these offerings, emphasizing that there is no essential difference between the purification process of a rich leper and that of a poor one.

Third aliya (Fifth aliya) ²¹**If the leper is impoverished, and his means do not suffice** for all the above offerings, **he shall take one lamb as a guilt offering for waving, to atone for him** as would the offering of a wealthy individual, **and** only **one-tenth,** not three-tenths, **of an ephah of choice flour mixed with oil as a meal offering, and a log of oil.** ²²**And** he shall bring **two turtledoves or two young pigeons, for which his means suffice,** that he can afford; **one** of them **shall be a sin offering and** the other **one a burnt offering.** ²³**He shall bring them,** the sheep and the two birds, **on the eighth day of his**

purification, to the priest, to the entrance of the Tent of Meeting, before the Lord.

²⁴The priest shall take the lamb of the guilt offering and the log of oil, and the priest shall wave them as a wave offering before the Lord. ²⁵He shall slaughter the lamb of the guilt offering, and the priest shall take from the blood of the guilt offering, and place it on the tip of the right ear of the one being purified, and on the thumb of his right hand, and on the big toe of his right foot. ²⁶The priest shall pour from the oil on the left palm of the priest. ²⁷The priest shall sprinkle with his right finger from the oil that is on his left palm seven times before the Lord. ²⁸The priest shall place from the oil that is on his palm on the tip of the right ear of the one being purified, and on the thumb of his right hand, and on the big toe of his right foot, on the place of the blood of the guilt offering. ²⁹The remainder of the oil that is on the priest's palm he shall place on the head of the one being purified, to atone for him before the Lord.

³⁰He shall offer one of the turtledoves or one of the young pigeons, from that which his means suffice. ³¹The priest shall sacrifice that for which his means suffice, one as a sin offering and one as a burnt offering, with, in addition to, the meal offering; the priest shall thereby atone for the one being purified before the Lord. ³²This is the law of one in whom there is a mark of leprosy, whose means do not suffice in his purification.

📖 **Further reading:** The Sages emphasize God's love for the offering of a poor person in particular; see *A Concise Guide to the Sages*, p. 134.

Leprosy of the House

Leprosy can also appear on the walls of a person's house. The affliction is deemed to be leprosy if the lesions on the walls spread. In order to conduct his inspection, the priest quarantines the house for seven days. If, at the end of the week, the priest determines that the spots have spread, the affected stones are removed and replaced. If, upon reexamination, the affliction has returned, the entire house must be dismantled.

ourth aliya (Sixth aliya) ³³The Lord spoke to Moses and to Aaron, saying: ³⁴When you come to the land of Canaan, which I give to you as a portion, an inheritance, if I shall place a mark of leprosy on a house, that is, on one of the houses, in the land of your ancestral portion,

Leviticus

³⁵**he to whom the house belongs shall come and tell to the priest, saying: Something like a mark seems to me to be on the house.** Since only a priest can diagnose the plague, the owner of the house can only assert his suspicion that there is leprosy in his house. ³⁶**The priest shall command and they shall empty the house** of any vessels **before the priest shall come to see the mark, so** that **all that is in the house shall not become impure** if the priest determines that it is leprosy; **and afterward the priest shall come to see the house.** ³⁷**He,** the priest, **shall examine the mark, and behold, if the mark is,** or appears to be, **recessed in the walls of the house,** giving the impression of **deep green or deep reddish** recesses, **and their appearance is lower than the wall;** due to their color, they appear to be sunken below the plane of the wall's surface, ³⁸**the priest shall exit the house** and proceed **to the entrance of the house, and he shall quarantine the house,** instructing that it be sealed, for **seven days.**

³⁹**The priest shall return on the seventh day, and shall examine it; and behold, if the mark has spread on the walls of the house,** ⁴⁰**the priest shall command, and they shall remove the stones on which there is a mark. And they shall dispose of them,** as they are ritually impure, **in an impure place outside the city,** an area designated for the disposal of impure objects. ⁴¹**And** as for **the house, he shall scrape** and remove the layer of plaster **from inside all around. And they shall pour out the plaster that they scraped outside the city in an impure place.** ⁴²**They shall take other stones, and they shall bring them in the place of the stones** that they removed from the wall; **and he shall take other plaster, and** then **he shall plaster the house.**

⁴³**If** these actions are ineffective, and **the mark returns and erupts** again **in the house after removing the stones, and after scraping the house and after plastering it,** ⁴⁴**the priest shall come and examine; and if, behold, the mark has spread** again **in the house, it is a malignant leprosy in the house** that affects the entire house and has no repair, and **it is impure.** ⁴⁵**He,** that is, anyone, **shall demolish the** entire **house, its stones, and its timber, and all the plaster of the house, and he shall take it,** all these materials, **outside the city to an impure place.**

⁴⁶Special laws of impurity apply to a leprous house: **One who comes into the house all the days that it is quarantined shall be impure until the evening.** ⁴⁷**One who sleeps in the house shall wash his garments** that he is wearing, **and one who eats in the house shall wash his garments.**

⁴⁸If, alternatively, **the priest shall come and examine, and behold, the mark did not spread in the house** after the plastering of the house, the **priest shall pronounce the house pure, because the mark was healed.** ⁴⁹He shall take, to cleanse, purify, the house, **two birds, cedar wood, scarlet wool, and hyssop.** ⁵⁰He shall slaughter one of the birds in an **earthenware vessel over spring water.** ⁵¹He shall take the cedar wood, **and the hyssop, and the scarlet wool, and the living bird, and dip them in the blood of the slaughtered bird and in the spring water, and he shall sprinkle on the house seven times.** ⁵²He shall thereby **cleanse the house with the blood of the bird, and with the spring water, and with the living bird, and with the cedar wood, and with the hyssop, and with the scarlet wool.** ⁵³He shall dispatch the living bird outside the city out **on the field,** setting it free; **and he shall atone for the house,** cleansing it of its impurity, **and it shall be purified.**

Fifth aliya ⁵⁴**This is the law for any leprous mark,** which appears primarily on the skin, **and for a scall,** leprosy of the head or the beard, ⁵⁵**and for leprosy of the garment, and of the house,** ⁵⁶**and** for the following marks: **for the spot, and for the scab, and for the pale spot.** ⁵⁷**To teach on which day it is impure, and on which day it is pure; this is the law of leprosy.**

Ritual Impurity Connected to Bodily Discharges

A *zav*, a man suffering from gonorrhea, an infectious sexually transmitted disease, is ritually impure. He imparts impurity to articles by touching or moving them, and the articles on which he sits or lies become a primary source of impurity just like him. After seven days with no secretions, he must immerse in spring water and bring a special purification sacrifice in order to achieve full atonement.

15 ¹**The Lord spoke to Moses and to Aaron, saying:** ²**Speak to the children of Israel, and say to them: Any man, when he has a discharge from his flesh,** his member, **his discharge is impure.** ³**This shall be his impurity with his discharge: Whether his flesh,** member, **emits his discharge** of fluid, **or his flesh is blocked from his discharge,** the discharge being thick and blocking the orifice, either way **it is his impurity.**

⁴**Any bedding** or article of furniture designed for reclining **on which the one who has a discharge lies, shall be impure,** even if his body did not come into direct contact with it; **and,** similarly, **any item on which he sits,** any object fashioned for sitting, **shall be impure.** ⁵**A man who will touch his bedding shall wash his garments and bathe in water, and he is impure until the evening.** ⁶Furthermore, **one who sits on an article on**

which the one who has a discharge sat, he too **shall wash his garments and bathe in water, and he is impure until the evening.**

[7]In addition, **one who touches the flesh,** any part of the body, **of the one who has a discharge shall wash his garments and bathe in water, and he is impure until the evening.** [8]**If the one who has a discharge shall spit on one who is pure,** the latter **shall wash his garments and bathe in water, and he is impure until the evening.**

[9]**Any saddle on which the one who has a discharge shall ride shall be impure,** even if it did not come into direct contact with his body.

[10]**Anyone who touches any item that was underneath him,** the one who has a discharge, such as the aforementioned articles used for bedding, sitting, and riding, **shall be impure until the evening. And one who carries them,** one of these articles, even if he does not touch it, **shall wash his garments and bathe in water, and he is impure until the evening.**

[11]**Anyone whom the one who has a discharge shall touch when he,** the latter, **did not rinse his hands in water,** if he has yet to immerse himself from his impurity, **he shall wash his garments and bathe in water, and he is impure until the evening.** [12]**And an earthenware vessel,** which cannot be purified, **that the one who has a discharge shall touch, shall be broken; and every wooden implement shall be rinsed in water,** they are immersed in a ritual bath and are thereby purified.

[13]The chapter turns to the purification of the *zav.* **When the one who has a discharge shall be cleansed from his discharge,** after he is healed, **he shall count for himself seven days from his cleansing,** seven days on which he examines himself and finds no emission. **And he shall wash,** immerse in water, **his garments,** those he wore when he was a *zav,* **and he shall bathe his flesh in spring water,** water connected to its source. **And he is** thereby **purified.** [14]**On the eighth day, he shall take for himself two turtledoves or two young pigeons, and come before the Lord to the entrance of the Tent of Meeting,** as he is not yet fit to enter the Tabernacle until he completes his atonement, **and he shall give them to the priest.** [15]**The priest shall offer them, one as a sin offering, and one as a burnt offering; and the priest shall atone for him before the Lord from his discharge.**

Sixth
aliya
(Seventh
aliya) [16]The chapter mentions another type of impurity: **And a man, when semen is emitted from him, shall bathe,** immerse all his flesh in water, and he is impure until the evening. [17]**Every garment and any leather skin**

upon which there shall be semen shall be washed in water, and it is impure until the evening. [18]And a woman with whom a man shall lie with the emission of semen, the man and woman engaging in marital relations, they shall bathe in water, and they are impure until the evening.

The Ritual Impurity of a Menstruating Woman and a Zava

According to Torah law, a menstruating woman counts seven days from the beginning of her menstrual bleeding, after which she immerses herself and becomes pure. In contrast, a *zava*, a woman who experiences uterine bleeding during the time of the month when she does not expect to experience menstrual bleeding, must count seven clean days on which there is no bleeding, and only then does she become purified with immersion and the offering of special sacrifices. In a later generation, the Sages became more stringent about a menstruating woman and applied the laws governing a *zava* to her.

[19]**A woman, if she has a discharge,** not an illness, but **her discharge from her flesh being** the **blood** of her menstrual cycle, **seven days she shall be in** the ritual impurity of **her menstrual state. Anyone who touches her** on those days **shall be impure until the evening.** [20]**Anything on which she lies in her menstrual state shall be impure, and anything on which she sits shall be impure,** whether or not she touches them directly. [21]**Anyone who touches her bedding shall wash his garments and bathe in water, and he is impure until the evening.** [22]**Anyone who touches any article on which she sits shall wash his garments and bathe in water, and he is impure until the evening.** [23]**If he,** a ritually pure person, **is on the bedding, or on any article on which she sits,** in touching it he shall be impure until the evening.

[24]**If a man lies with her** during her menstrual period, or afterward but before she has immersed, **then** the impurity of **her menstrual status shall be upon him,** he will have the same level of impurity as she does. **And,** therefore, **he shall be impure seven days; and** also **any bedding on which he lies shall be impure.**

[25]**And,** with regard to **a woman, if her discharge of blood shall flow many days not at the time of her menstruation,** or alternatively, **if it shall flow beyond,** in addition to **her menstruation, for all the days of the discharge of her impurity,** as long as she is bleeding, **she shall be like during the days of her menstruation; she is impure.** Such a woman is known as a *zava*. [26]**Consequently, any bedding on which she lies all the days of her discharge shall be for her like the bedding of her menstruation** with regard to ritual impurity, **and any article on which she shall sit shall**

Leviticus

be impure, like the impurity of her menstruation. ²⁷**And anyone who touches them,** the vessels, furniture, or bedsheets on which she had sat or lain, **shall become impure, and he shall wash his garments and bathe in water, and he is impure until the evening.**

²⁸**But if she was cleansed from her discharge** and the blood flow ended, **she shall count for herself seven days** on which she experiences no

Seventh aliya bleeding, **and then she shall** immerse and **be pure.** ²⁹**And on the eighth day, she shall take for herself two turtledoves or two young pigeons, and she shall bring them to the priest, to the entrance of the Tent of Meeting.** ³⁰**The priest shall perform one as a sin offering, and one as a burnt offering; and the priest shall atone for her before the Lord for the discharge of her impurity.**

Maftir ³¹**You shall separate,** distance, **the children of Israel from their impurity, that they shall not die in their impurity, by their rendering My Tabernacle that is in their midst impure.** For if they are impure, there is concern that they might enter the Tabernacle or touch a consecrated object in their impure state and become liable for the death penalty.

³²The chapter concludes: **This is the law of the one who has a discharge, and of one from whom semen will be emitted, to become impure through it;** ³³and the law **of she who is suffering with her menstruation,** at the time of her period, **and** the law for **one who has a discharge, for a man or for a woman; and,** likewise, **for one who lies with an impure woman,** whether she is a menstruating woman, a *zava*, or has given birth.

📖 **Further reading:** Laws relating to the impurity and purification of a menstruating woman appear in *A Concise Guide to Halakha*, p. 574.

Parashat Aharei Mot

The people of Israel are commanded to guard the sanctity of the Sanctuary. There are rules as to when entry will be permitted. The most sacred area is the Holy of Holies, which even the High Priest is only permitted to enter on Yom Kippur. The High Priest's service on Yom Kippur will atone for the people's sins throughout the year. The *parasha* continues with the laws governing the eating of meat, and with an admonition to refrain from engaging in forbidden sexual relations and other abominable behaviors practiced by the Canaanite nations living in the Land of Israel.

The High Priest's Entry into the Holy of Holies

The High Priest's entry into the Holy of Holies is accompanied by the burning of incense and the sprinkling of the blood of sin offerings that atone for the sins of the people of Israel and the defilement of the Temple. The sins are symbolically placed on a goat, which is sent off to the wilderness. The High Priest's rite in the Holy of Holies atones for the people's sins and restores their relationship with God.

16 ¹**The Lord spoke to Moses after the death of the two sons of Aaron, when they approached before the Lord,** entering the Holy of Holies without permission, **and they died.** ²**The Lord said to Moses: Speak to Aaron, your brother, that he shall not come at all times,** whenever he wishes, **into the Sanctum** that is **within,** behind, **the curtain,** the Holy of Holies, **before the cover that is upon the ark, that he not die; for I will appear in the cloud upon the cover** of the ark. The Divine Presence rests on the cover of the ark, and therefore even the High Priest is generally forbidden to enter.

³**With this,** with the following rites and offerings, **shall Aaron come into the Sanctum: with a young bull as a sin offering and a ram as a burnt offering.** ⁴**He shall don a sacred linen tunic, and linen trousers shall be on his flesh, and he shall gird himself with a linen belt, and he shall wear a linen mitre,** a long piece of fabric that is wound around the head. These were the four simple garments ordinarily worn by the common priests, all of which were made from white linen. **They are sacred vestments, and**

therefore **he shall bathe his flesh in water, and** only then shall he **don them.**

📖 **Further reading:** For more on the significance and laws of Yom Kippur see *A Concise Guide to the Sages*, p. 285; *A Concise Guide to Mahshava*, p. 66; *A Concise Guide to Halakha*, p. 167.

[5]**From the congregation of the children of Israel he shall take two** identical **goats as a sin offering and one ram as a burnt offering.** [6]**Aaron shall present,** bring into the Tabernacle courtyard, **the bull of the sin offering that is for him,** which he purchased with his own private funds, **and** place his hands on the bull and recite a confession, and thereby **atone for himself and for his household,** his immediate family.

[7]**He shall** then **take the two goats** that were set aside to atone for the entire people, **and he shall set them before the Lord at the entrance of the Tent of Meeting.** [8]**Aaron shall place** the **lots** that he drew to determine each animal's fate **on** the heads of **the two goats.** On **one lot** it shall say: **for the Lord, and** on **the other lot** shall be written the phrase: **for Azazel,** a place or metaphysical entity representing chaos and the wilderness.

[9]**Aaron shall present the goat on which fell the lot for the Lord and render it a sin offering** by consecrating it for this purpose. [10]**The** second **goat, on which fell the lot for Azazel, shall** first **be set alive before the Lord, to atone with it** through placing hands upon it and reciting a confession, and afterward, **to dispatch it to Azazel, to the wilderness.**

[11]Afterward, **Aaron shall present the bull of the sin offering that is for him, and he shall atone for himself and for his household** by placing his hands on the bull a second time and confessing his own sins and those of all the priests; **and he shall** then **slaughter the bull of the sin offering that is for him.**

[12]Before sprinkling the blood, **he shall take a fire-pan,** a small shovel used for scooping and transporting embers, **full of smoldering coals** taken **from upon the** outer **altar, from before the Lord, and his hands full of finely ground fragrant incense,** as much incense as he can hold in his two hands cupped together, **and bring it within the curtain,** to the Holy of Holies. [13]**He shall place the incense on the fire,** on the smoldering coals in the fire-pan, **before the Lord, and the cloud,** the smoke, **of the incense shall obscure the cover that is upon the** ark of **testimony, and he shall not die.** The cloud produced by the burning incense conceals the revelation of

God, and thus protects the High Priest from death. ¹⁴**He shall** then **take the vessel** that contains the **blood of the bull** he had slaughtered previously, enter the Holy of Holies, **and sprinkle it with his finger upon the cover toward the east,** toward the eastern side of the cover; **and** after that, **before the cover,** toward the floor in front of the ark, **he shall sprinkle from the blood with his finger seven times.**

📖 **Further reading:** A description of the High Priest's service on Yom Kippur is read during the Yom Kippur *Musaf* service; see *A Concise Guide to Halakha*, p. 172.

¹⁵**He shall** then go to the Tabernacle courtyard and **slaughter the goat of the sin offering that is for the people,** the goat upon which fell the lot for the Lord, **and he shall bring its blood** in a vessel **within the curtain,** to the Holy of Holies, **and he shall do with its blood as he did with the blood of the bull, and sprinkle it upon the cover and before the cover.**

¹⁶By sprinkling the blood of the offerings in the Holy of Holies, **he shall atone for the Sanctum from the impurity of the children of Israel,** which marred its sanctity, **and from their transgressions, for** the general impurity of **all their sins; and so shall he do,** the same sprinklings, **for the Tent of Meeting that dwells with them in the midst of** and despite **their impurity.** ¹⁷No other **man shall be in the Tent of Meeting from** the time of **his entry to atone in the Sanctum until his emergence, and he,** the High Priest, **shall** thereby **atone for himself, for his household, and for the entire assembly of Israel.**

Second
aliya ¹⁸**He,** the High Priest, **shall** then **go out** of the Holy of Holies **to the altar that is before the Lord,** the golden, inner altar, **and he shall atone for it** in the following manner: **And he shall take from the blood of the bull and from the blood of the goat, and place it on the horns of the altar all around.** ¹⁹**He shall** then **sprinkle from the blood on it,** the golden altar, **with his finger seven times, and he shall purify it and sanctify it from the impurity of the children of Israel.**

²⁰**He shall conclude atoning for the Sanctum, and** for **the Tent of Meeting, and** for **the altar, and he shall present the living goat,** which is ready to be sent to the wilderness. ²¹**Aaron shall lay both his hands on the head of the living goat, and he shall confess over it all the iniquities of the children of Israel, and all their transgressions, for all their sins; and he shall place** those transgressions and sins **upon the head of the goat, and he shall dispatch it in the hand of a designated man to**

Leviticus

the wilderness. [22]The goat shall bear upon it all their iniquities to a precipitous, or desolate land, and he shall dispatch the goat into the wilderness.

[23]Afterward, Aaron shall come into the Tent of Meeting and remove the linen vestments that he donned with his entry into the Sanctum, and he shall leave them there. [24]He shall bathe his flesh in water in a holy place, in a ritual bath in the Temple compound, and don his vestments, the eight vestments generally worn by the High Priest to perform the Temple service. And he shall emerge and perform his burnt offering and the burnt offering of the people, and atone for himself and for the people. [25]The fat of the aforementioned sin offering, the bull and the goat, the blood of which was brought into the Holy of Holies, he shall burn on the altar.

Third aliya (Second aliya)

[26]Because the dispatching of the goat to Azazel involves some degree of contact with impure forces, the one who dispatches the goat to Azazel shall wash his garments and bathe his flesh in water, and only afterward shall he come into the camp.

[27]The carcass of the bull of the sin offering of Aaron and the goat of the sin offering of the nation, whose blood was brought in to atone in the Sanctum, he shall take outside the camp, and they shall burn in fire their hides, their flesh, and their dung. [28]The one who burns them shall wash his garments and bathe his flesh in water, and afterward he shall come into the camp.

[29]It shall be for you an eternal statute: During the seventh month, which later became known as Tishrei, on the tenth of the month, Yom Kippur, you shall afflict yourselves by refraining from eating, drinking, and other specific forms of physical pleasure. Furthermore, you shall not perform all labor, the native and the stranger that resides among you, that is, converts who have joined the children of Israel. [30]For on this day he shall atone for you, to purify you; from all your sins before the Lord you shall be purified. [31]It is a sabbatical rest for you, a day of total rest, like the Sabbath, and you shall afflict yourselves; it is an eternal statute.

📖 **Further reading:** For more on the afflictions required on Yom Kippur see *A Concise Guide to the Sages*, p. 286; *A Concise Guide to Halakha*, p. 163.

[32]The priest who shall be anointed and who shall be ordained to serve in his father's stead as the High Priest, shall atone and shall don linen

vestments, the sacred vestments, special white garments for the Yom Kippur service. [33]**He shall atone for the sacred Sanctum,** the most sacred part of the Sanctuary, the Holy of Holies, **and for the Tent of Meeting and for the altar he shall atone; and for the priests and for all the people of the assembly he shall atone.** [34]**This shall be an eternal statute for you, to atone for the children of Israel for all their sins once in the year.** When Yom Kippur came, **he,** Aaron, **did as the Lord** had **commanded Moses.**

Eating Meat

The life force of an animal is in its blood, and therefore eating blood is prohibited. An animal's blood may be used to atone for an individual's sins when the animal is offered to God in the Tabernacle. Because life in the wilderness revolved around the Tabernacle, one who wanted to eat meat had to first offer the animal as a peace offering. If the animal was of a species unfit to be offered on the altar, after slaughtering its blood had to be removed and covered with dirt.

17 [1]**The Lord spoke to Moses, saying:** [2]**Speak to Aaron, to his sons, and**
urth aliya
to all the children of Israel, and say to them: This is the matter that the Lord has commanded, saying: [3]**Any man from the house of Israel who shall slaughter a bull or a sheep or a goat in the camp, or who slaugh-ters it,** such an animal, **outside the camp,** for its meat, [4]**and he did not bring it to the entrance of the Tent of Meeting to present an offering to the Lord before the Tabernacle of the Lord, it will be accounted as blood,** as killing, **for that man; he has shed blood,** by killing an animal instead of presenting it as an offering, **and that man shall be** punished by God and **excised from among his people.**

[5]This is **so that the children of Israel shall bring their slaughtered ani-mals that they** currently **slaughter in the open field, and they shall bring them to the Lord, to the entrance of the Tent of Meeting, to the priest, and they shall slaughter peace offerings to the Lord,** most of the meat of which will then be eaten by the individual who brings the offering. [6]**The priest shall cast the blood on the altar of the Lord** that is **at the entrance of the Tent of Meeting and burn the fat for a pleasing aroma to the Lord.** [7]**That they shall no longer slaughter their offerings to the demons, after whom they go astray.** This prohibition against bringing offerings to demons **shall be an eternal statute for them, for their gen-erations.**

📖 **Further reading:** For more on Judaism's approach to eating meat and to vegetarianism, see *A Concise Guide to Mahshava,* p. 121.

Leviticus

Fifth
aliya
(Third
aliya) **⁸And to them,** the children of Israel, **you shall** also **say** the following: **Any man from the house of Israel, or from the strangers who reside among them, who offers up a burnt offering,** which is entirely consumed on the altar, **or a feast offering,** much of which is eaten by people, **⁹and to the entrance of the Tent of Meeting does not bring it to present it to the Lord,** but rather offers it as a sacrifice outside the Tabernacle, **that man shall be excised from his people.**

¹⁰Any man from the house of Israel, or from the stranger who resides among them, who eats any blood, I will direct My attention to the person who eats the blood, in the form of retribution, **and I will excise him from the midst of his people. ¹¹For the life of the flesh,** the life force, **is in the blood, and I have given it to you** only to sacrifice **on the altar to atone for your souls, as it is the blood that shall atone for the life** of the individual who slaughters the animal as an offering to God. **¹²Therefore I said to the children of Israel: Every person among you shall not eat blood, and the stranger who resides among you shall not eat blood.**

¹³A related commandment: **Any man from the children of Israel, or from the strangers that reside among them, who shall hunt game of a beast or a bird that may be eaten** according to the criteria specified elsewhere, but that is not fit to be offered on the altar, **he shall** slaughter the animal and **pour out its blood and cover it with dirt. ¹⁴For the life** force **of all flesh, its blood is with its life; therefore, I said to the children of Israel: The blood of all flesh you shall not eat, because the life of all flesh is its blood,** and consequently, **anyone who eats it shall be excised.**

¹⁵One more law regarding the eating of meat: **Any person who shall eat an unslaughtered carcass or a mauled animal** that has suffered a fatal injury, **whether he is native or stranger, he shall wash his garments and bathe in water, and he is impure until the evening, and he shall be purified. ¹⁶But if he does not wash and he does not bathe his flesh, he shall bear his iniquity** and be punished, if he enters the Tabernacle in an impure state.

Forbidden Sexual Relations

The types of sexual relations forbidden here were a central feature of ancient Canaanite culture. The Land of Israel will no longer tolerate such moral debasement; the people of Israel who are being awarded the land in their place must preserve its sanctity and not defile it.

18 ¹The Lord spoke to Moses, saying: ²Speak to the children of Israel and say to them: I am the Lord your God. ³You shall not follow the practices

of the land of Egypt in which you lived, and you shall not follow the practices of the land of Canaan, where I am bringing you, and you shall not follow their statutes, their ways and mores. ⁴Rather, **My ordinances you shall perform, and My statutes you shall observe, to follow them; I am the Lord your God.** ⁵**You shall observe My statutes and My ordinances, which a man shall perform and live by them. I am the Lord.**

Sixth
aliya ⁶**Any man of you shall not approach his kin to uncover nakedness,** to engage in sexual relations; **I am the Lord.** ⁷**The nakedness of your father and the nakedness of your mother you shall not uncover.** She is your mother, and sexual relations with her would bring shame and embarrassment to both parents; **you shall not uncover her nakedness.** ⁸**The nakedness of your father's wife,** even if she is not your mother, **you shall not uncover; it is your father's nakedness;** sexual relations with your father's wife would cause the father shame and embarrassment. ⁹**The nakedness of your sister,** even if she is only a half-sister, **the daughter of your father or the daughter of your mother,** whether she is **born into the household** in the framework of marriage **or** she is **born outside** of wedlock, **you shall not uncover their nakedness,** as they are your relatives. ¹⁰**The nakedness of the daughter of your son, or of the daughter of your daughter, you shall not uncover their nakedness, for it is your nakedness** and personal shame. ¹¹**The nakedness of the daughter of your father's wife,** who was **born to your father** and not necessarily to your mother, **she is your sister;** therefore, **you shall not uncover her nakedness.** ¹²**The nakedness of your father's sister you shall not uncover; she is your father's kin,** blood relative. ¹³**The nakedness of your mother's sister you shall not uncover, as she is your mother's kin.** ¹⁴**The nakedness of your father's brother, you shall not uncover; you shall not approach his wife; she is your aunt.** Since she is married to your uncle, even an aunt who is not a blood relative is prohibited. ¹⁵The Torah lists further prohibitions involving relatives through marriage. **The nakedness of your daughter-in-law you shall not uncover; she is your son's wife.** Therefore, **you shall not uncover her nakedness.** ¹⁶**The nakedness of your brother's wife you shall not uncover; it is your brother's nakedness.** ¹⁷Some prohibitions focus on a preexisting relationship with a female relative that renders her forbidden. **The nakedness of a woman and her daughter you shall not uncover.** Even her granddaughter, **her son's daughter or her daughter's daughter, you shall not take to uncover her nakedness.** Once a man has already been married to a woman, he may never marry her daughter or granddaughter. **They**

Leviticus

are kin; it is lewdness. ¹⁸Similarly, **a woman with her sister you shall not take, to be rivals, to uncover her nakedness through her in her lifetime.** A man may not marry his wife's sister if his wife is still alive, even if he has divorced her. But if his wife has died, her sister is permitted to him.

¹⁹The following sexual relationships are prohibited for reasons other than familial connections: **To a woman in her state of menstrual impurity you shall not approach to uncover her nakedness.** ²⁰**And with the wife of your counterpart,** another Jewish man, **you shall not engage in sexual relations, to defile yourself with her.** ²¹The Torah now turns to a different type of prohibition: **You shall not give from your offspring to pass** him through fire as a symbolic or an actual offering **to Molekh,** the name of a particular idol or cult that was widespread at the time. **And you shall not** worship God with the sacrifice of children, as this would **profane the name of your God; I am the Lord.**

📖 **Further reading:** For more on the severity of the prohibition against forbidden sexual relations, see *A Concise Guide to the Sages*, p. 150.

Seventh aliya (Fourth aliya) ²²**You shall not lie with a male in the manner of lying with a woman; it is an abomination.** ²³**You shall not engage sexually with any animal to defile yourself with it. And a woman shall not stand before an animal for it to copulate with her; it is a perversion.**

²⁴**Do not** spiritually debase and **defile yourselves in any of these** prohibitions, **for in all these were defiled the nations that I am sending forth from before you.** ²⁵**The land was defiled** in the wake of these immoral behaviors, **and I visited its iniquity upon it,** punishing the people who contaminated it. **And the land spewed out its inhabitants** from its midst. ²⁶In contrast to those nations, **you,** the children of Israel, **shall observe My statutes and My ordinances. You shall not perform any of these abominations, the native and the stranger,** the convert **who** joins the people of Israel and **resides among you.** ²⁷**For all these abominations were performed by the people of the land, who were** living there **before you,** the **Maftir** Canaanites, **and the land was defiled** through these acts. ²⁸If you do not sin, **the land will not expel you by your defiling it, as it spewed out the nation that was before you.**

²⁹**For anyone who shall perform any of these abominations** listed above, **the people who perform them shall be excised from among their people.** ³⁰**You shall keep My commission to refrain from performing any**

of the abominable practices that were performed before you by the Canaanite nations, **and you shall not defile yourselves through them; I am the Lord your God.**

📖 **Further reading:** For more on the distinction between statutes and ordinances, see *A Concise Guide to the Sages*, p. 150.

Parashat Kedoshim

The demand made of the people of Israel that they be holy does not exhaust itself with a general requirement of holiness. The Torah spells out in detail many different commandments in a variety of areas, the careful observance of which creates a sacred lifestyle. The Torah presents a multitude of commandments that surround a person on all sides. The lack of order in the structure of this Torah portion might reflect the need to relate to the portion as a whole, the entirety of which creates the desired holiness.

The Commandment regarding Holiness

First, the Torah describes the preservation of holiness through a series of commandments governing the relationship between man and God – observance of Shabbat, the prohibition of idolatry, and the proper way to bring a peace offering. The commandment to revere one's parents is included in this unit, alluding to the connection between reverence for one's parents and reverence for God.

19 **¹The Lord spoke to Moses, saying: ²Speak to the entire congregation of the children of Israel, and say to them: You shall be holy,** set apart in your actions, **for I, the Lord your God, am holy,** set apart, beyond the limits of the material universe.

³Each of you shall revere his mother and his father, and you shall observe My Sabbaths: I am the Lord your God.

📖 **Further reading:** What does the mitzva of honoring one's parents entail? See *A Concise Guide to Halakha*, p. 609.

⁴Do not turn to the false gods, idols, **and do not fashion for yourselves cast gods** with shape and form; **I am the Lord your God.**

⁵And when you slaughter a peace offering to the Lord, for your propitiation you shall offer it, in order to find favor in God's eyes. **⁶On the day of your slaughter it shall be eaten, and on the next day, and the leftover until the third day, it shall be burned in fire. ⁷And if it,** the offering, **is eaten on the third day, it is detestable,** and **it shall not be accepted** by God. **⁸And he who eats it shall bear** responsibility and punishment for

Leviticus

his iniquity, because he profaned that which is sacred to the Lord; and that person shall be excised from his people.

Commandments Governing the Relationship between Man and His Fellow

Holiness is not limited to actions connected to man's relationship with God. God also requires of man that he behave with justice and integrity toward other people. The words, "I am the Lord," which repeat themselves again and again in the verses that follow, emphasize that it is a divine command to avoid social injustices, and that even if others are unaware, God sees when injustice is perpetrated.

⁹**When you reap the harvest of your land, you shall not finish reaping the corner of your field;** do not harvest the corners. **And the gleanings of your harvest,** the sheaves that fall from the sickle during the harvest, **you shall not gather.** ¹⁰**Your vineyard you shall not harvest completely;** do not gather the small, incompletely formed clusters of grapes, **and** similarly, **the fallen fruit of your vineyard,** the grapes that have separated and fallen off the cluster, **you shall not gather. For the poor and for the stranger,** who is financially unstable, **you shall leave them,** all this produce: **I am the Lord your God.**

¹¹**You shall not steal, nor shall you falsely deny a claim** that you owe another money, **nor shall you lie to one another** and collect money based on false claims. ¹²**You shall not take an oath in My name falsely, as you will profane the name of your God** by using it for wrongdoing: **I am the Lord.** ¹³**You shall not** use your power, status, or authority to **exploit your neighbor, and you shall not rob** someone of that which belongs to him; **you shall not keep the wages of a hired laborer with you overnight until morning.** You must pay your employees without delay.

¹⁴**You shall not curse a deaf person; you shall not place an obstacle before the blind.** Even though the injured parties in these cases would be unaware of who harmed them, **you shall fear your God,** before whom all actions and intentions are revealed: **I am the Lord.**

ond
ifth
iya) ¹⁵**You shall not perform injustice in judgment** and issue an unjust ruling; **you shall not favor the impoverished** out of pity for his situation, and, conversely, **you shall not defer to the great; with** absolute **righteousness you shall judge your counterpart.**

¹⁶**You shall not go as a gossip among your people** and relate one person's private matters to others. Additionally, **you shall not stand by the blood**

of your neighbor, refraining from coming to his assistance when he is in danger or distress. **I am the Lord.** ¹⁷**You shall not hate your brother in your heart.** Rather, **you shall rebuke your neighbor** and tell him how he wronged you, **and** thereby **you shall not bear a sin because of him.** ¹⁸**You shall not take vengeance** upon someone who has wronged you by treating him as he treated you. **You shall not** even **bear any grudge** in your heart **against members of your people. You shall love your neighbor as yourself,** relate to your neighbor as you wish others would relate to you: **I am the Lord.**

📖 **Further reading:** For more on the centrality of the injunction to love one's fellow Jew, see *A Concise Guide to the Sages*, p. 373; *A Concise Guide to Mahshava*, p. 113. Laws concerning how people are to relate to one another appear in *A Concise Guide to Halakha*, pp. 597ff.

Statutes and Decrees

After presenting various commandments that fall into the category of ordinances – rational laws that structure social interactions – the Torah introduces several commandments that are divine decrees. These laws cannot be derived by human reason and a person's adherence to them is entirely based on acceptance of divine authority.

¹⁹**You shall observe My statutes; you shall not breed your animal with diverse kinds,** you shall not crossbreed. Likewise, **you shall not sow your field with diverse kinds** of seeds, **and a garment that is a mixture of diverse kinds,** of wool and linen, **shall not be put on by you.**

²⁰**A man, if he lies sexually with a woman, and she is a maidservant, designated for a man;** a Canaanite slave wed to a Jewish slave, **and she was not redeemed** with money, **and** full **freedom was not granted her, there shall be an inspection;** while they might be punished, **they shall not be put to death, because she,** the maidservant, **was not freed,** and therefore, despite her relationship with the Hebrew slave, this act is not considered regular adultery. ²¹Nevertheless, since the man who lies with such a woman has sinned, **he shall bring his guilt offering to the Lord, to the entrance of the Tent of Meeting, a ram of a guilt offering.** ²²**The priest shall atone for him with the ram of the guilt offering before the Lord for his sin that he has sinned; and he shall be forgiven for his sin that he has sinned.**

Third aliya ²³**When you come into the land and plant any food tree** that bears edible fruit **then you shall seal,** consider as forbidden, **its fruit.** For the first **three years it,** the fruit, **shall be sealed for you; it shall not be eaten.**

²⁴**And in the fourth year, all its fruit shall be sacred,** set aside, **for praise to the Lord;** it must be eaten in Jerusalem in an atmosphere of holiness and praise. ²⁵**And in the fifth year, you may eat of its fruit** in your houses in an ordinary manner. As reward for observing My commandments, I will cause the tree **to increase its yield for you. I am the Lord your God.**

Separating from the Practices of the Nations

Separating from the customary practices of the gentile nations creates the sanctity of Israel. These customs, whether they involve actual idolatry or they are simply unmistakably non-Jewish practices, are strictly forbidden.

²⁶**You shall not eat** an animal **over,** alongside, **the blood** that was spilled in its slaughter. **You shall not practice divination** with the help of instruments or rituals. **And you shall not practice soothsaying,** predicting the future by looking at the clouds.

²⁷**You shall not round the edge of your head,** cut off your sideburns. **And you shall not mar the edge of your beard,** completely shave off the hair of your beard. ²⁸**You shall not make a laceration for the dead,** as a sign of mourning, **in your flesh. And the imprint of a tattoo you shall not place upon you. I am the Lord.**

²⁹**Do not profane your daughter, to pander her as a harlot;** do not hand over your daughter to prostitution, so **that the land does not become licentious and the land** not **be filled with lewdness** from such promiscuous sexual relationships.

³⁰**You shall observe My Sabbaths and you shall revere** and honor **My Sanctuary: I am the Lord.**

³¹**Do not turn to mediums or to necromancers,** who communicate with the dead. **Do not seek** answers from them, which will bring you **to be defiled by them: I am the Lord your God.**

Additional Commandments That Govern the Relationship between Man and His Fellow

The Torah lists other commandments governing how a person should behave in the company of others; he must pay proper respect to dignitaries and elders, and must not exploit his position to harm the weak, or those who are ignorant about a particular matter.

³²**You shall rise** out of respect **before the graybeard,** an old person, **and show deference before the elderly,** a person who has acquired wisdom. **You shall fear your God; I am the Lord.**

Leviticus

📖 **Further reading:** For more on the obligation to respect elders and sages, see *A Concise Guide to Halakha*, p. 612.

Fourth aliya (Sixth aliya) ³³**If a stranger,** someone of foreign origin, **resides with you in your land, you shall not mistreat him** through hurtful comments or by cheating him. ³⁴**Like a native of your own** land **shall be for you the stranger that resides with you.** You must treat him like one of your own, **and you shall love him as yourself, since you were strangers in the land of Egypt: I am the Lord your God.**

³⁵**You shall do no injustice,** deviating from the truth when you engage **in judgment.** Similarly, there may be no injustice or deviation **in measure,** measurements of area or volume, **in weight, or in** liquid **volume.** ³⁶**Accurate scales, accurate weights, an accurate dry measure, and an accurate liquid measure, you shall have.** All such measuring implements must be precise. **I am the Lord your God, who took you out of the land of Egypt.** ³⁷**You shall observe all My statutes, and all My ordinances, and perform them: I am the Lord.**

The Punishments for Transgressions Involving Forbidden Sexual Relationships

The laws governing forbidden sexual relationships were already mentioned in *Parashat Aharei Mot*. Here the Torah spells out the punishments that are to be administered by human courts to transgressors in this realm.

20 ¹**The Lord spoke to Moses, saying:** ²**And to the children of Israel you** *Fifth aliya* **shall say: Each man from the children of Israel, or from the strangers that reside in Israel, who gives of his offspring to** the worship of **Molekh,** passing them through fire in its service, **he shall be put to death; the people of the land,** the community, **shall stone him with stones.** ³Meanwhile, I too **shall direct My attention to that man, and I will excise him from the midst of his people, because he gave of his offspring to Molekh, in order to defile My Sanctuary, and to profane My sacred name.** ⁴**If the people of the land avert their eyes from that man, when he gives of his offspring to Molekh, and do not put him to death;** that is, if they do not fulfill their duty to execute him, ⁵**I will direct My attention to that man and to his family, and I will excise him and everyone who strays after him, to stray after Molekh, from the midst of their people.** ⁶**The person who turns to the mediums or to the necromancers,** who communicate with the dead, **to stray after them** by seeking their council, **I will direct**

Leviticus

My attention to that person and will excise him from the midst of his people.

⁷**You shall sanctify yourselves, and you shall be holy, for I am the Lord your God,** and therefore you must be committed to this sanctity.

⁸**You shall observe My statutes and perform them: I am the Lord who sanctifies you,** and therefore you must observe My commandments.

⁹**For each man who curses his father or his mother shall be put to death; he cursed his father or his mother; his blood is upon him,** on his own hands; he brought death upon himself.

¹⁰**A man who commits adultery with a married woman,** that is, **who commits adultery with the wife of his neighbor; the adulterer and** also **the adulteress shall be put to death.**

¹¹**The man that lies with his father's wife, he has uncovered his father's nakedness,** the act is shameful and disgraceful to his father; **both of them,** the son and the wife, **shall be put to death; their blood is upon them.** ¹²**If a man lies with his daughter-in-law, both of them shall be put to death; they have performed a perversion; their blood is upon them.**

¹³**A man who lies with a male in the manner that one lies with a woman, both of them have performed an abomination. They shall be put to death** by stoning; **their blood is upon them.**

¹⁴**A man who takes a woman and her mother, it is lewdness,** both women being intermingled in his thoughts and imagination. **He and they shall be burned in fire, and there shall be no lewdness among you.**

¹⁵**A man who copulates with an animal, he shall be put to death, and the animal you shall kill.** ¹⁶Similarly, **a woman who approaches any animal** in order for it **to copulate with her, you shall kill the woman and the animal. They shall be put to death** by stoning; **their blood is upon them.**

¹⁷**A man who takes his sister, daughter of his father or daughter of his mother,** meaning even if she is only his half-sister, **and he sees her nakedness, and she sees his nakedness,** the two of them being consenting adults who are aware of their actions, **it is a disgrace. And they shall be excised in the sight of the members of their people; he has uncovered his sister's nakedness; he shall bear his iniquity.**

¹⁸**A man who lies with a menstruating woman, and he uncovered her nakedness, he has probed her source** of blood, **and she has exposed the source of her blood,** the two of them acting knowingly and willingly. **Both of them shall be excised from the midst of their people.**

¹⁹The nakedness of the sister of your mother and the sister of your father you shall not uncover; for he exposed his kin, as they are blood relatives; they shall both bear their iniquity. ²⁰A man who lies with his aunt, the wife of his father's brother or mother's brother, he exposed his uncle's nakedness; they shall bear their sin; they shall die childless.

²¹A man who takes his brother's wife, even if she is no longer married to the brother, i.e., they divorced or the brother died, it is an abhorrent act; he exposed his brother's nakedness; they shall be childless. For an exception to this prohibition if the brother died childless, see Deut. 25:5-6.

Further reading: For more on the severity of the prohibition against forbidden sexual relations, see *A Concise Guide to the Sages*, p. 150.

The Conclusion of the Section Dealing with Israel's Special Sanctity
Observing the totality of the commandments, refraining from emulating the actions of gentile nations, and abstaining from forbidden foods are what shape and preserve the sanctity of the people of Israel, a sanctity which lies in their separation from the other nations and their belonging to God.

²²You shall observe all My statutes and all My ordinances, and you shall perform them, and the land to which I am bringing you to live there *Seventh* will not spew you out. ²³And you shall not follow the practices of the *aliya* nation which I am sending forth from before you; as they did all these prohibited acts, and I abhorred them. ²⁴I said to you: You shall inherit their land, and I will give it to you to inherit it, a land flowing with milk and honey. I am the Lord your God, who has distinguished you from the peoples.

Further reading: The sanctity of the Land of Israel is the basis for the high moral standards to which its inhabitants are held; see *A Concise Guide to Mahshava*, p. 132.

Maftir ²⁵You shall distinguish between the pure animal, that which is permitted for consumption, and the non-pure, which may not be eaten, and between the non-pure birds and the pure. And you shall not render yourselves detestable by means of consuming the animals or the birds, or by consuming any creature that creeps on the ground, which I have distinguished for you to be non-pure and therefore prohibited. ²⁶You shall be holy to Me, for I, the Lord, am holy. And I have distinguished you from the peoples to be Mine. ²⁷And a man or a woman, if they are a medium or a necromancer, they shall be put to death; with stones they shall stone them; their blood is upon them.

Parashat Emor

In the previous *parashiyot* the Torah elaborated on the commandments regarding holiness that pertain to all of Israel. This *parasha* deals with different forms of sanctity: the sanctity of the priests; the sanctity of sacred spaces, such as the Tabernacle; and the sanctity of time, as manifest on Shabbat and the festivals.

The priests, due to their sacred role and status, are given commandments that pertain to them alone. They are forbidden to defile themselves by coming into contact with a corpse, and they can only marry women whose personal status is worthy of their elevated rank. In the case of the High Priest, the restrictions are even more severe. The Tabernacle, the resting place of the Divine Presence, is a holy place. The Torah determines who is fit to perform the divine service, and prohibits the offering of blemished sacrifices. In the dimension of time, as well, there are times that bear special sanctity: the Sabbath, which commemorates the creation of the universe; the festivals, which are connected to historical events; and the Day of Atonement. In addition to all this, the *parasha* also describes two elements of the regular service in the Tent of Meeting: the lighting of the lamp and the setting of the showbread on the table. The end of the *parasha*, which records the story of the blasphemer, serves as an opening for commands concerning the sanctity of God and damage to people and property.

Leviticus

The Sanctity of the Priests

Because of the service that they perform in the Tabernacle, the priests must preserve their sanctity. They are forbidden to defile themselves through contact with the corpse of a person who is not a close relative, and they may not marry women whose personal status is not in keeping with their higher standing. The people of Israel are also commanded to relate to the priests with special holiness and respect.

21 ¹**The Lord said to Moses: Speak to the priests, sons of Aaron, and** inform them of the following commandments that pertain to them, **say to them: He,** a priest, **shall not become impure from a corpse among his people.** It is prohibited for a priest to come into contact with a corpse or participate in its burial. ²Except **only for his** deceased **kin, who is close to him; for his mother, for his father, for his son, for his daughter,** and **for his brother,** all of whom are first-degree blood relations. ³He may also become impure **for his virgin sister, who is close to him, who has not**

been with a man, neither married nor betrothed to one; **for her, he may become impure.** [4]The priest is **an important man among his people;** therefore, he **shall not become impure, to profane himself** for a person who is not a close relative.

📖 **Further reading:** For details and implications of the prohibition against priests becoming impure, see *A Concise Guide to Halakha*, p. 102.

[5]**They shall not create a bald spot on their head** by tearing out their hair as a sign of mourning, **and the corner of their beard they shall not shave, and in their flesh they shall not make a laceration** as an expression of sorrow and pain.

[6]**They shall be holy to their God, and they shall not profane the name of their God, for the fire offerings of the Lord, the food of their God, they offer; they shall be holy** and bear these special restrictions that give expression to their sanctity.

[7]**A licentious woman,** one who engaged in prohibited sexual relations, **or a profaned woman,** e.g., a woman who is the child of a priest and a woman forbidden to him, **they,** the priests, **shall not marry. And a woman divorced from her husband they shall not marry, for he is holy to his God.**

[8]**You,** all Jews, **shall sanctify him,** the priest, treating him with reverence and ensuring that he maintains his sanctity, **for he presents the food of your God. He shall be holy to you, for I, the Lord your sanctifier, am holy.**

[9]**The** married **daughter of a man who is a priest, if she shall profane herself by acting licentiously, she profanes** and humiliates **her father; she shall be burned in fire.**

The Sanctity of the High Priest

The priests have a higher level of sanctity than that of the holy people of Israel. Among the priests, the High Priest has an even higher level of sanctity, which is expressed in the additional constraints imposed upon him. He may not defile himself for any corpse, not even that of a relative, and he may only marry a woman who has never before been married.

[10]**The priest who is greater than his brethren, that the anointing oil will be poured on his head** in order to appoint him as the High Priest, **and who is ordained to don the** unique **vestments** of the High Priest, **he shall not grow out the hair of his head** during a period of mourning, **and he**

shall not rend his garments. **¹¹He shall not go near any dead people.** He is prohibited from coming into contact with a corpse under any circumstances. **He shall not become impure** even **for his father and for his mother. ¹²He shall not emerge from the Sanctuary** to participate in a funeral, so **that he not profane the Sanctuary of his God.** He must maintain his sanctity, **for the crown of the anointing oil of his God,** his unique appointment, **is upon him. I am the Lord.**

¹³He, the High Priest, **shall marry** only **a woman with her virginity** intact. **¹⁴A widow, or a divorcée, or a profaned woman, or a licentious woman, these he shall not marry. Only a virgin from his people he shall take as a wife. ¹⁵In** this way, **he shall not profane his offspring among his people, for I am the Lord, his sanctifier.**

A Priest with a Blemish

The sacrificial service in the Tabernacle must meet certain standards of beauty and ceremony. Priests with physical blemishes are not permitted to serve in the Tabernacle. However, blemishes do not remove the priest from the priesthood altogether; while he is prohibited from serving, he is permitted to eat of consecrated sacrificial meat.

ond
liya
¹⁶The Lord spoke to Moses, saying: ¹⁷Speak to Aaron, saying: Any man from your descendants, throughout their generations, that is, any priest, **in whom there shall be a blemish shall not approach to offer** sacrifices that are like **the food of his God.**

¹⁸For any man in whom there is a blemish shall not approach the Sanctuary. This includes: **a blind man, or lame, or with a sunken nose,** or with a disproportionately **protruding limb, ¹⁹or a man with a broken foot or a broken hand** that has not yet healed, **²⁰or a hunchback, or a dwarf, or** a man **with a cataract,** a white spot **in his eye, or scabbed, or with a skin eruption,** certain forms of skin diseases, **or with crushed testicles. ²¹Any man in whom there is a blemish from the descendants of Aaron the priest shall not approach to present the fire offerings of the Lord; he has a blemish, and the food of his God he shall not approach to offer.**

²²The food of his God from the sacred sacraments and from the sacraments of lesser sanctity **he may** nevertheless **eat. ²³However, he shall not come to** the Sanctuary, behind **the curtain,** where the showbread, the candelabrum, and the incense altar are, **and he may not approach the altar** to offer sacrifices in the manner of all priests, **because there is a blemish in**

Leviticus

him. And he shall not profane the offerings brought in **My Sanctuary, for I am the Lord, their sanctifier.** [24]**Moses spoke** these words **to Aaron, and to his sons, and to all the children of Israel.**

The Priests Who Are Fit to Eat Sacrificial Food

The consecrated gifts of the priesthood, which include the portions of the offerings that are given to the priests, and *teruma*, the portions of produce that are given to the priests, must be treated with sanctity and reverence; a priest is therefore forbidden to eat of them while he is in a state of ritual impurity. The *teruma* that a priest may eat in his home is permitted to him and his household, but is forbidden to other non-priests.

22 [1]**The Lord spoke to Moses, saying:** [2]**Speak to Aaron and to his sons, that they shall refrain,** in the cases described below, **from** approaching **the sacred items of the children of Israel that they consecrate to Me, and they shall not profane My holy name. I am the Lord.** [3]**Say to them: Throughout your generations, any man from all your descendants who approaches** to eat **the sacred items that the children of Israel consecrate to the Lord with his impurity upon him,** while he is in a state of ritual impurity, **that person shall be excised from before Me. I am the Lord.**

[4]**Any man from the descendants of Aaron who is a leper, or has a** gonorrhea-like **discharge, he shall not partake of the sacred items until he is purified. And** the following individuals are also forbidden to partake of consecrated food: **one who touches anyone impure from a corpse,** and all the more so one who himself comes into contact with a corpse, **or a man from whom semen has been emitted,** [5]**or a man who touches any** dead **swarming creature that renders him impure, or** who shall touch **a man that renders him impure, whatever his** form of **impurity.** [6]**A person who touches him,** the impure person or thing, **shall be impure until the evening. And he shall not partake of the sacred items unless he bathes his flesh in water,** immersing in a ritual bath. [7]**After he immerses, he must wait** until **the sun shall set, and** only then **he shall be purified. Then he may** once again **partake of the sacred items, because it is his food,** an important part of the priest's sustenance.

[8]**He shall not eat an unslaughtered carcass or a mauled animal,** one that suffered a fatal injury, **to render himself impure with it. I am the Lord.**

[9]**They,** the priests, **shall keep My commission,** keeping charge of the sacred food that is given to them. If they maintain the sanctity of their charge, **they shall not bear sin for it and die on its account.** However, if they

partake of sacred food in a state of ritual impurity, they will be punished by death at the hands of Heaven, **because they profane it. I am the Lord their sanctifier.**

10No non-priest shall partake of sacred items, the sacred portion of the produce given to the priests. Even **one who resides** for a lengthy period **with a priest or a** priest's **hired laborer shall not partake of sacred items. 11But if a priest acquires a person,** a Canaanite slave, as **an acquisition of his silver, he,** the slave, **may partake of it. And** similarly, with regard to **one born into his household,** Canaanite slaves born in the priest's possession, **they may partake of his** sacred **food.**

12If the daughter of a priest is married, or even betrothed, **to a non-priest, she shall not partake from that which is separated of the sacred items,** the consecrated gifts of the priesthood. **13But if a priest's daughter** who married a non-priest **is** now **a widow or a divorcée, and she has no offspring** from that husband, **and she returns to her father's house, as in her youth,** before she married, **from the** sacred **food of her father,** the sacred portions given to the priest from the produce and offerings, **she may partake. But no non-priest,** including a child born to her from her Israelite husband, **may partake of it.**

14If a man, a non-priest, **shall eat a sacred item,** the portion that is separated from the crop and given to a priest, **unwittingly, he shall add its one-fifth to it,** as a fine, **and he shall give** the fifth **to the priest** in addition to the value of **the sacred item** that he ate.

15They shall not profane the sacraments of the children of Israel that they separate for the Lord. 16They will cause them, the priests will cause themselves, **to bear the iniquity of guilt,** if they are negligent **when they eat their sacred items; for I am the Lord, their sanctifier.**

Offerings with Blemishes

Just as the priests serving in the Tabernacle had to be free of blemishes, so too, the offerings brought on the altar had to be free of physical defects. The Torah provides a detailed list of defects that disqualify animals from being offered on the altar.

Third aliya **17The Lord spoke to Moses, saying: 18Speak to Aaron, and to his sons, and to all the children of Israel, and say to them:** The following laws pertain to **any man from the house of Israel, or from the strangers in Israel,** converts who join the Jewish people, **who presents his offering, for** the fulfillment of **any of their vows,** when they vowed to bring an offering, **or**

for any of their pledges, when they pledged a specific animal as a voluntary offering, **that they shall bring to the Lord as a burnt offering,** all of which are offered to God on the altar. [19]In order for the offering to be brought **for your propitiation,** and for you to find favor in God's eyes, it must be **an unblemished male of cattle, of sheep, or of goats.** [20]Any animal **in which there is a blemish you shall not offer, as it shall not be accepted for you,** and you will not achieve propitiation.

[21]**If a man shall present a peace offering to the Lord,** portions of which are eaten by the priests and the owners, **to fulfill a vow,** when one vowed to bring an offering, **or as a pledge,** where a specific animal was designated as an offering, **of the cattle or of the flock, it shall be unblemished to be accepted. No blemish shall be in it.** [22]The following blemishes render an animal unfit to be presented as an offering: a **blind** animal; **or** an animal with a **broken** limb; **or maimed,** with a cracked or damaged limb; **or** an animal **with a cyst; or** a **scabbed** animal **or** one **with a skin eruption,** types of boils on the animal's skin; **you shall not offer these to the Lord, and you shall not place them as a fire offering upon the altar to the Lord.** [23]**A bull or a sheep with an extended limb or a truncated limb, as a pledge** to the Sanctuary treasury **you may present it,** so that it may be sold and the proceeds used for Sanctuary maintenance. **But as a vow** offering **it shall not be accepted.** [24]**Those** animals, the testicles of **which are bruised, or crushed, or torn, or cut, you shall not present to the Lord. And** furthermore, **you shall not do so in your land.** It is prohibited to castrate any animal, even one not designated as an offering. [25]Even **from the hand of a foreigner you shall not present the food of your God from any of these** castrated animals, **because their defect is in them, a blemish is in them; they shall not be accepted for you.**

🕮 **Further reading:** For the meaning behind the selection of certain animals as being worthy of sacrifice, see *A Concise Guide to the Sages,* pp. 134, 156.

Additional Laws Connected to Offerings

In addition to the requirement that an offering be free of any disqualifying blemish, there are other laws that govern the manner in which the offering must be brought: it is prohibited to slaughter an animal during the first seven days of its life; it is forbidden to slaughter an animal and its offspring on the same day; and one must be careful to eat the sacrificial meat within the designated time.

[26]**The Lord spoke to Moses, saying:** [27]**An ox or a sheep or a goat, when it is born, shall be seven days under its mother.** It may not be slaughtered

for any purpose during this time. Only **from the eighth day on, it shall be accepted as a fire offering to the Lord.**

[28]**An ox or a sheep, it and its offspring you shall not slaughter on one day** for any purpose, not only as offerings.

[29]**When you slaughter a thanks offering to the Lord, for your propitiation you shall slaughter it.** [30]**On that day** on which it is slaughtered **it shall be eaten; you shall not leave from it until** the next **morning. I am the Lord.**

[31]**You,** priests and non-priests alike, **shall observe My commandments and perform them. I am the Lord.** [32]Moreover, **you shall not profane My holy name** by committing transgressions or by performing the service in an inappropriate manner. **And I shall be sanctified among the children of Israel. I am the Lord your sanctifier.** [33]I am the Lord **who took you out of the land of Egypt to be your God. I am the Lord** who sanctifies you and obligates you to maintain your sanctity.

The Laws of the Appointed Times

The Torah moves on now from the sanctity of the priests and the sacrificial service to discuss sanctified time, i.e., Shabbat and festivals. These days are proclaimed as "holy convocations," days on which the congregation gathers to mark the unique sanctity of the day. Each day has its own special sacrifices. The festivals are listed in accordance with the order in which they occur during the calendar year. The first appointed time in this review is Shabbat, the weekly day of sabbatical rest.

23 [1]**The Lord spoke to Moses, saying:** [2]**Speak to the children of Israel, and** *Fourth* **say to them: The appointed times of the Lord that you shall proclaim as** *aliya* **holy convocations,** gatherings, **these are My appointed times.**

[3]**Six days labor shall be performed;** during the six days of the week work is permitted. **And on the seventh day, a sabbatical rest,** a complete rest from all types of labor. It is **a holy convocation,** a sacred gathering for the acceptance of the sanctity of the Sabbath. **You shall not perform any labor. It is the Sabbath to the Lord in all your dwellings,** wherever you are.

The Festival of Passover

From the laws of Shabbat, the Torah proceeds to the festival of Passover, the first festival on the Jewish calendar, which begins in the month of Nisan.

[4]**These are the appointed times of the Lord, holy convocations, that you shall proclaim at their** precise **appointed time.**

Leviticus

⁵**During the first month,** Nisan, **on the fourteenth of the month in the afternoon, there is** the Festival of **a Paschal Lamb to the Lord.** ⁶**On the fifteenth day of that month it is the Festival of Unleavened Bread to the Lord,** Passover; **seven days you shall eat unleavened bread.** ⁷**On the first day** of the seven days of Passover, **it shall be a holy convocation for you. You shall not perform any toilsome labor,** labor that is not required for the immediate preparation of food to be eaten on the festival. ⁸**You shall present a fire offering,** an offering that is wholly burnt on the altar, **to the Lord** on each of the **seven days. On the seventh day** too, it shall be **a holy convocation; you shall not perform any toilsome labor.**

The Counting of the *Omer*

The counting of the *omer* begins with the *omer* offering, which is brought on the second day of Passover. This is followed by the counting of forty-nine days until the Festival of Weeks.

⁹**The Lord spoke to Moses, saying:** ¹⁰**Speak to the children of Israel, and say to them: When you come to the land that I am giving to you, and you will reap its harvest, then you shall bring a sheaf** of barley, from which one can extract one-tenth of an ephah of fine flour, **of the first of your** grain **harvest to the priest** in the Sanctuary. ¹¹**He,** the priest, **shall wave the sheaf before the Lord, for your propitiation,** in order to find favor in God's eyes. **On the day after the sabbath,** which refers here to the first day of Passover, that is, on the sixteenth of Nisan, **the priest shall wave it.** ¹²**You shall present, on the day of your waving of the sheaf, an unblemished lamb in its first year as a burnt offering to the Lord.** ¹³**Its** accompanying **meal offering is two-tenths of an ephah of choice flour mixed with oil.** The offering is brought **as a fire offering to the Lord for a pleasing aroma, and its** accompanying **libation is wine, one-fourth of a hin.** ¹⁴Before you bring the sheaf offering you shall not eat **bread, roasted grain, or fresh kernels,** raw grain that has not yet dried. **You shall not eat** the new produce in any form **until that very day, until your bringing of the** sheaf **offering of your God; it is an eternal statute for your generations in all your dwellings.**

¹⁵**You shall count for yourselves from the day after the sabbath, from the day of your bringing of the sheaf of the waving, seven weeks; they shall be complete.** ¹⁶**Until the day after the seventh week, you shall count up to fifty days,** not including the fiftieth day, and **then,** on the

fiftieth day, **you shall present a new meal offering,** a meal offering from the new produce, **to the Lord.**

 Further reading: For more on the counting of the *omer*, see *A Concise Guide to the Sages*, p. 158; *A Concise Guide to Halakha*, p. 331.

The Festival of *Shavuot*

At the conclusion of the counting of the *omer*, the Festival of Weeks is celebrated. The central commandment on that day involves the offering of the two loaves, a meal offering from the new wheat crop.

¹⁷**From your dwellings you shall bring two loaves of waving,** two meal offerings, **from two-tenths of an ephah,** one-tenth of an ephah for each loaf. Of **choice** wheat **flour they shall be, baked as leavened bread, a first offering** from the new crop of wheat **to the Lord.** ¹⁸**You shall offer with the bread seven unblemished lambs in their first year, and one young bull, and two rams. They shall** all **be a burnt offering to the Lord, and their meal offering and their libations,** in accordance with the quantities stated elsewhere in the Torah, shall be **a fire offering of a pleasing aroma to the Lord.** ¹⁹**You shall** also **present one goat as a sin offering, and two lambs in the first year as a peace offering.** ²⁰**The priest shall wave them,** the lambs, **with the loaves of the first offering as a wave offering before the Lord,** the loaves placed **with,** or on, **the two lambs. They shall be sacred to the Lord,** and their flesh shall be given as a portion **for the priest.**

²¹**You shall proclaim on that very day,** the fiftieth day, **that it is a festival; a holy convocation it shall be for you; you shall not perform any toilsome labor, it is an eternal statute in all your dwellings for your generations.**

²²**When you reap the harvest of your land, you shall not finish the corner of your field in your reaping;** rather, you shall leave an unharvested area. **And the gleanings of your harvest,** the sheaves that fall during the harvest, **you shall not gather. For the poor and for the stranger you shall leave them. I am the Lord your God.**

New Year

The central commandment on the New Year is the blowing of the shofar.

Fifth aliya ²³**The Lord spoke to Moses, saying:** ²⁴**Speak to the children of Israel, saying: In the seventh month,** Tishrei, **on the first day of the month,** it **shall be a** day of **rest for you, a remembrance by means of an alarm blast,** the blast of the shofar. This day is also **a holy convocation.** ²⁵**You**

shall not perform on this day any toilsome labor, and you shall present a fire offering to the Lord.

The Day of Atonement
Yom Kippur, the Day of Atonement, is called a sabbatical rest. In addition to the commandment to rest, the people are also commanded to afflict themselves on this day.

²⁶The Lord spoke to Moses, saying: ²⁷In general, the festivals are times of feasting and rejoicing. However, on the tenth day of this seventh month, Tishrei, is the Day of Atonement for the Jewish people. A holy convocation it shall be for you. And you shall afflict yourselves; you shall abstain from food, drink, and other common forms of physical pleasure. And you shall bring a fire offering to the Lord. ²⁸You shall not perform any labor on that very day. All forms of labor are prohibited, just as they are prohibited on the Sabbath, as it is a day of atonement, to atone for you before the Lord your God. ²⁹For any person who is not afflicted on that very day shall be excised from his people. ³⁰And any person who performs any labor on that very day, I shall destroy that person from among his people. ³¹You shall not perform any labor; it is an eternal statute for your generations in all your dwellings. ³²It, the Day of Atonement, is a sabbatical rest for you, and you shall afflict yourselves on it. On the ninth of the month, at the conclusion of the day, in the evening, from evening to evening, for a full twenty-four hours, you shall rest on your sabbath.

The Festival of Sukkot
The festival of Sukkot is celebrated for seven days, and then followed by an eighth day of sabbatical rest, Shemini Atzeret. The special commandments of the festival are dwelling in the sukka and taking the four species.

Sixth aliya ³³The Lord spoke to Moses, saying: ³⁴Speak to the children of Israel, saying: On the fifteenth day of this seventh month, Tishrei, is the Festival of Tabernacles for seven days to the Lord. ³⁵On the first day is a holy convocation; you shall not perform any toilsome labor. ³⁶For seven days you shall present a fire offering to the Lord each day, as detailed elsewhere. On the eighth day shall be a holy convocation for you, and you shall bring a fire offering to the Lord. It is an assembly, a general gathering for God and the Jewish people. You shall not perform any toilsome labor on this day.

³⁷These are the appointed times of the Lord, which you shall proclaim and observe as holy convocations, to present a fire offering to the Lord:

a burnt offering and a meal offering, a feast offering and libations, each day's matter, the offerings prescribed for that day, on its day. [38]The festival offerings are besides the offerings of the Sabbaths of the Lord, and besides your gifts to the Sanctuary, and besides all your vows, and besides all your pledges that you give to the Lord even at other times of the year.

[39]However, on the fifteenth day of the seventh month, at the end of the period when you gather the produce of the land, you shall celebrate the Festival of the Lord seven days. On the first day there shall be a day of rest, when toilsome labor is forbidden, and similarly on the eighth day there shall be a day of rest.

[40]You shall take for you on the first day: the fruit of a pleasant tree, identified by tradition as the citron, an *etrog*; branches of date palms, identified by tradition as the *lulav*, a young branch of a date palm; a bough of a leafy tree, a myrtle branch; and branches of willows of the brook, a species of tree that typically grows next to streams. You shall rejoice with these four species before the Lord your God, in the Sanctuary, seven days. [41]You shall celebrate it as a festival to the Lord seven days in the year, an eternal statute for your generations; in the seventh month you shall celebrate it. [42]During this Festival of Tabernacles you shall live in booths, temporary dwellings, for seven days. Every native, every permanent resident, in Israel shall live in booths. [43]You shall dwell in booths so that your generations will know that I had the children of Israel live in booths when I took them out of the land of Egypt and led them through the wilderness. I am the Lord your God. [44]Moses spoke to the children of Israel the appointed times of the Lord.

> Further reading: For more on the mitzvot of the festival of *Sukkot*, dwelling in the *sukka*, and taking *lulav* and *etrog*, see *A Concise Guide to the Sages*, p. 290; *A Concise Guide to Mahshava*, pp. 72ff; *A Concise Guide to Halakha*, p. 176.

Lighting the Lamp and Arranging the Table in the Sanctuary

Here the Torah describes two rites of the regularly performed service in the Tabernacle that were not part of the sacrificial service: the lighting of the lamps of the golden candelabrum, and the setting of the showbread on the table in the Tent of Meeting.

24 [1]The Lord spoke to Moses, saying: [2]Command the children of Israel,
seventh aliya
and they shall take to you pure olive oil, beaten for the lighting, the first oil to issue from the crushed olives, to kindle a lamp continually. [3]Outside the curtain which conceals the Ark of the Testimony in the Holy of Holies, in the Tent of Meeting, Aaron shall arrange it, the lamps,

Leviticus

so that they will remain alight **from evening until morning before the Lord continually.** This commandment is **an eternal statute for your generations.** **⁴On the pure candelabrum,** on the candelabrum made of pure gold, he, Aaron, **shall arrange the lamps before the Lord continuously.** **⁵You shall take choice flour and bake with it twelve loaves; two-tenths of an ephah** of flour **shall be one loaf.** **⁶You shall place them,** the twelve loaves, **in two arrangements, six** loaves **to the arrangement, on the pure table, before the Lord.** **⁷You shall place pure frankincense on,** or next to, **the arrangement. And it,** the frankincense, **shall be a memorial portion for the bread, a fire offering to the Lord.** The frankincense is burned upon the altar as a remembrance for the bread, which is not burned. **⁸Each and every Sabbath day he shall arrange it,** twelve fresh loaves of showbread, **before the Lord continuously.** The showbread is a gift **from the children of Israel,** as **an eternal covenant.** **⁹It,** the showbread, **shall be for Aaron and his sons, and they shall eat it in a holy place,** in the Tabernacle, **for it is a sacred sacrament for him from the fire offerings of the Lord, an eternal statute.**

The Story of the Blasphemer

A quarrel that broke out between two people in the wilderness led one of them to curse the name of God. As a result, instructions were given regarding the law governing a person who cursed the name of God, as well as laws relating to damages.

¹⁰The son of an Israelite woman, and he was the son of an Egyptian man, that is to say, he was of mixed Jewish and non-Jewish descent, **went out among the children of Israel. And the son of the Israelite woman and the Israelite man,** one who was of solely Jewish descent, **fought in the camp.** **¹¹The son of the Israelite woman blasphemed,** mentioning **the** explicit **Name** of God, **and** he **cursed** God, speaking derogatively and mockingly about Him. **They,** the witnesses who heard him, **brought him to Moses. And the name of his mother was Shelomit, daughter of Divri, of the tribe of Dan.** **¹²They placed him in custody,** and waited for Moses **to clarify** his punishment **for them according to the Lord.**

¹³The Lord spoke to Moses, saying: **¹⁴Take the one who cursed outside the camp, and all** those **who heard** him curse God **shall lay their hands upon his head. And** then **the entire congregation shall stone him** to death.

¹⁵To the children of Israel you shall speak, saying: Each and every man who curses his God, then he shall bear his sin and be appropriately

punished. ¹⁶**One who blasphemes the** explicit **Name of the Lord shall be put to death; the entire congregation shall stone him.** The same law applies to **the stranger,** that is, the convert, **and native alike, when he blasphemes the** explicit **Name he shall be put to death.**

¹⁷**If a man smites the life of a person,** killing him, **he shall be put to death** by the court. ¹⁸**One who smites the life of an animal** that belongs to another **shall pay for it, a life for a life.** He must pay the value of an animal to replace the animal that he killed. ¹⁹**If a man inflicts** a wound and thus causes **a defect on his counterpart, as he did, so shall be done to him:** he shall be punished in accordance with the damage that he caused. ²⁰**A break for a break, an eye for an eye, a tooth for a tooth; as he inflicted a defect on the person, so shall be inflicted on him.** This is the punishment that he deserves, though in practice he pays for the damage.

📖 **Further reading:** For the Sages' interpretation of the expression "an eye for an eye," see *A Concise Guide to the Sages*, p. 113.

Maftir ²¹**One who smites an animal shall pay for it. And one who smites a person shall be put to death.** Again, the verse indicates that he is deserving of death. ²²**There shall be one law for you, the stranger and native alike, for I am the Lord your God.**

²³**Moses spoke to the children of Israel,** teaching them all of the aforementioned commandments. **And they took the one who cursed outside the camp and stoned him with stones.** From then on **the children of Israel did as the Lord had commanded Moses** with regard to the laws stated here.

Parashat Behar

The two main commandments that appear in this section, concerning the Sabbatical Year and the Jubilee, are intertwined. The Sabbatical Year is the seventh and last year of each Sabbatical cycle, and the Jubilee is the fiftieth year, the one following seven Sabbatical cycles. Both express the idea that the land and its inhabitants belong to God. During the Sabbatical Year, the owner must relinquish his ownership of his land, and he is prohibited to work it. All produce that does grow is ownerless, and must be left unguarded in the fields, so that any creature, including wild animals, can have ready access to it.

Similarly, the Jubilee Year restores the division of basic resources to its original state. All slaves go free and all land returns to its original owners. The sale of land is, therefore, in effect, only a lease, for a period of up to fifty years. The sale of a person, and therefore their status as a slave, is also not absolute. Their release in the Jubilee Year bestows upon them a status similar to that of hired hands who work for a living. Owners are not permitted to saddle slaves with hard labor.

Even before the Jubilee Year, the sale of an ancestral portion or of a person can be reversed. A person's relatives, or even the person themselves, can redeem their inheritance or buy themselves out of slavery by refunding the payment that had been received for the years remaining until the Jubilee Year.

The Sabbatical and Jubilee Years

During the Sabbatical Year, which occurs every seven years, working the land is forbidden for the entire year, and produce that grows is ownerless and may be eaten by anybody. During the Jubilee Year, which falls out after every seven Sabbatical cycles, ancestral portions are returned to their original owners and slaves are set free. God promises that the sixth year will yield an abundant crop that will suffice also for the Sabbatical and Jubilee Years.

25 ¹**The Lord spoke to Moses** when the Israelites were still camped **at Mount Sinai, saying:** ²**Speak to the children of Israel, and say to them: When you come into the land that I am giving you,** the Land of Israel, **the land shall rest, a Sabbath to the Lord.**

³**Six years you will sow your field, and six years you will prune your vineyard, and you will gather its produce.** ⁴**In the seventh year, it shall**

be a sabbatical rest for the land, just as the weekly Sabbath is a rest for people, a Sabbath for the Lord; your field you shall not sow, and your vineyard you shall not prune. ⁵The aftergrowth of your reaping, the produce that grows by itself from the remnants that fell to the ground during the previous harvest, you shall not reap in the normal manner of an owner in his field. And the uncultivated grapes of your vine, you shall not gather. It shall be a Sabbatical Year for the land.

📖 **Further reading:** For the significance of the Sabbatical Year and its rationale, see *A Concise Guide to the Sages*, p. 161. The practical implications for people who are not farmers appear in *A Concise Guide to Halakha*, p. 570.

⁶**The Sabbath of the land,** the produce that grows during the seventh year, **shall be yours for eating, for you, and for your slave, and for your maidservant, and for your hired laborer, and for your resident alien who reside with you,** all the inhabitants of the Land of Israel. ⁷**And for your animals,** your livestock, **and for the** wild **beasts, that are in your land, all of its,** the year's, **produce shall be to eat.**

⁸**You shall count for yourselves seven Sabbatical Years, seven years seven times, and they shall be to you the days of the seven Sabbatical Years,** a total of **forty-nine years.** ⁹After forty-nine years, **you shall sound an alarm blast of the shofar during the seventh month, on the tenth day; on the Day of Atonement** of the fiftieth year **you shall sound the shofar throughout your land,** to make it known that it is the Jubilee Year.

¹⁰**You shall sanctify the fiftieth year, and proclaim** full **liberty in the land for all its inhabitants,** freeing all slaves from their bonds. **It shall be a Jubilee** Year, a year of blowing the shofar, **to you; each man shall return to his ancestral portion, and each man,** each slave, **shall return to his family.** ¹¹**It is a Jubilee, the fiftieth year shall be for you; you shall not sow, and you shall not reap its aftergrowth, and you shall not gather its uncultivated grapes.** ¹²**Since it is a Jubilee, it shall be sacred for you;** you shall abstain from working the land and reaping its produce in the manner of an owner. **From the field you shall eat its produce,** taking a little at a time, and not gathering it into your house. ¹³**In this Jubilee Year you shall return each man to his ancestral portion.**

Second aliya ¹⁴**If you sell a sale item to your counterpart,** another citizen, **or acquire** an article **from the hand of your counterpart, you shall not exploit one another** by cheating. ¹⁵**On the basis of the number of years after,** or until,

the Jubilee you shall acquire from your counterpart. The price of the land should be calculated based on the number of years that the sale will last. **On the basis of the number of crop years,** excluding the Sabbatical Years, **he shall sell to you.** ¹⁶**According to the abundance of the years,** if there are many years until the Jubilee, **you shall increase its price, and according to the paucity of the years,** if there are only a few years until the Jubilee, **you shall decrease its price, as it is the number of crops,** the right to the land's produce, **he is selling to you,** and not the land itself. ¹⁷**You shall not wrong one another, and you shall fear your God; for I am the Lord your God.**

¹⁸**You shall perform My statutes, and My ordinances you shall observe, and perform them, and** then **you shall live on the land in security.**

⌐ **Further reading:** For more on the prohibition against fraud, and its practical implications, see *A Concise Guide to Halakha*, p. 599.

Third ¹⁹**The land shall yield its produce, and you shall eat your fill** and be sati-
aliya ated by it, **and you shall live in security upon it.**
(Second
aliya) ²⁰**If you shall say: What shall we eat during the seventh year,** for **behold,** due to these prohibitions, **we shall not sow, nor shall we gather our harvest.** ²¹**I will command My blessing for you in the sixth year, and it shall generate the produce** so abundantly that it will provide food **for the three years:** the sixth year, the seventh year, and part of the eighth year. ²²**You shall sow the eighth year,** after the Sabbatical Year, **and** meanwhile you will **eat of the old produce** from the sixth year, **until the ninth year, until the arrival of its produce** that you planted in the eighth year, **you shall eat the old.**

⌐ **Further reading:** For more on trust in God, see *A Concise Guide to Mahshava*, p. 154.

²³**The land,** the Land of Israel, **shall not be sold in perpetuity, as the land is Mine; for you are strangers and resident aliens with Me,** as you live in My land under a special agreement, but it does not belong to you. ²⁴**In all the land of your ancestral portion, you shall provide redemption for the land** by returning all properties to their original owners.

Selling Land in the Land of Israel
The sale of an ancestral portion is not absolute, and the seller or his relatives can redeem the property and bring it back into the possession of the family. On the other hand, the sale of

a house located in a walled city is permanent, unless the house is redeemed in the first year after the sale. However, in the case of Levites, who did not receive agricultural land, such houses can be redeemed at any time.

ourth
aliya **²⁵If your brother becomes poor and sells** property **from his ancestral portion, his redeemer,** a family member **who is close to him, shall come and redeem the sale of his brother.** This relative has the right to buy back the property. **²⁶If a man shall have no redeemer** who is able to exercise this right, **and** after a period of time **he,** the original owner, **acquires the means and finds enough** money **for its redemption, ²⁷he shall calculate the years of its sale,** the total number of years that the land would have remained in the buyer's possession from the time of sale until the Jubilee Year, and subtract the number of years that it was actually under the buyer's control, **and return the balance,** the money for the remaining years, **to the man to whom he sold it** until the Jubilee Year. **And he shall return to his ancestral portion. ²⁸But if he does not acquire enough** money **for its return to him,** then **his sale,** the property, **shall remain in the possession of the buyer until the Jubilee Year, and it shall be released** to the seller **in the Jubilee** without redemption, **and he shall return to his ancestral portion.**

Fifth
aliya
Third
aliya) **²⁹**On the other hand, **if a man sells a house of residence in a walled city,** its right **of redemption** by the seller **shall be until the conclusion of the year of its sale; its redemption shall be for** exactly **one year. ³⁰If it,** the house, **shall not be redeemed until the completion of one full year for it, the house that is in the city that has a wall shall be established in perpetuity to the one who bought it for his generations; it shall not be released in the Jubilee** to its original owner.

³¹But the houses in open cities that have no wall surrounding them shall be reckoned like the fields of the land; it, such a house, **shall have redemption** like a field, **and in the Jubilee it shall be released.**

³²As for **the cities of the Levites,** with regard to **the houses of the cities of their ancestral portion,** houses owned by Levites within their walled cities, **there shall be eternal redemption for the Levites.** Houses in the cities of Levites cannot be sold permanently, even if those cities are walled. **³³**Therefore, **one who buys from the Levites, the sale of the house in the city of his ancestral property shall be released in the Jubilee, for the houses of the cities of the Levites are their ancestral portion in the midst of the children of Israel. ³⁴But the fields of the open land of their cities,** surrounding them, common property of all the residents of the city

rather than of individual Levites, **shall not be sold, as it is their eternal ancestral portion.**

The Prohibition of Lending Money at Interest

Selling ancestral property or selling oneself into slavery is the last resort of a person who has fallen into dire financial circumstances. The people of Israel are commanded to help the poor before they reach these situations, and they are prohibited to lend their money at interest.

[35]**If your brother should become poor, and his means fail** while living **with you, you shall** help and **support him,** not only your brother but any **stranger or resident alien, and he shall live with you.** [36]**Do not take interest,** that is, do not lend money on the condition that the longer the borrower delays repayment the more he is forced to pay, **or increase,** demand a fixed fee that must be paid in addition to the loan, **from him; you shall fear your God. And your brother shall live with you.** [37]**Your silver you shall not give him with interest, and with increase you shall not give him** even **your food.** The prohibition applies to loans of all items, not only money. [38]**I am the Lord your God who brought you out of the land of Egypt, to give you the land of Canaan, to be your God.**

📖 **Further reading:** For more on how the prohibition against taking interest is practiced today, see *A Concise Guide to Halakha*, p. 619.

A Hebrew Slave

An Israelite who falls into poverty and is sold into slavery is not an absolute slave. His release from slavery in the Jubilee Year attests to the fact that his sale was not an absolute sale. Similarly, his master may not burden him with hard labor, and his relatives are commanded to ensure that he is redeemed. The only true slaves who are the property of their owners are gentile slaves.

Sixth
aliya
(Fourth
aliya)

[39]**If your brother shall become poor with you and is sold to you** as a slave, **you shall not work him as a slave** by forcing him to perform menial tasks. [40]**As a hired laborer, as a resident** of your area, who can choose what work he is willing to perform, **he,** the slave, **shall be with you.** Furthermore, **until the Jubilee Year he shall work with you.** [41]Then **he shall be released from you, he and his children with him.** As long as he was your slave, you were responsible for his family's support; when the slave goes free, his family leaves with him. **He shall return to his family, and to the ancestral portion of his fathers he shall return.** [42]Israelites may not be sold permanently, **for they are My servants, whom I brought out of the land of**

Egypt, and therefore **they shall** also **not be sold** in a despicable manner, **as slaves** that are sold in a slave market. ⁴³Furthermore, **you shall not oppress him with** uncommonly **hard labor; you shall fear your God.**

⁴⁴**But your slaves and your maidservants whom you shall have from the nations that surround you: From them,** but not from your fellow Israelites, **you may buy a slave or a maidservant.** ⁴⁵**Also from the children of the resident aliens who reside with you,** gentiles who reside within the boundaries of the Land of Israel, **from them you shall buy** a slave, **and from their families that are with you, which they have begotten in your land; they shall be an ancestral portion for you.** ⁴⁶**Furthermore, you shall bequeath them to your children after you, to inherit as an ancestral portion; you shall enslave them forever;** there is no set date when you must emancipate them. **But with regard to your brethren the children of Israel, one to another, you shall not oppress him with hard labor.** You must treat them gently and with respect.

⁴⁷**If a stranger who is a resident with you,** a gentile from a different nation who resides among you and who does not worship idolatry, **shall acquire means, and your brother becomes poor with,** in comparison to, **him and he is sold to** that wealthy **stranger who is a resident with you, or to an offshoot of a stranger's family** who does worship other gods, ⁴⁸in both such cases, the sale is valid. However, **after he,** the Israelite, **is sold** as a slave, **he shall have redemption; one of his brothers shall redeem him** and do his utmost to buy his freedom. ⁴⁹**Or his uncle or his cousin shall redeem him, or** another relative **from his close kin from his family shall redeem him; or if he** himself **acquires** the **means, he shall be redeemed** with his own money. ⁵⁰**He shall calculate with his buyer from the year of his sale to him until the Jubilee Year, and his sale price shall be accord-**ing **to the number of years. As the time of a hired laborer, he,** the slave, **shall be with him.** ⁵¹**If there are still many years** for the slave to work until the Jubilee, **in accordance with them he shall repay the cost of his re-demption from the silver of his purchase.** ⁵²**If a few remain of the years until the Jubilee Year, he shall calculate for him; in accordance with his years he shall repay the cost of his redemption.** ⁵³**As a yearly hired la-borer he shall be with him.** Even gentiles residing in the Land of Israel are obligated to treat Israelite slaves with the respect accorded to hired work-ers. **He,** the gentile master, **shall not oppress him with hard labor before your eyes.** ⁵⁴**If he shall not be redeemed by** one of **these** relatives, or by

himself, nevertheless **he shall be released in the Jubilee Year; he, and his children with him.**

Maftir **⁵⁵For to Me the children of Israel are slaves; they are My slaves whom I took out of the land of Egypt. I am the Lord your God.** Since God is the Master of Israel, the buyer's authority is limited.

26 **¹You shall not make for you false gods, and you shall not establish for you an idol or a pillar. And an ornamented stone you shall not place in your land, to prostrate yourself upon it,** the way that idol worshippers bow down on a mosaic floor. **For I am the Lord your God. ²You shall observe My Sabbaths,** the Sabbath and the festivals, **and you shall** honor and **revere My Sanctuary. I am the Lord.**

Further reading: For more on Shabbat and its meaning, see *A Concise Guide to the Sages*, p. 275; *A Concise Guide to Mahshava*, p. 33; *A Concise Guide to Halakha*, p. 379.

Parashat
Behukotai

After clarifying the details of many commandments in the book of Leviticus, the Torah now addresses the covenant between God and the people of Israel. The observance of God's commandments underlies Israel's right to live in the Land of Israel and to receive God's abundance and blessings, while the non-observance of the commandments and rejection of God's word will lead to more and more severe punishments, culminating in Israel's exile from their land.

The promise that following all of their hardships the people of Israel will repent and return to their land, testifies to the eternal validity of the covenant.

The second part of the *parasha* deals with the consecration of property to the Sanctuary. A person can consecrate his fields, his house, and his animals, and he can also pledge his own value or the value of another person. The Torah explains the laws relating to the consecration of various types of property.

Strengthening the Covenant of Sinai
The Torah promises blessing and good life to the people of Israel if they keep the word of God. It then continues with a description of the heavy punishments that will be meted out to Israel if they forsake the Torah and its commandments.

³If you follow My statutes and observe My commandments that I have made known to you, **and perform them, ⁴I will provide your rains in their season,** when they are needed and desired, **and the land shall yield its produce, and the tree of the field shall yield its fruit.** ⁵Owing to the abundance of your crops, **your threshing,** which starts at the beginning of the summer months, **shall reach until grape harvest** in the fall, **and the grape harvest shall reach until sowing** at the beginning of the next agricultural year. In a year of blessing, each one of these stages shall follow in an uninterrupted sequence. **You shall eat your food to repletion, and you shall live in your land in security** with no fear of enemies.

Second aliya **⁶I shall grant peace in the land, and you shall lie** asleep at night **without threat** of an enemy attack; **and I will banish wild beasts from the land. A sword shall not pass in your land.** Foreign forces will not dare even to pass through your territory. **⁷You shall pursue your enemies, and they**

shall fall before you by the sword. ⁸**Five of you shall pursue** and cause to flee **one hundred** of the enemy, **and one hundred of you shall pursue ten thousand; and your enemies shall fall before you by the sword.**

Further reading: For more on reward and punishment, see *A Concise Guide to the Sages*, p. 165; *A Concise Guide to Mahshava*, p. 256.

⁹**I will turn to you** with a special blessing **and make you fruitful, and multiply you,** granting you many children; **and I will fulfill My covenant** and all its promises **with you.** ¹⁰**You shall eat old produce, and you shall remove the old from before the new.** You will have to take out the excess old produce in order to make room for the new.

Third aliya (Fifth aliya)

¹¹**I will place My dwelling in your midst, and My Self shall not reject you;** I shall not distance My presence from you. ¹²**I shall walk in your midst, I shall be your God, and you shall be My people.** The mutual relationship between the nation and its God will be apparent. ¹³**I am the Lord your God, who took you out of the land of Egypt, from being slaves to them; I broke the beams of your yoke,** ending your bondage, **and caused you to** lift up your heads and **walk upright.**

Further reading: For more on the meaning of the blessings in this *parasha*, see *A Concise Guide to the Sages*, pp. 165ff.

¹⁴**And if you do not heed Me, and do not perform all these commandments,** ¹⁵**and if you despise My statutes, and if your soul rejects** and abhors **My ordinances, failing to perform all My commandments, in your violating** and annulling **My covenant,** ¹⁶**so** too, I will not fulfill My obligations stemming from the covenant, and **I will do this to you: I will appoint over you panic,** existential anxiety. I will also bring upon you diseases: **consumption and fever, causing the eyes to seek and the soul to despair** with continuous suffering. **And you shall sow your seed in vain, and your enemies shall eat** the produce growing from **it.** ¹⁷**I shall direct My attention** and anger **against you, and you shall be smitten** in combat **before your enemies; those who hate you shall subjugate you, and you shall flee** even **with no one pursuing you.**

¹⁸**And if** even **after these** troubles **you do not heed Me, I will amplify** chastising you, I will punish you **sevenfold for your sins.** ¹⁹**I will break the pride of your power,** your sense of strength, **and I will render your sky like iron** so no water issues from it, **and your earth like bronze,** so

that nothing will grow. **²⁰Your strength shall be** entirely **expended in vain; all your** efforts to grow crops shall be for naught: **And your land shall not yield its produce and the tree of the land shall not yield its fruit.**

²¹And if you walk contrarily with Me, in rebellion, **and you do not** wish to **heed Me, then I will amplify My blow upon you sevenfold, in accordance with your sins. ²²I will send the beast of the field against you. It will bereave you of your children,** the easiest prey, **and destroy your cattle, and diminish you; and your roads shall become desolate** due to the reduced number of people using them.

²³And if with these, too, **you are not chastised by Me,** by accepting My reproof, **and you walk contrarily with Me; ²⁴so I also will walk with you contrarily,** in the same harsh and forceful manner, **and I will also smite you sevenfold for your sins. ²⁵I will bring upon you the sword of vengeance for the** broken **covenant; you shall be gathered into your cities,** to hide from the enemy, and there **I will send forth pestilence among you. And** eventually **you shall be delivered into the hand of an enemy. ²⁶When I break for you the staff,** your support **of bread, ten women shall bake your bread in one oven,** owing to the small quantity of bread being baked. **And they shall return your bread by weight,** to determine exactly what belongs to them and what belongs to their neighbor. **And** then **you shall eat, but you shall not be satisfied.**

²⁷And if even with this, actual hunger, with the hardships and disasters increasing, you **do not heed Me, and you walk contrarily with Me, ²⁸I will walk with you in furious contrariness. I will also chastise you sevenfold for your sins. ²⁹You shall eat the flesh of your sons, and the flesh of your daughters you shall eat. ³⁰I will destroy your high places,** the tall structures that serve as altars, **and destroy your sun idols,** images and monuments for the worship of the sun, **and I shall cast your carcasses on the carcasses of your idols.** You too will die, along with your shattered idols. **And My soul shall reject you;** I will remove My presence from among you. **³¹I will render your cities ruins, I will make your sanctuaries desolate, and I will not smell your pleasing aroma.** I will not be appeased with your offerings. **³²I will make the land desolate, and your enemies who live in it shall be desolate upon it.** Even those who try to settle the land after you are gone will be unable to make it thrive and bloom. **³³As for you, I will scatter you among the nations, and I will draw the sword after you,** and it will pursue and kill you. **Your land shall be desolate, and your cities shall be ruins.**

📖 **Further reading:** Why does the Torah not mention spiritual repercussions? Several possibilities are presented in *A Concise Guide to Mahshava*, p. 257.

³⁴**Then the land shall be repaid for its sabbaths,** the Sabbatical Years during which it should have rested, **all the days of its desolation, and you are in the land of your enemies; then the land shall rest and will repay its sabbaths.** ³⁵**All the days of its desolation it,** the land, **shall rest** from yielding produce; **that which it did not rest during your sabbaths, when you lived upon it.**

³⁶**For the survivors among you, I will bring cowardice,** weakness and spinelessness, **in their hearts** when they are **in the lands of their enemies;** even **the sound of a driven leaf,** or a falling or rustling leaf, **shall pursue them.** Every slight noise will send them into a panic. Consequently, **they shall flee, as one flees the sword, and they shall fall** while running **with no pursuer.** ³⁷**They shall stumble over one another** during their flight, **as before a sword,** like those who flee from war, hurting each other in their rush to escape, **with no pursuer. You shall have no recourse before your enemies.** You will be unable to rise up and face enemy attackers. ³⁸Moreover, **you shall perish among the nations, and the land of your enemies shall consume you.** ³⁹**The survivors among you shall molder in,** due to, **their iniquity, in the lands of your enemies, and also in the iniquities of their fathers** which they shall continue, **with them they shall molder.**

⁴⁰Ultimately, **they shall** recognize their sins and **confess their iniquity and the iniquity of their fathers, in their trespass,** betrayal, **that they committed against Me, and also that they walked contrarily with Me.** ⁴¹**I too will** respond harshly and **walk contrarily with them, and I will bring them into the land of their enemies,** the ultimate punishment of exile; **only then,** when they have been exiled from their land, **their sealed hearts,** which had refused to listen to Me, **will be humbled. And then they will be repaid for their iniquity;** exile will atone for their sins.

⁴²**I will remember My covenant** that I enacted **with Jacob, and also My covenant with Isaac, and also My covenant with Abraham I will remember, and the land** that I chose to give to you, the Land of Israel, **I will remember.**

⁴³**The land shall be forsaken of them** during their exile, **and shall be repaid for her sabbaths** that they failed to observe **in** the fact of **its desolation from them; and they shall repay** the debt of **their iniquity** through

their punishment, **because they despised My ordinances, and their soul rejected** and abhorred **My statutes.**

[44]**Despite this,** after all the transgressions and punishments, even **when they are in the land of their enemies, I will not have despised them and will not have rejected them** in order **to destroy them** entirely, and thereby **to violate My covenant with them, as I am the Lord their God.** [45]**I shall remember for them,** those who will live after many generations, **the covenant of their ancestors, that I took them out of the land of Egypt, before the eyes of the nations,** in public display, with grand miracles, **to be their God. I am the Lord.**

[46]**These are the statutes and ordinances and laws which the Lord gave between Him and the children of Israel at Mount Sinai,** before their many journeys in the wilderness, **at the hand of Moses.**

The Laws of Consecration

Nearly anything can be consecrated as a donation to the Sanctuary. If these items are not useful as part of the sacrificial service, they are redeemed, and the funds received are used to provide for the upkeep of the Sanctuary. In a few cases, consecrated items are not redeemed at their market value as determined by priestly appraisal; the Torah sets fixed values for their redemption. Consecrated animals that are fit for the altar cannot be redeemed at all, and must be brought as an offering to God.

27 [1]**The Lord spoke to Moses, saying:** [2]**Speak to the children of Israel, and**
urth
•liya
•ixth
iya)
say to them: If a man articulates a vow in accordance with the valuation of persons to the Lord, obligating himself to give to God the monetary equivalent of the value of a certain person, [3]**the valuation shall be: For the male twenty years old until sixty years old, the valuation** with regard to this form of dedication **shall be fifty shekels of silver of the sacred shekel.** [4]**And if it is for a female** in the same age range of twenty years old to sixty, **the valuation shall be thirty shekels.** [5]**And if from five years old until twenty years old, the valuation shall be: The male twenty shekels, and for the female ten shekels.** [6]**And if from one month old until five years old, the valuation shall be: The male five shekels of silver, and for the female, the valuation three shekels of silver.** [7]**And if from sixty years old and above: If a male, the valuation shall be fifteen shekels, and for the female ten shekels.** [8]**And if he,** the one who vowed, **is too poor** to pay **for the valuation, he shall be set before the priest, and the priest shall assess him;** on the basis of what the one who vowed can afford to pay, **the priest shall assess him.**

⁹**And if it,** the object one vowed to donate, **is a** type of **animal from which one would present an offering to the Lord,** an animal fit for the altar, **any that one gives of it to the Lord shall be sacred.** The sanctity of the vow applies to the body of the animal itself. ¹⁰**Consequently, one shall not exchange it, and not substitute it,** replacing a **good** animal **with** a **bad** one, or even a **bad** one **with** a **good** one; **if he substitutes an animal for an animal, it and its substitute shall be sacred;** the sanctity will apply to both animals.

¹¹**And if** a man consecrates an animal, and **it is any type of non-pure animal, from which one does not present an offering to the Lord, he shall set the animal before the priest.** ¹²**The priest shall assess it, whether good or bad; as the priest's valuation, so shall it be.** ¹³**If,** after the owner consecrates the non-pure animal, **he redeems it, he shall add one-fifth to the valuation** of its worth.

¹⁴**And when a man consecrates his house to be sacred to the Lord, then the priest shall assess it, whether good or bad; as the priest assesses it, so shall it stand.** ¹⁵**And if the one who consecrated it redeems his house** himself, **he shall add one-fifth the silver of the valuation to it,** and **then** the house **shall be his.**

Fifth aliya (Seventh aliya) ¹⁶**If from the field of his ancestral portion,** land belonging to his family, **a man consecrates to the Lord, the valuation,** the value of the field for the purpose of redemption, **shall be according to its seed,** its growing cycles. Since the field is not sold forever, its value for this purpose is based on following formula: **An area** that is required to be **sown with a ḥomer,** a measure of volume **of barley,** shall be redeemed **for fifty shekels of silver.** ¹⁷**If he consecrates his field from,** that is, immediately after, **the Jubilee Year, the valuation shall stand.** It shall be redeemed in accordance with the full sum. ¹⁸**And if he consecrates his field after the Jubilee,** i.e., at some point after the first year of the next cycle, **the priest shall calculate for him the silver according to the remaining years until the Jubilee Year, and it shall be deducted from the valuation.** Slightly more than one shekel must be deducted from the total sum for each year that has passed.

¹⁹**And if the one who consecrated it** himself **redeems the field, he shall add one-fifth of the silver of the valuation to it** in order to redeem it, **and it shall be his.** ²⁰**And if he does not redeem the field** from Sanctuary property in all the years of the Jubilee cycle, **or if,** in the meantime, **he,** the Sanctuary treasurer, **sold the field to another man, it shall no longer be**

redeemed by the original owner. **²¹And when the field is released in the Jubilee** and leaves the possession of the buyer, **it shall be sacred to the Lord** and become Sanctuary property. It is considered **like a proscribed field,** as explained below, verse 28; **his portion shall belong to the priest.**

xth **²²And if he consecrates to the Lord a field of his acquisition,** a field that
liya he purchased from another, **that is not a field of his ancestral portion,** part of his family's property, **²³the priest shall calculate for him the sum of the valuation until the Jubilee Year,** the valuation in accordance with the number of years remaining until the Jubilee, and **he shall give the valuation as of that day** on which he comes to redeem it, and **it,** the payment, **is sacred to the Lord. ²⁴In the Jubilee Year, the field shall return to the one from whom he acquired it, to the one whose ancestral portion of the land it is,** the original seller.

²⁵Every payment of **valuation** discussed above **shall be in the sacred shekel; twenty gera shall be** the value of **the shekel.**

²⁶However, with regard to **a male firstborn that is born first to the Lord, from an animal, no man shall consecrate it,** there being no need to consecrate it, **whether it is an ox or a sheep,** because **it is the Lord's,** sacred from birth, and must be brought as an offering. **²⁷And if it,** the firstborn animal, **is a non-pure beast,** which cannot be brought as an offering, **he,** the owner, **shall redeem it according to the valuation,** by paying the animal's worth, **and he shall add one additional fifth of it,** of its value, **to it. And if it is not redeemed** by the owner, **it shall be sold** by the Sanctuary treasury **for the** amount of the **valuation.**

²⁸However, anything proscribed that a man proscribes for the Lord, i.e., dedicates to God by declaring it forbidden property, **from all that is his, whether man,** e.g., one of his slaves, **or animal, or the field of his ancestral portion,** which is in the absolute possession of its owner, **shall not be sold and shall not be redeemed** in any situation; **anything proscribed**
nth **is a sacred sacrament to the Lord. ²⁹Anything proscribed with regard**
liya **to people,** e.g., captives of war who have been proscribed, **shall not be redeemed; he shall be put to death.**

³⁰All the tithe of the land, the second tithe that is separated **from the seed of the land,** such as wheat or barley, **or from the fruit of the tree, is the Lord's; it is sacred to the Lord,** and must be eaten in close proximity to the Sanctuary in a state of ritual purity. **³¹And if a man shall redeem from**

his tithe, if he wants to reacquire his tithe and be permitted to treat his produce like regular produce, **he shall add one-fifth of it to it.**

^{Maftir} ³²**And all the tithe of cattle or the flock,** a tenth of the animals born each year, **any that passes under the rod,** the herdsman's staff, **the tenth** that passes under the rod **shall be sacred to the Lord.** ³³**He shall not distinguish between good and bad, nor shall he substitute it,** replacing the tenth animal that passed under the rod with a leaner animal. **And if he substitutes it, it and its substitute,** the original animal and that which was meant to replace it, **shall be sacred; it shall not be redeemed.** The tithe remains consecrated to God; one may not redeem it. ³⁴**These are the commandments that the Lord commanded Moses for the children of Israel on Mount Sinai.**

📖 Further reading: How does one separate tithes today? See *A Concise Guide to Halakha*, p. 564.

Numbers

Parashat Bemidbar

This Torah portion addresses the census of the Israelites that is conducted at God's command. The census is performed according to family and tribal affiliation. In addition, the configuration of the Israelite encampment during their stay in the wilderness, and the special role of the tribe of Levi in safeguarding and tending to the Tabernacle, are addressed.

The Census of the Israelites

God commands Moses to count all the males of an age fit for conscription, according to their families and patrilineal houses. The census is conducted with the assistance of the tribal princes, who had been appointed at the word of God. The tribe of Levi is the only tribe not included in the census due to their designated role of safeguarding the Tabernacle.

1 **¹The Lord spoke to Moses in the wilderness of Sinai, in the Tent of Meeting** in the Tabernacle, **on the first of the second month, in the second year of their exodus from the land of Egypt, saying: ²Take a census of the entire congregation of the children of Israel, by their families, by their patrilineal house, according to the number of names, every male, by their head count. ³From twenty years old and above, all those fit for military service in Israel: You shall count them according to their hosts, you and Aaron. ⁴With you** in charge of the census **shall be a man for each tribe, each** of them **is the head of his patrilineal house.**

📖 **Further reading:** For more on the significance of the census, see *A Concise Guide to the Sages*, p. 172.

⁵These are the names of the men, the princes of the tribes, **who shall stand with you** to perform the census, beginning with the tribes that were sons of Leah. **For Reuben, Elitzur son of Shede'ur. ⁶For Simeon, Shelumiel son of Tzurishadai. ⁷For Judah, Nahshon son of Aminadav. ⁸For Issachar, Netanel son of Tzuar. ⁹For Zebulun, Eliav son of Helon. ¹⁰From** the sons of Rachel, **for the sons of Joseph: for Ephraim, Elishama son of Amihud; for Manasseh, Gamliel son of Pedatzur. ¹¹For**

Benjamin, Avidan son of Gidoni. [12]From the sons of the maidservants, for Dan, Ahiezer son of Amishadai. [13]For Asher, Pagiel son of Okhran. [14]For Gad, Elyasaf son of De'uel. [15]For Naphtali, Ahira son of Einan.

[16]These are the distinguished officials of the congregation, the princes of the tribes of their fathers; they are the heads of the thousands of Israel. [17]Moses and Aaron took these men, who were designated by name by God. [18]They assembled the entire congregation on the first of the second month, and they verified their lineages by their families, by their patrilineal house, according to the number of names, from twenty years old and above, by their head count. [19]As the Lord had commanded Moses, he counted them in the wilderness of Sinai.

Second aliya [20]These were the the children of Reuben, Israel's firstborn, their descendants, by their families, by their patrilineal house, according to the number of names, by their head count, every male from twenty years old and above, all those fit for military service; [21]those counted for the tribe of Reuben were forty-six thousand five hundred.

[22]For the children of Simeon, their descendants, by their families, by their patrilineal house, those counted, according to the number of names, by their head count, every male from twenty years old and above, all those fit for military service; [23]those counted for the tribe of Simeon were fifty-nine thousand three hundred.

[24]For the children of Gad, their descendants, by their families, by their patrilineal house, according to the number of names, from twenty years old and above, all those fit for military service; [25]those counted for the tribe of Gad were forty-five thousand six hundred and fifty.

[26]For the children of Judah, their descendants, by their families, by their patrilineal house, according to the number of names, from twenty years old and above, all those fit for military service; [27]those counted for the tribe of Judah were seventy-four thousand six hundred.

[28]For the children of Issachar, their descendants, by their families, by their patrilineal house, according to the number of names, from twenty years old and above, all those fit for military service; [29]those counted for the tribe of Issachar were fifty-four thousand four hundred.

[30]For the children of Zebulun, their descendants, by their families, by their patrilineal house, according to the number of names, from twenty years old and above, all those fit for military service; [31]those counted for the tribe of Zebulun were fifty-seven thousand four hundred.

³²For the children of Joseph, for the children of Ephraim, their descendants, by their families, by their patrilineal house, according to the number of names, from twenty years old and above, all those fit for military service; ³³those counted for the tribe of Ephraim were forty thousand five hundred.

³⁴For the children of Manasseh, their descendants, by their families, by their patrilineal house, according to the number of names, from twenty years old and above, all those fit for military service; ³⁵those counted for the tribe of Manasseh were thirty-two thousand two hundred.

³⁶For the children of Benjamin, their descendants, by their families, by their patrilineal house, according to the number of names, from twenty years old and above, all those fit for military service; ³⁷those counted for the tribe of Benjamin were thirty-five thousand four hundred.

³⁸For the children of Dan, their descendants, by their families, by their patrilineal house, according to the number of names, from twenty years old and above, all those fit for military service; ³⁹those counted for the tribe of Dan were sixty-two thousand seven hundred.

⁴⁰For the children of Asher, their descendants, by their families, by their patrilineal house, according to the number of names, from twenty years old and above, all those fit for military service; ⁴¹those counted for the tribe of Asher were forty-one thousand five hundred.

⁴²For the children of Naphtali, their descendants, by their families, by their patrilineal house, according to the number of names, from twenty years old and above, all those fit for military service; ⁴³those counted for the tribe of Naphtali were fifty-three thousand four hundred.

⁴⁴These are the counted that Moses, Aaron, and the princes of Israel counted; they were twelve men, one each for his patrilineal house. ⁴⁵These were all the counted of the children of Israel by their patrilineal house, from twenty years old and above, all those fit for military service in Israel. ⁴⁶All the counted were six hundred thousand three thousand five hundred and fifty. ⁴⁷But the Levites by the tribe of their fathers were not counted among them.

⁴⁸The Lord spoke to Moses, saying: ⁴⁹Indeed, the tribe of Levi you shall not count, and you shall not take a census of them among the children of Israel. ⁵⁰But you, appoint the Levites as officials over the Tabernacle of the Testimony, over all its vessels, and over everything that is associated with it. They shall bear the Tabernacle and all its vessels, and

they shall minister to it; around the Tabernacle they shall encamp. [51]When the Tabernacle travels, the Levites shall dismantle it, and when the Tabernacle encamps, the Levites shall erect it; and the non-Levite stranger, who approaches the Tabernacle to dismantle or erect it, shall be put to death. [52]The children of Israel shall encamp, each of them in his camp, and each of them at his banner, according to their hosts. [53]The Levites shall encamp around the Tabernacle of the Testimony, and there shall not be divine rage against the congregation of the children of Israel, and the Levites shall protect the integrity of the Tabernacle of the Testimony, to prevent the approach of non-Levites. [54]The children of Israel did according to everything that the Lord had commanded Moses, so they did.

The Configuration of the Encampment

After the census of the Israelite males, God commands Moses and Aaron regarding the configuration of the encampment. The tribes are organized into four groups that encamp on the four sides of the Tabernacle. The tribe of Levi encamps in the center of the encampment, between the tribes and the Tabernacle.

2 [1]The Lord spoke to Moses and to Aaron, saying: [2]Each according to his banner, the groups of three tribes into which the camp was divided, with the insignias of their patrilineal house, shall the children of Israel encamp; at a distance, around the Tent of Meeting, they shall encamp. [3]The encamped at the front, to the east of the Tabernacle, shall be the banner of the camp of Judah, according to their hosts; and the prince of the children of Judah is Nahshon son of Aminadav. [4]Its host and those counted were seventy-four thousand six hundred. [5]The encamped with it shall be the tribe of Issachar; and the prince of the children of Issachar was Netanel son of Tzuar. [6]Its host and its count was fifty-four thousand four hundred. [7]Alongside them shall be the tribe of Zebulun; and the prince of the children of Zebulun was Eliav son of Helon. [8]Its host and its count was fifty-seven thousand four hundred. [9]All the counted for the camp of Judah, including the tribes of Issachar and Zebulun, were one hundred thousand eighty thousand six thousand four hundred, according to their hosts; they shall travel first.

Third aliya

Illustrations: See depiction of how the children of Israel were arranged while encamped in the wilderness, p. 529.

¹⁰The banner of the camp of Reuben shall be to the south according to their hosts; and the prince of the children of Reuben was Elitzur son of Shede'ur. ¹¹Its host and its count was forty-six thousand five hundred. ¹²The encamped with it shall be the tribe of Simeon; and the prince of the children of Simeon was Shelumiel son of Tzurishadai. ¹³Its host and those counted were fifty-nine thousand three hundred. ¹⁴And the tribe of Gad; and the prince of the children of Gad was Elyasaf son of Re'uel. ¹⁵Its host and those counted were forty-five thousand six hundred and fifty. ¹⁶All the counted for the camp of Reuben were one hundred thousand fifty-one thousand four hundred and fifty, according to their hosts; and they shall travel second, after the camp of Judah.

¹⁷The Tent of Meeting and the adjacent Levite camp shall travel in the midst of the camps; as they encamp so shall they travel, every man in his designated place, according to their banners.

¹⁸The banner of the camp of Ephraim according to their hosts shall be to the west; and the prince of the children of Ephraim was Elishama son of Amihud. ¹⁹Its host and those counted were forty thousand five hundred. ²⁰With it shall be the tribe of Manasseh; and the prince of the children of Manasseh was Gamliel son of Pedatzur. ²¹Its host and those counted were thirty-two thousand two hundred. ²²And the tribe of Benjamin; and the prince of the children of Benjamin was Avidan son of Gidoni. ²³Its host and those counted were thirty-five thousand four hundred. ²⁴All those counted for the camp of Ephraim were one hundred thousand eight thousand one hundred, according to their hosts; and they shall travel third.

²⁵The banner of the camp of Dan shall be to the north according to their hosts; and the prince of the children of Dan was Ahiezer son of Amishadai. ²⁶Its host and those counted were sixty-two thousand seven en hundred. ²⁷And the encamped with it shall be the tribe of Asher; and the prince of the children of Asher was Pagiel son of Okhran. ²⁸Its host and those counted were forty-one thousand five hundred. ²⁹And the tribe of Naphtali; and the prince of the children of Naphtali was Ahira son of Einan. ³⁰Its host and those counted were fifty-three thousand four hundred. ³¹All those counted for the camp of Dan were one hundred thousand fifty-seven thousand six hundred; they shall travel last by their banners.

³²These are those who were counted of the children of Israel by their patrilineal house; all those counted of the camps according to their hosts were six hundred thousand three thousand five hundred and fifty. ³³The Levites were not counted among the children of Israel, as the Lord had commanded Moses. The unusual form for the words "were not counted" [*hotpakdu*] indicates that they did not count themselves, nor did others count them. ³⁴The children of Israel did according to everything that the Lord had commanded Moses, so they encamped according to their banners, and so they traveled, each of them according to his families, by his patrilineal house.

The Commission of the Tribe of Levi

The tribe of Levi is placed in charge of the service in the Tabernacle, and its safeguarding. The descendants of Aaron are the officials appointed over the Tabernacle service, and the role of the rest of the tribe of Levi is to assist them. The Levites are appointed as keepers of the commission of the sacred in place of all Israelite firstborns, who had originally been designated for the role when they were spared from the plague of the firstborn in Egypt.

3 ¹These are the descendants of Aaron and Moses on the day that the
Fourth Lord spoke with Moses on Mount Sinai. ²These are the names of the
aliya sons of Aaron: the firstborn, Nadav, and Avihu, Elazar, and Itamar.
³These are the names of the sons of Aaron, the anointed priests, whom he invested to serve as priests. ⁴Nadav and Avihu died before the Lord in the Tabernacle **when they presented strange fire,** offerings that they were not commanded to sacrifice, **before the Lord, in the wilderness of Sinai, and they had no children; and Elazar and Itamar served as priests in the presence of Aaron, their father.**

⁵The Lord spoke to Moses, saying: ⁶Bring the tribe of Levi near, and stand it before Aaron the priest, and they shall serve him, and assist the priests in the Tabernacle service. ⁷They shall keep his commission in safeguarding the Temple, and the commission of the entire congregation before the Tent of Meeting, to perform the service of the Tabernacle. ⁸They shall safeguard all the vessels of the Tent of Meeting, and the commission of the children of Israel, to perform the service of the Tabernacle. ⁹You shall give the Levites to Aaron and to his sons** to be subordinate to their authority; **they are given to him** to assist him **from the children of Israel,** as their representatives. ¹⁰You shall count Aaron and his sons, and they shall observe their priesthood, and the stranger who approaches shall be put to death.**

[11]The Lord spoke to Moses, saying: [12]I have hereby taken the Levites from among the children of Israel in place of every firstborn, first issue of the womb from the children of Israel, and the Levites shall be Mine. [13]For every firstborn is Mine; on the day that I smote all the firstborn in the land of Egypt I designated and sanctified to Me every firstborn in Israel, from man to animal; they shall be Mine, I am the Lord.

The Families of the Tribe of Levi and Their Tasks

The Torah details at length the three Levite families, their numbers, and their tasks in bearing the Tabernacle when the Israelite camp travels, as well as the location of their encampment when the Israelites encamp.

Fifth aliya [14]The Lord spoke to Moses in the wilderness of Sinai, saying: [15]Count the children of Levi by their patrilineal house, by their families; every male from one month old and above you shall count them. [16]Moses counted them according to the directive of the Lord, as he was commanded. [17]These were the sons of Levi by their names: Gershon, Kehat, and Merari. [18]These were the names of the sons of Gershon by their families: Livni and Shimi. [19]The sons of Kehat by their families: Amram, Yitzhar, Hebron, and Uziel. [20]The sons of Merari by their families: Mahli and Mushi. These are the families of the Levites by their patrilineal house.

[21]For Gershon, the family of the Livnites and the family of the Shimiites; these are the families of the Gershonites. [22]Those counted, according to the number of all males from one month old and above; those counted were seven thousand five hundred. [23]The families of the Gershonites shall encamp behind the Tabernacle to the west. [24]The prince of the patrilineal house of the Gershonites was Elyasaf son of Lael. [25]The commission of the sons of Gershon in the Tent of Meeting was the Tabernacle, and the Tent, the two lower coverings, its upper, outer covering, and the screen of the entrance of the Tent of Meeting, [26]and the hangings of the courtyard, and the screen of the entrance of the courtyard that is near the Tabernacle, and near the altar surrounding, and its cords, which hold the hangings in place, for all its work, all the other accessories of the Tabernacle.

[27]For Kehat, the family of the Amramites, the family of the Yitzharites, the family of the Hebronites, and the family of the Uzielites; these are the families of the Kehatites. [28]According to the number of all males, from one month old and above, eight thousand six hundred, keepers

of the commission of the sacred. They were entrusted with the task of carrying the Tabernacle vessels. ²⁹The families of the sons of Kehat shall encamp on the side of the Tabernacle to the south. ³⁰The prince of the patrilineal house of the families of the Kehatites was Elitzafan son of Uziel. ³¹Their commission includes carrying the ark, the table, the candelabrum, the altars, and the sacred vessels, with which they would serve, and the screen, the partition of the Holy of Holies from the Sanctuary, and all its work, all the other accessories of the Tabernacle. ³²The prince of the princes of the Levites was Elazar son of Aaron the priest, who received the appointment over the keepers of the commission of the sacred.

³³For Merari, the family of the Mahlites and the family of the Mushites; these are the families of Merari. ³⁴Those counted, according to the number of all males, from one month old and above, were six thousand two hundred. ³⁵The prince of the patrilineal house of the families of Merari was Tzuriel son of Avihayil; they shall encamp on the side of the Tabernacle to the north. ³⁶The appointed commission of the sons of Merari included responsibility for the beams of the Tabernacle, its bars, its pillars, its sockets, all its accompanying instruments, and all its work, ³⁷and the pillars of the courtyard all around, their sockets, their pegs, and their cords.

Illustrations: See images of the Tabernacle, its components, and its vessels, pp. 523–526.

³⁸Those encamped in front of the Tabernacle, to the east, in front of the Tent of Meeting: Moses, and Aaron and his sons, keeping the commission of the Sanctuary for the commission of the children of Israel; and the stranger who approaches shall be put to death.

Redemption of the Firstborn in Exchange for the Levites

Previously there was brief mention of the fact that the Levites were to replace the firstborns in the performance of the Tabernacle service. Here the Torah details how this "redemption" took place; replacing each firstborn, a Levite is appointed to perform the service.

³⁹All those counted of the Levites, whom Moses and Aaron counted by the mandate of the Lord, by their families, all males from one month old and above, were twenty-two thousand. ⁴⁰The Lord said to Moses: Count all the firstborn males of the children of Israel from one month old and above, and take the number of their names. ⁴¹You shall take the

Sixth
aliya

Levites for Me, I am the Lord, in place of all the firstborn among the children of Israel, and the animals of the Levites in place of all the consecrated firstborn among the animals of the children of Israel. ⁴²Moses counted, as the Lord had commanded him, all firstborn among the children of Israel. ⁴³All the firstborn males according to the number of names, from one month old and above, by their count, were twenty-two thousand two hundred and seventy-three.

⁴⁴The Lord spoke to Moses, saying: ⁴⁵Take the Levites in place of all the firstborn among the children of Israel, and the animals of the Levites instead of their animals, and the Levites shall be Mine, I am the Lord. ⁴⁶For the redemptions of the two hundred and seventy-three of the firstborn of the children of Israel who exceed the number of the Levites, ⁴⁷you shall take five shekels each by head, for each additional firstborn beyond those who match the number of the Levites. In the sacred shekel you shall take; twenty gera is the shekel. ⁴⁸You shall give the silver to Aaron and to his sons as the redemptions of those among them, the firstborn, who exceed the number of the Levites. ⁴⁹Moses took the silver of the redemption from those who remain beyond the redemptions of the Levites. ⁵⁰From the firstborn of the children of Israel he took the silver: One thousand three hundred and sixty-five shekels, in the sacred shekels. ⁵¹Moses gave the silver of the redemption to Aaron and to his sons, according to the directive of the Lord, as the Lord had commanded Moses.

Carrying the Tabernacle

Here the division of labor between the Levite families in carrying the Tabernacle is detailed. Extra vigilance is required of the Kehatites, who carry the sacred vessels, to refrain from being present when the priests cover the vessels, and to enter the Tabernacle only after the priests have completed that task.

4 ¹The Lord spoke to Moses and to Aaron, saying: ²Take the census of the sons of Kehat, and designate them from among the sons of Levi, by their families, by their patrilineal house. ³From thirty years old and above and until fifty years old, all those enlisted for duty, to perform labor in the Tent of Meeting. ⁴This is the work of the sons of Kehat in the Tent of Meeting: the sacred sacraments. ⁵Aaron and his sons shall come when the camp travels, before the departure, and they shall remove the curtain that screens, that divides the Sanctuary from the Holy of Holies,

venth
aliya

Numbers

and with it they shall cover the Ark of the Testimony. ⁶They shall place upon it a covering of the hide of a taḥash, and they shall spread a cloth entirely of sky-blue wool over it, and they shall fasten its staves to facilitate carrying it. ⁷On the table for the showbread they shall spread a cloth of sky-blue wool, and place upon it the bowls and the spoons, the supports, and the covering tubes, the vessels used in the preparation and placement of the showbread, and the perpetual bread shall remain upon it. ⁸They shall spread upon them a cloth of scarlet wool, and they shall cover it with a covering of the hide of a taḥash, and shall place its staves to facilitate carrying it. ⁹They shall take a cloth of sky-blue wool, and cover the candelabrum of the light, its lamps, its tongs, to remove the wicks, its fire-pans, to clean the candelabrum, and all its oil vessels with which they serve it, kindle it. ¹⁰They shall place it and all its vessels into a covering of the hide of a taḥash, and shall place it on a pole to carry it. ¹¹Upon the golden altar they shall spread a cloth of sky-blue wool, and cover it with a covering of the hide of a taḥash, and they shall place its staves. ¹²They shall take all the service vessels with which they serve in the Sanctuary, and they shall place them in a cloth of sky-blue wool, and cover them with a covering of the hide of a taḥash, and they shall place them on the pole. ¹³They shall remove the ashes, remnants of the offerings, from the altar, and spread a cloth of purple wool over it. ¹⁴They shall place upon it all its vessels with which they serve upon it: the fire-pans, the forks, the shovels, and the basins, all the vessels utilized in the service of the altar; and they shall spread upon it a covering of the hide of a taḥash, and place its staves for carrying the altar. ¹⁵Aaron and his sons shall conclude to cover the sacred, and all the sacred vessels, when the camp travels. And only thereafter, the sons of Kehat shall come to bear them, so that they shall not touch the sacred and die. These are the burden of the sons of Kehat in the Tent of Meeting. ¹⁶The charge of Elazar son of Aaron the priest is the illuminating oil, the fragrant incense, the meal offering of the daily offering, and the anointing oil; the charge of the entire Tabernacle, and of all that is in it, in the sacred, and in its vessels.

Maftir ¹⁷The Lord spoke to Moses and to Aaron, saying: ¹⁸Do not excise, cause the elimination of, the tribe of the families of the Kehatites from among the Levites. ¹⁹But this do for them, and they will live, and will not die, upon their approach to the Holy of Holies. Aaron and his sons shall

come before them **and assign them,** summon the Levites to enter, **each man to his work and to his burden.** [20]**They shall not come to see while the sacred is** being **covered,** as if they do **that, they will die.**

Parashat Naso

This *parasha* concludes detailing the tasks of the Levite families in carrying the Tabernacle, after which laws relating to the camp and its sanctity are cited. The *parasha* continues with the laws of the *sota*, a woman whose husband suspects her of adultery, and of the nazirite. It concludes with a description of the dedication of the altar, which was accomplished with the sacrifice of the offerings of the princes of the tribes over the course of twelve days.

Carrying the Tabernacle

The Torah details at length the roles of the Gershonites and Merarites in carrying the Tabernacle.

²¹**The Lord spoke to Moses saying:** ²²**Take the census of the sons of Gershon as well,** in addition to Kehat, **by their patrilineal house, by their families.** ²³**From thirty years old and above until fifty years old you shall count them** and designate them: **Everyone enlisted to perform a duty, to perform work in the Tent of Meeting.** ²⁴**This is the work of the families of the Gershonites, to work,** perform unspecified tasks, in the Tabernacle **and for bearing** burdens when the camp traveled. ²⁵**They shall bear the sheet,** the bottom, woven covering **of the Tabernacle; and the Tent of Meeting,** the middle covering made of goatskins; and **its covering** of ram skins dyed red; **and the covering of the taḥash that is upon it from above; and the screen for the entrance of the Tent of Meeting;** ²⁶and **the hangings of the courtyard; and the screen for the entrance of the gate of the courtyard, that is near the Tabernacle, and near the altar, all around; and their cords** to affix the hangings; **and all the instruments of their work and everything that shall be fashioned for them; and they shall serve.** ²⁷**According to the directive of Aaron and his sons shall be all the work of the sons of the Gershonites, for all their burden, and for all their work; you shall assign them all of their burden as a commission.** ²⁸**This is the work of the families of the sons of the Gershonites in the Tent of Meeting; and their commission shall be in the hand of Itamar son of Aaron the priest.**

²⁹The sons of Merari, by their families, by their patrilineal house, you shall count them. ³⁰From thirty years old and above until fifty years old you shall count them, everyone that enlists for the duty, to perform the work of the Tent of Meeting. ³¹This is the commission of their burden for all their work in the Tent of Meeting: the beams of the Tabernacle, its bars, its pillars, and its sockets, ³²and the pillars of the courtyard all around, their sockets, their pegs, and their cords, with all their instruments, and for all their work. You shall assign by name the articles of the commission of their burden so that each member of Merarites would be familiar with his specific responsibility. ³³This is the work of the families of the sons of Merari, for all their work in the Tent of Meeting, in the hand of Itamar son of Aaron the priest.

Census of the Levite Families

The families of the tribe of Levi are now counted in order to ascertain the number of Levites eligible to participate in labor in the Tabernacle. All the males between the ages of thirty and fifty are counted in the census.

³⁴Moses, and Aaron, and the princes of the congregation counted the sons of the Kehatites by their families, and by their patrilineal house, ³⁵from thirty years old and above until fifty years old, everyone who enlisted for duty, for work in the Tent of Meeting. ³⁶Those counted, by their families, were two thousand seven hundred and fifty. ³⁷These are the counted of the families of the Kehatites, all who worked in the Tent of Meeting, whom Moses and Aaron counted according to the directive of the Lord at the hand of Moses.

Second
aliya ³⁸The counted of the sons of Gershon, by their families, and by their patrilineal house, ³⁹from thirty years old and above until fifty years old, everyone who enlisted for duty, for work in the Tent of Meeting. ⁴⁰Those counted, by their families, by their patrilineal house, were two thousand six hundred and thirty. ⁴¹These are the counted of the families of the sons of Gershon, all who worked in the Tent of Meeting, whom Moses and Aaron counted according to the directive of the Lord.

⁴²The counted of the families of the sons of Merari, by their families, by their patrilineal house, ⁴³from thirty years old and above until fifty years old, everyone who enlisted for duty, for work in the Tent of Meeting, ⁴⁴those counted by their families were three thousand two hundred. ⁴⁵These are the counted of the families of the sons of Merari,

whom Moses and Aaron counted according to the directive of the Lord at the hand of Moses.

⁴⁶All the counted, whom Moses and Aaron and the princes of Israel counted of the Levites, by their families, and by their patrilineal house, ⁴⁷from thirty years old and above until fifty years old, everyone who came to perform the service of work and the service of bearing in the Tent of Meeting, ⁴⁸those counted were eight thousand five hundred and eighty. ⁴⁹According to the directive of the Lord he counted them, at the hand of Moses, each man to his work and to his burden, and his count was performed as the Lord commanded Moses.

The Sanctity of the Camp

At the conclusion of the long description of the structure of the Israelite camp and the configuration of the tribes in it comes a general law instructing all the ritually impure to remain outside the camp until they regain purity.

5 ¹The Lord spoke to Moses, saying: ²Command the children of Israel:
Third aliya They shall send out from the camp every leper [*tzarua*], and anyone with a discharge [*zav*], and anyone impure by means of a corpse. ³Male and female alike you shall send out, outside the camp you shall send them; and they shall not render impure their camp, in which I dwell in their midst. ⁴The children of Israel did so, and sent them outside the camp; as the Lord spoke to Moses, so the children of Israel did.

📖 **Further reading:** See p. 278 for more on the impurity of a leper, and p. 289 for impurity due to a discharge.

Various Laws

This section repeats the law concerning the guilt offering brought by a person who stole an object and took an oath that he had not. When he does admit his crime, he must pay restitution, plus an added one-fifth (see Leviticus 5:20-26). Here the Torah adds that in a case where the victim of the theft has died, restitution is made to his heirs. If he has no heirs, then the restitution goes to the priests.

⁵The Lord spoke to Moses, saying: ⁶Speak to the children of Israel: A man or woman, when they commit any human sin that involves committing a trespass, misappropriating the property of another, which is also a sin against the Lord, and that person acknowledges that he or she is guilty, ⁷they shall confess their sin that they had committed; and he shall make restitution in its principal, of the sum stolen, and he shall add one-fifth of it to it, and he shall give it to the one to whom

he is guilty, the person whose property he misappropriated. ⁸If the person whose property he took dies before restitution, he returns the misappropriated property to his heirs. **But if the man has no redeeeer to make restitution to him, the restitution is returned to the Lord,** and is given **to the priest.** This is **besides the ram of atonement,** a guilt offering **with which he will atone for it,** his sin.

⁹**Any gift, of any of the sacred items** other than actual offerings, **of the children of Israel that they shall present to the priest,** e.g., fines or first fruits, **shall be his.** ¹⁰**A man's sacred items shall be his,** in the sense that **anything that a man gives the priest** he has chosen **shall be his;** it will belong to that priest.

The Portion of the Sota

The system of laws delineated here addresses the situation of a husband who suspects his wife of infidelity. He can bring her to the Temple, where she must undergo a rite whose purpose is to determine whether or not there was a basis for his suspicion.

Fourth aliya ¹¹**The Lord spoke to Moses, saying:** ¹²**Speak to the children of Israel, and say to them: If any man's wife shall go astray and commit a trespass against him,** betraying him, ¹³**and a man lay with her sexually, and it was hidden from the eyes of her husband, and she was secluded** with the man **and she was defiled** by engaging in intercourse with him, **and there is no witness** to testify **against her, and she was not coerced.** ¹⁴**And a spirit of jealousy overcame him,** the husband, **and he was jealous with regard to his wife, and she was defiled, or a spirit of jealousy overcame him, and he was jealous with regard to his wife, and she was not defiled;**

¹⁵**the man shall bring his wife to the priest. And he shall bring her offering for her, one-tenth of an ephah,** which is 2–4 liters, **of barley flour. He shall not pour oil upon it, and he shall not place frankincense upon it, for it is a meal offering of jealousy, a meal offering of remembrance, a recollection of iniquity,** and not a thanks or gift offering. ¹⁶**The priest shall bring her near, and cause her to stand before the Lord,** in the Temple. ¹⁷**The priest shall take sacred water** from the laver **in an earthenware vessel, and the priest shall take from the dirt that is on the floor of the Tabernacle, and he shall place it into the water.** ¹⁸**The priest shall cause the woman to stand before the Lord,** opposite the Tabernacle's entrance, **and he shall expose the woman's head, and he shall place on her palms the meal offering of remembrance, it is the meal offering of**

Numbers

jealousy; and in the hand of the priest shall be the imprecatory water of bitterness.

¹⁹The priest shall administer an oath to her, and he shall say to the woman: If no man has lain with you, and if you have not gone astray in an act of defilement while subject to your husband, be absolved of this imprecatory water of bitterness. ²⁰But you, if you have gone astray while subject to your husband, and if you were defiled, and a man has lain sexually with you, other than your husband, the water of bitterness will cause your death. ²¹The priest shall administer to the woman the oath of the curse, in which she accepts the consequences of the curse if she sinned, and the priest shall say to the woman: May the Lord render you as a curse and an oath among your people, when the Lord causes your thigh to shrivel and fall, and your belly to distend. ²²May this imprecatory water enter your intestines to cause a belly to distend, and a thigh to fall. The woman shall say: Amen, amen.

📖 **Further reading:** For more on the rite in which the priest gives the woman the water of bitterness to drink, see *A Concise Guide to the Sages*, p. 176.

²³The priest shall write these curses in the scroll, and he shall dissolve them, the words written in ink, into the water of bitterness. ²⁴He shall give the woman to drink the imprecatory water of bitterness and the imprecatory water shall enter her for bitterness. ²⁵The priest shall take the meal offering of jealousy from the woman's hand, and he shall wave the meal offering before the Lord, and bring it near to the altar. ²⁶The priest shall take a handful from the meal offering, its memorial portion, and burn it upon the altar, and then he shall give the woman to drink the water. ²⁷He shall give her to drink the water, and it shall be, if she was defiled, and committed a trespass against her husband, the imprecatory water shall enter her for bitterness, and her belly shall distend, and her thigh shall fall, and the woman shall become a curse among her people. ²⁸But if the woman was not defiled, and is untainted, she will be absolved from any suspicion, and will conceive offspring. ²⁹This is the law of jealousy, when a woman goes astray while subject to her husband and becomes defiled, ³⁰or when a man is overcome with the spirit of jealousy and is jealous with regard to his wife and causes the woman to stand before the Lord, the priest shall perform for her this entire ritual. ³¹The man shall be clear from iniquity, and that woman shall bear her iniquity.

The Portion of the Nazirite

This section addresses the case of one who wishes to sanctify himself as a nazirite to God. The laws of naziriteship detailed here include certain limitations on the nazirite's behavior, the *halakha* when these limitations are violated unintentionally, and the rite of purification of the nazirite at the end of the period of naziriteship.

6 ¹**The Lord spoke to Moses, saying:** ²**Speak to the children of Israel, and say to them: When a man or a woman articulates** the intent **to vow a vow of a nazirite, to abstain for the Lord,** ³**he shall abstain from wine and intoxicating drink: Vinegar of wine and vinegar of intoxicating drink he shall not drink; he shall not drink anything in which grapes were soaked; and grapes, fresh or dried, he shall not eat.** ⁴**All the days of his naziriteship, from anything that may be derived from the grapevine, from pits to skin, he shall not eat.** ⁵**All the days of his vow of naziriteship, a razor shall not pass on his head. Until completion of the days that he shall abstain for the Lord, he shall be holy; the hair of his head shall be grown out.** ⁶**All the days of his abstinence to the Lord, he shall not approach a corpse,** ⁷**even to his father and to his mother, to his brother and to his sister, he shall not become impure for them upon their death, since the crown of his God,** his long hair symbolizing his naziriteship, **is upon his head.** ⁸**All the days of his naziriteship he is holy to the Lord.**

⁹**If a corpse dies near him with unexpected suddenness and,** despite his best efforts, **renders the head of his naziriteship impure, he shall shave his head on the day of his purification,** as impurity imparted by a corpse lasts seven days; **on the seventh day shall he shave it.** ¹⁰**And on the eighth day he shall bring two turtledoves, or two young pigeons, to the priest, to the entrance of the Tent of Meeting.** ¹¹**The priest shall prepare one as a sin offering, and** the other **one as a burnt offering, and** shall **atone for him,** the nazirite, **for that which he sinned with regard to the corpse. And he shall sanctify his head,** reassume his naziriteship, **on that day,** the eighth day. ¹²**He shall dedicate to the Lord the days of his naziriteship,** commencing his period of naziriteship anew, **and shall bring a sheep in its first year as a guilt offering, and the first days,** prior to his naziriteship, **shall be void, as his naziriteship is impure.**

¹³**And this is the law of the nazirite, on the day of the completion of the days of his naziriteship: He shall bring it,** the set of offerings listed below, **to the entrance of the Tent of Meeting.** Alternatively, the verse means that he shall bring himself to the entrance of the Tent of Meeting. ¹⁴**He shall**

Numbers

present his offering to the Lord: one unblemished lamb in its first year as a burnt offering, one unblemished ewe in its first year as a sin offering, and one unblemished ram as a peace offering, [15]and a basket of unleavened bread: loaves of choice flour mixed with oil, and wafers of unleavened bread spread with oil, and their standard meal offering, and their libations. [16]The priest shall bring them before the Lord, and shall perform his sin offering, and his burnt offering. [17]He shall make the ram a peace offering to the Lord, with the basket of unleavened bread; and the priest shall perform its meal offering and its libation. [18]Then the nazirite shall shave the head of his naziriteship at the entrance of the Tent of Meeting and shall take the hair of the head of his naziriteship, and he shall place it on the fire that is beneath the peace offering. [19]The priest shall take the cooked foreleg of the ram, and one loaf of unleavened bread from the basket, and one wafer of unleavened bread, and he shall place them on the palms of the nazirite, after he shaved the head of his naziriteship. [20]The priest shall wave them as a wave offering before the Lord, it is sacred for the priest, as one of the gifts of the priesthood, with the breast of waving and with the haunch of lifting that are given to the priest from every peace offering, and then the nazirite may drink wine, as his naziriteship has concluded. [21]This is the law of the nazirite who vows his offering to the Lord for his naziriteship. The aforementioned offerings are required of every nazirite. Besides, he whose means suffice, if the nazirite vowed to bring other offerings and can afford to, then in accordance with his vow that he vows, so shall he do, along with what is required by the law of his naziriteship. The nazirite is subject to all the regular laws of offerings and his bringing the offerings to conclude his naziriteship does not absolve him of fulfilling any other vows.

> Further reading: Is naziriteship seen as something positive or negative? See *A Concise Guide to the Sages*, p. 178.

The Priestly Benediction

The priests, in addition to being sacred servants and overseers of the labor in the Temple, were also given the command, and the ability, to bless the Israelites in the name of God. Their blessing generates God's direct blessing of His people.

[22]The Lord spoke to Moses, saying: [23]Speak to Aaron and to his sons, saying: So shall you bless the children of Israel, say to them: [24]The Lord shall bless you, and keep you. [25]The Lord shall shine His countenance toward you, and be gracious to you, you will find favor in His

eyes. [26]The Lord shall lift His countenance to you, giving you preferential treatment, and grant you peace. [27]They, with this blessing, shall place My name upon the children of Israel, and I shall bless them.

Dedication of the Altar

Now that the long process of building the Tabernacle has been completed, the Torah reports on the dedication ceremony, in which the altar is used for the first time. The princes of all the tribes brought the offerings for these first days of use, and also donated various vessels to be used in the Tabernacle.

7 [1]It was on the day that Moses concluded erecting the Tabernacle that *Fifth* he anointed it with the anointing oil and sanctified it, all its vessels and *aliya* the altar and all its vessels; he anointed them and sanctified them. [2]The princes of Israel, the heads of their patrilineal houses, brought offerings, they were the princes of the tribes, they were those who stood over those who were counted, the officials who had conducted the census (1:4–15). [3]They brought their offering before the Lord, six covered wagons, and twelve cattle, a wagon for each two princes and an ox for each one, and they brought them before the Tabernacle. [4]The Lord spoke to Moses, saying: [5]Take these from them, and they shall be to perform the service of the Tent of Meeting, and you shall give them to the Levites, each according to his work. [6]Moses took the wagons and the cattle, and gave them to the Levites. [7]Two of the wagons and four of the cattle, he gave to the sons of Gershon, according to their work. [8]Four of the wagons and eight of the cattle he gave to the sons of Merari, according to their work, in the hand of Itamar son of Aaron the priest. [9]But he did not give any to the sons of Kehat, because the sacred service, bearing the sacred Tabernacle vessels, is upon them; they shall bear them on the shoulder.

The Offerings of the Princes

Over the course of twelve days, the princes of the tribes presented offerings on the altar and different gifts for use in the Tabernacle. The offerings of all the princes were identical.

[10]The princes brought their offering for the dedication of the altar on the day that it was anointed; and each of the princes brought their own offering before the altar. [11]The Lord said to Moses: One prince on each day shall present their offering for the dedication of the altar.

[12]The one who presented his offering on the first day was Nahshon son of Aminadav, of the tribe of Judah. [13]His offering was: one silver dish,

Numbers

its weight one hundred and thirty silver shekels; one silver basin with a weight of seventy shekels, in the sacred shekel; both of them were full of choice flour mixed with oil as a meal offering; [14]one ladle with a weight of ten shekels of gold, full of incense; [15]one young bull, one ram, one lamb in its first year, as a burnt offering; [16]one goat as a sin offering; [17]and for the peace offering: two cattle, five rams, five goats, and five sheep in their first year. This was the offering of Nahshon son of Aminadav.

[18]On the second day presented Netanel son of Tzuar, prince of Issachar. [19]He presented his offering: One silver dish, its weight one hundred and thirty; one silver basin of seventy shekels, in the sacred shekel; both of them full of choice flour mixed with oil as a meal offering; [20]one ladle of ten shekels of gold, full of incense; [21]one young bull, one ram, one lamb in its first year, as a burnt offering; [22]one goat as a sin offering; [23]and for the peace offering: two cattle, five rams, five goats, and five sheep in their first year. This was the offering of Netanel son of Tzuar.

[24]On the third day was the prince of the children of Zebulun, Eliav son of Helon. [25]His offering was one silver dish, its weight one hundred and thirty; one silver basin of seventy shekels, in the sacred shekel; both of them full of choice flour mixed with oil as a meal offering; [26]one ladle of ten shekels of gold, full of incense; [27]one young bull, one ram, one lamb in its first year, as a burnt offering; [28]one goat as a sin offering; [29]and for the peace offering: two cattle, five rams, five goats, and five sheep in their first year. This was the offering of Eliav son of Helon.

[30]On the fourth day was the prince of the children of Reuben, Elitzur son of Shede'ur. [31]His offering was one silver dish, its weight one hundred and thirty; one silver basin of seventy shekels, in the sacred shekel; both of them full of choice flour mixed with oil as a meal offering; [32]one ladle of ten shekels of gold, full of incense; [33]one young bull, one ram, one lamb in its first year, as a burnt offering; [34]one goat as a sin offering; [35]and for the peace offering: two cattle, five rams, five goats, and five sheep in their first year. This was the offering of Elitzur son of Shede'ur.

[36]On the fifth day was the prince of the children of Simeon, Shelumiel son of Tzurishadai. [37]His offering was one silver dish, its weight one hundred and thirty; one silver basin of seventy shekels, in the sacred

shekel; both of them full of choice flour mixed with oil as a meal offering; [38]one ladle of ten shekels of gold, full of incense; [39]one young bull, one ram, one lamb in its first year, as a burnt offering; [40]one goat as a sin offering; [41]and for the peace offering: two cattle, five rams, five goats, and five sheep in their first year. This was the offering of Shelumiel son of Tzurishadai.

Sixth
aliya [42]On the sixth day was the prince of the children of Gad, Elyasaf son of De'uel. [43]His offering was one silver dish, its weight one hundred and thirty; one silver basin of seventy shekels, in the sacred shekel; both of them full of choice flour mixed with oil as a meal offering; [44]one ladle of ten shekels of gold, full of incense; [45]one young bull, one ram, one lamb in its first year, as a burnt offering; [46]one goat as a sin offering; [47]and for the peace offering: two cattle, five rams, five goats, and five sheep in their first year. This was the offering of Elyasaf son of De'uel.

[48]On the seventh day was the prince of the children of Ephraim, Elishama son of Amihud. [49]His offering was one silver dish, its weight one hundred and thirty; one silver basin of seventy shekels, in the sacred shekel; both of them full of choice flour mixed with oil as a meal offering; [50]one ladle of ten shekels of gold, full of incense; [51]one young bull, one ram, one lamb in its first year, as a burnt offering; [52]one goat as a sin offering; [53]and for the peace offering: two cattle, five rams, five goats, and five sheep in their first year. This was the offering of Elishama son of Amihud.

[54]On the eighth day was the prince of the children of Manasseh, Gamliel son of Pedatzur. [55]His offering was one silver dish, its weight one hundred and thirty; one silver basin of seventy shekels, in the sacred shekel; both of them full of choice flour mixed with oil as a meal offering; [56]one ladle of ten shekels of gold, full of incense; [57]one young bull, one ram, one lamb in its first year, as a burnt offering; [58]one goat as a sin offering; [59]and for the peace offering: two cattle, five rams, five goats, and five sheep in their first year. This was the offering of Gamliel son of Pedatzur.

[60]On the ninth day was the prince of the children of Benjamin, Avidan son of Gidoni. [61]His offering was one silver dish, its weight one hundred and thirty; one silver basin of seventy shekels, in the sacred shekel; both of them full of choice flour mixed with oil as a meal offering; [62]one ladle of ten shekels of gold, full of incense; [63]one young

Numbers

bull, one ram, one lamb in its first year, as a burnt offering; ⁶⁴one goat as a sin offering; ⁶⁵and for the peace offering: two cattle, five rams, five goats, and five sheep in their first year. This was the offering of Avidan son of Gidoni.

⁶⁶On the tenth day was the prince of the children of Dan, Ahiezer son of Amishadai. ⁶⁷His offering was one silver dish, its weight one hundred and thirty; one silver basin of seventy shekels, in the sacred shekel; both of them full of choice flour mixed with oil as a meal offering; ⁶⁸one ladle of ten shekels of gold, full of incense; ⁶⁹one young bull, one ram, one lamb in its first year, as a burnt offering; ⁷⁰one goat as a sin offering; ⁷¹and for the peace offering: two cattle, five rams, five goats, and five sheep in their first year. This was the offering of Ahiezer son of Amishadai.

Seventh aliya ⁷²On the eleventh day was the prince of the children of Asher, Pagiel son of Okhran. ⁷³His offering was one silver dish, its weight one hundred and thirty; one silver basin of seventy shekels, in the sacred shekel; both of them full of choice flour mixed with oil as a meal offering; ⁷⁴one ladle of ten shekels of gold, full of incense; ⁷⁵one young bull, one ram, one lamb in its first year, as a burnt offering; ⁷⁶one goat as a sin offering; ⁷⁷and for the peace offering: two cattle, five rams, five goats, and five sheep in their first year. This was the offering of Pagiel son of Okhran.

⁷⁸On the twelfth day was the prince of the children of Naphtali, Ahira son of Einan. ⁷⁹His offering was one silver dish, its weight one hundred and thirty; one silver basin of seventy shekels, in the sacred shekel; both of them full of choice flour mixed with oil as a meal offering; ⁸⁰one ladle of ten shekels of gold, full of incense; ⁸¹one young bull, one ram, one lamb in its first year, as a burnt offering; ⁸²one goat as a sin offering; ⁸³and for the peace offering: two cattle, five rams, five goats, and five sheep in their first year. This was the offering of Ahira son of Einan.

⁸⁴This was the dedication of the altar, on the day when it was anointed, from the princes of Israel: twelve silver dishes, twelve silver basins, twelve golden ladles. ⁸⁵One hundred and thirty shekels was the weight of each silver dish and seventy shekels was the weight of each basin. All the silver of the vessels was two thousand and four hundred, in the sacred shekel. ⁸⁶Twelve golden ladles, full of incense, ten shekels was the

weight of **each ladle, in the sacred shekel; all the gold of the ladles was**
aftir **one hundred and twenty** shekels. [87]**All the cattle for the burnt offer-**
ing totalled **twelve bulls, twelve rams,** and **twelve sheep in their first
year, and their meal offering, and twelve goats as a sin offering.** [88]**All
the cattle of the peace offerings were twenty-four bulls, sixty rams,
sixty goats, and sixty sheep in their first year. This was the dedication
of the altar, after it was anointed.** [89]**When Moses went into the Tent of
Meeting to speak with Him, he heard the voice speaking to him from
above the ark cover that was upon the Ark of the Testimony, from between the two cherubs, and He,** God, **spoke to him.**

Further reading: Upon the conclusion of the dedication of the Tabernacle with the offerings of the tribal princes, the Divine Presence rested in the Tabernacle. For more on
the return of the Divine Presence to the world, see *A Concise Guide to the Sages*, p. 179;
A Concise Guide to Mahshava, p. 162.

Numbers

Parashat Behaalotekha

This *parasha* completes the description that was started at the beginning of the book of Numbers, regarding the structure of the Israelite camp and the order of its travels. There is also a description of the designation of the tribe of Levi as representatives of the entire people. Several commandments appear within this context, e.g., the kindling of the candelabrum of the Tabernacle and the laws of the Second *Pesaḥ*. In the second half of the Torah portion we read the story of the troubles and adversity that the Israelites encountered in the wilderness, conveying the difficulties of that period.

The Kindling of the Candelabrum

Aaron is commanded to kindle the lamps of the candelabrum so that they all face toward the middle lamp. The verse then relates that the candelabrum was crafted precisely in accordance with the instructions that Moses received on Mount Sinai.

8 **¹The Lord spoke to Moses, saying: ²Speak to Aaron, and say to him: When you kindle the lamps, the seven lamps shall illuminate toward the front of the candelabrum,** its central branch. **³Aaron did so; toward the front of the candelabrum he kindled its lamps, as the Lord had commanded Moses. ⁴This is the craftsmanship of the candelabrum: Hammered gold; from its base to its flowers,** from a single piece of gold **it is hammered;** just **like the vision that the Lord showed Moses, so he crafted the candelabrum.**

📖 **Further reading:** For more on the candelabrum and its significance, see *A Concise Guide to the Sages*, p. 181.

Designation of the Levites for Service

The description of the preparation of the Tabernacle and the Israelite camp continues with the designation of the Levites for service in the Tabernacle. They must undergo a special rite of purification and sanctification, and they become representatives of the Israelites in their performance of the sacred service.

⁵The Lord spoke to Moses, saying: ⁶Take the Levites from among the children of Israel and purify them. ⁷So shall you do to them, to purify

Numbers

them: Sprinkle upon them purification water mixed with the ashes of the red heifer (see 19:1–13), and they shall pass a razor over all their flesh, shaving all their hair, and they shall wash their clothes, and become pure through immersion in a ritual bath. ⁸They, the Levites, shall take a young bull as a burnt offering, and its associated meal offering of choice flour mixed with oil; and a second young bull you, Moses, shall take as a sin offering. ⁹You shall bring the Levites before the Tent of Meeting and you shall assemble the entire congregation of the children of Israel.

¹⁰You shall bring the Levites before the Lord, and the representatives of the children of Israel shall lay their hands upon the Levites. ¹¹Aaron shall wave the Levites as a wave offering before the Lord from the children of Israel, and they shall be designated to perform the service of the Lord. ¹²The Levites shall lay their hands upon the heads of the bulls, and you shall perform the one as a sin offering, and the other as a burnt offering, to the Lord, to atone for the Levites. ¹³You shall have the Levites stand before Aaron and before his sons, and you, Moses, shall wave them as a wave offering to the Lord. ¹⁴You shall separate the Levites from the midst of the children of Israel, as their representa-

ond
liya

tives, and the Levites shall be Mine. ¹⁵Thereafter the Levites shall come to serve in the Tent of Meeting; you shall purify them, and before they come to serve, wave them as a wave offering.

¹⁶For they are given to Me from among the children of Israel. In place of the one that emerges first from each womb, the firstborn, of all the children of Israel, I have taken them for Myself. ¹⁷For all the firstborn among the children of Israel are Mine, man and animal; on the day that I smote all the firstborn in the land of Egypt I sanctified them for Myself, to serve Me. ¹⁸I have taken the Levites in place of all the first-born among the children of Israel. ¹⁹I have given the Levites, given to Aaron and to his sons from among the children of Israel, to perform the service of the children of Israel in the Tent of Meeting, and to atone for the children of Israel, and accordingly there shall not be a stroke against the children of Israel when the children of Israel approach the Sanctuary. ²⁰Moses, Aaron, and the entire congregation of the children of Israel did to the Levites in accordance with everything that the Lord commanded Moses with regard to the Levites; so the children of Israel did to them. ²¹The Levites purified themselves, and they washed their clothes, and Aaron waved them as a wave offering before the Lord. Aaron atoned for them to purify them. ²²Thereafter the Levites came

Numbers

to perform their service in the Tent of Meeting before Aaron, and before his sons; as the Lord had commanded Moses with regard to the Levites, so they did to them.

²³The Lord spoke to Moses, saying: ²⁴This is with regard to the Levites: From twenty-five years and above one shall enlist to perform duty in the work of the Tent of Meeting. ²⁵From fifty years old, he shall return from the duty of the work, and he shall work no more in physically demanding labor. ²⁶He shall serve with his brethren in the Tent of Meeting, to stand a watch in the Tabernacle, but work he shall not perform. So shall you do with the Levites with regard to their watches.

The Paschal Offering in the Wilderness

With the approach of the one-year anniversary of the Israelites' exodus from Egypt, they are commanded to perform the rite of the paschal lamb in accordance with its requirements.

9 ¹The Lord spoke to Moses in the wilderness of Sinai during the second *Third* year, one year since their exodus from the land of Egypt, in the first *aliya* month, Nisan, saying: ²The children of Israel shall offer the paschal lamb at its appointed time. ³On the fourteenth day of that month, in the afternoon, you shall offer it at its appointed time; in accordance with all its statutes and in accordance with all its ordinances, you shall offer it. ⁴Moses spoke to the children of Israel, to offer the paschal lamb. ⁵They offered the paschal lamb during the first month, on the fourteenth day of the month, in the afternoon, in the wilderness of Sinai; in accordance with everything that the Lord commanded Moses, so the children of Israel did.

The Second *Pesaḥ*

People who were prevented from offering the paschal lamb at the correct time came to Moses, seeking a solution that would enable them to participate in the performance of the mitzva. They were commanded to offer the paschal lamb one month later.

⁶There were men who were impure by means of a corpse, and they were unable to offer the paschal lamb on that day of *Pesaḥ*; and they approached Moses and Aaron on that day. ⁷Those men said to him: We are impure by means of a corpse; why shall we be deprived and not present the offering of the Lord at its appointed time among the children of Israel? ⁸Moses said to them: Stand, and I will hear what the Lord will command you.

⁹The Lord spoke to Moses, saying: ¹⁰Speak to the children of Israel, saying: When any man shall be impure by means of a corpse, or on a distant journey from the Temple, for you or for your future genera- tions, he shall offer the paschal lamb to the Lord. ¹¹During the second month, Iyar, on the fourteenth day, in the afternoon, they shall offer it; with unleavened bread and bitter herbs they shall eat it, the flesh of the paschal lamb. ¹²They shall not leave from it until the morning, and they shall not break a bone in it; in accordance with the entire statute of the paschal lamb they shall do it. ¹³But the man who is pure, and was not on a journey, and refrains from offering the paschal lamb, that person shall be excised from his people; because he did not present the offer- ing of the Lord at its appointed time, that man shall bear his sin. ¹⁴If a stranger who converted from another nation shall reside among you, and will offer the paschal lamb to the Lord, in accordance with the statute of the paschal lamb, and in accordance with its ordinance, so shall he do; there shall be one statute for you, for the stranger, and for the na- tive of the land.

The Journey of the Nation at the Directive of the Lord

The Israelite camp moves and travels by the guidance of the cloud over the Tabernacle. When it ascends from upon the Tabernacle they move, and when the cloud comes to a halt, they reassemble the camp, with the Tabernacle at its center, under the cloud.

urth *aliya* ¹⁵On the day that the Tabernacle was erected, the cloud covered the Tabernacle to the Tent of the Testimony, which housed the Tablets of the Testimony, and in the evening there would be upon the Tabernacle as the appearance of fire, until morning. ¹⁶So it would be always: The cloud would cover it by day, and the appearance of fire at night. ¹⁷In ac- cordance with the ascent of the cloud from upon the Tent, thereafter the children of Israel would travel, and in the place where the cloud would stop, there the children of Israel would encamp. ¹⁸According to the directive of the Lord the children of Israel would travel, and according to the directive of the Lord they encamped; as all the days that the cloud would rest upon the Tabernacle, they would encamp. ¹⁹When the cloud lingered upon the Tabernacle many days, the chil- dren of Israel kept the commission of the Lord, and did not travel. ²⁰At times, the cloud would be several days upon the Tabernacle; accord- ing to the directive of the Lord they would encamp, and according to the directive of the Lord they would travel. ²¹At times the cloud would

Numbers

be in place only **from evening until morning; the cloud would ascend in the morning, and they would travel; or** it would be in place for **a day and a night, and the cloud would ascend and they would travel.** ²²**Or two days, or one month, or one year; when the cloud lingered upon the Tabernacle, to rest upon it, the children of Israel would encamp, and would not travel; with its ascent, they would travel.** ²³**At the directive of the Lord they would camp, and at the directive of the Lord they would travel; the commission of the Lord they kept, according to the directive of the Lord at the hand of Moses.**

The Silver Trumpets

Moses was commanded to prepare two trumpets to be utilized in summoning the elders and the entire congregation, and in announcing the travel of the encampment. In addition, the priests were commanded to sound the trumpets while sacrificing offerings and when going out to war.

10 ¹**The Lord spoke to Moses, saying:** ²**Craft for you two silver trumpets; hammered** from one piece of silver **you shall craft them, they shall be for you for summoning the congregation, and for causing the camps to travel** by instructing them. ³**They shall sound them, and the entire congregation shall assemble to you at the entrance of the Tent of Meeting.** ⁴**If they shall sound one** trumpet, **the princes, the heads of the thousands of Israel, shall assemble to you.** ⁵**You shall sound an alarm, and the camps that encamp to the east,** the camp of Judah, **shall travel.** ⁶**You shall sound an alarm again, and the camps that encamp to the south,** the camp of Reuben, **shall travel; they shall sound an alarm for their travels.** ⁷**When assembling the assembly you shall sound a blast, but you shall not sound an alarm.** ⁸**The sons of Aaron, the priests, shall sound the trumpets; they shall be for you as an eternal statute for your generations.** ⁹**When you go to war in your land against the enemy who oppresses you, you shall sound an alarm with the trumpets; and you shall be remembered before the Lord your God, and you shall be delivered from your enemies.** ¹⁰**On the day of your rejoicing, at your appointed times, and on your New Moons, you shall sound the trumpets over your** communal **burnt offerings and over your** communal **peace offerings; they shall be a remembrance for you before your God, I am the Lord your God.**

The Journey of the Encampments

After the lengthy, detailed description of the configuration of the Israelite camp and the manner of its travel, the Israelites travel for the first time from the wilderness of Sinai. Moses requests that his father-in-law, who had accompanied them until then, continue to tie his destiny to the destiny of the Israelites, but he declines. The Israelites leave Mount Sinai, thereby beginning their journey to the Land of Israel.

fth
liya

[11]It was during the second year, in the second month, Iyar, on the twentieth of the month, the cloud ascended from upon the Tabernacle of the Testimony. [12]The children of Israel traveled on their journeys from the wilderness of Sinai; the cloud rested in the wilderness of Paran. [13]They traveled from the beginning according to the directive of the Lord, at the hand of Moses, under his leadership. [14]The banner of the camp of the sons of Judah traveled first according to their hosts; and over its host was Nahshon son of Aminadav. [15]Over the host of the tribe of the children of Issachar was Netanel son of Tzuar. [16]Over the host of the tribe of the children of Zebulun was Eliav son of Helon. [17]Then the Tabernacle was dismantled, and the sons of Gershon and the sons of Merari, the bearers of the Tabernacle, traveled. [18]The banner of the camp of Reuben traveled according to their hosts; and over its host was Elitzur son of Shede'ur. [19]Over the host of the tribe of the children of Simeon was Shelumiel son of Tzurishadai. [20]Over the host of the tribe of the children of Gad was Elyasaf son of De'uel. [21]Then the Kehatites, bearers of the sacred vessels of the Sanctuary traveled; they, the Gershonites and Merarites who were traveling ahead of the Kehatites, erected the Tabernacle before their arrival. [22]The banner of the camp of the children of Ephraim traveled according to their hosts; and over its host was Elishama son of Amihud. [23]Over the host of the tribe of the children of Manasseh was Gamliel son of Pedatzur. [24]Over the host of the tribe of the children of Benjamin was Avidan son of Gidoni. [25]The banner of the camp of the children of Dan, the rear guard of all the camps, traveled according to their hosts; and over its host was Ahiezer son of Amishadai. [26]Over the host of the tribe of the children of Asher was Pagiel son of Okhran. [27]Over the host of the tribe of the children of Naphtali was Ahira son of Einan. [28]These are the travels of the children of Israel according to their hosts; and they traveled.

[29]Moses said to Hovav son of Re'uel the Midyanite, father-in-law of Moses: We are traveling to the place that the Lord said: I will give it to you; come with us, and we will be good to you and give you a portion

in the land, **as the Lord has spoken good about Israel.** [30]**He,** Hovav, **said to him: I will not go** with you; **rather, to my land, and to the land of my birth, I will go.** [31]**He,** Moses, **said: Please do not leave us, for since you know** the challenges of **our encampment in the wilderness, you shall be for us as eyes;** your presence will benefit us. [32]**It will be that if you go with us, that good that the Lord will bestow upon us will be, and we will be good to you.**

[33]**They traveled from the mountain of the Lord a journey of three days, and the Ark of the Covenant of the Lord was traveling before them, a journey of three days, to scout for them a resting place.** [34]**The cloud of**

Sixth aliya

the Lord was upon them by day, when they traveled from the camp. [35]**It was when the ark traveled, Moses said: Arise Lord, and may Your enemies be dispersed and may those who hate You flee from before You.** [36]**When it rested, he said: Repose O Lord,** among **the myriad thousands of Israel.**

The Israelites' Complaints regarding the Manna

Here begins a description of the hardships of the Israelites in the wilderness. The people are embittered and complain about the lack of the prosperity that they had enjoyed in Egypt. God becomes angry and ignites a fire in their midst. Moses, too, becomes angry, and says to God that he is not capable of bearing the burden of the people alone.

11 [1]**The people were** expressing their distress, **as** do **mourners; it was evil in the ears of the Lord. The Lord heard it, His wrath was enflamed, and the fire of the Lord burned in their midst, and consumed the edge of the camp.** [2]**The people cried out to Moses; Moses prayed to the Lord, and the fire subsided.** [3]**He called the name of that place Tavera, because the fire of the Lord burned** [*baara*] **in their midst.** [4]**The mob that was in their midst,** those who joined the Israelites upon their exodus from Egypt, **expressed a craving; and the children of Israel responded,** joined them, **and wept as well, and said: Who will feed us meat?** [5]**We remember the fish that we would eat in Egypt for free, and the cucumbers, the watermelons, the leeks, the onions, and the garlic.** [6]**But now our soul is parched, there is nothing at all; nothing but the manna before our eyes.**

[7]**The manna was** round **like coriander seed, and its appearance was** white **like the appearance of bdellium.** [8]**The people roamed about and gathered and ground it in a mill, or crushed it in a mortar, or boiled it in a pot, and made it into cakes, and its taste was like the taste of a cake**

moist with oil. ⁹With the falling of the dew upon the camp at night, the manna fell upon it.

¹⁰Moses heard the people weeping, according to their families, each man at the entrance of his tent. The wrath of the Lord was greatly enflamed and in the eyes of Moses it was bad. ¹¹Moses said to the Lord: Why have You mistreated Your servant and why have I not found favor in Your eyes, to place the burden of this entire people upon me? ¹²Did I conceive this entire people; did I give birth to it, that You should say to me: Carry it in your bosom, as a nurse carries the suckling babe, to the land with regard to which You took an oath to its forefathers? ¹³From where do I have meat to give to this entire people that they cry to me, saying: Give us meat, and we shall eat. ¹⁴I cannot bear this entire people alone, because it is too heavy for me. ¹⁵If this is what You do to me, please kill me, if I have found favor in Your eyes, and let me not see my wretchedness.

Delegating Prophecy to the Seventy Elders

God requests that Moses assemble for Him seventy elders, to share with him the task of tending to the Israelite people. As the people have complained at the lack of meat, God promises to provide meat until they grow sick of it. Ultimately, he afflicts the people with a plague that kills those among them who craved meat.

¹⁶The Lord said to Moses: Gather to Me seventy men of the elders of Israel, whom you know to be the elders of the people, and its officers; and you shall take them to the Tent of Meeting, and they will stand there with you. ¹⁷I will descend and speak with you there, and I will draw from the spirit of prophecy that is upon you, and I will place it upon them; they shall bear with you the burden of the people, and you shall not bear it alone. ¹⁸To the people you shall say: Prepare yourselves for tomorrow, and you shall eat meat, for you have wept in the ears of the Lord, saying: Who will feed us meat, as it is better for us in Egypt; and the Lord will give you meat, and you shall eat. ¹⁹You shall eat not for one day, nor two days, nor five days, nor ten days, nor twenty days. ²⁰Until a month of days, until it comes out of your nose and it shall be loathsome for you, because you despised the Lord who is in your midst, and you wept before Him, saying: Why is it that we left Egypt? ²¹Moses said: Six hundred thousand men on foot is the people that I am in their midst, and You said: I will give them meat, and they will eat for a month of days. ²²Will enough flocks and cattle be slain for

them and it suffice for them? If all the fish of the sea will be gathered for them, will it suffice for them? ²³The Lord said to Moses: Shall the hand of the Lord be inadequate? Now you will see whether My statement will transpire for you or not. ²⁴Moses emerged and spoke the words of the Lord to the people; he gathered seventy men of the elders of the people, and he had them stand around the Tent. ²⁵The Lord descended in the cloud, and spoke to him, and drew from the spirit that was upon him, and put it upon the seventy elders; it was, as the spirit rested upon them they prophesied, but did not continue.

📖 **Further reading:** For more on the complaints of the children of Israel and the subsequent emanation of Moses' prophetic spirit, see *A Concise Guide to the Sages*, pp. 183ff.

²⁶Two men remained in the camp; the name of the one was Eldad, and the name of the second was Meidad; the spirit rested upon them, and they were among those written, selected as leaders, but they did not go out to the Tent and they prophesied in the camp. ²⁷The young man ran and told Moses, and he said: Eldad and Meidad are prophesying in the camp. ²⁸Joshua son of Nun, servant of Moses from his youth, spoke up and said: My lord Moses, incarcerate them. ²⁹Moses said to him: Are you zealous on my behalf? Would that all the people of the Lord be prophets, that the Lord would place His spirit upon them.

Seventh aliya ³⁰Moses returned to the camp, he and the elders of Israel. ³¹A wind went from the Lord, and displaced quail from flying over the sea, and dispersed them over the camp, extending approximately a day's journey here, in one direction, and approximately a day's journey there, in the other direction, around the camp, and they were piled up approximately two cubits above the face of the earth. ³²The people arose all that day, all the night, and all the next day, and they gathered the quail; he who did the least, gathered ten piles, and they spread them around the camp. ³³The meat was still between their teeth, it was not yet finished, and the wrath of the Lord was enflamed against the people, and the Lord struck the people with a very great blow. ³⁴He called the name of that place Kivrot Hataava, because there they buried [*kaveru*] the people that had craved [*hamitavim*] meat. ³⁵From Kivrot Hataava the people traveled to Hatzerot, and they were in Hatzerot.

Miriam Speaks about Moses

Miriam and Aaron speak critically about Moses between themselves. God summons them and explains Moses' distinct virtue; his relationship with God is unique among the prophets. Miriam is punished with leprosy and is banished from the camp for seven days.

12 ¹**Miriam and Aaron spoke against Moses, with regard to the Kushite woman whom he had married** and from whom he had apparently separated; **for he had married a Kushite woman,** in the sense that just as a Kushite woman is undoubtedly black, so Tzipora, his wife, was obviously beautiful. ²**They said: Was it only with Moses that the Lord spoke; didn't he speak with us as well? The Lord heard.** ³**And the man Moses was very humble, more than any person on the face of the earth.**

⁴**The Lord said suddenly to Moses, to Aaron, and to Miriam: Go out the three of you to the Tent of Meeting. The three of them went out.** ⁵**The Lord descended in a pillar of cloud, and stood at the entrance of the Tent. He called Aaron and Miriam and both of them came out.** ⁶**He said: Hear now My words: If your prophet is of the Lord, I will reveal Myself to him** indirectly **in a vision, in a dream I will speak to him.** ⁷**Not so My servant Moses; in all My house he is** the only one absolutely **trusted.** ⁸**Mouth to mouth I will speak with him** directly, **and** in a clear **vision, that is not in riddles, and the image of the Lord he will behold. Why did you not fear to speak against My servant, against Moses?** ⁹**The wrath of the Lord was enflamed against them and He departed.** ¹⁰**The cloud withdrew from upon the Tent, and behold, Miriam was leprous like snow. Aaron turned to Miriam; and behold, she was leprous.** ¹¹**Aaron said to Moses: Please my lord, do not place sin upon us, as we have been foolish, and we have sinned.** ¹²**Please, let her not be as** one born **a corpse, who when he emerges from his mother's womb, half his flesh was consumed.** ¹³**Moses cried out to the Lord, saying: God, please, heal her now.**

ᵃftir ¹⁴**The Lord said to Moses: If her father spit in her face,** humiliating her, **wouldn't she be ashamed for seven days? She shall be quarantined outside the camp seven days** as a leper, **and then she shall be readmitted to the camp.** ¹⁵**Miriam was quarantined outside the camp seven days,** in accordance with the law of a leper, **and the people did not travel until Miriam's readmission.** ¹⁶**Then, the people traveled from Hatzerot, and encamped in the wilderness of Paran.**

Numbers

Parashat Shelah

Parashat Shelah deals primarily with the story of the scouts and its dramatic consequences. The Israelites were led astray by the scouts, and that entire generation was condemned to wander in the wilderness for forty years, and not allowed to enter the land. The second half of the Torah portion contains several mitzvot, including meal offerings, separating *halla* from dough, and wearing ritual fringes [*tzitzit*].

The Incident of the Scouts

God commands Moses to dispatch people to the land of Canaan and to bring back information about it, as a prelude to its conquest. Twelve scouts go on this mission.

13 ¹The Lord spoke to Moses, saying: ²**Send you men, that they may scout the land of Canaan that I am giving to the children of Israel; you shall send one man each** as a representative **for the tribe of his fathers, every one a prince among them.** ³**Moses sent them from the wilderness of Paran, according to the directive of the Lord; all of them were personages, they were heads of the children of Israel.** ⁴**These were their names: For the tribe of Reuben, Shamua son of Zakur.** ⁵**For the tribe of Simeon, Shafat son of Hori.** ⁶**For the tribe of Judah, Caleb son of Yefuneh.** ⁷**For the tribe of Issachar, Yigal son of Joseph.** ⁸**For the tribe of Ephraim, Hoshe'a son of Nun.** ⁹**For the tribe of Benjamin, Palti son of Rafu.** ¹⁰**For the tribe of Zebulun, Gadiel son of Sodi.** ¹¹**For the tribe of Joseph: For the tribe of Manasseh, Gadi son of Susi.** ¹²**For the tribe of Dan, Amiel son of Gemali.** ¹³**For the tribe of Asher, Setur son of Mikhael.** ¹⁴**For the tribe of Naphtali, Nahbi son of Vofsi.** ¹⁵**For the tribe of Gad, Ge'uel son of Makhi.** ¹⁶**These are the names of the men whom Moses sent to scout the land. Moses called Hoshe'a son of Nun, Joshua [Yehoshua].** Moses added the letter *yod* to his name as a prayer that God would come to his aid.

Further reading: For more on the scouts' journey and its fateful result, see *A Concise Guide to the Sages*, p. 187.

¹⁷Moses sent them to scout the land of Canaan, and he said to them: Go up there in the South, and climb the highland. ¹⁸You shall see the land, what it is like. And the people that live in it, are they strong or weak? Are they few or many? ¹⁹What of the land in which they, the people, live, is it good or bad? What are the cities in which they live? Are they in unwalled **camps**, or in cities with **fortifications**? ²⁰What of the land, is it fat or lean? Are there trees in it, or not? You shall strengthen yourselves, and you shall take from the fruit of the land. The days were the days of the first grapes.

²¹They went up and scouted the land from the wilderness of Tzin to Rehov, at Levo Hamat, the approach to the city of Hamat. ²²They went up in the South, and came to Hebron. And Ahiman, Sheshai, and Talmai, children of the giant, were there. Hebron was built seven years before the city Tzo'an of Egypt. ²³They came to the Eshkol Ravine, and cut from there a vine with one cluster of grapes, and two of them bore it upon a pole, and they also took from the pomegranates, and from the figs. ²⁴That place he called the Eshkol Ravine, because of the cluster [eshkol] that the children of Israel cut from there. ²⁵They returned from scouting the land at the conclusion of forty days.

Illustrations: See map of places the scouts traveled, p. 529.

The Scouts Return to the Wilderness

Upon their return to the wilderness, the scouts bring the fruit of the land and speak its praises; however, they also engender fear and sow panic about entering the land. Caleb and Joshua attempt to encourage the people, telling them that with God's help they can conquer the land, but the other scouts' claims are more convincing. The fear is so great that some even suggest that they should appoint a new leader and return to Egypt. At the moment that the people are about to stone Caleb and Joshua, the glory of God appears in the Tent of Meeting.

God initially tells Moses that He will destroy the entire people and make a new people from Moses' descendants. Moses begs God for forgiveness, mentioning the fact that it will appear as if God was incapable of bringing about the conquest of the land, and invoking the divine attributes of mercy. God relents and agrees not to destroy the people.

²⁶They went and came to Moses, and to Aaron, and to the entire congregation of the children of Israel, to the wilderness of Paran, to Kadesh, and brought back word to them and to the entire congregation, and showed them the fruit of the land. ²⁷They related to him, Moses, and said: We came to the land to which you sent us, and indeed it is flowing

with milk and honey, and this is its fruit. ²⁸Only, the people that lives in the land is mighty, and the cities are fortified, very great; we also saw the children of the giant there. ²⁹Amalek lives in the southern region, and the Hitites, the Yevusites, and the Emorites live in the highland, and the Canaanites live along the sea and alongside the Jordan. ³⁰Caleb silenced the people toward Moses, and said: We shall go up and inherit it, conquer the land, for we can prevail over it. ³¹But the men who went up to the land with him said: We will not be able to go up against the people, for they are stronger than we are. ³²They promulgated a slanderous report of the land that they had scouted to the children of Israel, saying: The land which we passed through to scout it is a land that devours its inhabitants, and all the people whom we saw in it were people of great size. ³³There we saw the Nefilim, sons of a giant, from among the Nefilim, an ancient race of giants. We were as grasshoppers in our eyes, and so we were in their eyes.

14 ¹The entire congregation raised and sounded their voice; and the people wept that night. ²All the children of Israel complained against Moses and against Aaron; and the entire congregation said to them: If only we had died in the land of Egypt, or in this wilderness; if only we had died. ³Why does the Lord bring us to this land, Canaan, to fall by the sword? Our wives and our children will be for loot, they will be taken captive. Isn't it better for us to return to Egypt? ⁴They said, one to another: Let us appoint a leader and set our course to return to Egypt. ⁵Moses and Aaron fell upon their faces before the entire assembly of the congregation of the children of Israel.

⁶Joshua son of Nun and Caleb son of Yefuneh, from those who had scouted the land, rent their garments. ⁷They said to the entire congregation of the children of Israel, saying: The land through which we *Third* passed to scout it, the land is exceedingly good. ⁸If the Lord is favor-*aliya* ably disposed to us, He will bring us to this land and will give it to us, a land flowing with milk and honey. ⁹However, do not rebel against the Lord, and you, do not fear the people of the land, as they are like our bread; we will consume them easily. Their protection has withdrawn from them, and the Lord is with us; do not fear them. ¹⁰The entire congregation said to stone them, Joshua and Caleb, with stones, and the glory of the Lord appeared in the Tent of Meeting, to all the children of Israel. ¹¹The Lord said to Moses: Until when will this people scorn and anger Me, and until when will they not believe in Me, with

all the signs and miracles **that I have performed in their midst?** ¹²**I will smite them with the pestilence, and I will destroy them, and will make you,** Moses, **into a nation greater and mightier than they.** ¹³**Moses said to the Lord: Egypt will hear – for You took up this people with Your might from its midst,** ¹⁴**and they will say to the inhabitants of this land,** Canaan, that **they,** the Egyptians, **had heard that You, the Lord, are in the midst of this people; that with their very eyes You, the Lord, were seen, and Your cloud stands over them; and in a pillar of cloud You go before them by day, and in a pillar of fire by night.** ¹⁵**But,** nevertheless, **if You kill this people as one man, the nations that have heard of Your renown will say, saying:** ¹⁶**The Lord lacks the ability to bring this people into the land with regard to which He took an oath to them, and** therefore **He slaughtered them in the wilderness.** ¹⁷**Now, please, let the might of my Lord be great, as You spoke, saying:** ¹⁸**The Lord is** patient and **slow to anger, and abounding in kindness, bearing iniquity and transgression. But He will not** completely **exonerate** the penitent; rather, He will continue **reckoning the iniquity of the fathers upon the children, upon the third and upon the fourth generation.** ¹⁹**Please pardon the iniquity of this people in accordance with the greatness of Your kindness, and as You have** patiently **borne** and forgiven **this people, from Egypt until now.**

²⁰The Lord said: I have pardoned in accordance with your word.

The Punishment for the Sin of the Scouts

Although God, in response to Moses' prayer, has agreed not to destroy the people, He decrees that the entire generation who experienced the exodus will not enter the land, with the exception of Caleb and Joshua. The other scouts die immediately in a plague. Instead of accepting God's decree, the people then attempt to enter the land by force, but are routed in a battle with the Emorites.

²¹**However, as I live,** an oath, **the entire earth shall be filled with the glory of the Lord:** ²²**For, all the people who have seen My glory, and My signs which I performed in Egypt and in the wilderness, and have tested Me these ten times, and have not heeded My voice,** ²³**they shall not see the land with regard to which I took an oath to their fathers. And all those who scorn Me shall not see it.** ²⁴**But My servant Caleb, because another spirit was with him, and he followed Me wholeheartedly, I will bring him to the land into which he came, and his descendants shall take possession of it.** ²⁵**The Amalekites and the Canaanites dwell**

in the valley; tomorrow, turn and travel you to the wilderness by way of the Red Sea.

Fourth aliya ²⁶The Lord spoke to Moses and to Aaron, saying: ²⁷How long will it be with this evil congregation, that they bring complaints against Me? I have heard the complaints of the children of Israel that they have brought against Me. ²⁸Say to them: As I live – the utterance of the Lord – surely as you spoke in My ears your complaints, so I shall do to you. ²⁹Your carcasses shall fall in this wilderness, and all those of you who were counted in any of your censuses from twenty years old and above, who brought complaints against Me; ³⁰you shall not come into the land with regard to which I raised My hand and took an oath **that I would settle you in it, except for Caleb son of Yefuneh and Joshua son of Nun.** ³¹Your children, about whom you said they would be for **loot,** taken captive, **I will bring them** into the land, **and they shall know the land that you have despised.** ³²But your carcasses, you, shall fall in this wilderness. ³³Your children shall be wandering in the wilderness for **forty years, and** they **shall bear** the consequences of **your harlotry,** your betrayal, **until the demise of your carcasses in the wilderness.** ³⁴In accordance with the number of the days that you scouted the land, forty days; each day for a year you shall bear your iniquities, forty years, and you shall know the extent of **My estrangement.** ³⁵I am the Lord, I have spoken; surely, I will do this to this entire evil congregation that congregated against Me; in this wilderness they shall expire, and there they shall die.

³⁶The men whom Moses sent to scout the land and returned and brought the entire congregation to complain against him, to promulgate a slanderous report of the land; ³⁷the men, promulgators of the evil slanderous report of the land, died in the plague before the Lord. ³⁸But Joshua son of Nun and Caleb son of Yefuneh lived, from among those men who went to scout the land. ³⁹Moses spoke these words to all the children of Israel, and the people mourned greatly. ⁴⁰They awoke early in the morning, and went up to the top of the mountain, saying: Here we are, and we will go up to the place that the Lord said, because we acknowledge that we have sinned. ⁴¹Moses said: Why are you violating the directive of the Lord? It shall not succeed. ⁴²Do not go up, as the Lord is not in your midst, that you will not be struck down before your enemies. ⁴³For the Amalekites and the Canaanites are there before you, and you shall fall by the sword since you have withdrawn

from following the Lord, and the Lord will not be with you. ⁴⁴They ventured to go up to the top of the mountain, but the Ark of the Covenant of the Lord, and Moses, did not move from the midst of the camp. ⁴⁵The Amalekites and the Canaanites who lived on that mountain came down and smote them and crushed them, until their demise in a place known as Horma.

Meal Offerings That Accompany Animal Offerings

Every animal offering must be accompanied by a meal offering and a wine libation poured on the altar. Here, the different meal offerings and their measures are detailed for each offering respectively.

15 ¹The Lord spoke to Moses, saying: ²Speak to the children of Israel, and say to them: When you will come into the land of your dwellings that I am giving to you, ³and you will perform a fire offering to the Lord, a burnt offering or a peace offering to fulfill a vow, or as a pledge, a gift offering, or at your appointed times, to create a pleasing aroma to the Lord, from the cattle, or from the flock; ⁴the one who presents his offering to the Lord shall present a meal offering: One-tenth of an ephah of choice flour mixed with one-fourth of a hin of oil, ⁵and wine as the libation: One-fourth of a hin you shall make with the burnt offering or for the peace offering, for one sheep. ⁶Or for a ram, you shall perform a meal offering of two-tenths of an ephah of choice flour mixed with one-third of a hin of oil. ⁷And you shall present wine as the libation: One-third of a hin, a pleasing aroma to the Lord. ⁸When you render a young bull a burnt offering, or a peace offering, to fulfill a vow or a peace offering to the Lord, ⁹one shall present with the young bull a meal offering: Three-tenths of an ephah of choice flour, mixed with one-half a hin of oil. ¹⁰And you shall present wine as the libation: One-half a hin as a fire offering of a pleasing aroma to the Lord. ¹¹So shall be done for one bull, or for one ram, or for a lamb, or for a kid. ¹²According to the number of offerings that you shall do, so shall you do for each according to their number. ¹³Every native shall do these in this manner, to present a fire offering of a pleasing aroma to the Lord. These are the fixed amounts for the meal offerings and libations brought with the offerings. ¹⁴If a stranger who converts will reside with you, or one who is in your midst for your generations, and will perform a fire offering of a pleasing aroma to the Lord, as you do, so he shall do. ¹⁵The assembly: One statute shall be for you and for the stranger who resides,

Fifth aliya

Numbers

an eternal statute for your generations; like you, so the stranger shall be before the Lord. ¹⁶One law and one ordinance shall be for you and for the stranger who resides with you.

Separating *Halla*

Similar to *teruma*, that is separated from grain and given to priests, the Israelites are commanded to separate *halla* from their dough.

Sixth aliya ¹⁷The Lord spoke to Moses, saying: ¹⁸Speak to the children of Israel, and say to them: When you come to the land that I am bringing you there, ¹⁹it shall be, when you eat from the bread of the land, you shall separate a gift for the Lord. ²⁰The first of your kneading basket you shall separate a loaf [*halla*] as a gift, like the gift, *teruma*, from the threshing floor, so shall you separate it. ²¹From the first of your kneading basket you shall give to the Lord a gift for your generations.

Unwitting Idol Worship

A special offering is brought for an unwitting act of idol worship, and there is a special provision for a case where the entire congregation errs.

²²If you act unwittingly and do not observe all these commandments that the Lord spoke to Moses, ²³everything that the Lord commanded to you at the hand of Moses, from the day that the Lord commanded and onward, for your generations. ²⁴It shall be, if from the eyes of the congregation it was performed unwittingly, as a result of an erroneous ruling by the court, the entire congregation, the court, shall render one young bull as a burnt offering for a pleasing aroma to the Lord, and its meal offering and its libation according to the ordinance, and one goat as a sin offering. ²⁵The priest shall atone for the entire congregation of the children of Israel, and it will be forgiven for them, as it was an unwitting act, and they brought their offering, a fire offering to the Lord, and their sin offering before the Lord, for their unwitting act. ²⁶The entire congregation of the children of Israel shall be forgiven, and the stranger that resides in their midst, as it was unwitting for the entire people.

Seventh aliya ²⁷If one person will sin unwittingly, he shall present a female goat in its first year as a sin offering. ²⁸The priest shall atone for the unwitting person when he sins unwittingly, before the Lord, to atone for him; and it shall be forgiven for him. ²⁹The native of the children of Israel and for the stranger that resides in their midst: There shall be one law for you,

for one who acts unwittingly. ³⁰The person that acts with a high hand, defiantly, whether native or stranger, it is the Lord that he blasphemes, and that person shall be excised from among his people. ³¹Because he scorned the word of the Lord, and he violated His commandment; that person shall be excised; his iniquity is upon him.

📖 **Further reading:** For more on sin offerings, see p. 252.

The Gatherer

For the first time, the Israelites encounter a person who publicly desecrates Shabbat, and they must ascertain his sentence.

³²The children of Israel were in the wilderness and they found a man gathering wood on the Sabbath day. ³³Those who found him gathering wood brought him to Moses and Aaron, and to the entire congregation. ³⁴They placed him in custody, because it had not been explicated what should be done to him.

³⁵The Lord said to Moses: The man shall be put to death; the entire congregation shall stone him with stones outside the camp. ³⁶The entire congregation took him outside the camp, and they stoned him with stones, and he died, as the Lord had commanded Moses.

The Mitzva of Ritual Fringes

The Israelites are commanded to attach ritual fringes to their garments. This special commandment is designated to serve as an eternal daily reminder of all the mitzvot.

Maftir ³⁷The Lord spoke to Moses, saying: ³⁸Speak to the children of Israel, and say to them: They shall make for themselves a fringe consisting of hanging threads on the corners of their garments for their generations, and they shall put on the fringe of the corner a sky-blue thread. ³⁹It shall be for you a fringe, and you shall see it and remember all the commandments of the Lord, and perform them, and you shall not rove after your heart and after your eyes, after which you stray; ⁴⁰so that you shall remember and perform all My commandments and be holy to your God. ⁴¹I am the Lord your God, who took you out of the land of Egypt, to be your God: I am the Lord your God.

📖 **Further reading:** For more on the mitzva of ritual fringes, see *A Concise Guide to the Sages*, p. 190; *A Concise Guide to Halakha*, p. 580.

Parashat Korah

This Torah portion addresses the role of the priests and the Levites, and the struggle over that role. Korah and his congregation rebelled against the priestly class and the dispute ended with a harsh punishment. The Torah underscores the role of the priests as overseers of the Tabernacle, and the role of the Levites as their assistants. The Torah portion concludes with the details of the gifts that the Israelites are required to give the priests and the Levites in exchange for their devotion to their vocation.

The Episode of Korah and His Congregation

Korah, a member of the tribe of Levi, challenges the leadership of Moses and Aaron, and then also demands that the service in the Tabernacle be divided among the entire nation. Moses refers the decision to God, who determines the apportionment of positions among the Israelites. The reaction is swift – the earth opens its mouth and swallows Korah and his congregation, and fire incinerates his people, who sought to offer incense.

16 ¹**Korah son of Yitzhar, son of Kehat, son of Levi, and Datan and Aviram sons of Eliav, and On son of Pelet,** who were **sons of Reuben, took** themselves and their associates; ²**they arose before Moses, and two hundred and fifty people from the children of Israel, princes of the congregation, the distinguished of the convocation, people of renown,** ³**assembled against Moses and against Aaron, and said to them:** What you have taken, **it is too much for you, as the entire congregation, all of them are holy, and the Lord is among them; why do you elevate yourselves over the assembly of the Lord** and monopolize all the leadership positions? ⁴**Moses heard and he fell upon his face.** ⁵**He spoke to Korah and to his entire congregation, saying: In the morning the Lord will disclose who is His, and who is holy, and will bring him near to Him; whom He shall choose, He will bring near to Him.** ⁶**This you shall do: Take for you fire-pans, Korah and all his congregation.** ⁷**Place fire in them, and place incense upon them before the Lord tomorrow; it shall be the man whom the Lord will choose, he is the holy one. It is too much for you, sons of Levi,** you should be content with the roles that have been assigned to you.

📖 **Further reading:** Why did Moses put off Korah and his congregation until the next day?
See *A Concise Guide to the Sages*, p. 193.

⁸Moses said to Korah: Hear now, sons of Levi: ⁹Is it not enough for you that the God of Israel has distinguished you from the congregation of Israel, to bring you near to Him, to perform the service of the Tabernacle of the Lord, and to stand before the congregation to serve them? ¹⁰He brought you near, and all your brethren the sons of Levi with you, and will you seek the priesthood as well? ¹¹In fact, you and all your congregation are congregated and complaining against the Lord; and Aaron, what is it that he has done, that you bring complaints against him? ¹²Moses sent to summon Datan and Aviram, sons of Eliav, and they said: We will not go up and come to you. ¹³Is it not enough that you brought us up from a land flowing with milk and honey, Egypt, to kill us in the wilderness? Will you also reign over us? ¹⁴Yet you did not take us to a land flowing with milk and honey, and give us an inheritance of field and vineyard. Will you gouge out the eyes of these men; do you think you can conceal this failure from us? We will not go up. ¹⁵Moses was very incensed, and said to the Lord: Do not turn to and accept their offering; not one donkey did I take from them unjustly, nor did I wrong one of them.

Second aliya

¹⁶Moses said to Korah: You and all your congregation, be before the Lord: You, and they, and Aaron, tomorrow. ¹⁷Each of you take his fire-pan and place incense upon them, and each of you shall bring his fire-pan before the Lord, two hundred and fifty fire-pans; and you and Aaron, each his fire-pan. ¹⁸Each man took up his fire-pan; they put fire on them and placed incense on them, and stood at the entrance of the Tent of Meeting with Moses and Aaron. ¹⁹Korah assembled the entire congregation against them to the entrance of the Tent of Meeting, and the glory of the Lord appeared to the entire congregation.

Third aliya

²⁰The Lord spoke to Moses and to Aaron, saying: ²¹Separate yourselves from the midst of this congregation, and I will destroy them in a moment. ²²They fell upon their faces and said: God, God who knows of the spirits of all flesh, shall one man sin, and You will rage against the entire congregation?

²³The Lord spoke to Moses, saying: ²⁴Speak to the congregation, saying: Depart from around the dwelling of Korah, Datan, and Aviram. ²⁵Moses arose and went to Datan and Aviram, and the elders of Israel followed him. ²⁶He spoke to the congregation saying: Depart now from

Numbers

near the tents of these wicked men, and do not touch anything that is theirs, lest you be destroyed for all their sins. [27]They departed from around the dwelling of Korah, Datan, and Aviram. Datan and Aviram emerged and stood at the entrance of their tents with their wives, their sons, and their children. [28]Moses said: With this you will know that the Lord has sent me to perform all these actions, as it is not from my heart, it is not my initiative. [29]If these die like the death of all people, and the destiny of all people is visited upon them, natural deaths, the Lord has not sent me. [30]But if the Lord creates a creation, and the ground opens its mouth and swallows them and everything that is theirs, and they descend alive into the abyss, you shall know that these people have scorned the Lord.

[31]It was as he concluded to speak all these words that the ground that was beneath them split. [32]The earth opened its mouth and swallowed them, their households, all the people who were with Korah, and all the property. [33]They and everything that was theirs descended alive into the abyss. The earth covered them and they were lost from the midst of the assembly. [34]All Israel that were around them fled at their cry, the screams of those swallowed up by the earth, as they said: Lest the earth swallow us. [35]Fire emerged from the Lord, and consumed the two hundred and fifty men, the presenters of the incense.

📖 **Further reading:** For more on the manner in which the earth swallowed Korah and his congregation, see *A Concise Guide to the Sages*, p. 194.

17 [1]The Lord spoke to Moses, saying: [2]Say to Elazar son of Aaron the priest that he shall lift up the fire-pans from the midst of the fire, and the fire that was still burning in the coals, he shall **cast** and scatter **about, for they,** the fire-pans, **have become holy** and their use is prohibited. [3]The fire-pans of these sinners, who are liable to pay **with their lives, they shall render them beaten sheet metal, a covering for the altar, for they brought them before the Lord, and they became holy; they shall be as a sign to the children of Israel.** [4]Elazar the priest took the bronze fire-pans that those who were burned had **brought, and they beat them as a covering for the altar.** [5]A remembrance to the children of Israel, so that a non-priestly man who is not from the descendants of Aaron shall not draw near to burn incense before the Lord, and he will not be like Korah and like his congregation, as the Lord spoke with regard **to him at the hand of Moses.**

The Complaint and the Plague

The Israelites complain about what was done to Korah and his congregation, and God afflicts them with a plague.

⁶The entire congregation of the children of Israel complained against Moses and against Aaron the next day, saying: You have killed the people of the Lord. ⁷It was when the congregation was assembled against Moses and against Aaron, they turned toward the entrance of the Tent of Meeting and behold, the cloud covered it, and the glory of the Lord appeared. ⁸Moses and Aaron came before the Tent of Meeting.

Fourth aliya ⁹The Lord spoke to Moses, saying: ¹⁰Remove yourselves from among this congregation, and I will destroy them in a moment. They, Moses and Aaron, fell upon their faces in prayer. ¹¹Moses said to Aaron: Take the fire-pan, put fire on it from upon the altar and place incense, so the people will realize that incense saves and does not kill, and go quickly to the congregation and atone for them, for the rage has emerged from before the Lord: The plague has begun. ¹²Aaron took a fire-pan, as Moses had spoken, and ran to the midst of the assembly, and behold, the plague had begun among the people; he placed the incense, and atoned for the people. ¹³He stood between the dead and the living; and the plague was stopped. ¹⁴The dead in the plague were fourteen thousand seven hundred besides, not including, the dead over the matter of Korah. ¹⁵Aaron returned to Moses, to the entrance of the Tent of Meeting, and the plague was stopped.

Aaron's Staff

In order to underscore God's selection of Aaron's family for the priesthood, God commands all the princes of the tribes to deposit their staffs in the Tabernacle, and miraculously, Aaron's staff blossoms and produces fruit overnight.

Fifth aliya ¹⁶The Lord spoke to Moses, saying: ¹⁷Speak to the children of Israel, and take from them one staff for each patrilineal house, from each of their princes according to their patrilineal house, twelve staffs; each man's name you shall write upon his staff. ¹⁸You shall write Aaron's name upon the staff of Levi, for there shall be one staff for the head of their patrilineal house. ¹⁹You shall place them in the Tent of Meeting before the Testimony, the Ark of the Covenant, where I will meet with you. ²⁰It shall be that the man whom I shall choose, his staff will blossom, and I will quell from upon Me the complaints of the children of Israel that they bring against you.

Numbers

²¹**Moses spoke** these matters **to the children of Israel, and all their princes gave him one staff for each prince according to their patrilineal house, twelve staffs; and the staff of Aaron was among their staffs.** ²²**Moses placed the staffs before the Lord in the Tent of the Testimony.** ²³**It was on the next day, and Moses came into the Tent of the Testimony and behold, the staff of Aaron of the house of Levi had blossomed; it had produced a blossom, and had sprouted a bud, and had brought forth almonds.** ²⁴**Moses took out all the staffs from before the Lord to all the children of Israel, and they saw, and each took his staff.**

Sixth aliya ²⁵**The Lord said to Moses: Return the staff of Aaron before the Testimony for safekeeping, as a sign for the defiant ones, and their complaints will cease from Me, and they will not die** as punishment for their complaints. ²⁶**Moses did as the Lord had commanded him; so he did.**

> **Further reading:** For more on the wonder performed with Aaron's staff, see *A Concise Guide to the Sages*, p. 195.

Preservation of the Sanctity of the Sanctuary

As a result of recent events, the Israelites are wary of approaching the Tabernacle of God. God explains that the priests are appointed as overseers of the Sanctuary; therefore, they bear the responsibility of preserving its sanctity. The role of the Levites is to assist the priests and ensure that no non-priest will approach the Sanctuary.

²⁷**The children of Israel spoke to Moses, saying: Behold, we perish, we are lost, all of us are lost.** ²⁸**Anyone who approaches the Tabernacle of the Lord will die. Have we ceased to perish,** or are we doomed?

18 ¹**The Lord said to Aaron: You, and your sons, and your patrilineal house with you, shall bear** responsibility for **the iniquity of** any unauthorized approach to **the Sanctuary. And you and your sons with you shall bear the iniquity for** any sins relating to **your priesthood.** ²**Also your brethren, the tribe of Levi, the tribe of your father, bring near with you, and they shall accompany you, and serve you. And** only **you and your sons with you,** not the Levites, will serve **before the Tent of the Testimony.** ³**They,** the Levites, **shall keep your commission, and the commission of all the Tent; however, they shall not come close to the sacred vessels and to the altar, and neither they nor you will die.** ⁴**They shall accompany you** and the priests, **and keep the commission of the Tent of Meeting, for all the service of the Tent; a non-priest shall not approach you.** ⁵**You shall**

keep the commission of the sacred and the commission of the altar, and there will be no more rage against the children of Israel. ⁶And I, behold, I have taken your brethren the Levites from among the children of Israel; to you they are given as a gift for the Lord, to perform the service of the Tent of Meeting. ⁷You and your sons with you shall keep your priesthood with regard to any matter of the altar, and with regard to that which is within the curtain, and you shall serve. As a service that is a gift, not an imposition, I give you your priesthood, whereas the non-priest who approaches shall be put to death.

Priestly Gifts

In exchange for the devotion of the priests to the Tabernacle service, they receive the "priestly gifts." These include being allowed to eat the flesh of offerings, receiving the first fruits, and the firstborn sons of people – who are redeemed – and the firstborn males of animals.

⁸The Lord spoke to Aaron: Behold, I have given you the commission of My gifts; with regard to all the consecrated items of the children of Israel I have given them to you for prominence, and to your sons, as an eternal allotment. ⁹This shall be for you from the sacred sacraments, the offerings of the most sacred order, from the fire on the altar: Every offering of theirs, every meal offering of theirs, every sin offering of theirs, and every guilt offering of theirs that they shall return to Me; it is a sacred sacrament for you and for your sons. ¹⁰In the sacred sanctum, the Tabernacle courtyard, shall you eat it, the offerings of the most sacred order; every male may eat it; it shall be sacred to you. ¹¹This is yours: The separation of their gift, for all the wave offerings from the peace offerings of the children of Israel, I have given them to you, and to your sons and to your daughters with you, as an eternal allotment; all pure in your household may eat it, as they are offerings of lesser sanctity. ¹²All the best of the oil, and all the best of the wine and of the grain, the first of them that they will give to the Lord, to you have I given them. ¹³The first fruits of all that is in their land that they bring to the Lord shall be yours; all pure, male and female, in your household may eat it. ¹⁴Everything proscribed in Israel, property that was consecrated, shall be yours.

¹⁵Every first issue of the womb of all flesh, which they offer to the Lord, of man and of animal, shall be yours; however, the firstborn of man you shall redeem with money, and the firstborn of the impure animal,

the donkey, **you shall redeem.** ¹⁶**Its redeemed,** a woman's firstborn son, **from one month old shall you redeem, with a value of five shekels of silver in the sacred shekel; it is twenty gera,** twice the value of a regular shekel. ¹⁷**However, the firstborn of an ox, or the firstborn of a sheep, or the firstborn of a goat, you shall not redeem; they are sacred. You shall sprinkle their blood on the altar, and you shall burn their fat as a fire offering for a pleasing aroma to the Lord.** ¹⁸**Their meat, though, shall be for you; like the breast of the waving and like the right haunch** of peace offerings, **it shall be yours.** ¹⁹**All the gifts of the consecrated items that the children of Israel separate for the Lord, I have given you, and your sons and your daughters with you, as an eternal allotment; it is an everlasting covenant of salt before the Lord to you and to your descendants with you.** ²⁰**The Lord said to Aaron: You shall not inherit in their land, and you shall not have a portion in their midst; I am your portion and your inheritance among the children of Israel.**

📖 **Further reading:** For more on how redemption of the firstborn son is practiced, see *A Concise Guide to Halakha*, p. 17.

Levite Gifts

The Levites, like the priests, do not receive an agricultural portion in the Land of Israel, and are assigned to the commission of the Tabernacle. Therefore, they too receive certain gifts, tithes from agricultural produce.

Seventh ²¹**To the children of Levi, behold, I have given the entire tithe,** one-tenth
aliya of all produce **in Israel, as an inheritance, in exchange for their service that they perform, the service of the Tent of Meeting.** ²²**The children of Israel shall not approach the Tent of Meeting anymore, to bear sin, to die.** ²³**The Levite himself shall perform the service of the Tent of Meeting, and they shall bear their iniquity,** they bear responsibility for others approaching the Tabernacle. **It shall be an eternal statute for your generations, and among the children of Israel, they shall not inherit an inheritance.** ²⁴**For the tithe of the children of Israel that they will separate to the Lord as a gift, I have given to the Levites as an inheritance; therefore, I said to them: In the midst of the children of Israel they shall not inherit an inheritance.**

²⁵**The Lord spoke to Moses, saying:** ²⁶**To the Levites you shall speak, and say to them: When you take from the children of Israel the tithe that I have given you from them for your inheritance, you shall separate**

from it a gift to the Lord, a tithe from the tithe. ²⁷Your gift to the priest shall be considered for you like the grain from the threshing floor, and like the fill of the winepress, as though you gave it from produce that grew in your land. ²⁸So you too shall separate the gift of the Lord from all your tithes that you receive from the children of Israel; you shall give from it the gift of the Lord to Aaron the priest and his descendants. ²⁹From all your gifts that you receive you shall separate all the gifts of the Lord; of all its finest, you must give the priest its sacred part from

Maftir it. ³⁰You shall say to them: When you separate its finest from it, it shall be considered for the Levites like the produce of the threshing floor, and like the produce of the winepress. The remainder of the tithe has the status of nonsacred produce. ³¹You may eat it, the tithe, in any place, you and your households, for it is your wage in exchange for your service in the Tent of Meeting. ³²You shall not bear sin on its account when you separate its finest from it. The sacred items of the children of Israel you shall not profane, and you will not die.

📖 **Further reading:** For more on how the mitzvot of tithes and gifts are observed today, see *A Concise Guide to Halakha,* p. 564.

Numbers

Parashat Hukat

This *parasha* opens with the laws of the red heifer, and the laws governing the impurity that is contracted through contact with a corpse and how one purifies oneself, and then continues the story of the Israelites in the wilderness. At the end of the *parasha* the Torah begins its account of the Israelites approaching the Promised Land, and tells of their first encounters with the peoples living in the neighboring lands.

The Red Heifer

The rite that purifies someone who has had contact with a corpse involves the sprinkling of water into which was mixed the ashes of a red heifer. Therefore, to perform such a rite the people of Israel must locate a red heifer, an exceedingly rare animal, burn it in a special ceremony, and mix its ashes with spring water. These ashes were preserved within the Temple for generations.

19 **¹The Lord spoke to Moses and to Aaron, saying: ²This is the statute of the law that the Lord had commanded, saying: Speak to the children of Israel, and they shall take to you an unflawed red heifer,** a heifer of a rare color **in which there is no** physical **blemish, and upon which a yoke was not placed** for any sort of work in the field. **³You shall give it to Elazar the priest, and he shall take it out of the camp, and one shall slaughter** it **before him. ⁴Elazar the priest shall take from its blood with his finger, and sprinkle from its blood toward the front of the Tent of Meeting,** its opening, **seven times. ⁵One shall burn the heifer before his eyes,** in his presence: **Its skin, its flesh, and its blood, with its dung in its bowels, he shall burn. ⁶The priest shall take cedarwood,** a twig of **hyssop, and a scarlet thread, and** he shall **cast** these items **into the burning of the heifer. ⁷The priest** involved in this ritual **shall wash his garments, and he shall bathe,** immerse, **his flesh in water, and then he may come to the camp. The priest shall be impure until the evening;** only then does he return to a state of purity. **⁸He who burns it shall** also **wash his garments in water, and bathe his flesh in water, and he shall be impure until the evening. ⁹A pure man** who was not involved in the burning of the heifer **shall gather the ashes of the heifer, and place them outside the camp**

in a pure place, and it, this collection of ashes, **shall be for the congregation of the children of Israel a keepsake, as a water of sprinkling; it,** the heifer, **is** a means of **purification.** [10]**He who gathers the ashes of the heifer shall** also **wash his garments, and he shall be impure until the evening; it shall be for the children of Israel, and to the stranger who resides among them, for an eternal statute.**

📖 **Further reading:** Even King Solomon, the wisest person of all, found the rationale for the mitzva of the red heifer difficult to understand; see *A Concise Guide to the Sages*, p. 196.

[11]**One who touches the corpse of any person shall be impure** for at least seven days, the minimum number of days required for the purification process. [12]**He shall purify himself with it,** the mixture of water and ashes, **on the third day and on the seventh day** of his impurity, and then **he shall be pure; however, if he does not purify himself on the third day and on the seventh day, he shall not be pure** even after seven days have elapsed. [13]**Anyone who touches a corpse of a person who has died and does not purify himself,** and enters the Tabernacle, **has defiled the Tabernacle of the Lord; that person shall be excised from Israel because the water of sprinkling,** the mixture of water and ashes, **was not sprinkled upon him; he shall be impure,** his impurity is still upon him.

[14]**This is the law: When a man dies in a tent,** or in any roofed structure, **anyone who comes into the tent** while the corpse is there, **and anything that is in the tent** while the corpse is there, **shall be impure seven days,** even if the person or object does not touch the corpse. [15]**Any open vessel** in the tent **that does not have a tight-fitting lid upon it is impure.** [16]**Anyone who will touch in the open field,** in an unroofed area, **one slain with a sword, or one who died** through other means, **or a bone of a man, or a grave** of a person, **shall be impure seven days.** [17]In order to purify him, **they shall take for the impure** person **from the ashes of the burning of the purification,** the ashes of the heifer, **and he shall place** pure **spring water upon it,** the ashes, **in a vessel.** [18]**A pure person shall take hyssop, and dip it in the water, and sprinkle it on the tent, and on all the vessels, and on the people who were there, and on one who touched the bone, or the slain, or the dead, or the grave.** [19]**The pure shall sprinkle upon the impure on the third day and on the seventh day, and he shall purify him,** complete the purification process, **on the seventh day; he,** the one undergoing purification, **shall then wash his garments, and bathe,** immerse, **in water, and be pure in the evening.**

📖 **Further reading:** Today the *halakhot* pertaining to impurity imparted by a corpse apply only to a *kohen*. See *A Concise Guide to Halakha*, p. 102.

²⁰**A man who is impure, and does not purify himself,** and nevertheless enters the Temple or eats from sacrificial items, **that person shall be excised from the midst of the assembly because he has rendered the Sanctuary of the Lord impure; the water of sprinkling has not been sprinkled on him, he is impure.** ²¹**It shall be an eternal statute for them,** the people of Israel; **he,** the priest **who sprinkles the water of sprinkling, shall wash his garments,** as he is rendered impure, **and he who touches the water of sprinkling,** even if he does not use it, **shall** also **be impure until the evening.** ²²**Anything that the impure person** who came into contact with the water of sprinkling **shall touch shall be impure, and the person who touches** an individual who came into contact with a corpse **shall** himself **be impure until the evening.**

The Sin of Moses and Aaron

At this point the narrative shifts to the children of Israel's final year in the desert. The generation that left Egypt has died; everything that follows relates to the generation of men who were not yet twenty years of age at the time of the sin of the scouts (Numbers 13–14). Now the Torah records the death of Miriam, followed by the sin of Moses and Aaron which precludes them from entering the land. When the Israelites complain that they have no water, God commands Moses to speak to the rock, but instead, Moses strikes it. For this, both Moses and Aaron are barred from entering the Land of Israel.

20 ¹**The children of Israel, the entire congregation, came to the wilderness of Tzin during the first month, and the people** stopped to camp and **lived in Kadesh. Miriam died there, and she was buried there.** ²**There was no water for the congregation, and they assembled** to complain **against Moses and against Aaron.** ³**The people quarreled with Moses, and they said, saying: If only we had perished in the perishing of our brethren before the Lord.** ⁴**Why did you bring the assembly of the Lord to this wilderness, that we and our animals should die there?** ⁵**Why did you bring us up from Egypt, to bring us to this wretched place? It is not a place of seed, or figs, or vines, or pomegranates, and there is no water to drink.** ⁶**Moses and Aaron came from before the assembly,** retreated from it, and were forced by the angry crowd **to the entrance of the Tent of Meeting, and** there they **fell upon their faces** in prayer, **and the glory of the Lord appeared to them.**

Third aliya
(Second aliya)

7The Lord spoke to Moses, saying: 8Take the staff with which you per-formed all the miracles and wonders **and assemble the congregation, you, and Aaron your brother, and speak to the rock before their eyes,** in their presence, **and it,** the rock, **will provide its water.** You will thereby **extract water for them from the rock, and you shall give drink to the congregation and their animals. 9Moses took the staff from before the Lord, as He had commanded him. 10Moses and Aaron assembled the assembly before the rock, and said to them: Hear now, defiant ones:** From this rock **will we bring out water for you?** Is it possible for us to do so? **11Moses raised his hand, and he struck the rock with his staff twice; a great deal of water came out, and the congregation and their animals drank.**

12The Lord said to Moses and Aaron: Because you did not cause the people to **have faith in Me, to sanctify Me before the eyes of the children of Israel, therefore you shall not** merit to **bring this assembly into the land that I have given them. 13These are the waters of dispute, where the children of Israel quarreled with the Lord, and He was sanctified through them.** God was sanctified through the execution of judgment upon Moses and Aaron.

The Land of Edom

The people of Israel continue on their journey, drawing closer to the Land of Israel. Along the way, they reach the land of Edom, a land which they had been commanded not to conquer. They ask the Edomites for permission to pass through their land, but their request is denied, and they are forced to take a longer route to circumvent it.

Fourth aliya

14Moses sent messengers from Kadesh to the king of Edom: So said your brother, Israel: You know all the travail that we have encountered. 15Our ancestors descended to Egypt, and we lived in Egypt many years; the Egyptians mistreated us and our ancestors. **16We cried to the Lord and He heard our voice, sent an angel, and took us out of Egypt; behold,** we are now **in Kadesh, a city at the edge of your border. 17**Therefore, we ask: **Please, let us pass through your land; we will not pass in a field or in a vineyard,** in your settled areas, **and we will not drink well water; we will go on the king's way,** the main thoroughfare. **We will not turn** from it **right or left until we will pass your border** without causing any damage. **18**The king of **Edom said to him,** Moses, or the nation of Israel: **You shall not pass through me, lest I come out toward you with the sword** and wage war against you. **19The children of Israel said to him: If** you do

Numbers

not permit us to use the king's road, which is in the valley, **we will go up on the** mountain **highway. And if we drink your water, I or my cattle, I will give its price; only it is no matter,** no harm will be caused, **let me pass on foot,** not in military chariots. [20]**He,** Edom, **said: You shall not pass. Edom came out toward him with a great** armed **multitude, and with a powerful hand.** [21]**Edom refused to allow Israel to pass in his border, and** so **Israel turned from him** to bypass the land.

The Death of Aaron

The time arrives for Aaron the priest to die. God instructs Moses and Aaron to go up Hor Mountain with Elazar, Aaron's son. Before his death, Aaron's priestly vestments are removed and are placed on Elazar, as a ceremonial transfer to him of the high priesthood. This ritual, of the new High Priest donning the vestments of his predecessor, became part of the ceremony of inaugurating a High Priest.

Fifth aliya (Third aliya) [22]**They traveled from Kadesh, and the children of Israel, the entire congregation, came to Hor Mountain.** [23]**The Lord spoke to Moses and Aaron at Hor Mountain, on the border of the land of Edom, saying:** [24]**Aaron shall be gathered to his people;** the time has come for him to die. **For he shall not come into the land that I gave to the children of Israel because you defied My directive at** the incident involving **the waters of dispute.** [25]**Take Aaron and Elazar his son, and take them up Hor Mountain.** [26]**Undress Aaron of his** priestly **vestments, and dress Elazar his son in them. Aaron will be gathered** to his people, **and** he will **die there.** [27]**Moses did as the Lord had commanded, and they went up to Hor Mountain before the eyes of the entire congregation.** [28]**Moses undressed Aaron of his vestments, and dressed Elazar his son in them, and Aaron died there at the top of the mountain, and Moses and Elazar descended from the mountain.** [29]**The entire congregation saw that Aaron,** who did not return with Moses and Elazar, **had perished. And they wept** in mourning **for Aaron thirty days, the entire house of Israel.**

📖 **Further reading:** For more on Aaron's death and the people's great distress, see *A Concise Guide to the Sages*, p. 201.

The War against the Canaanites

This is the first military clash between the people of Israel and the peoples currently living in the Land of Israel; with the help of God, the people of Israel emerge victorious.

21 [1]**The Canaanite, king of Arad, who lives in the South, heard that Israel came via Atarim,** a route that crosses important routes into Canaan. **And**

he fought against Israel, and took a captive, a group of captives, from them. ²Israel took a vow to the Lord, and said: If You will deliver this people into my hand, I will destroy their cities, and take no spoils. ³The Lord heeded the voice of Israel, and delivered the Canaanites into their hands; it, the nation, destroyed them and their cities; and from then onward it called the name of the place Horma, after the destruction.

The Bronze Serpent

The Israelites once again complain about God and about Moses, and they are punished with an attack of venomous serpents. They recognize their sin and seek atonement, and a remedy arrives for them in the form of a miraculous bronze serpent; whoever looks at it is healed.

⁴They, the children of Israel, traveled from Hor Mountain via the Red Sea in order to circumvent the land of Edom; the soul of the people grew restive on the way. ⁵The people spoke harshly against God and against Moses: Why did you bring us up from Egypt to die in the wilderness, for there is no real bread and there is no natural water, and our soul loathes this insubstantial bread, the manna. ⁶The Lord sent the venomous fiery serpents against the people, and they bit the people, and a large multitude of Israel died. ⁷The people then came to Moses, and they said contritely: We sinned, for we spoke against the Lord, and against you; pray to the Lord, and He will remove the serpents from us. Moses prayed on behalf of the people. ⁸The Lord said to Moses: Craft for yourself the image of a fiery, poisonous serpent, and place it upon a tall standard; it shall be that anyone who was bitten by a serpent will see it and live, be healed. ⁹Moses crafted a bronze serpent, and Moses placed it on the standard, and it was, that if a serpent bit a man, he would look at the bronze serpent and live.

📖 Further reading: What was the power of the bronze serpent? See *A Concise Guide to the Sages*, p. 202.

The Journeys of the Children of Israel

The Israelites continue their journey on the eastern side of the Jordan, circumventing the lands of Edom and Moav, which they were not permitted to conquer.

Sixth aliya ¹⁰The children of Israel traveled and encamped in Ovot. ¹¹Then they traveled from Ovot, and encamped at Iyei HaAvarim, in the wilderness that is before Moav, toward the rising sun, to the east. ¹²From there they traveled north and encamped in the Zered Ravine, which descends

Numbers

from the mountains of modern-day Jordan. **¹³From there they traveled and encamped across the Arnon** Ravine, **which is in the wilderness that emerges from the border of the Emorites, for Arnon is the border of Moav, between Moav and the Emorites. ¹⁴Therefore, it is said in the book of the Wars of the Lord: Vahev,** the name of a place, the children of Israel conquered **by storm, and** also **the tributaries of the Arnon; ¹⁵the outpouring of the streams that tended toward the settled area of Ar,** an important Moavite city, **and** this estuary **abuts the border of Moav. ¹⁶From there** Israel traveled **to the well; that is the well where the Lord said to Moses: Assemble the people, and I will give them water.**

The Song of the Well
The Israelites sing a song of gratitude to God for the well of water that He provides for them in the heart of the wilderness.

¹⁷Then, at the time of the incident involving the well, **Israel sang this song: Rise,** O water of the **well; give voice** and sing **for it,** in honor of the well. **¹⁸A well that princes dug; the nobles of the people excavated with a ruler's staff,** meaning with the staffs in their hands, which symbolize their leadership, and **with their canes.** This was not a typical well dug by common laborers. **And from the wilderness** they journeyed **to** a place called **Matana,** perhaps because of the abundance that was found there. **¹⁹And from Matana** they came **to** a place called **Nahaliel,** after its streams, **and from Nahaliel to Bamot,** which was probably an elevated area, like a platform; **²⁰and from Bamot** they traveled **to the canyon that is in the field of Moav** and, **at the top of the peak** above, one could see Moav on one side, **and** the other side **overlooks the surface of the desert,** east of Moav.

The Wars against Sihon and Og
Here an account is provided of the first two major wars of the conquest of the land. The land of the Emorites once belonged to Moav, but it had been conquered by Sihon, the king of the Emorites. The *parasha* ends with the Israelites reaching the point from which they would eventually enter the western portion of the Land of Israel, opposite the city of Jericho.

Seventh aliya (Fourth aliya) **²¹Israel sent messengers to Sihon, king of the Emorites, saying: ²²Let me pass in your land; we will not turn to a field or to a vineyard; we will not drink well water** from your wells; **we will go on the king's way,** the main thoroughfare, **until we will pass your border** on the way to Canaan. **²³But Sihon did not allow Israel to pass in his border.** Rather, **Sihon gathered his entire people and came out toward Israel, to the**

wilderness; he came to Yahatz and he fought against Israel. ²⁴Israel smote him by sword, killing all of his army, and took possession of his land from the Arnon, on the border of Moav, until the Yabok Ravine, until the children of Amon; for the border of the children of Amon was strongly defended and closed to them. ²⁵Israel took all these cities in Sihon's land, and Israel dwelt in all the cities of the Emorites, in the city of Heshbon, and in all its environs. ²⁶For Heshbon was the city of Sihon, king of the Emorites; he, Sihon, had fought against the first king of Moav, and took all his land from his possession until Arnon, including the city of Heshbon.

²⁷Therefore, in the wake of the conquest of Heshbon from the Moavites, the Emorite allegorists would say: Let us go to Heshbon. May the city of Sihon be built and established in this place. ²⁸For a fire emerged from Heshbon, a flame from the city of Sihon. The allegorist imagines the conquest of the land of Moav, which will spread from Heshbon to other Moavite cities. It consumed Ar, a city of Moav, and the shrines of the high places of Arnon. ²⁹Woe to you, Moav, for your land has been conquered by Sihon; you are lost, people of Kemosh, the god of Moav. He, Sihon, has rendered his, Kemosh's, sons refugees, and his daughters are in captivity to the Emorite king, Sihon. ³⁰Their, the Moavite, fields were lost from Heshbon until Divon, another Moavite city. And we, the Emorites, laid waste till Nofah that reaches to Medva.

³¹Israel dwelt in the land of the Emorites. ³²Moses sent to spy out Yazer. They captured its environs, the small settlements surrounding the city, and dispossessed, conquered and exiled, the Emorites who were there.

³³They turned and ascended via the Bashan. And Og, king of Bashan, another king of the Emorites, came out against them, he and his entire *aftir* people, to the battle against Israel at the city of Edre'i. ³⁴The Lord said to Moses: Do not fear him, for I have delivered him into your hand, him and his entire people, and his land; you shall do to him as you did to Sihon, king of the Emorites, who lives in Heshbon. ³⁵They smote him, and his sons, and his entire people, until they left no remnant of 22 him; and they took possession of his land. ¹The children of Israel traveled southward, and encamped on the plains of Moav across the Jordan River from Jericho.

📖 **Further reading:** Why was Moses trepidatious about war with Og? See *A Concise Guide to the Sages*, p. 203.

Parashat Balak

The victory of the Israelites over the kings of the Emorites, Sihon and Og, worries Balak, king of Moav. He tries to enlist Bilam the sorcerer in a different kind of war against the Jewish people, hiring him to curse them. Bilam and Balak try with all their might to curse Israel, but without success. Bilam is forced to admit that it is beyond his power to act against the will of God, and instead of cursing he blesses the people with special blessings and with a prophecy about their future. Another challenge, however, awaits the Israelites. They are drawn after the daughters of Moav, and their behavior has disastrous results, until Pinhas takes an extreme step to save the people.

Moav's Fear of Israel

The king of Moav, who sees how the Israelites easily conquered the Emorite kings in his vicinity, is overcome with fear. He turns to Bilam the sorcerer, and pleads with him to impose a curse upon them.

²**Balak son of Tzipor,** king of Moav, **saw all that Israel had done to the Emorites.** ³**Moav was very alarmed by the people because they were numerous, and,** furthermore, **Moav was disgusted by the children of Israel.** ⁴**Moav said to the elders,** the leaders **of Midyan,** with whom they were allied: **Now this** large **assembly** of Israel **will lick clean,** consume, **all** the food in **our surroundings, as the ox licks clean** and eats **the grass of the field. Balak son of Tzipor was king of Moav at that time.** ⁵**Therefore, he,** Balak, **sent messengers to Bilam son of Beor, to** a place called **Petor that is by the** Euphrates **River,** far north of Moav, **in the land of the members of his,** Balak's, **people, to summon him, saying: Behold, a people emerged from Egypt; behold, it has covered the face of the earth. And it,** this nation, **dwells** now **across from me.** ⁶**Now, please, come curse this people for me, as they are too mighty for me; perhaps I will be able to smite them. And I will drive them from the land, for I know that he whom you bless is blessed, and he whom you curse is cursed.** As a great sorcerer and prophet, your blessings and curses come to pass.

📖 **Further reading:** For more on the cooperation between Moav and Midyan, heretofore sworn enemies, see *A Concise Guide to the Sages*, p. 204.

Balak's Messengers Persuade Bilam

Balak's emissaries go off to bring Bilam, but they fail in their mission to persuade him to come and curse Israel. Bilam answers that he can only do what God commands, and He does not want Bilam to curse Israel. After additional entreaties, and after God allows him to go, he sets out, and then an angel of God reveals himself to Bilam, reproaches him, and reminds him that even though he is going on a mission organized by the Moavites, he must say only what God instructs him to say.

⁷**The elders of Moav and the elders of Midyan went with the tools of sorcery in their hand** to persuade Bilam to come back with them. **And they came to Bilam, and spoke to him the words of Balak.** ⁸**He,** Bilam, **said to them,** the elders of Moav and Midyan: **Spend the night here, and** in the morning **I will reply to you, as the Lord will speak to me** in a nightly vision. **The princes of Moav stayed** overnight **with Bilam.** ⁹Indeed, **God came to Bilam, and said: Who are these men with you?** ¹⁰**Bilam said to God: Balak son of Tzipor, king of Moav, sent** messengers **to me,** and they said: ¹¹**Behold the people that has come out of Egypt and it has covered the face of the earth; now, come curse them for me; perhaps I will be able to make war against them, and I will drive them away.** ¹²**God said to Bilam: You shall not go with them; you shall not** succeed in fulfilling Balak's desire to **curse the people, as it is blessed.**

cond aliya Fifth liya) ¹³**Bilam arose in the morning, and said to the princes of Balak: Go to your land, as the Lord refused to allow me to go with you.** ¹⁴**The princes of Moav rose, and they came to Balak, and they said: Bilam refused to go with us.** ¹⁵**Balak continued sending additional princes, more numerous and more prestigious than those** he had sent before. ¹⁶**They came to Bilam and said to him: So said Balak son of Tzipor: Please, do not refrain from going to me.** ¹⁷**For I will honor you greatly, and anything that you say to me I will do;** just **please go curse this people for me.** ¹⁸**Bilam answered and said to the servants of Balak:** Even **if Balak were to give me his house full of silver and gold, I would be unable to violate the directive of the Lord my God,** whether **to perform a small or a great matter.** ¹⁹**Now, please, you too, remain here also this night, and I will know more what the Lord will speak to me,** which I will relay to you. ²⁰**God came to Bilam at night, and He said** a different message **to him: If the people came to summon you,** then **rise, go with them. However, only the matter that I will speak to you shall you do.** You are permitted to go to Moav, but you are still obligated to fulfill My bidding.

Numbers

⊜ **Further reading:** For more on Bilam's character and abilities, see *A Concise Guide to the Sages*, p. 205.

The Journey to Balak

Bilam sets out with Balak's emissaries, but on the way it becomes clear to them that God alone will dictate the conditions of his mission.

Third aliya ²¹**Bilam arose in the morning, saddled his donkey,** readying it for the journey, **and went off with the princes of Moav.** ²²**God's wrath was enflamed because he was going, and the angel of the Lord stood on the way, as an impediment to him. He,** Bilam, **was riding on his donkey, and his two servants were with him.** ²³**The donkey saw the angel of the Lord standing on the way, and his sword was drawn in his hand. And the donkey turned from the way, and went into the field. Bilam struck the donkey, to turn it** back **to the way.** ²⁴**The angel of the Lord** then **stood in the** narrow **path of the vineyards, a** vineyard **fence on this side** of the path, **and a** vineyard **fence on that side** of the path, with the angel in between. ²⁵**The donkey saw the angel of the Lord, and it,** the donkey, **was pressed to the wall,** to bypass the angel, **and it pressed Bilam's foot against the wall; and he carried on striking it.** ²⁶**The angel of the Lord continued passing** before him, **and stood in a narrow place, where there is no way to turn right or left.** ²⁷**The donkey saw the angel of the Lord, and it lay down underneath Bilam,** with Bilam still upon it. **Bilam's wrath was enflamed, and he struck the donkey with the staff.** ²⁸**The Lord** then **opened the mouth of the donkey,** and enabled it to speak, **and it said to Bilam: What did I do to you that you struck me these three times?** ²⁹**Bilam said to the donkey: Because you abused** and afflicted **me; if only there were a sword in my hand, I would have killed you now.** ³⁰**The donkey said to Bilam: Am I not your donkey that you have ridden upon me from your start,** from your youth, **until this day? Have I made it a habit to do so,** to act in this manner, **to you? He said: No.**

³¹**The Lord uncovered the eyes of Bilam,** allowing him to see, **and he saw the angel of the Lord standing on the way, and his sword was drawn in his hand; he,** Bilam, **bowed his head, and he prostrated himself to him,** the angel. ³²**The angel of the Lord said to him: For what** reason **did you smite your donkey these three times? Behold, I came out to be an obstacle** and block your path, **because the path** that you have taken **was altered against me,** it is not good in my eyes. ³³**The donkey saw me, and turned from before me these three times; had it not turned from before**

Numbers

me, but continued to advance, **then now I would have indeed slain you
and spared it.** ³⁴**Bilam said to the angel of the Lord: I have sinned, for
I did not know that you were standing opposite me on the way; now, if
it,** my journey to Balak, **is wrong in your eyes, I will return** home. ³⁵**The
angel of the Lord said to Bilam: Go with the men,** as God said to you in
the nighttime vision; **but only the matter that I will speak to you shall
you speak. Bilam went** on **with the princes of Balak.**

Bilam's Prophecies

Balak is pleased that Bilam arrives to curse Israel, but he is quickly disappointed, for instead
of cursing the Jewish people, Bilam blesses them time after time. Prophecy rests upon
Bilam, and he even adds extra blessings on his own initiative.

³⁶**Balak heard** from messengers **that Bilam had come, and came out
to meet him, to the city of Moav,** the city **which is on the border of
the Arnon** Stream, **which is on the edge of the border.** ³⁷**Balak said to
Bilam: Did I not send to you to summon you** once before? **Why didn't
you come to me** on the first occasion? **Is it true that** you thought **I cannot**
properly **honor you?** ³⁸**Bilam said to Balak: Behold, I have come to you;
now,** what do you assume? **Will I be able to speak anything** that I choose?
The matter that God places in my mouth, that alone **I will** be able to

ırth
liya
ixth
ʾya)

speak; I am merely God's mouthpiece. ³⁹**Bilam went with Balak, and they
came to Kiryat Hutzot,** a large city. ⁴⁰**Balak slaughtered cattle and sheep,
and sent to Bilam and to the princes who were with him.**

⁴¹**It was in the morning, and Balak took Bilam, and brought him up
to the heights of Baal,** a ritual site dedicated to the service of Baal at the
top of a mountain, **and he saw from there the edge of** the camp of **the
23 people** of Israel. ¹**Bilam said to Balak: Build me,** right **here** and now, **seven altars, and prepare me here seven bulls and seven rams** as offerings.
²**Balak did as Bilam had spoken; Balak and Bilam** together **offered up
a bull and a ram on each altar.** ³**Bilam said to Balak: Stand with your
burnt offering** and wait for me, **and I will go** from here; **perhaps the Lord
will happen upon me** and reveal Himself to me, **and He will show me
some matter and I will tell you. He went** off **alone** quietly. ⁴**Indeed, God
happened upon Bilam, and he,** Bilam, **said to Him: The seven altars I
have prepared, and I offered up a bull and a ram on each altar.** ⁵**The
Lord placed speech in Bilam's mouth,** instructing him what to say, **and
He said: Return to Balak, and so,** as I have said to you, **you shall speak.**

Numbers

⁶**He returned to him, and behold, he,** Balak, **was standing with his burnt offering** next to the altar, **he, and all the princes of Moav.** ⁷**He launched his oration,** or his poetic allegory, **and said: From Aram,** as Bilam lived in Aram, **Balak leads me,** calls me, **the king of Moav from the highlands of the east,** saying: **Go, curse Jacob for me, and go, censure Israel;** issue pronouncements of rage against the nation of Israel. ⁸**How will I curse,** when **God has not cursed? How will I censure,** when **the Lord has not censured?** I am unable to fulfill Balak's request to curse and censure if God does not allow me to do so. ⁹**For from the top of precipices I will see it,** the nation of Israel, **and from hills I behold it. Behold, it is a people that shall dwell alone, and shall not be reckoned among the nations.** This people is not part of the family of nations. ¹⁰**Who has counted the dust of Jacob?** Who can count the descendants of Jacob? They are as numerous as the dust. **Or** who has **tallied** even **one quarter of Israel? Let me die the death of the upright, and let my end be like his,** like one of the children of Israel.

📖 **Further reading:** For suggested interpretations of Bilam's prophecies, see *A Concise Guide to the Sages,* p. 207; *A Concise Guide to Mahshava,* p. 210.

¹¹**Balak said to Bilam,** in shock: **What have you done to me? To curse my enemies I took you, and behold, you have blessed them.** ¹²**He,** Bilam, **answered and said: Is it not that which the Lord will place in my mouth, that I will take care to speak?** I cannot speak according to your will. ¹³**Balak said to him: Please, go with me to another place, that you may see them,** the Israelites, **from there; you will see only their edge, but you will not see all of them; curse them for me from there.** ¹⁴**He took him to the field of Tzofim,** again **to the top of the peak,** where he had a good view of the Israelites, **and he built seven altars, and offered up a bull and a ram on each altar.** ¹⁵**He said to Balak: Stand here** as you are, **with your burnt offering, and I will be happened upon there.** I will walk until I receive a prophecy. ¹⁶**The Lord happened upon Bilam, and** again **placed speech in his mouth, and said: Return to Balak, and so you shall speak.**

¹⁷**He came to him,** Balak, **and behold, he was standing with his burnt offering,** as Bilam had instructed, **and the princes of Moav** were there **with him. Balak said to him: What did the Lord speak?** ¹⁸**He launched his oration, and said: Rise, Balak, and hear; listen to me, son of Tzipor.** ¹⁹**God is not a man that He will lie** and not fulfill His promises, **or the son**

Fifth aliya

of man, who changes his mind, **that He will reconsider; will He say and not perform, or speak and not fulfill** His word? [20]**Behold,** says God, **for blessing I have taken him,** Bilam, **and he will bless, and I will not retract it.** [21]**One has not beheld evil in Jacob, and not seen sin in Israel.** When God looks upon His people, He sees nothing reprehensible in them. **The Lord his God is with him, and the blast of the King is in its midst.** [22]**It is God who took them out of Egypt.** He is exalted **as if He had the** great **horns of the wild ox.** [23]**For there is no divination** that can have an effect **in Jacob, and no sorcery in Israel.** No sorcery, divination, or magic that I might perform will have any effect upon Israel, as God sees no flaw in them. **Now, what God has** directly **wrought** in their regard **is what shall be said of Jacob and of Israel.** [24]**Behold, a people will rise like a great cat, and like a lion will raise itself; it will not lie** down again **until it will devour prey, and** until **the blood of the slain it will drink.**

[25]**Balak said to Bilam: Do not curse them; also do not bless them.** If you refuse to curse them, at least do not bless them. [26]**Bilam answered and said to Balak: Did I not speak to you** and warn you, **saying: Everything that the Lord speaks, that I will do?** [27]**Balak said to Bilam: Come, please, I will take you to another place; perhaps it will be proper in the eyes of God and you will curse it,** the people of Israel, **for me from there.** [28]**Balak took Bilam to the top of Peor,** once again to a mountain peak, **to one that overlooks upon the wilderness.** [29]**Yet** again, **Bilam said to Balak: Build me here seven altars, and prepare me here seven bulls and seven rams.** [30]**Balak did as Bilam said, and offered up a bull and a ram on each altar.**

Sixth aliya
(Seventh aliya)

24 [1]**Bilam saw that it was good in the eyes of the Lord to bless Israel, and** therefore **he did not go as each other time,** the two previous times, **toward a divination,** in the hope that God would reveal Himself to him in that manner, **but he set his face to the wilderness.** [2]**Bilam raised his eyes, and he saw Israel dwelling** quietly, ordered **according to its tribes, and** then **the spirit of God was upon him.** [3]**He launched his oration, and said: The utterance of Bilam son of Beor; the utterance of the open-eyed man** who sees. [4]**The utterance of one who hears the sayings of God; the vision of the Almighty he will see, he falls** when he receives a vision due to the overwhelming force of the prophecy, but nevertheless he receives the revelation **with uncovered eyes,** as the message is revealed to him: [5]**How goodly are your tents, Jacob, your dwellings, Israel.** [6]**Like streams they,** the tents of Israel, **diverged,** spreading out from one area to another, **like gardens** that thrive **beside a river; like marigolds planted**

Numbers

by the Lord, like cedars beside the water. ⁷Water will flow over from its, Israel's, drawings, from its wells, because they will be in such abundance, and its seed shall sprout and further spread in many waters; its king shall rise above and be stronger than Agag, king of the Amalekites, and its kingdom shall be exalted. ⁸God, who took it out of Egypt, is like the lofty, powerful, and prominent horns of the wild ox for it. He will consume nations of its adversaries; He will crush their bones, and break its arrows. ⁹It, Israel, crouched, it lay like a lion, and like a great cat, who shall rouse it? Nobody would dare provoke them, as those who bless you are blessed, and those who curse you are cursed.

¹⁰Balak's wrath was enflamed against Bilam, and he clapped his hands in despair, and Balak said to Bilam: I called you to curse my enemies and behold, you have blessed them these three times. ¹¹Now flee to your place. Go home. For I said that if you succeeded, I would honor you, and behold, the Lord, who speaks through your mouth, has precluded you from receiving honor. ¹²Bilam said to Balak: You have no cause to be angry with me, for did I not also speak to your messengers that you sent me, saying: ¹³Even if Balak gives me his house full of silver and gold, I will be unable to violate the directive of the Lord, to perform good or bad on my own; that which the Lord will speak, I will speak?

📖 **Further reading:** For more on curses that were transformed into blessings, see *A Concise Guide to the Sages*, p. 342.

Seventh aliya ¹⁴Now, behold, I am going to my people. However, come, I will advise you. I will tell you what this people will do to your people at the end of days. ¹⁵He launched his oration, and said: The utterance of Bilam son of Beor; the utterance of the open-eyed man. ¹⁶The utterance of one who hears the sayings of God and knows the knowledge of the Most High; he shall see the vision of the Almighty, he falls with uncovered eyes during his revelations. ¹⁷I see him in a vision of future events, but not now. I behold him, but he will not rise in the near future. A star, a sparkling leader, shall rise from Jacob, and a ruling scepter shall rise from Israel, and shall crush the outskirts of Moav, and destroy all the descendants of Seth, all of the other nations. ¹⁸Edom shall be a possession for Israel, and a possession shall be Se'ir, Edom, for Israel, as they are its enemies; Israel will achieve success. ¹⁹One ruler shall rule from Jacob, and will rid a remnant from the city, destroying the city to its foundations. ²⁰He saw Amalek and other nations from his lookout point, and he launched

his oration, and said: **Amalek was the first of the nations** to attack Israel; **and its end will be oblivion.** ²¹**He saw the Kenites,** Yitro's children and family, **and launched his oration, and said: Firm** and stable **is your dwelling. Place your nest in the rock,** from where it cannot be removed, as you are a friend of Israel. ²²**Nevertheless,** when **Kayin shall** eventually **be expelled, until when will Assyria take you captive?** You will be captured by Assyria only temporarily, and then you will return to your place. ²³**He launched his oration, and said: Alas, who shall live after God's implementation** of His plan? In those future days, distant nations will come to conquer the region: ²⁴**Seafarers** will emerge **from Kitim,** Rome or Greece, and they **will afflict Assyria, and afflict the riverbank,** the residents of the western side of the Euphrates River, **and** yet **it, too,** this nation that metes out affliction, **will end in oblivion.** ²⁵**Bilam rose, and went, and returned to his place** without receiving any reward, **and Balak too went on his way,** dissatisfied and frustrated.

The Daughters of Midyan

For the first time, the Israelites come into close contact with the peoples of the land. They cannot resist the temptation to adopt their gods and cohabit with their women. The situation reaches an extreme in the defiant conduct of one of the most distinguished members of the people when he brings the Midyanite woman to whom he had attached himself into the heart of the camp. Pinhas, the grandson of Aaron the High Priest, stabs him to death, and the plague that had begun to spread among the people is stopped.

25 ¹**Israel was living in Shitim,** a place near Moav, **and the people began to engage in licentiousness with the daughters of Moav.** ²As a result, **they,** the Midyanites, **invited the people,** the Israelites, **to the offerings of their gods; the people** participated in the idolatrous rites, **ate** of the offerings, **and prostrated themselves to their gods.** ³Ultimately, **Israel adhered to Baal Peor,** the Moavite god, **and the wrath of the Lord was enflamed against Israel,** for their licentiousness and idol worship. ⁴**The Lord said to Moses: Take all the leaders of the people** who participated in the sin, **and hang them for the Lord, opposite the sun,** in a public manner, **and** then **the enflamed wrath of the Lord will be withdrawn from Israel.** ⁵**Moses said to the judges,** the leaders **of Israel: Each of you, kill his men,** the members of his own tribe, **who are adhering to Baal Peor.** ⁶**Behold,** an important **man from the children of Israel came and brought near to his brethren the Midyanite woman** with whom he had become involved, and brought her to the tent, **before the eyes of Moses, and before the eyes of**

the entire congregation of the children of Israel. And they, the Israelites, were weeping at the entrance of the Tent of Meeting, feeling helpless *Maftir* and knowing not what to do. ⁷**Pinhas, son of Elazar, son of Aaron the High Priest, saw** this act, **and he rose from among the congregation, and he took a spear in his hand.** ⁸**He went after the man of Israel** who had brought the Midyanite woman **into the tent, and stabbed both of them** as they were engaged in the act, **the man of Israel, and the woman through her abdomen,** in the area of her sexual organs. **The plague,** which had started because of God's wrath, **was stopped from the children of Israel,** because of this stabbing. ⁹**Those who died in the plague were twenty-four thousand.**

> 📖 **Further reading:** A midrash suggests that Bilam was the one who recommended tempting the people to sin; see *A Concise Guide to the Sages*, p. 208.

Numbers

Parashat Pinhas

Pinhas, whose act of zealotry was related at the end of the previous Torah portion, receives his reward. As the conclusion of the wilderness era approaches and the tribal portions are allotted, the people are counted again. The daughters of Tzelofhad, who had no sons, demand the right to inherit from their father, and thereby establish a precedent for the generations. In preparation for their entry into the land, Joshua is ordained by Moses to lead the people. The second half of the Torah portion lists in detail the fixed communal offerings to be brought on weekdays, Shabbatot, *Rosh Hodesh*, and festivals.

Reward for the Act of Zealotry

At the end of the previous Torah portion, the Torah related the sin of the Israelites with the daughters of Midyan, and the act of Pinhas, who was zealous on behalf of God and killed the leaders of the sinners. Here, Pinhas receives praise from God for his action, and the priesthood is granted to him and his family.

[10]The Lord spoke to Moses, saying: [11]Pinhas, son of Elazar, son of Aaron the priest, has caused My wrath to be withdrawn from the children of Israel, in that he was zealous on my behalf among them; so that I did not destroy the children of Israel in My zealotry. [12]Therefore, say: Behold, I am giving him My covenant of peace. [13]It shall be for him, and for his descendants after him, a covenant of an eternal priesthood, because he was zealous for his God, and he atoned for the children of Israel. [14]The name of the man of Israel who was slain, who was slain with the Midyanite woman, was Zimri son of Salu, prince of a patrilineal house of the Simeonites. [15]The name of the Midyanite woman who was slain was Kozbi daughter of Tzur; he was tribal head of a significant patrilineal house in Midyan.

[16]The Lord spoke to Moses, saying: [17]Bear enmity to the Midyanites, and smite them, [18]because they are enemies to you, with their deceits that they deceived you in the matter of Peor, and in the matter of Kozbi, daughter of the prince of Midyan, their sister, who was slain on the day of the plague in the matter of Peor.

📖 **Further reading:** The people reacted negatively to Pinhas's action. For God's response, see *A Concise Guide to the Sages*, p. 209.

The Census of the People

After the plague that killed many, and in preparation for entry into the land, Moses and Elazar are commanded to again count the Israelites, just as they were counted at the beginning of their time in the wilderness. This census was to be a determining factor in the allotment of tribal portions after the conquest of the land.

26 ¹**It was after the plague, and the Lord said to Moses and to Elazar son of Aaron the priest, saying:** ²**Take a census of the entire congregation of the children of Israel, from twenty years old and above, by their patrilineal house, all those fit for military service in Israel.** ³**Moses and Elazar the priest spoke with them on the plains of Moav along the Jordan, opposite Jericho, saying:** ⁴**From twenty years old and above, as the Lord had commanded Moses and the children of Israel when coming out from the land of Egypt;**

Second aliya ⁵**Reuben, the firstborn of Israel: The sons of Reuben: Hanokh, the family of the Hanokhites; for Palu, the family of the Paluites;** ⁶**for Hetzron, the family of the Hetzronites; for Karmi, the family of the Karmites.** ⁷**These are the families of the Reubenites; those counted were forty-three thousand seven hundred and thirty.** ⁸**And the sons of Palu: Eliav.** ⁹**And the sons of Eliav** were **Nemuel, Datan, and Aviram. This is Datan and Aviram, the distinguished of the congregation, who incited against Moses and against Aaron in the congregation of Korah, when they incited against the Lord.** ¹⁰**The earth opened its mouth, and swallowed them and Korah, with the death of the congregation, when the fire devoured two hundred and fifty men, and they became a sign.** ¹¹**The sons of Korah,** who did not participate in the dispute, **did not die.**

📖 **Further reading:** The story of Korah's challenge to authority appears above, from p. 380.

¹²**The sons of Simeon by their families: for Nemuel, the family of the Nemuelites; for Yamin, the family of the Yaminites; for Yakhin, the family of the Yakhinites;** ¹³**for Zerah, the family of the Zerahites; for Shaul, the family of the Shaulites.** ¹⁴**These are the families of the Simeonites, twenty-two thousand two hundred.**

¹⁵**The sons of Gad by their families: for Tzefon, the family of the Tzefonites; for Hagi, the family of the Hagites; for Shuni, the family of the Shunites;** ¹⁶**for Ozni, the family of the Oznites; for Eri, the family**

of the Erites; [17]for Arod, the family of the Arodites; for Areli, the family of the Arelites. [18]These are the families of the sons of Gad by their count, forty thousand five hundred.

[19]The sons of Judah: Er and Onan. Er and Onan died in the land of Canaan, before Jacob and his family descended to Egypt. [20]The sons of Judah by their families were: for Shela, the family of the Shelanites; for Peretz, the family of the Peretzites; for Zerah, the family of the Zerahites. [21]The sons of Peretz were for Hetzron, the family of the Hetzronites; for Hamul, the family of the Hamulites. [22]These are the families of Judah by their count, seventy-six thousand five hundred.

[23]The sons of Issachar by their families: for Tola, the family of the Tola'ites; for Puva, the family of the Punites; [24]for Yashuv, the family of the Yashuvites; for Shimron, the family of the Shimronites. [25]These are the families of Issachar by their count, sixty-four thousand three hundred.

[26]The sons of Zebulun by their families: for Sered, the family of the Seredites; for Elon, the family of the Elonites; for Yahle'el, the family of the Yahle'elites. [27]These are the families of the Zebulunites by their count, sixty thousand five hundred.

[28]The sons of Joseph by their families: Manasseh and Ephraim. [29]The sons of Manasseh: for Makhir, the family of the Makhirites, and Makhir begot Gilad; for Gilad, the family of the Giladites. [30]These are the sons of Gilad: for Iezer, the family of the Iezerites; for Helek, the family of the Helekites; [31]Asriel, the family of the Asrielites; Shekhem, the family of the Shekhemites; [32]Shemida, the family of the Shemida'ites; Hefer, the family of the Heferites. [33]Tzelofhad son of Hefer did not have sons, but daughters. The names of the daughters of Tzelofhad were Mahla, Noa, Hogla, Milka, and Tirtza. [34]These are the families of Manasseh; those counted were fifty-two thousand seven hundred.

[35]These are the sons of Ephraim by their families: for Shutelah, the family of the Shutelahites; for Bekher, the family of the Bekherites; for Tahan, the family of the Tahanites. [36]These are the sons of Shutelah: for Eran, the family of the Eranites. [37]These are the families of the sons of Ephraim by their count, thirty-two thousand five hundred. These are the sons of Joseph by their families.

[38]The sons of Benjamin by their families: for Bela, the family of the Bela'ites; for Ashbel, the family of the Ashbelites; for Ahiram, the

family of the Ahiramites; ³⁹for Shefufam, the family of the Shufamites; for Hufam, the family of the Hufamites. ⁴⁰The sons of Bela were Ard and Naaman; the family of the Ardites; for Naaman, the family of the Naamites. ⁴¹These are the sons of Benjamin by their families; and their counted were forty-five thousand six hundred.

⁴²These are the sons of Dan by their families: for Shuham, the family of the Shuhamites. These are the families of Dan by their families. ⁴³All the families of the Shuhamites, by their count, were sixty-four thousand four hundred.

⁴⁴The sons of Asher by their families: for Yimna, the family of the Yimnites; for Yishvi, the family of the Yishvites; for Beria, the family of the Beriites. ⁴⁵For the sons of Beria: for Hever, the family of the Heverites; for Malkiel, the family of the Malkielites. ⁴⁶The name of the daughter of Asher: Serah. ⁴⁷These are the families of the sons of Asher by their count, fifty-three thousand four hundred.

⁴⁸The sons of Naphtali by their families: for Yahtze'el, the family of the Yahtze'elites; for Guni, the family of the Gunites; ⁴⁹for Yetzer, the family of the Yetzerites; for Shilem, the family of the Shilemites. ⁵⁰These are the families of Naphtali by their families; their counted were forty-five thousand four hundred.

⁵¹These are the counted of the children of Israel, six hundred thousand one thousand seven hundred and thirty.

Third aliya ⁵²The Lord spoke to Moses, saying: ⁵³To these families the land shall be divided as an inheritance, according to the number of names. ⁵⁴To the greater in number you shall increase its inheritance, and to the lesser in number you shall decrease its inheritance; each, according to its counted, its inheritance shall be given. ⁵⁵However, by lot the land shall be divided; according to the names of the tribes of their fathers they shall inherit. ⁵⁶Their inheritance shall be divided by lot whether the many or the few.

The Number of the Levites

The members of the tribe of Levi are not allotted a tribal portion in the Land of Israel and are counted separately.

⁵⁷These are the counted of the Levites according to their families: for Gershon, the family of the Gershonites; for Kehat, the family of the Kehatites; for Merari, the family of the Merarites. ⁵⁸These are

the families of Levi: the family of the Livnites, the family of the Hebronites, the family of the Mahlites, the family of the Mushites, the family of the Korahites. Kehat begot Amram. ⁵⁹The name of Amram's wife was Yokheved daughter of Levi, who was born to Levi in Egypt; she bore to Amram: Aaron, Moses, and Miriam their sister. ⁶⁰To Aaron were born: Nadav, Avihu, Elazar, and Itamar. ⁶¹Nadav and Avihu died when they offered strange fire before the Lord. ⁶²Those counted were twenty-three thousand, each male from one month old and above. For they, the Levites, were not counted among the children of Israel, as no inheritance was given to them among the children of Israel.

⁶³These are the counted of Moses and Elazar the priest, who counted the children of Israel on the plains of Moav by the Jordan opposite Jericho. ⁶⁴Among these there was not a man still alive from the counted of Moses and Aaron the priest, who counted the children of Israel in the wilderness of Sinai prior to the sin of the scouts. ⁶⁵As the Lord said of them: They will die in the wilderness. No man was left of them, except Caleb son of Yefuneh, and Joshua son of Nun.

Tzelofhad's Daughters

Tzelofhad had died with no sons to inherit land on behalf of his family. His daughters seek to establish a precedent and inherit themselves. Their request is brought before God, and is granted, establishing a legal precedent for the generations.

27 ¹The daughters of Tzelofhad son of Hefer, son of Gilad, son of Makhir, son of Manasseh, from the families of Manasseh son of Joseph, approached; these are the names of his daughters: Mahla, Noa, Hogla, Milka, and Tirtza. ²They stood before Moses, before Elazar the priest, before the princes and the entire congregation, at the entrance of the Tent of Meeting, saying: ³Our father died in the wilderness, and he was not among the congregation of those who congregated against the Lord in the congregation of Korah, as he died for his own sin; and he had no sons. ⁴Why should the name of our father be subtracted from among his family because he had no son? Give us a portion among the brothers of our father. ⁵Moses brought their case before the Lord.

ourth
aliya
⁶The Lord spoke to Moses, saying: ⁷The daughters of Tzelofhad speak justly: You shall give them a portion for inheritance among their father's brothers and you shall convey the inheritance of their father to them. ⁸To the children of Israel, you shall speak, saying: If a man will die, and he has no son, you shall convey his inheritance to his daughter.

Numbers

⁹If he has no daughter, you shall give his inheritance to his brothers. ¹⁰If he has no brothers, you shall give his inheritance to his father's brothers. ¹¹If his father has no brothers, you shall give his inheritance to his next of kin from his family, and he shall take possession of it. It shall be for the children of Israel a statute of justice, as the Lord had commanded Moses.

Passing the Leadership to Joshua

It had been decreed that Moses would not enter the land in the wake of his sin with the waters of dispute. Now, with his death approaching, he requests of God that he appoint a man worthy of leading the people in his place; Joshua is appointed and ordained to assume that position.

¹²The Lord said to Moses: Ascend to this highlands of Avarim, from which there is a view in many directons [avarim], and see the land that I have given to the children of Israel. ¹³You will see it, and you also will be gathered to your people, as Aaron your brother was gathered, ¹⁴because you defied My directive in the wilderness of Tzin, in the dispute of the congregation, to sanctify Me with the water before their eyes. It is the water of dispute in Kadesh in the wilderness of Tzin.

¹⁵Moses spoke to the Lord, saying: ¹⁶May the Lord, God of the spirits of all flesh, appoint a man over the congregation ¹⁷who will go out before them to war, who will come before them, who will take them out, and who will bring them in, so that the congregation of the Lord will not be like a flock that has no shepherd. ¹⁸The Lord said to Moses: Take you Joshua son of Nun, a man in whom there is spirit, the appropriate temperament, and lay your hand upon him to transfer your authority to him. ¹⁹Stand him before Elazar the priest, and before the entire congregation, and command him before their eyes, so that they will accept his leadership. ²⁰You shall confer from your grandeur, your radiant face and your prophetic spirit, upon him, so that the entire congregation of the children of Israel will heed, and accept his leadership. ²¹Before Elazar the priest he shall stand, and he, Elazar, will inquire for him, Joshua, regarding the judgment of the Urim before the Lord; at his, Elazar's, directive they shall go out to war, and at his directive they shall come, he and all the children of Israel with him, and the entire congregation. ²²Moses did as the Lord had commanded him; he took Joshua, and stood him before Elazar the priest, and before the entire congregation. ²³He laid

his hands upon him, and commanded him, as the Lord spoke at the hand of Moses.

📖 **Further reading:** For more on the laws of inheritance and the proper way to write a will, see *A Concise Guide to Halakha*, p. 75.

Communal Offerings

From this point until the end of the *parasha*, the Torah addresses the matter of the fixed communal offerings brought in the Tabernacle, beginning with the continual offering, sacrificed twice daily, and continuing with the offerings brought on Shabbat and *Rosh Hodesh* and festivals throughout the year.

28 ¹The Lord spoke to Moses, saying: ²Command the children of Israel,
Fifth aliya and say to them: My offering, My food for My fires, burned on the altar, My pleasing aroma; you shall take care to present to Me at its appointed time. ³You shall say to them: This is the fire offering that you shall bring to the Lord: Unblemished lambs in the first year, two each day, a continual burnt offering. ⁴The one lamb you shall offer in the morning, and the second lamb you shall offer in the afternoon. ⁵Bring with it one-tenth of an ephah of choice flour as a meal offering, mixed with one-fourth of a hin of high quality virgin oil. ⁶It is a continual burnt offering that was done at Mount Sinai, as a pleasing aroma, a fire offering to the Lord. ⁷And its libation is one-fourth of a hin for the one lamb; in the holy place, pour a libation of intoxicating drink, wine, to the Lord. ⁸The other lamb you shall offer in the afternoon; like the meal offering of the morning, and like its libation, you shall offer a fire offering of a pleasing aroma to the Lord.

⁹On the Sabbath day, two unblemished lambs in the first year, two-tenths of an ephah of choice flour as a meal offering, mixed with oil, and its libation. ¹⁰This is the burnt offering of each Sabbath on its Sabbath, with the continual burnt offering and its libation.

¹¹On your New Moons you shall present a burnt offering to the Lord: Two young bulls, and one ram, and seven lambs in the first year, unblemished. ¹²Three-tenths of an ephah of choice flour as a meal offering, mixed with oil, for each bull, and two-tenths of an ephah of choice flour as a meal offering, mixed with oil, for the one ram. ¹³One-tenth of an ephah of choice flour mixed with oil as a meal offering for each lamb; a burnt offering of a pleasing aroma, a fire offering to the Lord. ¹⁴Their libations shall be one-half of a hin of wine for a bull, and one-third of

a hin for the ram, and one-fourth of a hin for a lamb. This is the burnt offering of the New Moon for each New Moon for the months of the year. ¹⁵One goat shall be as a sin offering to the Lord; with the continual burnt offering and its libation it shall be offered.

Sixth
aliya

¹⁶In the first month, Nisan, on the fourteenth day of the month, is the paschal lamb offered to the Lord. ¹⁷On the fifteenth day of that month shall be a festival; seven days unleavened bread shall be eaten. ¹⁸On the first day there shall be a holy convocation of the nation: You shall not perform any toilsome labor. ¹⁹You shall present a fire offering, a burnt offering to the Lord: Two young bulls, and one ram, and seven lambs in the first year; they shall be unblemished for you; ²⁰and their meal offering: Choice flour mixed with oil; three-tenths for a bull, and two-tenths for the ram; ²¹one-tenth shall you offer for each lamb for the seven lambs. ²²And one goat as a sin offering, to atone for you. ²³Besides the burnt offering of the morning that is for the continual burnt offering, you shall offer these. ²⁴Like these you shall offer for each day, for seven days: It is the food of the fire offering, a pleasing aroma to the Lord; with the continual burnt offering, and its libation, it shall be offered. ²⁵On the seventh day, it shall be a holy convocation for you; you shall not perform any toilsome labor.

²⁶On the day of the first fruits, when you present a new meal offering to the Lord, the offering of the two loaves, which is the first offering of the year that is brought from the new crop of wheat, on your Festival of Weeks [Shavuot], at the conclusion of the seven-week counting of the omer, it shall be a holy convocation for you; you shall not perform any toilsome labor. ²⁷You shall present a burnt offering for a pleasing aroma to the Lord: Two young bulls, one ram, and seven lambs in the first year; ²⁸and their meal offering: Choice flour mixed with oil, three-tenths for each bull, two-tenths for the one ram, ²⁹one-tenth for each lamb for the seven lambs; ³⁰and one goat, to atone for you. ³¹Besides the continual burnt offering, and its meal offering, you shall offer these; they shall be unblemished for you, and their libations.

29 ¹In the seventh month, Tishrei, on the first of the month, Rosh HaShana, it shall be a holy convocation for you; you shall not perform any toilsome labor; a day of sounding the alarm with the shofar it shall be for you. ²You shall perform a burnt offering for a pleasing aroma to the Lord: One young bull, one ram, and seven lambs in the first year, unblemished; ³and their meal offering: Choice flour mixed with oil,

three-tenths for the bull, two-tenths for the ram, ⁴and one-tenth for each lamb for the seven lambs, ⁵and one goat as a sin offering, to atone for you. ⁶These are besides the burnt offering of the New Moon and its meal offering, as this festival occurs on the first of the month, and the continual burnt offering and its meal offering, and their libations, in accordance with their ordinance, for a pleasing aroma, a fire offering to the Lord.

⁷On the tenth of this seventh month, Yom Kippur, it shall be a holy convocation for you; you shall afflict your souls by fasting and other afflictions; you shall not perform any labor. ⁸You shall present a burnt offering to the Lord, a pleasing aroma: One young bull, one ram, and seven lambs in the first year, unblemished. ⁹And their meal offering: Choice flour mixed with oil, three-tenths for the bull, two-tenths for the one ram, ¹⁰one-tenth for each lamb for the seven lambs. ¹¹One goat as a sin offering, besides the bull and goat brought as a sin offering of atonement, and the continual burnt offering, and its meal offering, and their libations.

eventh
aliya ¹²On the fifteenth day of the seventh month it shall be a holy convocation, *Sukkot,* for you; you shall not perform any toilsome labor, and you shall celebrate a festival to the Lord seven days. ¹³You shall present a burnt offering, a fire offering, a pleasing aroma to the Lord: Thirteen young bulls, two rams, fourteen lambs of the first year, they shall be unblemished; ¹⁴and their meal offering: Choice flour mixed with oil, three-tenths for each bull for the thirteen bulls, two-tenths for each ram for the two rams, ¹⁵and one-tenth for each lamb for the fourteen lambs. ¹⁶And one goat as a sin offering; besides the continual burnt offering, its meal offering, and its libation.

📖 **Further reading:** For more on the significance of the *Sukkot* offerings, see *A Concise Guide to the Sages,* p. 294.

¹⁷On the second day, twelve young bulls, two rams, fourteen lambs in the first year, unblemished; ¹⁸and their meal offering and their libations for the bulls, for the rams, and for the lambs, according to their number, in accordance with the ordinance. ¹⁹And one goat as a sin offering; besides the continual burnt offering, and its meal offering, and their libations.

Numbers

²⁰On the third day, eleven bulls, two rams, fourteen lambs in the first year, unblemished; ²¹and their meal offering and their libations for the bulls, for the rams, and for the lambs, according to their number, in accordance with the ordinance. ²²And one goat as a sin offering; besides the continual burnt offering, and its meal offering, and its libation.

²³On the fourth day, ten bulls, two rams, fourteen lambs in the first year, unblemished; ²⁴their meal offering and their libations for the bulls, for the rams, and for the lambs, according to their number, in accordance with the ordinance. ²⁵And one goat as a sin offering; besides the continual burnt offering, its meal offering, and its libation.

²⁶On the fifth day, nine bulls, two rams, fourteen lambs in the first year, unblemished; ²⁷and their meal offering and their libations for the bulls, for the rams, and for the lambs, according to their number, in accordance with the ordinance. ²⁸And one goat as a sin offering; besides the continual burnt offering, and its meal offering, and its libation.

²⁹On the sixth day, eight bulls, two rams, fourteen lambs in the first year, unblemished; ³⁰and their meal offering and their libations for the bulls, for the rams, and for the lambs, according to their number, in accordance with the ordinance. ³¹And one goat as a sin offering; besides the continual burnt offering, and its meal offering, and its libations.

³²On the seventh day, seven bulls, two rams, fourteen lambs in the first year, unblemished; ³³and their meal offering and their libations for the bulls, for the rams, and for the lambs, according to their number, in accordance with their ordinance. ³⁴And one goat for a sin offering; besides the continual burnt offering, its meal offering, and its libation.

Maftir ³⁵On the eighth [shemini] day it shall be an assembly [atzeret] for you, an additional festival day, Shemini Atzeret; you shall not perform any toilsome labor. ³⁶You shall present a burnt offering, a fire offering, a pleasing aroma to the Lord: One bull, one ram, seven lambs in the first year, unblemished; ³⁷their meal offering and their libations for the bull, for the ram, and for the lambs, according to their number, in accordance with the ordinance. ³⁸And one goat as a sin offering; besides the continual burnt offering, and its meal offering, and its libation.

³⁹These communal offerings you shall offer to the Lord in your appointed times, besides your vows, and your pledges, for your burnt offerings, and for your meal offerings, and for your libations, and for your peace

30 offerings. ¹Moses said to the children of Israel in accordance with everything that the Lord commanded Moses.

📖 **Further reading:** For more on the festival of *Shemini Atzeret* and its laws, see *A Concise Guide to Halakha*, p. 221.

Parashat Matot

The *parasha* opens with the laws of vows. Next, we read about the war of vengeance against Midyan, which was the final task that was incumbent upon Moses to carry out before his death.The *parasha* concludes with the request of the Reubenites and the Gadites to receive their tribal lands east of the Jordan, and Moses' agreement provided they first participate in the conquest of the land.

The Laws of Vows

A person may assume commitments beyond those required by the Torah by taking a vow or oath, and these are as binding as Torah prohibitions. However, when a young woman takes a vow, her father has the power to nullify it. Moreover, when a married woman takes a vow that involves her afflicting herself, or otherwise affects her relationship with her husband, he can nullify it as long as he does so on the same day he hears about it.

²Moses spoke to the heads of the tribes of the children of Israel saying: This is the matter that the Lord commanded. ³If a man takes a vow to the Lord to give something to God, or to do something for Him, **or takes an oath to impose a prohibition upon himself, he shall not profane his word, he shall act in accordance with everything that emerges from his mouth.**

📖 **Further reading:** For more on vows and the importance of being careful with them, see *A Concise Guide to the Sages*, p. 213.

⁴If a woman takes a vow to the Lord and imposes a prohibition upon herself **in her father's house,** unmarried, **in her youth, ⁵and her father hears her vow and her prohibition that she imposed upon herself, and her father keeps silent toward her,** not expressing opposition to the vow, **all her vows shall be upheld, and every prohibition that she imposed upon herself shall be upheld,** and obligate her. **⁶But if her father prevented her,** nullifying her vow **on the day of his hearing, all her vows and her prohibitions that she imposed upon herself shall not be upheld,** they are voided; **and the Lord will forgive her because her father prevented**

her, i.e., she is not liable if she behaves in a manner inconsistent with her vow since her father has voided it.

⁷**If** a young woman vows, and then **she is** betrothed **to a husband, and her vows are upon her, or the expression of her lips with which she prohibited herself,** ⁸**and her husband hears** of those vows, **and keeps silent toward her on the day of his hearing, her vows shall be upheld, and her prohibitions that she imposed upon herself shall be upheld.** ⁹**But if, on the day of her husband's hearing, he prevents her and nullifies her vow that is upon her, or the expression of her lips that she imposed upon herself, the Lord will forgive her.** ¹⁰**But the vow of a widow or a divorcée,** such a woman not being subject to the authority of her father or her husband; **anything that she imposed upon herself shall be upheld for her.**

¹¹**If she vowed in her husband's house,** after marriage, **or imposed a prohibition upon herself with an oath,** ¹²**and her husband heard and kept silent toward her, he did not prevent her, then all her vows shall be upheld, and every prohibition that she imposed upon herself shall be upheld.** ¹³**But if her husband nullifies them on the day of his hearing, anything that emerges from her lips for her vows or for the prohibitions of herself shall not be upheld: Her husband has nullified them and the Lord will forgive her.** ¹⁴**Every vow and every oath of prohibition to afflict the soul, her husband shall uphold it, and her husband shall nullify it.** ¹⁵**But if her husband keeps silent toward her from day to day, and he upholds all her vows, or all her prohibitions that are upon her, he has upheld them,** and the vows can no longer be nullified, **because he kept silent toward her on the day that he heard them.** ¹⁶**But if he nullifies them after** the day of **his hearing** them, **he shall bear her iniquity.**

¹⁷**These are the statutes that the Lord commanded Moses, between a man and his wife, between a father and his daughter, in her youth, in her father's house.**

The War against Midyan

Moses' final task as the leader of the children of Israel is to send them to fight against Midyan, to take vengeance for the Midyanites' seduction of the Israelites at Baal Peor. The war and the details of the division of the spoils are described in detail.

31 ¹**The Lord spoke to Moses, saying:** ²**Execute the children of Israel's vengeance against the Midyanites** for the episode with the Midyanite women at Baal Peor (chap. 25); **then you shall be gathered to your people,** i.e.,

die. ³Moses spoke to the people, saying: Select from among you men for the army, and they shall be against Midyan, to execute the vengeance of the Lord against Midyan. ⁴One thousand from each tribe, from all the tribes of Israel, you shall send to the army. ⁵One thousand per tribe from the thousands of Israel were provided; twelve thousand mobilized soldiers. ⁶Moses sent them, one thousand per tribe, to the army, them and Pinhas son of Elazar the priest, to the army, with the holy vessels and the trumpets of alarm in his hand. ⁷They campaigned against Midyan as the Lord had commanded Moses, and they killed every male. ⁸They killed the kings of Midyan among those they slayed: Evi, Rekem, Tzur, Hur, and Reva, the five kings of Midyan; and Bilam son of Beor, they killed with the sword. ⁹The children of Israel took the women of Midyan and their children captive; all their animals, all their livestock, and all their wealth, they looted. ¹⁰All their cities, in their dwellings and all their fortresses, they burned with fire. ¹¹They took all the spoils and all the plunder of man and of animal. ¹²They brought these to Moses and to Elazar the priest and to the congregation of the children of Israel; the captives, the plunder, and the spoils, to the camp, to the plains of Moav, which are along the Jordan at Jericho.

Third aliya (Second aliya) ¹³Moses, Elazar the priest, and all the princes of the congregation came out toward them, to outside the camp. ¹⁴Moses became angry at the commanders of the army, the officers of the thousands and the officers of the hundreds, who came from the army of the battle. ¹⁵Moses said to them: Did you keep all the females alive? ¹⁶Behold, they were for the children of Israel, by the word of Bilam, the cause to commit trespass against the Lord in the matter of Peor, and the result was that the plague was among the congregation of the Lord. ¹⁷Now, kill every male among the children, and kill every woman who has reached the appropriate age to have known a man by lying with a male. ¹⁸However, all the children among the women, who have not reached the appropriate age to have known lying with a male, keep alive for yourselves as captives. ¹⁹And you, encamp outside the camp seven days; anyone who killed a person and anyone who touched a dead body shall purify yourselves with the waters of purification of the red heifer, on the third day and on the seventh day, you and your captives. ²⁰Every garment, every vessel of hide, anything fabricated from goats, and every wooden vessel that was similarly impurified, you shall purify.

²¹Elazar the priest said to the men of the army who came to the battle: This is the statute of the law that the Lord has commanded Moses: ²²Even the gold, the silver, the bronze, the iron, the tin, and the lead vessels; ²³everything that comes through fire, every utensil that comes into direct contact with fire, you shall pass through fire, and it shall thereby be purified; all traces of non-kosher food that had been absorbed into it will be purged. However, it shall also be purified from ritual impurity with the water of sprinkling, the waters of purification; and everything that does not come through fire, you shall pass through water, purge it with boiling water. ²⁴You shall wash your garments on the seventh day, and you shall be purified, and only then you shall come to the camp.

📖 Further reading: The halakhot of rendering vessels kosher and immersing them are derived from these verses; see A Concise Guide to Halakha, pp. 560ff.

Fourth aliya ²⁵The Lord spoke to Moses, saying: ²⁶Take a census of the plunder of the captives, of human and of animal; you, Elazar the priest, and the clan heads of the congregation. ²⁷You shall divide the plunder in half, between those who took part in the war, who went out with the army, and the entire congregation. ²⁸You shall separate a levy to the Lord from the men of war that go out with the army: One individual from each five hundred, from the persons, from the cattle, from the donkeys, and from the flocks; ²⁹from their half, you shall take one five-hundredth and give it to Elazar the priest, a gift for the Lord. ³⁰From the half of the children of Israel, you shall take one part drawn from fifty, from the persons, from the cattle, from the donkeys, from the flocks, from all the animals, and you shall give them to the Levites, keepers of the commission of the Tabernacle of the Lord. ³¹Moses and Elazar the priest did as the Lord had commanded Moses.

³²The plunder, not including the rest of the loot, smaller items that the men of the army looted for themselves and weren't brought before Moses for the separation of the tax, was: flocks, six hundred and seventy-five thousand; ³³and cattle, seventy-two thousand; ³⁴and donkeys, sixty-one thousand; ³⁵and human beings, from the women who had not known lying with a male, thirty-two thousand. ³⁶The half, the portion of those who went out in the army, the number of the flock was three hundred thirty-seven thousand five hundred. ³⁷The levy to the Lord from the sheep was six hundred and seventy-five. ³⁸And the cattle, thirty-six thousand, and their levy to the Lord, seventy-two. ³⁹And

the donkeys, thirty thousand five hundred, and their levy to the Lord, sixty-one. ⁴⁰And human beings, sixteen thousand, and their levy to the Lord, thirty-two people.

⁴¹Moses gave the levy, the gift to the Lord, to Elazar the priest, as the Lord had commanded Moses. ⁴²And from the half of the plunder to be given to the children of Israel, that Moses had divided, taken, from the men who campaigned, ⁴³the half of the congregation, from the flock was three hundred thirty-seven thousand five hundred; ⁴⁴and cattle, thirty-six thousand; ⁴⁵and donkeys, thirty thousand five hundred; ⁴⁶and human beings, sixteen thousand. ⁴⁷Moses took from the half of the children of Israel the one drawn from fifty, from the humans and from the animals, and he gave them to the Levites, keepers of the commission of the Tabernacle of the Lord, as the Lord had commanded Moses.

Fifth aliya

⁴⁸Those appointed over the thousands of the army, the officers of thousands and the officers of hundreds, approached Moses. ⁴⁹They said to Moses: Your servants took a census of the men of war in our charge, and not one man is missing from us. ⁵⁰We have brought the offering of the Lord: Any man who found a gold ornament, a bangle or a bracelet, a ring, an earring, or a girdle, has brought it to atone for our souls before the Lord, for miraculously delivering us. ⁵¹Moses and Elazar the priest took the gold from them, all wrought vessels. ⁵²All the gold of the gift that they donated to the Lord was sixteen thousand seven hundred and fifty shekels, from the officers of the thousands, and from the officers of the hundreds. ⁵³Each of the rest of the men of the army looted for himself. ⁵⁴Moses and Elazar the priest took the gold of the officers of the thousands and of the hundreds and brought it to the Tent of Meeting, a remembrance for the children of Israel before the Lord.

The Gadites and the Reubenites

The Gadites and the Reubenites seek to receive their tribal portion east of the Jordan. Their wish is granted, provided that they join the rest of the people in the conquest of the land first, and return to their assigned tribal lands only when the conquest has been completed.

32 ¹The children of Reuben and the children of Gad had much livestock; it was very considerable. They saw the land of Yazer and the land of Gilad, and behold, the place was a good place for the grazing of livestock. ²The children of Gad and the children of Reuben came and said

Sixth aliya
(Third aliya)

to Moses, to Elazar the priest, and to the princes of the congregation, saying: [3]Atarot, Divon, Yazer, Nimra, Heshbon, Elaleh, Sevam, Nevo, and Beon, [4]the land that the Lord smote before the congregation of Israel, it is a land of livestock, and your servants have livestock.

[5]They said: If we have found favor in your eyes, may this land be given to your servants as an ancestral portion; do not take us across the Jordan.

[6]Moses said to the children of Gad and to the children of Reuben: Will your brethren go to the war, and you will sit here? [7]And why will you dishearten the children of Israel from crossing into the land that the Lord has given them? [8]So did your fathers, the spies, when I sent them from Kadesh Barnea to see the land. [9]They went up until the Eshkol Ravine, and they saw the land, and they disheartened the children of Israel, so as not to come to the land that the Lord had given them. [10]The Lord's anger was enflamed on that day, and He took an oath, saying: [11]The men who came up from Egypt, from twenty years old and above, shall not see the land about which I took an oath to Abraham, to Isaac, and to Jacob, because they did not wholeheartedly follow Me, [12]except Caleb son of Yefuneh the Kenizite, and Joshua son of Nun; because they wholeheartedly followed the Lord. [13]The Lord's anger was enflamed against Israel, and He caused them to wander in the wilderness forty years, until the end of the entire generation that did evil in the eyes of the Lord. [14]And behold, you have risen in place of your fathers, a breed of sinful men, to further exacerbate the enflamed wrath of the Lord against Israel. [15]If you will turn from following Him, He will continue to leave them in the wilderness, and so you will bring harm to this entire people.

[16]They approached him, Moses, and said: We will build sheep enclosures for our livestock here, and cities, for our children. [17]And we will swiftly set out as a vanguard before the children of Israel, until we have taken them to their place; our children shall live in the fortified cities, due to the inhabitants of the land. [18]We will not return to our homes until each of the children of Israel has inherited his inheritance, [19]as we will not inherit with them across the Jordan and beyond, as our inheritance has come to us on the east side of the Jordan.

Numbers

²⁰Moses said to them: If you will do this matter; if you will be a vanguard before the Lord to the war, ²¹all of the vanguard from you will cross the Jordan before the Lord, until His dispossession of His enemies from before Him, ²²the land will be conquered before the Lord, and then you will return; and you shall be absolved before the Lord and before Israel, and this land shall be for you as an ancestral portion before the Lord. ²³But if you will not do so, behold, you have sinned to the Lord; and know your sin and your punishment that will find you. ²⁴Build cities for your children and enclosures for your flocks, and that which comes out of your mouth you shall do.

²⁵The children of Gad and the children of Reuben said to Moses, saying: Your servants will do as my lord commands. ²⁶Our children, our wives, our livestock, and all our animals will be there, in the cities of Gilad. ²⁷And your servants will cross, all the vanguard soldiers, before the Lord to war, as my lord speaks. ²⁸Moses commanded Elazar the priest, and Joshua son of Nun, and the clan heads of the tribes of the children of Israel in their regard. ²⁹Moses said to them: If the children of Gad and the children of Reuben will cross the Jordan with you, all the vanguard to war before the Lord, and the land will be conquered before you, you shall give them the land of Gilad as a portion. ³⁰But if they will not cross as a vanguard with you, they will receive their portion in your midst, in the land of Canaan. ³¹The children of Gad and the children of Reuben answered, saying: That which the Lord has spoken to your servants, so we will do. ³²We will cross as a vanguard before the Lord into the land of Canaan, and for us the portion of our inheritance will be across the Jordan.

³³Moses gave to them, to the children of Gad, to the children of Reuben, and to half the tribe of Manasseh son of Joseph, the kingdom of Sihon, king of the Emorites, and the kingdom of Og, king of Bashan, the land with its cities, within the borders of the cities of the land all around. ³⁴The children of Gad built Divon, Atarot, Aroer, ³⁵Atrot Shofan, Yazer, Yogbeha, ³⁶Beit Nimra, and Beit Haran, fortified cities and enclosures for sheep. ³⁷The children of Reuben built Heshbon, Elaleh, and Kiryatayim, ³⁸and Nevo and Baal Meon, with changed names, and Sivma, and they designated names for the cities that they built. ³⁹The children of Makhir son of Manasseh went to Gilad and conquered it, and dispossessed the Emorites who were in it. ⁴⁰Moses gave the Gilad to Makhir son of Manasseh, and he dwelt in it. ⁴¹Ya'ir son of Manasseh

went and captured their ranches [*havot*], and he called them Havot Ya'ir. ⁴²And Novah went and captured Kenat, and its environs, and he called it Novah, after his name.

Illustrations: See map of the land east of the Jordan, p. 530.

Parashat Masei

This *parasha* concludes the account of the wilderness era. In it we find a list of the stations where the Israelites encamped over the course of their forty-year journey. The rest of the *parasha* is devoted to different matters relating to the imminent entry of the people into the Land of Israel: the command to destroy the Canaanite gods, delineating the borders of the Promised Land, the Levite cities and the cities of refuge, and the laws of inheritance.

The Journeys of the Israelites

A review of the Israelites' journeys in the wilderness and the sites of their encampments, from their exodus from Egypt until their arrival at the borders of the Land of Israel.

33 ¹These are the journeys of the children of Israel, who came out from the land of Egypt according to their hosts, at the hand of Moses and Aaron. ²Moses wrote their points of origin for their journeys according to the directive of the Lord; these are their journeys from their points of origin:

> 📖 **Further reading:** For more on the inner reasons for reviewing the stations of the people's journey through the wilderness, see *A Concise Guide to the Sages*, p. 218.

³They traveled from Rameses in the first month, on the fifteenth day of the first month; on the day after the Passover, the offering of the paschal lamb, the children of Israel exited with a high hand, triumphantly, before the eyes of all Egypt. ⁴The Egyptians were burying those whom the Lord had smitten among them, all their firstborn; and furthermore, on their gods, the Lord had administered punishments. ⁵The children of Israel traveled from Rameses, and encamped in Sukot. ⁶They traveled from Sukot, and encamped in Etam, which is at the edge of the wilderness. ⁷They traveled from Etam, and went back to Pi HaHirot, which is before Baal Tzefon, and they encamped before Migdol. ⁸They traveled from Penei HaHirot, and they crossed in the midst of the Red Sea to the wilderness, and they took a three-day journey in the wilderness

Numbers

of Etam, and they encamped in Mara. ⁹They traveled from Mara, and came to Eilim, and in Eilim were twelve springs of water and seventy palm trees; and they encamped there. ¹⁰They traveled from Eilim, and *cond aliya* encamped near the Red Sea. ¹¹They traveled from the Red Sea, and encamped in the wilderness of Sin. ¹²They traveled from the wilderness of Sin, and encamped in Dofka. ¹³They traveled from Dofka, and encamped in Alush. ¹⁴They traveled from Alush, and encamped in Refidim; there was no water for the people to drink there. ¹⁵They traveled from Refidim, and encamped in the wilderness of Sinai. ¹⁶They traveled from the wilderness of Sinai, and encamped in Kivrot HaTaava, where they buried the people who lusted for meat. ¹⁷They traveled from Kivrot HaTaava, and encamped in Hatzerot. ¹⁸They traveled from Hatzerot, and encamped in Ritma. ¹⁹They traveled from Ritma, and encamped in Rimon Peretz. ²⁰They traveled from Rimon Peretz, and encamped in Livna. ²¹They traveled from Livna, and encamped in Risa. ²²They traveled from Risa, and encamped in Kehelata. ²³They traveled from Kehelata, and encamped at Mount Shefer. ²⁴They traveled from Mount Shefer, and encamped in Harada. ²⁵They traveled from Harada, and encamped in Mak'helot. ²⁶They traveled from Mak'helot, and encamped in Tahat. ²⁷They traveled from Tahat, and encamped in Terah. ²⁸They traveled from Terah, and encamped in Mitka. ²⁹They traveled from Mitka, and encamped in Hashmona. ³⁰They traveled from Hashmona, and encamped in Moserot. ³¹They traveled from Moserot, and encamped in Benei Yaakan. ³²They traveled from Benei Yaakan, and encamped at Hor HaGidgad. ³³They traveled from Hor HaGidgad, and encamped in Yotvata. ³⁴They traveled from Yotvata, and encamped in Avrona. ³⁵They traveled from Avrona, and encamped in Etzyon Gever. ³⁶They traveled from Etzyon Gever, and encamped in the wilderness of Tzin; that is, Kadesh. ³⁷They traveled from Kadesh, and encamped at Hor Mountain, at the edge of the land of Edom.

³⁸Aaron the priest ascended Hor Mountain at the directive of the Lord, and he died there, in the fortieth year of the exodus of the children of Israel from the land of Egypt, in the fifth month, on the first of the month. ³⁹Aaron was one hundred twenty and three years old when he died on Hor Mountain.

⁴⁰The Canaanite king of Arad, who lived in the south in the land of Canaan, heard of the arrival of the children of Israel. ⁴¹They traveled from Hor Mountain, and encamped in Tzalmona. ⁴²They traveled from

Numbers

Tzalmona, and encamped in Punon. ⁴³They traveled from Punon, and encamped in Ovot. ⁴⁴They traveled from Ovot, and encamped in Iyei Avarim at the border of Moav. ⁴⁵They traveled from Iyim, and encamped in Divon Gad. ⁴⁶They traveled from Divon Gad, and encamped in Almon Divlataim. ⁴⁷They traveled from Almon Divlataim, and encamped in the highlands of Avarim, before Nevo. ⁴⁸They traveled from the highlands of Avarim, and encamped on the plains of Moav along the Jordan at, across from, Jericho. ⁴⁹They encamped along the Jordan, from Beit Yeshimot until Avel Shitim, on the plains of Moav.

Destruction of the Idols

God commands the Israelites to destroy all the trappings of idolatry in the Land of Israel once they enter it.

Third aliya (Fifth aliya) ⁵⁰The Lord spoke to Moses on the plains of Moav along the Jordan at Jericho, saying: ⁵¹Speak to the children of Israel, and say to them: When you cross the Jordan to the land of Canaan, ⁵²you shall dispossess all the inhabitants of the land from before you, and you shall destroy all their ornamented stones used in their idolatrous rites, and all their cast images, idols, you shall destroy, and all their high places, altars, you shall demolish. ⁵³You shall take possession of the land and you shall settle in it, as to you I have given the land to take possession of it. ⁵⁴You shall allocate the land by lot according to the size of your families: To the greater you shall increase his allocation, and to the lesser you shall decrease his allocation; wherever the lot shall fall for him, it shall be his; according to the tribes of your fathers you shall allocate. ⁵⁵But if you will not dispossess the inhabitants of the land from before you, it shall be that those who you will leave from them in the land will be as thorns in your eyes, and as sharp stones in your sides, and they will bear enmity to you in the land in which you dwell. ⁵⁶It shall be that as I had planned to do to them, to drive them from the land, I will do to you.

The Borders of the Land

In preparation for the allocation of the land to the tribes, the Torah gives a detailed description of its borders, and men are appointed to implement the allocation.

Illustrations: See map of the territories in the Land of Israel to be allocated to each tribe, p. 531.

34 ¹The Lord spoke to Moses, saying: ²Command the children of Israel, and say to them: When you come to the land of Canaan, this shall be

the land that shall fall to you as an inheritance, the land of Canaan according to its borders: ³The southern side shall be for you from the wilderness of Tzin alongside Edom, and your southern border shall begin at the edge of the Dead Sea eastward. ⁴Your border shall turn westward south of Maaleh Akrabim, and pass toward Tzin, and its terminus shall be south of Kadesh Barnea, and it shall emerge to Hatzar Adar, and pass toward Atzmon. ⁵The border shall turn from Atzmon toward the Ravine of Egypt, and its terminus shall be at the Mediterranean Sea. ⁶The western border shall be for you the Great Sea, the Mediterranean, and its coast; this shall be the western border for you. ⁷This shall be the northern border for you; from the Great Sea, you shall veer toward Hor Mountain. ⁸From Hor Mountain you shall veer toward the approach to Hamat, and the terminus of the border shall be toward Tzedad. ⁹The border shall go out toward Zifrona, and its terminus shall be Hatzar Einan; this shall be your northern border. ¹⁰You shall veer toward the east border, from Hatzar Einan to Shefam. ¹¹The border shall descend from Shefam to Rivla, east of the spring, and the border shall descend and shall converge upon the bank of the Sea of Galilee eastward. ¹²The border shall descend to the Jordan, and its terminus shall be at the Dead Sea; this shall be your land according to its borders all around.

¹³Moses commanded the children of Israel, saying: This is the land that you shall allocate by lot, that the Lord commanded to give to the nine tribes, and to half the tribe; ¹⁴for the tribe of the children of Reuben, according to their patrilineal houses, and the tribe of the children of Gad, according to their patrilineal houses, have taken, and half the tribe of Manasseh has taken their inheritance. ¹⁵The two tribes and the half tribe have taken their inheritance across the Jordan from Jericho, to the east.

urth
aliya
sixth
liya)
¹⁶The Lord spoke to Moses, saying: ¹⁷These are the names of the men who shall allocate the land on your behalf: Elazar the High Priest, and Joshua son of Nun. ¹⁸You shall take one prince from each tribe to allocate the land. ¹⁹These are the names of the men: From the tribe of Judah, Caleb son of Yefuneh. ²⁰From the tribe of the children of Simeon, Shmuel son of Amihud. ²¹From the tribe of Benjamin, Elidad son of Kislon. ²²From the tribe of the children of Dan, a prince, Buki son of Yogli. ²³From the children of Joseph: From the tribe of the children of Manasseh, a prince, Haniel son of Efod; ²⁴from the tribe of

the children of Ephraim, a prince, Kemuel son of Shiftan. ²⁵From the tribe of the children of Zebulun, a prince, Elitzafan son of Parnakh. ²⁶From the tribe of the children of Issachar, a prince, Paltiel the son of Azan. ²⁷From the tribe of the children of Asher, a prince, Ahihud son of Shelomi. ²⁸From the tribe of the children of Naphtali, a prince, Pedahel son of Amihud. ²⁹These are those whom the Lord commanded to allocate the inheritance to the children of Israel in the land of Canaan.

The Levite Cities

Although the Levites do not receive a tribal portion in the land, they receive cities in which to reside. These come at the expense of the other tribal portions, proportionate to their size.

35 ¹The Lord spoke to Moses on the plains of Moav along the Jordan at Jericho, saying: ²Command the children of Israel, and they shall give to the Levites, from the allocation of their ancestral portion, cities in which to live, and perimeter fields for the cities around them; you shall give to the Levites. ³The cities shall be for them to live, and their perimeter fields shall be for their animals, and for their property, and for all their provisions. ⁴The perimeter fields of the cities that you shall give to the Levites, from the wall of the city and outward, one thousand cubits all around. ⁵You shall measure outside the city: the eastern side two thousand cubits, and the southern side two thousand cubits, and the western side two thousand cubits, and the northern side two thousand cubits, and the city in the middle. This shall be for them the perimeter fields of the cities. ⁶The cities that you shall give to the Levites: The six cities of refuge that you shall give for the murderer to flee there and with them you shall give forty-two more cities. ⁷All the cities that you shall give to the Levites are forty-eight cities; them, and their perimeter fields. ⁸The cities which you shall give from the portion of the children of Israel, from the greater tribes you shall increase the number of Levite cities, and from the lesser tribes, you shall decrease that number; each tribe according to its inheritance that it will inherit shall give from its cities to the Levites.

Fifth aliya

Cities of Refuge

The Israelites are commanded to designate cities that will serve as a refuge for a person who unwittingly killed someone, to protect him from the vengeance of the victim's relatives. The distinction between unwitting and intentional killing is detailed here, as well as additional related laws.

Sixth
aliya
enth
aliya)
⁹The Lord spoke to Moses, saying: ¹⁰Speak to the children of Israel, and say to them: When you cross the Jordan to the land of Canaan, ¹¹you shall designate cities, cities of refuge they shall be for you; and the murderer who smites a person unwittingly shall flee there. ¹²The cities shall be for you for refuge from the blood redeemer, a relative of the victim seeking vengeance, so that the murderer shall not die, until he stands before the congregation for judgment. ¹³The cities that you shall give, six cities of refuge you shall have. ¹⁴Three cities you shall place across the Jordan, and three cities you shall give in the land of Canaan; they shall be cities of refuge. ¹⁵For the children of Israel, and for the stranger and for the resident alien among them, these six cities shall be for refuge to flee there, anyone who kills a person unwittingly.

> 📖 **Further reading:** The institution of cities of refuge carries a profound message. See *A Concise Guide to the Sages*, p. 219.

¹⁶But if he smote him with an instrument of iron and he died, he is a murderer; the murderer shall be put to death. ¹⁷If he smote him with a hand-sized stone, by means of which one may die, and he died, he is a murderer; the murderer shall be put to death. ¹⁸Or if he smote him with a hand-sized weapon of wood, by means of which one may die, and he died, he is a murderer; the murderer shall be put to death. ¹⁹The blood redeemer, he shall put the murderer to death; when he encounters him, he shall put him to death, he may kill the murderer. ²⁰If he shoved him with enmity, or cast an object upon him intentionally, and he died; ²¹or he smote him with his hand with animosity, and he died; the assailant shall be put to death; he is a murderer; the blood redeemer shall put the murderer to death when he encounters him.

²²But if there is no apparent reason to suspect that he meant to kill him, e.g., he shoved him suddenly, without animosity, or he cast upon him any vessel without intention, ²³or with any stone by means of which one may die, without seeing him, and he dropped it upon him, and he died, and he did not bear enmity to him nor did he seek his harm, ²⁴the congregation of Israel, the court, shall judge between the assailant and the blood redeemer according to these ordinances. ²⁵If it is established that he killed unwittingly, the congregation shall deliver the murderer from the hand of the blood redeemer, and the congregation shall restore him to the city of his refuge, where he fled, and he shall live in it until the death of the High Priest, who was anointed with the sacred

Numbers

oil. ²⁶But if the murderer emerges from the border of the city of his refuge to which he flees, ²⁷and the blood redeemer finds him outside the border of the city of his refuge, and the blood redeemer murders the murderer; he has no bloodguilt. ²⁸Because he shall live within the city of his refuge until the death of the High Priest; and after the death of the High Priest the murderer shall return to the land of his ancestral portion.

²⁹These laws of the murderer shall be for you as a statute of justice for your generations in all your dwellings. ³⁰Anyone who kills a person, on the basis of witnesses one shall murder the murderer, but one witness shall not testify against a person to die. ³¹You shall not take ransom for the life of a murderer who is condemned to die; as, rather, he shall be put to death. ³²You shall not take ransom from one who fled to the city of his refuge to allow him to return and to live in the land; he may not return until the death of the High Priest. ³³You shall not tarnish the land in which you are, as the blood whose shedder is not punished will tarnish the land, and the land will not be atoned for the blood that is shed in it except through the blood of its shedder. ³⁴You shall not defile the land in which you live, in the midst of which I rest, for I am the Lord, who rests in the midst of the children of Israel.

The Inheritance of Tzelofhad's Daughters

The legal precedent set in the matter of the daughters of Tzelofhad, which deemed them entitled to inherit from their father, who had died without sons, arouses the opposition of the members of their tribe. They are concerned that when these women marry, the tribal portion that they inherited will be transferred to their husbands' tribes. A rider is attached to the law requiring Tzelofhad's daughters to marry within their tribe.

36 ¹The clan heads of the family of the children of Gilad, son of Makhir, *Seventh aliya* son of Manasseh, from the families of the sons of Joseph, approached, and they spoke before Moses, and before the princes, the clan heads of the children of Israel. ²They said: The Lord commanded my lord, Moses, to give the land as inheritance by lot to the children of Israel, and my lord was commanded by the Lord to give the inheritance of Tzelofhad our brother to his daughters. ³They express their concern: They will become the wives of the sons of the other tribes of the children of Israel, and their inheritance will be deducted from the inheritance of our fathers, and it will be added to the inheritance of the tribe to which they will be joined through marriage, and from the lot of

our inheritance it shall be deducted. ⁴When the Jubilee, the fiftieth year, that occurs after seven Sabbatical cycles, **will be for the children of Israel, their inheritance will be added to the inheritance of the tribe to which they will be** joined in marriage, **and from the inheritance of the tribe of our fathers, their inheritance will be deducted.** Since the children will belong to their fathers' tribe, the land they inherit from their mothers will be transferred to that tribe.

⁵Moses commanded the children of Israel according to the directive of the Lord, saying: The tribe of the sons of Joseph speaks justly. ⁶This is the matter that the Lord commanded with regard to the daughters of Tzelofhad, saying: To whomever is good in their eyes they shall be wives; however, they shall be wives only to the family of the tribe of their father. ⁷No inheritance of the children of Israel shall pass from tribe to tribe, as each of the children of Israel shall cleave to the inheritance of the tribe of his fathers. ⁸Every daughter who inherits an inheritance from the tribes of the children of Israel shall be a wife to one from the families of the tribe of her father, so that each of the children of Israel will inherit the inheritance of his fathers. ⁹No inheritance shall pass from tribe to tribe, as each of the children of Israel shall cleave to his inheritance. ¹⁰As the Lord commanded Moses, so the daughters of Tzelofhad did. ¹¹Mahla, Tirtza, Hogla, Milka, and Noa, daughters of Tzelofhad, were married to the sons of their uncles. ¹²They were married into the families of the sons of Manasseh son of Joseph, and their inheritance was with the tribe of the family of their father.

¹³These are the commandments and the ordinances which the Lord commanded at the hand of Moses to the children of Israel on the plains of Moav along the Jordan at Jericho.

▭ **Further reading:** For more on the laws of inheritance and wills, see *A Concise Guide to Halakha*, p. 75.

Deuteronomy

Parashat Devarim

The book of Deuteronomy consists of Moses' addresses to the nation before his passing. He delivers them on the eastern bank of the Jordan River, during the fortieth year since the exodus from Egypt, just prior to the Israelites' entry into the land of Canaan. The book begins with an account of the events that befell them throughout their time in the wilderness, continues with a review of many mitzvot, and concludes with an extended description of how the people's behavior will affect their lives in the Land of Israel. If they keep the covenant they will prosper, and if they do not, they will suffer terribly.

In this *parasha*, Moses mentions certain events and omit others. He describes the process of establishing the judicial hierarchy after the giving of the Torah, the episode of the spies and the story of those who sought to enter the Land of Israel in its wake, and the conquest of the lands of the Emorites on the eastern side of the Jordan. These depictions are interwoven with encouragement of the people as they are on the brink of entering the land and living in it. The final verse of the *parasha* concludes with words of support for Joshua and the people as they prepare for the conquest and settlement of the land.

Introduction to Moses' Speech
The Israelites are at the conclusion of the wilderness period, after a journey of forty years and the conquest of the lands of Sihon and Og on the eastern side of the Jordan. Prior to their entry into the Land of Israel Moses takes his leave of them with a long speech.

1 ¹**These are the words that Moses spoke to all Israel,** when they were **beyond the Jordan, in the wilderness in the Arava opposite the Red Sea, between Paran and Tofel, and Lavan, and Hatzerot, and Di Zahav.** All these are the names of places. ²It is **eleven days from Horev,** Mount Sinai, **via Mount Se'ir to Kadesh Barnea.** Although the nation was located a distance of only eleven days travel from Sinai, the Israelites' journey had lasted forty years.

³**It was in the fortieth year** since the exodus from Egypt, **in the eleventh month, on the first of the month,** that **Moses spoke to the children of Israel, in accordance with everything that the Lord had commanded him for them.** ⁴**After his smiting of Sihon, king of the Emorites, who lived in Heshbon, and Og, king of Bashan, who lived in Ashtarot, at**

Deuteronomy

Edre'i, ⁵beyond the Jordan, in the land of Moav, Moses began expounding, teaching and interpreting, this Torah, saying:

The Command to Proceed to the Land of Israel

Moses relates how, after the revelation at Sinai, God commanded the Israelites to travel to the Land of Israel, which was promised to the Israelites as an inheritance.

⁶The Lord our God spoke to us when we were at Horev, saying: Enough of your living at this mountain; you have stayed here long enough, ⁷turn from Horev, and set out for yourselves, and come to the highlands of the Emorites and all their neighbors, on the plain, on the highlands, in the lowlands, in the south, and on the seashore, the land of the Canaanites, and the Lebanon, to the great river, the Euphrates River. This is a delineation of the borders of the Land of Israel. ⁸See, I have placed the land before you. Come and take possession of and conquer the land about which the Lord took an oath to your fathers, to Abraham, to Isaac, and to Jacob, to give it to them and to their descendants after them.

Establishment of the Judicial System

Moses relates that when he realized he was unable to bear the burden of leading the people alone, he asked that distinguished members of the nation gather, whom he would be able to appoint as judges and officers. He commanded them to judge justly and uprightly, fearlessly, and without favoritism.

⁹I spoke to you at that time, saying: I am unable to bear you, judge you, alone. ¹⁰The Lord your God has multiplied you, and behold, you are today as numerous as the stars of the heavens in abundance. ¹¹The Lord, God of your fathers, shall add to you one thousand times as many as you are now, and He will bless you, as He spoke to you. ¹²How shall I be able to bear alone your troubles, your burdens, and your quarrels?

Second aliya

¹³Get for you men, wise and understanding, and who are well known to your tribes, and I will place them at your head. I will appoint them as judges over you. ¹⁴You answered me and said: The matter is good that you have spoken to do. ¹⁵I took the heads of your tribes, men wise and known, and I placed them as heads over you, leaders of thousands, and leaders of hundreds, and leaders of fifties, and leaders of tens, and officers for your tribes. I appointed judges over segments of the population, as well as officers to implement their rulings.

¹⁶I commanded your judges at that time, saying: Hear the claims between your brethren, and only then judge righteousness between man

and his brother, and a stranger to him, who appended himself to the people of Israel. [17]**You shall not give preference in judgment; small and great alike you shall hear** equally, listening to both without regard to their status. **You shall not fear due to,** because of, **any man,** even one who is intimidating, **as judgment is God's.** Therefore, judge without concern. **And the matter that is too difficult for you,** you will be unable to reach a decision, **you shall bring near to me, and I will hear it** and resolve the matter. [18]**I commanded you at that time all the matters that you shall do.**

The Narrative of the Spies and Those Who Sought to Enter the Land against God's Will

Moses describes how, when the Israelites approached the land, they asked that spies be sent before them, in preparation for their entry into the land. Twelve spies were sent, and upon their return they brought fruit from the land and sang its praises. The people, however, refused to enter the land for fear of its residents; God decreed that the generation which had left Egypt would therefore die in the desert and only their children would be allowed to enter the land. The people, upon hearing the decree, had a change of heart and attempted to begin conquering the land against God's will, and were routed in battle by the Emorites.

[19]**We traveled from Horev, and we went through the entire great and awesome wilderness that you saw, via the Emorite highlands, as the Lord our God had commanded us, and we came to Kadesh Barnea.** [20]**I said to you: You have come to the Emorite highlands, which the Lord our God is giving us.** [21]**See, the Lord your God has placed the land before you; ascend, take possession,** enter and conquer the land, **as the Lord, God of your fathers, spoke to you; do not fear, and do not be frightened.**

Third aliya [22]**You all approached me and said: Let us send men before us, and they will spy the land for us, and they will return word to us** about the land: The way that we will ascend, and the cities at which we will arrive. [23]**The matter was good in my eyes; and I took from you twelve men, one man** as a representative **for each tribe.** [24]**They turned and they ascended to the highlands, and they came to the Eshkol Ravine, and spied it.** [25]**They took in their hand from the fruit of the land and brought it down to us; they brought back word to us, and said: The land that the Lord our God is giving to us is good.**

[26]**But you were not willing to ascend, and you defied the directive of the Lord your God.** [27]**You murmured** your complaints **in your tents, and you said: In the Lord's hatred of us, He took us out of the land of**

Deuteronomy

Egypt, to deliver us into the hand of the Emorites, to destroy us. God is sending us to Canaan only because He wants to destroy us. ²⁸**Where are we ascending? Our brethren,** the spies, **have dissolved our heart,** frightened us, **saying:** We have seen **a people greater and taller than we; cities great and fortified,** whose fortifications reach **to the heavens, and we have also seen the sons of giants there.**

²⁹**I said to you: Do not be intimidated and do not fear them.** ³⁰**The Lord your God who goes before you, He will make war for you, like everything that He did for you in Egypt before your eyes,** that you saw yourselves, ³¹**and in the wilderness, where you saw that the Lord your God bore you as a man would bear his** young **son,** seeing to his needs, **in the entire path that you went, until you came to this place.** ³²**But in this matter** of conquering the land, **you do not have faith in the Lord your God,** ³³**who goes before you on the way, to scout for you a place for your encampment with fire by night, to show you the path on which you shall go, and in the cloud by day.**

> **Further reading:** While Moses bears great love for Israel, it is he who rebukes them; see *A Concise Guide to the Sages,* p. 223.

³⁴**The Lord heard the sound of your words, and He was enraged and took an oath, saying:** ³⁵**No man among these men, this wicked generation, will see the good land about which I took an oath to give to your fathers,** ³⁶**except** for **Caleb son of Yefuneh, he shall see it,** the land; **and to him I will give the land in which he trod, and to his children, because he followed the** instruction of the **Lord wholeheartedly,** and provided an accurate description of the land, while assuring the people that they could conquer it. ³⁷**Also the Lord was incensed with me,** Moses, **because of you, saying: You too shall not come there.** ³⁸**Joshua son of Nun, who stands before you, he shall come there; strengthen him, for he shall bequeath** Fourth aliya **it to Israel.** ³⁹**And your children, whom you said would be captives** and die in the wilderness, **and your sons, who today** are too young and **do not know** to distinguish between **good and evil, they will come there, and to them I will give it,** the land, **and they will take possession of it.** ⁴⁰**And you, turn** around **and travel into the wilderness via the Red Sea.**

⁴¹**You answered and you said to me: We sinned against the Lord, we will go up and make war, in accordance with everything that the Lord our God had commanded;** each of you girded his weapons of war, and

decided, or dared, **to go up to the highland.** The southern part of the land of Israel is an elevated plateau. **⁴²The Lord said to me: Say to them: Do not go up and do not make war, as I am not in your midst, so that you not be routed before your enemies.** I do not support this endeavor and you will be defeated. **⁴³I spoke to you, but you did not heed, and you defied the directive of the Lord, and you intentionally went up to the highland,** contrary to the will of God. **⁴⁴The Emorites who live on that highland came out toward you, and pursued you, as** a swarm of **bees would do** when pursuing a person, **and they beat you,** routed you, **in Se'ir until Horma.** The location of their defeat came to be called *horma*, meaning destruction. **⁴⁵You returned and wept before the Lord, but the Lord did not heed your voice, and He did not listen to you. ⁴⁶You lived in Kadesh many days, like the days that you lived there.** You know how long you lived there.

Passage Via Se'ir, Moav, and Amon

Moses describes how in the course of the years of their travels in the wilderness, the Israelites passed adjacent to certain lands east of the Jordan which they were commanded not to conquer, as they were given as inheritances to the descendants of Esau and Lot (Amon and Moav). During that period, all those who left Egypt died. The time therefore arrived to conquer the land.

2 **¹We turned and we traveled** back **into the wilderness via the Red Sea, as the Lord spoke to me; and we circled Mount Se'ir for many days.**

Fifth
aliya **²The Lord said to me, saying: ³Enough for you circling this mountain, turn you to the north. ⁴Command the people, saying: You are passing through the border of your brethren, the children of Esau, who live in Se'ir; they will be afraid of you, and** even so, **you shall be very careful. ⁵Do not provoke them, for I will not give you** territory equivalent **even to the tread of the sole of a foot from their land, because I have given Mount Se'ir to be an inheritance to Esau. ⁶You shall purchase from them food with silver, and eat, and also water you shall purchase from them with silver, and drink. ⁷For the Lord your God blessed you in all your handiwork, He has known** your needs in **your walking through this great wilderness; these forty years the Lord your God has been with you, you have not lacked anything. ⁸We passed, away from our brethren the children of Esau, who live in Se'ir, from the way of the Arava, from Eilat and from Etzyon Gever, and we turned** northward **and passed via the wilderness of Moav.**

Deuteronomy

⁹The Lord said to me: Do not besiege and harass **Moav, and do not provoke war with them, as I will not give you from his land a possession, because to the children of Lot I have given Ar,** in Moav, **as a possession.** ¹⁰The Emim dwelt there previously, a people great, numerous, and tall, like giants. ¹¹Refa'im would also be regarded as giants; but the Moavites would call them Emim. ¹²In Se'ir the Horites lived previously, and the children of Esau took possession from them and they destroyed them from before them, and dwelled in their place, as Israel did to the land of its possession, the land of Sihon and Og, on the eastern side of the Jordan, **which the Lord gave to them.**

¹³**Now,** the Lord continued, **rise, and cross the Zered Ravine. And we crossed the Zered Ravine.** ¹⁴**The days that we went from Kadesh Barnea until we crossed the Zered Ravine were thirty-eight years, until the demise of the entire generation, the men of war from the midst of the camp, as the Lord swore to them.** ¹⁵**The hand of the Lord was also among them, to destroy them from the midst of the camp, until their demise.** God accelerated the process.

¹⁶**It was when the dying of all the men of war from among the people was completed.**

¹⁷**The Lord spoke to me, saying:** ¹⁸**You are passing today the border of Moav, Ar;** ¹⁹**you will approach opposite the children of Amon; do not besiege them and do not provoke them** to battle, **as I will not give you from the land of the children of Amon as a possession, because to the children of Lot I have given it as a possession.** ²⁰**It, too, is considered a land of Refaim,** a land of the mighty, as **Refaim lived in it previously, and the Amonites call them Zamzumim.** ²¹**A people great, and numerous, and tall as the giants; the Lord destroyed them from before them, and they took possession from them, and settled** in their land **in their place,** ²²**as He did for the children of Esau, who live in Se'ir, in that He destroyed the Horites from before them and dispossessed them, and they,** the children of Esau, **settled in their place until this day.** ²³**And the Avim, who lived in unwalled cities approaching,** in the vicinity of, **Gaza: Kaftorim, who emerged from Kaftor,** Crete, **destroyed them,** the Avim, **and settled in their place.**

²⁴**Rise, and travel, and cross the Arnon Stream; see, I have placed Sihon, king of Heshbon, the Emorite, and his land in your hand; begin** conquering and **taking possession, and provoke war with him.** ²⁵**This**

day, I will begin to place terror of you and fear of you upon the peoples under all the heavens, who will hear your reputation and will tremble, and be in trepidation because of you.

The Conquests East of the Jordan

Moses relates how the people waged war against Sihon and Og, and conquered their lands.

²⁶I sent messengers from the wilderness of Kedemot, in the east [*kedem*], to Sihon king of Heshbon, with words of peace, saying: ²⁷Let me pass through your land, I will go only on the designated path, I will not diverge right or left. ²⁸You will sell me food for silver, and I will eat, and you will give me water for silver, and I will drink; only let me pass on my feet, ²⁹like the children of Esau, who live in Se'ir, and the Moavites, who live in Ar, did for me, until I cross the Jordan into the land that the Lord our God is giving us. ³⁰But Sihon, king of Heshbon, was unwilling to let us pass through it, his land, for the Lord your God had hardened his spirit, and made his heart obstinate, in order to deliver him into your hand, like it is this day. You have conquered his land and destroyed him.

📖 Further reading: Although Moses had been commanded to wage war, he nevertheless chose to open the interaction peacefully; see *A Concise Guide to the Sages*, p. 226.

Sixth
aliya
³¹The Lord said to me: See, I have begun delivering before you Sihon and his land; begin taking possession of his land. ³²Sihon came out to war toward us, he and his entire people, to Yahatz. ³³The Lord our God delivered him before us and we smote him, and his sons, and his entire people. ³⁴We captured all his cities at that time, and we destroyed every inhabited city, and the women, and the children. We left no remnant of its inhabitants. ³⁵Only the animals we looted for ourselves, and the spoils of the cities that we captured. ³⁶From Aroer, which is on the northern edge of the Arnon Ravine, and the city that is in the ravine, until the Gilad, there was no city that was too high, strong, for us to conquer; everything, the Lord our God delivered before us. ³⁷Only to the land of the children of Amon you did not approach, all the area adjacent to the Yabok Ravine, and the cities of the highlands, and everywhere that the Lord our God had commanded us.

3 ¹We turned, and went up northward toward the Bashan, and Og, king of the Bashan, came out toward us, he and his entire people, to war at the city of Edre'i. ²The Lord said to me: Do not fear him, as I have delivered

him and his entire people and his land into your hand; you shall do to him as you did to Sihon, king of the Emorites, who lives in Heshbon. ³The Lord our God also delivered into our hand Og, king of Bashan, and all his people, and we smote him until we left him no remnant. ⁴We took all his cities at that time; there was no city that we did not take from them, sixty cities which constitute the entire region of Argov, the kingdom of Og in the Bashan. ⁵All these were fortified cities, surrounded by a high wall, with gates and a bar, besides the very many unwalled cities that we conquered. ⁶We destroyed them, as we did to Sihon, king of Heshbon, destroying every inhabited city, the women, and the children. ⁷But all the animals, and the spoils of the cities, we looted for ourselves.

⁸We took, at that time, the land from the hand of the two kings of the Emorites, Sihon and Og, that is beyond the Jordan, from the Arnon Stream to Mount Hermon. ⁹Sidonians would call Hermon, Siryon, and the Emorites would call it Senir. ¹⁰All the cities of the plain, and all the Gilad, and all the Bashan, until Salkha and Edre'i, cities of the kingdom of Og in the Bashan. ¹¹For only Og, king of the Bashan, remained from the rest of the Refaim. Behold, his bed was a bed of iron; isn't it in Raba, of the children of Amon? Nine cubits is its length, and four cubits its width, by the cubit of a man. A cubit is the length of a normal man's forearm.

Allotment of the Land East of the Jordan

Moses describes the allotment of the land already conquered as the tribal inheritance of two and a half tribes. He made this allocation contingent on the mobilization of the military-ready men of those tribes, together with the rest of the tribes, for the conquest of the western Land of Israel. Only at the conclusion of the wars are they to be permitted to return to their families and their lands. The Torah portion concludes with Moses' words of encouragement to Joshua prior to his assuming leadership.

¹²This land we took possession of at that time, from Aroer, which is near the Arnon Stream, and half of Mount Gilad, and its cities, I gave to the Reubenite and to the Gadite tribes. ¹³The rest of Gilad, and all the Bashan, the kingdom of Og, I gave to half the tribe of Manasseh; the whole region of Argov of the entire Bashan, that is called the land of Refaim. ¹⁴Ya'ir son of Manasseh took the entire region of Argov up to the border of the Geshurite and the Maakhatite, and he called them *Seventh* after his name; the Bashan is called Havot Ya'ir to this day. ¹⁵To Makhir, *aliya*

I gave Gilad as an inheritance. ¹⁶To the Reubenites and to the Gadites I gave from the Gilad up to the Arnon Stream, within the ravine and its border, up to the Yabok Ravine, the border of the children of Amon, ¹⁷and the plain, and the Jordan, and its border, from the Sea of Galilee up to the sea of the plain, the Dead Sea, under the waterfalls of the peak to the east.

Illustrations: See map of the land east of the Jordan, p. 530.

¹⁸I commanded you, the men of the two and a half tribes, at that time, saying: The Lord your God gave you this land to take possession of it; all those mobilized shall pass as the vanguard before your brethren the children of Israel; all capable military men. ¹⁹Only your wives, and your children, and your livestock, your herds of cows and flocks of sheep; I know that you have much livestock, they shall live in your cities that I *Maftir* gave you, ²⁰until the Lord will give rest to your brethren, like He did to you, and they too will take possession of the land that the Lord your God is giving them beyond the Jordan, to the west. Each of you shall only then return to his possession that I gave you.

²¹I commanded Joshua at that time, saying: It is your eyes that have seen everything that the Lord your God has done to these two kings; so shall the Lord do to all the kingdoms where you are crossing. ²²You shall not fear them, as it is the Lord your God who makes war for you, on your behalf.

Parashat Va'ethanan

In this Torah portion, Moses continues to describe the significant events that transpired during the wilderness period, including his punishment, that he would not be allowed to enter the land, and his attempts to alleviate the severity of the punishment. He then moves on to encouragement regarding observance of the Torah in the face of the challenges that will confront the Israelites when they enter the land. He relates the revelation at Sinai, and what may be learned from it. He concludes with additional words of rebuke, and with the command to eliminate the sinful nations that reside in the land of Canaan.

Moses Will Not Enter the Land

Moses describes pleading before God that He revoke His decree that Moses would not enter the land, and the rejection of his plea.

²³I pleaded with the Lord at that time, saying: ²⁴My Lord God, You began to show Your servant Your greatness and Your mighty hand, your power; for what other god is in the heavens or on the earth who can perform like Your actions, and like Your mighty deeds? ²⁵Please, let me cross, and I will see the good land that is beyond the Jordan, that good mountain, the highlands in the land's interior, and the Lebanon mountains.

📖 Further reading: For more on Moses' plea to enter the Land of Israel, see *A Concise Guide to the Sages*, p. 228.

²⁶The Lord was irate with me because of you, and did not heed me, and the Lord said to me: Enough for you, do not continue speaking to Me anymore about this matter. ²⁷Ascend to the top of the peak, and lift your eyes to the west, and to the north, and to the south, and to the east, and see the land with your eyes, as you will not cross this Jordan. ²⁸Command Joshua, and strengthen him and encourage him, as he will cross before this people and lead them, and he will conquer and allocate

to them the land that you will see. ²⁹We dwelled in the canyon opposite Beit Peor.

Encouragement to Observe the Commandments

Prior to their entry into the land, Moses cautions the Israelites regarding their following the Torah and keeping the mitzvot. The primary challenge facing them is refraining from idol worship, in which the current residents of the land are steeped. Moses reminds them of the great deeds that God performed for them, in choosing them and in the revelation at Sinai, and the obligation that this imposes upon them. In his address, he accentuates the differences between them and the other nations.

4 ¹Now, Israel, heed the statutes and the ordinances that I am teaching you to perform, so that you will live, and you will come and take possession of the land that the Lord, God of your fathers, is giving you. ²You shall not add to the matter that I am commanding you, and you shall not subtract from it, to observe the commandments of the Lord your God that I am commanding you. ³It is your eyes that have seen that which the Lord recently did concerning Baal Peor, an idol that they worshipped, as every man who followed Baal Peor, the Lord your God destroyed him from your midst. ⁴But you, who cleave and are loyal to the Lord your God, all of you live today.

^{Second aliya} ⁵See, I have taught you statutes and ordinances, as the Lord my God had commanded me: to do so in the midst of the land that you are coming there to take possession of it. ⁶You shall observe and you shall perform, as this, the observance of the mitzvot, is your wisdom and your understanding in the eyes of the peoples; when they hear all these statutes, they will say: It is a particularly wise and understanding people, this great nation. ⁷For who is a great nation that has God near it, as the Lord our God, who is close to us in all of our calling to Him? ⁸Who is a great nation that has righteous statutes and ordinances, like this entire Torah that I place before you today?

⁹Only beware, and protect yourself greatly, lest you forget the matters that your eyes saw, and lest they move from your heart all the days of your life. And you shall impart them to your children and to your children's children. ¹⁰The day that you stood before the Lord your God at Horev, at Mount Sinai, when the Lord said to me: Assemble the people for Me, and I will have them hear My words, so that they will learn to fear Me all the days that they live on the earth, and so that they will also teach their children. ¹¹You approached and stood at the foot of the mountain,

Deuteronomy

and the mountain was burning with fire to the heart of the heavens, shrouded in **darkness, cloud, and fog.** [12]The **Lord spoke to you from the midst of the fire; the sound of words you were hearing, but an image you were not seeing, only a sound.** [13]**He told you His covenant that He commanded you to perform, the Ten Commandments, and He inscribed them on two tablets of stone.** [14]**To me, the Lord commanded at that time to teach you statutes and ordinances, to have you perform them in the land that you are crossing** there **to take possession of it.**

> **Further reading:** The giving of the Torah is constantly renewed and constitutes an eternal memory; see *A Concise Guide to Mahshava*, p. 103.

[15]**You shall greatly beware for your lives, as you did not see any image on the day that the Lord your God spoke to you at Horev from the midst of the fire,** [16]**lest you act corruptly, and make for yourselves an idol, the image of any shape; the form of a male or a female** person, [17]**the form of any beast that is on the earth, the form of any winged bird that flies in the heavens,** [18]**the form of any being that creeps on the ground,** or **the form of any fish that is in the water under the earth.** [19]**And** beware **lest you lift your eyes to** look toward **the heavens, and see the sun and the moon and the stars, all the host of the heavens,** the heavenly bodies, **and you are led astray and prostrate yourselves to them, and serve them which the Lord your God has allotted to all the peoples** that live throughout the world, **under all the heavens.** [20]**And you, the Lord has taken, and He took you out from the iron crucible, from Egypt, to be for Him a people of inheritance, as** you are **this day.**

[21]**The Lord was incensed with me because of your deeds and He took an oath that I not cross the Jordan, and not come to the good land which the Lord your God is giving you as an inheritance.** [22]**For I will die in this land; I am not crossing the Jordan, and you are crossing** without me, **and you will take possession of that good land.** [23]**Therefore, beware, lest you forget the covenant of the Lord your God which He made with you, and you make for yourselves an idol, the image of anything that the Lord your God has commanded you** not to make. [24]**For the Lord your God is** like **a consuming fire, a zealous God** vis-à-vis any betrayal of Him.

[25]**When you will beget children, and children's children, and you will have been long in the land, and you** will **act corruptly and make an idol,**

the image of anything, and you will perform evil in the eyes of the Lord your God, to anger Him, ²⁶I call today to the heavens and earth to bear witness against you, that I warned you, and if you do this you will be quickly eradicated, expelled, from upon the land that you are crossing the Jordan there to take possession of it; you will not extend your days upon it, as you will be destroyed, expelled.

²⁷The Lord will disperse you among the peoples, and you will remain few in number among the nations where the Lord will lead you. ²⁸You will serve gods there, the handiwork of man, wood and stone, which have the capacity neither to see, nor hear, nor eat, nor smell. ²⁹You will seek from there the Lord your God, and you will find Him, when you search for Him with all your heart and with all your soul. ³⁰When you are in distress and all these matters befall you, by the end of days, in the distant future, you will return to the Lord your God, and you will heed His voice. ³¹As the Lord your God is a merciful God, He will neither forsake you, nor destroy you, nor forget the covenant of your fathers with regard to which He took an oath to them.

³²For ask now of the early days that were before you, from the day that God created man upon the earth, and from the end of the heavens to the end of the heavens: Has there been anything like this great thing, or has anything been heard like it? ³³Has a people heard the voice of God speaking from the midst of the fire, as you heard, and lived? ³⁴Or has a god sought to come and take for himself a nation from the midst of a nation, with wondrous tribulations, with signs, and with wonders, and with war, and with a mighty hand, and with an outstretched arm, and with fearsome deeds, like everything that the Lord your God did for you in Egypt, before your eyes?

³⁵You have been shown in order to know that the Lord, He is the God; there is no other besides Him. ³⁶From the heavens He had you hear His voice, to chastise you, and upon earth He showed you His great fire and you heard His words from the midst of the fire. ³⁷Because He loved your forefathers, He chose their descendants after them, and He took you out before Him with His great power, from Egypt, ³⁸to dispossess nations greater and mightier than you from before you, to bring you, to give you their land as an inheritance, as it is this day, as it will be soon. ³⁹You shall know this day, and restore to your heart, that the Lord, He is the God in the heavens above and upon the earth below; there is no other. ⁴⁰You shall observe His statutes and His commandments, which

I am commanding you this day, so that then He will do good to you, and to your children after you, and so that you may extend your days upon the land that the Lord your God is giving you, forever.

📖 **Further reading:** For more on how miracles and signs can function as a basis of belief in God, see *A Concise Guide to Mahshava*, p. 213.

Cities of Refuge

Moses designates three cities east of the Jordan to serve as cities of refuge for unwitting murderers fleeing from the vengeance of a relative of the victim. This relative is referred to as 'the blood redeemer.'

Third aliya [41]Then Moses designated three cities beyond the Jordan, toward the eastern sunrise, on the east bank, [42]for the murderer to flee there, one who will kill his neighbor unwittingly, and he does not hate him previously; he shall flee to one of these cities and live. He will be protected there from the blood redeemer. [43]He designated Betzer in the wilderness, in the land of the plain, for the members of the tribe of the Reubenites in their tribal region; and Ramot in Gilad, for the members of the Gadites; and Golan in the Bashan for the members of the Manassites. [44]This is the Torah that Moses placed before the children of Israel.

Summary of the Historical Section

Moses concludes the section of his speech devoted to the events of the past, ending with the place and time that these matters were stated.

[45]These are the testimonies, and the statutes, and the ordinances which Moses spoke to the children of Israel, when they emerged from Egypt, [46]beyond the Jordan, in the canyon opposite Beit Peor, in the land of Sihon king of the Emorites, who lived in Heshbon, whom Moses and the children of Israel smote and overcame, upon their emergence from Egypt. [47]They took possession of his land, and the land of Og king of the Bashan, the two kings of the Emorites, lands which are beyond the Jordan, toward the eastern sunrise, [48]from Aroer, which is on the bank of the Arnon Stream, up to Mount Sion, which is Hermon, [49]and all the plain beyond the Jordan to the east, up to the sea of the plain, the Dead Sea, under the waterfalls of the peak.

Description of the Revelation at Sinai

Moses reminds the people of the revelation at Sinai, where the Ten Commandments were given. He relates how the Israelites reacted to this direct divine revelation, and the lesson that may be learned from it.

5 ¹Moses called all Israel, and said to them: Hear, Israel, the statutes and the ordinances that I am speaking in your ears today, and you shall learn them, and you shall take care to perform them. ²The Lord our God established a covenant with us at Horev, Sinai. ³Not with our forefathers alone did the Lord establish this covenant, but with us, we who are here, all of us alive today. ⁴Face-to-face the Lord spoke with you at the mountain, from the midst of the fire. ⁵I was standing as an intermediary between the Lord and you at that time, to tell you the word of the Lord, because you were afraid due to the fire, and you did not ascend the mountain. These were God's words, saying:

⁶I am the Lord your God, who took you out of the land of Egypt, from the house of bondage. ⁷You shall have no other gods before Me. I am the only being worthy of worship. ⁸You shall not make for you an idol, or any image of that which is in the heavens above, or that which is on the earth below, or that which is in the water beneath the earth. ⁹You shall not prostrate yourself to them, and you shall not worship them, because I am the Lord your God, a zealous God, who reckons the iniquity of the fathers against the children, and against the third generation, and against the fourth generation, to those who hate Me, ¹⁰and engages in kindness for the thousands of generations, for those who love Me and observe My commandments.

¹¹You shall not take the name of the Lord your God in vain, as the Lord will not absolve one who takes His name in vain.

¹²Observe the Sabbath day to keep it holy, as a sacred day, as the Lord your God commanded you. ¹³Six days you shall work and perform all your labor. ¹⁴The seventh day is a Sabbath to the Lord your God. You shall not perform any labor; you, and your son, and your daughter, and your slave, and your maidservant, and your ox, and your donkey, and all your animals, and your gentile stranger who is within your city gates, so that your slave and your maidservant may rest like you. ¹⁵You shall remember that you were a slave in the land of Egypt, and the Lord your God resolutely took you out from there with a mighty hand and with

Fourth aliya

Deuteronomy

an outstretched arm; therefore, the Lord your God commanded you to observe the Sabbath day.

¹⁶Honor your father and your mother, as the Lord your God commanded you, so that your days will be extended and so that it will be good for you on the land which the Lord your God gives you. ¹⁷You shall not murder. And you shall not commit adultery or engage in forbidden sexual relations. And you shall not steal. And you shall not bear false witness, unsubstantiated testimony, against your neighbor. ¹⁸You shall not covet your neighbor's wife, and you shall not desire your neighbor's house, his field, or his slave, or his maidservant, his ox, or his donkey, or anything that is your neighbor's.

Fifth aliya ¹⁹These words the Lord spoke to your entire assembly at the mountain, Mount Sinai, from the midst of the fire, the cloud, and the fog, a great voice that did not cease, and He inscribed them on two stone tablets, and He gave them to me. ²⁰It was when you heard the voice from the midst of the darkness, and the mountain was burning with fire, that you approached me, all the heads of your tribes, and your elders. ²¹You said: Behold, the Lord our God has shown us His glory and His greatness, and His voice we heard from the midst of the fire; this day we have seen, have come to realize, that God will speak with man, and he may live. ²²And now, why should we die, when this great fire will consume us? If we continue to hear the voice of the Lord our God, we shall die. ²³For who of all flesh, all people, that heard the voice of the living God speaking from the midst of the fire, like us, has lived? ²⁴You approach and hear everything that the Lord our God will say, and you will speak to us everything that the Lord our God will speak to you, and we will hear it and we will perform it.

²⁵The Lord heard the sound of your words upon your speaking to me, and the Lord said to me: I heard the sound of the words of this people that they spoke to you; they did well in everything that they spoke. ²⁶Would that this shall be their heart: To fear Me and to observe all My commandments for all days, so that it will be good for them and for their children forever. ²⁷Go say to them: Return to your tents, ²⁸But you, Moses, stand here with Me, and I will speak to you all the commandment, and the statutes, and the ordinances that you will teach them, and they will perform them in the land that I am giving them to take possession of it.

More Encouragement to Keep the Mitzvot

Moses again encourages the Israelites to follow the Torah, for which they will be rewarded with long life and an established presence in the Land of Israel. He reminds them of the all the good that God had performed on their behalf in the course of the exodus from Egypt, and that He will perform on their behalf in the Land of Israel, and he encourages them to cultivate a sense of gratitude and love of God.

²⁹You shall take care to act as the Lord your God commanded you; you shall not deviate right or left. ³⁰In the entire path that the Lord your God commanded you, you shall walk, so that you will live, and that it will be good for you, and you will extend your days in the land of which

6 you will take possession. ¹And this is the commandment, the statutes, and the ordinances that the Lord your God commanded to teach you, to perform them in the land into which you are crossing to take possession of it, ²so that you will fear the Lord your God, to observe all His statutes and His commandments that I am commanding you: You, your son, and your son's son, all the days of your life; and so that your days will be extended. ³You shall hear, Israel, and you shall take care to perform, so that it will be good for you, and so that you will increase greatly, as the Lord, the God of your forefathers, spoke to you, in a land flowing with milk and honey.

^{Sixth} ⁴Hear, Israel: The Lord is our God, the Lord is one. ⁵You shall love the
^{aliya} Lord your God with all your heart, and with all your soul, and with all your might. ⁶These matters that I command you today shall be upon your heart; you shall focus your attention on them. ⁷You shall inculcate them in your children, and you shall speak of them, engage in them, while you are sitting in your house, and while you are walking on the way, and while you are lying down to sleep, and while you are rising. ⁸You shall bind them as a sign in the phylactery on your arm, the *tefillin* of the arm, and they shall be for ornaments in the *tefillin* between your eyes, on your head. ⁹You shall write them on the doorposts of your house, and on your gates, of courtyards and city walls.

📖 **Further reading:** For more on the profound significance of *Shema*, see *A Concise Guide to the Sages*, p. 231; the *halakhot* of reciting *Shema* appear in *A Concise Guide to Halakha*, pp. 486, 498.

¹⁰It shall be, when the Lord your God will take you into the land with regard to which He took an oath to your forefathers, to Abraham, to Isaac, and to Jacob, to give to you, you will find great and good cities

Deuteronomy

that you did not build, ¹¹and houses full of everything good that you did not fill, and hewn water cisterns that you did not hew, vineyards and olive trees that you did not plant, and you shall eat and you shall be satisfied. ¹²Beware, lest you forget the Lord, who took you out of the land of Egypt, from the house of bondage. ¹³You shall fear the Lord your God, and Him you shall serve, and by His name you shall swear. ¹⁴You shall not follow other gods from the gods of the peoples that are around you. ¹⁵For the Lord your God is a zealous God in your midst, lest the wrath of the Lord your God will be enflamed against you, and He will destroy you from upon the face of the earth.

¹⁶You shall not test the Lord your God; do not make requests from Him to determine whether He will meet your needs, as you tested Him in Masa (see Exodus 17:1–7). ¹⁷You shall observe the commandments of the Lord your God, and His testimonies, and His statutes that He commanded you. ¹⁸You shall do the right and the good in the eyes of the Lord, so that it will be good for you, and you will come and you will take possession of the good land with regard to which the Lord took an oath to your forefathers, ¹⁹to cast all your enemies from before you and overcome them, as the Lord spoke.

²⁰When your son asks you tomorrow, saying: What are the testimonies, and the statutes, and the ordinances that the Lord our God commanded you; what is the nature of these various forms of mitzvot? ²¹You shall say to your son: We were slaves to Pharaoh in Egypt, and the Lord resolutely took us out of Egypt with a mighty hand. ²²The Lord provided signs and wonders, great and awful, against Egypt, against Pharaoh, and against his entire household, before our eyes. ²³He took us out of there so that He would bring us to give us the land with regard to which He took an oath to our forefathers. ²⁴The Lord commanded us to perform all these statutes, to fear the Lord our God, for our good always, to keep us alive, as we are this day. ²⁵Justice and merit will be had for us, if we take care to perform all of this commandment before the Lord our God, as He commanded us.

The Seven Nations

Moses commanded the Israelites to keep absolute distance from the seven Canaanite nations that were steeped in idol worship. The Israelites were privileged to be selected as the distinguished people of God, who is zealous in His love for them, and therefore, he expects absolute loyalty from them.

7 ¹When the Lord your God will bring you to the land into which you are

Seventh aliya coming to take possession of it, and He will banish many nations from before you: the Hitites, the Girgashites, the Emorites, the Canaanites, the Perizites, the Hivites, and the Yevusites, seven nations greater and mightier than you. ²The Lord your God will deliver them before you, and you will smite them. You shall destroy them; you shall not establish a covenant with them, and you shall not show them favor or have mercy upon them. ³You shall not marry them; your daughter you shall not give to his son, and his daughter you shall not take for your son; ⁴he will divert your son from following Me, and they will serve other gods, and the wrath of the Lord will be enflamed against you, and He will destroy you quickly. ⁵Rather, so you shall do to them: Their altars you shall smash, and their stone monuments you shall shatter, and their sacred trees for idol worship you shall cut down, and their idols you shall burn in fire.

⁶For you are a holy people to the Lord your God; the Lord your God has chosen you to be His people of distinction, from all the peoples that are on the face of the earth. ⁷It is not for your multitude that the Lord desired you and chose you, as you are the fewest of all the peoples. ⁸Rather, it is from the Lord's love of you, and from His observance of the oath that He took to your forefathers that the Lord took you out with a mighty hand, and He redeemed you from the house of bondage,

Maftir from the hand of Pharaoh king of Egypt. ⁹You shall know, and internalize, that the Lord your God, He is the God, the faithful God, who maintains the covenant and the kindness to those who love Him and those who observe His commandments, for as many as one thousand generations. ¹⁰And He repays His enemies to their face, He punishes him immediately, to destroy them. He will not delay for His enemy; to his face He will repay him. ¹¹You shall observe the commandment, and the statutes, and the ordinances that I command you today, to perform them.

Further reading: For more on reward and punishment, see *A Concise Guide to the Sages,* p. 165; *A Concise Guide to Mahshava,* p. 256.

Deuteronomy

Parashat Ekev

In *Parashat Ekev*, Moses continues his admonition of the people regarding observance of the mitzvot, and describes the anticipated reward for it. He continues his encouragement of the Israelites prior to their conquest of the Land of Israel, and reminds them, again, of the wonders that God has performed for them up to this point. Upon their entry into the Land of Israel, it will be incumbent upon them to remember that their possession of it is not due to their merit, but rather to God's kindness. Moses relates the story of the sin of the Golden Calf, and other sins from the era of the wilderness, at length.

The Reward for Keeping the Mitzvot
Thanks to the observance of the ordinances of the Torah, the Israelites will merit blessing and prosperity in their inheritance of their land.

¹²**It shall be, because you heed these ordinances, and observe and perform them, the Lord your God will maintain for you the covenant and the kindness with regard to which He took an oath to your forefathers.** ¹³**He will love you, bless you, and multiply you; He will bless the fruit of your womb,** your offspring, **and the fruit of your land,** your crops, **your grain, your wine, and your** olive **oil, the calves of your herds and the lambs of your flock, in the land with regard to which He took an oath to your forefathers to give to you.** ¹⁴**You shall be blessed more than all peoples: There shall not be an infertile male or a barren female among you, or among your animals.** ¹⁵**The Lord will remove from you all illness, and all of the evil maladies of Egypt that you knew,** that you saw firsthand, **he will not place them among you; rather, he will give them to your enemies.** ¹⁶**You shall consume all the peoples that the Lord your God shall deliver to you; your eye shall not pity them, and you shall not serve their gods, for it is a snare for you.**

📖 **Further reading:** For more on divine providence, see *A Concise Guide to Mahshava*, p. 173.

Remembering Divine Providence

With wars of conquest lying ahead for the Israelites, Moses encourages them, reminding them of the kindnesses and the miracles that God has performed for them in the past. If they scrupulously distance themselves from the ways of the nations of the land, they will continue to merit assistance.

¹⁷**If you shall say in your heart: These nations are more numerous than I; how can I dispossess them?** ¹⁸**You shall not fear them; remember that which the Lord your God did to Pharaoh, and to all of Egypt.** ¹⁹**The great tests,** miracles, **that your eyes saw, and the signs, and the wonders, and the mighty hand, and the outstretched arm, with which the Lord your God took you out; so will the Lord your God do to all the peoples whom you fear.** ²⁰**The hornets, too, the Lord your God will dispatch among them,** driving them out of their hiding places, **until the annihilation of those remaining and those hiding from before you.** ²¹**Do not be broken before them,** fear them, **as the Lord your God is in your midst, the great and awesome God.** ²²**The Lord your God will banish those nations from before you little by little; you will be unable to eliminate them quickly, lest the beasts of the field increase against you.** If the land is emptied of its population too quickly, it will be overrun by wild beasts. ²³**The Lord your God will deliver them before you, and He will confound them;** they will suffer **a great confusion, until their destruction.** ²⁴**He shall deliver their kings into your hand, and you will eradicate their name from under the heavens. No man will stand before you.** You will prevail **until you have destroyed them.**

²⁵**The idols of their gods you shall burn in fire; you shall not covet silver or gold that is on them** as ornamentation **and take it for you, lest you be ensnared by it, as it is an abomination to the Lord your God.** ²⁶**You shall not bring an abomination into your house, or you will be proscribed** and abominated **like it; you shall detest it, and you shall abhor it,** and you shall distance yourself from it, **as it is proscribed** and revolting.

8 ¹**All the commandment that I command you this day, you shall take care to perform, so that you will live and you will multiply and come and take possession of the land with regard to which the Lord took an oath to your forefathers.** ²**You shall remember the entire way that the Lord your God led you these forty years in the wilderness, to afflict you** in order **to test you, to know** and assess **what is in your heart: Will you keep His commandments or not.** ³**He afflicted you, and starved you, and fed you the manna that you did not know, and your fathers did not**

Deuteronomy

know, in order to impart to you that man does not live by bread alone; rather, it is by everything that emanates from the mouth of the Lord that man lives. [4]Your garment did not grow worn from upon you, and your foot did not swell, despite the strenuous travels of these forty years. [5]You shall know in your heart that as a man chastises and challenges his son, so the Lord your God chastises you. [6]You shall observe the commandments of the Lord your God, to walk in His ways, and to fear Him.

The Danger of Forgetting God When Times Are Good

On the verge of their entry into the Land of Israel, anticipating the prosperity the people will enjoy there, Moses cautions them not to forget God's providence and kindness. It is not thanks to them, or their merit, that they are taking possession of the land, but rather due to an ancient promise that was made to the patriarchs.

[7]For the Lord your God is bringing you to a good land, a land of streams of water, of springs and depths, coming out in the valley and on the highlands. [8]A land of wheat and barley, grapevines, figs, pomegranates, a land of oil extracted from olives, and date honey; [9]a land in which you shall eat bread without poverty, you shall not lack anything in it; a land whose stones are iron, and from whose hills you will excavate copper. [10]You will eat and be satisfied, and you shall bless the Lord your God for the good land that He gave you. [11]Beware, lest you forget the Lord your God, to not observe His commandments, and His ordinances, and His statutes that I am commanding you today.

Second aliya

[12]Lest you eat and be satisfied, and build good houses, and settle in them, [13]and your cattle and your flocks increase, and silver and gold increase for you, and everything that is yours increases following your settlement of the land; [14]and your heart will grow haughty, and you will forget the Lord your God who took you out of the land of Egypt, from the house of bondage, [15]who guides you in the great and awesome wilderness, where there is snake, fiery, poisonous, serpent, and scorpion, and thirst where there is no water; who took water for you from the hard rock of flint; [16]who feeds you manna from the heavens in the wilderness, which your fathers did not know, in order to afflict you, and in order to test you, to do good for you in your future. [17]And you will say in your heart, you are liable to say to yourself: My power and the might of my hand made me these riches. [18]Moses charges them: You shall remember the Lord your God, as it is He who gives you power to generate

riches, in order to fulfill His covenant with regard to which He took an oath to your forefathers, as it is this day.

¹⁹It shall be, if you shall forget the Lord your God, and you shall follow other gods, and serve them, and prostrate yourself before them, I am warning you today that you shall be annihilated. ²⁰Like the nations that the Lord annihilates from before you, so will you be annihilated, because you would not heed the voice of the Lord your God.

9 ¹Hear, Israel: You are crossing the Jordan today to come to take possession from nations greater and mightier than you, cities great and fortified, with battlements reaching to the heavens; ²a people great, powerful, and tall, sons of giants, about whom you knew and you heard: Who can stand before the sons of giants? ³You shall know today that the Lord your God is He who passes before you, leading you in war; He is a devouring fire; He will destroy them, and He will subdue them before you, and you will conquer them, dispossess them, and eradicate them quickly, as the Lord spoke to you. ⁴Do not say in your heart, when the Lord your God casts them from before you, saying: It is due to my righteousness that the Lord has brought me to take possession of this land and due to the wickedness of these nations that the Lord dispossesses them from before you. ⁵It is not due to your righteousness, or due to the uprightness of your heart, that you are coming to take possession of their land; rather, it is due to the wickedness of these nations that the Lord your God dispossesses them from before you, and in order to keep the word with regard to which the Lord took an oath to your forefathers, to Abraham, to Isaac, and to Jacob.

Third aliya (margin, beside verse 3–4)

Account of the Sin of the Golden Calf

Moses describes the Israelites' sins during the wilderness era at length, especially the sin of the Golden Calf and its consequences. This account is intended to remind the Israelites that they are inheriting the land due to God's kindness, not due to their merit.

⁶You should know that it is not due to your righteousness that the Lord your God is giving you this good land to take possession of it, as you are a stiff-necked, stubborn people. ⁷Remember; do not forget that you infuriated the Lord your God in the wilderness. From the day that you emerged from the land of Egypt until your arrival at this place, you have been defiant against the Lord.

⁸At Horev, Mount Sinai, you provoked the Lord, and the Lord was incensed with you, to destroy you, ⁹when I had ascended to the

mountaintop to take the tablets of stone, the Tablets of the Covenant that the Lord made with you; I remained on the mountain forty days and forty nights, bread I did not eat and water I did not drink. ¹⁰The Lord gave me the two tablets of stone inscribed with the finger of God, and on them all the words that the Lord spoke with you on the mountain from the midst of the fire on the day of the assembly, when you assembled for the revelation at Sinai. ¹¹It was at the end of forty days and forty nights, the Lord gave me the two tablets of stone, the Tablets of the Covenant. ¹²The Lord said to me: Rise, descend quickly from here, as your people that you took out of Egypt acted corruptly; they deviated quickly from the path that I had commanded them, they made for them a cast figure, an idol.

¹³The Lord said to me, saying: I have seen this people, and behold, it is a stiff-necked, stubborn people. ¹⁴Let Me, and I will destroy them and I will erase their name from under the heavens and I will make you a nation mightier and more numerous than they. ¹⁵I turned and descended the mountain, and the mountain was burning in fire, and the two Tablets of the Covenant were in my two hands. ¹⁶I saw, and, behold, you had sinned against the Lord your God, you made yourselves a cast figure of a calf; you quickly deviated from the path that the Lord had commanded you. ¹⁷I grasped the two tablets, I cast them from my two hands, and I shattered them before your eyes.

¹⁸I fell before the Lord in prayer, as at the first time I went up on Sinai, for forty days and forty nights; bread I did not eat and water I did not drink, for all of your sin that you sinned, to perform evil in the eyes of the Lord, to anger Him. ¹⁹For I was daunted due to the wrath and the fury that the Lord raged against you, to destroy you, and the Lord heeded me that time as well. ²⁰And the Lord was incensed with Aaron, to destroy him, and I prayed for Aaron too, at that time. ²¹I took your sin that you made, the calf, and I burned it in fire; I pulverized it until it was well ground, into dust, and I cast its dust into the ravine that descends from the mountain.

²²In Tavera, and in Masa, and in Kivrot HaTaava, places where the Israelites encamped in the wilderness, you enraged the Lord. ²³Upon the Lord's sending you from Kadesh Barnea, saying: Go up and take possession of the land that I have given you, you defied the directive of the Lord your God; you did not trust Him, and you did not heed His voice. ²⁴You have been defiant of the Lord from the day that I knew you.

Deuteronomy

²⁵I fell before the Lord in prayer the forty days and forty nights that I fell, because the Lord had said to destroy you. ²⁶I prayed to the Lord, and said: My Lord God, do not destroy Your people and Your inheritance, Your people that You have redeemed in Your greatness, that You took out of Egypt with a mighty hand. ²⁷Remember Your servants, Abraham, Isaac, and Jacob; do not turn to, focus on, the stubbornness of this people, or to its wickedness, or to its sin, ²⁸lest the inhabitants of the land that You took us out from there say: It is due to the lack of the ability of the Lord to bring them to the land with regard to which He spoke to them, and due to His hatred of them that He took them out to kill them in the wilderness.

10 ¹At that time the Lord said to me: Carve for yourself two tablets of
ᴼᵘʳᵗʰ stone like the first tablets, and ascend to Me to the mountain, and make
ᵃˡⁱʸᵃ for yourself a wooden ark. ²I will inscribe on the tablets the statements that were on the first tablets that you shattered, and you shall place them in the ark.

³I made an ark of acacia wood, I carved two tablets of stone like the first, and I ascended to the mountaintop, and the two tablets were in my hand. ⁴He, God, inscribed on the tablets like the first inscription, the Ten Commandments that the Lord spoke to you on the mountain from the midst of the fire on the day of the assembly, on the day of the revelation at Sinai, and the Lord gave them to me. ⁵I turned and I descended from the mount, and I placed the tablets in the ark that I had made and they were there, as the Lord had commanded me.

📖 **Further reading:** For more on the Tablets of the Covenant, see *A Concise Guide to the Sages*, pp. 105, 122.

⁶The children of Israel traveled from Be'erot Benei Yaakan to Mosera; there Aaron died, and he was buried there, and Elazar his son served as priest in his place. ⁷From there they traveled to Gudgod, and from Gudgod to Yotvata, a land of streams of water. ⁸At that time, the Lord designated the tribe of Levi to carry the Ark of the Covenant of the Lord, to stand before the Lord to serve Him, and to bless in His name to this day. ⁹Therefore Levi did not have a portion or an inheritance with his brethren; the Lord is his inheritance, as the Lord your God spoke to him. ¹⁰I stayed on the mountain like I did the first time, forty days and forty nights, and the Lord heeded me that time as well; the

Deuteronomy

Lord was unwilling to destroy you. [11]The Lord said to me: Rise, go on a journey before the people, and they will come and take possession of the land with regard to which I took an oath to their forefathers to give to them.

Encouraging Observance of the Mitzvot
Moses again encourages the people to observe the commandments and the Torah, to behave justly and ethically, and to love and fear God.

Fifth aliya [12]Now, Israel, what does the Lord your God ask of you? Only to fear the Lord your God, to walk in all His ways, and to love Him, and to serve the Lord your God with all your heart and with all your soul, [13]to observe the commandments of the Lord, and His statutes that I command you today, for your good.

[14]Behold, to the Lord your God are the heavens, and the heavens of heavens, the earth and everything that is in it. [15]Yet the Lord desired your forefathers, to love them, and He chose their descendants after them, you, from all the peoples, as this day. [16]Remove the metaphorical obstruction of your heart that prevents your heart from feeling, and do not stiffen your neck, be stubborn, anymore. [17]For the Lord your God, He is the God of gods, and the Lord of lords, the great, the valorous, and the awesome God, who will not show favor in judgment, and will not take a bribe. [18]He executes justice for the orphan and the widow, and loves the stranger, to give him food and garment. [19]You shall love the stranger, as you were strangers in the land of Egypt. [20]The Lord your God you shall fear, Him you shall serve, and to Him you shall cleave, and in His name you shall take an oath. [21]He is your glory, and He is your God, who performed for you these great and awesome deeds that your eyes saw. [22]With seventy people your ancestors descended to Egypt, and now the Lord your God has rendered you as the stars of the heavens in abundance.

11 [1]You shall love the Lord your God, and observe His charge, and His statutes, and His ordinances, and His commandments, always.

[2]You shall know today that it is not with your children that I am speaking, who did not know, and who have not seen the chastising of the Lord your God, His greatness, His mighty hand, and His outstretched arm, [3]and His signs, and His actions that He performed in the midst of Egypt to Pharaoh king of Egypt, and to his entire land, [4]and what

He did to the army of Egypt, to its horses, and to its chariots; that He inundated the water of the Red Sea upon them in their pursuit of you, and the Lord annihilated them to this day; ⁵and what He did for you in the wilderness, until you arrived at this place; ⁶and what He did to Datan and Aviram, sons of Eliav son of Reuben; that the earth opened its mouth, swallowed them, their households, their tents, and all the property that was at their feet in the midst of all Israel. ⁷Rather, it is your eyes that see all the great work of the Lord that He performed. ⁸You shall observe the entire commandment that I command you this day, so that you will be strong, and come and take possession of the land, that you are crossing there to take possession of it, ⁹and so that you may extend your days upon the land with regard to which the Lord took an oath to your forefathers to give to them and to their descendants, a land flowing with milk and honey.

God Is Present in the Land of Israel

The Land of Israel is unique because it is subject to the special providence of God, whose attention is perpetually directed toward it. Therefore, the reward and punishment cycle there is instantaneous. Observing the path of the Torah will translate into prosperity and blessing for the Israelites in their land.

Sixth aliya ¹⁰For the land that you are coming there to take possession of it is not like the land of Egypt, from which you emerged, where, due to the abundance of water, you would sow your seed, and water it on foot, i.e., by irrigation, like a vegetable garden. ¹¹Rather, the land that you are crossing there to take possession of it is a land of mountains and valleys; by the rain of the heavens it drinks water. ¹²It is a land that the Lord your God seeks; always the eyes of the Lord your God are upon it, from the beginning of the year until the end of the year.

¹³It shall be, if you will heed My commandments that I command you today, to love the Lord your God, and to serve Him with all your heart and with all your soul, ¹⁴I will provide the rain of your land at its appointed time, the early rain and the late rain, and you will gather your grain, and your wine, and your oil. ¹⁵I will provide grass in your field for your animals, and you will eat and you will be satisfied. ¹⁶Beware, lest your heart be seduced, and you stray and serve other gods, and prostrate yourself before them. ¹⁷The wrath of the Lord will be enflamed against you, and He will curb the heavens and there will be no rain, and the ground will not yield its produce, and you will be quickly

Deuteronomy

eradicated from upon the good land that the Lord is giving you. [18]You shall place these words of Mine upon your heart and upon your soul, and you shall bind them as a sign in the *tefillin* upon your arm, And they shall be as ornaments in the *tefillin* between your eyes, on your head. [19]You shall teach them to your children, to speak of them while you are sitting in your house and while you are walking on the way, [20]and you shall write them on the doorposts of your house, and on your gates; [21]so that your days will be increased, and the days of your children, on the land with regard to which the Lord took an oath to your forefathers to give them, like the days of the heavens above the earth since the creation of the world.

> **Further reading:** For more on the mitzvot of *mezuza* and *tefillin*, see *A Concise Guide to Halakha*, pp. 539, 589.

Seventh aliya, Maftir [22]For if you shall observe this entire commandment that I command you to perform it, to love the Lord your God, to walk in all His ways, and to cleave to Him, [23]the Lord will dispossess all these nations from before you, and you will take possession from nations greater and mightier than you. [24]Every place upon which the sole of your foot shall tread will be yours, from the wilderness and the Lebanon, from the river, the Euphrates River, up to the last sea will be your border. [25]No man will stand before you, the Lord your God will place terror of you and fear of you upon the entire land on which you will tread, as He spoke to you.

Deuteronomy

Parashat Re'eh

Parashat Re'eh marks the conclusion of the survey of the events that transpired during the wilderness era with which Moses began his great address. Here he moves on to a survey of the mitzvot, beginning with the assertion that the choice regarding fulfillment of the mitzvot is essentially a choice between blessing and curse. Among the mitzvot surveyed in this Torah portion is the prohibition against idol worship, including the restriction of sacrificial worship to the Holy Temple, as well as other mitzvot – the laws of which foods are permitted and prohibited, and different social commandments, e.g., the laws of the Hebrew slave and the Sabbatical Year, and the laws concerning the three pilgrimage festivals.

Blessing and Curse

Moses places a choice before the people: blessing or curse. The blessing entails listening to God and walking in His ways. The curse is abandoning service of God, and instead worshipping false gods. Moses alludes to a ceremony, to be described later, which will take place on Mount Gerizim and Mount Eival after the people cross the Jordan River.

²⁶**See, I put before you this day** the choice between **a blessing and a curse.** ²⁷**The blessing, if you heed the commandments of the Lord your God, that I am commanding you today,** ²⁸**and the curse, if you will not heed the commandments of the Lord your God, and you stray from the path that I am commanding you today, to follow other gods that you did not know.**

📖 **Further reading:** For more on the granting of free will to human beings, see *A Concise Guide to Mahshava*, p. 138.

²⁹**It shall be when the Lord your God brings you into the land that you are coming there to take possession of it, you shall deliver the blessing on Mount Gerizim, and the curse on Mount Eival.** ³⁰**Are they not beyond,** west of, **the Jordan, after the path of the setting of the sun, in the land of the Canaanite that lives in the plain, opposite the Gilgal, beside the plains of Moreh?**

Destroying Idols and Designating a Place to Worship God

Entry into the Land of Israel intensifies the significant challenge for the Israelites of distancing themselves from idol worship. Moses again emphasizes the commands regarding destruction of idols. In contrast to idol worship, which is performed anywhere, God will designate a place for His service, and only there will it be permitted to sacrifice offerings and consume sacrificial food. In this context, the consumption of non-sacred food, which may be eaten anywhere, and the laws governing it, are mentioned.

³¹**For you are crossing the Jordan to come to take possession of the land that the Lord your God is giving you, and you shall take possession of it, and you shall reside in it.** ³²**You shall take care to perform all the statutes and the ordinances that I put before you today.**

12 ¹**These are the statutes and the ordinances that you shall take care to perform in the land that the Lord, God of your fathers, has given you to take possession of it, all the days that you live on the earth.** ²**You shall eradicate all the places where the nations from whom you are taking possession served their gods: on the high mountains, and on the hills, and under every flourishing,** unhewn, **tree.** ³**You shall smash their altars, and you shall shatter their monuments, and their sacred trees you shall burn in fire, and the idols of their gods you shall cut down; and you shall eradicate their name** and their memory **from that place.**

⁴**You shall not do so to the Lord your God;** you shall not bring offerings to Him just anywhere. Alternatively, this is an explicit prohibition to destroy places sanctified to God. ⁵**Rather, to the place that the Lord your God will choose from all your tribes to place His name there, you shall seek for His resting place and you shall come there.** ⁶**You shall bring there your burnt offerings,** burned in their entirety on the altar, **and your peace offerings,** most of which are eaten by you, **and your tithes and the gift of your hand** from your produce and your animals, **and your vows and your pledges** to bring gift offerings, **and the firstborn of your cattle and of your flocks.** ⁷**You shall eat there before the Lord your God, and you shall rejoice in all your endeavors, you, and your households with which the Lord your God has blessed you.**

⁸**When you settle the land you shall not do like all that we are doing here today, each man anything that is right in his eyes,** sacrificing offerings wherever you please. ⁹**For you have not yet come to the haven and to the inheritance,** the Land of Israel, **that the Lord your God is giving you.** ¹⁰**You shall cross the Jordan, and you will live in the land that the Lord your God is bequeathing to you, and He will give you respite from all**

Second
aliya your enemies around, and you will live securely. ¹¹It shall be the place that the Lord your God will choose to rest His name there; there, you shall bring everything that I command you: your burnt offerings, and your peace offerings, your tithes, and the gifts of your hand, and all your choice vows that you vow to the Lord. ¹²You shall rejoice before the Lord your God, you, and your sons, and your daughters, and your slaves, and your maidservants, and the Levite who is within your city gates, as he has no share and inheritance with you.

📖 **Further reading:** For more on "the place that God will choose," i.e., the Temple, see *A Concise Guide to Mahshava*, p. 160.

¹³Beware, lest you offer up your burnt offerings in any place that you see. ¹⁴Rather, in the place that the Lord will choose, in one of your tribes, there you shall offer up your burnt offerings, and there you shall do everything that I command you. ¹⁵Only, with all of your heart's desire, you may slaughter and eat meat in accordance with the blessing of prosperity **of the Lord your God that He gave you within all your gates,** wherever you live. Both **the pure and the impure,** who are prohibited from eating from offerings, **may eat it.** If you slaughter domesticated animals not as sacrifices, you may eat the meat, **like** that of **the gazelle and like** that of **the deer,** undomesticated animals which are ineligible to be sacrificed as offerings. ¹⁶Only the blood you shall not eat; you shall pour it on the ground like water. ¹⁷You may not eat within your gates the tithe of your grain and your wine and your oil, or the firstborn of your cattle and of your flocks, or any of your vows that you will vow, or your pledges, or the gift of your hand. ¹⁸Rather, before the Lord your God you shall eat them, in the place that the Lord your God will choose; you, and your son, and your daughter, and your slave, and your maidservant, and the Levite who is within your gates; and you shall rejoice before the Lord your God in all your endeavors. ¹⁹Beware, lest you forsake the Levite all your days upon your land.

²⁰When the Lord your God will expand your border, as He spoke to you, and you will say: I will eat meat, because your heart will desire to eat meat; with all your heart's desire, you may eat meat. ²¹If the place that the Lord your God will choose to place His name there will be far from you, you shall slaughter from your herd and from your flock that the Lord gave you, as I commanded you, and you shall eat within your city gates, with all your heart's desire. ²²However, just as the gazelle or

the deer is eaten, so you shall eat it; the pure and the impure may eat it together. ²³Only be strong and resolute to not eat the blood, as the blood is the life, and you shall not eat the life with the meat. ²⁴You shall not eat it; you shall pour it on the earth like water. ²⁵You shall not eat it, so that it will be good for you and for your children after you, when you will do that which is right in the eyes of the Lord. ²⁶Only your sacraments, your obligatory offerings that you will have, and your vows, your gift offerings, you shall carry, and come to the place that the Lord will choose. ²⁷You shall perform your burnt offerings, the meat and the blood, on the altar of the Lord your God, and the blood of your offerings shall be poured on the altar of the Lord your God, and the meat you shall eat.

²⁸Observe and heed all these matters that I command you, so that it will be good for you and for your children after you forever, when you perform the good and the right in the eyes of the Lord your God.

Prohibitions Related to Idolatry

The people are warned to stamp out not only idol worship itself, but how to respond to related pitfalls: a false prophet, one who entices others to worship false gods, and an entire city that has gone astray to idolatry.

Third aliya ²⁹When the Lord your God will excise the nations that you are coming there to take possession from them from before you, and you will take possession from them and live in their land, ³⁰beware, lest you be ensnared after them, their ways, after they are destroyed from before you, and lest you seek their gods, saying: How do these nations serve their gods? I will do so as well. ³¹You shall not do so to the Lord your God, as every abomination of the Lord that He hates they have done to their gods, as they also burn their sons and their daughters in the fire to their gods.

13 ¹All this matter that I command you, you shall take care to perform; you shall not add to it and you shall not subtract from it. ²If a prophet rises in your midst, or a dreamer of a dream that he claims is prophetic, and he provides you with a sign or a wonder, ³and the sign or the wonder that he spoke to you comes to pass, saying: Let us follow other gods that you did not previously know, and serve them; ⁴You shall not heed the words of that prophet, or that dreamer of a dream, as the Lord your God is testing you, to know whether you love the Lord your God with all your heart and with all your soul. ⁵You shall follow the

Lord your God, and Him you shall fear, and His commandments you shall observe, and His voice you shall heed, and Him you shall serve, and to Him you shall cleave. [6]That prophet, or that dreamer of a dream, shall be put to death, because he spoke fabrication about the Lord your God, who took you out of the land of Egypt and redeemed you from the house of bondage, to lead you astray from the path on which the Lord your God commanded you to walk; and you shall eliminate the evil from your midst.

[7]If your brother, son of your mother, or your son, or your daughter, or the wife of your bosom, or your close friend who is like your own soul, entices you secretly, saying: Let us go and serve other gods that you did not know, you and your fathers, [8]from the gods of the peoples that are around you, that are near to you, or that are far from you, from one end of the earth to the other, [9]you shall not accede to him, and you shall not heed him, and your eye shall not pity him, and you shall not be compassionate, and you shall not cover up for him. [10]Rather, you, who are close to him, shall kill him; your hand shall be against him first to put him to death, and the hand of all the people last. Those closest to someone who would entice others to idolatry bear the responsibility of ensuring he is punished. [11]You shall stone him with stones and he shall die because he sought to lead you astray from the Lord your God who took you out of the land of Egypt, from the house of bondage. [12]All Israel shall hear and shall fear, and they will not continue to perform any act like this evil matter in your midst.

[13]If you shall hear, in one of your cities that the Lord your God is giving you to live there, saying: [14]Wicked people have emerged from your midst, and have led the inhabitants of their city astray, saying: Let us go and serve other gods that you did not know, [15]you shall inquire, and interrogate, and ask diligently, and behold, if it is true, the matter is correct, this abomination was performed in your midst, [16]you shall smite the inhabitants of that city by sword; destroy it, and all that is in it, and its animals, by sword. [17]You shall gather all its spoils into the midst of its square, and you shall burn in fire the city and all its spoils, completely, to the Lord your God, and it shall be an eternal mound; it shall not be rebuilt. [18]Nothing of the proscribed property shall cleave to your hand, so that the Lord will abandon His enflamed wrath, and He will give you mercy and be merciful to you, and multiply you, as He took an oath to your fathers, [19]when you will heed the voice of the Lord

Deuteronomy

your God, to observe all His commandments that I am commanding you today, to perform the right in the eyes of the Lord your God.

Various Mitzvot

Moses moves on to a general survey of the mitzvot, some related to the identity of the Israelites as the people of God, a people of distinction, e.g., the laws of permitted and forbidden foods, and some social mitzvot, e.g., the laws of the Hebrew slave, the Sabbatical Year, and more.

14 ¹You are children to the Lord your God; you shall not cut yourselves
Fourth aliya and you shall not place a bald spot between your eyes, on your head, as an expression of mourning **for the dead.** ²For you are a holy people to the Lord your God, and you the Lord chose to be His people of distinction, beloved from all the peoples that are on the face of the earth.

³You shall not eat any item that is an **abomination.** ⁴These are the animals that you may eat: an ox, a sheep, and a goat; ⁵a deer, a gazelle, a fallow deer, a wild goat, an oryx, an aurochs, and a mouflon sheep. ⁶Any animal that has hooves, and the two hooves are split, and that brings up the cud; among the animals, that you may eat. ⁷However, these you shall not eat from those that bring up the cud or from those with a split hoof: the camel, and the hare, and the hyrax, because they bring up the cud but do not have hooves; they are impure for you; ⁸and the pig, because it has split hooves but does not bring up the cud, it is impure for you, and therefore from their meat you shall not eat, and their carcasses you shall not touch.

Illustrations: See photograph of split hooves, p. 528.

⁹This you may eat from all that is in the water: Anything that has fins and scales you may eat, ¹⁰and anything that does not have fins and scales you may not eat; it is impure for you.

¹¹All pure birds you may eat. ¹²This is that which you may not eat from them: the griffon vulture, the bearded vulture, and the lappet-faced vulture; ¹³the glede, the buzzard, and the kite, after its kinds; ¹⁴every raven after its kinds; ¹⁵the ostrich, the swift, the seagull, and the sparrow hawk after its kinds; ¹⁶the little owl, the short-eared owl, and the barn owl, ¹⁷the eagle owl, the roller, and the fish owl, ¹⁸the stork, the heron after its kinds, the hoopoe, and the bat. ¹⁹Every flying swarming

creature is impure for you; they shall not be eaten. ²⁰All pure flying creatures you may eat.

²¹You shall not eat any unslaughtered carcass, an animal that was not ritually slaughtered; to the gentile stranger who is within your gates you may give it and he will eat it, or you may sell it to a foreigner, as you are a holy people for the Lord your God. You shall not cook a kid in its mother's milk.

Fifth aliya ²²You shall tithe the entire crop of your sowing that comes out in the field year by year. ²³You shall eat before the Lord your God, in the place which He will choose to rest His name there, in Jerusalem, proximate to the Temple, the tithe of your grain, your wine, and your oil, and the firstborn of your cattle and your flocks, so that you will learn to fear the Lord your God always. ²⁴If the way is too great for you as you are unable to carry it; if the journey is too long to carry the tithe of your produce because the place that the Lord your God will choose to place His name there is too far from you, when the Lord your God blesses you with an expansive land, ²⁵you shall exchange it for silver, and you shall bind the silver in your hand, and you shall go to the place that the Lord your God will choose. ²⁶You shall spend the silver for whatever your heart desires, for cattle, or for sheep, or for wine, or for intoxicating drink, or for whatever your heart shall wish, and you shall eat it there before the Lord your God, and you shall rejoice, you and your household. ²⁷The Levite who is within your city gates, you shall not forsake him, as he has no portion or inheritance with you.

²⁸At the end of every three years, you shall take out all the tithe of your crop in that year, and you shall deposit it within your gates. ²⁹The Levite, because he has no portion or inheritance with you, and the stranger and the orphan and the widow who are within your gates, all of whom have no agricultural source of income, shall come, and they shall eat and be satisfied, so that the Lord your God will bless you in all your endeavors that you do.

15 ¹At the end of seven years you shall perform a remittal. ²This is the *Sixth aliya* matter of the remittal: Every creditor that has extended credit to his neighbor shall remit; shall abrogate his right to demand repayment. He shall not demand it from his neighbor or his brother, because remittal has been proclaimed for the Lord. ³From the foreigner you may demand it, but that which you will have with your brother, you shall

Deuteronomy

remit your claim. ⁴It, the hope, is only that there will be no indigent among you, as the Lord will bless you in the land that the Lord your God is giving you as an inheritance to take possession of it, ⁵if you only heed the voice of the Lord your God, to take care to perform this entire commandment that I command you today. ⁶For the Lord your God has blessed you, as He spoke to you, and you will lend to many nations but you will not borrow, and you will rule many nations, but they will not rule you.

⁷If there is among you an indigent from your brethren within your gates, in your land that the Lord your God is giving you, you shall not harden your heart and you shall not close your hand from your indigent brother. ⁸Rather, you shall open your hand to him, and you shall lend him money with collateral, enough for his need that will be lacking for him. ⁹Beware, lest there be a wicked thought in your heart, saying: The seventh year, the year of remittal, is approaching, and your eye will be miserly toward your indigent brother, and you will not give him, and he will cry to the Lord against you, and it will be a sin for you. ¹⁰You shall give him the loan, and your heart shall not be miserly when you give to him. Because due to this matter, the Lord your God will bless you in all your actions, and in all your endeavors. ¹¹For the reality is that the indigent will never cease from the land; therefore, I command you, saying: You shall open your hand to your brother, to your poor, and to your indigent in your land.

Further reading: For more on the mitzva of charity, see *A Concise Guide to the Sages*, pp. 240, 245, 426; *A Concise Guide to Mahshava*, p. 248; *A Concise Guide to Halakha*, p. 615.

¹²If your brother, a Hebrew man, or a Hebrew woman is sold to you as a slave, he shall serve you six years, and in the seventh year you shall set him free from you. ¹³When you set him free from you, you shall not release him empty-handed. ¹⁴You shall grant him from your flock, and from your threshing floor, and from your winepress that the Lord your God has blessed you, you shall give him. ¹⁵You shall remember that you were a slave in the land of Egypt, and the Lord your God redeemed you; therefore I command you this matter today. ¹⁶It shall be that if he says to you: I will not leave you after six years, because he loves you and your household, because it is good for him with you; ¹⁷You shall take the awl, a tool for piercing hides, and you shall place it through and pierce

his ear and the door post, and he shall be an eternal slave to you, and so to your maidservant you shall do likewise. [18]It shall not be difficult in your eyes in your setting him free from you, as twice above and beyond the wage of a hired man he has served you six years. and the Lord your God will bless you in all that you will do.

venth
aliya [19]Any firstborn that shall be born of your cattle and of your flocks, you shall sanctify the males to the Lord your God; you shall not work the field with the firstborn of your ox, and you shall not shear the wool of the firstborn of your flock. [20]You shall eat it before the Lord your God year by year, each year, in the place that the Lord shall choose, you and your household. [21]And if there is a blemish on it, lameness, or blindness, or any severe blemish, you shall not slaughter it to the Lord your God. [22]You shall eat it within your gates, the impure and the pure alike, because it is non-sacred, like the flesh of the gazelle and like the flesh of the deer, which are ineligible for sacrifice as offerings. [23]Only its blood you shall not eat; you shall pour it on the ground like water.

The Three Pilgrimage Festivals

Moses describes the festivals of Passover, Shavuot, and Sukkot. These are days of rejoicing and thanksgiving associated with the harvests of different crops in the Land of Israel. Moses emphasizes the obligation to include the weaker members of society in the celebration of the festivals.

16 [1]Observe the month of ripening, ensuring that the festival of Passover occurs in the spring and you shall perform the paschal offering to the Lord your God, for in the month of ripening the Lord your God took you out of Egypt at night. [2]You shall slaughter the paschal offering to the Lord your God, sheep and cattle for the festive meal and other offerings that accompany it, in the place that the Lord shall choose to rest His name there. [3]You shall not eat with it leavened bread; seven days you shall eat with it unleavened bread, the bread of affliction, or the bread of poverty, that which is eaten by the poor, as in haste you came out from the land of Egypt and therefore did not have time to allow the dough to rise; do this so that you will remember the day of your exodus from the land of Egypt all the days of your life. [4]No leaven [se'or] shall be seen by you within all your borders for seven days. And the meat of the paschal lamb that you slaughter in the evening on the first day shall not remain overnight until morning of the first day of the festival.

⁵You may not slaughter the paschal lamb within any of your gates that the Lord your God is giving you, ⁶except at the place that the Lord your God shall choose to rest His name; there you shall slaughter the paschal lamb in the evening, as the sun sets, the appointed time of your exodus from Egypt. ⁷You shall cook and eat it in the place that the Lord your God shall choose, and you shall turn away in the morning, and only then go to your tents. ⁸Six days you shall eat unleavened bread, and on the seventh day, in addition to eating unleavened bread, there shall be a solemn assembly to the Lord your God, you shall perform no labor.

⁹You shall count seven weeks for you; from the start of the sickle in the standing grain, from the beginning of the harvest, you shall start to count seven weeks. ¹⁰You shall hold the Festival of Weeks to the Lord your God; the measure of your personal pledge which you give will be as the Lord your God will bless you, commensurate with your prosperity. ¹¹You shall rejoice before the Lord your God, you, your son, your daughter, your slave, your maidservant, and the Levite who is within your gates, and the stranger, the orphan, and the widow who are in your midst, in the place that the Lord your God shall rest His name there. ¹²You shall remember that you were a slave in Egypt, and you shall observe and you shall perform these statutes.

Maftir ¹³You shall hold the Festival of Tabernacles seven days, upon your gathering produce from your threshing floor and from your winepress. ¹⁴You shall rejoice on your festival, you, your son, your daughter, your slave, your maidservant, and the Levite, and the stranger, the orphan, and the widow who are within your gates. ¹⁵Seven days you shall celebrate to the Lord your God in the place that the Lord shall choose, as the Lord your God will bless you in your entire crop, and in all your endeavors, and you shall be completely joyous. ¹⁶Three times in the year all your males shall appear before the Lord your God in the place that He shall choose: On the Festival of Unleavened Bread, and on the Festival of Weeks, and on the Festival of Tabernacles, and they shall not appear before the Lord empty-handed. ¹⁷Each man shall bring according to the gift of his hand, as he sees fit, in accordance with the blessing of the Lord your God that He gave you.

📖 **Further reading:** For more on the three pilgrimage Festivals – Passover, *Shavuot*, and *Sukkot* – see *A Concise Guide to the Sages*, pp. 290, 306, 309; *A Concise Guide to Mahshava*, pp. 72, 93, 99; *A Concise Guide to Halakha*, pp. 176, 274, 340.

Parashat Shofetim

In *Parashat Shofetim* the general survey of mitzvot continues. Many diverse mitzvot are cited in it, some relating to the necessary attitude toward the peoples of the land and the need for the Israelites to distance themselves from their ways, and some to the configuration of the judicial system. In addition, laws related to war and murder are cited.

Establishing the Judicial System

Moses describes the obligation to establish a judicial system and with it, the necessity of obeying the rulings of the judges and the punishments that will ensue for one who defies them. In addition, laws related to idol worship are cited.

¹⁸Judges and officers you shall place for you within all your gates that the Lord your God is giving you for your tribes. And they shall judge the people, a fair judgment. ¹⁹You judges shall not distort judgment, you shall not give preference, and you shall not take a bribe, as the bribe will blind the eyes of the wise and corrupt the words of the righteous. ²⁰Justice, justice you shall pursue, so that you will live and take possession of the land that the Lord your God is giving you.

> **Further reading:** For more on what characterizes a worthy judge and what constitutes justice, see *A Concise Guide to the Sages*, pp. 103, 183, 225, 243, 477ff.

²¹You shall not plant for you any kind of sacred tree next to the altar of the Lord your God that you shall make for you. ²²You shall not establish for you a commemorative **monument, which the Lord your God hates.**

17 ¹You shall not slaughter to the Lord your God an ox or a lamb in which there is a blemish, any bad thing, as that is an abomination of the Lord your God.

²If there will be found in your midst, within any of your city gates that the Lord your God is giving you, a man or a woman who will perform evil in the eyes of the Lord your God, to violate His covenant; ³he went

and served other gods, and prostrated himself before them, or to the sun, or to the moon, or to any of the host of the heavens that I did not command to worship them, [4]and it will be told to you, and you will hear, and you shall inquire, examine, and clarify diligently, and behold, it is true, the matter is correct, this abomination was performed in Israel; [5]you shall take out that man or that woman who has performed this evil thing to your gates, the man or the woman; you shall stone them with stones, and they will die. [6]At the word of two witnesses, or three witnesses, a person shall be put to death. He shall not be put to death at the word of one witness. [7]The hand of the witnesses shall be first upon him to put him to death, and the hand of all the rest of the people last, after the witnesses, and you shall eliminate the evil from your midst.

[8]If a matter of judgment will be obscure to you, between blood that is ritually pure and blood that is ritually impure, e.g., from a menstruating woman, or between one case of monetary law and another case, or between one leprous mark and another mark, matters of dispute within your gates; you shall arise, and you shall go up to the place that the Lord your God shall choose. [9]You shall come to the priests, the Levites, and to the judge, the head of the Great Sanhedrin, who shall be in those days, and you shall inquire, and they shall tell you the statement of judgment. [10]You shall do according to the statement that they will tell you from that place that the Lord shall choose, and you shall take care to perform in accordance with everything that they will instruct you. [11]On the basis of the law that they will instruct you, and the judgment that they will say to you, you shall act; you shall not deviate from the matter that they will tell you, right or left. [12]The man who shall perform with intent to not heed the High Priest who stands to serve the Lord your God there, or the judge; that man shall die, and you shall eliminate the evil from Israel. [13]All the people shall hear and they shall fear, and they will not act defiantly with intent anymore.

The Monarchy

With the Israelites' entry into the land and their resumption of a routine life, they will seek to institute a monarchy. The Torah allows this, but only with the restrictions enumerated here.

Second aliya [14]When you will come to the land that the Lord your God is giving you, and you shall take possession of it, and you shall live in it, and you shall say: I will place a king over me, like all the nations that are around me; [15]you shall place a king over you whom the Lord your God shall choose.

From among your brethren you shall place a king over you; you may not place over you a foreign man, who is not your brother. [16]Only he shall not amass horses for himself, and he shall not return the people to Egypt in order to amass horses, as the Lord said to you: You shall not return again on that way anymore. [17]He shall not amass wives, and his heart will not stray, and silver and gold he shall not amass greatly. [18]It shall be upon his sitting on the throne of his kingdom, he shall write for himself a copy of this Torah in a scroll, from that which is before the priests, the Levites. [19]It shall be with him, and he shall read from it all the days of his life, so that he will learn to fear the Lord his God, to observe all the words of this Torah and these statutes, in order to perform them, [20]that his heart will not be elevated above his brethren, and that he will **not deviate from the commandment right or left,** so that he may extend his days over his kingdom, he and his sons, in the midst of Israel.

Priestly Gifts

Since the priests do not receive a portion of the land like the members of the tribes, the people of Israel must take care of them, and they are entitled to certain benefits. In this section the priestly gifts are listed, alongside the rights of the priests to serve in the Temple and to receive a portion of the meat of the offerings.

18 [1]There shall not be for the priests the Levites, the entire tribe of Levi,
Third aliya a portion and an inheritance with Israel; the fire offerings of the Lord and His inheritance they shall eat. [2]He shall not have an inheritance among his brethren; the Lord is their inheritance, just as He had spoken to him, them.

[3]This shall be the allocation of the priests to which they are entitled from the people: From those who perform non-sacred slaughter, if it is an ox or if it is a lamb, he shall give the priest the foreleg, and the jaw, and the stomach. [4]You shall give him the first fruits of your grain, of your wine, and of your oil as *teruma,* and the first of the fleece of your flock. [5]For the Lord your God has chosen him from all your tribes, to stand and to serve in the name of the Lord, he and his sons all the days.

Fourth aliya [6]And if a Levite priest shall come from one of your gates, from all of Israel where he resides, and he comes with all the desire of his heart, when he wishes, to the place that the Lord will choose, [7]he shall serve in the name of the Lord his God, like all his brethren the Levites who stand there before the Lord during their assigned watch. [8]Portion by

portion they shall eat equally, the Levite who is volunteering, and the members of the assigned watch, **except for that which was sold by the ancestors.** If their ancestors had agreed on a permanent division of certain offerings, that agreement will remain in effect.

The Prohibition against Sorcery and Witchcraft

Once again, the primary challenge facing the Israelites upon their entry into the Land of Israel is emphasized; they are warned not to imitate the behavior of the peoples of the land. Here, Moses addresses witchcraft and sorcery, in which those peoples were steeped. Such attempts at manipulation of the spiritual world stand in direct opposition to the prophetic connection with God that the Israelites are privileged to enjoy.

⁹**When you come into the land that the Lord your God is giving you, you shall not learn to act in accordance with the abominations of those nations.** ¹⁰**There shall not be found among you any one who passes his son or his daughter through the fire,** an idolatrous rite, **or a sorcerer, a soothsayer** [*me'onen*] who makes predictions on the basis of the clouds [*ananim*], **or a diviner, or a warlock,** ¹¹**or an enchanter, or a medium, or an oracle, or a necromancer.** All of these seek to foretell the future or reveal secrets through sorcery or contact with the spirits of the dead. ¹²**For anyone who performs these is an abomination to the Lord, and due to these abominations the Lord your God dispossesses them from before you.**

¹³**You,** though, **shall be wholehearted with the Lord your God,** and not employ these measures.

Fifth aliya ¹⁴**For these nations from whom you are taking possession heed soothsayers and sorcerers; but you, not so did the Lord your God give to you.** ¹⁵**A prophet from your midst, from your brethren, like me,** Moses, **the Lord your God will establish for you; him you shall heed,** ¹⁶**in accordance with everything that you asked of the Lord your God at Horev on the day of the assembly,** at the revelation at Sinai, **saying: I will not continue to hear the voice of the Lord my God, and I will not see this great fire anymore so that I will not die.** ¹⁷**The Lord said to me: They did well in that which they spoke.** ¹⁸**I will establish a prophet for them from among their brethren, like you, and I will place My words in his mouth, and he will speak to them everything that I will command him.** ¹⁹**It shall be that the man who will not heed My words that he will speak in My name, I will demand it from him.** I will take vengeance upon him. ²⁰**However, the prophet who will speak with intent a matter in My name**

that I did not command him to speak, or who will speak in the name of other gods, that prophet shall die. ²¹If you say in your heart, how shall we know the matter that the Lord did not speak? ²²That which a prophet will speak in the name of the Lord, and the matter will not be and will not come to pass, that is the matter that the Lord did not speak; the prophet spoke with malicious intent, you shall not be daunted by him, do not fear punishing him.

The Laws of the Murderer

Moses describes the system of cities of refuge, whose role is to enable one who kills by accident; an unwitting murderer, to escape the vengeance of the relatives of the victim. Asylum should not be provided to intentional murderers in cities of refuge; those should be judged severely. In this context, the laws of testimony are also cited.

19 ¹**When the Lord your God shall excise the nations that the Lord your God is giving you their land, and you take possession from them and live in their cities and in their houses,** ²**you shall separate three cities for you in the midst of your land that the Lord your God is giving you to take possession of it.** ³**You shall prepare for yourselves the path, and you shall divide the boundaries of your land that the Lord your God will bequeath to you into three parts,** so that the cities are equally accessible from all parts of the land, **and it shall be for every** unwitting **murderer to flee there.**

⁴**This is the matter of the murderer who shall flee there and live; he who will kill his neighbor without knowledge,** premeditated intent, **and he does not hate him previously.** ⁵**One who will come with his neighbor in the forest to hew trees, and his hand will slip from the axe while chopping the tree, and the blade comes off the wood** handle **and finds** and strikes **his neighbor, and he dies; he** who caused this death inadvertently **shall flee to one of these cities and he shall live.** ⁶You must make these cities accessible **lest the blood redeemer pursue the murderer because his heart is incensed, and he will overtake him because the way** to the city of refuge **is great, and he will smite him mortally. And** yet **for him,** the unwitting murderer, **there is no sentence of death, as he does not hate him,** his victim, **previously.** ⁷**Therefore, I command you, saying: You shall separate three cities for you,** to serve as asylum for unwitting murderers.

⁸**When the Lord your God will expand your border** of inheritance beyond the land of Canaan as delineated in Numbers 34:1–12, **as He has**

Deuteronomy

taken an oath to your forefathers, and He will give you the entire land that He spoke to give to your forefathers (see Genesis 15:18); **⁹because you will observe this entire commandment to perform it, that I am commanding you today, to love the Lord your God, and to walk in His ways always, you shall add for you three more cities with these three,** west of the Jordan, which, in turn, were in addition to the three east of the Jordan, for a total of nine. **¹⁰Innocent blood will be not spilled in the midst of your land that the Lord your God is giving you as an inheritance, and** if blood is spilled because of your failure to establish these cities of refuge and to ensure access to them, **the blood will be upon you;** you will be responsible.

¹¹But if there will be a man who hates his neighbor, and he ambushed him and rose against him, and smote him mortally and he died, and he, this intentional murderer, **flees to one of these cities** of refuge for asylum, **¹²the elders of his city shall send and take him from there and will place him into the hand of the blood redeemer** to stand trial **and he will die** once his death sentence has been pronounced. **¹³Your eye shall not pity him,** the murderer; **you shall eliminate the** spiller of the **blood of the innocent from Israel, and it will be good for you.**

Sixth aliya **¹⁴You shall not move your neighbor's boundary that the predecessors demarcated, in your inheritance that you will inherit, in the land that the Lord your God is giving you to take possession of it.**

¹⁵One witness shall not stand against a man for any iniquity, or for any sin, in any sin that he may sin; according to two witnesses, or according to three witnesses, a matter shall be established. ¹⁶If a corrupt, false, **witness shall stand against a man to testify a fabrication against him,** to accuse him falsely, **¹⁷both the men between whom there is a dispute shall stand before the Lord, before the priests and the judges who will be in those days. ¹⁸The judges shall inquire diligently and behold,** if they discover that **the witness is a false witness; he testified falsehood** against his brother, **¹⁹you shall do to him as he had conspired to do to his brother, and you shall eliminate the evil from your midst. ²⁰The survivors** who witnessed the proceedings **shall hear, and fear, and shall not continue to do like this evil matter in your midst anymore. ²¹Your eye shall not pity** him, **a life for a life, an eye for an eye, a tooth for a tooth, a hand for a hand, a foot for a foot;** the punishment that they sought to have administered shall be administered to them.

Deuteronomy

The Laws of War

Prior to engaging in battle, warriors will hear words of encouragement from the High Priest, after which those exempt from battle will return to their homes. The Torah mentions the obligation to offer peace to a city before conquering it, as well as guidelines as to how to treat a conquered city. The Torah portion concludes with instructions on the procedure to follow if a murder victim is found in a field.

20 ¹**When you go out to war against your enemies, and you shall see horses and chariots, a people more numerous than you, you shall not fear them, as the Lord your God is with you, who took you up from the land of Egypt.** ²**It will be when you advance to the war,** the battlefield, **the priest** appointed specifically for this purpose **shall approach and speak to the people.** ³**He shall say to them: Hear, Israel. You are advancing today to war against your enemies; let your heart not be faint, do not fear, do not panic, and do not be broken before them,** ⁴**for it is the Lord your God who goes with you to wage war for you against your enemies, to save you.** ⁵**The officers shall speak to the people, saying: Who is the man who** has **built a new house, and did not dedicate it,** has not yet dwelt there? **Let him go and return to his house, lest he die in the war and another man dedicate it.** ⁶**And who is the man who** has **planted a vineyard and did not celebrate it,** did not yet eat of its fruit? **Let him go and return to his house, lest he die in the war, and another man will celebrate it.** ⁷**And who is the man who is betrothed** to a woman, **and has not** yet **married her? Let him go and return to his house, lest he die in the war, and another man will marry her.** ⁸**The officers shall continue to speak to the people, and they shall say: Who is the man who is fearful and fainthearted? Let him go and return to his house, that he shall not dissolve his brethren's heart like his heart.** ⁹**It shall be, when the officers conclude to speak to the people, and they appoint the captains of the guard at the head of the people,** and the army goes out to war,

Seventh aliya ¹⁰**when you approach a city to wage war against it, you shall call to it for peace,** offer them the option of avoiding war. ¹¹**It shall be, if it responds** with **peace to you,** and accepts your offer, **and it opens** its gates **for you, the entire people that is found in it shall be for tribute for you, and they shall serve you.** ¹²**If it will not make peace with you, but will wage war against you and you besiege it,** ¹³**the Lord your God will deliver it into your hand, and you shall smite all its males by sword.** ¹⁴**Only the women, and the** young **children, and the animals, and everything that is in the city, all its spoils, you shall loot for you, and you shall consume the**

479

spoils of your enemies that the Lord your God has given you. ¹⁵So you shall do to all the cities that are very far from you, that are not from the cities of these Canaanite nations; ¹⁶however, from the cities of these peoples that the Lord your God is giving you as inheritance, you shall not keep any person alive. ¹⁷Rather, you shall destroy them, the Hitites, and the Emorites, the Canaanites, and the Perizites, the Hivites, and the Yevusites, as the Lord your God has commanded you, ¹⁸so that they will not teach you to do like all their abominations, their idol worship, that they performed with their gods, and you will sin against the Lord your God.

¹⁹When you will besiege a city many days to wage war against it to seize it, you shall not destroy its fruit trees, to wield an axe against them, as from them you will eat, and you shall not cut them down. For is the tree of the field a man, to retreat from you during the siege? ²⁰Only a tree that you will know that it is not a food tree, it you may destroy and cut down. It is sometimes difficult to distinguish between a fruit-bearing tree whose fruit has fallen off or has yet to sprout, and a tree that does not bear fruit. Consequently, the Torah stresses that one may destroy only those trees one knows for certain are not fruit trees. And you will build with the wood of those trees a siege against the city that makes war with you, until its fall, meaning until the city's defeat or until its walls fall.

21 ¹If a dead body of someone who has been murdered will be found in the land that the Lord your God is giving you to take possession of it, fallen in the field, and it is not known who smote him, ²your elders and your judges shall go out, and they shall measure from the body to the cities that are surrounding the body. ³It shall be that the city that is nearest to the body, the elders of that city shall take a calf of the herd with which work was not performed, and which has not drawn a yoke. ⁴The elders of that city shall take the calf down to a harsh ravine with a constant stream of water, in which work will not be done and it will not be sown, and they shall behead the calf there in the ravine. ⁵The priests, sons of Levi, shall approach, as the Lord your God chose them to serve Him and to bless in the name of the Lord, and by their word shall be judged every dispute and every affliction. ⁶And all the elders of that city who are nearest to the body shall wash their hands over the calf that was be-

Maftir headed in the ravine. ⁷They shall proclaim and say: Our hands did not shed this blood, and our eyes did not see who committed the murder. ⁸Absolve Your people Israel, whom You have redeemed, Lord, and do

not let there be innocent blood in the midst of your people Israel, and the bloodshed will be atoned for them. ⁹You shall eliminate the spiller of innocent blood from your midst when you shall do the right in the eyes of the Lord.

Parashat Ki Tetze

This Torah portion contains a survey of numerous and diverse mitzvot, including the laws of marriage and family and the laws relating to interpersonal relationships, including the obligation to care for the stranger and the unfortunate.

Family Matters

The Torah portion begins with a series of laws related to marriage and children, beginning with the law of one who desires a female captive and continuing to questions of inheritance and preferring one son over another, and concluding with what should be done when a son descends into extreme rebelliousness and his parents lose control over him.

¹⁰When you go out to war against your enemies, and the Lord your God delivers them into your hand, and you capture its captives, ¹¹and you see among the captives a beautiful woman, and you desire her, and you take her for you as a wife; ¹²you shall bring her into your house, and she shall shave her head, and she shall do her nails. ¹³She shall remove the garment of her captivity, which she wore when taken, **from her, and she shall remain in your house, and she shall lament her father and her mother a month of days, and** only **thereafter you may consort with her, and engage in intercourse with her, and she shall be a wife to you. ¹⁴It shall be** that **if you do not desire her, you shall release her on her own, you shall not sell her for silver; you shall not enslave her, because you afflicted her.**

¹⁵If a man has two wives, the one beloved, and the one hated, and they bear him children, the beloved and the hated, and the firstborn son is of the hated, ¹⁶it shall be on the day that he bequeaths to his sons that property **which he has, he may not prefer the** younger **son of the beloved over the son of the of the hated, the firstborn. ¹⁷Rather, he shall acknowledge the firstborn, son of the hated, to give him double from everything that is found with him, as he is the first of his potency, his is the right of the firstborn.**

📖 **Further reading:** For more on inheritance laws and preference among children, see *A Concise Guide to the Sages,* pp. 55, 405; *A Concise Guide to Halakha,* p. 75.

[18]If a man has a defiant and rebellious son, who does not heed the voice of his father, or the voice of his mother, and they chastise him, and he still **does not heed them,** [19]his father and his mother shall seize him, and they shall take him out to the elders of his city, to the gate of his place. [20]They shall say to the elders of his city: This son of ours is defiant and rebellious; he does not heed our voice; he is a glutton and a drunkard. [21]All the men of his city shall stone him with stones, and he shall die, and you shall eliminate the evil from your midst, and all Israel shall hear and fear.

Various Mitzvot

Moses enumerates a series of mitzvot: returning a lost item, dispatching a mother bird from the nest, the prohibition against mixtures of diverse kinds, and the prohibition against a man or a woman wearing the garments of the other gender.

Second aliya [22]If there is in a man a sin with a death sentence, and he is put to death, you shall hang him on a tree after his execution. [23]His carcass shall not remain overnight upon the tree; rather you shall bury him on that same day, as one hanged is a curse, a disgrace, of God, and you shall not defile your land that the Lord your God is giving you as an inheritance.

22 [1]You shall not see your Israelite **brother's ox or his sheep wandering and disregard them; you shall return them to your brother.** [2]If your brother who owns the animal **is not near to you, and you do not know him, you shall gather it,** the ox or sheep, **into your house, and it shall be with you until your brother seeks it, and you shall return it to him.** [3]So you shall do with his donkey, and so you shall do with his garment, and so you shall do with every lost item of your brother that shall be lost from him; and you found it, you shall not disregard.

[4]You shall not see your brother's donkey or his ox fallen on the road from the weight of its burden, **and disregard them; you shall raise it with him.** You must help a fellow Jew with his animal.

[5]A man's garment or accessory **shall not be on a woman, and a man shall not wear a woman's garment, as it is an abomination to the Lord your God anyone who does these.**

[6]If a bird's nest will happen before you on the way, on any tree or on the ground, with fledglings or eggs, and the mother is crouching on

Deuteronomy

the fledglings or on the eggs, you shall not take the mother with the offspring. ⁷You shall send forth the mother, and the offspring take for yourself, so that it will be good for you, and you will extend your days.

Third aliya ⁸If you build a new house, you shall make a parapet for your roof, and by doing so you shall not place blood, cause bloodshed, in your house, if someone falls from it.

⁹You shall not sow your vineyard with diverse kinds, plant other crops in your vineyard, lest the growth be forbidden, both the seed that you will sow, and the produce of the vineyard.

¹⁰You shall not plow with an ox and a donkey together, pulling the same plow. ¹¹You shall not wear a garment with a mixture of fibers, wool and linen together.

¹²You shall make for yourself twisted threads on the four corners of your garment with which you cover yourself.

Laws Relating to Marriage

Now the Torah cites a series of matters related to the structure of the family: what to do in the case of a husband's suspicions regarding the fidelity of his wife; cases of rape or promiscuity; and, finally, a list of people or members of foreign nations who are ineligible for marriage with the Israelites.

¹³If a man takes, marries, a wife, and consorts with her, and he hates her. ¹⁴And he proffers a libelous matter against her, and disseminated an evil name about her, and said: I took this woman, and I approached her, and contrary to expectations, I did not find signs of her virginity. ¹⁵The father of the young woman and her mother take and bring the signs of the virginity of the young woman, the bedsheet or garment stained with blood, out to the elders of the city, to the city gate, the courthouse. ¹⁶The father of the young woman shall say to the elders: I gave my daughter to this man for a wife, and he hated her. ¹⁷Behold, he proffered libelous words, saying: I did not find signs of virginity for your daughter, but these are the signs of virginity of my daughter. They shall spread the garment before the elders of the city. ¹⁸The elders of that city shall take the man and they shall chastise him with lashes. ¹⁹They shall punish him with a fine of one hundred shekels of silver, and they shall give it to the father of the young woman because he disseminated an evil name about a virgin of Israel. And she shall be a wife to him; he may not release her, divorce her against her will, all his days. ²⁰But, if

this matter was true, and the signs of virginity were not found for the **daughter,** and it was proven that the bride committed adultery during the period between betrothal and marriage, **²¹they shall take the young woman out to the entrance of her father's house, and the people of her city shall stone her with stones and she shall die, because she performed a despicable act in Israel, to engage in licentiousness** while residing **in her father's house, and you shall eliminate the evil from your midst.**

²²If a man shall be found lying with a woman married to a husband, the two of them shall die, the man who lay with the woman, and the woman.

²³If there is a young virgin betrothed to a man, and a man finds her in the city, and lies with her, ²⁴you shall take the two of them out to be judged at **the gate of that city, and you shall stone them with stones and they shall die. The young woman because she did not cry out** for help **in the city** where, presumably, had she cried out, her cry would have been heard, **and the man, because he afflicted the wife of his neighbor, and you shall eliminate the evil from your midst.**

²⁵But if the man shall find the betrothed young woman in the field, and the man seized her, and lay with her, the man who lay with her shall die alone. ²⁶But to the young woman you shall do nothing; the young woman has no sin worthy of death, as just like a man rises against his neighbor and murders him, so is this matter. Rape is tantamount to murder. **²⁷For he found her in the field; the betrothed young woman** presumably **cried out, and there is no rescuer for her.**

²⁸If a man finds a young virgin who is not betrothed, and he seizes her forcibly, **and lies with her, and they are found, ²⁹the man who lay with her** is not executed; rather, he **shall give to the young woman's father fifty silver shekels,** the set bride price in biblical times, **and she shall be a wife to him, because he afflicted her; he may not release her,** divorce her against her will, **all his days.**

23 **¹A man shall not take his father's wife,** even after his father dies or divorces her, **and he shall not uncover the edge of his father's garment,** his father's nakedness.

²One with crushed testicles and one with a severed or severely damaged **penis shall not enter into the assembly of the Lord** through marriage.

Deuteronomy

485

³A child born from incest or adultery shall not enter into the assembly of the Lord through marriage; even the tenth generation and beyond, he shall not enter into the assembly of the Lord forever.

⁴An Amonite or a Moavite convert shall not enter into the assembly of the Lord, i.e., marry a Jewish woman who is not a convert herself; even the tenth generation and beyond shall not enter into the assembly of the Lord forever, ⁵because they did not even greet you with bread and with water on the way, upon your exodus from Egypt (see 2:1–19). And because he, the king of Moav, hired against you Bilam son of Beor, from Petor, Aram Naharayim, to curse you. ⁶But the Lord your God was unwilling to heed Bilam, and the Lord your God transformed for you the curse into a blessing, because the Lord your God loved you. ⁷You shall

Fourth
aliya

not seek their peace or their welfare all your days, forever. ⁸You shall not despise an Edomite, as he is your brother. You shall not despise an Egyptian, as you were a stranger in his land. Your treatment of converts from these two nations should be less extreme than your treatment of converts from Amon and Moav. ⁹Children that will be born to them, Egyptian and Edomite converts, in the third generation, shall enter into the assembly of the Lord, can marry a Jew by birth.

📖 **Further reading:** For more on Bilam and his curses that turned into blessings, see p. 396.

Various Mitzvot

From this point until the end of the Torah portion, a long list of mitzvot is cited, most of them in brief although some at greater length, among them several mitzvot relating to the social fabric of society, and concern for the weak and the defenseless. Others deal with the sanctity of the military camp, the laws of divorce and levirate marriage, and, in conclusion, the mitzva of remembering Amalek.

¹⁰When you go out in a military camp against your enemies, you shall be vigilant from every evil thing. ¹¹If there is among you a man who will not be pure due to a nocturnal incident, a seminal emission, he shall go outside the camp, he shall not come into the midst of, into the sanctified areas of, the camp. ¹²It shall be that toward evening he shall bathe in water, in a ritual bath, and with the setting of the sun, he shall come into the camp. ¹³A place shall be designated for you outside the camp, and you shall go out there to relieve yourself. ¹⁴You shall have a spade for yourselves with your weapons, and it shall be used upon your sitting outside to relieve yourself; you shall dig with it and you shall return and

cover your excrement. ¹⁵As the Lord your God walks in the midst of your camp to save you, and to deliver your enemies before you, your camp shall be holy, and He shall not see a shameful matter among you, and turn from behind you, forsake you.

¹⁶You shall not hand over to his master a Canaanite slave who has escaped to you from his master. ¹⁷With you he shall reside, in your midst, in the place that he will choose within one of your gates in which it is good for him; you shall not mistreat him.

¹⁸There shall not be a prostitute from the daughters of Israel, and there shall not be a male prostitute from the sons of Israel.

¹⁹You shall not bring an item given as the fee of a harlot, or received as the price of a dog, to the House of the Lord your God for fulfillment of any vow to God, for the two of them are an abomination to the Lord your God.

²⁰You shall not lend with interest to your Jewish brother; interest of silver, interest of food, or interest of any item that is lent with interest. ²¹To the foreigner, a gentile, you shall, it is permitted to, lend with interest, but to your Jewish brother you shall not lend with interest, so that the Lord your God will bless you in all your endeavors on the land that you are coming there to take possession of it.

²²When you shall take a vow to the Temple of the Lord your God, you shall not delay to pay it; if you delay payment, the Lord your God will seek it from you, and there will be a sin in you. ²³If you shall refrain from vowing, there will be no sin in you. ²⁴That which emerges from your lips, your commitments, you shall observe and you shall perform, as you vowed a pledge to the Lord your God that you spoke with your mouth.

Fifth aliya ²⁵When you come into your neighbor's vineyard, you may eat grapes as you desire, to your contentment, but into your vessel you shall not place them. ²⁶When you come into your neighbor's standing grain you may pick ripe stalks with your hand, but you shall not wield a sickle on your neighbor's standing grain.

24 ¹When a man takes a wife, and engages in intercourse with her, it shall be that if she does not find favor in his eyes, because he found in her an indecent matter, immoral behavior, and he wrote her a bill of divorce, and he placed it in her hand, and he sent her from his house, ²and she departed from his house, and she went and was married to another

man, ³and if the latter man hated her, and he wrote her a bill of divorce and placed it in her hand, and sent her from his house, or if the latter man, who took her as his wife, died, ⁴her former husband, who sent her, may not take her again to be a wife for him after she was defiled, married to another man, as it is an abomination before the Lord to facilitate exchange of wives; and you shall not bring sin to the land that the Lord your God is giving you as an inheritance.

Sixth aliya ⁵When a man takes a new wife, he shall not go out to serve in the army, and for no civil matter shall he be obligated; he shall be free for his house for one year and shall cause his wife, whom he took, to rejoice.

⁶One shall not take the lower millstone or the upper millstone as collateral, as he takes a life as collateral; it would be removing the means for making a living.

⁷If a man is found abducting any of his brethren of the children of Israel, and he enslaved, abused, him, and sold him into slavery, that thief shall die, and you shall eliminate the evil from your midst.

⁸Be careful with the mark of leprosy, to greatly take care and to act in accordance with all its laws and with everything that the priests, the Levites, will instruct you; as I had commanded them, you shall take care to perform. ⁹Remember that which the Lord your God did to Miriam, who was afflicted with leprosy, on the way upon your exodus from Egypt.

¹⁰When you lend your neighbor a loan of any amount, you shall not go into his house to take his collateral. ¹¹Outside you shall stand, and the man to whom you lend shall bring the collateral to you outside. ¹²If he, the borrower, is a poor man, you shall not sleep with his collateral, if it is a garment or a blanket. ¹³Return him the collateral with the setting of the sun and he will sleep in his garment, and he will bless you and for you it will be considered righteousness before the Lord your God.

📖 **Further reading:** The *halakhot* concerning lending money with interest appear in *A Concise Guide to Halakha*, p. 619.

Seventh aliya ¹⁴You shall not exploit a poor or indigent hired laborer from your brethren, or from your stranger who is in your land within your gates. ¹⁵On his work day you shall give him his wage, and the sun shall not set upon it, as he is poor, and he anticipates it; pay him that same day lest

he cry out against you to the Lord and it will be a sin in you for having caused injustice.

[16]**Fathers shall not be put to death for** the sins of **sons, and sons shall not be put to death for** the sins of **fathers; each** one **shall be put to death for his** own **sin.**

[17]**You shall not distort the judgment against a stranger or an orphan, and you shall not take a widow's garment as collateral.** [18]**You shall remember that you were a slave in Egypt, and the Lord your God redeemed you from there; therefore, I command you to do this thing.**

[19]**When you reap your harvest in your field, and you forget a sheaf in the field, you shall not return to take it; for the stranger, the orphan, and the widow it shall be, so that the Lord your God will bless you in all your endeavors.**

[20]**When you beat your olive tree** to harvest olives, **you shall not search the boughs again** to gather the remaining olives; **for the stranger, the orphan, and the widow it shall be.** [21]**When you harvest your vineyard, you shall not glean** the individual grapes not in large clusters **behind you; for the stranger, the orphan, and the widow it shall be.** [22]**You shall remember that you were a slave in Egypt; therefore I command you to perform this matter.**

25 [1]**When there is a quarrel between men, and they approach to judgment, and they judge them, and they exonerate the righteous, and they convict the wicked,** [2]**if the wicked man will be liable for flogging, the judge shall cast him down, and he shall flog him before him, in accordance with his wickedness, by number.** [3]**Forty he shall flog him; he shall not continue, lest he continue to flog him beyond these, a great blow, and your brother will be degraded before your eyes.**

[4]**You shall not muzzle an ox,** preventing it from eating, **in its threshing.**

[5]**If** paternal **brothers will live together, and one of them dies, and he has no child, the wife of the dead** man **shall not be married outside** the family, **to a strange man; her husband's brother shall consort with her, and take her as a wife, and perform levirate marriage with her.** [6]**It shall be that the firstborn that she will bear will perpetuate the name of his dead brother,** will be treated as the child of the brother who died, **and his name will not be expunged from Israel** because he has no descendants. [7]**If** the man does not wish to take his brother's widow, his brother's widow **shall go up to the gate,** to the court, **to the elders, and say: My husband's**

brother refused to perpetuate a name for his brother in Israel; he is unwilling to perform levirate marriage with me. [8]The elders of his city shall call him and speak to him, and he shall stand, and he shall say: I do not wish to take her. [9]His brother's widow shall approach him before the eyes of the elders, and she shall remove his shoe from his foot, and spit on the ground before him, and she shall proclaim and say: So shall be done to the man who will not build the house of his brother. [10]His name, his family, shall be called in Israel: The house of one whose shoe was removed.

[11]If men fight together, one with another, and the wife of the one approaches to rescue her husband from the hand of the one who is striking him, and she extends her hand, and grabs his genitals, [12]you shall sever her hand, she is obligated to pay for humiliating him, your eye shall not pity her.

[13]You shall not have in your pouch different weights, great and small that appear identical. [14]You shall not have in your house different measures of volume, great for purchase and small for sale. [15]You shall have a whole and just weight, you shall have a whole and just measure, so that your days will be extended on the land that the Lord your God is giving you, [16]as it is an abomination to the Lord your God, all who do these; all who do injustice.

> Further reading: For more on fair trade and the prohibition against fraud, see *A Concise Guide to Halakha*, pp. 599ff.

Maftir [17]Remember that which Amalek did to you on the way, upon your exodus from Egypt. [18]That he encountered you on the way, and he attacked from behind you all the weak stragglers stumbling behind you when you were faint and weary, and he did not fear God. [19]It shall be, when the Lord your God gives you rest from the wars with, and the conquest of all your surrounding enemies, in the land that the Lord your God gives you as an inheritance to take possession of it, you shall expunge the memory of Amalek from under the heavens, you shall not forget.

Parashat
Ki Tavo

The bulk of the Torah portion of *Ki Tavo* addresses the topic of "the blessing and the curse." First, there is a command to stage a special ceremony upon the Israelites' entry into the land, involving the establishment of a stone altar upon which the words of the Torah will be inscribed. Later, the Torah presents an extensive list of the blessings destined to be bestowed upon Israel if they observe the covenant and, alternatively, the curses that will be poured upon them if they fail to observe it. The Torah portion begins with two mitzvot relating to the obligation to thank God for the good that he performed for the nation in bequeathing them the land.

First Fruits and Disposal of Tithes

The *parasha* begins with the obligation to bring the first fruits of the season to the Temple, and to recite there a festive formula of thanksgiving to God. Then the Torah details the obligation to remove all tithes from one's house after the third year of the Sabbatical cycle and give them to the poor. This act, too, is to be accompanied by a declaration, and a prayer blessing God.

26 ¹It shall be, when you will come into the land that the Lord your God is giving you as an inheritance, and you take possession of it, and live in it. ²You shall take from the first of all the fruit of the ground that you bring, harvest, **from your land that the Lord your God is giving you. And you shall place it in a basket, and you shall go to the place that the Lord your God will choose to rest His name there.** ³You shall come to the priest who will be in those days, and you shall say to him: I am telling today to the Lord your God that I have come to the land with regard to which the Lord took an oath to our fathers to give to us. ⁴The priest shall take the basket from your hand, and he shall place it before the altar of the Lord your God. ⁵You shall proclaim and you shall say before the Lord your God: A wandering Aramean was my father** Jacob, or alternatively, Laban the Aramean sought to annihilate my father Jacob. **And he descended to Egypt, and resided there, few in number, and he became there a nation, great, mighty, and numerous.** ⁶The Egyptians mistreated us, and afflicted us, and imposed upon us hard labor. ⁷We cried out

to the Lord, God of our fathers, and the Lord heard our voice, and He saw our affliction and our toil, and our oppression. ⁸The Lord took us out of Egypt with a mighty hand, and with an outstretched arm, and with great awe, and with signs, and with wonders. ⁹He brought us to this place, and He gave us this land, a land flowing with milk and honey. ¹⁰Now, behold, I have brought the first of the fruit of the land that You have given me, Lord. You shall place it before the Lord your God, and you shall prostrate yourself before the Lord your God. ¹¹You shall rejoice in all the good that the Lord your God has given to you and to your household: you, and the Levite, and the stranger who is in your midst.

📖 **Further reading:** For more on the ceremony of bringing the first fruits, see *A Concise Guide to the Sages*, p. 253.

Second aliya ¹²**When you finish tithing all the tithes of your produce in the third year** of the Sabbatical cycle, which is **the year of the** poor man's **tithe, and you have given it,** your tithes, **to the Levite, to the stranger, to the orphan, and to the widow, and they ate within your gates, and were satisfied;** ¹³**you shall say before the Lord your God: I have disposed of the consecrated,** the tithes, **from my house, and also I gave them to the Levite, and to the stranger, to the orphan, and to the widow, in accordance with all Your commandment that You commanded me; I did not violate any of Your commandments, and I did not forget.** ¹⁴The following part of the declaration refers specifically to the second tithe: **I did not eat from it during my** times of acute **mourning,** before my relative was buried, **and I did not dispose of it,** separate it, **in a state of impurity, and I did not give from it for the** needs of the **dead. I heeded the voice of the Lord my God, I have acted in accordance with everything that You commanded me.** ¹⁵**Look from Your holy abode, from the heavens, and bless Your people Israel, and the land that You gave us, as You took an oath to our fathers, a land flowing with milk and honey.**

📖 **Further reading:** How are tithes separated today? See *A Concise Guide to Halakha*, p. 564.

Third aliya ¹⁶Moses continues: **This day, the Lord your God is commanding you to perform these statutes, and the ordinances, and you shall observe and you shall perform them with all your heart, and with all your soul.** ¹⁷**You have exalted the Lord today, to be your God, to walk in His ways,**

to observe His statutes, His commandments, and His ordinances, and to heed His voice. [18]And the Lord has exalted you today to be a people of distinction for Him, a treasured nation, just as He spoke to you, and to observe all His commandments, [19]to place you uppermost over all the nations that He made, for praise, and for renown, and for splendor, and for you to be a holy people to the Lord your God, as He spoke.

Mount Gerizim and Mount Eival

Upon their crossing of the Jordan and entry into the Land of Israel, the Israelites are commanded to stage a one-time ceremony of entering into a covenant and making an oath. At the first stage, it will be incumbent upon them to build an altar of twelve stones and to inscribe the words of the Torah upon them. Then the tribes will stand facing each other on two adjacent mountains, while the Levites read aloud a list of transgressions whose violators will be declared to be cursed, and the people will answer: Amen.

27 [1]Moses and the elders of Israel commanded the people, saying: *Fourth aliya* Observe the entire commandment that I am commanding you today. [2]It shall be, on the day that you will cross the Jordan to the land that the Lord your God is giving you, you shall erect for you great stones, and plaster them with lime. [3]You shall write on them all the words of this Torah, upon your crossing, so that you will come to the land that the Lord your God is giving you, a land flowing with milk and honey, as the Lord, God of your fathers, spoke to you. [4]It shall be upon your crossing of the Jordan, you shall erect these stones that I am commanding you today on Mount Eival, and you shall plaster them with lime. [5]You shall build there an altar to the Lord your God, an altar of stones, you shall not wield iron upon them. [6]Of whole stones, not chiseled, you shall build the altar of the Lord your God, and you shall offer up on it burnt offerings to the Lord your God. [7]You shall slaughter peace offerings, and you shall eat them there, and you shall rejoice before the Lord your God. [8]You shall write on the stones all the words of this Torah, very clearly, accessible to all.

[9]Moses and the priests, the Levites, spoke to all Israel, saying: Listen and heed, Israel, this day you have become a people for the Lord your God. [10]You shall heed the voice of the Lord your God, and you shall perform His commandments and His statutes that I am commanding you today.

Fifth aliya [11]Moses commanded the people on that day, saying: [12]Members of these tribes shall stand to bless the people upon Mount Gerizim, upon your

Deuteronomy

crossing of the Jordan: Simeon, and Levi, and Judah, and Issachar, and Joseph, and Benjamin. ¹³And these shall stand for the curse upon Mount Eival: Reuben, Gad, and Asher, and Zebulun, Dan, and Naphtali. ¹⁴The Levites shall proclaim and say to every man of Israel in a loud voice:

¹⁵Cursed is the man who makes an idol or a cast figure of a face, an abomination of the Lord, the handiwork of a craftsman, and places it in secret. And the entire people shall answer and say: Amen.

¹⁶Cursed is one who demeans his father or his mother, and the entire people shall say: Amen. ¹⁷Cursed is one who moves his neighbor's boundary, and the entire people shall say: Amen. ¹⁸Cursed is one who misleads the blind on the way, and the entire people shall say: Amen. ¹⁹Cursed is one who distorts the judgment against a stranger, an orphan, or a widow, and the entire people shall say: Amen. ²⁰Cursed is one who lies with the wife of his father, as he exposed the edge of his father's garment, his father's nakedness, and the entire people shall say: Amen. ²¹Cursed is one who lies with any beast, and the entire people shall say: Amen. ²²Cursed is one who lies with his sister, the daughter of his father, or the daughter of his mother, and the entire people shall say: Amen. ²³Cursed is one who lies with his mother-in-law, and the entire people shall say: Amen. ²⁴Cursed is one who smites his neighbor in secret, and the entire people shall say: Amen. ²⁵Cursed is one who takes a bribe to slay a person of innocent blood, and the entire people shall say: Amen. ²⁶Cursed is one who will not take action to uphold the matters of this Torah to perform them, and the entire people shall say: Amen.

The Blessing and the Curse

In the second part of the making of the covenant before the people enter the Land of Israel, Moses details to them the blessings they will enjoy if they follow the Torah and, in contrast, the punishments they will receive if they abandon God's path.

28 ¹It shall be, if you shall heed the voice of the Lord your God to take care to perform all His commandments that I am commanding you today, the Lord your God will place you uppermost over all the nations of the earth. ²All these blessings will come upon you, and reach you, if you shall heed the voice of the Lord your God. ³Blessed are you in the city and blessed are you in the field. ⁴Blessed is the fruit of your womb, your offspring, and the fruit of your land, your produce, and the fruit of

your animals: the calving of your cattle, and the lambing of your flock. [5]Blessed is your fruit basket and your kneading bowl. [6]Blessed are you upon your arrival, and blessed are you upon your departure.

Sixth aliya [7]The Lord will render your enemies who rise against you routed, fleeing from before you. On one path they will emerge united toward you, and on seven paths they will flee before you. [8]The Lord will command for you the blessing in your silos, and in all your endeavors, and He will bless you in the land that the Lord your God is giving you. [9]The Lord will establish you as a holy people to Him, as He took an oath to you, if you shall observe the commandments of the Lord your God, and walk in His ways. [10]All the peoples of the earth will see that the name of the Lord is invoked upon you, is identified with you, and they shall fear you. [11]The Lord will increase you for good in the fruit of your womb, and in the fruit of your animals, and in the fruit of your land, on the land with regard to which the Lord took an oath to your fathers to give you. [12]The Lord will open for you His good storehouse, the heavens, to provide the rain of your land at its time, and to bless all your handiwork; you shall have the ability to lend to many nations, but you shall not borrow. [13]The Lord will set you as a head, and not as a tail. You will lead and not follow. And you will be only above, and you will not be below, if you shall heed the commandments of the Lord your God that I am commanding you today, to observe and to perform. [14]You shall not stray from any of the matters that I am commanding you today, right or left, to follow other gods to serve them.

[15]It shall be, if you do not heed the voice of the Lord your God, to take care to perform all His commandments and His statutes that I am commanding you today, all these curses will come upon you and find you. [16]Cursed are you in the city, and cursed are you in the field. [17]Cursed is your basket and your kneading bowl. [18]Cursed is the fruit of your womb, and the fruit of your land, the calving of your cattle, and the lambing of your flock. [19]Cursed are you upon your arrival, and cursed are you upon your departure. [20]The Lord will release among you the curse, the confusion, disorder, and the diminution in all your endeavors that you will perform, until your destruction and until your swift annihilation, because of the wickedness of your deeds, that you forsook Me. [21]The Lord will attach the pestilence to you, until it eradicates you from upon the land that you are coming there to take possession of it. [22]The Lord will smite you with consumption, and with fever, and

Deuteronomy

with inflammation, and with desiccation, thirst, and with the sword, and with blight and with mildew, crop diseases. And they shall pursue you until your annihilation. [23]Your heavens that are over your head will be as impenetrable as bronze and will not produce rain, and the earth that is beneath you, like iron. [24]The Lord will render the rain of your land dust and dirt; from the heavens it will descend upon you, until your destruction. [25]The Lord will render you routed before your enemies; on one path you will go out toward him, and on seven paths you will flee before him. You will be a horror, a paradigm of failure, to all the kingdoms of the earth. [26]Your carcass will be for food, for every bird of the heavens and for the animals of the earth, and there is none to frighten them and prevent them from feasting upon your remains.

[27]The Lord will smite you with the rash of Egypt, a skin disease, and with hemorrhoids, with skin eruptions, and with dry boils, skin diseases, from which you will be unable to be healed. [28]The Lord will smite you with madness, and with blindness, and with confusion of the heart, disorientation. [29]You shall grope at noon as the blind gropes in the dark, and you will not succeed on, in finding, your way, and you will only be exploited and robbed always, and there is no savior.

[30]You will betroth a woman and another man will lie with, marry, her; you will build a house and you will not live in it; you will plant a vineyard, and you will not celebrate it; you will not eat its fruit. [31]Your ox is slaughtered before your eyes, and you will not eat from it; your donkey is robbed from before you and will not return to you; your flock is given to your enemies and there is no savior for you. [32]Your sons and your daughters are given, enslaved, to another people, and your eyes see and long for them all day, and you are powerless. [33]A nation that you did not know will eat the fruit of your land and the fruit of all your toil, and you will be only exploited and broken always. [34]You will be mad from the sight of your eyes that you will see.

[35]The Lord will smite you with a terrible rash on the knees and on the shins from which you will be unable to be healed, from the sole of your foot to the top of your head. [36]The Lord will lead you and your king whom you will establish over you to a nation that you did not know, you or your ancestors, and you will serve there other gods, of wood and stone. [37]You will become an astonishment, a proverb, and an adage among all the peoples that the Lord will lead you there. You will be the prototype for failure about whom everyone will speak.

[38]**Much seed you will take out to the field** for sowing, **and little will you gather** during the harvest, **as the locust will consume it.** [39]**Vineyards you will plant and till, and you will not drink wine and you will not store it,** as the worm will eat them. [40]**Olive trees you will have within all your borders, and** yet **you will not anoint** your skin with **oil as your olives will fall** to the ground. [41]**Sons and daughters will you beget and they will not be for you, as they will go into captivity.** [42]**All your trees and the fruit of your land, the worm will deplete.** [43]**The stranger who is in your midst will ascend over you higher and higher, and you will descend lower and lower.** [44]**He will** have the means to **lend to you and you will not lend to him; he will be as a head, and you will be as a tail.**

📖 **Further reading:** For more on reward and punishment, see *A Concise Guide to the Sages*, p. 165; *A Concise Guide to Mahshava*, p. 256.

[45]**All these curses will come upon you, and will pursue you, and will find you until your destruction, because you did not heed the voice of the Lord your God, to observe His commandments and His statutes that He commanded you.** [46]**They,** all these troubles and plagues, **will be against you as a sign and as a wonder** for others **and against your descendants forever,**

[47]**because you did not serve the Lord your God with joy and with gladness of heart, due to the abundance of everything,** instead of showing gratitude for the abundance given you, and serving God with joy, you became spoiled and entitled; therefore, [48]**you will** be forced to **serve your enemies, whom the Lord will dispatch against you, in** a state of **hunger, and in thirst, and in nakedness, and in the lack of everything; and he will place an iron yoke on your neck until he destroys you.** [49]**The Lord will bring a nation against you from afar, from the end of the earth, which will swoop down** upon you **like an eagle, a nation whose language you will not understand.** [50]**A brazen nation that will not show favor to the elderly, and will not have mercy on the young.** [51]**It will eat the fruit of your animals and the fruit of your land, until your destruction;** it will be a nation **which will not leave you grain, wine, or oil, the calving of your cattle, or the lambing of your flock, until it annihilates you.** [52]**It will besiege you** and torment you **at all your gates, until the downfall of your high and fortified walls upon which you rely throughout your land, and it will besiege you at all your gates throughout your land that the Lord your God gave you.** [53]**You shall eat the fruit of your womb, the**

flesh of your sons and your daughters that the Lord your God gave you, in siege, and in distress that your enemy will distress you. ⁵⁴The man among you who is tender and very delicate will be selfish toward his brother, and toward the wife of his bosom, and toward the remaining children that he will leave, ⁵⁵rather than give to one of them from the flesh of his children that he will eat, not leaving anything for him, his relative, in the siege and in the distress that your enemy will distress you within all your gates. ⁵⁶The tender and delicate woman among you, who did not venture setting the sole of her foot on the ground due to delicacy and due to tenderness, will be selfish toward the husband of her bosom, and toward her son, and toward her daughter, ⁵⁷and toward her afterbirth that emerges from between her legs, her babies, and toward her children whom she will bear, as she will eat them in the lack of everything, in secret, in the siege and in the distress that your enemy will distress you at your gates.

⁵⁸If you will not take care to perform all the words of this Torah that are written in this book, to fear this revered and awesome name, the Lord your God, ⁵⁹the Lord will intensify your blows, and the blows of your descendants, great and profound blows, and dire and profound illnesses. ⁶⁰He will return to you all the afflictions of Egypt of which you were terrified, and they will cleave to you. ⁶¹Also, every illness and every blow that is not written in the book of this Torah, the Lord will pile them upon you, until your destruction. ⁶²You shall remain few in number, instead of your having been like the stars of the heavens in plenitude, because you did not heed the voice of the Lord your God. ⁶³It shall be that, as the Lord exulted over you to do you good, and to multiply you, the Lord will cause others to exult over you to annihilate you and to destroy you, and you will be expelled from upon the land that you are coming there to take possession of it. ⁶⁴The Lord will disperse you among all the peoples from the end of the earth to the end of the earth. ⁶⁵Among these nations you will not be calm, and there will be no rest for the sole of your foot, the Lord will give you there a trembling heart, and yearning eyes, longing for respite, and desolation of the soul, sadness. ⁶⁶Your life will be dangling precariously before you, and you will fear night and day, and you will not believe in your life. ⁶⁷In the morning you will say: Would that it were evening, and in the evening you will say: Would that it were morning, from your heart's fear that you will feel, and from your eyes' sight that you will see. ⁶⁸The Lord will

return you to Egypt in ships, on the way, the route, with regard to which I said to you: You will not see it ever again (see 17:16). And you will seek to sell yourselves there to your enemies as slaves and as maidservants, and there is no buyer.

69These are the words of the covenant that the Lord commanded Moses to make with the children of Israel in the land of Moav, besides the covenant that He made with them at Horev.

Words of Admonishment
Moses moves on to the final part of his address. From this point until the end of the following Torah portion, he implores the Israelites to acknowledge the wonders that God performed on their behalf throughout their years in the wilderness, and to understand the necessity of observing the mitzvot and cleaving to God.

29 **Seventh aliya** 1Moses summoned all of Israel and he said to them: You have seen everything that the Lord performed before your eyes in the land of Egypt, to Pharaoh, and to all his servants, and to his entire land; 2the great trials and miracles that your eyes saw, the signs and those great wonders. 3But the Lord has not given you a heart to know and internalize, and eyes to see, and ears to hear, until this day. 4Moses now speaks as God's voice: I led you forty years in the wilderness; your garments did not wear out from upon you, and your shoe did not wear out from upon your foot. **Maftir** 5Bread you did not eat, and wine and intoxicating drink you did not drink, so that you will know that I am the Lord your God. 6You came to this place and Sihon king of Heshbon and Og king of Bashan emerged against us to war, and we smote them and routed them. 7We took their land and we gave it as an inheritance to the Reubenite, and to the Gadite, and to half the tribe of the Manassite. 8You shall observe the words of this covenant and you shall perform them, so that you will succeed in everything that you do.

Further reading: For more on the accord with the tribes of Reuben and Gad, see p. 420.

Deuteronomy

Parashat Nitzavim

Moses continues the final part of his great address, in which he continues to implore the Israelites to faithfully fulfill the Torah.

Making the Covenant

Moses explains to the Israelites that they are now making a covenant with God to be loyal to Him throughout the generations. God, in turn, will render them His people, as He promised the patriarchs.

⁹**You are standing today, all of you, before the Lord your God: Your heads,** leaders of **your tribes; your elders,** officials; **and your officers,** and **every man of Israel,** ¹⁰**your children, your wives, and your stranger who is in the midst of your camp, from the hewer of your wood to the drawer of your water,** ¹¹**to pass you into the covenant of the Lord your God and into His oath that the Lord your God is making with you**

Second aliya **today,** ¹²**in order to establish you today for Him as a people, and He will be your God, as He spoke to you, and as He took an oath to your forefathers, to Abraham, to Isaac, and to Jacob.** ¹³**But not with you by yourselves do I make this covenant and this oath;** ¹⁴**rather, with him who is here with us standing today before the Lord our God, and with him who is not here with us today,** but who will be born in the future.

📖 **Further reading:** It is when the people of Israel are united that the covenant and the promise are in effect; see *A Concise Guide to the Sages*, p. 257.

The Sin and the Exile

Violating the covenant will cause all the curses mentioned in the previous chapters to befall them, and the Israelites will be exiled from their land.

Third aliya ¹⁵**For you know how we lived in the land of Egypt, and how we passed in the midst of the nations that you passed.** ¹⁶**You saw their detestable things,** their gods, **and their idols** of **wood and stone, silver and gold, that were with them.** ¹⁷**Lest there is among you a man, or a woman, or a family, or a tribe, whose heart turns,** is enticed, **today from the Lord**

our God, to go to serve the gods of those nations; lest there is among you a root producing gall and wormwood, bitter and poisonous plants; [18]and it will be that upon his hearing the words of this curse, he will bless himself in his heart, saying: Peace will be with me, as the curse will not affect me, I will follow the desire of my heart, doing as I please, so that the watered, the sins he performs deliberately will be added to the dry, the sins he performs unwittingly; [19]the Lord will be unwilling to forgive him, as then the wrath of the Lord and His zealotry will smoke against that man, and the entire curse that is written in this book shall rest upon him, and the Lord will expunge his name from under the heavens. [20]The Lord will separate him for evil from all the tribes of Israel, in accordance with all the curses of the covenant that is written in this book of the Torah.

[21]The latter generation, your children who will arise after you, and the foreigner who will come from a distant land, they will see the afflictions of that land, and the illnesses with which the Lord has blighted it, and they will say: [22]Sulfur and salt, its, Israel's, entire land afire. It will not be sown and will not produce, and no vegetation will grow in it, like the aftermath of the upheaval of Sodom and Gomorrah, Adma and Tzevoyim, which the Lord overturned in His wrath and in His fury. [23]All the nations will say: For what reason did the Lord do thus to this land? What is the cause of this great enflamed wrath? [24]They will say: It is because they forsook the covenant of the Lord, God of their fathers, which He made with them when He took them out of the land of Egypt. [25]They went and served other gods and prostrated themselves before them, gods that they did not know them and He did not allot to them. [26]The wrath of the Lord was enflamed against that land, to bring upon it the entire curse that is written in this book. [27]The Lord uprooted them from upon their land with wrath, and with fury, and with great rage, and He cast them to another land, as they are to this day. [28]The concealed sins are for the Lord our God to punish, but the revealed sins are our responsibility, for us and for our children forever, to perform all the matters of this Torah.

Repentance

Moses presents the possibility of repentance to the nation. Even in the worst case scenario, where the Israelites do sin, and are exiled from their land, they will still have the ability to return to the Lord with all their hearts, and then He will gather them from all the lands of their dispersion and renew His ties of love with them.

30 *Fourth aliya (Second aliya)* ¹**It shall be, when all these matters will come upon you, the blessing and the curse that I have placed before you, you shall restore to your heart,** you will reflect **among all the nations that the Lord your God has banished you there.** ²**You shall return to the Lord your God, and heed His voice, in accordance with everything that I command you today, you and your children, with all your heart, and with all your soul.** ³**The Lord your God will restore your returnees and He will be merciful to you, and He will return and gather you from all the peoples, that the Lord your God dispersed you there.** ⁴**If your banished** brethren **will be at the ends of the heavens, from there the Lord your God will gather you, and from there He will take you.** ⁵**The Lord your God will bring you to the land of which your fathers took possession, and you shall take possession of it and He will do good to you, and increase you beyond your fathers.** ⁶**The Lord your God will remove the obstruction from your heart and the heart of your descendants, to love the Lord your God with all your heart, and with all your soul, for the sake of** *Fifth aliya (Third aliya)* **your life.** ⁷**The Lord your God will place all these curses upon your enemies and upon those who hate you, who pursued you.** ⁸**You shall return and you shall heed the voice of the Lord, and you shall perform all His commandments that I command you today.** ⁹**The Lord your God will increase you,** grant you success, **in all your endeavors: In the fruit of your womb,** your children; **and in the fruit of your animals,** their offspring; **and in the fruit,** the produce, **of your land, for good, as the Lord will return to rejoice over you for good as He rejoiced over your fathers,** ¹⁰**if you will heed the voice of the Lord your God, to observe His commandments and His statutes that are written in this book of the Torah, when you will return to the Lord your God with all your heart, and with all your soul.**

Sixth aliya ¹¹**For this commandment that I command you today, it is not obscured from you, and it is not distant.** ¹²**It is not in the heavens,** which might lead one **to say: Who will ascend for us,** on our behalf, **to the heavens, and take it for us and communicate it to us, that we will perform it?** ¹³**It is not across the sea,** which might lead one **to say: Who will cross**

for us to the other side of the sea, and take it for us and communicate it to us, that we will perform it? [14]**Rather, the matter** of the Torah and its commandments **is very near to you,** and its fulfillment attainable; **in your mouth** to speak it, **and in your heart** to understand it, **to perform it.**

Choosing Life

The Israelites now understand the choice placed before them. Moses implores them to choose life; the path of good and right, which will lead them to a life of stability and prosperity in the Land of Israel.

venth aliya, Maftir ourth aliya) [15]**See, I have placed before you today, life and good, and death and evil,** [16]**that I command you today to love the Lord your God, to walk in His ways and to observe His commandments, His statutes, and His ordinances; you will live and you will multiply, and the Lord your God will bless you in the land that you are coming there to take possession of it.** [17]**But if your heart will turn away,** will be enticed, **and you will not heed** these matters, **and you go astray and prostrate yourself before other gods and serve them,** [18]**I am telling you today that you will be annihilated; you will not extend your days upon the land that you are crossing the Jordan to go there to take possession of it.** [19]**I call today to the heavens and the earth to bear witness to you: I have placed life and death before you, the blessing and the curse; you shall choose life, so that you and your descendants will live,** [20]**to love the Lord your God, to heed His voice, and to cleave to Him, for He is your life and the length of your days, so that you may live in the land with regard to which the Lord took an oath to your forefathers, to Abraham, to Isaac, and to Jacob, to give to them.**

📖 **Further reading:** For more on free will as a human inheritance, see *A Concise Guide to Mahshava,* p. 138.

Deuteronomy

Parashat Vayelekh

This *parasha* consists of a description of Moses' preparations for taking his leave from the Israelites, and for his death, and an introduction to the poem that is his final warning to them.

Transfer of Leadership

Moses officially transfers the mantle of leadership to Joshua. He encourages and reassures Joshua and the people with regard to the wars of conquest they are about to embark upon.

31 ¹**Moses went and spoke these words to all Israel.** ²**He said to them: I am one hundred and twenty years old today, I will no longer be able, allowed, to go and come,** to lead you, **and the Lord said to me: You shall not cross this Jordan.** ³**The Lord your God, He is crossing before you; He will destroy these nations from before you, and you will take possession from them. Joshua, he is crossing before you, as the Lord** Second aliya **spoke.** ⁴**The Lord will do to them as He did to Sihon and to Og, kings of the Emorites, and to their land, that He destroyed them.** ⁵**The Lord will deliver them before you, and you shall do to them in accordance with the entire commandment that I commanded you.** ⁶**Be strong and courageous; do not fear or be intimidated before them, as the Lord your God, it is He who goes with you; He will not fail you,** loosen His grip on you, **and He will not forsake you.**

Third aliya (Fifth aliya) ⁷**Moses summoned Joshua, and said to him before the eyes of all Israel: Be strong and courageous, as you will come with** and bring **this people into the land with regard to which the Lord took an oath to their forefathers to give them, and you will bequeath it to them.** ⁸**The Lord, it is He who goes before you, He will be with you, He will not fail you, and He will not forsake you; do not fear and do not be frightened.**

Further reading: The Sages say that Moses requested to have the mantle of leadership pass to Joshua and that he himself would live with Joshua as leader; see *A Concise Guide to the Sages*, p. 262.

Deuteronomy

The Mitzva of Assembly

With the death of Moses approaching, he passes to the Israelites the Torah that they received at Sinai. He writes it and gives it to the Levites and the princes and commands them to stage a public ceremony, reading and studying it once every seven years.

⁹Moses wrote this Torah, and he gave it to the priests, sons of Levi, who carry the Ark of the Covenant of the Lord, and to all the elders of Israel. ¹⁰Moses commanded them, saying: At the end of seven years in the appointed time of the year of remittal, during the Festival of the Tabernacles, ¹¹upon the arrival of all of Israel to appear before the Lord your God in the place that He will choose, you, Joshua, shall read this Torah before all Israel in their ears. ¹²Assemble the people, the men and the women and the children, and your gentile stranger who is within your gates, so that they will hear, and so that they will learn, and they will fear the Lord your God, and they will take care to perform all the matters of this Torah. ¹³Their children, who do not know the Torah, **they will hear, and they will learn to fear the Lord your God,** all the days that you live on the land that you are crossing the Jordan to there, to take possession of it.

Fourth aliya is marked in the margin.

God's Words to Moses

At this point, God speaks to Moses for the last time, and appoints Joshua as his replacement. He anticipates that the Israelites will sin in the future, and commands Moses to teach them the poem recorded in the next Torah portion – to serve as an admonition when they are punished. In conclusion, God encourages and reassures Joshua prior to the entry into the land.

Fifth aliya (Sixth aliya) is marked in the margin.

¹⁴The Lord said to Moses: Behold, your days are drawing near for you to die. Summon Joshua, and stand in the Tent of Meeting, the Tabernacle, and I will command him. Moses and Joshua went and stood in the Tent of Meeting. ¹⁵The Lord appeared in the tent in a pillar of cloud, and the pillar of cloud stood over the entrance of the tent. ¹⁶The Lord said to Moses: Behold, you will lie with your fathers, you are going to die, and **this people will rise, and it will stray after the foreign gods of the land that it is coming there into their midst, and it will forsake Me, and it will breach My covenant that I made with it.** ¹⁷My wrath will be enflamed against it on that day, and I will forsake them, and I will hide My face from them, and it, the nation, **will be for consumption,** subject to persecution, and **many evils and troubles will find it, and it will say on that day: Is it not because my God is not in my midst that these evils**

Deuteronomy

found me? [18]I will conceal My face on that day, because of all the evil that it performed as it turned to other gods.

[19]Now, write this poem, *Haazinu*, for yourselves, and teach it to the children of Israel, place it in their mouths until they can recite it by heart, so that this poem will be a witness for Me for the children of Israel that they have been warned. [20]For I will bring them to the land with regard to which I took an oath to their forefathers, a land flowing with milk and honey, and they will eat, and will be satisfied, and they will grow fat, prosperous, and they will turn to other gods, and will serve them, and scorn Me, and will breach My covenant. [21]It will be, when many evils and troubles find them, that this poem will testify before them as a witness, as it will not be forgotten from the mouths of their descendants; this is necessary as I know their inclination to sin from what they do today, before I will bring them to the land with regard to which I took an oath.

Sixth aliya (Seventh aliya)

[22]Moses wrote this poem on that day, and he taught it to the children of Israel. [23]He, God, commanded Joshua son of Nun, and he said: Be strong and courageous, as you shall bring the children of Israel into the land with regard to which I took an oath to them; and I will be with you.

📖 **Further reading:** For more on the transfer of leadership to Joshua, see *A Concise Guide to the Sages*, pp. 212, 263.

Reciting the Song

Moses concludes his writing of the Torah and he hands it to the Levites for safekeeping. He assembles the people to hear the poem of *Haazinu*.

Seventh aliya

[24]It was, as Moses finished writing the words of this Torah in a book, until their conclusion. [25]Moses commanded the Levites, bearers of the Ark of the Covenant of the Lord, saying: [26]Take this book of the Torah, and place it at the side of the Ark of the Covenant of the Lord your God, and it will be there as a witness for you. [27]For I know your defiance, and your stiff neck, your stubbornness; behold, while I am still alive with you today, you have been defiant with the Lord, and so too,

Maftir

all the more so, after my death. [28]Assemble to me all the elders of your tribes, and your officers, and I will speak these words in their ears, and I will call the heavens and the earth to testify for them. [29]For I know after my death you will act corruptly, and you will deviate from the path

Deuteronomy

that I commanded you and evil will befall you at the end of days, in the future, because you will do that which is evil in the eyes of the Lord, to anger Him with your handiwork. [30]Moses spoke in the ears of the entire assembly of Israel the words of this poem, until their conclusion.

Parashat Haazinu

In this *parasha* the poem of *Haazinu* is recorded, warning the Israelites of the troubles that will arise from future sins. The poem is addressed to the Israel of the future, which will prosper and then grow rebellious, bringing about disaster. Along with this message, however, is a promise of vengeance against the nations that will torment Israel. The Torah portion concludes with God inviting Moses to ascend Mount Nevo and see the Land of Israel, into which he was forbidden from entering.

Foreword to the Poem

Moses opens the poem by petitioning the heavens and the earth to serve as witnesses.

32 **¹Listen, the heavens, and I will speak, and the earth will hear the sayings of my mouth. ²My moral lesson will fall as the rain, my saying will flow like dew; like rainstorms on grass, and like raindrops on vegetation. ³When I proclaim the name of the Lord, acclaim greatness to our God.**

📖 **Further reading:** For more on the significance of choosing the heavens and earth as witnesses for the poem, see *A Concise Guide to the Sages*, p. 264.

God's Righteousness and Goodness

Moses reminds the Israelites of the future of the upright ways of God and all the good acts that He has performed on behalf of His people. The problems that have arisen are due to their corrupt ways, and cannot be blamed on God.

⁴The Rock, a metaphor for God, His actions are perfect, as all His ways are justice: He is a faithful God, and there is no injustice; righteous and upright is He. ⁵Corruption is not from Him; His children, it is their blemish, they are a crooked and twisted generation. ⁶Will you repay the Lord like this? How can you do so, crude and unwise people? Is He not your Father, your Redeemer? He made you, and He established you.⁷Remember the days of yore; examine the years of each generation. Ask your father, and he will tell you; your elders, and they will say to you. ⁸When the Most High bequeathed lands to the nations, when

Second aliya

Deuteronomy

He separated the children of man into nations, He set the borders of the peoples according to the number of the children of Israel; seventy nations, corresponding to the seventy souls who descended with Jacob to Egypt. **⁹For the portion of the Lord is His people; Jacob is the allotment of His inheritance.** Israel is God's distinctive nation. **¹⁰He would find him, Jacob, in a wilderness land, and in emptiness, a howling wasteland. He would** protectively **encircle him, He would grant him understanding, He preserved him like the pupil of His eye. ¹¹Like an eagle that would rouse** those within **its nest, over its fledglings it would hover, it would spread its wings and take them, carrying them on its pinions.** God carried Israel through the wilderness in this manner. **¹²The Lord alone would**
Third **lead him, and there was no foreign god with Him. ¹³He would mount**
aliya **him on the elevations of the earth, and he,** Israel, **ate the yield of the field; He suckled him honey from a stone, and oil from a flinty rock. ¹⁴Butter of cattle, and milk of sheep, with fat of lambs and rams of the Bashan** region, **and goats, with wheat** that is as **fat as kidneys; and the blood of,** the juice of, red **grapes you would drink** as wine.

Betrayal of God

Despite the great prosperity with which the Israelites will be blessed, they will rebel against God and turn to idols.

¹⁵Yeshurun, the Israelites, **grew fat** enjoying all this bounty, **and kicked,** rebelled against God; **you became fat, you thickened, you grew obese; he forsook God his Maker, and reviled the Rock of his salvation. ¹⁶They,** the Israelites, **would infuriate Him with** their worship of the idols of **strangers, with abominations they anger Him. ¹⁷They would slaughter to demons, to a non-god, to gods that they did not know, new ones that came recently; your fathers did not consider them. ¹⁸The Rock that gave birth to you, you forsook, and you forgot God, your Originator.**

📖 **Further reading:** Rebellion against God specifically in situations of tranquility and prosperity is a familiar phenomenon in Jewish history; see *A Concise Guide to the Sages*, p. 265.

God's Anger

God will become angry at the Israelites and punish them severely. He will prevent their total destruction only so that the nations of the world will not say that He abandoned His people.

Fourth **¹⁹The Lord saw and scorned** them, **out of anger for His sons and His**
aliya **daughters,** the anger they caused Him. **²⁰He said: I will conceal My face**

Deuteronomy

from them, I will see what their end is, as they are a generation of fickleness, children in whom there is no faithfulness. [21]They have infuriated Me with a non-god, by worshipping false gods, they angered Me with their futilities of idolatry, sorcery, and witchcraft, and I will infuriate them with a non-people, a mixture of several nations, with a crude, base and dishonorable, nation I will anger them. [22]For a fire of rage blazed in My nostrils, and it burned to the lowest depths, to Gehenna, and it consumed the earth and its produce, and set ablaze the foundations of mountains. [23]I will add evils upon them, I will exhaust My arrows on them. [24]They will be wasted from hunger, and consumed by fire demons and evil spirits, and the teeth of animals I will dispatch at them, with the venom of crawlers in the dust. [25]Outside, the sword will bereave, and there will be terror within; for youth and maiden alike, the suckling babe with the gray-haired man.

[26]I said I would scatter them, I would terminate their memory from man, [27]were it not that I dread the enemy's anger, lest their adversaries misapprehend, lest they say: We defeated Israel because our hand is mighty, and it is not the Lord who did all this. [28]For they are a nation void of counsel, and there is no understanding in them.

> **Further reading:** Why are punishments in the World to Come not mentioned in the Torah? See *A Concise Guide to Mahshava*, p. 257.

Fifth aliya [29]If they were wise they would comprehend this, they would understand their end, the real cause of Israel's punishment. [30]How does one pursue one thousand of Israel, and two cause ten thousand to flee, if not that their Rock, God, sold them and the Lord handed them over to their enemies?

[31]For our Rock is not like their rock, and our enemies are our judges, carry out God's punishment upon us. [32]For their, our enemy's, vine, their actions, is from the vine of Sodom, and from the fields of Gomorrah; their grapes are grapes of poison, noxious clusters for them. [33]The venom of serpents is their wine, and the cruel poison from the head of vipers. [34]Is this, their sins, not concealed with Me, sealed in My treasuries?

God's Vengeance at the End of Days

The poem concludes with God's promise to take vengeance upon the enemies that afflicted His people, Israel.

³⁵**Vengeance and recompense are Mine, at the time that their foot will collapse; for the day of their calamity is near, and the future is rushing toward them.** ³⁶**When the Lord judges His people, and He reconsiders with regard to** the punishment that was imposed on **His servants, as He sees that their,** his people's, **power is gone, and there is none protected or fortified,** there is no one to help them, ³⁷**He,** God, **will say: Where are their gods** in whom they placed their trust, **the rock in whom they sought refuge,** ³⁸**the fat of whose offerings they would eat, the wine of whose libations they would drink?** Do you believe that **they will arise and help you;** that **it will be shelter over you?** ³⁹**See now that I, I am He, and there is no god with,** other than, **Me. I will kill and I will give life, I crushed and I will heal, and there is no rescuer from My hand;** everything is under My control. ⁴⁰**When I raise My hand** in oath **to the heavens and say: As I live forever.** The Lord takes an oath, as it were, by His own life. ⁴¹**Surely I will hone** and display **My flashing sword, and My hand will grasp judgment, I will return vengeance to My enemies, and to those who hate Me I will recompense.** ⁴²**I will intoxicate My arrows with blood, and My sword will devour flesh, from the blood of the slain and the captive, from the heads of the enemy raiders.** ⁴³**Nations, acclaim His people, as He will avenge the blood of His servants, and He will return vengeance to His adversaries, and He will make expiation for His land** and **His people.**

📖 **Further reading:** For more on resurrection of the dead, see *A Concise Guide to Mahshava*, p. 295.

Seventh aliya ⁴⁴**Moses came and he spoke all the words of this poem in the ears of the people, he, and Hoshe'a son of Nun.** ⁴⁵**Moses finished speaking all these matters to all Israel.** ⁴⁶**He said to them: Set your heart to all the matters that I attest to you today,** so that you will command them to your children, to take care to perform all the words of this Torah. ⁴⁷**For it is not an empty thing for you, as it is your life, and through this matter you will extend** your **days on the land that you are crossing the Jordan to take possession of it.**

Mount Nevo

At the conclusion of the poem and a short while before his death, God invites Moses to ascend to the peak of Mount Nevo and look from there to the Promised Land – into which he will not be privileged to enter.

Maftir ⁴⁸**The Lord spoke to Moses on that very day** that the poem of *Haazinu* was first recited, **saying:** ⁴⁹**Ascend to this highland of Avarim,** a mountain from which all its sides [*avarav*] are visible, **Mount Nevo, which is in the land of Moav, which is opposite Jericho, and see the land of Canaan that I am giving to the children of Israel as a portion.** ⁵⁰**Die on the mountain that you are ascending there, and be gathered to your people, as Aaron your brother died on Hor Mountain, and he was gathered to his people,** ⁵¹**because you trespassed against Me in the midst of the children of Israel at the waters of dispute of Kadesh, in the wilderness of Tzin; because you did not sanctify Me in the midst of the children of Israel.** ⁵²**For from a distance you will see the land, but there you will not come, to the land that I am giving to the children of Israel.**

📖 **Further reading:** For more on the sin of striking the rock, see p. 390.

Deuteronomy

Parashat
Vezot HaBerakha

The final portion of the Torah contains Moses' blessings upon the tribes prior to their entry into the Land of Israel, and a description of his unique death.

Moses' Blessing

Moses begins his final blessing of the Israelites with mention of the most significant event in their history, the revelation at Sinai.

33 ¹**This is the blessing that Moses, the man of God,** the prophet, **blessed the children of Israel before his death.** ²**He said,** in describing the manifestations of the revelation at Sinai: **The Lord came from Sinai, and shone from Se'ir for them, He appeared from Mount Paran, and He came from the holy myriads,** the angels; **from His right** He gave **a fiery law to them.** ³**Indeed, He loves** all **the peoples; all His holy ones,** the myriad of holy angels above and the Israelites below, are **in Your hand; and they fell at Your feet, and they received Your sayings.** ⁴**Torah, Moses commanded us, a heritage of the assembly of Jacob.** ⁵The revelation at Sinai transpired when **He,** God, **became King in Yeshurun,** over Israel, **when the heads of the people were assembled, the tribes of Israel,** the entire people, **together.**

📖 **Further reading:** For more on the Torah as Israel's inheritance, see *A Concise Guide to the Sages*, p. 268.

The Blessings of the Tribes

At this point, Moses begins blessing each of the tribes individually. Some of the blessings are brief and some are longer. Most relate to the tribal territory that the Israelites are destined to receive in the Land of Israel.

⁶**May Reuben live and not die, and may his people be numerous.**

⁷**And this** is the blessing designated **for Judah, and he,** Moses, **said: Hear, Lord, the voice of Judah, and to his people bring him** back from the battlefield unharmed; **his hands are mighty for him** in his many battles, **and You will be a helper against his adversaries.**

📖 **Further reading:** Jacob also blessed his sons, progenitors of the tribes, before his death; see p. 126. For a comparison of the character of the two sets of blessings, see *A Concise Guide to Mahshava*, p. 215.

Second aliya **⁸And of Levi he said: Your Tumim and Your Urim,** the *Urim veTumim,* **symbols of the priesthood, for Your virtuous one,** Aaron and his descendants, **whom You tested at Masa; You challenged him at the waters of Meriva,** the ordeal at Masa and Meriva, where Moses and Aaron sinned. **⁹**In the wake of the sin of the Golden Calf, the Levites were mustered by Moses to kill the sinners (see Exodus 32:27-28). Doing so required them to overcome their family attachments: **Who said of his father, and of his mother: I did not see him; and his brothers he did not recognize, and his children he did not know, because they observed Your saying,** Your commandment, **and Your covenant they upheld. ¹⁰They,** the Levites, and the priests in particular, **shall teach Your ordinances to Jacob and Your law to Israel; they shall place incense before You, and entire offerings on Your altar. ¹¹Bless, Lord, his might, and the work of his hands accept. Crush the loins of those who rise against him, and his enemies,** prevent them **from rising.**

¹²Of Benjamin he said: Benjamin, **the beloved** of the Lord, He will dwell **in safety with him,** God's dwelling will be in Benjamin's portion. **He,** God's presence, rests over Benjamin and **hovers over him all day, and He rests between his shoulders.** This is a prophetic allusion to the Temple that would be in Benjamin's portion.

Third aliya **¹³And of Joseph he said: Blessed of the Lord is his land, from the sweetness of heaven, from dew, and from** the groundwater of **the depths lying below, ¹⁴and from the sweetness of the crops of the sun,** that ripen in the sun, **and from the sweetness of the yield of the moons,** those that ripen with the help of the moon, **¹⁵and from the tops of the ancient,** or eastern, **mountains, and from the sweetness of the eternal hills, ¹⁶and from the sweetness of the earth and its fullness, and the will of He who rested in the bush** [*seneh*]; **it shall come upon the head of Joseph, upon the top of the head of the crowned of his brothers. ¹⁷He has glory like a firstborn bull; his horns are the** large, impressive **horns of aurochs. With them together, he will gore the peoples at the ends of the earth. And** the tribe of Joseph is divided into two branches: **They are the myriads of Ephraim, and they are the thousands of Manasseh.**

Fourth aliya ¹⁸**And of Zebulun he said: Rejoice, Zebulun, in your departure** to engage in commerce, **and Issachar,** rejoice **in your tents.** ¹⁹**They,** the children of Zebulun, **will call** other **peoples to** worship at **the mountain** of God; **there shall they,** those peoples, **slaughter offerings of righteousness, because they,** the children of Zebulun, **will be nourished by the bounty of** fish and commerce via **the seas, and** they will uncover **the hidden treasures of the sand.**

²⁰**And of Gad he said: Blessed is He who expands** the tribal land of **Gad** east of the Jordan. **Like a lion he rests,** confident in his power, **and mauls the arm, even the top of the head.** Like a lion that breaks the leg and head of its prey. ²¹**He saw the first** region that Israel conquered, east of the Jordan, and chose it **for himself, as there** is **the** burial **plot of the lawgiver,** where Moses **is hidden.** Moses will be buried on the eastern side of the Jordan but no one will know where his grave is. **He brings the heads of the people** of Israel to the land of Canaan, as the vanguard in conquest of the land. **He performed the righteousness of the Lord, and His ordinances, with Israel.**

Fifth aliya ²²**And of Dan he said: Dan is a lion cub that leaps from the** adjacent **Bashan.**

²³**And of Naphtali he said: Naphtali, his desire is satisfied,** because his land is fertile **and full with the blessing of the Lord; he will take possession of the sea and south.** Naphtali will inherit the Sea of Galilee, and the fertile land to its south.

²⁴**And of Asher he said: Blessed of sons is Asher,** the tribe will be blessed with many sons. **He will be the beloved of his brothers,** they will not begrudge him, **and he dips his foot in oil,** his tribal land will produce much olive oil. ²⁵**Iron and copper** will be **your padlocks;** your land, Asher, will be fortified and protected, **and like your days shall be your flow,** you will enjoy prosperity all your days.

> 🕮 **Further reading:** *Parashat Vezot HaBerakha* is read in a unique way, as the year's Torah reading is concluded on *Simhat Torah*; see *A Concise Guide to Halakha,* p. 234.

A General Blessing for the Israelites

Moses concludes with general words of blessing for the Israelites. God watches over them closely; they dwell alone, and will dominate the surrounding nations.

Deuteronomy

²⁶**Yeshurun,** Israel, **there is none like** the **God** of Israel, **who rides the heavens in your assistance, and in His majesty** rules **the sky.**

Hatan
Torah ²⁷**An abode** for Israel **is the God of eternity, and below,** God embraces you with **eternal arms. He banished the enemy from before you, and He said: Destroy** the enemy. ²⁸**Israel dwelled securely. Alone is the spring,** the descendants, **of Jacob,** after coming **to a land of grain and wine. His heavens drip dew.** ²⁹**Happy are you, Israel; who is like you? A people saved by the Lord,** who is **the shield of your assistance, and who is the sword of your honor. Your enemies will** seek to **deceive you, and you will tread on their high places** and defeat them.

Moses' Death

The final section of the Torah describes the death of Moses, the servant of God. God shows him the Promised Land, into which he is not privileged to enter. Moses dies not as a result of sickness, or the infirmity of old age, but in accordance with the edict of God.

34 ¹**Moses ascended from the plains of Moav to Mount Nevo, the top of the peak, that is opposite Jericho, and the Lord showed him the entire land, the Gilad until Dan,** ²**and all of Naphtali, and the land of Ephraim and Manasseh, and the entire land of Judah until the last sea,** the Mediterranean, ³**and the South, and the Plain, the Valley of Jericho, city of the date palms, until Tzo'ar.** ⁴**The Lord said to him: This is the land with regard to which I took an oath to Abraham, to Isaac, and to Jacob, saying: To your descendants I will give it; I have shown it to you with your eyes, but there you will not cross.**

⁵**Moses, servant of the Lord, died there in the land of Moav, at the directive of the Lord.** ⁶**He buried him,** Moses buried himself, or God buried Moses, **in the canyon in the land of Moav opposite Beit Peor, and no man knows** the location of **his grave to this day.** ⁷**Moses was one hundred and twenty years old upon his death; his eye had not dimmed, and his vitality had not departed.** He displayed no outward indications of aging. ⁸**The children of Israel wept for Moses in the plains of Moav thirty days, and** then **the days of weeping of the mourning of Moses concluded.**

⁹**Joshua son of Nun was full of the spirit of wisdom, as Moses had placed his hands upon him; and the children of Israel heeded him, and acted as the Lord commanded Moses.** ¹⁰**There has not risen another prophet in Israel like Moses, whom the Lord knew face-to-face,** ¹¹**with all the**

signs and the wonders that the Lord sent him to perform in the land of Egypt, to Pharaoh, and to all his servants, and to all his land; [12]and with all the mighty hand, and with all the actions that inspired great awe, that Moses performed before the eyes of all Israel.

📖 **Further reading:** For more on Moses' wondrous death, see *A Concise Guide to the Sages*, p. 270.

Illustrations

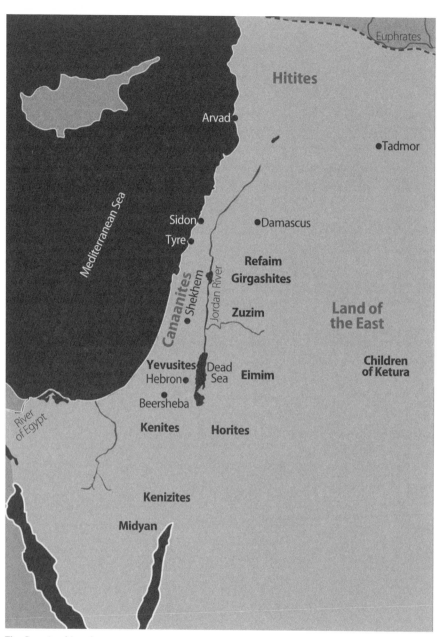

The Promised Land

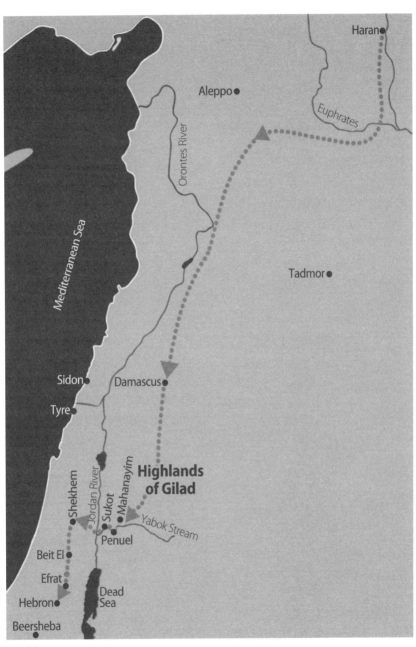

Jacob's route

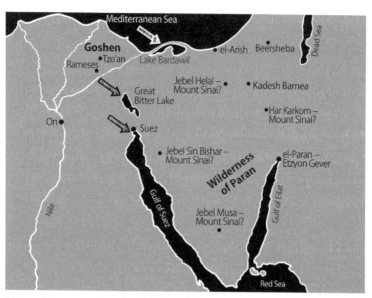

Main opinions on where the children of Israel crossed the sea, indicated by arrows

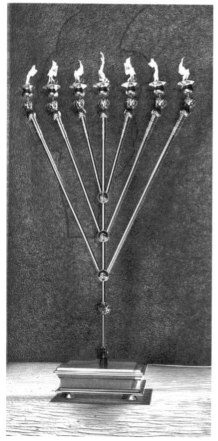

Candelabrum

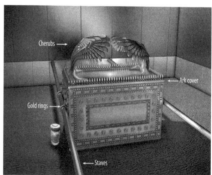

Ark of the Covenant

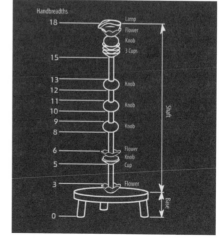

Detail of the central branch of the candelabrum

523

Sockets

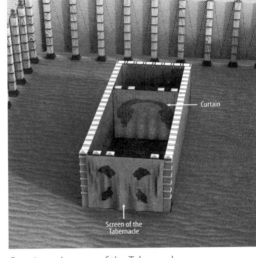

Curtain and screen of the Tabernacle

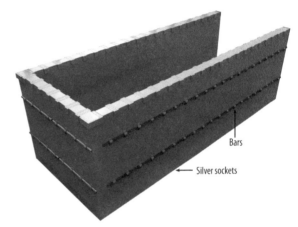

Boards and bars

Walls of the Tabernacle

Tabernacle and courtyard

Basin for collecting the blood of an offering

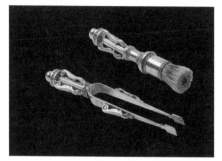

Tongs and brush for handling wicks and cleaning out oil lamps

Altar

Labels on Altar image: Horn, Arrangement of the firewood, Ledge, Mesh, Base

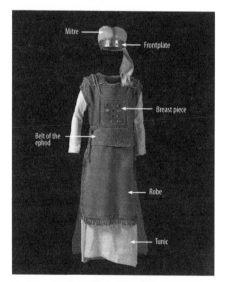

Vestments of the High Priest

Labels on Vestments image: Mitre, Frontplate, Breast piece, Belt of the ephod, Robe, Tunic

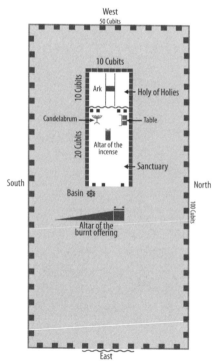

Placement of Tabernacle vessels

Labels on Tabernacle diagram: West, 50 Cubits, 10 Cubits, Ark, Holy of Holies, Candelabrum, Table, 10 Cubits, 20 Cubits, Altar of the incense, Sanctuary, South, North, Basin, 100 Cubits, Altar of the burnt offering, East

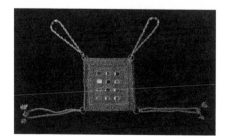

Breast piece

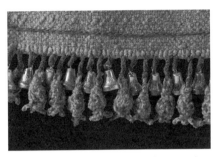

Hem of the High Priest's robe, decorated
with pomegranates and bells

Diadem

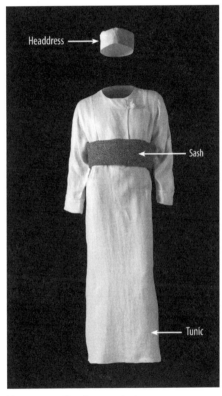

Small incense altar

Vestments of ordinary priests

Basin

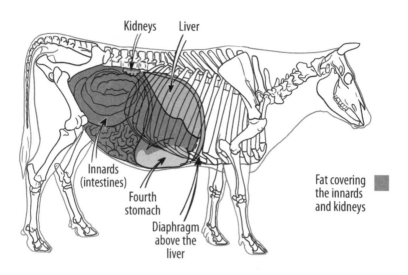

Fats from cattle burned on the altar

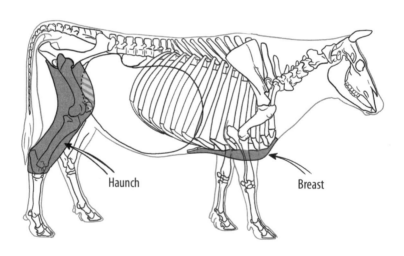

Breast of waving and haunch of lifting

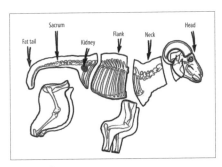

Pieces of a ram

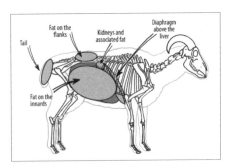

Sacrificial portions of a sheep

Split hooves

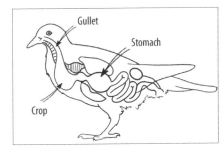

Digestive tract of a bird

Grasshopper with jointed leg

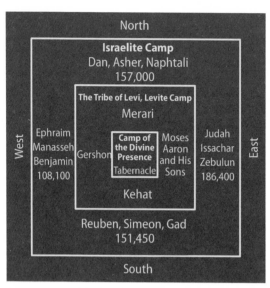

Arrangement of the Israelite camps

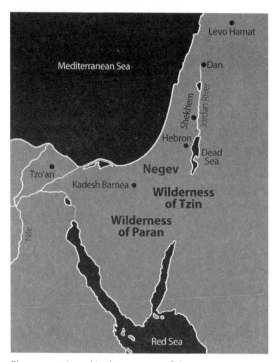

Places mentioned in the account of the scouts

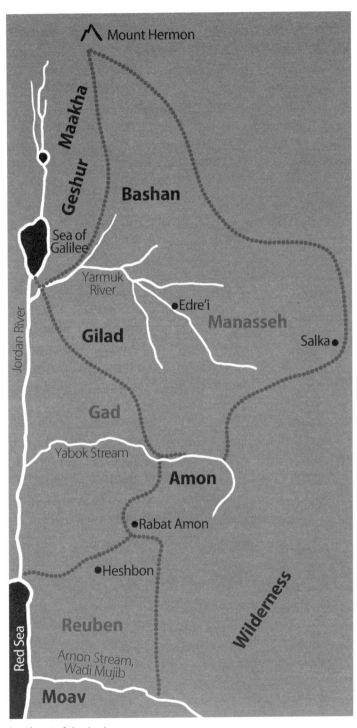

Land east of the Jordan

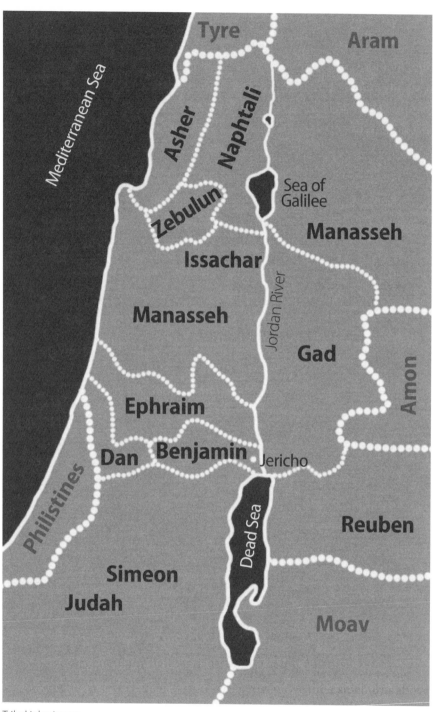

Tribal inheritance

Glossary

Glossary

Adar – Month of the Jewish calendar, occurring during February/March.

afikoman – Part of the middle matza at the Passover Seder, which is set aside during *Yahatz* and eaten at *Tzafun*, after the meal.

aggada (pl. aggadot) – Rabbinic story meant to impart an educational lesson.

Al HaNisim – Lit. "for the miracles"; a paragraph added to the *Amida* and the Grace after Meals on Purim and Hanukkah, thanking God for the miracles He wrought on behalf of the Jewish people.

aliya – Subdivision of the weekly Torah portion; the honor of being called up to the Torah for the reading of such a subdivision.

Amen – A response to a blessing indicating agreement with it and belief in its content..

Amida – A prayer comprising nineteen blessings that forms the central part of the prayer service. Also known as *Shemoneh Esreh* (lit. eighteen), because its original formulation had eighteen blessings.

arava (pl. aravot) – Willow branch, one of the four species taken on *Sukkot*.

ark – Repository in the prayer hall for Torah scrolls.

Ashkenazim (adj. Ashkenazic) – Segment of the Jewish population; broadly, Jews of European descent.

aufruf – Yiddish for "calling up." In Ashkenazic custom, a groom is called up to the Torah on the Shabbat before his wedding. This is observed as a celebratory event.

Av – Month of the Jewish calendar, occurring during July/August.

bar mitzva, bat mitzva – When a Jewish child reaches maturity and becomes formally obligated in mitzva observance. For a boy this occurs at the age of thirteen, for a girl at twelve.

baraita – A tannaitic statement that does not appear in the Mishna.

Barekhu – An invitation by the prayer leader to the congregation to recite a blessing. This marks the beginning of the blessings before *Shema* and of the blessings recited when one is called up to the Torah.

bima – The table in the synagogue upon which the Torah scroll is placed for Torah reading.

Birkot HaShahar – Morning Blessings.

Blessings over the Torah – Blessings said as part of the Morning Blessings, thanking God for the Torah and requesting His assistance to cleave to it.

brit – Circumcision ritual in which the baby is given his name.

dreidel – A four-sided spinning top played with on Hanukkah.

Edot HaMizrah – A general term for Sephardic congregations or the version of liturgy they use in their prayer services.

eiruv – A solution instituted by the Sages with regard to Shabbat prohibitions against carrying between domains and against walking far out of one's town; commonly used to refer to one type of *eiruv, eiruv hatzerot*.

eiruv hatzerot – The symbolic joining of private domains belonging to different people, thereby allowing them to carry from one place to another on Shabbat. This is accomplished when food belonging to the different residents is placed in one location.

eiruv tavshilin – When Shabbat falls on the day after a festival day, one must set aside bread and a cooked dish for a Shabbat meal before the festival begins. This allows him to cook or to carry out other preparations for Shabbat on the festival.

eiruv tehumin – The placement of food in a particular location, which establishes that location as a person's Shabbat residence. This allows him to travel two thousand cubits, the maximum distance one may travel on Shabbat (see *tehum Shabbat*), from that new location, rather than from his home.

Elul – Month of the Jewish calendar, occurring during August/September.

etrog – Citron, one of the four species taken on *Sukkot*.

farbrengen – Gathering of Chabad hasidim that may include the teaching of hasidic ideas, the telling of stories, and the singing of songs, as well as refreshments.

Full Kaddish – An Aramaic prayer of praise of God that is recited in the synagogue service, often by mourners.

gabbai – The synagogue sexton, who oversees the services.

gebrokts – Yiddish term for matza that has come into contact with liquid. Many Jews of hasidic descent have a custom not to eat *gebrokts* on Passover.

gematriya – A system in which each Hebrew letter is given a numerical value. It often highlights connections, sometimes mystical ones, between words.

geniza – Storeroom or repository in a synagogue used for discarded, damaged, or defective sacred books, papers, and objects.

Grace after Meals – Blessings recited after eating bread. Known in Hebrew as *Birkat HaMazon* and in Yiddish as *Bentching*.

hadas – Myrtle branch, one of the four species taken on *Sukkot*.

haftara – A portion from the Prophets read after the Torah reading on Shabbat, festivals, and public fasts.

haggada (pl. *haggadot*) – The text that presents the order of the Passover Seder. It contains instructions for the different parts of the Seder, and includes the text traditionally recited as fulfillment of the mitzva to retell the story of the redemption from Egypt.

HaGomel – Blessing said by one who is saved from a dangerous situation.

hakafot sheniyot – The seven rotations taken with the Torah, accompanied by music and dancing, on the night following *Simhat Torah*. This is customary in some communities.

halaka – Ceremonial first haircut, given to boys at age three; means haircut in Arabic. The Yiddish term is *upsherin*.

halakha (pl. halakhot) – Jewish law.

halakhic hour – One-twelfth of the period of daylight, may be longer or shorter than ordinary hours.

Half Kaddish – A shortened version of the Kaddish prayer (see Full Kaddish) that is recited by the prayer leader at certain points in the synagogue prayer service.

halla (pl. hallot) – Braided bread eaten on Shabbat and festivals. The name derives from the mitzva of *halla*, which is to separate a piece of dough and give it to a priest. Nowadays, however, the dough is destroyed.

Hallel – A series of psalms of praise recited on festivals.

hametz – Leavened grain products, which are prohibited for consumption on Passover.

HaMotzi – The blessing before eating bread.

Hanukkah – Eight-day holiday in the winter commemorating the victory of the Hasmoneans over the Seleucid Empire and the rededication of the Temple. On each day candles are lit.

hanukkiya – Hanukkah menora, the eight- or nine-branched candelabrum on which Hanukkah candles are lit.

hasid – Literally, a pious person. A member of the hasidic movement founded by the Baal Shem Tov in the eighteenth century.

hasidic – Having to do with Hasidism.

Hasidism – Pietist, anti-elitist movement founded by Rabbi Yisrael Baal Shem Tov in the eighteenth century. Hasidism emphasizes the service of God in all of one's actions, especially through ecstatic prayer and celebration, and the connection to God through the intervention of a *tzaddik*, a saintly person. Within a generation, Hasidism also became an intellectual movement, applying kabbalistic thought to an individual's religious life.

hatan me'ona – The name given in Sephardic communities to the penultimate *aliya* to the Torah before concluding the Torah on *Simhat Torah*.

hatan Torah – Literally, bridegroom of the Torah. The person who receives the *aliya* for the reading of the last section of the Torah on *Simhat Torah*.

Havdala – The ceremony for concluding the Sabbath. The blessing is said over a cup of wine, and with a candle and sweet-smelling spices.

hazan – Prayer leader in the synagogue, cantor.

hevra kadisha – Burial society, responsible for both preparing the deceased for burial and the actual interment.

hitbodedut – Seclusion practiced by Breslov hasidim for personal communication with God.

hitbonenut – Deep contemplation or meditation on one matter until the person has a spiritual experience regarding that matter. *Hitbonenut* combines intellectual study and spiritual passion.

Hol HaMoed – Intermediate days of *Sukkot* and Passover. On these days certain activities are prohibited, but there is no general prohibition of performing labor.

Hoshana Rabba – The seventh day of *Sukkot,* called *Hoshana Rabba* due to the custom of circling the *bima* seven times in a procession while reciting prayers that begin with the word *hoshana.*

huppa – Literally wedding canopy; *huppa* also refers to the wedding ceremony as a whole.

Isru Hag – The day after Passover, *Shavuot,* and *Sukkot.*

Iyar – Month of the Jewish calendar, occurring during April/May.

Kabbala – The Jewish tradition of mystical theory and practice.

Kabbalat Shabbat – The prayer service said at the onset of Shabbat on Friday night, as instituted by the Sages of Safed in the sixteenth century.

kabbalists – Thinkers who make use of the traditions of Kabbala

Kaddish – Prayer praising God that is said at particular intervals during the prayer service. See Mourner's Kaddish, Half Kaddish, and Rabbis' Kaddish.

kasher – To render a pot or a utensil kosher, usually by immersing it in boiling water or by heating it directly.

kashrut – The theory and practice of ritually kosher food.

Kedusha – Literally, sanctification. In this prayer, said during the repetition of the *Amida,* Israel joins forces with the angels in sanctifying God.

keli rishon – Primary vessel (lit. "first vessel"). The vessel in which something is cooked, even after it has been removed from a heat source.

kelipa (pl. kelipot) – Literally, husk. The kabbalistic term for those elements of existence that are forces of evil that need to be removed.

ketuba – A marriage contract that guarantees the wife a certain sum of money in the event of divorce or her husband's death.

kezayit – Olive-bulk, a halakhic measure of volume that generally corre-

sponds to the amount of food one needs to consume in order to fulfill a mitzva or be liable to punishment for a transgression. According to the most prevalent halakhic opinion, an olive-bulk is about 27 ml.

Kiddush – The blessing made over wine at the beginning of Shabbat and festival meals. The *Kiddush* said on Friday night includes a blessing consecrating Shabbat.

kiddush – Light meal at which *Kiddush* is said on Shabbat morning.

Kiddush Levana – The blessing said once a month at the appearance of the new moon. Usually said on Saturday night at the close of Shabbat.

kiddushin – The part of the wedding ceremony involving the groom giving the ring to the bride. Once *kiddushin* has been performed they are formally married.

kimha depis'ha – Aramaic for "Passover flour," also known as *ma'ot hittin* (lit. "money for wheat"). Charity given before Passover to enable the poor to buy food for the holiday.

kinnot – The liturgical poems that lament the destruction of the Temple and other tragedies, recited on *Tisha BeAv*.

Kislev – Month of the Jewish calendar, occurring during November/December.

kitniyot – Foods derived from edible seeds such as rice, beans, and lentils. These are not *hametz,* but are prohibited on Passover in the Ashkenazic tradition.

kittel – A white robe worn by many married men on Yom Kippur, Seder night and other occasions.

kohen (pl. kohanim) – A person of priestly lineage, a descendant of Aaron.

kol hane'arim – The *aliya* on *Simhat Torah* in which all the children of the community are called to the Torah. An adult recites the blessing.

Kol Nidrei – The prayer said at the onset of Yom Kippur in which the prayer leader asks to nullify all the vows made in the community that year.

Lag BaOmer – The thirty-third day of the *omer,* the eighteenth of the month of Iyar. *Lag BaOmer* is the day of the passing of Rabbi Shimon bar Yohai and also, in many customs, the end of the mourning period of the *omer.*

Various customs of *Lag BaOmer* include lighting bonfires and visiting Rabbi Shimon's grave at Meron.

lehem mishneh – Two whole loaves of bread that are used for the blessing at the beginning of a Shabbat meal.

Lekha Dodi – Liturgical poem composed by Rabbi Shlomo Alkabetz that is traditionally sung on Friday evening during *Kabbalat Shabbat*.

lulav – Palm branch, one of the four species that are taken together on *Sukkot*. Often, *lulav* is used to refer to all four species.

Ma'ariv – The evening prayer.

maftir – The additional reading at the conclusion of the Torah reading on Shabbat, festivals, and fast days. The person who receives the *maftir aliya* also reads the *haftara*.

maggid – In Eastern Europe before the Holocaust, a *maggid* was a person who gave sermons and admonished the community, e.g., the Maggid of Koznitz.

mahzor – Prayer book for festivals, Rosh HaShana, or Yom Kippur.

Marheshvan – Month of the Jewish calendar, occurring during October/ November.

mashgiah – (1) *Kashrut* supervisor; (2) In many yeshivot, the person in charge of the spiritual development of the students.

matanot la'evyonim – Literally, gifts to the poor. Giving a gift to at least two poor people is one of the obligations of Purim.

matza (pl. matzot) – Unleavened bread that is eaten on Passover.

matza sheruya – See *gebrokts*.

megilla – Literally, scroll; often refers to the book of Esther.

melakha – Productive, creative activity (lit. "labor"), which is prohibited on Shabbat.

melaveh malka – Literally, "accompanying the queen." The meal customarily served on Saturday night to acknowledge the end of Shabbat.

messiah – Literally, "the anointed one." The anointed king from the house of David who will appear at the end of days and rule Israel righteously.

mezuza (pl. mezuzot) – The scroll affixed to the doorposts of a Jewish home

containing the verses beginning *Shema Yisrael.*

mikva – Ritual bath. Food utensils acquired from gentiles must be immersed in a *mikva* before being used. A woman immerses herself in a *mikva* a week after her menstrual period before she resumes relations with her husband. Some men have the practice of immersing themselves in a *mikva* either every morning or every week.

Minha – The afternoon prayer service.

minyan – The quorum of ten men required for public prayer and Torah reading.

mishlo'ah manot – Gifts of food given on Purim.

mishnayot – Plural of mishna.

mishteh – Feast, one of the mitzvot on Purim.

mitnagged (pl. mitnaggedim) – Opponents of Hasidism. The original *mitnaggedim* fiercely opposed the innovations of the Baal Shem Tov and his followers. Once Hasidism became established, the *mitnaggedim* became a competing ideological movement that was centered in the great yeshivot of Eastern Europe.

mitzva (pl. mitzvot) – Literally, commandment. Traditionally there are 613 commandments in the Torah. Mitzva is often also used more loosely to refer to any religious obligation.

mohel – One who performs a ritual circumcision.

molad – The moment when the new moon becomes visible. See *Kiddush Levana.*

Morning Blessings – Blessings said upon rising in the morning celebrating the beginning of a new day.

Mourner's Kaddish – Kaddish said by mourners, usually by children for a parent, commemorating and elevating the soul of the deceased. See Kaddish.

muktze – An item that may not be handled on Shabbat or festivals. An item is *muktze* either because it serves no purpose (e.g., sticks and stones) or because its purpose involves a prohibited action on Shabbat or a festival (e.g., a pen).

Musaf – The additional prayer service said after the morning service on Shabbat and holidays.

Musar – (1) A type of Jewish literature devoted to moral development and spiritual and psychological growth; (2) A movement begun in the second half of the nineteenth century by Rabbi Yisrael Salanter that emphasized moral reflection and self-improvement, often through the study of Musar literature.

Ne'ila – The closing prayer service on Yom Kippur.

Nisan – Month of the Jewish calendar, occurring during March/April.

nisu'in – The second part of the Jewish marriage ceremony, in which blessings are recited under the wedding canopy.

nolad – An item that has just come into being. This concept is used in various *halakhot*, including those of festivals.

nusah – Version of a prayer used by a particular community.

Nusah Sefarad – Version of the prayer service used by those of hasidic heritage.

Old Yishuv – Ultra-Orthodox communities that were present in the Land of Israel prior to the various waves of Zionist immigration in the nineteenth and early twentieth centuries.

omer – An offering brought from the new crop of barley on the sixteenth of Nisan; the period from the sixteenth of Nisan until *Shavuot*.

onen – An acute mourner, one whose close relative has died but has not yet been buried. An *onen* does not perform any positive mitzvot.

panim hadashot – Literally, a new face. In order to recite the seven blessings celebrating the bride and groom during the week following the wedding, there must be *panim hadashot,* a person who was not present at the wedding.

parasha – The weekly Torah portion.

pareve – Food containing neither dairy nor meat ingredients.

pe'ot – Sideburns. Jewish men are forbidden to remove their sideburns above about half the ear. Some hasidic groups have the custom of growing their *pe'ot* long.

pesik reisha – Performing an action that will unintentionally bring about the performance of labor on Shabbat or a holiday is permitted. However, if such an unintentional result will necessarily occur, the action is called a *pesik reisha* and is prohibited. For example, it is prohibited to open a refrigerator on Shabbat if that action will necessarily cause an incandescent light bulb to be lit in the refrigerator, even if one opened the refrigerator with no intention of turning on the light.

Pesukei DeZimra – The psalms said at the beginning of the morning service.

pidyon haben – Redemption of the firstborn, performed on firstborn sons of Israelite lineage on the thirtieth day of life.

pikuah nefesh – Saving a life. Saving a life overrides all mitzvot in the Torah except for the prohibitions against murder, illicit sexual relations, and idolatry.

prozbol – Legal transfer of the responsibility for the collection of one's debts to the court. *Prozbol* is performed during the Sabbatical Year in order to avoid the cancellation of those debts.

Rabbis' Kaddish – The Kaddish prayer that is said after studying Torah. It includes a passage praying for the welfare of Torah scholars and their students.

Retzeh – (1) The third-to-last blessing of the *Amida*, in which we pray for the renewal of the Temple service; (2) The addition to Grace after Meals for Shabbat.

Rosh Hodesh – The first of the month, which is a minor holiday. Jewish months have either 29 or 30 days. When the preceding month had 30 days, *Rosh Hodesh* is celebrated on the 30th day of the preceding month and the first of the new month. When the preceding month had 29 days, *Rosh Hodesh* is celebrated only on the first of the new month.

sandak – The person at a circumcision ceremony who holds the baby during the actual circumcision. To be *sandak* is regarded as an honor, often given to one of the newborn's grandfathers.

Sanhedrin – The High Court of the Jewish people, composed of 71 members. The Sanhedrin continued to exist after the destruction of the Second Temple for about 350 years.

seder – Literally, order; one of the six sections of the Mishna.

Seder – Ceremonial Passover meal in which four cups of wine are drunk, matza and bitter herbs are eaten, and those present read the haggada.

sefer Torah – Torah scroll, in which the entire Pentateuch is written by hand, using special calligraphy.

Sefira (pl. Sefirot) – The ten different manifestations of the Divine according to Kabbala. The *Sefirot* bear structured relationships with one another, and the relationships between them serve to explain every aspect of Being.

Sefirat HaOmer – The counting of the *omer,* the mitzva to count the days and weeks beginning on the second day of Passover and concluding on the day before *Shavuot.*

segula – An object or practice that serves as a favorable omen or a talisman for receiving some benefit.

sekhakh – *Sukka roofing. Sekhakh must be made from a plant that is no longer attached to the earth and is not edible or any sort of utensil (and therefore is not subject to ritual impurity).*

Selihot – Prayers, mostly composed as liturgical poems, that petition God for mercy and forgiveness. *Selihot* are said on fast days, during the days before and between Rosh HaShana and Yom Kippur, and on Yom Kippur itself.

Sephardim (adj. Sephardic) – Jews who trace their traditions and liturgy back to medieval Spain and Portugal. Today, most Sephardic families trace their more recent origins to Middle Eastern countries, from Morocco in the west to Iran in the east.

seuda shelishit – The third Shabbat meal.

seudat havra'a – The meal prepared for mourners upon their return from the funeral, by their friends and neighbors.

seudat mitzva – A celebratory meal held in honor of the performance of a mitzva, including a wedding, bar mitzva, circumcision, and *siyum.*

Shabbat (pl. Shabbatot) – Saturday. Shabbat is the day of rest and the *halakha* proscribes thirty-nine specific labors on that day.

Glossary

Shabbat Hatan – Literally, groom's Shabbat. On the Shabbat either immediately before or after a wedding the groom's family and friends gather to celebrate. The groom usually receives an *aliya* to the Torah.

Shaharit – The morning prayer service.

Shalom Zakhar – Traditional Ashkenazic ceremony in which family and friends gather on the Friday evening after the birth of a baby boy to sing, share words of Torah, and celebrate the birth.

Sheheheyanu – The blessing recited on the occasion of a new experience: when one makes a significant purchase, upon eating a fruit or vegetable that was previously out of season, the first time one performs a mitzva, and at the beginning of holidays.

Shekhina – The Divine Presence, the manifestation of God in the world. In Kabbalistic thought, the *Shekhina* is identified with the *Sefira* of *Malkhut*.

sheloshim – The thirty-day period of mourning after the death of a close relative.

Shema – The verse "Hear, Israel: the Lord is our God, the Lord is one" (Deut. 6:4). It is a mitzva to recite the *Shema* (along with other verses) every morning and evening. The *Shema* is a declaration of one's acceptance of the yoke of Heaven and is the ultimate expression of a Jew's loyalty to and faith in God. As such it has often been recited by martyrs at their deaths.

Shemini Atzeret – The eighth day of the festival of *Sukkot*, which is in many ways a separate holiday, as the mitzvot of *Sukkot* such as *lulav* and *sukka* do not apply to it.

sheva berakhot – The seven blessings recited at a wedding and at subsequent meals made for the couple in celebration of their wedding in the following week.

Shevat – Month of the Jewish calendar, occurring during January/February.

shevut – Actions on Shabbat that the Sages prohibited beyond those prohibited by Torah law.

shiva – The seven-day mourning period observed after the death of a close relative.

shofar – A hollowed-out ram's horn that is sounded on Rosh HaShana.

siddur – Jewish prayer book.

Simhat Beit HaSho'eva – The celebration of the drawing of the water, a celebration that took place in the Temple on *Sukkot* in honor of the water libation that was brought on that festival. *Simhat Beit HaSho'eva* has become a general term for a celebration held on the festival of *Sukkot.*

Simhat Torah – The last day of the festival of *Sukkot.* In Israel, *Simhat Torah* is celebrated on *Shemini Atzeret,* while in the diaspora it is celebrated on the following day. On this day the yearly cycle of Torah reading is completed and begun again.

sitra ahra – Literally, the other side. In kabbalistic thought, the *sitra ahra* is the metaphysical locus of the forces of evil.

Sivan – Month of the Jewish calendar, occurring during May/June.

siyum – A celebration marking the completion of the study of a talmudic tractate or some other significant work of Torah literature.

sukka – A covered booth (see *sekhakh*). On *Sukkot,* it is a mitzva to dwell in a *sukka* rather than in one's house.

Sukkot – The festival beginning on the fifteenth of Tishrei, in which we are commanded to dwell in *Sukkot* and to take up the four species. *Sukkot* lasts seven days, concluding on the eighth day with *Shemini Atzeret* and in the diaspora extending a ninth day with *Simhat Torah.*

Tahanun – A petitionary prayer recited on weekdays following the *Amida* in both the morning and afternoon services. It is the custom in Ashkenazic (and some Sephardic) synagogues to lean over and cover one's face with one's arm during this prayer.

tallit – A prayer shawl, a four-cornered garment with *tzitzit* that is worn by men during the morning service.

Tamuz – Month of the Jewish calendar, occurring during June/July.

tanna – A Sage of the period of the Mishna.

tefillin – Phylacteries, leather boxes containing scrolls upon which are written passages from the Torah. The boxes are attached to one's forehead and one's upper arm with leather straps. *Tefillin* are worn by Jewish men during weekday morning prayers.

tehum Shabbat – The Shabbat limit, the maximum distance one may travel on Shabbat: two thousand cubits beyond one's place of dwelling, or in a city, from the city limit.

tena'im – Literally, conditions. The contract explicating the monetary commitments of both sides in a marriage and the consequences for each side if they do not go through with the marriage. In many communites today, this is not done at all or if it is, it is merely a ritualized formality.

tereifa – An animal that has a certain type of physical defect that renders it non-kosher. The most common type of defect is a hole in the lung.

Tevet – Month of the Jewish calendar, occurring during December/January.

Three Weeks – The three-week period between the Seventeenth of Tammuz and Tisha BeAv, a period of mourning for the destruction of the two Temples.

tikkun – A set text of prayers and readings from the Bible and from rabbinic and kabbalistic works, read on evenings when it is customary to study Torah at night. These occasions include *Shavuot, Hoshana Rabba*, and the eve of the seventh day of Passover. Each day has its own *tikkun*.

tisch – Literally, table. A gathering of hasidim around their rebbe, with singing and Torah discourses.

Tisha BeAv – The ninth day of the month of Av, which is the anniversary of the destruction of both the first and second Temples. as well as of other disasters that befell the Jewish people. *Tisha BeAv* is a day of mourning and a fast day.

Tishrei – Month of the Jewish calendar, occurring during September/October.

Tu BeAv – The fifteenth of the month of Av. It is a minor holiday in commemoration of an ancient practice recorded in the Mishna (*Ta'anit* 4:8) whereby young women would dance in the vineyards in search of a bridegroom.

Tu BeShvat – The fifteenth of the month of Shevat, known as the New Year for the trees. This date has halakhic significance in terms of the calculation of the year for the purpose of tithes. Many have the custom to hold special celebrations on this day.

Glossary

tza'ar ba'alei hayim – Causing unnecessary pain to animals. Not only is this forbidden, but one is also obligated to alleviate the pain of animals in one's possession.

tzadik (pl. tzadikim) – In general, a *tzadik* is a righteous person. In Hasidism, a *tzadik* is an extraordinary individual who has a special connection to God. Ordinary people can connect to God through a *tzadik*, either by becoming his hasidim, his followers, or by his acting as an intermediary for them.

tzedaka – Charity, or more generally, righteousness. *Tzedaka* is used specifically to denote monetary gifts to the poor.

tzedaka box – A small box into which people put small amounts of money for charity.

tzimtzum – Literally, contraction. The kabbalistic/theological principle that God "contracted" Himself in order to create a "space" for the universe to exist.

tzitzit – Ritual fringes that one is commanded to place at the corners of a four-cornered garment.

Wayfarer's Prayer – A prayer one recites when he travels between cities, to request divine protection.

Ya'aleh VeYavo – The prayer inserted into the *Amida* and Grace after Meals on Rosh Hodesh and festivals.

yad soledet bo – The temperature at which one's hand spontaneously recoils from an item's heat. Used for *halakhot* of Shabbat and *kashrut*.

yahrzeit – The anniversary of someone's death. On that day Kaddish is recited by his or her children.

Yedid Nefesh – A liturgical hymn composed by Rabbi Elazar Azikri in the sixteenth century. In many communities it is sung at the beginning of Friday night prayers. It is also often sung at the third meal on Shabbat.

yeshiva – A traditional institution for Torah study. The focus of the curriculum is usually the Talmud.

yetzer hara – The evil inclination, the aspect of the human personality that desires to sin. In some contexts the *yetzer hara* is conceived of as a metaphysical force.

Glossary

yihud room – The room in which the bride and groom briefly seclude themselves following their wedding ceremony.

Yizkor – A prayer said in memory of the deceased. Usually said by his or her children on the last day of each festival and on Yom Kippur.

Zeved HaBat – Celebration for the birth of a girl.

zimmun – The invitation to recite Grace after Meals, added when three men (or three women) eat together.

A Concise Guide to the Torah

Rabbi Adin Even-Israel Steinsaltz

altz Center

English Edition

Executive Director, Steinsaltz Center
Rabbi Meni Even-Israel

Editor in Chief
Rabbi Jason Rappoport

Executive Editors
Rabbi Joshua Amaru
Rabbi Joshua Schreier

Translators
Ilana Sobel
Rabbi David Strauss

Editor
Deborah Meghnagi Bailey

Copy Editors
Caryn Meltz, Manager
Dvora Rhein
Ilana Sobel
Avi Steinhart

Technical Staff

Adena Frazer
Adina Mann

Hebrew Edition

Senior Editors
Menachem Brod
Amechaye Even-Israel

Editors
Meir Klein
Genesis
Ezra Shekel
Exodus
Avraham Branner
Leviticus
Israel Malkiel
Numbers; Deuteronomy

Designer
Eliyahu Misgav

Typesetters
Rina Ben-Gal
Estie Dishon

MW00612086